THE SOCIAL
INVESTMENT ALMANAC

THE

SOCIAL

INVESTMENT

ALMANAC

**A COMPREHENSIVE GUIDE TO
SOCIALLY RESPONSIBLE INVESTING**

EDITED BY

PETER D. KINDER

STEVEN D. LYDENBERG

AMY L. DOMINI

A Henry Holt Reference Book

HENRY HOLT AND COMPANY   NEW YORK

Copyright ©1992 by Kinder, Lydenberg, Domini & Co., Inc.
A Henry Holt Reference Book
Published by Henry Holt and Company, Inc.,
115 West 18th Street, New York, New York 10011.
Published in Canada by Fitzhenry & Whiteside Limited,
91 Granton Drive, Richmond Hill, Ontario L4B 2N5.

Owing to limitations of space, acknowledgments
for permission to reprint previously published
materials may be found before the indexes on p. 857.

Library of Congress Cataloging-in-Publication Data
Kinder, Peter D.
The social investment almanac / Peter D. Kinder, Steven D.
Lydenberg, and Amy L. Domini.
    p.   cm.
Includes indexes.
    1. Investments—Social aspects—Handbooks, manuals, etc.
2. Investments—Social aspects—Directories. 3. Investments—Social
aspects—Bibliography 4. Investments—Social aspects—Terminology.
I. Lydenberg, Steven D.   II. Domini, Amy L.   III. Title.
HG4527.K525 1992
332.6'78—dc20   91–36732
ISBN 0-8050-1769-0   CIP
Henry Holt Reference Books are available at special discounts
for bulk purchases for sales promotions, premiums,
fund-raising, or educational use. Special editions
or book excerpts can also be created to specification.
For details contact:
Special Sales Director, Henry Holt and Company, Inc.,
115 West 18th Street, New York, New York 10011.

First Edition—1992

Designed by Ann Gold
Printed in the United States of America
Recognizing the importance of preserving the written word,
Henry Holt and Company, Inc., by policy, prints all of its
first editions on acid-free paper. ∞
10 9 8 7 6 5 4 3 2 1

This book is dedicated to eight people who made social investing in the United States what it is today:

Joan Bavaria; Alice Tepper Marlin; Milton Moskowitz; Robert Schwartz; Joan Shapiro; Timothy Smith; the Reverend Leon Sullivan; and Robert Zevin.

C O N T E N T S

III. CORPORATE SOCIAL ACCOUNTABILITY RESEARCH

IV. THE SOCIAL PORTFOLIO

V. COMMUNITY DEVELOPMENT INVESTING

VI. CONSUMER AND EMPLOYMENT ISSUES AFFECTING SOCIAL INVESTING

ACKNOWLEDGMENTS

When a book has fifty-one contributors, it is very hard to single out individuals for thanks. Making this task still more difficult is the invaluable aid we received from perhaps twice that number of people who happened to have *just* the bit of data we needed.

But, our contributors made this book possible. They supplied us with excellent manuscripts, which we proceeded to misunderstand. To each round of pettifogging editorial queries, they responded patiently and quickly. We cannot thank them enough.

In the preparation of this almanac, we have been overwhelmed by the generosity of the experts on social investing. No book on social investing would be authoritative without the assistance of Tim Smith, executive director of the Interfaith Center on Corporate Responsibility (ICCR). We have had the benefit not only of his extensive essays on shareholder activism but also of his advice on the almanac's structure and content. Indeed, this book is much richer for the contributions of many people affiliated with ICCR.

Alan Miller of Financial Platforms in London gave us the keys to social investing in Europe. Then he and his wife, Lynn, opened doors for us in London. With great patience, he responded to our many queries. Tessa Tennant of the Merlin Research Unit supplied us with much information and several key introductions.

Sometimes material comes through pure chance. Alison MacDonald of the Concorde Unternehmensgruppe heard about the almanac and called us. We received the benefit not only of her encyclopedic knowledge of screened investment on the Continent but also of her exceptional understanding of what we as a movement are—and should be—about. Chris McKenzie called to ask us to review his article for the *Columbia Journal of Environmental Law*. To make a long story short, he gave us permission to reprint his extraordinary paper on environmental investing.

Chris heard about us from Brad Lehrman, then the executive director of the Social Investment Forum. And he and our other friends in Minneapolis, John Schultz and Joan Kanavich, came through when we needed them.

Joan Shapiro of South Shore Bank, Patrick McVeigh of Franklin Research & Development, and Steve Bennett of the Bennett Information Group took considerable time out of their killing schedules to produce chapters for us and to tell us where we should be heading.

Special recognition must go to James Rowley of Lincoln Benefits Group and Veronica Froelich, who made significant contributions to the genesis of this work.

One problem we did not anticipate was the wealth of information and articles we would receive. For reasons of space, some excellent articles had to be dropped. We hope to be able to include them in the next edition.

Several people at Loring, Wolcott & Coolidge were of great help. The support and encouragement of Lawrence Coolidge and the other trustees made a great difference to us. Carolyn Free always seemed to have the answer to every problem. We could not have done the almanac without her.

At Kinder, Lydenberg, Domini & Company, we have been blessed with an extraordinary team of employees. Lloyd Kurtz has been with us since the beginning. His loyalty and good humor have pulled us through many a difficult time. The chapters on the Domini Social Index and our research methodology, as well as the tables of corporate social performance, owe much to him. Adrienne Turcott has coped with more tasks cryptically described than all of the heroes in *Grimm's Fairy Tales*. She brought not the luck of the Irish to this project but the persistence—thank heavens! By now the number of books in which Holly Grano's contributions are acknowledged probably has hit three figures. She is at once secretary, critic, friend, and indispensable collaborator. Carolyn Dever, Jack Kranefuss, Kathryn Kunkel, Adrienne Toomey, Lisa Loveland, Annica Lydenberg, Jack Maxwell, and Tony Rousmaniere added their support at critical moments.

Last but not least, we want to thank our friends at Henry Holt, especially Paula Kakalecik. They had the idea for this book and the patience to see the project through.

Six hundred years ago astrologers compiled almanacs of information about the movement of the moon and the planets so that their clients would know what the stars were telling them to do. By the time Benjamin Franklin began producing *Poor Richard's Almanac*, the moon's phases were still featured, but the emphasis had shifted to practical knowledge—when to sow, when to reap—and entertainment. Today's almanacs lack guides to predicting the future (fortunately) and most of their entertainment value (unfortunately). Instead an almanac is a basic reference tool containing current and historical information loosely organized by topic. And such is *The Social Investment Almanac: A Comprehensive Guide to Socially Responsible Investing*.

| GUIDING PRINCIPLES

An understanding of what we set out to do will help you use this book efficiently. We had three goals. First, we aspired to survey the entire field of social investing in the United States. Second, we wanted to transfer social investment techniques to a broad audience of investors and managers. And third, we intended to provoke debate not only about how social investing is done but about its nature and its future.

Completeness
The Social Investment Almanac: A Comprehensive Guide to Socially Responsible Investing is the first attempt to survey the entire field of social investment. Therefore, our first goal was completeness.

We have produced the most thorough treatment of social investing to date. However, we will save the reader the task of discovering that we failed to cover everything. We admit it. From the start we wanted to encompass all of the forms social investing takes, from microloan funds to institutional mutual funds. We had not aspired to a global scope, but through luck we have been able to include the most extensive survey of international activity available in the United States.

Information Transfer

Our second goal was the transference of social investment techniques to a broad audience of managers and financial advisers. To accomplish that, we asked experts to contribute articles. We also asked vendors of mutual funds and research services, among others, to prepare descriptions of their products. Our purpose here was to let the vendors speak for themselves so that readers can compare for themselves. When we began to receive material from outside the United States, we realized that this approach had another benefit: it allowed comparisons of several types of screens and screening techniques.

Provoke Debate

Our third goal was to provoke debate over social investing. Such debate is part of a much larger discussion about what we as a society aspire to and what we define as "justice." Socially responsible investors share a commitment to positive social change. Social change advocates must struggle constantly against their great enemy, complacency. Keeping the debate alive is the best weapon here.

To that end, we have devoted considerable space to the issues of fiduciary responsibility, the performance of socially screened portfolios, and the nature of the issues social investors are presenting. Some of the views we present are not ones to which we subscribe. But they are opinions that every social investment professional must be prepared to confront.

| FINDING WHAT YOU NEED

Almanac users want specific information. They rate usefulness by how quickly they can find what they are looking for. *The Social Investment Almanac* offers three ways to find material: a table of contents and two distinct indexes.

The topical articles often contain discussions of particular firms or people in the field they cover. In many cases you will find more particular descriptions in other sections of the book. For a variety of practical reasons, we could not do comprehensive cross-referencing—something we hope to add in future editions.

Topical Analysis

The Social Investment Almanac is designed to be a desk reference for investment professionals. Its purpose is to provide its users with quick access to information and to direct them to resources they may need.

To that end, each chapter has a single focus. We tried to group related articles together so that, for instance, someone interested in stocks quickly could reach articles on evaluating portfolio performance. However, not all topics could be neatly consigned to a single chapter or even to a single unit.

For example, the most difficult questions that confront social investment professionals relate to screens: how are they formed? how are they implemented? The almanac addresses these questions in several ways. First, the chapters on shareholder activism describe the central issues confronting social investors today. Second, the chapters on social research identify techniques for implementing screens. And third, the chapters describing performance evaluation and those profiling social investment vehicles here and abroad illustrate how screens are applied in practice. Similarly, environmental investing receives attention in every unit, though from quite different perspectives.

So it will pay readers to look beyond the chapter that seems to fit their needs to related topics.

INDEXES. The table of contents has been designed to offer readers quick access to topics they want. However, for locating more particular bits of information, thorough indexes are a must. We have provided two: a subject matter index and an index to publicly traded companies, funds, and bonds.

DIRECTORIES AND RESOURCE LISTS. Although we have tried to anticipate nearly every question a reader might have, we could not possibly succeed in this effort. For that reason, we have included eight directories composed of more than 450 individuals, companies, and nonprofits organized by their fields.

Many chapters end with extensive resource lists. The chapter on employee stock ownership plans (ESOPs) has a particularly extensive list of publications. The chapters in part III, Corporate Social Accountability Research, contain comprehensive discussions of publications useful for investigating particular topics and detailed descriptions of some of the specialized research services and publications catering to social investors.

Glossary

One of the major frustrations encountered in reference books is a lack of definitions. For that reason, we have erred on the side of inclusiveness in constructing a glossary. With the help of several of our contributors, we have tried to define terms unique to social investing. Social investing as we are experiencing it is a new phenomenon, and it lacks a commonly accepted vocabulary. We hope these definitions attract criticism and new word lists.

Social Performance Tables

Managers looking for an initial universe of screened companies can start with the Domini Social Index. We have included in appendix A a table that lists all four hundred companies on the index and identifies their areas of strength and weakness across our principal screens. The table is current as of April 30, 1991.

I SELECTION PROCESS

Whenever we write on social investing, people ask, "Why didn't you include him/her/it/them?" and "Why *did* you include him/her/it/them?"

Why They Are Not Here

We began the process of writing by sending out requests for submissions from all of the research vendors and mutual funds we knew of in the United States and Canada. We wrote again to those who did not respond. We wrote to everyone we thought would want to be included in our directories. As we write the last pieces of the book—eight weeks after our deadline to contributors and well after the publisher's due date—we are still receiving submissions and directory entries.

In short, if they are not in this book, then either we have never heard of them or, more likely, we never heard from them.

Why They *Are* Here

Since its beginning, the Social Investment Forum has confronted the issue of qualifications for membership. Should the Forum establish tests of its members' commitments? For both practical and philosophical reasons, the Forum has not imposed qualifications. Membership is open to anyone who wants to join.

We used the same criterion. Mutual funds that said they screened are included, as are consultants who said they handled social clients. We did not attempt to verify what vendors of services and financial products claimed about themselves or their products. Rather, we asked them to supply information with which readers could evaluate them. Several of the articles discuss them as well.

How to Get In

We've already begun preparing for the next edition. Send us your suggestions, directory entries, and proposals for articles. Write or fax:

> Kinder, Lydenberg, Domini & Company
> Seven Dana Street
> Cambridge, Mass. 02138
> (617) 354-5353 (fax)

Our annual deadline is easy to remember: April 15.

P A R T   O N E

SOCIAL INVESTING:

ITS ORIGINS

Social investing is neither a new concept nor a new movement. Even the views of social investors held (until recently) by the investment community are not new. Consider how George Fox, one of the founders of the Quakers and therefore of social investing, was regarded in seventeenth-century London. Lord Macaulay put it well when he described Fox as having "an intellect in the most unhappy of all states, that is to say, too much disordered for liberty and not sufficiently disordered for Bedlam."

One can trace the origins of socially responsible investing (SRI) from at least the Quakers and other Anabaptists into the most established of our churches during the era of the Social Gospel in the late nineteenth and early twentieth centuries. But the first formal expression of the concept probably came in the 1910s and 1920s from the churches that chose not to invest in companies that made alcohol or tobacco products. They deliberately set about to make their investments consistent with their ethics. From that insight came today's social investment movement.

As Amy Domini points out, today's social investors span a spectrum that ranges from traditional stockholders to innovative community-oriented investors. No small part of the strength of SRI comes from this diversity of approaches. Joan Shapiro brings us up to date with a look at the modern movement, that is, the movement given impetus by Vietnam, the consumer revolution, and South Africa. We are part of a great tradition that has accomplished much and aspires to do more.

Karen Paul and Dominic Aquila look specifically at the effect of social investing on the struggle against apartheid. Many lessons for the future lie in that chapter. Chris McKenzie, too, offers a look at the future when he describes the history and legal status of environmental investing. His chapter also introduces the controversy over the application of fiduciary standards to screened investments.

Marcy Murninghan outlines the history of the corporation. Many who argue that corporations have no duty other than to make the best possible return for their investors willfully ignore the history of why the corporate form exists at all. Corporations exist to confer a benefit on society as a whole, not merely to enrich a few members of it.

These first few chapters mark the beginning, we hope, of a serious examination of the history of social investment. We insist that individual investors examine the impact of their investments. We should know the context of our movement.

WHAT IS SOCIAL INVESTING?
WHO ARE SOCIAL INVESTORS?

Amy L. Domini Loring, Wolcott & Coolidge

Six blind men, each touching a different part of an elephant, sought to describe the beast. The man who touched its tusks found the elephant entirely different from the man who touched its tail, who in turn found it different from the man who touched its knees.

Social investing, socially responsible investing, socially constrained investing, shareholder activism, alternative investing, community development investing, program-related investing, and alternative investing are phrases that describe a financial creation of the past two decades. Social investment encompasses many complementary, though different, concepts. But the various parts of social investment share a common fundamental theme: the integration of social or ethical criteria into the investment decision-making process.

SOCIAL INVESTING'S THREE FORMS

Historically, social investing has manifested itself in three distinct but related forms: shareholder activism, guideline portfolio investment, and community development investing. Each nourishes the others.

How this symbiosis works may be seen in the experience of the Episcopal Church, the first church to sponsor a shareholder resolution. In 1971 the Presiding Bishop of the Episcopal Church presented General Motors Corporation with a resolution asking the company to withdraw from South Africa. Two years later the church's social justice mission led it to commit a portion of its available funds to venture capital investments promoting community development, particularly in minority communities. In 1985, after years of frustration over the dialogue with U.S. corporations on South Africa, the church divested its portfolio of U.S. corporations doing business in that country. By then the church's shareholder activism had expanded to four or five social issue proxy resolutions each year, and its governing body was investigating ways in which its mission and money could be more directly connected. In 1990 the church entered its second phase of community investing with a program of direct community investments. The church also entered a second phase of guideline portfolio investing when it voted to divest its tobacco stocks. And the church continues an active dialogue with corporations on a variety of social issues. Many individuals and institutions have passed through similar processes over the last several years.

| THE PATH TO SOCIAL INVESTING

Whether social investors are individuals or institutions, one of two basic motivations lies behind their choices: the integration of money and ideals, and social change. The first social investors were motivated by the desire to avoid sin. If it was a sin to drink, then it was a sin to make money from the production of alcohol. If it was a sin to smoke, then it was a sin to profit from making cigarettes. This deeply personal motivation reflected a desire for institutional or individual consistency and the integration of money with moral purpose.

Often socially responsible investors express the impetus to manage their money under social criteria as a desire for an "integration of money into one's self and into the self one wishes to become." An institution may strive for consistency between its mission and the way it achieves that mission. In both instances, this motivation comes from within. The provost of a Quaker college was asked why his college did not invest in the manufacturers of armaments. Did the board of trustees think it was going to stop the armaments buildup? "No," he responded, "our board isn't out to change the world. We're seeking a oneness between ourselves and our Lord."

Currently approximately $650 billion is restricted from investing freely in U.S. corporations doing business in South Africa. Major pension funds—California, New Jersey, TIAA-CREF, and New York City among them—have imposed such restrictions. California is not, however, seeking a oneness between itself and its Lord. Rather it has responded to its constituency and used its pension portfolio to join a boycott of stocks of U.S. corporations with operations in South Africa. This boycott has as its goal social change, a motivation that increasingly drives social investors.

SOCIAL INVESTING'S IMPACT

It is the goal of many social investors to define—and to hold up as a model—an ideal of sound corporate management. The definition of sound corporate management includes corporations' impact on communities, employees, customers, shareholders, and the environment.

Each of the three major approaches to social investing addresses these issues differently. Shareholder activists directly pressure corporations to improve their performance in certain specific areas. When shareholders ask a corporation to provide better reporting on its environmental impact, they are not solely interested in the details of a company's current action. They also hope to affect its future.

Community investors look beyond the immediate corporate concerns to broader concerns about our society. They address the absence of economic building blocks needed to cope with our society's critical needs for shelter, food, and capital for the disadvantaged. Venture capital too can promote entrepreneurship in, say, appropriate technologies as an additional benefit.

Guideline investing—managing stock and bond portfolios within social constraints—has its impact not so much through the movement of money but rather through the infrastructure it builds. Investors, money managers, and research firms engage in dialogue with corporations. They can point to opportunities for inspired corporate citizenship or to strengths and weaknesses among corporate peers. Because of investor demand for social screening, public scrutiny and corporate accountability follow. Social investing provides one framework within which this scrutiny can take place.

CONCLUSION

Social investing has many names but a single purpose: the integration of a broad range of social criteria into the investment decision-making process. Through shareholder activism, community development investing, and guideline portfolio investing, individuals and institutions hope both to achieve personal integrity and to bring about social change.

CHAPTER 2

THE MOVEMENT SINCE 1970

Joan Shapiro Senior Vice President,
South Shore Bank of Chicago

In February 1988, during the second year of my tenure as president of the Social Investment Forum, I was asked to speak at a conference in Chicago on ethics and investing. My task was to present a short history of the social investment movement in this country, to identify key issues and opportunities, and to set the context for the day-long deliberations attended by corporate executives, members of the religious community, investment professionals, managers of institutional resources, researchers, and interested individuals, including prospective social investors. In my speech, I identified social investing not as a movement but as a permanent, integral part of the investment industry.

I am reproducing that speech here because as I reviewed it I realized that it summed up my views of the movement in its first two decades. Also, the consensus I outline for the movement is more relevant today than it was in 1988. I have updated the speech with a few footnotes and interstitial notes.

Joan Shapiro is senior vice president of both the South Shore Bank of Chicago and its holding company, Shorebank Corporation. She joined the corporation in 1976 and in 1981 took over management of Development Deposits,ˢᵐ the bank's SRI deposit portfolio held by socially concerned individuals and institutions from all fifty states. Under her management the portfolio has grown from $20 million to $95 million. On the founding board of the Social Investment Forum, Shapiro was president for two years and serves on its Executive Committee. She is an adviser to the Council on Economic Priorities and to the Center for Economic Conversion, a director of the National Association of Community Development Loan Funds, and a trustee of the Parnassus Income Fund and the International House of the University of Chicago.

| MY 1988 SPEECH

A year ago this April over five hundred investment professionals, investors, researchers, interested observers, and the press gathered at New York University Graduate School of Business on Wall Street for an all-day conference and trade fair on socially responsible investing. That conference was organized by the Social Investment Forum, a national trade association incorporated in 1985 to promote the concept and practice of socially responsible investing. It represented the largest of an increasing number of such gatherings organized across the country beginning in 1984. On the plane to New York that week I read of Harvard University's latest and largest first: $10 million to support an ethics curriculum in its business school.

Some of you may recall that the 1985 commencement address at the University of California's School of Business Administration was given by a gentleman who, according to those present, brought the house down with this advice to the graduating class: "Greed is all right. . . . Greed is healthy. You can be greedy and still feel good about yourself." With no malice of intent, but simply because he was on a mailing list, the Forum office sent this man a conference brochure. It was returned to us stamped by the post office, "Moved. Not forwardable. New York City." The addressee: Ivan Boesky. April 1987—the high-water mark of an era when self-interest was king, and the beginning of a deluge that has yet to run its course.

Since then, we have watched as insider trading scandals have rocked Wall Street; we've read about multimillion-dollar fines assessed by corporations that pollute the environment; and we've witnessed, if not participated in, the casino days of Wall Street that culminated—or did they?—on October 19, 1987. At the same time, we can no longer ignore:

- the existence and growth, in this richest of all countries, of America's newly described underclass; or
- Jonathan Kozol's devastating exposé (first published in the *New Yorker* and now a book) about homelessness ("homeless," incidentally, defined not as derelict men panhandling on corners, but as children and their mothers and sometimes their fathers, on the street because the recent loss of jobs has meant losing their homes); or

- the plight of thousands of workers whose plants close, sometimes on less than a day's notice; or
- skilled workers of the land with few opportunities for retraining or predictable employment.

The list goes on and on.

Each of these issues relates in significant ways to the allocation of the still vast capital resources at our disposal in this country, and to choices about how and where those resources are invested. This is not to claim that socially responsible investing is the panacea to these myriad, complex problems. Or that all the experience is in place. It is, however, to suggest that there may be different approaches to allocating our investable resources more in line with ethical behavior and more conducive to addressing critical social needs.

In April 1985 the Social Investment Forum documented $40 billion under professional management with some social criteria. We put that number three years later conservatively at $350 to $400 billion. See figure 2-1. That impressive increase was fueled primarily by public sector employees' retirement funds and other major institutional investors, such as colleges and universities divesting their holdings in stocks of companies doing business in South Africa. These figures include divestments by the State of California and the New York City retirement systems. The growth of socially responsible investing has been exponential, the performance credible and competitive. What was once viewed by the investment community as a curious phenomenon is now an emerging force in the financial marketplace. It is demanding the attention of increasing numbers of individual and institutional investors and, through them, professional money managers.

What is socially responsible investing? Why and how has it developed? What are the issues and opportunities that challenge the field?

Socially Responsible Investing Defined

Socially responsible investing (SRI) is the practice of making investment decisions based on both financial and social performance. It is the concept of investing in concert with your principles. The SRI strategy asserts that investing is not value neutral and that there are significant ethical and social, as well as economic, consequences in how we invest our money. It is a commitment, if you will, to achieving social good through investment. Seeking what some call

FIGURE 2-1
THE GROWTH OF SOCIALLY SCREENED INVESTMENTS
IN THE UNITED STATES

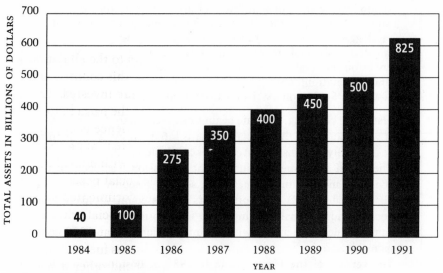

SOURCE: Social Investment Forum.

NOTE: The best estimate is that $625 billion were invested subject to social screens by the end of the first quarter of 1991.

the "double bottom line," or what we at South Shore Bank have for fifteen years called the "social dividend," is proving to be a prudent, legitimate long-term investment strategy.

Beyond this general definition, SRI means different things to different people depending on the social concerns or objectives they want to achieve, e.g., environmental impact; peace; human and, more recently, animal rights; employee relations; South Africa divestment; military conversion; product safety and quality; economic development; low-income housing. All agree that there is no 100 percent clean, or pure, investment, social or otherwise. At the same time, SRI practitioners are demonstrating that responsible business practices, environmentally safe products, rehabilitated housing, and cooperative or small business enterprise can be supported through investments.

BOX 2-1
THE SOCIAL INVESTMENT FORUM

Brad Lehrman

Behind every tract of rain forest cleared, every factory that is
shut and locked due to a hostile takeover and every beach that
is clogged, there lies an investment decision. It may have paid
big dividends to shareholders and large capital gains to former
investors, but it also may have affected our economy, our society
and our environment.
—Gelvin Stevenson, Assistant Comptroller, City of New York

Investors are changing. They are beginning to realize the opportunities
that will incorporate their social concerns into their investment portfolios. Socially responsible investing is available to all.

The Social Investment Forum is the professional association for
individuals and institutions active in socially responsible investing
(SRI). Formed in 1981, the Forum acts as this country's facilitator,
advocate, and national clearinghouse for information on SRI. The
Forum provides its members with the information they need to invest
responsibly.

The genesis of the Forum came in 1981 in Boston when a few
visionary financial professionals met to discuss issues that would
incorporate their social agendas into their financial and business activities. Joan Bavaria, the first president of the Social Investment
Forum, recalls meeting in restaurants and members' living rooms to
discuss with like-minded financial specialists a broad range of social
and financial issues. They needed a forum to discuss concerns such
as women's rights, the environment, South African divestiture, corporate ethics, and community investments. This small core created
an information network that they shared with other professionals.

THE GROWTH OF SOCIALLY SCREENED INVESTMENTS
Soon the discussion group blossomed into an association of concerned
investors and financial advisers. In 1985 the Social Investment Forum
was incorporated as a 501(c)(6) nonprofit tax-exempt trade association.

Brad Lehrman was executive director of the Social Investment Forum from
1987 to 1991. He received a degree in economics from Carleton College in
1977 and received his law degree from William Mitchell College of Law in
1981. The author gratefully thanks the following contributing Forum members
for insight in the presentation of this history: Joan Bavaria, Joan Shapiro, and
John Schultz.

Its mission is to increase awareness of the opportunity to apply ethical values and constructive social goals to investment decisions. The Forum assists investors in establishing criteria for responsible investments and encouraging investments in entities or organizations that respect the environment and human and civil rights, improve occupational health and safety of workers, and cooperate with other organizations with like purposes. The Forum promotes the concept and methodology of socially responsible investing among its membership, the public, and governmental bodies.

The Forum's first executive director was Gordon Davidson. During his tenure, Franklin Research & Development Corporation generously supplied the Forum with office space and other resources. It is no exaggeration to say that there would be no Forum without the generosity of Don Falvey and Joan Bavaria.

The Forum's first task was to build a membership base. This effort was greatly strengthened by an active board and a broad base of founding members who had devoted themselves to social investing.

From its inception, the Forum has offered a wide variety of membership services, including a comprehensive directory that includes listing of members in the community investment field, financial institutions, financial planners, investment advisers and money managers, information providers, socially responsible organizations and services, venture capitalists, and mutual and money market funds. The Forum also began educational outreach meetings four times a year throughout the country in addition to providing quarterly newsletters and updates to its members.

In September 1989 the Forum announced the CERES Project, a broad coalition of environmentalists and socially responsible investors that created the Valdez Principles, a guideline for U.S. corporations for environmentally sound policies. Modeled on the Sullivan Principles on South Africa (now called the Statement of Principles), the Valdez Principles stress sustainable use of natural resources, waste minimization and recycling, the wise use of energy, the marketing of safe products and services, and protection of the biosphere.

The Forum's membership grew 113 percent between 1988 and 1990. It had established itself as the pivotal national resource in the field of social investing. Aided by the twentieth anniversary of Earth Day in April 1990 and an aging baby boom population concerned about ethical issues, the Forum has become the leading voice in the $650 billion social investing industry. The Forum now has local chapters in the following areas: Boston, Chicago, Long Island, Los Angeles, Minneapolis, Pacific Northwest, and San Francisco.

> Social investing is no longer a peripheral strategy. The Social Investment Forum continues to give investors the opportunity to become visionaries by increasing awareness of the interrelationship between our economic power as investors and society at large.

Development of the Field Since 1970

How and why has this field developed? Socially responsible investing is not new. South Africa divestment has certainly catapulted it into national attention. But the earliest social investment probably dates to when a single investor chose not to buy a "sin" stock—shares in companies producing tobacco, liquor, or gambling. Contemporary social investing started with shareholder resolutions in 1970; the first South Africa resolution was recorded in 1971. The Interfaith Center for Corporate Responsibility, a coalition of national religious denominations headquartered in New York City, has, under Tim Smith, provided stellar leadership in this area.

In that same year, 1971, a group of Methodist clergy established Pax World Fund, the first mutual fund to screen for social issues. John Simon, professor of law at Yale University, published his seminal position paper for foundations on SRI, "The Ethical Investor," in 1972; he and Lou Kinnock at the Ford Foundation independently developed the concept of program-related investments at the same time.

Also, in the early 1970s, two investment managers—Dr. Robert Schwartz in New York and Robert Zevin in Boston—began managing portfolios with social criteria for selected institutional investors and individuals.* In 1973 the South Shore Bank became the

---

*Zevin takes little credit for the innovation, frankly acknowledging the debt he owes to one client who on principle did not want nuclear utilities in his portfolio but who also believed that "nuclear" was simply a poor investment. An economist by training, Zevin became convinced after doing the economic analysis. His earliest commentaries on SRI stress that a poor investment decision from the point of view of a social analysis will also make a poor financial decision, to wit, "a good social rule can also be a very good investment rule" ("83–84 Funding Exchange Directory of Socially Responsible Investments"). Schwartz, also an economist, recognized and discussed with several organizations he was advising the contradictions between their beliefs and their investments. That is, some of his religious organizational clients held stocks in companies supplying the war effort while they strenuously opposed the war in Vietnam, and some of his union clients were investing their pension funds in overseas companies whose practices or products undermined the very industries in which they worked.

nation's first private development bank; in 1974 it began offering one of the nation's first social investment products—Development Deposits—market rate bank deposits combining competitive returns with the social dividend of renewing distressed minority neighborhoods.

Other pioneering organizations include the Council on Economic Priorities, headed by Alice Tepper Marlin. CEP's research on corporate and government responsibility brings the Pentagon to press conferences, and its recent book, *Rating America's Corporate Conscience*, is drawing significant attention and highlighting a new segment of the SRI industry—consumerism. (A three-by-six-inch pocket edition, *Shopping for a Better World*, has sold nearly one million copies.) Co-op America has also made important contributions in this area, cataloging products and services offered by cooperatively owned and managed businesses. Franklin Research & Development, founded by Joan Bavaria and Don Falvey, spearheaded the creation of the Social Investment Forum in the early 1980s.* Calvert Social Investment Fund, created by Wayne Silby and John Guffey, offered the first socially responsible money market fund; Working Assets Money Fund, organized by Jerry Dodson, soon after introduced the first social credit card; and the Institute for Community Economics (ICE), under Chuck Matthei's leadership, inspired the creation of the national community revolving loan fund movement.

I cannot name all the innovators here. Fortunately, today there are many books, guides, and newsletters for novices and professionals alike that chart the development of this field and track the growing number of investment opportunities. Among the first of the "SRI roadshows" was one in 1984 that Jerry Dodson, George Pillsbury, and I did. We spoke at two conferences over one weekend, the first in Seattle, sponsored by the Commonwealth Fund, and the second

---

*A few of us who later participated in the founding board of the Forum met for the first time in New York City early in 1983. It was held in the faculty house of Columbia University. About a dozen people, known mainly to one another by name and organization, sat in an unadorned room around a small conference table, envisaging a national trade organization whose structure and operations were still vague but whose purpose was clear—to promote the concept and practice of socially responsible investing. My boss, Ronald Grzywinski, chairman of Shorebank, could not go and left it to me to decide the extent of South Shore Bank's involvement. I never regretted my decision to attend.

in Portland, sponsored by the MacKenzie River Gathering. Since then, all over the country there have been hundreds of meetings on SRI, ranging from small seminars to conferences such as this one. In addition, press coverage of the field is approaching some balance. Hostility is not the rule anymore, and TV—"MacNeil Lehrer," "Wall Street Week," "Today's Business"—is beginning to cover the industry.

BOX 2-2
SOCIAL INVESTING'S FOUR PHASES

1. *1920 to the Early 1970s: The Forerunners.* The earliest avoidance investors; the first South Africa resolution; the founding of PAX World Fund, Dreyfus Third Century Fund, Council on Economic Priorities, and the South Shore Bank of Chicago. PRIs (program-related investments) are described simultaneously at Yale University and the Ford Foundation; and the first two money managers apply social screens to investment portfolios.

2. *The 1980s: Launching the Movement.* Meetings in the early eighties of the founding members and first board of the Social Investment Forum; Forum incorporates in 1985; Franklin Research & Development and U.S. Trust of Boston emerge as trendsetting SRI portfolio management firms, spurring the formation of other SRI financial management and brokerage companies; Calvert Social Investment Funds and Working Assets Money Fund incorporate; *Ethical Investing* (Amy Domini and Peter Kinder) and several SRI newsletters (most notably, *GOOD MONEY, Insight, Catalyst,* and *Clean Yield*) are published; the Investor Responsibility Research Center (IRRC) begins marketing its social research; the Institute for Community Economics (ICE) and Industrial Cooperative Association (ICA) stimulate the founding of other community-based revolving loan funds and the formation of a national association. ACCION heightens interest in microlending enterprises in South America; and the National Association of Community Development Credit Unions and Self-Help Credit Union bring attention to loan and investment opportunities through local, cooperatively owned financial institutions.

3. *Late 1980s to the Present: Entering the Mainstream.* Driven by the success of the South Africa divestiture movement, individual and institutional investors routinely request social investment products,

and SRI is generally recognized as a prudent, long-term investment strategy producing comparable returns in a balanced portfolio. While negative screens predominate, there is increasing interest and demand for positive, proactive investments such as those long provided by South Shore Bank and the loan funds. Dramatic, new participation by brokers around the country nationally heralds the marketing of social funds by mainstream brokerage firms. SRI consumerism gains momentum, a network of social venture businesses is formed, and the media provides more balanced coverage of SRI. CERES (the Coalition for Environmentally Responsible Economies), begun as a project of the Social Investment Forum, creates the Valdez Principles. Enhanced by international environmental awareness, environmental investing replaces divestment as the second international SRI issue.

4. *The Twenty-first Century: SRI Is Business As Usual.*

Initially South Africa divestment drove the growth of the SRI industry. But SRI is not going to fade away with apartheid. Other issues have entered the debate as investors begin to question time-honored, sacrosanct investment strategies. And SRI is growing. This time the growth is driven, not just by softhearted baby boomers or guilty 1960s radicals, but by people in their fifties, by the elderly, and by institutional investors, such as municipalities, unions, universities, and pension funds, which control—and own, through you—the majority of the investment resources in this country. All of these investors are coming to the conclusion that there may be different and better ways to do business.

Issues and Opportunities

I would like to conclude by addressing some of the more interesting issues and opportunities about SRI that you may not find in the primers.

THIS IS A MARKET-DRIVEN INDUSTRY. This in no way detracts from the pioneers and innovators. It simply acknowledges that today the largest investment houses managing screened portfolios are doing so because their biggest institutional clients are demanding it. To my knowledge, only one national brokerage house offers a social fund.*

---

*Of course, within a couple of months of my making this speech in February 1988, this situation had changed dramatically.

Yet stockbrokers are getting calls every day from customers requesting screened investments. And banks are being challenged increasingly under the Community Reinvestment Act (CRA).

We are dealing with a generation of new clients. If we choose to ignore them, it is our loss—in terms of business and, more importantly, in terms of the opportunity they give us to create and direct a new industry. Investors are demanding product and performance. We have to provide both, professionally and predictably, not only to get, but to keep, their loyalty.

SRI IS NOT AN EASY BUSINESS. Take, for example, the business I know best—development banking. It has taken us a decade to demonstrate that banks can rebuild neighborhoods. Why, we are frequently asked, haven't hundreds of other banks followed South Shore's lead? The fact is that doing development for low- and moderate-income people is not the easiest way to make money, especially if shareholders and directors are monitoring only short-term profits and results. My colleague Beate Klein Becker, formerly of U.S. Trust in Boston, pointed out at a recent seminar that managing money with social criteria means not only learning new techniques, but it demands more homework on an ongoing basis. You have to be informed about significant social issues.

SRI IS A LONG-TERM, NOT A SHORT-TERM, INVESTMENT STRATEGY. SRI is neither easy, nor quick, nor the final answer. It is, however, a thoughtful, comprehensive approach to achieving specific social objectives without undue sacrifice of investment return—if indeed there is any sacrifice at all.

THOSE IN THE SRI BUSINESS CANNOT BE COMPLACENT ABOUT THE DIRECTION OF ITS GROWTH. The vast majority of the billions in screened accounts are invested in publicly traded securities—securities chosen as a result of negative social screens and an "avoidance" strategy. They represent decisions to "get out" or "not to buy." An insignificant portion of the billions divested from South Africa has gone into affirmative social investments. Thus, the flip side of divestment is far from what it could or should be: "the positive reallocation of capital."*

*In September 1989 the Social Investment Forum published its "Survey on Alternative Investments," a report funded by a grant from the Ford Foundation. While most of

THE PLIGHT OF THE HOMELESS AND THE JOBLESS CANNOT BE "FIXED" THROUGH CONVENTIONAL WALL STREET INVESTMENTS. That challenge is left to the targeted or community investment professionals—those operating outside the marketplace of paper and securities—through companies such as development banks, community-based revolving loan funds, credit unions, worker cooperatives, social venture firms, and foundations making program-related investments.* If actual social investment dollars—compared to the daily trading volume on Wall Street—is small, then the amount in this arena is a mere trickle.

THERE CONTINUES TO BE A SIGNIFICANT AND TROUBLING IMBALANCE WITHIN THE SRI INDUSTRY. Not only are more social investments negatively screened, but among those that are not, only a tiny percentage go into direct community investment. This is the area where people are most directly affected and where our most critical social and economic needs will be met.

YOU CAN'T HAVE IT ALL, ALL THE TIME, WITH SRI. You can't expect maximum social impact *and* maximum profit all the time. There

---

the conventional money managers surveyed expressed enthusiasm and support for alternative investments—that is, investments designed to deliver a socially beneficial product or remedy a social ill—the actual proportion of their firms' SRI assets in this area of investing was minuscule, less than one-tenth of 1 percent. (See Beate Klein Becker's chapter in part IV of this almanac for further discussion of this dilemma.)

*In 1986 the John D. and Catherine T. MacArthur Foundation made a large program-related investment (PRI) in Shorebank Corporation. That capital, allocated by the holding company to its various development subsidiaries, resulted in the following "alternative investments": First, equity in the real estate company City Lands Corp. allowed it to proceed with its development of a $10 million, 110,000-square-foot shopping center, the first commercial development in the community for twenty-five years. Second, the shopping center, Jeffery Plaza, had as its anchor tenant a large, quality supermarket chain that needed to hire 250 workers. The Neighborhood Institute, Shorebank's nonprofit affiliate and a recipient of part of the MacArthur PRI, was engaged to screen and process job applicants. Working with the supermarket, it succeeded in identifying the majority of new employees from the community; most of these residents had been out of work for months. Finally, part of the PRI was made in the form of a Rehab CD, South Shore Bank's below market rate deposit that directly supports rehabilitation of deteriorated apartments into decent, affordable housing units for low- and moderate-income minority residents in the bank's target neighborhoods. All are examples of alternative investment strategies that, in this case, resulted from a foundation PRI.

may be trade-offs, depending on the issue and the investment. But the social investor, like all investors, makes choices while seeking a balanced, diversified portfolio to achieve both financial and social returns.

EVERY INVESTMENT PROFESSIONAL LIMITS CHOICES. The argument that the social investment professional necessarily does more poorly because he or she screens or limits the universe of investments is simply not borne out by the facts. The principal variable in investment performance is management expertise.

INVESTORS CAN NO LONGER PLEAD IGNORANCE OR HELPLESSNESS. I think of a parallel in the medical profession. How many of us a decade ago would have seriously challenged our doctor, his diagnosis, or his cure? We do it all the time today. Investment professionals don't have the truth. They should be questioned and challenged. If you don't like the way they do things, find another planner, banker, or adviser.

BEFORE QUESTIONING YOUR ADVISER, QUESTION YOURSELF. Try objectively and realistically to examine your attitudes toward money, capital accumulation, and your responsibilities for managing and allocating those assets.

Conclusion

I ask you to think about the following issues: Can we do better with our investments than we are doing now? Can the SRI industry, through continued, competitive, and professional performance, and through the conscious application of ethical and social principles, change the rules so that the financial markets cease to be, as described by the former chairman of the Bank of Tokyo, "a kind of money game in which the funds available for potential investment chase around the world in search of the highest possible rates of return, with little relationship to the real economy"?

Can we create and promote investment opportunities that support productive public purposes? How can we prudently and profitably make our personal and organizational self-interest—our private gain, if you will—coincide with the public good?

| EPILOGUE

Since this speech was given a few months after the October 1987 crash, it is a useful benchmark. What it omits, the rest of this almanac will fill in. The growth of SRI has been dramatic and dynamic, and the Social Investment Forum has joined the ranks of many small organizations whose influence is far greater than their size or resources.

As recently as four years ago, the recurring question was, Is social investing just a fad? Today investors recognize that the answer to the question of whether we can ignore the social consequences of our financial decisions comes from neither morality nor ideology, but economics—real costs and lost opportunities. The local and national media cover social investing daily; meetings and conferences across the country have introduced the concept to thousands of professionals and the investing public; many of the largest brokerage houses now aggressively market social investment products; and corporations are eager to be recognized for exemplary performance in product quality, employment practices, philanthropic activities, or other aspects of their businesses that relate to the social good. Corporate social responsibility and social investing are here to stay.

Yet critical issues remain, and the legacy of this industry lies in their resolution. SRI had its origins in ethics and the religious stewardship of finite resources. It was, and for many continues to be, grounded in the principle that we, as investors, can no more suspend our values or morals when dealing with money than we can when dealing with any other important part of our lives. In the early 1970s a couple of portfolio managers tested that idea with a new investment approach; a research group exposed the social costs of certain corporate products and practices; and a bank set a new standard by measuring performance in two ways—social impact and financial return.

Social investment has entered the mainstream. Yet the gap between some of its rhetoric and the actual impact on sectors outside of the conventional Wall Street marketplace continues to be daunting. A few pension funds, national religious denominations, foundations, mutual funds, and community-based investment organizations are exploring solutions and testing pilot programs. If, however, the early SRI rallying cry "Doing well by doing good" is its only legacy, then we will have trivialized a historic international economic opportunity. The gap between a powerful new marketing tool for selling paper on the one hand and, on the other, ensuring measurable, long-term impact on people must be filled. Only then will social investing merit broad support from the hearts and minds—as well as the pocketbooks—of Americans and investors abroad and fulfill its extraordinary promise.

RESOURCES

PEOPLE AND GROUPS

Social Investment Forum Directors 1991

Bonnie Albion
Albion Financial Associates
2560 Ninth Street, Suite 209B
Berkeley, Calif. 94710
(415) 486-8333

Joan Bavaria
Franklin Research & Development
711 Atlantic Avenue
Boston, Mass. 02111
(617) 423-6655

Carol Coston, O.P.
Common Good Loan Fund
1320 Fenwick Lane, #600
Silver Spring, Md. 20910
(301) 565-0053

George Crocker
North American Water Office
P.O. Box 174
Lake Elmo, Minn. 55042
(612) 770-3861

Jerome L. Dodson
Parnassus Fund
244 California Street
San Francisco, Calif. 94111
(415) 362-3505

Marjorie Fine
North Star Fund
666 Broadway, Suite 500
New York, N.Y. 10012
(212) 460-5511

Carsten Henningsen
Progressive Securities Financial
  Services
5200 Macadam SW, Suite 350
Portland, Oreg. 97201
(503) 224-7828

Joan Kanavich
Acting Executive Director
Social Investment Forum
430 First Avenue North, Suite 290
Minneapolis, Minn. 55401
(612) 333-8338

Hugh Kelley
SRI Group, Inc.
Candler Building, Suite 622
127 Peachtree Street NE
Atlanta, Ga. 30303
(404) 577-3635

Elizabeth Kent Glenshaw
Loring, Wolcott & Coolidge
230 Congress Street
Boston, Mass. 02110
(617) 523-6531

Peter D. Kinder
Kinder, Lydenberg, Domini &
  Company
Seven Dana Street
Cambridge, Mass. 02138
(617) 547-7479

Jim Phillips
Progressive Asset Management
8489 West Third Street
Los Angeles, Calif. 90048
(213) 655-4277

Greg Ramm
Institute for Community Economics
57 School Street
Springfield, Mass. 01105
(413) 746-8660

Steve Schueth
Calvert Group
4550 Montgomery Avenue
Bethesda, Md. 20814
(301) 951-4820

John E. Schultz
Ethical Investments, Inc.
430 First Avenue North, Suite 204
Minneapolis, Minn. 55401
(612) 339-3939

Howard Shapiro
American Bank Building
621 Morrison SW, Suite 600
Portland, Oreg. 97205
(503) 222-6613

John Shapiro
South Shore Bank
7054 Jeffrey Boulevard
Chicago, Ill. 60649
(312) 753-5636

Frank Tsai
2426 Thirty-third Avenue
San Francisco, Calif. 94116
(415) 564-5956

TRADE SANCTIONS, ETHICAL INVESTING, AND SOCIAL CHANGE IN SOUTH AFRICA

Karen Paul Professor of Business Environment, Florida International University

Dominic Aquila Lecturer, Rochester Institute of Technology

Ed. Note: *An earlier version of this article, "Political Consequences of Ethical Investing: The Case of South Africa," appeared in* Journal of Business Ethics 7 (1988): 691–97, *copyright © 1988 by Kluwer Academic Publishers. That article was adapted with the permission of Kluwer Academic Publishers.*

Ethical investing and trade sanctions began as improvisary tactics more than a generation ago. Since then, institutional mechanisms have developed that systematically present moral and social demands to corporate managers, government officials who deal with

Dr. Karen Paul is professor of Business Environment at Florida International University. She received her Ph.D. from Emory University in 1974. She has published and presented widely on the subject of business ethics and business and public policy. Her current research interest in business and South Africa has taken her to South Africa on a Fulbright Fellowship. Paul was named a Radcliffe Peace Fellow for 1987–88. She is the editor of *Business Environment and Business Ethics: The Social, Moral, and Political Dimensions of Management* (Ballinger Press, 1987).

Dominic Aquila has been a full-time lecturer at the Rochester Institute of Technology since 1984. He received his M.B.A. degree from New York University in 1980 and is just finishing his Ph.D. in American history at the University of Rochester. Aquila was awarded the David Parker Memorial Prize in History by the University of Rochester in 1986.

trade and tax issues, and investors themselves. Corporations are being asked to use their capital, products and services, access to markets, and other resources to realize social objectives. The arena in which these demands have reached their most systematic development is in their use to oppose apartheid in South Africa.

| THE USE OF TRADE SANCTIONS

The use of economic force to oppose apartheid goes back to the system's early days. Apartheid usually is said to have been institutionalized in South Africa during the years following the 1948 election in which the National party assumed control of the South African government. However, removal of Indian nationals from property they owned, which was claimed by whites, dates from before this election.

In the early years international pressure came from the government of India through its objections to the treatment of Indian nationals in South Africa. In 1946 India imposed the first trade sanctions against South Africa. By the end of the 1950s, trade sanctions were being used to punish companies doing business in South Africa and to harm the economic status of the country, thereby perhaps in time influencing that government to abolish apartheid. One U.S. business leader, Walter Krieger, following a fact-finding mission to judge investment prospects in South Africa, concluded, "I wouldn't invest a dime in your country in its present circumstances," adding that South Africa had lost millions of dollars in potential U.S. investments because of apartheid.[1]

In May 1959 the African National Congress called for a boycott of South African potatoes. Picking up on the idea of using the boycott to pressure South Africa, African trade unions in the east African nations of Kenya, Uganda, Tanganyika, and Zanzibar announced a boycott of South African goods. At the end of 1959, Great Britain's largest labor organization, the Trades Union Congress, announced that its nine million members would boycott South African goods as a protest against apartheid. In Brussels the International Confederation of Free Trade Unions also called for a boycott of South African goods, at the same time condemning segregation in U.S. schools. The call for an international consumer boycott of South African goods was taken up in Sweden, the home of the newly elected head of the Brussels organization. Jamaica also ordered a boycott of all South African goods.

In 1960 the action moved to the local level in Great Britain when the Liverpool Municipal Council voted to boycott South African goods. In the United States, citizens' groups began to speak out against apartheid. The American Committee on Africa issued a Declaration of Conscience protesting white supremacy and racial discrimination in South Africa. The South African government responded that these protests were the work of left-wing circles.

| THE IMPACT OF SHARPEVILLE

On March 21, 1960, police opened fire on unarmed black demonstrators at a police station in Sharpeville, a town just south of Johannesburg. The protesters were objecting to a law requiring blacks to carry passes at all times, a measure that made it possible for the white authorities to maintain strict control over where blacks could live, visit, or even seek employment. This measure had resulted in the arrest and imprisonment of thousands of blacks each year and effectively kept most blacks out of urban areas where they might find jobs in the modern sector of the economy. Reports indicated that possibly fifty unarmed demonstrators had been killed by the police in Sharpeville and that more deaths had occurred in Langa, a black township in the Cape Town region.

In the next two months, foreign investors grew uneasy about their holdings in South Africa and withdrew about $64 million from the country. By the end of the year this sum was to grow to $224 million. Gold reserves of South Africa declined every week for the three months following the shootings and were down almost 50 percent by the end of the year. In the two months following the shootings, exporters lost $1 million as a result of boycotts, and they anticipated that $15 million more would be lost by the end of the year. The value of shares traded on the Johannesburg Stock Exchange had fallen sharply. For a developing country such as South Africa, foreign investment is absolutely required to build up modern industry and commerce, and exports are a vital source of funds from abroad.

South African businessmen began to speak out on the necessity that the government examine its race relations policies and reconsider its stand on apartheid. Leaders of the Johannesburg Stock Exchange spoke out, urging the government to reconsider how the status of blacks could be improved. In May five major business organizations sent delegations to the South African government, asking the prime minister to liberalize the country's policy toward blacks. They recommended that blacks no longer be required to carry identity passes, allowing blacks to move from rural areas to urban areas, the abolition of curfews for blacks, and legalizing the sale of alcoholic beverages to blacks. In response the government issued a statement by B. J. Vorster indicating that the businessmen "would be well advised to attend to their own affairs and leave the governing of the country in the hands of the Government."[2]

U.S. companies began to renew their investments in South Africa. Newmont Mining Corporation, a major holder in several South African mining companies, announced that it intended to expand its investments in that country by $30 million. General Motors, Ford, and International Harvester also announced that they intended to expand their facilities in South Africa. These actions were powerful signals that the outside world was again willing to look the other way, to give the South African government another chance, to put aside concern over the exploitation and repression of blacks.

| THE DEVELOPMENT OF ETHICAL INVESTING

In 1932 A. A. Berle and Gardner C. Means, in their influential book *The Modern Corporation and Private Property*, showed that modern corporations no longer were controlled by their owners. Corporations had been turned over to professional managers and in the process had become unaccountable to a specific, interested constituency. Formally the shareholders of the corporation are such a constituency, their mechanism of control being the elected board of directors. But in practice, as writers as ideologically apart as Peter Drucker and John Kenneth Galbraith argue, boards (usually identical to the slate that management has put up for election) have not represented the shareholders' interest, and shareholders, for their part, would sooner sell their interest in a company whose management they disapprove than challenge the management. Increasingly, over the past fifty-five years, writers, social activists, and labor leaders have tried to change these practices and to mobilize shareholders to exercise the control over management that proceeds from ownership.[3]

In 1934 the United States Congress provided the formal mechanism for shareholder participation in the major financial decisions of the country's publicly held corporations. In the process of creating the Securities and Exchange Commission (SEC), Congress declared that "fair corporate suffrage is an important right that should be attached to every equity security bought on a public exchange."[4] In 1942 the SEC broadened the meaning of suffrage by requiring companies to include shareholder resolutions in their proxy statements.

While the government was making sure that shareholders could play a more active role in corporate business, Wall Street and corporate managers tried to broaden the base of corporate shareholders. The New York Stock Exchange during the early 1950s began its "People's Capitalism" program, whose aim was "to make the great majority of American wage earners 'capitalists' and owners of common stock through the Wall Street mechanism."[5]

Around the same time, Charles Wilson, then president of General Motors, proposed to the United Auto Workers that General Motors create a pension fund for its workers that would hold mostly equity instruments. Heretofore pension funds held mostly credit instruments—government and corporate bonds and mortgages. Wilson's plan had workers invest, and hence become interested parties, in corporate growth. By the end of 1951, eight thousand new pension plans were written; all of them included Wilson's innovation. Pension funds quickly became the largest holders of American corporate stock—"the revolution no one noticed."[6] Worker ownership, the ever-elusive goal of socialists around the world, came to America silently, through the back door. But workers have shown little interest in exercising the control that comes with ownership. Indeed, in Drucker's words, "not one in a thousand seems to realize that through his pension plan he actually owns American business."[7]

Ironically, the first attempt to exercise control over a corporation came from outside the corporation, from people with only a small stake in the company's equity. In 1967 as a spontaneous tactic in their confrontations with Eastman Kodak over jobs and recognition for the poor blacks of Rochester, New York, Saul Alinsky and the community organization FIGHT purchased a few shares of Kodak stock in order to gain entrance into its shareholder meeting in Flemington, New Jersey. Alinsky's intent was to get national publicity for what had been mostly a local conflict. He was by his own admission interested in no other end. Yet his very opportunistic tactic made the corporation into a direct instrument of social reform and drew attention to the link between its ownership and control.[8]

"There are two kinds of social radicalism in America," says Paul Berman, "the conventional and the hip."[9] Those who subscribe to the former, like populists of the 1890s, educate, plan, and organize; those who prefer the latter, in fine Emersonian tradition, cultivate an eccentric, if ephemeral, critique of the mainstream. Before it becomes passé, the hip usually delivers a blow to society's received wisdom, and in so doing provides the conventional with new perspectives and opportunities. In this way, the hip radicals of the 1960s forced conventional radicals to see something as commonplace and upstanding as one's equity investments in a corporation in a brand-new light. Out of this new insight emerged the practice of ethical investing.

Alinsky straddled hip and conventional radicalism. He honed a caustic critique of the American establishment, yet he understood that using shareholder proxies to force corporate managers to discharge their social responsibility was a strategy with appeal to many members of the same establishment.[10] As letters of enthusiasm for his "proxies for people" organization poured into his offices, Alinsky waxed philosophical about the possibilities of shareholder activism. Still, Alinsky saw shareholders only as a countervailing power set against corporate managers and their loyal shareholders. He never discussed, for instance, the use of shareholder resolutions, the tactic that eventually became the centerpiece of the ethical investor movement.

Alinsky's conception, crude though it was, was a watershed in the history of shareholder activism. It was the first direct demand by well-organized citizens for a large corporation to solve a social problem. Heretofore such demands were made on the state. Moreover, he formulated a relationship between the citizen and the corporation that mirrored the relationship between the citizen and the modern pluralistic state.

Since the 1950s, to get a hearing from the state, citizens have had to identify themselves with an interest group, which makes its claim on the state on the citizens' behalf. The state acts as a broker of competing interests.[11] The corporation now finds itself at the center of competing claimant groups and, like the state, has assumed the role of a broker of interests.

Just after Alinsky provided the political framework for shareholder activism, a group of young lawyers formed the Project on Corporate Responsibility (PCR) and tested the mechanism for that activism—the shareholder resolution. In February 1970 PCR's founders called a press conference to announce Campaign GM. Those involved in the campaign presented nine resolutions to General Motors for inclusion in its proxy statements. Unlike prior resolutions, these addressed social issues—the demands of minorities, workers, and consumers. Arguing that these resolutions were inappropriate, GM initially refused to include them on its proxy statements. But after fourteen months of public debate, the SEC ruled that two of the nine resolutions had to be included. Neither resolution received the necessary 3 percent of the shareholders' votes in order for the resolutions to be reconsidered the following year. Although this has been the outcome of numerous shareholder submissions since 1970, the proxy resolution remains the favored mechanism for shareholder activism.[12]

Once the door had been opened to proxy resolutions directed at social reform, churches, foundations, universities, and some pension funds, many with significant equity holdings, began to submit similar resolutions. The National Council of Churches rejected shareholder activism as too radical in the late sixties, but in the 1970s it, along with various Catholic religious orders and the American Jewish Congress, submitted more proxy resolutions than other institutional investors.[13]

In 1972 the Interfaith Center on Corporate Responsibility (ICCR), an outgrowth of the National Council of Churches' Committee on Social Responsibility in Investments, was established in New York City. ICCR gained prominence through the central role it played in the boycott of Nestlé's products. Nestlé's marketing of infant formula to mothers in less-developed countries had violated the marketing code established by the World Health Organization. Nestlé was a Swiss multinational corporation, with no stock traded in the United States and therefore beyond the reach of the investors' pressure. For that reason, many Americans chose the boycott to protest Nestlé's unethical practices. In the same year, 1972, a group of major universities and foundations founded the Investor Responsibility Research Center in Washington, D.C., to study shareholder resolutions. Approximately 170 institutions now subscribe to its research services. Finally, John Simon and his associates in *The Ethical Investor* gave the movement a sense of urgency by arguing that under certain conditions, shareholders have a duty to submit resolutions to their fellow shareholders to correct irresponsible corporate policies.

The Council on Economic Priorities also was formed during this period. This New York–based organization, founded in 1969, has achieved considerable effectiveness in industry studies and reports on special topics of interest to consumers, activist groups, and public policy analysts. *Rating America's Corporate Conscience*[14] is a fairly recent compilation of assessments that gives the relative performance of 130 U.S. corporations on a variety of social dimensions, including investment in South Africa.

A new form of organizational pressure on corporations evolved in the mid-1980s. In 1985 Jesse Unruh, the state treasurer of California and a trustee of the two largest pension funds in California, led the formation of the Council of Institutional Investors. The council provides a forum where managers of more than forty institutional portfolios with combined assets of more than $200 billion discuss the economic and social performance of America's corporations.[15] Its efforts have focused mainly on challenging antitakeover, poison pill–type mechanisms adopted in the 1980s by a number of companies. However, this organization provides a new forum in which issues of ethical investing can be considered routinely and expectations of a key corporate constituency put forward.

| THE INSTITUTIONALIZATION OF ETHICAL INVESTING

Ethical investing has now developed to the point where individual conviction and concern have coalesced into a focused political movement with the requisite organizations, communication systems, and institutions. The organization of this movement, and especially its political impact, can be seen most clearly in the mobilization to challenge the South African government and to create pressure for the end of apartheid.

Divestment is the term used to refer to the requirement that portfolios be structured in a way that eliminates companies with holdings in South Africa, or companies that have performed poorly on the Sullivan Principles.[16] *Disinvestment* refers to the withdrawal of corporations from South Africa. Disinvestment has several facets. One is the withdrawal of new capital, either in the form of new corporate investment or in the form of capital available from banks that operate internationally.

In 1985 international banks withdrew the extension of further credit from South Africa, effectively cutting off the inflow of capital.

However, in 1987 they agreed to a restructuring of South Africa's debt and granted a restoration of credit, and no political demands were pressed by the banks. Another form of disinvestment is the selling off of operating units in South Africa by multinational corporations based in other countries. Yet another form is the cutting off of operations in South Africa completely, eliminating not only holdings but also trade. Only Eastman Kodak has adopted this latter policy, but it can be anticipated that if apartheid continues, the demands of the ethical investing movement will escalate so that not only eliminating holdings but also eliminating trade will become a demand in the future.*

State legislative bodies and municipalities have been presented with resolutions that restrict pension funds and other funds from investing in companies that place new investment in South Africa, or companies that rank poorly on the Sullivan Principles. The largest of these, California, began in January 1987 to restructure its investments so that $90 billion would be divested of companies doing business in South Africa by the end of 1990. Colleges and universities, unions, churches and religious groups, and some foundations also have been pressured to divest, and many of them have indicated their intent to do so, generally in a phased process.

Several investment funds have been marketed on the basis of their not having holdings in companies doing business in South Africa, for example, New Alternatives, Calvert Social Investment Managed Growth Portfolio, Pioneer, Pioneer II, Pioneer III, Pioneer Bond, Parnassus, Pax World, and Dreyfus Third Century. Conventional financial wisdom has it that restricting a portfolio in any way would limit the potential for maximizing return, but in practice this has not been the case in the issue of ethical investing insofar as the South Africa–free portfolios are concerned.[17]

Restrictions on portfolios that require that they divest themselves of stocks in companies doing business in South Africa have been challenged in the courts. In a recent test case the trustees of the Baltimore, Maryland, retirement system sued the mayor and city council in an attempt to overturn a 1986 divestment ordinance. The

*In the case of South Africa, another form of ethical investing exists on a theoretical level. This might be termed "contingent investing" and has been proposed by British Petroleum. This company has announced that it will contribute 100 million rand toward the reconstruction of District 6 in Cape Town provided that the government does whatever necessary to make it possible for this area to be developed as a racially mixed residential area.

trustees charged that compliance would violate their legal obligation to invest prudently and would subject the portfolio to unnecessary and substantial selling costs. As a parallel argument, they claimed that the city's divestment law was an intrusion on the federal government's constitutional role in conducting foreign affairs.

The courts upheld the divestment ordinance. Trial court Judge Martin B. Greenfeld ruled that the selling costs would not be significant and went on to state, "Even if the impairment were more significant, it would be insubstantial when compared to the salutary moral principle which generated the ordinance."[18] Furthermore, the judge held that the requirement did not impinge on the federal prerogative in conducting foreign policy. Previous Supreme Court rulings had held that such local laws were constitutional so long as they had only an incidental or indirect effect in foreign countries.[19]

| SANCTIONS

An associated political outcome of the ethical investing movement is the Comprehensive Anti-Apartheid Act of 1986, which mandates economic sanctions on South Africa. The Act prohibits new corporate investment in South Africa. The legislative approach to sanctions is particularly interesting because in most cases where the United States has imposed sanctions, it has been by executive order. Furthermore, the Act has several innovative features, including a projected tightening of sanctions after one year if substantial progress was not made toward eliminating apartheid. On the other hand, changes in South Africa would allow the sanctions to be eliminated by executive order, as they were in August 1991.

The cumulative, long-term, and interactive effects of ethical investing, divestment, disinvestment, and sanctions on South Africa are somewhat speculative at the present time. Indeed, the South African government initially stated that in fact sanctions might have positive effects, as the country proceeded toward economic self-sufficiency, "inward industrialization" (development of the domestic economy), and export replacement. However, through the 1980s, the South African consumer price index rose while real income per capita for South African workers (excluding blacks, who are nominally citizens of the "native homelands") fell.[20] Unemployment was high, and for the first time since the rural-urban migration following World War II, it became a problem for the white population as well as the nonwhite.

From 1984 through 1987, withdrawals of numerous multinational corporations occurred, and new international lending nearly stopped. The conditions of withdrawal have varied. Many companies retained licensing and distribution networks, while others sold their South African holdings to South African investors (often former managers of the multinational itself), and only one—Eastman Kodak—indicated an intent to cut off trade as well as investment. Although new loans were cut off, old loans were rescheduled.

The Johannesburg Stock Exchange prospered, however, with stock averages increasing sharply after the sanctions were imposed. Earnings for major companies were up, while economic concentration increased. The four largest South African corporations—Sanlam, Anglo-American, SA Mutual, and Rembrandt—now control at least 83 percent of the shares on the Johannesburg Stock Exchange. The value of the rand declined on international markets by over 50 percent from 1984 to 1986, but increased sharply in recent months, especially since March 1987, when banks restored international lending.[21]

The argument generally made for ethical investing, divestment, disinvestment, and sanctions was that these measures would isolate South Africa, cut its access to international markets, increase the cost of obtaining needed supplies, reduce or eliminate the import of capital, and in time create enough economic hardship so that the government would be forced to make concessions and eliminate apartheid. The changes in South Africa that occurred during the last years of the 1980s and the first of the 1990s surely were influenced by the gradual but progressive isolation of its economy. The sanctions were effective.*

| THE POLITICAL CONSEQUENCES OF ETHICAL INVESTING

The basic currency of government is legitimacy. The legitimacy of the present government in South Africa, and of the institution of

---

*This discussion of the economic and political dimensions of ethical investing does not treat the moral or philosophical basis of the movement, but rather it takes it as a given in the case of South Africa. Briefly, the most frequently used moral justification for divestment is that whatever the practical impact of this action, it is necessary to separate oneself from the kind of evil made manifest by apartheid. From this perspective, even if consequences other than those envisioned by the investor were to follow from ethical investing, it would still be the right thing to do.

apartheid, was in a steep decline among the population as a whole (although not necessarily the minority enfranchised) for several years prior to the election of F. W. de Klerk as state president in 1989. One contributing factor in the delegitimizing process is the moral suasion of the ethical investing movement. Any government whose citizens do not accept its legitimacy can still maintain power, but only with a high expenditure in surveillance, security, and the apparatus of state control. One political aspect of the ethical investing movement was to force the white communities of South Africa to assess the relative costs of maintaining control and maintaining apartheid or, alternatively, of instituting the kind of changes sought by blacks and their sympathizers.[22]

The basic legitimacy of the South African government came to be granted only among progressively narrower segments of the population. The approach of the whites-only election of May 1987 brought with it significant defections from the National party, including elected representatives of the party and its academic base at Stellenbosch University—the center of political thought and philosophy that gave apartheid its theoretical foundation—and prominent members of the Afrikaans press. The coloured and Asian populations, nominally included in the government since 1982, progressively withdrew their cooperation. A realization developed even in proapartheid circles that the maintenance of apartheid was going to involve greater and greater costs and more and more repression.

Another political effect of ethical investment is that it communicates a powerful message of progressive international condemnation. Cultural and sports boycotts created a situation in which South Africa was not permitted to participate in these types of activities in the international community. To a somewhat lesser extent, the same was true of international professional and scholarly associations. The withdrawal of multinational corporations from South Africa may not objectively have had a significant impact on local markets, but it intensified the feeling of vulnerability and isolation.

A third political effect of the ethical investing movement has been to challenge the most important suppliers of military goods to South Africa. The Comprehensive Anti-Apartheid Act of 1986 included the provision that suppliers of arms to South Africa would face sanctions in the form of reduced military aid. The main country to be affected by this threat was Israel, and, predictably, it resolved in March 1987 to cut off future arms shipments to South Africa.

This strategy of using indirect sanctions to extend the net of social control in the international community seems to have been an effective way of further isolating South Africa.

Finally, the signal that ethical investing has sent to the black population of South Africa can have a significant political impact during future years. If the end of apartheid comes, then it will have been good business from an economic viewpoint as well as from an ethical viewpoint for Western multinationals to have pulled out of South Africa.[23] It is possible that when power sharing or majority rule comes in South Africa, there will be little place for Western corporations. Perhaps capitalism will be renounced along with apartheid, and state-sponsored socialism will be instituted. In this case, those who have withdrawn from South Africa sooner rather than later, and under conditions that allowed for orderly planning with no risk of expropriation, will have made a good decision.

However, given the tendencies in other African nations, this path seems not quite so inevitable as it might have appeared a decade ago. There is a new appreciation for capitalism, even in the countries of the world that call themselves socialist. South Africa has the economic infrastructure to remain the central point for the economic development of the whole of southern Africa, particularly if change in apartheid comes sooner rather than later. Leaders of the African National Congress (ANC) have assured delegations from South Africa's white business community, from the black labor movement, and indeed from the U.S. government that there is a place for private enterprise in the future as envisioned by the ANC.[24]

However, it seems logical that this attitude would be somewhat contingent on the support or lack of support that Western multinationals have provided the present South African government. Paradoxically, what a corporation must do to transact business effectively under the current regime may be precisely the opposite of what should be done to prepare for the South Africa of the future, whether it turns out to be a capitalist or a socialist future. In this case, those speaking out for and working to implement ethical investing may be the best friends multinationals ever had in establishing the legitimacy of Western business for future participation in the economic affairs of southern Africa.

NOTES

1. "Racism Bars Capital, South Africans Told," *The New York Times*, July 10, 1956, p. 43.
2. "1,200 Face Curbs in South Africa," *The New York Times*, June 30, 1960, p. 3.
3. Drucker, *Unseen Revolution*.
4. Domini and Kinder, *Ethical Investing*.
5. Drucker, *Unseen Revolution*, 71.
6. Ibid., 7.
7. Ibid., 40.
8. Alinsky, *Rules for Radicals*.
9. Berman, "Politics of Hip," 33.
10. Alinsky, *Rules for Radicals*.
11. Lowi, "Public Philosophy"; Bachrach, *Democratic Elitism*; and Galbraith, *American Capitalism*.
12. Vogel, *Lobbying the Corporation*.
13. Ibid.
14. Lydenberg et al., *Rating America's Corporate Conscience*.
15. Heard, "Pension Funds."
16. Paul, "Sullivan Reporting."
17. See for example, Barrett and Ring.
18. The Baltimore case is discussed in detail in chapter 4.
19. Valentine, "Divestiture Law Upheld."
20. Innes, "Interest in Monopolies."
21. Ibid.
22. Savage, "Cost of Apartheid"; and Jenkins, *Economic Implications of Disinvestment*.
23. Sethi, "Beyond Apartheid."
24. O'Dowd, "South African Situation"; and Sampson, *Black and Gold*.

RESOURCES

PUBLICATIONS

Alinsky, S. D. 1971. *Rules for Radicals*. New York: Random House.

Bachrach, P. 1967. *The Theory of Democratic Elitism: A Critique*. Boston: Little, Brown.

Barrett, P. M. 1986. "Doing Good and Doing All Right: Investors Applying Ethical Values." *Wall Street Journal*, August 5.

Berle, A. A., and G. C. Means. 1932. *The Modern Corporation and Private Property*. New York: Macmillan.

Berman, P. 1985. "The Politics of Hip." *New Republic,* September 16 and 23.

Domini, A. L., and P. D. Kinder. 1984. *Ethical Investing.* Reading, Mass.: Addison-Wesley, p. 194.

Drucker, P. F. 1976. *The Unseen Revolution: How Pension Fund Socialism Came to America.* New York: Harper & Row.

Galbraith, J. K. 1952. *American Capitalism: The Concept of Countervailing Powers.* Cambridge, Mass.: Riverside Press.

Heard, J. E. 1987. "Pension Funds and Contests for Corporate Control." *California Management Review* 29(2):89–100.

Innes, D. 1987. "A Sudden Interest in Monopolies." *Weekly Mail,* March 13–19, p. 17.

Jenkins, C. 1986. *The Economic Implications of Disinvestment in South Africa.* Johannesburg, South Africa: South African Institute of International Affairs.

Lowi, T. 1967. "The Public Philosophy: Interest-Group Liberalism." *American Political Science Review* 61:5–24.

Lydenberg, S. D., et al. 1986. *Rating America's Corporate Conscience.* Reading, Mass.: Addison-Wesley.

O'Dowd, M. 1990. "Complexities of the South African Situation." *International Journal on World Peace* 1:25–41.

Paul, K. 1986. "The Inadequacy of Sullivan Reporting." *Business and Society Review* 57:61–65.

Ring, T. 1986. "S.A.-free Portfolios Down in '86." *Pensions and Investment Age,* March 9, p. 20.

Sampson, A. 1987. *Black and Gold: Tycoons, Revolutionaries, and Apartheid.* New York: Pantheon.

Savage, M. 1986. "The Cost of Apartheid." In *New Series #121.* South Africa: University of Cape Town.

Sethi, S. P. 1970. *Business Corporations and the Black Man: An Analysis of Social Conflict—The Kodak FIGHT Controversy.* New York: Harper & Row.

———. 1986. "South Africa Beyond Apartheid." Working paper no. SR-86-02. New York: Baruch College, Center for Management Development and Organization Research.

Simon, J., C. W. Powers, and J. P. Gunnemann. 1972. *The Ethical Investor.* New Haven, Conn.: Yale University Press.

Talner, L. 1983. *The Origins of Shareholder Activism.* Washington, D.C.: Investor Responsibility Research Center.

Valentine, P. W. 1987. "Baltimore Divestiture Law Upheld." *Washington Post,* July 18.

Vogel, D. 1978. *Lobbying the Corporation: Citizen Challenge to Business Authority.* New York: Basic Books.

ENVIRONMENTAL INVESTING: A SUGGESTION FOR STATE LEGISLATION

Christopher J. McKenzie

Few issues loom larger today than the problem of environmental degradation due to human activity. America has made considerable progress over the course of the past twenty years in reducing pollution from industrial sources. It also has seen the development of far-reaching and complex local, state, and federal regulatory structures designed to address this issue. Yet environmental irresponsibility continues in force worldwide, resulting in massive costs to life, property, and aesthetic values.

One of the many ways to encourage corporations to minimize their adverse effects on the environment is to require public employee pension fund trustees to consider the environmental responsibility of a company before investing capital in the securities of that company. Public pension funds control more than $700 billion of investment capital.[1] Their size allows these funds to exercise tremendous influence on corporate behavior. It also makes their investment policies an issue of great public importance.[2]

While a vast array of excellent articles has been written about divestment from corporations with operations in South Africa,[3] very little scholarship has emerged regarding the use of environmental criteria to make investment decisions. And what little has been written is relatively cursory.[4] This chapter attempts to fill that gap.

Christopher J. McKenzie is the editor of the *Columbia Journal of Environmental Law*, in which this chapter originally appeared.

It proposes state legislation that mandates that environmental criteria enter the investment process of public pension funds. In so doing, it seeks to promote the adoption of this legislation and to encourage corporate managers, who now enjoy considerable discretion in shaping and responding to social demands, to fulfill their social responsibilities at a time when action beyond current regulatory requirements is largely voluntary.[5]

The first part of this chapter defines environmental investing, explains how criteria are used to make investment decisions, and traces the development of social investing to the present, where social investment legislation is commonplace. Part II analyzes the three state legislative proposals that have, at this writing, been put forward and makes recommendations for future adoption. Part III examines the legal limitations that define the scope of environmental investing legislation by looking at its relationship to state law defining fiduciary obligations and by evaluating potential legal challenges based on federal law. Since no empirical evidence exists on the effects of environmental investing alone on portfolio performance, part IV bases much of its treatment of this issue on available analyses of other forms of social investing. Part V looks at some likely effects of the proposed legislation, if adopted. I conclude that environmental investment legislation is not only legally permissible, it is also a good idea that should be enacted into law.

I. ENVIRONMENTAL INVESTING AND PUBLIC PENSION FUNDS

"Environmental investing" is, very generally, the incorporation of environmental criteria into the investment decision-making process. As a form of "social investing,"[6] it benefits from being part of an investment strategy that has gained considerable support from the investment community over the last twenty years.

Social Investing

Most accounts of the development of the socially responsible investment industry as a major force begin in the early 1970s. At that time, religious groups commonly refused to invest in "sin stocks," securities of companies that manufactured tobacco or alcohol or that reaped profits from gambling.[7] In 1971 a number of religious groups joined to form the Interfaith Center on Corporate Responsibility and began voting proxies in blocks.[8] The first socially responsible mutual fund appeared as early as 1928,[9] but most of these funds appeared in the 1970s and 1980s.[10] In the mid-1980s popular support for the divestment of institutional funds from corporations doing business in South Africa transformed the socially responsible investment industry from a fringe activity into what is now a critical aspect of the money-management industry.[11] At that time, trustees of private mutual funds and state and municipal retirement funds began to pull investments out of "South Africa–related" companies, and even mainstream money managers offered "South Africa–free" investment plans.[12]

Today, various public pension plans, union pension plans, private mutual funds, and churches regularly use nonfinancial investment criteria in their investment decisions.[13] Many of these investors actually have divested their portfolios of certain securities for ethical reasons.[14] Social investing is now commonplace across the United States, and it will continue to greatly affect both investment trends and corporate activity in the 1990s.[15]

Environmental Investing

The first example of environmental criteria being used for investment decisions is the Pax World Fund, a mutual fund organized in 1970. Pax uses a number of criteria in its investment decisions, one of which is pollution control. At present there are five "environmental" funds on the *Barron's*/Lipper Gauge.[16] However, because of *Barron's* definition of an "environmental" fund,[17] this figure is misleading. A much larger number of funds actually use environmental criteria to make investment decisions.[18] Additional confusion may arise because of a distinction that is not included in *Barron's* definition.[19] Some "environmental" funds buy stocks according to the environmental services a company offers.[20] These "environmental sector" funds are not particularly socially or politically conscious and should not be confused with "green" funds.[21] Environmental sector funds do not examine the pollution records or policies of the companies whose stocks make up their portfolio so as to avoid the firms with poor environmental records.[22] Green funds, on the other hand, are funds that avoid investing in firms that pollute or that seek out firms with pollution control policies.[23] At present, two mutual funds consider only environmental and financial factors in making their investment decisions.[24]

Interest in the field of environmental investing is growing.[25] Financial advisers and investment managers involved in portfolio screening now claim that the environment has replaced South Africa as the most widespread ethical concern of investors.[26]

The Valdez Principles

One major step in the development of environmental investing was the introduction in early 1989 of the Valdez Principles. Authored by the Coalition for Environmentally Responsible Economies (CERES)[27] and modeled after the Sullivan Principles,[28] the Valdez Principles received their name from and were adopted shortly after the *Exxon Valdez* oil spill in Alaska on March 24, 1989. The Principles establish standards and procedures for evaluating the activities of corporations that directly or indirectly affect the earth's biosphere.[29] Such information is designed to aid investors in making informed decisions with regard to complex environmental issues.[30]

With the Valdez Principles, CERES intends to establish a voluntary mechanism of corporate self-governance that maintains business practices consistent with the goals of sustaining the natural environment for future generations.[31] Some writers claim that the Principles work by inducing companies to become signatories or risk losing investment dollars,[32] but this is not a stated mission of the code. Each signatory pays a first-year fee based on gross revenues and an annual administration fee, neither of which exceeds $15,000.[33] Then, each year, signatories complete an environmental report that is returned to CERES to be summarized and made available to the public.[34]

One of the main attractions to the Valdez Principles is their potential use by fund managers and individuals as investment criteria. Researching the environmental records of individual companies can be a complex and costly process, but it is more burdensome for smaller funds and individual investors than it is for large public employee pension funds. Once perfected and accepted by a critical mass of companies,[35] the Valdez Principles are likely to fulfill their intention to "help investors make informed decisions around environmental issues."[36] CERES will collect, monitor, and verify environmental compliance information so that social investors may use a signatory list as a simple test for environmentally responsible investment.

Opponents of the Principles have raised a number of criticisms.

Industry opposition has cited immediate adverse economic effects due to implementation costs, the nonexistence of an acceptable audit requirement, and the Principles' duplication of existing internal environmental programs.[37] But while these arguments may keep firms from signing, they do not discredit the Principles' utility when used by fund managers to judge environmental responsibility. Other criticisms include the vagueness of the Principles, the possibility that signatories will receive a disproportionate amount of negative media attention as compared with nonsignatories, and potential litigation arising from disclosure.[38] The problems identified by many of these criticisms would be addressed if an environmental investing statute were to consider whether a company is in compliance with the Principles rather than whether or not a company is a signatory.

The Use of Criteria in Environmental Investing

The Valdez Principles are only one example of a standard for evaluating the environmental responsibility of companies. Other criteria that might be used to make environmental investment decisions include pollution records;[39] the existence or efficacy of a company's policy for waste minimization; the existence or effectiveness of a company policy for employee and community information about toxic or hazardous materials used or manufactured by the firm; or a signatory list for a set of principles put forth by an industry association.[40] The severity of a given investment criterion may determine the degree to which environmental investing affects portfolio performance.[41] It also may determine its legality.[42]

Lacking an environmental screen using criteria that can be answered with a simple yes or no, environmental investing poses special problems for the investor.[43] Making decisions about the relative environmental soundness of different companies can be complex and difficult.[44] For example, certain industries pollute more than others, regardless of their managers' responsibility and diligence. Therefore, it is difficult to compare individual companies in different industries but easier to make these decisions within a given industry. Even when dealing with comparable companies, researching their environmental records often requires reporting and monitoring schemes, which are hard for both investors and individual companies to implement.[45] These difficulties argue for the desirability of a simple criterion, such as whether a company has signed the Valdez Principles.[46] They also point to the usefulness of a more thorough analysis, such as looking to see whether a firm complies with them.[47]

Once a set of criteria has been chosen, there are three ways in which those criteria can be used to make investment decisions.[48] The first is positive investment. This form of investment involves seeking out companies that have made exceptional strides on the environmental issues that concern the investor, thereby including only desirable companies in the portfolio.[49] For example, an investor concerned about waste disposal might invest in companies with progressive waste-reduction policies.

A second way in which an environmental criterion can be used is called negative investment. This kind of investing entails the avoidance or selling of stocks of companies that have products or practices incompatible with the values of the investor.[50] The South African divestment campaign is a good example of this kind of investment strategy.

Shareholder activism is the third way to invest with environmental principles. It involves creating change through filing shareholder resolutions and voting proxies.[51] This form of investing could mean including the securities of a company with an unattractive environmental record in order to exercise ownership rights to effect desired changes in corporate management behavior.[52]

| II. PROPOSED LEGISLATION

Current Developments

At this writing, interest in environmental investing, and, specifically, in using the Valdez Principles for this purpose, is growing.[53] For example, in 1990 major corporations, including American Express, Atlantic Richfield, Exxon, Kerr-McGee, and Union Pacific, were targets of shareholder resolutions requiring that the companies report on their compliance with the Valdez Principles.[54] The vote tallies were surprisingly high, ranging from 8.5 percent to 16.7 percent.[55] Their success is due at least in part to the votes of public pension and mutual funds, which are major shareholders in these companies.[56]

Among the proponents of the Principles are three public employee pension funds—the New York City Retirement System, California Public Employees' Retirement System, and California State Teachers' Retirement System.[57] Controlling large sums of investment capital, these funds are able to exercise considerable influence over the companies in which they invest.

Legislation requiring state fund managers to "give preference" to companies that are in compliance with the Valdez Principles has been introduced in New Jersey and New York.[58] California has passed a concurrent resolution[59] requesting fund managers to take shareholder action respecting the Valdez Principles. In addition, Connecticut, Michigan, and Wisconsin are reportedly studying the Principles, and several other states are known to be looking at the idea.[60] More than fifty cities, including New York, Los Angeles, and Philadelphia, also are researching the possibility of adopting the investment code for their pension fund assets.[61]

The Proposals
Four principal areas are covered by the New York and New Jersey bills and the California resolution. First is an investment preference for companies in compliance with the Valdez Principles. Second is shareholder action, in which the fund exercises shareholder rights in order to force the company to adopt the Principles. The next area is the use of environmental experts to determine a company's compliance with the Principles. Last, these legislative proposals include some reporting mechanism that allows the results of the first three activities to be compiled and updated. Both of the bills address all four of these items; the resolution deals only with shareholder action and reporting.

INVESTMENT PREFERENCE. An investment preference is exercised by the trustee of a state pension or annuity fund. Often more than one of these funds exists for state employees,[62] so a bill might address either a division of investment of a state treasury department, as does the New Jersey bill, or individual fund managers, as does the New York bill. The New Jersey bill describes the process as follows:

> When choosing corporations in which to invest the assets of any pension or annuity fund under its control, [the trustee] shall give preference to the stocks, securities or other obligations of corporations which have formally adopted and are complying with the Valdez Principles . . . or which are pursuing corporate policies which [the trustee] determines are in compliance with the Valdez Principles.[63]

While New Jersey's bill does not offer a definition of an investment preference, New York's bill does:

> When, after the various financial and other benefits of investing a portion of the assets of a fund in the stocks, securities and other obligations of two or more corporations have been estimated to be comparable, similar or approximately equal, the fund . . . invest[s] in the . . . corporation or corporations which have adopted or are in compliance with the Valdez Principles.[64]

New Jersey's failure to include a definition of preference could be seen as either a fiduciary shortcoming or an environmental benefit. As a fiduciary shortcoming, this absence leaves open the possibility of investment in companies with inferior financial records. The New York definition fills this gap by defining the preference as a nonfinancial means of making an investment decision between two financially comparable investments. Conversely, the absence of a definition could allow more leeway for a trustee to pursue environmental goals with the fund's resources.[65]

Neither of the bills requires divestment of any assets.

SHAREHOLDER ACTION. All three proposals include similar versions of shareholder activity as a means of encouraging compliance with the Valdez Principles. The New York bill explains that when a fund invests in a company that is not complying with the Principles,

> such fund shall, through formal written communications and through any other action deemed appropriate by such fund, encourage such corporation to comply with such Principles. Whenever feasible, such fund shall sponsor, cosponsor or support shareholder resolutions designed to encourage such corporations to adopt or to comply with the Valdez Principles.[66]

The California resolution merely requests its funds to consider using shareholder action to encourage adoption of the Principles and including the Principles "in the existing criteria for responsible voting of corporate shares owned by the [funds]."[67]

ENVIRONMENTAL EXPERTS. In the New Jersey bill, the State Investment Council, established by the original act in the Division of

Investment of the Treasury Department, is increased in size from ten to fifteen members.[68] All five of the new members must have experience or expertise in at least one of a series of environmental subjects. These subjects include environmental protection, environment science, land conservation, ecology, and waste management.[69]

Similarly, the New York bill directs the state comptroller to consult with the commissioner of environmental conservation before promulgating rules and regulations that "establish guidelines by which corporations shall be evaluated regarding their compliance with such Principles."[70] In addition to outlining investigation procedures, these rules and regulations presumably would set forth a rating system allowing trustees to rate the degree of compliance of individual companies.[71] The trustees may decide to use only their own compliance data or perhaps supplement their information with data published by CERES.[72]

ANNUAL REPORT. The New Jersey bill directs the State Investment Council to report on its compliance with the provisions of the act in its annual report to the governor, the legislature, and the state treasurer.[73] Similarly, the California resolution requires submission of proposed stockholder resolutions to the administrative board of the state pension funds.[74]

Providing much more specific guidance, the New York bill directs each of its pension funds to compile and publish an annual list of corporations in whose stocks, securities, or other obligations it has invested a portion of its assets.[75] Such a list must contain (a) information on whether each corporation has adopted or is in compliance with the Valdez Principles; (b) an assessment of whether corporations that have not adopted or are not in compliance with the Principles have taken significant action to comply with the Principles during the preceding year; and (c) information on whether the fund has taken any action to encourage each listed corporation to adopt or to comply with the Valdez Principles during the preceding year.[76]

RECOMMENDATION. A drafter of environmental investing legislation may desire to include less than all four of these elements in another bill or resolution, so as to more easily obtain bipartisan support in a state legislature.[77] A case in point is California's resolution. Merely calling for shareholder activism and minor reporting, it is the only legislation of this kind that has been passed. However, divestment is a far more effective way of achieving corporate environmental responsibility than are shareholder activism or investment preferences.[78] Therefore, divestment should at least be considered for legislative proposals, especially in cases where pursuing such a strategy will not harm the financial performance of the fund.[79]

The scheme used by the New York and New Jersey bills involves using investment preferences to choose new investments and using shareholder activism to request companies already invested in to comply with the Valdez Principles. A more effective strategy would be to employ investment preferences to choose new investments, specifying the degree of strictness of the preference in an unambiguous definition and then embarking on a careful policy of divestiture from irresponsible companies only after shareholder activism fails to influence irresponsible firms over a given period of time.

It would be wise to use an environmental selection criterion that includes enough relevant factors to be a meaningful test of the environmental responsibility of a firm. The criterion of compliance with the Valdez Principles certainly examines a considerable variety of matters relating to environmental responsibility,[80] but other guidelines, such as the factors used by the Franklin Research & Development Corporation,[81] would suffice.

The two remaining aspects of environmental investing legislation also deserve discussion. Implementation of an annual reporting provision like the one in the New York bill would require additional resources. But it would serve a critical role in monitoring the progress of the enactment. In addition, it would not be politically self-defeating, assuming compliance data were not released to the public.[82] For these reasons, it should be included in any proposal. Similarly, including environmental experts in the investment decision process is an easily implemented and effective way of helping trustees make informed decisions about compliance with investment criteria. Consequently, it is also an important element to include in any legislative proposal for environmental investing.

I III. LIMITATIONS ON ENVIRONMENTAL INVESTING BY PUBLIC PENSION FUNDS

State environmental investing legislation directs fiduciaries to employ nonfinancial factors in their investment decisions. As state legislation, it is not subject to an attack based on the violation of state common law on the subject of fiduciary duties.[83] It is nevertheless subject to a variety of relatively weak federal and state constitutional challenges and indirect trust law arguments.[84] All of these challenges are tempered by the fact that states have broad authority in dealing with their own funds.[85] Moreover, courts, wherever reasonably possible, will construe and apply statutes to avoid casting doubt on their constitutionality.[86] It should be noted that there is little case law dealing with challenges to social investing legislation and none addressing attacks on environmental investing legislation.

Impermissible Delegation

If a statute uses the Valdez Principles as an investment criterion and uses CERES's reports to determine which companies are environmentally responsible, it is subject to a challenge based on the argument that such reliance on the report of a private organization is an impermissible delegation of legislative power to a private entity. The reasoning is that delegation of legislative authority to private persons unaccountable to the general public is improper.[87]

The impermissible delegation argument is rarely successful. However, *Board of Trustees of the Employees' Retirement System v. Mayor of Baltimore*[88] is an example of one state court's willingness to apply the doctrine in certain circumstances. In that case, a city public employee pension fund's South Africa divestment statute was in issue. The court upheld the use of a private organization's list of companies "doing business in or with the Republic of South Africa."[89] The provision was upheld on the ground that the trustees of the fund were not bound by the organization's list.[90] It was "merely a reference."[91] According to the Court of Appeals of Maryland, there is no impermissible delegation when a legislature simply adopts a fixed standard promulgated by a private entity, because the entity's influence does not continue.[92] However, the adoption of a list that is subsequently revised by the private organization may constitute impermissible delegation.[93] Nevertheless, periodically revised standards may be used "in limited circumstances such as where the standards are issued by a well-recognized, independent authority, and provide guidance on technical and complex matters within the entity's area of expertise."[94] This language suggests that the use of a signatory list periodically updated by CERES may be permissible. As a project of the Social Investment Forum, composed of financial managers and experts in the field of social investing, CERES probably satisfies this standard.

By using only the guidelines that CERES created and not the private entity's research services, the bills proposed in part II completely avoid the impermissible delegation problem. These bills allow the trustees themselves, with the help of environmental experts, to determine whether a company is in compliance with the Principles. Further, the bills do not require companies to actually sign the code, but allow them merely to comply with it. By employing careful language, drafters of state legislation easily can steer clear of the impermissible delegation argument.

Contract Clause

If the environmental investment statute impairs obligations of the beneficiaries' pension contracts with the state, it may violate the contract clause of the United States Constitution.[95]

Analysis of a claim that a government action is invalid because it impairs contractual obligations involves a series of steps.[96] First, a contractual obligation must be found.[97] The court must then determine whether an obligation under that contract was impaired.[98] Last, the issue becomes whether the impairment violates the contract clause, "for it is not every modification of a contractual promise that impairs the obligation of contract under federal law."[99]

The threshold issue is whether any contractual duties exist for trustees or beneficiaries of pension plans.[100] State common law will usually determine whether pension plans create contractual duties toward persons with vested rights under the plans.[101] Statutes may also expressly recognize the existence of a contractual relationship.[102] Of course, if the court determines that no contractual obligations exist, then the contract clause is not violated.

The Supreme Court, in *Home Building and Loan Association v. Blaisdell*,[103] enunciated the constitutional standard for impairment of contracts: "The obligations of a contract are impaired by a law which renders them invalid, or releases or extinguishes them."[104] This constitutional prohibition is not absolute, because "the State also continues to possess authority to safeguard the vital interests of its people. It does not matter that legislation appropriate to that end 'has the result of modifying or abrogating contracts already in effect.' "[105] Despite the existence of a few more recent cases with broader readings of the contract clause,[106] the Supreme Court has remained reluctant, as it was in *Blaisdell*, to use the contract clause to invalidate state statutes.[107]

Since the state legislation proposed in part II does not alter the provisions in the pension plans concerning the amount of benefits a beneficiary is entitled to receive,[108] such an act does not directly change the state's pension contracts with the system's beneficiaries.

The statute may indirectly alter these contractual obligations by changing the manner in which the pension funds are invested.[109] Only an evidentiary inquiry can determine whether the ongoing costs of the statute will significantly jeopardize the amount or payment of defined benefits or future variable benefits.[110] Some changes are permissible: insignificant changes do not unconstitutionally impair the obligations of a contract.[111] In *Baltimore*, the trial court, after hearing extensive testimony, found the initial cost of divestiture to the beneficiaries to be so minimal that it did not even approach the constitutional standard for impairment.[112]

Another possible argument is that the contracts incorporate common-law trust duties of prudence and loyalty and that the statute alters those duties. For example, the *Baltimore* court agreed with the trustees that the pension contracts incorporated the trustees' fiduciary duties and assumed that "if legislation substantially alters those duties, the legislation should be viewed as changing the obligations of contract."[113] The trustees in that case did not convincingly prove such change.[114]

The duty of prudence provides that "In his management of the trust, the trustee is required to manifest the care, skill, prudence, and diligence of an ordinarily prudent man engaged in similar business affairs and with objectives similar to those of the trust in question."[115]

Although public pension funds are exempt from the Employee Retirement Income Security Act (ERISA)[116] as "governmental plans,"[117] some states nevertheless adopt the duty of prudence set forth in the act. ERISA's "prudent expert" standard is substantially similar to the standard set forth above, except that it assumes that the "prudent person" is "familiar with such matters."[118] In order to show an alteration of the duty of prudence, an opponent might allege that the statute substantially reduces the universe of eligible investments, thereby diminishing returns.[119] However, even under rigid divestiture programs, which are more radical than the New York or New Jersey bills, economically competitive substitute investments remain available,[120] allowing for the construction of a well-diversified portfolio that does not imprudently increase risk or decrease returns.[121] And as to the alteration of a trustee's management style, it cannot be said that there is a contractual right to a particular management style.[122] In addition, the existence of safeguards, such as the gradual introduction of the social investment strategy or a provision for suspensions, may help to ensure that environmental investing occurs only within the bounds of the trustee's duty of prudence.[123]

Another argument based on the duty of prudence is that by requiring the consideration of factors unrelated to investment performance, the statute alters that duty.[124] In the traditional formulation, the trustees' overriding purpose must be to provide the beneficiaries with their benefits.[125] Social considerations are permitted only if they have no adverse effect on the fund's finances.[126] This would appear to be the legal framework around which the New York and New Jersey investment preference bills[127] were drafted: opting for one of two investments with equal risk and return over the other based on a social preference would not offend the prudent investor rule.[128] But according to trust law experts and several courts, a trustee's duty is not necessarily to maximize the return on investments, it is to obtain a "reasonable" or "just" return while avoiding unnecessary risk.[129] Furthermore, by investing in businesses that exercise prudence in environmental matters, thus avoiding huge fines and long and costly liability disputes, trustees and drafters of legislation may reasonably believe that these businesses will best serve the beneficiaries' long-term interests and most effectively ensure the provision of future benefits.[130] As long as environmental investing results in competitive levels of risk and return, it does not alter the duty of prudence.[131]

The duty of loyalty also is established by state judicial decisions and statutes, which commonly adopt the ERISA formulation. A fiduciary must "discharge his duties with respect to a plan solely in the interest of the participants and beneficiaries and for the exclusive purpose of providing benefits to participants and their beneficiaries."[132] A challenger could argue that the environmental investing law alters the duty of loyalty by (1) requiring the trustees to consider the interests of the public rather than the interests only of the beneficiaries, and (2) directing them to invest the fund's assets for purposes other than merely providing benefits.[133] But where the costs of environmental investing are negligible, the obligation of loyalty can be reconciled with a trustee's taking the environmental implications of the fund's investments into account.[134] Alternatively, it can be argued that the duty of loyalty contemplates only the prohibition of transactions involving fiduciary conflicts of interest and not the consideration of social interests.[135]

Thus, the proposed form of environmental investing statute does not violate the strict common-law duties of prudence and loyalty. Furthermore, under the *Blaisdell* standard for impairment,[136] it can be forcibly argued that since the purpose of the proposed legislation is ultimately to safeguard the vital interests of state citizens, some modification of contractual obligations should be tolerated. Under any analysis, the proposed statute does not violate the contract clause.

Takings Clause

A takings clause attack of an environmental investing statute probably would be brought by beneficiaries. Assuming that the fund continues to deliver any defined minimum benefits,[137] the beneficiaries' only plausible argument would be that the initial and ongoing costs of such legislation reduce the pension fund's future earnings and thus the amount of their variable benefits,[138] amounting to a confiscation by the state. The state having taken their property without just compensation, the beneficiaries would be deprived of their constitutional right to due process under the takings clause of the Fifth and Fourteenth amendments.[139]

Beneficiaries' contractual right to receive benefits, if determined by state law to exist, may constitute property.[140] The drafter should under no circumstances assume the existence of these contractual rights. *United States Railroad Retirement Board v. Fritz*,[141] for example, upheld Congress's destruction of statutorily scheduled retirement benefits for a whole class of railroad employees. On the issue of the denial of retirement benefits that the plaintiff beneficiaries had spent years expecting and planning on, the Supreme Court unanimously held that there was no taking of property, "since railroad benefits, like social security benefits, are not contractual and may be altered or even eliminated at any time."[142] Professor Tribe notes that "for those who invest their time and toil in exchange for statutorily promised government pension benefits, 'the legislative determination provides all the process that is due.'"[143]

If property rights are found to exist and the fund neglects to deliver payments commensurate with the pension fund's earnings, then beneficiaries may be able to claim deprivation of a property right.[144] But a beneficiary's property interest in future benefits above any guaranteed minimum payments is not unconstitutionally taken in every instance where the fund trustees act in a way that might reduce those additional earnings.[145] As a general matter, unless there is a provision in the law to this effect, beneficiaries have no right to direct the investment of a pension system's assets.[146]

The Supreme Court has declined to develop any clear test for identifying a taking forbidden by the Fifth Amendment.[147] Instead it has conducted ad hoc factual inquiries into the circumstances of each particular case.[148] In *Penn Central Transportation Co. v. City of New York*, however, the court identified three factors having "particular significance."[149] They are (1) "the economic impact of the regulation on the claimant";[150] (2) "the extent to which the regulation has interfered with distinct investment-backed expectations";[151] and (3) "the character of the governmental action."[152]

The first two factors require an evidentiary inquiry into the degree to which beneficiaries are deprived of benefits they would otherwise receive in the absence of the statute.[153] Any provisions in the legislation that mitigate adverse impacts on benefits make the success of a takings challenge less likely.[154] If the legislation reduces defined benefits, beneficiaries may claim that the statute interferes with distinct investment-backed expectations. But the variable nature of anticipated future benefits above any guaranteed returns weakens an argument that loss of future profits interferes with distinct expectations.[155] The amount of interference necessary to constitute a violation of the takings clause is a matter for the court to decide. However, the evidence suggests that environmental investing will not significantly diminish benefits, if at all.[156]

Finally, in regard to the character of the government action, the proposed environmental investing legislation does not entail government appropriation of the beneficiaries' money for its own use or for the use of others. It attempts to promote the common good by regulating a pension system's investment policy. As stated by Professor Tribe, "government regulation—by definition—involves the adjustment of private rights for public benefit. To require compensation whenever the law curtailed the potential for economic exploitation 'would effectively compel the government to regulate by *purchase*.' It has long been recognized that such a regime would be unworkable."[157] Any reduction in benefits, which appears unlikely, is merely an incidental cost to these efforts and does not approach the kind of government action contemplated under the Fifth Amendment that requires compensation.[158]

Preemption

Another possible attack on environmental investing legislation could be that such a law is preempted by existing federal environmental laws. However, no federal statute exists that undertakes to regulate the investment of public monies in the securities of companies according to their level of environmental responsibility.[159]

There are three ways in which federal law preempts local law: (1) express congressional intent to do so,[160] (2) the existence of a scheme of federal regulation sufficiently comprehensive to occupy a given field or to make clear that Congress left no room for supplementary state legislation,[161] or (3) actual conflict of the state statute with federal law.[162] None of these doctrines applies to environmental investing legislation.

Moreover, in areas traditionally regulated by state and local governments, there is a strong presumption against finding federal preemption.[163] Since the state's proposed regulation of investments by its public employees' pension funds is arguably a matter of traditional local concern, the proposed statute enjoys this presumption against federal preemption. Therefore, a drafter need not work around a possible challenge on these grounds.

Commerce Clause

One other potential legal limitation on environmental investing legislation is the "dormant" or "negative" commerce clause. According to that doctrine, state regulations substantially affecting interstate commerce are impermissible. But by falling within the "market participant" exception, the state may be excepted from the scrutiny of the dormant commerce clause.

When a state government acts as a buyer or seller in a market rather than in its distinct governmental capacity, its behavior is not subject to the limitations of the dormant commerce clause.[164] Just as a private merchant may elect to deal with certain companies on the basis of their environmental responsibility, so may a state pension system make the same choice unhindered by the constraints of the negative commerce clause.[165] The limits of the market participant exception were delineated in *South-Central Timber Development, Inc. v. Wunnicke*:[166] "it allows a State to impose burdens on commerce within the market in which it is a participant, but ... the State may not impose conditions ... that have a substantial regulatory effect outside of that particular market."[167] Through its ownership of corporate securities, the state retains a continuing proprietary interest[168] in the firms in which it remains invested. By engaging in these ongoing commercial relationships and dealing only in the securities market, a state adopting an environmental investment statute falls within the market participant exception to the dormant commerce clause.[169]

In cases where the market participant exception does not apply, the proposed state legislation is subject to dormant commerce clause scrutiny under the Supreme Court's test in *Pike v. Bruce Church, Inc.*:[170] "Where the statute regulates evenhandedly to effectuate a legitimate local public interest, and its effects on interstate commerce are only incidental, it will be upheld unless the burden imposed on such commerce is clearly excessive in relation to the putative local benefits."[171] The court clarified when this standard applies in *Maine v. Taylor*,[172] noting that the appropriate standard to be applied depends on whether the statute's effect on interstate commerce is incidental or whether the statute affirmatively discriminates against interstate transactions.[173]

The proposed environmental investing statute neither facially nor in purpose favors residents of the state over residents of any other state.[174] Therefore, the question becomes whether the incidental burden on interstate commerce, if any, caused by the investment policies in the statute are "clearly excessive" in relation to the state's legitimate local interests.[175] A state's regulation of its own employees' pension funds is arguably a local interest appropriately addressed by the state. Whatever burden the investment guidelines adopted in the statute exert on the interstate sale of securities must be weighed against such compelling local interests. Given the financial evidence available, it is doubtful that even a powerful environmental investing statute with a reasonable divestment strategy would burden the securities market enough to be characterized as "clearly excessive" when compared with these local interests.

IV. THE EFFECT OF ENVIRONMENTAL INVESTING ON PORTFOLIO PERFORMANCE

No empirical studies have been conducted specifically on environmental investing. Therefore, all of the conclusions about the effect of environmental investing on portfolio performance must be drawn by analogy to studies on the effects of social investing in general and South Africa–related divestment in particular.[176] Information on socially screened mutual, money market, and trust funds, which use various investment criteria, including environmental responsibility, indicates that social investing can produce solid financial performance.[177] Similarly, according to the data on South Africa divestment, a portfolio may suffer no adverse effect from excluding all South Africa–related stocks.[178]

An environmental investment strategy may affect a portfolio in several ways. These aspects include composition, risk and return, transaction, liquidity and administrative costs, and management style.[179]

Composition, Risk, and Return[180]

The core of the composition issue is whether narrowing the range of potential investments by excluding a class of companies in the securities market will impede the construction of a viable portfolio.[181] Any investment strategy, other than "buying the market" according to an index scheme, reduces portfolio diversity to some extent, because it narrows the universe of potential investments.[182] Ultimately the social investment strategy's impact on portfolio composition depends on the number of stocks excluded, the kinds of stocks excluded, the operating and financial characteristics of included and excluded stocks, and whether excluded stocks have common characteristics that would irreversibly distort portfolio composition.[183]

There are two facts that suggest that composition will not suffer as a result of environmental investing. First, the universe of securities available to portfolio managers is huge.[184] While the strictness of the environmental criteria used to exclude companies will determine to what extent composition is affected, risk and return may not be harmed.[185] Second, very few industries or classes of companies are automatically excluded by a potent environmental investing strategy, namely chemicals, specialty chemicals, automobiles, and mineral extraction.[186] After eliminating these industries, the vast array of "clean" firms remaining is more than adequate to construct a well-diversified portfolio.[187]

The studies of South Africa–free portfolio performance found that South Africa–free portfolios were higher both in risk and in return than their unconstrained counterparts.[188] Adjusting these higher risk levels to equal the risk levels of unconstrained portfolios, researchers found that South Africa–free portfolios actually outperformed unconstrained portfolios by about twenty basis points[189] per year.[190] This is a significant margin when it is considered that performance represents annual return on the investment of billions of dollars in public pension funds. In summarizing the results of all of these studies, one set of authors concludes that in the area of portfolio risk and return, "South Africa–free portfolios can compete effectively with unconstrained portfolios because South Africa–free portfolios do not sacrifice return or increase risk."[191]

The data regarding social investment in general indicate that mutual funds using multiple screens, including the environment, have performed better, the same, and worse than unrestricted portfolios, depending on which fund is examined and over what time period.[192] Although almost all mutual funds performed poorly in 1990, most screened funds remained at or above the benchmark indexes—the Standard and Poor's 500 Index (S & P 500) and the Lipper equity fund average.[193] While three- or five-year results are more useful than a one-year perspective, some of these funds are too new to produce such a record.[194] Of the funds that have been around long enough, all but a few performed better or equal to the Lipper three- and five-year averages last year.[195]

Under one version of modern finance theory, the method of portfolio selection, whether it be by social criteria or otherwise, will have no effect on the portfolio's expected or average return if one ignores administrative costs, because "stock picking" is futile, and every stock of the same risk class is an equally good investment.[196] Assuming this theory is accurate, it tends to explain the competitive performance of social investing.

One very promising development with respect to the performance of socially screened portfolios is the Domini Social Index (DSI). Designed to represent the market of stocks most social investors buy from, the DSI acts as a standard by which to measure the performance of socially screened portfolios, just as the S & P 500 represents the market of large capitalization stocks most investors buy from.[197]

The DSI is a multiscreened, four hundred–company common stock index that, because of its screens, eliminates about 250 of the stocks that make up the S & P 500.[198] But despite their differences in composition, the returns of the DSI and the S & P 500 are very closely correlated, the former outperforming the latter in some months and underperforming it in others.[199] This similarity is based on approximately one year of actual performance data and about four years of backtested results.[200]

One difference between the two indexes is that the DSI appears slightly more volatile than the S & P 500, meaning that it dips somewhat lower in a down market and peaks somewhat higher in an up market.[201] When compared with the S & P 500, the DSI's stocks are slightly smaller, though still large, in terms of market capitalization, and this is one explanation for the increased volatility.[202] Although admittedly preliminary, these data suggest that there is no reason why an actively managed, multiscreened portfolio of large capitalization stocks should underperform the market.

But these data do not show definitively that funds using only environmental criteria to exclude stocks can achieve equivalent levels of risk and return. Differences in the size or other characteristics of firms whose stocks make up the environmental portfolio could produce different results. For example, a South Africa–free investment strategy tends to exclude many large firms, thus including more stocks from small firms in the portfolio.[203] Curiously, studies of this "small stock bias" show that the stocks of small firms tend to earn higher rates of return than would be expected.[204] This trend works in favor of South Africa–free portfolios. However, if environmental investment strategies are designed so that they produce less favorable effects on composition, the performance of the funds using these strategies may suffer.[205]

If environmental investors can track the market as the DSI does, or at least mimic the composition characteristics of other forms of social investing, then there is no reason to suspect that environmental screens will have any significant deleterious effects on risk and return.[206] The challenge for the investment manager of a fund using environmental criteria is to balance the need for a strategy that has enough bite to exert a positive effect on the firms whose stocks are held with the requirement that the strategy not impermissibly sacrifice return. The strategies put forth in the New York, New Jersey, and California bills do not require the exclusion of any potential investments.[207] They are therefore unlikely to affect portfolio performance. However, it remains to be seen whether conservative initiatives like the California resolution, or even the investment preferences in the other bills, will have the desired significant positive effects on industry.

Transaction, Liquidity, and Administrative Costs

In a fund pursuing an environmental divestment strategy, transaction costs are incurred first when the fund sells stock of companies that do not meet its environmental guidelines, and again when stocks of responsible companies are purchased as replacements.[208] Repeated transaction costs also may occur because of peculiarities in the way an environmental portfolio is managed,[209] such as a preference for large or small transactions. Studies have shown that the transaction costs of South Africa–free portfolios are smaller than had been previously expected.[210] No data are available on the size of these costs in environmental investing.

Liquidity costs, which are effects on price resulting from trading activities, are incurred when investors influence a stock's price by either buying or selling a large portion of the stock.[211] Liquidity costs could feasibly be affected by a fund's environmental investing strategy, thereby affecting return. But since no quantitative evidence exists on the effects of social investing on these costs, no definitive conclusions can be drawn as to how they will be affected.[212]

Administrative costs include the expenses of relying on security analysts to investigate the return prospects of stocks, compiling data and issuing reports, monitoring the environmental activities of firms, and organizing shareholder action.[213] They also include governmental fees, interest charges, taxes, fees and expenses of independent auditors and of legal counsel, and a host of other expenses.[214] Available estimates of the actual costs of environmental screening are quite low.[215] And of this amount, what percentage should be assigned to purely social criteria? Today's financial analyst cannot appraise a company without considering its potential environmental liabilities, and even lenders conduct environmental assessments because they have been drawn into the liability picture.[216] Therefore, it would be misleading to label all environmental research costs as social research costs, as many of these expenses would be incurred in the absence of any social agenda.

As a general matter, the larger and more actively managed the portfolio, the more likely that divestment will increase liquidity and transaction costs, thereby adversely affecting performance.[217] Because state public employee pension funds tend to be large,[218] these increased costs could become significant. On the other hand, a fund with a more passive than active management style[219] probably will incur only minimal transaction, liquidity, and administrative costs.[220]

I V. PRESUMED EFFECTS OF ENVIRONMENTAL INVESTMENT LEGISLATION

There are many foreseeable results of the proposed legislation. As previously explained, negative investment effects on individual funds are unlikely, as are successful attacks on the legality of the proposed laws. There are several other possible consequences that deserve attention. These include effects in the financial management industry, effects on the likelihood of passage of similar legislation in other states, economic effects on companies induced to adopt environmentally responsible policies, and environmental effects from changes in corporate practices.

In the financial management industry, the recent trend toward acceptance of the social investing concept[221] will be heightened by passage of environmental investing legislation. Such laws will allow fiduciaries to follow, rather than lead, others into an area of uncertain legality.[222] The passage of these statutes also should give environmental investing the boost it needs to become, as have other forms of social investing, a major force for change. If such legislation employs the Valdez Principles, it also will lend credibility to those guidelines and perhaps spur some firms into becoming signatories.

With regard to legislative developments, after one or a few states join California in its pioneering initiative, still other states will be encouraged to follow suit. Similarly, cities and municipalities may find opportunities to put forward their own ordinances. And by rallying public support for the environmental investing idea, these state and local measures could lead to the passage of federal legislation. Federal efforts might involve the regulation of all investment institutions or only federal employee pension plans, both of which would be based on Congress's powers under the interstate commerce clause[223] and, presumably, on the model of state initiatives.[224]

Extremely poor voter support for environmental ballot initiatives in November of 1990[225] may lend support to the notion that when the economic climate is poor, people are reluctant to spend for the environment. If the economic slump persists, some of the less environmentally responsible companies that are forced to adopt measures that are costly in the short run could be hard hit by environmental investing legislation. But over the long term, making these changes can save these firms a great deal of money in manufacturing costs as well as in regulatory fines and cleanup expenses.[226] In the words of Gray Davis, controller of the state of California, "The first kid on the block to embrace these principles will increase market share and profit substantially."[227] Thus, in the long run, adverse economic effects on companies due to positive changes in industrial hygiene and the like do not appear substantial.[228]

One uncertain yet possible effect of environmental investing statutes is that pension funds may experience difficulty obtaining insurance to protect beneficiaries from suits over the funds' investment practices.[229] If obtaining fiduciary liability coverage does become a problem, most likely it will be due to legal uncertainties in the area of social investing.[230] The passage of environmental investing statutes will help to clarify these legal uncertainties.[231]

Finally, we must consider the social effectiveness of environmental investing legislation. Still in its infancy, the environmental investing idea has hardly been tested. When enacted, environmental investing laws will embody a social consensus that investors are unwilling to use their capital to support destruction of the environment. The degree to which levels of pollution and other measurable effects on the physical environment are affected will depend both on the number of such statutes adopted and on the strictness of the legislation that is passed. Environmental investing will require extensive participation from governments, institutions, individuals, and money managers in order for it to make the impact that the current regulatory regime has, in many respects, failed to achieve.

I CONCLUSION

Huge sums of investment capital in state public employee pension funds create the opportunity for tremendous influence on corporate behavior in the area of the environment. Now is the time to take advantage of this opportunity. After twenty years of development, the concept of social investing has gained considerable acceptance in the investment community. The idea has been tested by individuals, institutions, and public and private pension funds in the context of divestment from companies doing business with South Africa, and the results are encouraging. Through legislation, state public pension funds can exert preferences for companies that are environmentally responsible by subjecting the potential pool of stocks to environmental responsibility criteria. I have shown that such legislation can be implemented without any serious legal challenges or negative effects on portfolio performance. Three states have taken this initiative; one succeeded, another experienced a setback, and the third is still trying. This chapter suggests that other states follow suit. The quality of our air, water, and soil demands it.

NOTES

Ed. Note: *The endnotes to this chapter amount to the first thorough bibliographical essay on socially responsive investing and its legal consequences. The case materials may be found in almost any courthouse law library and certainly any law school library. A full selection of legal treatises and law journals usually is available only in the latter. Those wishing to decode the citations should consult* A Uniform System of Citation *(commonly referred to as "the Blue Book"), published by the Harvard Law Review Association, Gannett House, Cambridge, Massachusetts 02138. It will be found in bookstores serving law students.*

1. The most recent estimate of the total amount of investment capital controlled by public employee pension funds is $734.2 billion. Telephone interview (Mar. 28, 1991) with Michael Clowes, editor of PENSIONS & INVESTMENTS (considered to be the biweekly bible of the investment industry). Another, less recent, source put the total at $700 billion. *See* Dolan, *Social Investing: Pressure Grows to Pump Pension Money into "Worthy" Causes,* 31 AARP BULLETIN, Oct. 1990, at 17.

As of April 1985, the estimated asset value of public employee pension funds was $340 billion, representing 18 percent of U.S. publicly traded stocks, while university endowment funds were estimated at $40 billion (2 percent) and corporate and union pension funds at $980 billion (52 percent). Jerry & Joy, *Social Investing and the Lessons of South Africa Divestment: Rethinking the Limitations on Fiduciary Discretion,* 66 OR. L. REV. 685, 731 (1987) (citing Smith, *American Stocks Shrug Off Anti-Apartheid Pressure,* WALL ST. J., Apr. 30, 1985, at 34, col. 1). Combined, these three types of funds comprised 72 percent of publicly traded stocks. One source estimated the total combined assets of public and private pension fund assets in the late 1980s at $2.3 trillion. E. JUDD, IN VESTING WITH A SOCIAL CONSCIENCE 11 (1989).

The growth in size and importance of pension funds is demonstrated by comparing more recent figures with those in 1980. In that year, public and private pension funds combined totaled only just over $550 billion, which translated into ownership of about 25 percent of all publicly traded stock and control of around 40 percent of all debt capital in the United States. Troyer, Slocombe & Boisture, *Divestment of South Africa Investments: The Legal Implications for Foundations, Other Charitable Institutions, and Pension Funds*, 74 GEO. L. J. 127, 154, n. 98 (1987) (citing McCarroll, *Socially Responsible Investment of Public Pension Funds: The South Africa Issue and State Law*, 10 REV. L. & SOC. CHANGE 407 [1981]).

2. Troyer, Slocombe, & Boisture, *supra* note 1, at 154. *See* Murrmann, Schaffer, & Wokutch, *Social Investing by State Public Employee Pension Funds*, 35 LAB. L. J. 360, 366 (1984); Lynn, *Investing Pension Funds for Social Goals Requires Changing the Law*, 53 U. COLO. L. REV. 101, 114 (1981).

3. For an excellent list of sources dealing with South Africa divestment and social investment generally, *see* Jerry & Joy, *supra* note 1, at 687–88, n. 5.

4. *See, e.g.*, A. SIMPSON, THE GREENING OF GLOBAL INVESTMENT, Economist Publications special report no. 2108 (1991) (dealing mainly with environmental issues in the European investment industry); Goldinger, *Investing in the Earth*, USAIR, Nov. 1990, at 18 (a short article geared toward individual investor interest in mutual funds); Current Development, *The Valdez Principles: A Corporate Self-Governance Code on Environmental Conduct*, 2 GEO. INT'L ENVTL. L. REV. 237 (1989) (a brief discussion of Valdez Principles).

5. *See* Silverstein, *Managing Corporate Social Responsibility in a Changing Legal Environment*, 25 AM. BUS. L. J. 523, 566 (1987) (encouraging early perception of and imaginative responses to potential legal problems by corporate managers in order to avoid more costly and burdensome regulation in the future.)

6. Social investing is simply the incorporation of social or ethical criteria into the investment decision-making process.

7. JUDD, *supra* note 1, at 10; *Franklin Research & Development Corporation*, Harvard Business School publication no. 9-390-027, at 3 (1989) (hereinafter *FRDC*]; Proffitt, *Ethical Investment Funds Proliferate, Set Tenor for Social Investing in the 1990s*, IRRC NEWS FOR INVESTORS, Dec. 1990, at 233, 235.

8. *FRDC, supra* note 7, at 3.

9. The Pioneer Fund was the first mutual fund designed specifically to accommodate the social objectives of religious groups. JUDD, *supra* note 1, at 10; Proffitt, *supra* note 7, at 235.

10. *See* Dunnan, *Investing in Good*, A.B.A. J., Aug. 1990, at 102; Proffitt, *supra* note 7, at 236–37.

11. JUDD, *supra* note 1, at 11; Harvey & Conner, *South Africa Turmoil Spawns Social Investment Growth Industry*, STRATEGY WEEKLY (a publication of Prudential-Bache Securities), Feb. 28, 1990, at 29; Sypher, *Some Investors Seek Clean Yields*, BURLINGTON FREE PRESS, May 17, 1987, at E1, col. 1; Bromberg, *Social Investing: The Good Guys Finish First*, BUS. & SOC'Y REV., Fall 1988, at 32.

12. JUDD, *supra* note 1, at 11; *FRDC, supra* note 7, at 3–4; Murrmann, Shaffer & Wokutch, *supra* note 2, at 361. An example of a mainstream money-management firm offering South Africa screens for its clients is The Boston Company, which offered its SAFE (South Africa Free Equity) Index. JUDD, *supra* note 1, at 11.

13. Currently about $625 billion are invested using ethical criteria by public and private pension funds, mutual funds, and individual portfolios, up from about $40 billion just seven years ago. Wang, *You Can Be Clean and Green by Investing in Ecology, Peace and Social Harmony and Still Finish First*, MONEY, June 1991, at 130.

The capital invested in socially screened mutual, money market, and trust funds totals just over $8 billion, a small fraction of the $625 billion figure. Proffitt, *supra*, note 7, at 238. More than 80 percent of this $625 billion screened assets total is controlled by institutional investors, like public pension funds, many of which are required by law to screen for South Africa connections. *Id.* *See also infra* note 15.

14. Playing leadership roles in the South Africa divestment trend were the retirement funds for the states of New York, California, Wisconsin, and Minnesota and the cities of Washington, Philadelphia, and New York. JUDD, *supra* note 1, at 11; Wise, *City Pension Fund Upheld on Anti-Apartheid Policy*, N.Y. L. J., Mar. 20, 1986, at 1, col. 3; Williams, *In Support of Azania: Divestiture of Public Pension Funds as One Answer to United States Private Investment in South Africa*, 9 BLACK L. J. 167, 178 (1985); Dobris, *Arguments in Favor of Fiduciary Divestment of "South African" Securities*, 65 NEB. L. REV. 209, 217–18 (1986). For a more detailed discussion of several state and local divestment initiatives, see Note, *The Constitutionality of State and Local Governments' Response to Apartheid: Divestment Legislation*, 13 FORDHAM URB. L. J. 763, 773–78 (1985).

15. Harvey & Conner, *supra* note 11, at 29. The extensive influence of the social investment industry is evidenced by the following data, compiled in February 1990:

- Mutual and money market funds claiming to be socially conscious investment vehicles (all including South Africa–related guidelines) managed an estimated $7.6 billion, up from $5.5 billion two years previously.
- A total of twenty-five states had passed legislation placing restrictions on the investment of public funds in firms with business ties in South Africa. These states accounted for over half of the $700 billion in tax-exempt state government employee benefit funds.

- At that time, seventeen counties and seventy-three cities had placed South Africa–related restrictions on the management of their funds.
- Major universities, labor unions, and private endowments were following suit, and demand for South Africa–free portfolio management by individual investors was growing steadily.

Id. at 29–30.

More specifically, these data demonstrate the institutionalization of the Sullivan Principles in the investment community. *Id.* at 30. Developed in 1977 by the Reverend Leon Sullivan, these principles served as a means to guide corporate behavior in South Africa. *Id. See* Weedon, *The Evolution of Sullivan Principle Compliance*, Bus. & Soc'y Rev., Spring 1986, at 56; Williams, *supra* note 14, at 176. Entities that subscribe to the principles agree to an annual evaluation of their efforts to positively affect the quality of life of "Blacks, Coloureds, and Asians" in and out of the workplace and to promote a more democratic government. *Id.* The Principles have been formally incorporated into many state and local South Africa–related investment laws and regulations. Harvey & Conner, *supra* note 11, at 30.

Twelve states have similar legislation related to the MacBride Principles governing corporate activity in Northern Ireland. Melcher, *Social Investing: The Changing Face of the Investment Community*, Strategy Weekly, Feb. 28, 1990, at 28.

The interest in social investing is so widespread that a national nonprofit professional association was established in Boston in 1981 and incorporated in 1985. The seven hundred–member Social Investment Forum is made up of money managers, brokers, bankers, analysts, and other social investors. It encourages social investing and serves as a clearinghouse of information on the subject. *See generally*, Social Investment Forum, Social Investment Services: A Guide to Forum Members (May 1, 1990, ed.).

16. Barron's, Nov. 12, 1990, at M38. The Barron's/Lipper Gauge is a relatively comprehensive list of mutual funds that provides financial performance information for each listed fund.

17. Barron's defines an "environmental" mutual fund as a fund that "invests at least 65% of its portfolio in stock and convertible securities of companies contributing to a cleaner environment, such as waste management and pollution control firms." Barron's, Nov. 12, 1990, at M41, col. 4. These five funds are: Fidelity Select Environment Fund, Freedom III Environmental Fund, Oppenheimer Global Environment Fund, Schield Progressive Environmental Fund, and SFT: Environmental Awareness Fund. *Id.* at M42–61.

18. *See, e.g.*, Social Investment Forum, Socially Responsible Mutual Funds, Aug. 1990 (unpublished information compiled from fund prospectuses) (hereinafter SIF information).

19. Proffitt, *supra* note 7, at 238.

20. Examples of such services include garbage and hazardous waste removal, paper recycling, pollution control response, water technology improvements, and alternative energy sources. *See* Dunnan, *supra* note 10, at 104. For a discussion of the growing profitability of companies offering these services, *see* Heller, *Know-How Cleans Up*, CHEMICAL WEEK, May 2, 1990, at 26.

21. Dunnan, *supra* note 10, at 104; Rauber, *The Stockbroker's Smile*, SIERRA, July–Aug. 1990, at 18–19.

22. *See* Fenn & Opheim, *Environmental Sector Funds*, IRRC INVES-TOR'S ENVTL. REP., Winter 1991, at 11. In addition to the Fidelity Select, Freedom III, and Oppenheimer Global funds, *see supra* note 17, the Alliance Global Environment Fund, Kemper Environmental Services Fund, and Merrill Lynch Environmental Technology Trusts 1 and 2 are of the "environmental sector" variety. *See* Dunnan, *supra* note 10, at 104; Fenn & Opheim, *supra*, at 10; Proffitt, *supra* note 7, at 245.

23. The green funds, other than Progressive Environmental and Environmental Awareness (*see supra* note 17) are: New Alternatives Fund (equity fund), Pax World Fund (balanced stock and bond fund), Parnassus Fund (equity), Calvert-Ariel Appreciation and Growth Funds, Calvert Social Investment Funds (equity, bond, managed growth, money market funds), Working Assets Fund (money market), Dreyfus Third Century Fund (equity), Merrill Lynch Ecological Trust, Alpine Catholic Income Trust, and Domini Social Index Trust. *See* Dunnan, *supra* note 10, at 104; Proffitt, *supra* note 7, at 239, 244; Rauber, *supra* note 21, at 18–19; SIF information, *supra* note 18. These funds use environmental protection, pollution control, or energy efficiency as one of a set of investment criteria. SIF information, *supra* note 18.

24. They are Schield Progressive Environmental Fund (positive and negative environmental screens) and SFT: Environmental Awareness Fund (positive environmental screens only). SIF information, *supra* note 18.

25. Harvey & Conner, *supra* note 11, at 31. *See* Burns, *Socially Responsible Investing*, PORTSMOUTH (N.H.) HERALD, Sept. 8, 1989, at C1, col. 1.

26. *See* Fenn & Opheim, *supra* note 22, at 10; P. Kinder, The Domini Social Index: Its Composition and Performance, at 12 (address delivered at the Social Investment Forum Workshops on Performance Evaluation, Mar. 4, 1991); Proffitt, *supra* note 7, at 233.

27. Formed by the Social Investment Forum (*see supra* note 15) along with national environmental organizations, including the Sierra Club and the National Audubon Society, CERES was created in order to draft the Valdez Principles.

28. *See supra* note 15.

29. CERES, 1990 GUIDE TO THE VALDEZ PRINCIPLES 7 (1990) (hereinafter VALDEZ GUIDE in this section). For the full text of the Valdez Principles, see box 10-1 in chapter 10.

30. VALDEZ GUIDE, *supra* note 29, at 7.

31. *Id.*

32. *See* Current Development, *supra* note 4, at 240; Sternberg, *New Pressure for Good Conduct*, CHEMICAL WEEK, Sept. 20, 1989, at 23.

33. VALDEZ GUIDE, *supra* note 29, at 21.

34. *Id.* at 7.

35. CERES worked closely with U.S. industry to assure that the guidelines were reasonable, and the signatory list is now growing. *See* Harvey & Conner, *supra* note 11, at 31. At the end of 1990, however, only seventeen small companies had actually signed on. *See* Cogan, *Shareholders Launch Valdez Principles Campaign*, IRRC INVESTOR'S ENVTL. REP., Winter 1991, at 5. Interest at the state level continues to expand. *See infra* notes 53–56 and accompanying text.

36. VALDEZ GUIDE, *supra* note 29, at 7.

37. *GM Shareholders Reject Adoption of Valdez Environmental Principles*, 22 ENV'T REP. (BNA) 260 (May 31, 1991); Kiesche, *Facing Up to Hidden Liabilities*, CHEMICAL WEEK, Feb. 14, 1990, at 58; Current Development, *supra* note 4, at 241–44; Feder, *Who Will Subscribe to the Valdez Principles?* THE NEW YORK TIMES, Sept. 10, 1989, at F6.

38. Current Development, *supra* note 4, at 241–44; Feder, *supra* note 37, at F6. Presumably as a response to some of these criticisms, the Global Environmental Management Initiative (GEMI), a coalition of twenty-one blue chip U.S. companies, is working to devise another code of corporate environmental conduct. Naimon, *GEMI: The Corporate Response*, IRRC INVESTOR'S ENVTL. REP., Winter 1991, at 8. Under the GEMI-sponsored code, companies make their own decisions about implementing the code, compliance information is not shared with the public, and the principles themselves are likely to be even more broad than the Valdez Principles. *Id.*

39. For example, an investor could discover the total amounts of fines levied against the company for environmental infractions or the total amounts of pollutants generated by the company as compared with other companies in the same industry.

40. For example, in 1988 the Chemical Manufacturers Association (CMA) adopted its Responsible Care program. CMA, RESPONSIBLE CARE: A PUBLIC COMMITMENT (1990) (association brochure). Responsible Care has six elements:
    1. Guiding Principles. A statement of the philosophy and commitment by all member companies regarding environmental, health, and safety responsibilities in the management of chemicals.

2. Codes of Management Practices. Codes focus on management practices in specific areas of chemical manufacturing, transporting, and handling that CMA member companies are to make continuous good-faith efforts to attain.

3. Public Advisory Panel. A group of environmental, health, and safety thought leaders assists the industry in identifying and developing programs and actions that are responsive to public concerns.

4. Member Self-Evaluations. Reports, measurements, and other demonstrations of program implementation document progress toward improved environmental, health, and safety performance in the responsible management of chemicals.

5. Executive Leadership Groups. In periodic regional meetings, senior industry representatives review Codes of Management Practices under development, discuss progress on implementing existing codes, and identify areas where assistance from CMA or other companies is needed.

6. Obligation of Membership. Bylaws obligate member companies to ascribe to the Guiding Principles, to participate in the development of the codes and programs, and to make good-faith efforts to implement the program elements of the Responsible Care initiative.

Id. This program is strikingly similar in form and content to the Valdez Principles. Another such set of principles is GEMI, discussed *supra* note 38.

41. For a detailed discussion of the effects of environmental investing on portfolio performance, *see infra* part IV.

42. For a detailed discussion of the legal limitations on environmental investing, *see infra* part III.

43. Proffitt, *supra* note 7, at 244–46. *See* P. Kinder, *supra* note 26, at 10.

44. Proffitt, *supra* note 7, at 244–46. Because assessing a firm's degree of commitment to the environment can be difficult, Franklin Research and Development, an investment management firm for clients concerned with socially responsible investing, attempts "to distinguish those companies that stand out within their industry for exceptional initiatives or consistent neglect." *FRDC, supra* note 7, at 17. The four questions that guide its analysis are:

1. Is the company in compliance with state and federal environmental regulations? Does it have major environmental lawsuits pending? Does it have a record of environmental controversy? Has it gone beyond the letter of the law in dealing with pollution problems?

2. Where comparative environmental studies of an industry have been conducted, how has the company in question performed relative to others in its industry?

3. What efforts has the company made in reducing the generation of hazardous, toxic, and hazardous [sic] wastes and in the proper disposal of those wastes it generates?

4. Does the company contribute to, or otherwise support, non-profit environmental protection organizations?

Id. The group rates the company on a scale of one to five. *Id.* These ratings are then used to screen out firms that are environmentally irresponsible. An investor's choice of which number to use as a cutoff point determines the severity of this investment criterion.

Some of Franklin's sources are the Center for Environmental Management of Tufts University, corporate annual reports and 10-K forms, and the Office of Technology Assessment. *Id.*

45. For example, irregularities and inadequacies in SEC disclosure requirements for 10-K forms and similar filings make using these sources for environmental responsibility information unreliable. Biersach, *Inside the 10-K*, IRRC INVESTOR'S ENVTL. REP., Winter 1991, at 1, 12–13. Investors must consult third-party sources, such as nonprofit research groups and government regulatory agencies, in addition to collecting their own information in order to obtain the information they need. *See FRDC, supra* note 7, at 6.

46. *Cf.* Slater, *Companies That Hide Behind the Sullivan Principles*, BUS. & SOC'Y REV., Spring 1984, at 15, 16, 18 (arguing against the use of a signatory list for investment decisions because of its inaccuracy as an indicator of social responsibility).

47. *See id.* at 18.

48. A. DOMINI & P. KINDER, ETHICAL INVESTING 2 (1986); JUDD, *supra* note 1, at 9. *Cf.* Jerry & Joy, *supra* note 1, at 690 (mentioning only positive and negative investing); Langbein & Posner, *Social Investing and the Law of Trusts*, 79 MICH L. REV. 72, 73 (1980) (mentioning two forms of social investing, basically positive and negative investing).

49. *FRDC, supra* note 7, at 5. *See* A. DOMINI & P. KINDER, *supra* note 48, at 2; Jerry & Joy, *supra* note 1, at 690; JUDD, *supra* note 1, at 9; Langbein & Posner, *supra* note 48, at 73.

50. *FRDC, supra* note 7, at 5. *See* A. DOMINI & P. KINDER, *supra* note 48, at 2; Jerry & Joy, *supra* note 1, at 690; JUDD, *supra* note 1, at 9; Langbein & Posner, *supra* note 48, at 73.

51. JUDD, *supra* note 1, at 10; *FRDC, supra* note 7, at 5. *See* A. DOMINI & P. KINDER, *supra* note 48, at 9. U.S. securities law allows any stockholder who holds at least 1 percent or $1,000 in market value of shares of a company for a year to introduce a proposal at that company's annual meeting. Securities and Exchange Act of 1934 Rule 14a-8(a)(1), 17 C.F.R. § 240.14a-8(a)(1) (1990).

52. *FRDC, supra* note 7, at 5.

53. *See* Cogan, *supra* note 35, at 5; Harvey & Conner, *supra* note 11, at 29–32; *Preliminary Listing of 1991 Shareholder Resolutions*, IRRC NEWS FOR INVESTORS, Dec. 1990, at 254, 254–59.

54. CERES, Valdez Principles Shareholder Resolutions Garner Record-breaking Totals, at 1 (press release, June 7, 1990). Other corporations that have been similarly targeted include Kodak and Polaroid. Snow, *Putting Mother Earth in the Boardroom*, WORLD PAPER, June 1990, Worlddiary sec., at 15. More than fifty such resolutions have been filed for the 1991 proxy season asking companies to sign or report on the Valdez Principles. Cogan, *supra* note 35, at 5; *Preliminary Listing, supra* note 53, at 254–59.

55. CERES, *supra* note 54, at 1. The totals were as follows: American Express, 8.5 percent (representing 35.5 million shares voting for the resolution); Atlantic Richfield, 14.2 percent (23.3 million shares); Exxon, 9.5 percent (119.8 million shares); Kerr-McGee, 16.7 percent (8.4 million shares); and Union Pacific, 13.6 percent (13.6 million shares). *Id.* According to CERES, a vote total exceeding 3 percent on a resolution introduced without company support is considered a success. *Id.* The average support level for these resolutions was 12.5 percent, the highest of any first-year shareholder initiative for the twenty-year history of proxy voting on social issues. Cogan, *supra* note 35, at 5.

56. For example, the Valdez referendum introduced at Exxon's annual meeting resulted primarily from the votes of the controller of California and comptroller of New York State. Snow, *supra* note 54, at 15. The Washington State Investment Board and trustees of public pension funds in Alaska also supported the motion. *Washington Fund Says Exxon's Environmental Record Jeopardizing Its Investment*, 68 PLATT'S OILGRAM NEWS, 4 (Apr. 9, 1990). Another participant was the public employee pension fund of Massachusetts. Heller, *The Buck Starts Here*, CHEMICAL WEEK, Apr. 18, 1990 (special report), at 28. Institutional support for the 1991 initiatives is likely to be influential as well. *See supra* note 54.

57. Cogan, *supra* note 35, at 5; Dolan, *supra* note 1, at 17.

58. The New Jersey bill, N.J. Ass. No. 2861, 204th Leg. Sess., was introduced on January 22, 1990. It was referred to the State Operations Committee and is still being considered there. The New York bill, N.Y. Ass. No. 9127—A, 213th Leg. Sess., was introduced on January 29, 1990. After being referred to the Government Employees Committee, which reported favorably on the bill, it was recommended to Ways and Means. Before any action was taken, the two-year bill period elapsed, so it is now dead. It is not clear whether it will be reintroduced next session.

59. Cal. S. Con. Res. 84, 1989–90 Leg. Sess. (1990).

60. Harvey & Conner, *supra* note 11, at 31.

61. *Politicians Support Valdez Principles*, PENSIONS & INVESTMENT AGE, Feb. 19, 1990, at 43.

62. New Jersey, for example, has seven. N.J. Ass. No. 2861, 204th Leg. Sess. § 2(a) (1990).

63. N.J. Ass. No. 2861, 204th Leg. Sess. § 3(a) (1990).

64. N.Y. Ass. No. 9127—A, 213th Leg. Sess. § 2(1) (1990).

65. For a detailed discussion of the financial aspects of environmental investing, see *infra* part IV.

66. N.Y. Ass. No. 9127—A, 213th Leg. Sess. § 2(2) (1990).

67. Cal. S. Con. Res. 84, 1989–90 Leg. Sess. at 3 (1990).

68. N.J. Ass. No. 2861, 204th Leg. Sess. § 6 (1990).

69. *Id.*

70. N.Y. Ass. No. 9127—A, 213th Leg. Sess. § 2(3) (1990).

71. For an example of such a rating system, *see supra* note 44.

72. For an explanation of CERES, *see supra* note 27 and accompanying text. For a discussion of potential legal problems arising when certain functions are legislatively delegated to private parties, *see infra* part III(A).

73. N.J. Ass. No. 2861, 204th Leg. Sess. § 5 (1990).

74. Cal. S. Con. Res. 84 1989–90 Leg. Sess. at 3 (1990).

75. N.Y. Ass. No. 9127—A, 213th Leg. Sess. § 2(4) (1990).

76. *Id.*

77. *See State May Ask Firms to Use Valdez Rules*, Los Angeles Times, Feb. 28, 1990, at D7, col. 1.

78. Compare, from the point of view of a publicly traded company that depends on investment capital, the threat of an unsuccessful (though significant) shareholder resolution to adopt or comply with the Valdez Principles with a threat of withdrawal of many millions of dollars in investment capital unless the company signs and/or follows the Principles.

79. For a detailed discussion of the effects of environmental investing on portfolio performance, see *infra* part IV.

80. *See* Valdez Principles in box 10-1 in chapter 10.

81. *See supra* note 44.

82. As of February 1990, one of California's pension funds, the Public Employees Retirement System, had agreed to ask twenty-seven major companies it invested its funds with to report how their policies compared to the Valdez Principles. *State May Ask Firms to Use Valdez Rules, supra* note 77, at D7, col. 1. At that time, eight companies had consented to this reporting plan. *Id.* They were such household names as Aetna, Amoco, Chevron, Eastman Kodak, Mobil, Texaco, and Union Carbide. *Id.*

83. State environmental investing legislation thus avoids many of the arguments that would be available against analogous local enactments.

84. One example of a state constitutional constraint is contained in article 5, section 7 of the New York State Constitution's "nonimpairment clause." Campbell & Josephson, *Public Pension Trustees' Pursuit of Social Goals*, 24 WASH. U. J. URB. & CONTEMP. L. 43, 118 (1983). That clause provides that "membership in any pension or retirement system of the state or of a civil division thereof shall be a contractual [sic] relationship, the benefits of which shall not be diminished or impaired." Such a clause entitles benefits under applicable plans to protection under the contracts clause of the federal constitution. *Id. See infra* part III(B).

There is some variation among state constitutions, but most state constitutional provisions parallel the federal provisions. In this section I will, therefore, address the legal constraints using the language of the federal document. Differences in state constitutional language could nevertheless be determinative in a legal dispute.

85. *See* Tron v. Condello, 427 F. Supp. 1175, 1187–87 (S.D.N.Y. 1976); Campbell & Josephson, *supra* note 84, at 118–19 (citing Sgaglione v. Levitt, 37 N.Y. 2d 507, 513, 337 N.E. 2d 592, 595, 375 N.Y.S.2d 79, 84 [1975]); Troyer & Slocombe, *supra* note 1, at 158.

86. *See* Ashwander v. Tennessee Valley Auth., 297 U.S. 288, 346 (1936).

87. *See, e.g.*, Bd. of Trustees of the Employees' Retirement Sys. v. Mayor of Baltimore, 317 Md. 72, 94, 562 A.2d 720, 730 (1989), *cert. denied*, 110 S. Ct. 1167 (1990).

88. *Id.*

89. *Id.* at 92, 562 A.2d at 730.

90. *Id.* at 98, 562 A.2d at 732.

91. *Id.*

92. *Id.* at 95, 562 A.2d at 731.

93. *Id.* at 95–96, 562 A.2d at 731.

94. *Id.* at 96–97, 562 A.2d at 731–32 and cases cited.

95. U.S. CONST., art 1 § 10 ("No State shall . . . pass any . . . law impairing the obligation of contracts").

96. *See* United States Trust Co. v. New Jersey, 431 U.S. 1, 17–21 (1977).

97. *See id.* at 17.

98. *See id.* at 21.

99. City of El Paso v. Simmons, 379 U.S. 497, 506–7 (1965).

100. This issue was cursorily addressed by the Supreme Court in United States R.R. Retirement Bd. v. Fritz, 449 U.S. 166 (1980), which held that railroad re-

tirement benefits, like social security benefits, were not contractual. *Id.* at 174. Although that case dealt with a Fifth Amendment takings clause challenge to a federal enactment and not a contract clause challenge to a state law, the court was unanimous in its characterization of these benefits as noncontractual.

101. *See, e.g.,* Bd. of Trustees of the Employees' Retirement Sys. v. Mayor of Baltimore, 317 Md. 72, 100, 562 A.2d 720, 733 (1989), *cert. denied,* 110 S. Ct. 1167 (1990). The states of Washington and Massachusetts have characterized benefits promised under public employee pension plans as contractual in nature. *See* Campbell & Josephson, *supra* note 84, at 118.

102. *See, e.g.,* BALTIMORE CITY CODE, art. 22, § 42 (1983).

103. 290 U.S. 398 (1933).

104. *Id.* at 431 (footnotes omitted).

105. *Id.* at 434–35 (footnote omitted) (quoting Stephenson v. Binford, 287 U.S. 251, 276 [1932]).

106. *See, e.g.,* Allied Structural Steel v. Spannaus, 438 U.S. 234 (1978); United States Trust Co. of New York v. New Jersey, 431 U.S. 1 (1977).

107. *See, e.g.,* Exxon Corp. v. Eagerton, 462 U.S. 176 (1983); Energy Reserves Group, Inc. v. Kansas Power & Light Co., 459 U.S. 400 (1983); United States R.R. Retirement Bd. v. Fritz, 449 U.S. 166 (1980); Usery v. Turner Elkhorn Mining Co., 428 U.S. 1 (1976).

108. More specifically, the proposed legislation does not change or replace explicit provisions in the plans that guarantee minimum earnings or that concern future benefits. *See infra* note 110.

109. *See Baltimore,* 317 Md., at 72, 100, 562 A.2d, at 720, 734.

110. Future variable benefits represent earnings in excess of any defined (guaranteed) minimum earnings. Defined benefits are fixed, and if they exist in a fund, they are explicitly guaranteed. Variable benefits fluctuate with market performance and thus cannot be guaranteed. Beneficiaries may claim contractual rights to both fixed and future variable benefits. *See id.* at 100 n. 26, 562 A.2d, at 733, n. 26.

111. Energy Reserves Group, Inc. v. Kansas Power & Light Co., 459 U.S. 400, 411 (1983); Allied Structural Steel v. Spannaus, 438 U.S. 234, 244–45 (1978).

112. *Baltimore,* 317 Md., at 101, 562 A.2d, at 734. The court found the initial cost of divestiture to the beneficiaries to be $750,000, which represented 1/32 of 1 percent of the total returns from the funds' invested assets, and the ongoing cost to be $1.2 million, which represented 1/20 of 1 percent of the total returns. *Id.*

113. *Id.* at 102, 562 A.2d, at 734.

114. *Id.*

115. G. G. Bogert & G. T. Bogert, The Law of Trusts and Trustees, § 541 (rev. 2d. ed., 1978).

There is considerable authority for the view that the duty of prudence (and also the duty of loyalty) is not obligatory, but that it can be set aside explicitly in the pension trust instrument or implicitly by consent of the beneficiaries to the fund's investment strategy. *See* 3 A. Scott, The Law of Trusts §§ 174, 227.14 (3d ed., 1967); Dobris, *supra* note 14, at 218, 236; Langbein & Posner, *supra* note 48, at 105–7; Lynn, *supra* note 2, at 110; Ravikoff & Curzan, *Social Responsibility in Investment Policy and the Prudent Man Rule*, 68 Cal. L. Rev. 518, 544–45 (1980). For one set of authors' thorough analysis of the prudent person standard applicable to a public pension fund, see Campbell & Josephson, *supra* note 84, at 48–50, 87–109.

116. 29 U.S.C. §§ 1001–1461 (1988).

117. 29 U.S.C. §§ 1002(32), 1003(b)(1) (1988).

118. 29 U.S.C. § 1104(a)(1) (1988).

119. *See, e.g., Baltimore*, 317 Md., at 72, 103, 562 A.2d, at 720, 735; Zelinsky, *The Dilemma of the Local Social Investment: An Essay on "Socially Responsible" Investing*, 6 Cardozo L. Rev. 111, 111 (1984); Dunlap, *Some Trustees Want City Pension Funds to Cut Pretoria Ties*, The New York Times, Mar. 7, 1984, at A1, col. 6, B24, col. 6. *See also* Ferris & Rykaczewski, *Social Investment and the Management of Pension Portfolios*, J. Am. Soc'y CLU & CHFC, Nov. 1986, at 62, 63 (making same argument with regard to private pension funds); *SAG Pension & Health Rejects South Africa Divestiture*, Screen Actor News, Dec. 1984, at 3 (trustees of private pension plan refused to divest because of imprudence) (cited in Note, *supra* note 14, at 772, n. 45).

120. For a discussion of data on this subject, see *infra* part IV.

121. *See Baltimore*, 317 Md., at 103–4, 562 A.2d, at 735; Zelinsky, *supra* note 119, at 111–12; Wise, *supra* note 14, at 16, col. 6. *But see* Broderick, *The Prudent Person vs. Divestment*, Directors & Boards, Summer 1984, at 4 (predicting, without data, lower rates of return and higher risks for pension funds subject to South Africa divestment statutes). Given the financial data available, there may be no reason to believe that companies with substantial ties to South Africa will necessarily have higher rates of return than firms with no ties to that country. *See* Zelinsky, *supra* note 119, at 111–12.

122. *Baltimore*, 317 Md., at 104, 562 A.2d, at 735.

123. *See id.* at 105, 562 A.2d, at 736.

124. *See, e.g., id.*: Dolan, *supra* note 1, at 17 ("pension funds are designed for one purpose—income for retirees") (quoting Bernard Jump, a pension expert at Syracuse University); Murrmann, Schaffer, & Wokutch, *supra* note 2, at 360.

125. Campbell & Josephson, *supra* note 84, at 45. *See* Lynn, *supra* note 2, at 102–3; Zelinsky, *supra* note 119, at 111, nn. 19–25 and accompanying text.

126. Langbein & Posner, *supra* note 48, at 98.

127. *See supra* part II.

128. Campbell & Josephson, *supra* note 84, at 46–47; Jerry & Joy, *supra* note 1, at 700.

129. *Baltimore*, 317 Md., at 72, 107, 562 A.2d, at 720, 737. *See* Withers v. Teachers' Retirement Sys., 447 F. Supp. 1248, 1254 (S.D.N.Y. 1978), *aff'd*, 595 F.2d 1210 (2d Cir. 1979); King v. Talbot, 40 N.Y. 76, 86 (1869); 3 A. SCOTT, THE LAW OF TRUSTS, § 227.3 (W. Fratcher, 4th ed., 1988); RESTATEMENT (SECOND) OF TRUSTS § 227 comment (e) (1957); Campbell & Josephson, *supra* note 84, at 92; Dobris, *supra* note 14, at 230, 232; Ravikoff & Curzan, *supra* note 115, at 519; Zelinsky, *supra* note 119, at 121–22. *But see* Campbell & Josephson, *supra* note 84, at 48; Langbein & Posner, *supra* note 48, at 98, 103; Lynn, *supra* note 2, at 102–3; Schotland, *Should Pension Funds Be Used to Achieve "Social" Goals?* (part 3 of 3), TRUSTS & ESTATES, Nov. 1980, at 33.

130. *See Baltimore*, 317 Md., at 106–7, 562 A.2d, at 738; 3 A. SCOTT, *supra* note 129, at § 227.17; *Do Good Ethics Ensure Good Profits?* BUS. & SOC'Y REV., Summer 1989, at 4, 9 (comment of Jerome L. Dodson, president of Parnassus Fund), 10 (comment of Maurice L. Shoenwald, president of New Alternatives Fund). *See also infra* note 226 and accompanying text.

Some indirect benefits of environmental investment, such as lowered health care costs or the adoption of an effective local emergency remediation plan, also may inure to the benefit of the fiduciary's beneficiaries, thus increasing the investment's overall rate of return. *See* Zelinsky, *supra* note 119, at 139, 146; Dobris, *supra* note 14, at 235. *See also* Ravikoff & Curzan, *supra* note 115, at 545–46. *But see* Campbell & Josephson, *supra* note 84, at 102 (indicating "no support" for theory permitting trustees of public employee pension funds to consider indirect benefits in the absence of necessity).

131. *Baltimore*, 317 Md., at 107, 562 A.2d, at 737. Some writers argue further that decreased fund productivity should be acceptable when lost in pursuit of social gain. *See* Dobris, *supra* note 14, 230; FRDC, *supra* note 7, at 11.

132. 29 U.S.C. § 1104(a)(1) (1988). For a detailed treatment of the duty of loyalty applicable to public pension funds, see Campbell & Josephson, *supra* note 84, at 67–87.

133. *See, e.g., Baltimore*, 317 Md., at 109, 562 A.2d, at 738. One author provides an interesting analysis to this problem, attributing to advocates of social investing a desire to redefine the fiduciary relationship as a three-party affair involving the fiduciary, the beneficiary, and society as a whole, as opposed to the bilateral focus of conventional fiduciary jurisprudence only on the relationship between the fiduciary and its beneficiary. *See* Zelinsky, *supra* note 119, at 120.

134. *See Baltimore*, 317 Md., at 110, 562 A.2d, at 738; 3 A. Scott, *supra* note 129, § 227.17; Campbell & Josephson, *supra* note 84, at 46–47; Dobris, *supra* note 14, at 233; Ravikoff & Curzan, *supra* note 115, at 523. *But see* Langbein & Posner, *supra* note 48, at 96, 98, 102; Lynn, *supra* note 2, at 105, 107 (criticizing Scott's view). While Langbein & Posner define the duty of loyalty in terms of exclusive benefit to the beneficiary, they go on to say that "some form of social-investing option could be created that would be consistent with the trust investment law and with ERISA." Langbein & Posner, *supra* note 48, at 106.

135. *See* Campbell & Josephson, *supra* note 84, at 68; Ravikoff & Curzan, *supra* note 115, at 531.

136. *See supra* notes 103–5 and accompanying text.

137. For a definition of this term, see *supra* note 110.

138. For a definition of this term, see *supra* note 110.

139. For an analogous, though unsuccessful, attack of South Africa divestment ordinances, see *Baltimore*, 317 Md., at 72, 110–11, 562 A.2d, at 720, 738–39.

140. *See, e.g., id.* at 111, 562 A.2d, at 739.

141. 449 U.S. 166 (1980).

142. *Id.* at 174.

143. L. Tribe, American Constitutional Law 627 (2d ed., 1988) (quoting *Fritz*, 449 U.S., at 174).

144. *See, e.g., Baltimore*, 317 Md., at 112, 562 A.2d, at 739.

145. *Id.*

146. Withers v. Teachers' Retirement Sys., 447 F. Supp. 1248, 1260 (S.D.N.Y. 1978) (stating that beneficiaries of a public retirement fund "have no entitlement to, or right to direct the retention of, the particular assets that are held for investment purposes in the pension fund"), *aff'd*, 595 F.2d 1210 (2d Cir. 1979); Crown v. Patrolmen's Variable Supp. Fund Trustees, 659 F. Supp. 318, 320 (S.D.N.Y. 1987) (citing *Withers*, 447 F. Supp., at 1260), *aff'd*, 819 F.2d 47 (2d Cir. 1987). See Tron v. Condello, 427 F. Supp. 1175, 1189–90 (S.D.N.Y. 1976) (beneficiary "has a vested right in receiving his pension benefits, but not in regulating the investment policies set by the Legislature and the Retirement Board").

Withers v. Teachers' Retirement Sys. is often cited to support socially constrained investments of public pension funds. In that case, the court upheld the decision of a fund's trustees to purchase New York City bonds (which had a high risk of default and left the pension fund undiversified) as part of the plan that ultimately prevented that city's bankruptcy in late 1975. The beneficiaries had claimed that the trustees acted more in the interest of the city than for the benefit of the beneficiaries themselves. *Withers*, 447 F. Supp., at 1254. The court disagreed, noting that the bond purchases were probably the most advantageous investment the fund could make on purely financial grounds, due to the fact that the city was the main contributor to the fund. *Id.* at 1256, 1259. *See* Jerry & Joy, *supra* note 1, at 701–3; Troyer & Slocombe, *supra* note 1, at 157, n. 110. Some writers view *Withers* as an affirmation of traditional law on fiduciary administration. *See* Campbell & Josephson, *supra* note 84, at 99–100; Langbein & Posner, *supra* note 48, at 101–2; Lynn, *supra* note 2, at 109. Others view it as a break from mainstream traditional law. *See* Ravikoff & Curzan, *supra* note 115, at 523.

147. Penn Central Transp. Co. v. City of New York, 438 U.S. 104, 124 (1978). See C. BERGER, LAND OWNERSHIP AND USE 712 (1983) (noting the continuing intractability of the taking issue).

148. *Penn Central*, 438 U.S., at 124.

149. *Id.*

150. *Id.*

151. *Id.*

152. *Id.*

153. *See, e.g., Baltimore,* 317 Md., at 72, 113, 562 A.2d, at 720, 739–40.

154. *See, e.g.,* Connolly v. Pension Benefit Guar. Corp., 475 U.S. 211, 225–26 (1986) (rejecting such a challenge in part because the statutory imposition of liability for employer withdrawal from a pension plan mitigated the economic impact on the individual employer); *Baltimore,* 317 Md., at 113, 562 A.2d, at 739–40 (noting that a provision allowing for the postponement of divestment until it can be done without substantial detrimental impact to the fund would mitigate adverse impacts on benefits).

155. *See* Andrus v. Allard, 444 U.S. 51, 66 (1979) (stating that "loss of future profits—unaccompanied by any physical property restriction—provides a slender reed on which to rest a takings claim"); *Baltimore,* 317 Md., at 113, 562 A.2d, at 740 ("Variable benefits are, as their name suggests, speculative and uncertain. Whatever diminution of variable benefits the Ordinances might cause cannot be said to interfere with a 'distinct . . . expectation' ").

156. For a discussion of the effects of environmental investing on portfolio performance, see *infra* part IV.

157. L. TRIBE, *supra* note 143, at 596–97 (footnotes omitted).

158. *See Connolly,* 475 U.S., at 225; *Baltimore,* 317 Md., at 113–14, 562 A.2d, at 740.

159. *Cf. Baltimore*, 317 Md., at 114–21, 562 A.2d, at 740–44, in which the court held that the city's South Africa divestment ordinance was not preempted by the Comprehensive Anti-Apartheid Act of 1986, Pub. L. No. 99–440, 100 Stat. 1086 (codified in relevant part at 22 U.S.C. §§ 2151, 2346[d], 5001–16 [1988]), which sets forth U.S. policy toward the government of South Africa and encourages action through economic, political, and diplomatic measures with the goal of establishing a nonracial democracy.

160. California v. ARC America Corp., 109 S. Ct. 1661, 1665 (1989); Hillsborough County v. Automated Medical Laboratory, Inc., 471 U.S. 707, 713 (1985); *Baltimore*, 317 Md., at 145, 562 A.2d, at 740–41.

161. *California v. ARC*, 109 S. Ct., at 1665; Pacific Gas & Electric v. Energy Resources Comm'n, 461 U.S. 190, 204 (1983); Rice v. Santa Fe Elevator Corp., 331 U.S. 218, 230 (1947); *Baltimore*, 317 Md., at 115, 562 A.2d, at 741.

162. *California v. ARC*, 109 S. Ct., at 1665; *Hillsborough County*, 471 U.S., at 713; *Baltimore*, 317 Md., at 115, 562 A.2d, at 741.

163. *California v. ARC*, 109 S. Ct., at 1665; *Hillsborough County*, 471 U.S., at 715–16; *Pacific Gas*, 461 U.S., at 206; San Diego Bldg. Trades Council v. Garmon, 359 U.S. 236, 244 (1959); *Baltimore*, 317 Md., at 116, 562 A.2d, at 741.

164. New Energy Co. of Indiana v. Limbach, 108 S. Ct. 1803, 1809 (1988); South-Central Timber Dev., Inc. v. Wunnicke, 467 U.S. 82, 93 (1984); *Baltimore*, 317 Md., at 131–33, 562 A.2d, at 749. *See* Wisconsin Dep't of Indus., Labor and Human Relations v. Gould, Inc., 475 U.S. 282, 289–91 (1986); United Bldg. & Construction Trades Council v. Mayor of Camden, 465 U.S. 208, 219–20 (1984); White v. Massachusetts Council of Construction Employers, Inc., 460 U.S. 204, 206–8 (1983); Reeves, Inc. v. Stake, 447 U.S. 429, 434–36 (1980); Hughes v. Alexandria Scrap Corp., 426 U.S. 794, 806 (1976); L. TRIBE, *supra* note 143, at 430–34.

It has been suggested that the Supreme Court, in Garcia v. San Antonio Metro. Transit Auth., 469 U.S. 528 (1985), by overruling Nat'l League of Cities v. Usery, 426 U.S. 833 (1976), repudiated the market participant doctrine. *See* Swin Resource Sys., Inc. v. Lycoming County, 883 F.2d 245, 260–61 (3d Cir. 1989) (C. J. Gibbons, dissenting), *cert. denied*, 110 S. Ct. 1127 (1990); Manheim, *New-Age Federalism and the Market Participant Doctrine*, 22 ARIZ. ST. L. J. 559, 562 (1990).

However, the court's reiteration of the rule after *Garcia* (see, *e.g.*, *Wisconsin v. Gould*, 475 U.S., at 289 [holding the doctrine inapplicable to the facts, but not invalidating it]; *New Energy v. Limbach*, 108 S. Ct., at 1809 [holding the doctrine inapplicable]) and the reasoning of *Garcia* itself indicate that the market participant exception remains a viable doctrine. *See Swin Resource Sys.*, 883 F.2d, at 254–55 (summarizing the majority's adoption of the market participant principle and criticism of Judge Gibbons's analysis); Evergreen Waste Sys., Inc. v. Metropolitan Serv. Dist., 643 F. Supp. 127, 132 (D. Or. 1986) (explicitly rejecting the argument that *Garcia* overruled the market participant exception), *aff'd*, 820 F.2d 1482 (9th Cir. 1987); Coenen, *Untangling the Market-Participant Exemption to the Dormant Commerce Clause*, 88 MICH. L. REV. 395, 407, n. 86, 429–30 (1989) (arguing that the federalist reasoning in *Garcia* both explains and validates the market participant doctrine).

165. *See* Reeves, Inc. v. Stake, 447 U.S., at 438–39 (noting "the long recognized right of trader or manufacturer, engaged in an entirely private business, freely to exercise his own independent discretion as to parties with whom he will deal") (quoting United States v. Colgate & Co., 250 U.S. 300, 307 [1919]); *Baltimore*, 317 Md. 133–35, 562 A.2d at 750.

166. 467 U.S. at 97–98.

167. *Id.* at 97.

168. Restrictions on an ongoing commercial relationship are distinct from restrictions on economic activities that take place between parties after their direct commercial obligations have ended. The former fall within the market participant exception; the latter do not. See *South-Central Timber*, 467 U.S., at 99 (distinguishing White v. Massachusetts Council of Construction Employers, Inc., 460 U.S. 204 [1983]).

169. *See Baltimore*, 317 Md., at 137, 562 A.2d, at 752; Note, *supra* note 14, at 790–91.

170. 397 U.S. 137 (1970).

171. *Id.* at 142.

172. 477 U.S. 131 (1986).

173. *Id.* at 138. Accord *Baltimore*, 317 Md., at 141–42, 562 A.2d, at 754.

174. *Cf.* Dean Milk Co. v. City of Madison, 340 U.S. 349, 353–56 (1951) (regulation in practical effect excluded from local distribution milk produced out of state, thus impermissibly protecting local industry against competition from without the state).

175. *See Baltimore*, 317 Md., at 143, 562 A.2d, at 754–55 (citing Pike v. Bruce Church, Inc., 397 U.S. 137 [1970]).

176. A thorough examination of the studies on the effect of South Africa divestment on portfolio performance can be found in Jerry & Joy, *supra* note 1, at 688, n. 7, 714–44.

177. *See* Bromberg, *supra* note 11, at 32–34; Proffitt, *supra* note 7, at 237. *See also* Meyer, *Ethics in Investing Takes Off*, KANSAS CITY STAR, June 5, 1990, at D15, col. 1 (noting that "you can make just as much money or more money by taking a socially responsible approach to investing as by taking a conventional one"). *But see* Wang, *A True Believer Who Does Well by Seeking to Do Good*, MONEY, May 1990, at 177 (citing no data, yet quoting a critic of social investing: "the long-term record of the socially responsible [mutual] funds is mediocre").

178. Jerry & Joy, *supra* note 1, at 745; Williams, *supra* note 14, at 181 (quoting Franklin Research and Development and United States Trust). The strength of this conclusion depends on the severity of the divestment criteria. For example, an extreme position of divesting the stock of any firm doing business in South Africa may give rise to disagreement about the effects of divestment. Jerry & Joy, *supra* note 1, at 744. A mild divestment position, such as excluding only South Africa–related firms not ranked in the top two compliance categories of the Sullivan Principles, would almost certainly cause no adverse effects on portfolio performance. *Id.* For an explanation of the Sullivan Code compliance categories, see Paul, *The Inadequacy of Sullivan Reporting*, BUS. & SOC'Y REV., Spring 1986, at 61–62.

179. *See* Dobris, *supra* note 14, at 233; Jerry & Joy, *supra* note 1, at 714.

180. This discussion of financial performance is limited mainly to the subject of returns from a fund's investments; it does not address other financial advantages, such as tax deductions, exemptions, exclusions, or deferrals available for beneficiaries of qualifying pension plans under the Internal Revenue Code and Treasury regulations. *See, e.g.,* I.R.C. § 401(a), 26 U.S.C. § 401(a) (1988) (offering favorable tax treatment for pension plans administered "for the exclusive benefit of . . . employees or their beneficiaries"). A discussion of these matters is contained in Campbell & Josephson, *supra* note 84, at 57–63, 83–87.

Other unexamined effects on rate of return in financial as well as nonfinancial terms include the indirect effects, such as improved health, that an environmental investing strategy confers on its beneficiaries. *See* Dobris, *supra* note 14, at 235; Zelinsky, *supra* note 119, at 139, 146. *See also supra* note 130.

181. *See* Jerry & Joy, *supra* note 1, at 715.

182. *See* Jerry & Joy, *supra* note 1, at 745; Langbein & Posner, *supra* note 48, at 85. Both socially responsible and traditional fund managers commonly operate with their personal "buy lists" from which they choose investments. The universe of potential investments is thus severely narrowed by selecting the stocks that make up this list. Letter from Peter D. Kinder, president of Kinder, Lydenberg, Domini & Co., to Christopher J. McKenzie (March 13, 1991).

183. Jerry & Joy, *supra* note 1, at 715–16. *Cf.* Langbein & Posner, *supra* note 48, at 85 (concluding, based on one hypothetical social investing portfolio study, that "a portfolio constructed in accordance with social principles will be less diversified").

184. Jerry & Joy, *supra* note 1, at 720.

185. See Jerry & Joy, *supra* note 1, at 717; Langbein & Posner, *supra* note 48, at 87, 89.

186. Kinder to McKenzie, *supra* note 182.

187. *Id.*

188. Jerry & Joy, *supra* note 1, at 724.

189. A basis point is 1/100 of 1 percent of a portfolio's rate of return. *Id.* at 725.

190. *Id.*

191. Jerry & Joy, *supra* note 1, at 743. *See* Langbein & Posner, *supra* note 48, at 92 (admitting that the average rate of return of portfolios using social investing will be the same as portfolios designed to maximize the financial well-being of the investment beneficiaries); *More Municipalities Joining Drive to Cut South Africa Links*, THE NEW YORK TIMES, Sept. 25, 1984, at A1, col. 6, A25, col. 1 (Connecticut and Michigan officials claiming they suffered no financial loss as a result of their South Africa divestment). *But see* Broderick, *supra* note 121, at 4 (concluding, in the absence of data, that South Africa divestment increases risk and decreases returns); Hutchinson & Cole, *Legal Standards Governing Investment of Pension Assets for Social and Political Goals*, 128 U. PA. L. REV. 1340, 1386 (1980) (reaching the conclusion of sacrificed safety or return by mere inference); Note, *Socially Responsible Investment of Public Pension Funds: The South African Issue and State Law*, 10 N.Y.U. REV. L. SOC. CHANGE 407, 416–18 (1980–81).

192. Proffitt, *supra* note 7, at 237.

193. *Id.*

194. *Id.* at 238.

195. *Id.* at 238–39.

196. Langbein & Posner, *supra* note 48, at 92.

197. P. Kinder, *supra* note 26, at 2.

198. *Id.* at 2–3.

199. *Id.* at 27–28.

200. *See id.* at 27.

201. *Id.* at 27.

202. *Id.*

203. *See* Jerry & Joy, *supra* note 1, at 718; Langbein & Posner, *supra* note 48, at 85.

204. Jerry & Joy, *supra* note 1, at 727.

205. An example of a short-term trend of this nature is Calvert's Ariel Growth and Appreciation funds, losing nearly one fourth of their value in 1990, allegedly due to their investment strategy of pursuing small capitalization companies, which usually suffer more in a down market. Proffitt, *supra* note 7, at 237. Such short-term trends are not necessarily indicative of long-term performance, however. *Id.*

206. This conclusion finds support even from the critics of social investing. *See, e.g.*, Langbein & Posner, *supra* note 48, at 95–96 (admitting that despite increased administrative costs and decreased diversification, a social investing fund's overall performance will not substantially differ from that of a fund following an optimal [purely financial] strategy).

207. *See supra* part II(B)(1).

208. *See* Jerry & Joy, *supra* note 1, at 737. It has been suggested that divestment sales actually can take place more cheaply than ordinary institutional sales. Dobris, *supra* note 14, at 234 (citing BALDWIN, ET AL., PENSION FUNDS AND ETHICAL INVESTMENT 114–16 [1980]).

209. Jerry & Joy, *supra* note 1, at 737.

210. *See id.* at 740. *But see* Chettle, *The Law & Policy Divestment of South African Stock*, 15 LAW & POL'Y INT'L BUS. 445, 445–46 (1983) ("the brokerage fees required to sell Harvard's shares in companies with South African investments might range from $5.7 million to $16.5 million").

211. Jerry & Joy, *supra* note 1, at 740.

212. *See id.* at 740–41.

213. Shareholder activism is not a normal part of most funds' activities. Kinder to McKenzie, *supra* note 182. It usually is accomplished collectively, thus spreading costs, by such organizations as the Investor Responsibility Research Center (IRRC) or the Interfaith Council on Corporate Responsibility (ICCR). *Id.* However, the proposed legislation calls for the fund to undertake shareholder action.

214. See DOMINI SOCIAL INDEX TRUST, PROSPECTUS 15–16 (1990).

215. Peter D. Kinder, of Kinder, Lydenberg, Domini & Co., a social research firm, estimates that the environmental screening costs for a thirty-company large capitalization portfolio will run between $10,000 and $15,000 annually, a modest amount. Kinder to McKenzie, *supra* note 182. *Cf.* Langbein & Posner, *supra* note 48, at 93 (concluding, in the absence of data, that "the administrative costs of a social-investment portfolio will be higher . . . than the administrative costs of a portfolio constructed in accordance with the principles of modern finance theory").

216. See, *e.g.*, United States v. Fleet Factors Corp., 901 F.2d 1550, 1557–58 (11th Cir. 1990), *cert. denied*, 111 S. Ct. 752 (1991).

217. Jerry & Joy, *supra* note 1, at 741. This trend is based on empirical data, the explanation of which is beyond the scope of this chapter. However, one example of this phenomenon is that as the size of the segment of the portfolio requiring divestment and reinvestment increases, so do transaction costs. *See id.* at 737–40.

218. For example, the combined assets of California's two largest pension funds, the Public Employees' Retirement System and State Teachers' Retirement System, total about $85 billion to $90 billion. *State May Ask Firms to Use Valdez Rules*, Los Angeles Times, Feb. 28, 1990, at D7, col. 1; Kirkpatrick, *Environmentalism: The New Crusade*, Fortune, Feb. 12, 1990, at 44, 47.

219. "An active management style involves continuous research, investigation, and trading in an effort to 'add value' " to the portfolio. Jerry & Joy, *supra* note 1, at 741. "A passive management style involves buying and holding stocks without adjusting the portfolio," often using a mechanical screen such as price-to-earnings ratio. *Id.* at 741–42.

220. *Id.* at 741–42.

221. *See supra* part I.

222. *See* Lynn, *supra* note 2, at 115.

223. U.S. Const., art. 1, § 8, cl. 3.

224. Other related federal proposals could include a statute requiring that all contractors receiving federal funds adhere to a set of environmental guidelines such as the Valdez Principles (based on the Buy American Act, 41 U.S.C. § 10[a] [1933] [requiring, where reasonable, the purchase of American-made products for use by the federal government]) and incorporating the Valdez Principles or a similar guideline into the Federal Acquisition Regulation (FAR), 48 Fed. Reg. 42102 (1983) (codified at 48 C.F.R. 1), which provides standard procedures and methods for the acquisition of products and services by the federal government. See Current Development, *supra* note 4, at 245–46.

225. Pear, *Voters Spurn Array of Plans for Protecting Environment*, The New York Times, Nov. 8, 1990, at B1, col. 5.

226. Cairncross, *The Environment: An Enemy and Yet a Friend*, The Economist, Sept. 8, 1990 (special survey section), at 9; Kirkpatrick, *supra* note 218, at 47. *See* Brackett, *EPA and Justice Department Step Up Enforcement Against Corporate Environmental Violators*, IRRC Investor's Envtl. Rep., Winter 1991, at 3–4 (noting record penalty assessments, Superfund contributions, and civil and criminal enforcement efforts in 1990). In fact, saving money is the principal reason companies such as Minnesota Mining & Manufacturing (3M) ("Pollution Prevention Pays [PPP]" policy), Chevron ("Save Money and Reduce Toxics [SMART]"), and Dow Chemical ("Waste Reduction Always Pays [WRAP]") have embarked on campaigns to reduce polluting waste. Cairncross, *supra*, at 9. *See* 136 Cong. Rec. S4686, 4687 (daily ed., Apr. 20, 1990) (statement of Senator Kerry); Naimon, *supra*, note 38, at 9 (noting savings and efficiency of environmental Total Quality Management [TQM] practices of E. I. DuPont de Nemours Co. and Florida Power & Light). In the fifteen years of its PPP program, 3M claims to have saved in excess of $482 million worldwide. Cairncross, *supra*, at 9.

227. Kirkpatrick, *supra* note 218, at 47.

228. *See* Barbera & McConnell, *The Impact of Environmental Regulations on Industry Productivity: Direct and Indirect Effects*, 18 J. ENVTL. ECON. & MGMT. 50, 62–63 (1990) (concluding that the net impact of environmental regulations on total factor productivity growth of the five most polluting industries is fairly small).

229. *See, e.g.*, Bottorff, *City Pension Board Cannot Get Insurance for Divestiture Plans*, LOS ANGELES DAILY J., Jan. 24, 1986, at B1, col. 1.

230. *See id.*

231. *See supra* note 222 and accompanying text.

CHAPTER 5

CORPORATIONS AND SOCIAL RESPONSIBILITY: A HISTORICAL PERSPECTIVE

Marcy Murninghan McCormack Institute of Public
Affairs, University of Massachusetts—Boston

This chapter provides a brief overview of the evolution of corporate
structure in Europe and the United States and examines the historical justification for claims that a corporation acts as a public moral,
as well as economic, agent. In addition, the chapter advances the
concept of a "corporate covenant"—that is, a mutually agreed-on
relationship of responsibility between a corporation and society voluntarily entered into, periodically renewed, and dedicated to the
common good. A contractual relationship, which can be broken or
renegotiated and tends to be past- and present-oriented, is dominated
by rules and focused on compliance and avoiding injury. In contrast,
a covenantal relationship recognizes the need for different levels of
accountability, is forward looking, is voluntary, and seeks to achieve
a more desirable state of being. Its essence is affirmative and
grounded in faith and trust rather than proscriptive and based on
fear and suspicion.

Marcy Murninghan is a senior associate at the McCormack Institute of Public
Affairs at the University of Massachusetts—Boston. For eight years she has been
a writer, teacher, and consultant on issues related to the interplay between moral
values and economic decision making. These issues include the ethical responsibility of corporation ownership, the role of philanthropy and voluntarism in
public life, and the democratization of economic enterprises. She has special
expertise with respect to investment policy and South Africa and Northern
Ireland. She holds a doctorate from Harvard University, a master's degree from
Antioch, and a bachelor's degree from Albion College.

CORPORATE HISTORY: FIVE STAGES

In the United States, the modern corporation is a product of the 1880s, a period when systems of mass production and mass distribution created new forms of industrial enterprise. The opening of national and international markets, made possible by a new transportation and communications infrastructure, triggered the reorganization of business into integrated, multifunctional structures with full-time salaried management. Before 1880, Western Union and Montgomery Ward were among the few large companies to operate throughout the country. By the end of the 1880s, numerous businesses marketed household products nationwide: American Tobacco Company, Diamond Match, Pillsbury Company (flour), Quaker Oats, H. J. Heinz, Campbell Soup, Borden (milk), Eastman Kodak, Procter & Gamble, General Electric, and Anheuser-Busch, to name a few. By the turn of the century, many more integrated, multifunctional firms were transforming both American life and the American economy. At the same time, these companies separated ownership from management, enabling the business enterprise to take on a life of its own.

This type of corporate structure is the fourth in a series of chronological stages of corporate evolution. It has prevailed throughout the twentieth century, but appears to be giving way to another in an era marked by global competition and institutional ownership. These two new factors promote greater application of the democratic principles of participation, power sharing, and accountability to corporate decision making. Ours, too, is an era when many investors believe that public moral and financial criteria are intertwined. Before describing this shift and its implications, it is useful to review the early stages in corporate history.

PHASE ONE: ROMAN AND MEDIEVAL PERIODS

The roots of corporate history can be traced to early Roman and Anglo-Saxon laws governing the conduct of groups. In those times, public responsibilities rested not merely with individuals but also with collectives, such as clans, families, or civic organizations. Structures that were neither public nor private evolved to produce what was necessary for the maintenance of the community. The rise of group law helped to formalize and legitimate these assumptions of corporate interdependence or "wholeness."

Within the Roman Empire, the management of villages, towns, and guilds was handled by formally established corporate bodies. Christianity introduced other collective entities—such as churches, monasteries, and abbeys—independent of both the traditional household and the existing regime. This initial phase of corporate evolution, lasting well into the Middle Ages, was characterized by the belief that institutions organized purely for business or financial purposes were morally inferior to institutions operating beyond economic self-interest. Businesses were "bad" because they were not connected to home and family, because they represented a departure from nature and spirituality, and because they took wealth out of the community. Entities granted a corporate charter—usually conferred by the reigning sovereign—were those perceived as contributing to the health and vitality of the community, such as universities, churches, guilds, and boroughs. They were viewed as promoting some legitimate common interest that advanced the common good. In this sense, then, corporations possessed a public moral dimension.

This public moral or civic dimension helped provide members of a corporation with a purpose in addition to profit. For members of the university, it was the generation of knowledge; for the church, it was religion; for a town or borough, it was shared political interests; for the guild, it was the identification of legitimate practitioners. The notion of "profit" was not viewed as intrinsically bad. It was viewed, in value-free terms, as the difference between assets and liabilities, something that could be used in new efforts to create wealth. As such, profit represented a calculation rather than an ideology or a cause. As such, it had a limited and precise meaning. More than merely profit-making entities, corporations were expected to make a highly valued civic contribution.

I PHASE TWO: SIXTEENTH TO EIGHTEENTH CENTURIES

The second period in the evolution of the corporation occurred during the years of global exploration and trade, particularly with the East and the New World. In contrast to the first, this phase saw the crown grant charters to groups formed for the express purpose of making money. Throughout the 1500s, the corporation functioned primarily as a passport for individuals with legitimate trading privileges. For example, a country's sovereign would grant special trading rights to a particular group, while both financial responsibilities and liability still resided in the corporation's individual members. The Russia Company and the Turkey Company were examples of such corporations.

But as exploration and trade increased, a prototype of the modern corporation emerged, with its emphasis on profit making, structural separation of ownership and management, and limited liability. Throughout the 1600s and well into the 1700s, major trading companies were organized as joint-stock enterprises. One of the first was the East India Company, with members pooling resources for the initial investment and agreeing to divide expected profits according to share ownership. In this structure, corporate authority was vested in a governor and his committee, and liability was distributed among stockholders. The Massachusetts Bay Company, the Hudson's Bay Company, and the Royal African Company were examples of profit-making companies functioning solely as de facto instruments of the crown. As such, they were viewed as quasi-governmental entities. Moreover, each enjoyed monopoly status in its respective business.

Despite this evolution, the idea of public moral or civic responsibility did not fade. In eighteenth-century England, the principle that private corporate activity should be undertaken for a public purpose was incorporated in the law. The language of many charters granted during this period—including that of the Bank of England—continued to include references to actions taken in the public interest in exchange for the monopoly power a charter bestowed.

| PHASE THREE: THE AMERICAN CORPORATION

By the time of the settlement of America, the tools and mechanics of incorporation had spread throughout Europe. In the early 1700s, corporate chartering was no longer restricted to Parliament or the crown. It became a process, available to different agents, which invited abuse. Eventually Parliament enacted reforms restoring charter-granting authority to the crown and requiring a demonstration of public purpose. Once again the process within Europe became more selective and the commitment to civic responsibility more secure.

Following Roman and medieval tradition, the corporation was

put to a public purpose during the American colonial era. Many nonindustrial structures were incorporated, including cities and towns, colleges, and churches. In fact, few businesses were incorporated until after the Revolution. Numerous corporations, however, were chartered. Between 1783 and 1801, nearly 350 enterprises were incorporated, primarily in New England. In contrast to the practice in Britain, chartering authority was democratic. It was granted by the sovereignty of the state rather than by the crown or the federal government. In fact, the Founding Fathers deliberately omitted federal charter-granting power from the Constitution, viewing it as a matter more appropriately left to the individual states.

The corporation in colonial times was notably democratic, adhering to the principles of accountability, participation, and power sharing. Because it was created by special act of a state legislature, was carefully scrutinized, and possessed a public-purpose orientation, the colonial corporation reflected the community's sense of itself. The colonial corporation's civic orientation helped to strengthen the community while keeping the size of government down. Moreover, the proliferation of corporations and general access to chartering reflected a pluralist orientation, a departure from the European elitist tradition.

The situation began to change, however, in the first half of the nineteenth century. During the decades following the Revolution, state legislatures continued to have the power to accept or reject corporate applications. But politicians sometimes attached special conditions to these charters, conditions that eventually became the subject of abuse and the target of criticism. As a result of reforms aimed at eliminating favoritism and corruption, the chartering process became bureaucratized and standardized. By 1850 the movement away from special charters to free incorporation gained momentum as various states passed laws that allowed groups to form corporations without special legislative action.

Reformers replaced the old system of special petition (typically accompanied by an uncertain and subjective review process) with general laws of incorporation. This shift opened up the process, thereby increasing participation—an important democratic principle. However, accountability—another important democratic principle—declined as corporate entities enjoyed greater autonomy and freedom from public control. Gone was the problem of government favoritism. Standardized procedures assured corporate status to any organization that could fill out forms and pay fees. Gone too, however, was the idea of government control and the expectation of corporate public moral or civic responsibility—a major departure from the earlier American and European tradition.

| PHASE FOUR: THE INDUSTRIAL REVOLUTION AND THE RISE OF THE MANAGERIAL ELITE

As the nation grew—with its railways, mills, refineries, and pipelines—the corporate form became essential to the efficient capitalization and management of large-scale, complex enterprises. In 1830 there were only 23 miles of railroad track; by 1890 there were 208,152 miles of track. As the national railroad system was built, the manufacturing sector quickly grew. With this growth came the invention of the multidivisional or multifunctional corporate structure, considered revolutionary in the history of corporate organization. No longer primarily a legal construct possessing quasi-public functions, the corporation became an inward-looking, private, organized social unit possessing—and breeding—considerable power.

Product or line divisions were separate from advisory or staff divisions. Hierarchies formed: top management, represented by the board, president, and executive committee; middle management, consisting of general staff and product line division offices; lower management, representing the functional offices within the divisions. These structures exploited economies of scale and were designed to facilitate efficient production, marketing, and distribution. As resources were transferred among divisions, they also functioned as internal capital markets. Finally, these corporate structures further separated ownership and control. The older custom of owner management and civic involvement was replaced by a managerial elite that became more entrenched as corporate structures became more complex and diversified. The rise of this managerial elite came to dominate the twentieth century and greatly undermined both corporate and public expectations for accountability and civic responsibility.

By midcentury, the managerial firm—that is, a corporation with governance and operations controlled by the managerial class—became the primary form of modern business enterprise throughout major sectors of the American economy. Several forces contributed to the emergence of this managerial capitalism. Corporate share ownership became more diffuse, thus reducing possibilities for direct owner participation in corporate affairs. Through mergers and internal growth, corporations became larger and more complex, thus increasing the need for centralized power and control. To effectively respond to greater corporate size and complexity, the managerial task became more professionalized and established—particularly in middle levels of the organization, where managers would supervise semiskilled and unskilled workers.

In spite of the dominance of the managerial elite, the concept of corporate civic responsibility surfaced again during this period. In some instances, corporate chief executive officers considered their role in public affairs to be a crucial one. In other instances, civic obligation was promoted from outside the corporate boardroom. Throughout the 1960s, 1970s, and 1980s, many arguments were advanced for corporate social responsibility by reformers utilizing various strategies—including boycotts, proxy campaigns, and governmental intervention. An extension of the tradition of American suspicion of consolidated power, these social responsibility efforts had little impact on the continued clout of the managerial elite. They did, however, help reinvigorate old assumptions about corporate duty and social obligation.

I PHASE FIVE: GLOBALISM, OWNERSHIP, AND THE CORPORATE COVENANT

At the end of this century, we seem to be entering a fifth phase in the history of the corporation, one that could produce greater levels of interdependence and accountability. Stimulating the evolution of this fifth stage are two forces: the rapid increase in global enterprise and international competition, and a dramatic increase in institutional corporate share ownership. The hallmark of this era is the multinational corporation, both U.S. and non-U.S. With the exception of nation-states, many people view multinational corporations as the most powerful organizations in the world. These corporations have proliferated in the last several decades. Direct investments abroad by American companies grew from $11.8 billion in 1950 to $232.7 billion in 1985, with much of that growth occurring since 1970. Over the same period, investment by foreign corporations in the United States grew rapidly.

By the end of the 1980s, free trade and private enterprise had become important means for stimulating the economies of communist and underdeveloped systems. And the collapse of trade barriers and reductions in tariffs and other forms of protectionism created a free-trade environment that facilitated a rapid increase in international commerce.

The Role of World Citizens

The resulting global competition and economic interdependence add a new dimension to the old dilemma of balancing private interests and the common good. For corporations, underlying public moral or civic questions related to rights, fairness, and justice take on fresh meaning when considered in this multinational context. These issues have attracted the attention of social investors and the media but have been relatively neglected by economists and business researchers. There are considerable difficulties in discerning civic obligation in a world community without falling into the quandary of cultural relativism. But as corporations become more global, defining their civic role becomes more important.

The Changing Nature of Ownership

The ownership of corporations also has changed dramatically over the past twenty years. In the United States, institutional shareholders now hold close to a majority of common stock. By the end of this decade, public and private pension plans alone are expected to become the majority shareholders in most American firms. During the 1980s, pension plans tripled in size; now they represent a combined value of more than $2 trillion. Other institutional investors, including trust funds, mutual funds, and endowments, have grown, fueled by federal tax policies granting special treatment to funds committed for retirement and charitable purposes.

Most institutional investors share underlying characteristics, even if they have different values and financial objectives. Their trust structures are similar, they display a preference for indexing or passive fund management, and they have a longer-term investment orientation. Increasingly, institutional owners are becoming permanent owners. This development has significant implications for their relationship to the companies they own. Rather than remaining passive owners, ignorant of corporate governance and corporate behavior, institutional owners are in a position to assert their power in ways that also advance the public interest. As majority owners of American corporations, they are in a position to restore some of the original ideas embedded in the earlier corporate tradition—ideas concerning corporate citizenship and public obligation. After all, institutional investors are fiduciaries for individuals who happen to be citizens as well as beneficiaries. Put another way, what is in their interest as owners can be considered in the public's interest as well. Most beneficiaries want to live in a world free from the ravages of poverty, illiteracy, crime, environmental abuse, and tyranny.

| A CORPORATE COVENANT

We come, then, full circle to ways in which the corporation might carry out its mission, enhancing its community as well as its immediate self-interest. Central to this new stage in corporate history is the idea of a *corporate covenant*—a voluntary, reciprocal, and periodically renewed relationship between a corporation and society. Such a covenant would be aimed at achieving a greater good.

Several changes in current practice must occur for the corporate covenant to succeed. They include: changes that gear the corporate governance system to the agenda of owners rather than of managers, thus removing impediments to shareholder action; changes in chartering that will reinvigorate earlier notions of civic duty and public accountability—perhaps through a federal law that sets minimum standards with improvements allowed at the state level; changes in the way in which fiduciary responsibility is defined and understood; and changes in the prevailing view of economic activity—that is, the incorporation of public moral and civic criteria into economic decision making.

PART TWO

SHAREHOLDER

ACTION

People who came of age in the 1960s and 1970s were shaped by television. Paladin, Emma Peel, the boys on Route 66, Donna Reed, and Matt Dillon always put everything right by the end of the show. Television news made positive social change look easy. File a lawsuit and win it, or push a law through Congress—backed up with a messy demonstration or two—and the world would change. With desegregation, the environment, and even Watergate, success seemed quick and final.

Now we know better.

Positive social change, which is what socially responsible investing is all about, takes a long time. It results from the work of millions, without whose efforts all of the court decisions and statutes would be worthless. And it comes in increments.

Changing things for the better usually takes a lot longer than changing things for the worse. Developing a vision for the future is the easy part. The hard work follows. There is a lot of "one step forward, two steps backward" before one sees progress. Patience, a sense of purpose, faith in the ultimate goodwill of fellow humans, and, most important, resilience—these characterize the successful reformer. The chapters in this section by shareholder activists reveal how necessary these characteristics are and how much has been accomplished.

This chapter's placement toward the beginning of the book may seem curious. After all, this is *The Social Investment Almanac*, and shareholder activism seems tangentially related to investing. But understanding how shareholder activism works and what its objectives are requires a knowledge of the corporation—at once, the entities we wish to reform *and* the engines of societal reform—and the issues shareholder activists are forcing society to confront. Those issues are, or in some cases will be, the social screens applied by investors.

Perhaps the other great lesson to the 1960s generation is that corporations are not implacable forces of evil that suck in drones and automatons to carry out their nefarious schemes. Instead they are small cultures within our larger culture. They are made up of people who think and react to the same things—the environment, crime, homelessness—that everyone else does. These people can be reached and they can be persuaded. And they can transform their corporations.

Shareholder activism plays a key role in this process of transformation.

Shareholder activism takes two forms. The form most in the news recently has been efforts by institutions—pension funds, primarily—to force corporations to act more in their interests. James Heard, one of the institutional activists' chief theorists, explains the hows and whys of this new force.

The remainder of this section explores shareholder activists whose causes are social. Tim Smith, executive director of the Interfaith Center on Corporate Responsibility, introduces the movement he has done as much as anyone to shape. Bill Somplatsky-Jarman outlines the South African situation, which now appears headed toward a resolution. The lessons learned in the South Africa divestiture movement are cited throughout this section.

One area that Americans seem to ignore willfully is Central America. But not all Americans, as Steve Koenig points out, are willing to allow the hideous struggles in El Salvador to pass unnoticed. The lever is coffee, and the targets include Procter & Gamble.

Since 1989 shareholder activists have moved strongly on environmental issues, as Ed Crane, Ariane van Buren, and Andy Smith point out in their survey. While the Valdez Principles (described by Joan Bavaria) are the centerpiece of this effort, other issues, like chlorofluorocarbons (CFCs) have not been forgotten.

In the euphoria of *glasnost* and the relaxation of superpower tensions, two byproducts of our century of hot and cold wars have run down the drain of consciousness. But international debt, used to buy friendship, and militarism, used to make sure friends stayed that way, are not issues of the past, as John Lind and Valerie Heinonen point out.

Indeed, the breaking down of international boundaries, especially in trade, has brought its own set of ethical dilemmas—the exploitation of foreign workers and consumers. The horrendous labor and environmental problems posed by the *maquiladoras* just across our border with Mexico, Amy Domini indicates, are not unique. As Regina Rowan and Michael Crosby show, the pharmaceutical and tobacco industries have pushed products in the third world that are banned elsewhere or known to cause serious health problems.

Has shareholder activism had any effect on corporations and society in general? Ed Crane and Tim Smith present evidence that it has and that its momentum is growing. But much remains to be done. As Larry O'Brien, the mastermind of many of the great legislative and political victories of the 1960s, put it, in social reform there are "no final victories."

FIDUCIARY DUTY AND INSTITUTIONAL SHAREHOLDER ACTIVISM

James E. Heard Senior Adviser, Institutional
Shareholder Services

The past five years have witnessed an extraordinary transformation in the role that institutional investors are playing as shareholders in major American corporations. Passive ownership has given way to active involvement. Institutional investors have begun to deter-

---

James E. Heard is senior adviser to Institutional Shareholder Services (ISS), where he counsels institutional investors on fiduciary issues affecting their investments. His clients include many of the largest pension funds and money managers in the United States. Mr. Heard has written and spoken widely on corporate governance issues and has given frequent testimony to Congress, state legislatures, and regulatory agencies on these issues. He also advises clients on social and political issues that affect investment policy. Mr. Heard previously held positions as managing director of Analysis Group, executive director of the United Shareholders Association, and deputy director of the Investor Responsibility Research Center. A graduate of Harvard College and George Washington University Law School and a member of the Bar Association of the District of Columbia, he also has served as an adjunct faculty member at Georgetown University's School of Business.

Institutional Shareholder Services is the nation's leading proxy advisory firm. Based in Washington, D.C., ISS provides research and consulting services to more than one hundred major institutional investors to assist them in meeting their fiduciary duties as shareholders in public corporations. The firm advises clients on legal and regulatory developments that affect them as fiduciaries, assists clients to vote proxies efficiently and on an informed basis, and conducts research on policy issues that affect institutional investors. The firm's clients include public and private pension funds, money managers, and endowments.

mine the outcome of shareholder proposals at corporate annual meetings, cast the decisive votes in proxy contests, reshape the structure and composition of boards of directors, and define the public agenda for corporate accountability in the 1990s.

Among institutional investors, public pension funds have been by far the most active, but they have not been alone. Other types of institutional investors have decided to reevaluate the role they play in corporate affairs through voting of their proxies.

The activism of the past five years has centered primarily on corporate governance issues, not questions of social responsibility. The most important reason for this emphasis is the determination by institutional investors that corporate governance issues affect their bottom lines. As fiduciaries, these institutions believe that they have a responsibility to preserve and enhance the rights of shareholders to participate in corporate affairs, because these issues have measurable economic effects on the companies in their portfolios. This position is supported by a substantial body of economic research as well as by recent U.S. Department of Labor directives to pension funds and their investment managers. The department has indicated that proxy voting is subject to the same fiduciary standards as other investment decisions.

In contrast, most institutional investors have tended to regard the social responsibility issues on which they are asked to vote as at best peripheral—at worst harmful—to the economic interests of the companies in which they invest. With the notable exceptions of endowments and a small number of public and labor union funds, institutional investors have shown far less interest in and concern about social issues than they have about corporate governance matters. The potential exists, however, to cast social issues in a different light. This is true particularly of environmental questions. If during the 1990s environmentalists and other social activists can frame shareholder campaigns in economic terms, they could receive high levels of support from institutional investors and increase their bargaining position with corporations whose policies they seek to influence.

This chapter describes the changes that have occurred in the role of institutional investors as shareholders during the past decade, explains the reasons for those changes, and suggests how the role of institutional investors is likely to evolve. The emphasis of the chapter is on proxy voting, the most visible manifestation of shareholder activism.

| VOTING POLICIES OF INSTITUTIONAL INVESTORS

Traditionally, institutional investors in the United States have played a passive role as shareholders. Most have followed the Wall Street Rule: support management in voting decisions; if serious disagreements arise, sell the stock. Adherence to the rule was the norm among institutional investors in the 1960s and during most of the 1970s.[1] Changes in voting policy during the 1980s resulted from three related developments.

One important development has been the phenomenal growth in the institutional ownership of common stocks. By various estimates, institutional investors—pension funds, mutual funds, insurance companies, endowments, and others—now own more than 45 percent of all publicly traded stock in the United States. Among larger companies, such as those in Fortune 500, it is not unusual for more than half of the stock to be owned by institutional investors.[2] Because they have a larger stake in a company, institutional investors have an economic incentive to become more attentive to actions that may affect the value of their investments.

A second reason for the change in voting behavior is that voting issues in the 1980s involved questions that clearly had an economic impact on shareholders. The proliferation of antitakeover amendments to corporate charters transferred important governance rights from shareholders to top management and their hand-picked boards of directors. The harmful economic effects of these amendments on shareholders have been documented in dozens of economic studies by academics and by the Securities and Exchange Commission (SEC).[3]

A third important reason why institutions have changed their voting policies is that the Department of Labor has advised pension funds and their investment managers that proxy voting is subject to federal fiduciary standards. The department administers the Employee Retirement Income Security Act of 1974. This statute governs the investment activities of private pension plans and their outside investment managers. And even though it does not apply directly to public pension funds, many public sector retirement systems model their policies on ERISA.

In a series of pronouncements in the late 1980s, the Labor Department stated that ERISA's requirements of prudence and loyalty apply to proxy voting. Prudence requires that due care be taken in making investment decisions; loyalty requires that all investment devisions be made for the exclusive benefit of pension plan participants. A basic premise of this policy is that voting issues can affect the value of stocks held by pension plans subject to ERISA. The department's top ERISA official said in 1988,

> A fiduciary who manages a portfolio has a duty to evaluate issues that can have an impact on the economic value of the stock in the portfolio and to vote on those issues. Shares should be voted based upon a careful analysis of the impact of the vote on the ultimate value of the plan's investment. . . .[4]

The Labor Department has backed up its words with a series of investigations aimed at pension plans, their investment managers, and other fiduciaries.[5] The result has been a much higher level of due diligence on proxy voting by institutions subject to Labor Department regulation.

Lower-level clerical employees no longer automatically cast votes in favor of management. Instead many institutions have developed independent voting policies and procedures and created high-level committees to monitor voting activities. Among the institutions that have adopted such policies and procedures are not only major public pension funds (which are not subject to ERISA), but also large financial institutions, such as Fidelity Investments, Alliance Capital Management, Citibank, and Bankers Trust Company, and corporate pension funds, such as AT & T. Institutions are doing more independent research, hiring outside experts to advise them on voting issues, and voting in an informed and independent manner.

| THE FOCUS OF INSTITUTIONAL CONCERN

The principal concern among institutional investors in regard to proxy voting has been on questions of corporate governance, structure, and control, because these issues affect the value of portfolio securities. Thus, most public pension funds that have become activists are so on proxy issues of these types. The Council of Institutional Investors, created in the mid-1980s by labor union and public pension funds, has concentrated exclusively on corporate governance and shareholder rights issues. The council has eschewed involvement in social issues. Similarly, institutions subject to the

Labor Department's standards frequently support proposals to protect shareholder rights but seldom vote for social issue resolutions. Endowments and religious organizations are much more likely to support social responsibility initiatives, but because they are much smaller, they are much less likely to affect voting outcomes.[6]

A comparison of voting outcomes on corporate governance issues with those for social responsibility issues illustrates the difference. In 1990, for example, proposals to establish confidential voting and independent tabulation of voting results and proposals to require shareholder approval of poison pill takeover defenses actually were approved at some companies. At many others, their levels of voting support exceeded 40 percent. In contrast, shareholder proposals asking companies to sever economic ties with South Africa received on average about 13 percent of the vote. Voting results on many other social responsibility issues were even lower.

While they have initiated shareholder campaigns to require confidential voting, more independent directors, and reasonable levels of management compensation, large institutional investors have, for the most part, chosen not to develop shareholder campaigns on social issues. The major exception to this rule has been South Africa. Some public pension funds, prodded by legislatures or public opinion, have undertaken shareholder initiatives. The principal purpose of these campaigns seems to have been defensive—to preempt pressure to sell securities by jawboning companies into leaving South Africa altogether.

| A SOCIAL AGENDA FOR THE 1990S

The 1990s present new opportunities to activists to generate support for their actions through proxy campaigns aimed at persuading institutional investors that social issues can have significant economic effects on portfolio companies. Much of the reluctance of institutional investors to become active supporters of shareholder initiatives on social issues could be overcome if campaigns—and specific shareholder proposals—were framed in credible economic terms.

The reluctance to date of institutional investors to support social initiatives is in many cases due to a stigma attached to terms such as "social investing" and "socially responsible investing." These terms have been widely understood to mean pursuit of noneconomic objectives, either as primary or ancillary investment objectives. An often-debated question is whether fiduciaries can reconcile social goals with their obligation to manage assets solely in the interest of those to whom they owe a fiduciary duty. This issue arises frequently in voting proxies, deciding whether to divest holdings for social reasons, or making targeted investments for social purposes— all forms of social investing in the minds of many fiduciaries.[7]

The debate over these issues is now more than two decades old. Both supporters and opponents of social investing have made credible arguments. Much of the debate is definitional: what is meant by "social investing"? Some is philosophical: do institutional investors or, at the least, certain types of institutional investors have ethical responsibilities as investors? But for many fiduciaries, the issue is economic: are the proposed actions consistent with the economic interests of those whom the fiduciary owes his or her duty?

Much of the opposition to social investing, however understood, evaporates when proponents of the proposed action can make a credible case that their actions are consistent with the economic welfare of those to whom fiduciaries are responsible. This applies to divestiture campaigns, to targeted economic investing programs, and to proxy voting. Shareholder proposals that ask companies to take actions for social reasons that are inimical to the economic interests of the corporation and its shareholders are unlikely to win support from most fiduciaries, even when the actions proposed may be in society's best interests. But, proposals that ask companies to take actions that advance the corporation's interests or protect their shareholders' interests will be treated seriously. A careful reading of the Labor Department's recent pronouncements strongly suggests that ERISA fiduciaries have an obligation to examine all such proposals to determine whether they are likely to have an economic impact on pension plan participants.

Fiduciaries are unlikely to vote for shareholder proposals that ask tobacco companies to go out of business, as voting results on such proposals suggest. But they will pay serious attention to proposals asking companies to curtail activities that can directly impact the bottom line. Environmental issues are especially conducive to being framed in economic terms. Institutional investors can hardly take a cavalier attitude toward environmental issues when Exxon faces cleanup costs exceeding $1 billion for the Alaskan oil spill. Among proposals likely to have broad appeal are requests to make special reports to shareholders on environmental impacts, to add environmentalists or scientists to boards of directors, to create environmental committees of boards to endorse environmental codes of conduct, and to agree to independent third-party auditing of environmental activities. Well-framed proposals that address company-specific concerns are likely to elicit significant levels of support. When this happens, corporations are willing to negotiate seriously with proponents. In 1990 and 1991, for example, dozens of companies agreed to adopt confidential proxy voting and independent third-party tabulation of voting results. It is no coincidence that this occurred in the aftermath of a campaign by major public pension funds in which shareholders had given very high levels of support to confidential voting shareholder proposals at many Fortune 500 companies.

Environmentally conscious investors already have initiated a shareholder campaign aimed at persuading U.S. corporations to curtail harmful environmental impacts associated with their business. So far the campaign has focused on asking companies to support the Valdez Principles, a ten-point environmental code developed by a coalition of environmental groups and socially conscious investors. In 1990 and 1991, a number of companies were asked either to report to their shareholders on their compliance with the code or to sign the code. Voting results are quite encouraging. Requests that companies report to their shareholders on the environmental impacts of their actions have generated respectable, though modest, levels of support. For example, a proposal to Armstrong World Industries requesting that it report to its shareholders on the environmental impact of its operations received more than 13 percent of the vote at the company's 1991 annual meeting. Requests that companies sign the Valdez Principles have encountered significant opposition, however. No major public company has yet signed the Principles, though several are considering doing so. A number of others have outlined in their 1991 annual meeting materials the actions that they have taken to protect the environment.

An important second step for environmental activists will be to frame proposals that address company-specific concerns or problems, and to frame the proposals in economic terms that speak to fiduciary concerns of institutional investors. Careful selection of companies, and development of recommendations that consider company-specific environmental impacts, is likely to generate significant levels of support among institutional investors. This in turn is likely to strengthen the bargaining position of environmentally conscious investors with corporate managements and boards of directors.

NOTES

1. An extensive literature exists documenting the voting policies of institutional investors and their adherence to the Wall Street Rule. See, for example, 20th Century Fund, *Abuse on Wall Street: Conflicts of Interest in the Securities Markets* (Westport, Conn.: Quorum Books, 1980); Securities and Exchange Commission, *Institutional Investor Study Report* (Washington, D.C.: GPO, 1971); Securities and Exchange Commission, *Staff Report on Corporate Accountability* (Washington, D.C.: GPO, 1980); James E. Heard and Howard D. Sherman, *Conflicts of Interest in the Proxy Voting System* (Washington, D.C.: Investor Responsibility Research Center, 1987).
2. These estimates are taken from testimony given to the Senate Banking Committee in 1989. See *The Impact of Institutional Investors on Corporate Governance, Takovers and the Capital Markets*, hearings before the Senate Banking Subcomittee on Securities, Oct. 3, 1989.
3. The literature on voting issues that affect shareholder value is enormous. Excellent summaries and citations are found throughout Robert A. G. Monks, Howard D. Sherman, and Nell Minow, *The ISS Proxy Voting Manual* (Washington, D.C.: Institutional Shareholder Services, 1991).
4. David M. Walker, Assistant Secretary of Labor, address to Pension Research Council, May 12, 1988.
5. See James E. Heard, "Labor Department Launches Proxy Voting Enforcement Program," *Insights* 2, no. 8 (August 1988): 17. See also *ISS Proxy Voting Manual*, chap. 1, "The Obligations of Fiduciary Shareholders in Proxy Voting and Other Aspects of Corporate Ownership."
6. The best source of information about voting results on shareholder proposals, and on how various types of institutional investors vote, can be found in the annual voting surveys conducted by the Investor Responsibility Research Center.
7. An excellent summary of fiduciary principles and a discussion of how they apply to social investing is contained in Betty Linn Krikorian's *Fiduciary Standards in Pension and Trust Fund Management* (Washington, D.C.: Butterworth Legal Publications, 1989).

SHAREHOLDER ACTIVISM

Timothy Smith Executive Director,
Interfaith Center on Corporate Responsibility

In 1971 the Episcopal Church took a historic step and filed the first church-sponsored shareholder resolution. The company was General Motors, the issue South Africa. The year before, the Project on Corporate Responsibility had broken ground and challenged General Motors with a series of shareholder resolutions on such issues as putting women and minorities on the board, the environment, corporate governance, and nondiscrimination in employment. A new era of corporate accountability had been born. Over the next twenty years, shareholder resolutions rose from a small handful to more than 350 sponsored in 1991.

TWENTY YEARS OF GROWTH

In the early 1970s, social shareholder resolutions were considered successful if they reached the 3 percent threshold vote allowing them

---

Timothy Smith is the longtime executive director of the Interfaith Center on Corporate Responsibility (ICCR), which is celebrating its twentieth anniversary this year. ICCR provides research and coordinates action for some 25 Protestant denominations and 230 Roman Catholic orders and dioceses active in bringing social concerns to corporate attention via dialogue with management, open letters, public hearings, stockholder resolutions, divestment of stock, and the like.

As executive director, it is Smith's responsibility to help translate statements of concern on corporate issues into action. ICCR has focused on questions of discrimination in employment, investments in and bank lending to South Africa, corporate involvement in the nuclear arms race and Star Wars, baby formula abuse, alternative investment opportunities, energy and the environment, and so on.

ICCR has a twelve-person program and administrative staff, and in 1990 had a budget of over $550,000.

to be resubmitted the next year.* In the 1990s many social resolutions are receiving 10 to 25 percent of votes, and corporate governance votes are gaining 20 to 50 percent.

The sponsors of the early resolutions were church investors whose work was coordinated by the ICCR. By 1991 shareholder resolution filers included some of America's largest pension funds, such as TIAA-CREF, the pension funds of New York City, New York State, and the states of California, Wisconsin, and Minnesota. In addition, hundreds of pension funds, universities, foundations, trade unions, and church investors have decided to sell their stock in companies that had socially objectionable policies on issues like South Africa and tobacco. Between the proactive approach and divestment, institutions with portfolios worth in excess of $600 billion are involved in challenging corporations.

The movement has evolved from the stage when shareholder resolutions were considered an annoying irritation by gadflies to one where only corporate executives with their heads in the sand would ignore the power—if not the sensibilities—of these investor petitioners. As one analyst stated, "The acoustics change at a stockholders meeting when the resolution is jointly sponsored by investors with one to three million shares."

However, the acoustics have been changing whether the sponsor has one hundred shares or one million shares. In the 1980s from one-quarter to one-third of the shareholder resolutions were withdrawn as part of negotiated agreements with companies. Many companies decided that it was better "to switch than fight." And shareholder activists had learned the art of compromise. The first resolution withdrawn as part of an agreement was a United Church of Christ resolution filed with Mobil in the early 1970s asking the company to report to shareholders on its South African operations. The first corporate report on a social issue was mailed to Mobil's hundreds of thousands of shareholders.

---

*The filing of a resolution is a relatively simple matter. The proponents must hold the stock for one year before the filing date (the specific deadline for resolutions for the following year is listed in the company's proxy statement). The filers must together hold a minimum of one thousand dollars' worth of stock. The resolution must be under five hundred words and fit within the rules of the Securities and Exchange Commission (SEC). The resolution is sent to the CEO or corporate secretary with proof of ownership from a broker or investment manager. In order for the resolution to be submitted again—assuming it lost—it must exceed a threshold vote: 3 percent the first year, 6 percent the second, and 10 percent the third and subsequent years.

Since then companies have prepared hundreds of reports on issues from South Africa to the environment, from infant formula abuse to equal employment opportunity (EEO). Information is a vital component in building corporate accountability, and these reports have become an essential ingredient.

Shareholder resolutions have led to substantial changes in corporate policies. These are much harder to negotiate than mere disclosure. Companies have agreed to resolutions asking them to cut ties in South Africa, end infant formula abuse, improve their EEO record, and support fair employment standards in Northern Ireland—to list a few.

| THE CHURCHES AND SHAREHOLDER ADVOCACY

Why are the churches in the United States involved in corporate social responsibility and shareholder advocacy work? We are concerned about corporations and how they affect our lives. We are concerned about economic and social justice. As investors we have a responsibility to look both at the bottom line that creates returns to our pensions and endowments and the "social bottom line," so that our values, our social concerns, and our religious traditions are on the same table with our investments and our economic decisions.

For many years, that was not the case. In the 1950s and 1960s the religious communities were official schizophrenics. They had their ethics in one pocket and their stock portfolios in the other, and never did the twain meet. Today's reality is very different.

Screened Investments

Some institutional investors also screen parts of their portfolio. New York City, for example, divested its stock in most companies that were in South Africa. California's pension funds, with over $100 billion, also have divested. California law dictates that the state pension funds be managed on a "South Africa–free" basis. TIAA-CREF has taken a slightly different approach. It does not screen out such investments. Instead it files shareholders resolutions for discussions with management and debate at the stockholders meeting.

So in the context of $600 billion of institutional and individual investor wealth, different approaches are being used toward common goals. The network has grown immensely, and the respect for the issues posed by shareholder resolutions has gained in the business community as well.

Alternative Investments

Using investments for a particular social purpose is a different kind of shareholder advocacy. Alternative investment or investment targeted for community economic development is the other side of the social investment coin. We do not have to invest our portfolios in a Mobil or an IBM. We can put money into a low-cost housing cooperative or a minority business in the inner city. In this way, our money does dual duty—making a return for the investor and helping to build that low-income housing cooperative, for example.

Alternative investment is growing, and not just among church investors. Insurance companies recently reported that they had $1.2 billion in "social investing," a term they use to describe putting money to work in areas like low-income housing projects. Their ten-year survey showed that they suffered remarkably few delinquencies while enjoying a reasonable return.

| 1991 RESOLUTION ISSUES

Some corporate social responsibility issues have a long history; others are relatively recent manifestations. Some are highly controversial; others are exceptionally reasonable. Corporate responsibility issues on proxy ballots in the spring of 1991 included:

- South Africa, an issue that has twenty years of history
- EEO—fair employment practices and nondiscrimination for women and ethnic minorities
- militarism and peace, and involvement in the nuclear arms race
- baby formula abuse, an issue that has been with us for more than fifteen years
- the environment
- third world debt—a most complex question
- tobacco-related issues
- fair employment in Northern Ireland
- corporate governance concerns
- *Maquiladoras*—how are U.S. companies in the north of Mexico treating their primarily female work force in terms of wages and working conditions, health and safety? What are they doing about the toxic waste that too often gets poured into border communities?

Let us examine some of these issues in more depth.

South Africa and the Banks

The issue of our banks' role in South Africa has been with us for two decades. Banking and financial pressure is especially important now. In 1990 and 1991 the press described the consensus that economic pressures and sanctions have been the key components in bringing about the changes to date. Even the conservative press and people inside South Africa indicate that these pressures were an important factor in pushing the South African government to the negotiating table. The South African government itself declared that financial sanctions have been very effective. It told the white electorate that if the 1990s were to be different and there was to be economic growth again, there must be substantial reforms. Nelson Mandela's message when he was in North America was unequivocal: keep the pressure on until apartheid is eradicated and a nonracial and nonsexist democracy is established. Our church colleagues in South Africa urge us to maintain this pressure as well.

We have won many victories in the United States as our banks have stopped lending to the government and to the private sector in South Africa and stopped selling South African gold in the United States. Nine banks in the last year have agreed to take a tougher position, cutting additional financial ties. We are in the last chapter of this struggle, and we will see it through to the end.

Tobacco

One of the more important issues of the nineties is the question of tobacco.

For more than three generations, some individuals and churches would not, on principle, own stock in tobacco companies. In the last twenty-five years, a new debate has arisen from the overwhelming evidence of the dangers of tobacco. Tobacco helps kill more than 400,000 people every year in the United States alone. Meanwhile, Philip Morris makes a 40 percent profit from its tobacco business. For investors, that makes it a very appealing stock. Nicotine is addictive, but profits may be even more addictive.

The debate over tobacco will ripple out beyond the current contestants. Insurance companies in the United States give preferential rates to nonsmokers. People who do not smoke have fewer health problems and longer lives. These same insurers own millions of shares of Philip Morris, Loews, and other tobacco companies. What is the insurer's responsibility when it knows the evidence and yet invests in these companies? What about companies like 3M and Gannett, who sell space on their billboards for ads that encourage young people to smoke?

The tobacco issue is going to open up a very interesting sector in the corporate responsibility debate.

The Environment

The top issue for the 1990s is the environment. A new energy, a new concern, and a new commitment have produced new approaches. The resurgence of the environment has come not just because we care about wildlife, but because we have reason to worry about the very survival of our planet.

In 1989 a remarkable coalition created a set of standards for environmental performance called the Valdez Principles. The coalition included:

- the comptroller of the City of New York;
- the controller of the state of California;
- a number of religious investors including ICCR;
- experts in social investment, such as Joan Bavaria of Franklin Research & Development;
- representatives of organized labor; and
- mainstream U.S. environmental groups.

In 1991 sixty companies received shareholder resolutions asking them to deal with the Valdez Principles, either by doing a report on the Principles or by signing them and agreeing to live up to them.

Ironically, the debate over the Valdez Principles arises out of a consensus; all agree that environmental issues must be addressed. The issue is whether companies like Mobil, AT & T, and Exxon will sign somebody else's set of principles. That becomes a point of corporate governance and corporate power.

Industry codes, such as those in the chemical and petroleum industries, have emerged so that companies can avoid this problem. If the prospect of principles imposed from the outside impels people to set up internal standards and work to live up to them, that is a very positive step.

Some of the results of the environmental debate to this point:

- Top management and boards of directors paying a lot more attention to the environment and their environmental responsibilities;
- Agreements to report much more fully to shareholders;
- Upgrading corporate standards on the environment;
- A number of companies seriously considering signing the Valdez Principles.

| SHAREHOLDER ACTIVIST IMPACT

Shareholder resolutions have considerable impact when used as a single rifle shot. However, they have a greater impact when they are part of a multipronged, concerted campaign.

Often resolutions are used in concert with other pressure. Some pressure comes in the form of gentle persuasion, as in dialogue sessions and letters. Some resolutions take the form of high-visibility efforts, such as media outreach, demonstrations, boycotts, and legal actions. Both approaches have had successes and failures. Obviously a company that understands a resolution to be in its self-interest— whether defined in financial or public relations terms—is more likely to respond positively.

CEOs have stated that we had convinced them of our position but they had to protect the interests of shareholders. The lesson for shareholder activists is clear: their case cannot consist only of an ethical appeal. It also must advance the company's interests.

Sometimes management uses a resolution to deal with a broader set of pressures from consumers and the public. It is easier to negotiate with a group of designated representatives to carve out an agreement on South Africa or the environment than it is to deal with an amorphous general public. Thus, escalating public pressure encourages a company to work out an agreement with concerned shareholders in a publicly acceptable environment.

In the 1990s shareholder actions will multiply, their effectiveness will increase, and the coalitions proposing them will expand. They will be used in single-shot efforts and in concerted campaigns. Shareholder advocacy efforts will parallel actions by investors to divest from offending companies or to avoid their stock in the first place. Shareholder activism will continue to be an important tool holding corporations accountable to their various stakeholders.

SOUTH AFRICA
SHAREHOLDER RESOLUTIONS

The Reverend William Somplatsky-Jarman
Committee on Mission Responsibility Through
Investment, Presbyterian Church (U.S.A.)

South African issues once again dominated the 1991 shareholder season. Debates raged over the extent to which the "winds of change" were blowing apartheid away.

| THE 1991 DEBATE

The debate over the significance of changes within South Africa formed the backdrop for this season of stockholder initiatives. During 1990 events were heralded as encouraging signs by antiapartheid church groups or as indicating apartheid's demise by many companies and government officials.

Events in South Africa
February 1990 saw the release of Nelson Mandela, just nine days after the government unbanned the antiapartheid organizations the African National Congress, the Pan African Congress, and the South African Communist party.

The government of South Africa ended emergency restrictions on

---

Reverend William Somplatsky-Jarman has staffed the Committee on Mission Responsibility Through Investment of the Presbyterian Church (U.S.A.) since 1984. In addition to attending numerous corporate annual meetings on South Africa, he helped develop a common position and coordinated strategy of U.S. and European churches to press their respective banks to extract maximum repayment of outstanding loans.

thirty-three political organizations, including the United Democratic Front and the Coalition of South African Trade Unions (COSATU). In March, Namibia formally was granted independence, marking the end of South Africa's attempts to interfere militarily with its neighbors. The African National Congress suspended its commitment to the armed struggle, thus permitting it to receive grants from the U.S. government. President F. W. de Klerk made public commitments to move toward an end to apartheid's legislative underpinnings, and indeed the Separate Amenities Act was repealed in October 1990. (Skeptics are quick to point out that the law covered public facilities only. Private facilities within South Africa remain almost entirely segregated.) In October the state of emergency imposed to squelch the growing unrest was lifted in all areas except Natal, and discussions began between representatives of the majority population and government officials over a number of issues.

The dramatic increase of black-on-black violence has added to the uncertainty. The situation is exacerbated by the proximity of migrant labor housing to the townships, the role of the police, and the political desires of Gatha Buthelezi and his Inkatha organization. Buthelezi, chief minister of the Kwa Zulu homeland, has been a vigorous opponent of the African National Congress. While denouncing apartheid, he has cooperated with the South African government and opposed disinvestment and sanctions. Whatever its impetus, the violence has withered support for the antiapartheid movement.

The Erosion of Sanctions
This political change brought about an erosion of the economic pressures placed on South Africa by the United States and European countries. The European Economic Community voted to relax its sanctions by lifting a ban on new investment and considered lifting trade restrictions on the importation of South African iron, steel, and gold coins. The Danish government balked at the iron and steel agreement, thwarting this change.

These moves indicate the waning ability of the antiapartheid movement to hold the line on sanctions. Some of the strongest supporters of the antiapartheid movement, such as Hungary, Poland, and Czechoslovakia, sent trading missions and explored diplomatic relationships with South Africa. The USSR Council of Ministers even sent a delegation to South Africa. And South Africa has established relations with several African countries. The African Development Bank invited the Development Bank of South Africa as an observer at its annual meeting. Most surprising of all, Angola hinted at the possible resumption of oil sales to South Africa should South Africa repudiate the UNITA coalition under Jonas Savimbi.

The financial press reported that European banks were actively involved in refinancing South African bond issues, particularly for Electricity Supply Commission (ESCOM), and hinted that new money was flowing into South Africa.

The Response in the United States

The Bush administration contends that South Africa has met three of the five preconditions in the Comprehensive Anti-Apartheid Act for lifting sanctions:

1. the release of all political prisoners, including Nelson Mandela;
2. the repeal of the state of emergency, including the release of any prisoners detained under the state of emergency;
3. the unbanning of political parties and the permission of full political participation for all South Africans;
4. the repeal of the Group Areas Act and the Population Registration Act; and
5. entering into good faith negotiations with representatives of the majority population.

The U.S. antiapartheid movement only concedes that condition two has been substantially met. Nonetheless, the Bush administration has lifted U.S. sanctions, galvanizing the antiapartheid movement to a degree not seen in the last few years. Whether the movement can put enough political pressure on Congress to override the president remains in doubt at this writing.

The churches have responded by noting that their South African ecumenical partners still call for sanctions and disinvestment until events signal that the process of change is irreversible. These events may include the removal of sovereign power from apartheid legislative structures and investing that power in a constituent assembly or some other agreed-on interim structure and clear assurance that the white minority cannot reverse or veto this process of change.

| THE 1991 SHAREHOLDER SEASON

As the debate raged, churches and other shareholders, including a number of public pension funds, pressed ahead with 1991 shareholder resolutions. Ninety-one shareholder resolutions were submitted to eighty-two U.S. companies. The resolutions took four basic forms:

1. withdrawal;
2. severance of nonequity ties, such as sales and services;
3. banking relationships;
4. disclosure of information about South Africa operations.

Most urged companies to withdraw from South Africa and/or sever any nonequity ties that they might have.

For the first time in many years, no resolutions specifically addressed the Signatory Program that grew out of the Sullivan Principles, a set of guidelines committing corporations to equal opportunity. The Reverend Leon Sullivan, who initiated the principles, later withdrew from the program, declaring it incapable of ending apartheid.

Withdrawal Resolutions

Proponents of withdrawal remain convinced that U.S. corporations cannot effectively address the South African political situation. Their spending on reforms in the workplace or on social actions in South Africa is dwarfed by the corporate income and sales taxes they pay the South African government. Black organizations in South Africa continue to call for sanctions.

Proponents of withdrawal also have argued that remaining in South Africa is not in the corporations' best interest because of its sluggish economy and political unrest. Continued presence subjects U.S. companies to selective purchasing legislation by city and state governments as well as increased taxation. Companies no longer are able to deduct the taxes paid to the South African government from their U.S. tax bill.

DISINVESTMENT CRITERIA. Over the years, withdrawal resolutions have broadened their focus to add criteria for the disinvestment process. Often they urge the corporation to involve trade unions in negotiations about the terms of withdrawal and to seek sales agreements that empower blacks, possibly giving them a role in the management of or an ownership position in the new company. Resolve clauses in such resolutions may ask the company to:

1. Sever all economic ties with South Africa, including direct investment; sales and purchases of products or parts; licensing, technology, distribution, management or franchise agreements, and servicing of products; or
2. Negotiate disinvestment—before taking action—with South African workers and unions in a way that protects their rights and recognitions and benefits the larger black communities; or
3. Relocate in the front-line states, if possible, in a way that aids the economies of those states while continuing to isolate South Africa.

Withdrawal resolutions of the first type may read that the company should "use all legal means to completely and expeditiously withdraw from South Africa, including termination of any agreements to continue, directly or indirectly, any business links there."

Withdrawal resolutions of the second type concern the sales and services to strategic entities, which by and large are the police or military or parastatal organizations, such as ESCOM or the recently privatized South African Coal, Oil and Gas Corporation (SASOL). Shareholders have focused on these relationships as the role of U.S. corporations has been particularly linked to the key sectors of the South African economy—energy, computer technology, and transportation. The companies argue that South African law makes it virtually impossible to restrict the linkages of companies to the government or to elements of the economy. The proponents believe that companies should refuse such business because it involves them in the worst aspects of the apartheid system.

SASOL is important because it represents the effort of the South Africans to gain energy independence, thus averting the impact of the oil embargo. SASOL now provides nearly 35 percent of South Africa's oil needs through a coal-to-gas process. South Africa's transportation sector depends heavily on oil, particularly for the police and military, so SASOL's importance cannot be overestimated. ESCOM generates 97 percent of South Africa's electricity. Electrification is an important factor of the modernization of any country, but the South African government uses it as a political weapon to punish dissenters and townships marked by unrest.

SALES RELATIONSHIPS. Most resolutions concerning sales relationships request that the companies terminate the activity. In some cases the stockholders ask for reports on the nature of sales and contractual relationships with SASOL or ESCOM. The leading proponents of such resolutions are the New York City pension funds. The Wisconsin State Board of Investment and church groups affiliated with the Interfaith Center on Corporate Responsibility (ICCR) often cosponsor these resolutions.

These resolutions have been addressed mainly to major U.S. corporations often found in the portfolios of large investors. Smaller companies that may have strategic importance to South Africa have been overlooked. For example, Convex Computer, which has developed highly sophisticated "mini-supercomputers," has entered into nonequity distributorship agreements in South Africa and has actively solicited business. Convex is not widely held and never has received a shareholder resolution about these relationships. Likewise, Amdahl Corporation maintains a distributorship agreement in South Africa, but it received only its second resolution in 1991.

Nonequity Ties
Corporations withdrawing from South Africa often maintain economic links through nonequity ties, such as contracts, sales agents, distributorships, manufacturing or assembly agreements, and licensing. The Investor Responsibility Research Center (IRRC) indicates that of the 162 U.S. corporations that have disinvested since 1986, 79 retained some nonequity links. The 1991 resolutions sponsored by New York State pension funds address the issue of direct assets in South Africa, while TIAA-CREF or the church groups affiliated with ICCR call on companies to withdraw their assets and sever any nonequity ties. The New York State pension funds, however, do co-file the broader resolution if a company has assets in South Africa.

Banking Relationships
Antiapartheid activists have long identified bank loans to South Africa as a major source of support for the South African economy and government. U.S. banks have been key players in these rela-

tionships over the years. However, in 1985 the South African government imposed a moratorium on the repayment of its short-term debts. New credit from U.S. banks dried up. This parched the country and, many analysts assert, contributed significantly to 1990's political developments. South Africa's decision to withdraw from Namibia and Angola stemmed in large part, they say, from an inability to pay for the military adventures.

Since September 1985 nearly $11 billion of capital investments have flowed out of South Africa. The government has resorted to import restrictions to maintain a satisfactory balance of payments. Since the moratorium suspended repayment, South Africa has negotiated three "interim agreements" with the international banking community governing the repayment schedule of loans falling due during the moratorium. Three U.S. banks (Citicorp, J. P. Morgan, and Manufacturers Hanover) have served on a technical committee negotiating those agreements.

Church shareholders pressured the three banks to extract as much money from South Africa as possible and to adopt formal policies against any lending until apartheid is ended. As other major U.S. banks also have been approached, the shareholder resolutions have been tailored to the recipient.

Church shareholders also have called on the banks to forego trade-related lending, conversion of their outstanding debt to long-term agreements with the South African government, or holding South Africans' deposits or accounts. They also have asked banks to sever any correspondent banking ties and to cease serving as depositaries for American depositary receipts (ADRs) that permit the investment in shares of South African companies. Just before its 1991 annual meeting, J. P. Morgan, the bank that handled the largest part of the South African ADR business, announced that it no longer would handle South African ADRs.

Information Resolutions

The fourth type of shareholder resolution asks for disclosure of South African involvement. In 1991 six companies received them. Often shareholders submit these resolutions after years of requesting the company to withdraw or to cut off sales relationships.

In 1991 the information requested included such things as the amount of South African taxes paid during the last three years, how much profit the company may have made and remitted to the United States, and the dollar amount spent on social programs. Companies also were asked: to disclose any contingency plans for disinvestment and their plans for negotiation of disinvestment with the workers and their unions; to report on any action they had taken to lobby against sanctions legislation in the United States; and to declare formally their position on sanctions. Finally, the companies were to provide an accounting for any business they may have lost because of state, county, or municipal purchasing restrictions.

The NCNB Resolution

A resolution submitted to NCNB (North Carolina National Bank) deserves note because of its unique nature. Several years ago, Royal Dutch Petroleum stockholders identified a procedure in the company's bylaws that permitted a special meeting to be called to address items of concern to the stockholders. Shareholders are trying to trigger these procedures because Royal Dutch never has permitted the filing of a formal South Africa resolution. The purpose of the meeting would be to submit a resolution to a vote calling on Royal Dutch to withdraw from South Africa. Church shareholders are soliciting the support of such institutional stockholders as NCNB, which has nearly three million shares of Royal Dutch. The 1991 NCNB resolution received 9.4 percent of the vote.

I CONCLUSION

The situation in South Africa makes it difficult to identify trends related to shareholder resolutions. The proponents are committed to the issue until antiapartheid organizations in South Africa or their ecumenical partners indicate that irreversible change is under way. The possibilities of such change are difficult to predict. It is significant that the African National Congress will hold a national meeting in the summer of 1991, when such issues will be vigorously debated. The South African Council of Churches also will be holding its meeting in the summer of 1991.

As this is written in June 1991, it is a bit early to analyze the 1991 shareholder votes. The banking resolutions seem to have received significant votes, while the withdrawal resolutions may have slipped by a few points. However, they still garner votes far in excess of those typically received on a shareholder resolution. Shareholder proposals for 1992 will be developed along the same lines and filed with the corporations during the fall of 1991. Political developments in South Africa and the erosion of economic sanctions may dictate some modifications made for 1992.

The Interfaith Center on Corporate Responsiblity is sending a delegation to South Africa in July 1991 to meet with the church's ecumenical partners to evaluate the situation and identify future steps for engagement of U.S. companies around the South Africa question. At least for the near term, South Africa will continue to be a major focus for church stockholders and others seeking to raise issues of social responsibility with U.S. corporations.

BEYOND SOUTH AFRICA— SHAREHOLDERS TARGET EL SALVADOR

Steven Koenig President, Informed Investors Group

Since the first proxy resolution on a social issue appeared in 1970, shareholders have paid particular attention to the controversy regarding apartheid in South Africa. Recently, as the situation in South Africa has changed dramatically, a new human rights issue has surfaced regarding the civil war in El Salvador. Highlighting that issue was a shareholder resolution filed with Procter & Gamble in 1990, asking that company to stop purchasing coffee from El Salvador.

HISTORY OF EL SALVADOR AND ITS CIVIL WAR

Investigative journalist Scott Armstrong states in his 1990 report on the Salvadoran coffee industry, "The story of the country of El Salvador is the history of the coffee industry of El Salvador." For the past sixty years El Salvador has been a country with no middle class, just the very wealthy and the very poor. The consolidation of land ownership has been the key factor in maintaining this disparity and has precipitated some of the worst violence in Central America. Even the deaths during the recent civil war in Nicaragua do not

---

Steven Koenig, a chartered financial analyst, is a Seattle portfolio manager specializing in social investing. An economist and a pension specialist, Koenig is a former senior pension adviser at Seafirst Bank, a pension investment adviser at Seattle Trust & Savings Bank, and an investment specialist with New England Mutual Life Insurance Company. Koenig has a B.S. from the University of Illinois and an M.S. from the University of Washington.

compare to the more than seventy thousand killed in El Salvador since 1980.

Since the coffee industry is the country's largest and its ownership remains concentrated among a small number of families, a struggle between the "haves" and the "have nots" is inevitable. Some claim that many of the large Salvadoran coffee growers are tied to death squad violence. Others blame leftist guerrillas for bomb attacks, political assassinations, and terrorism.

The Reagan and Bush administrations have supported conservative government forces in El Salvador with both military and humanitarian aid. Activist groups opposed to U.S. aid claim that this support helps maintain right-wing death squads. This aid is characterized as de facto sanctioning of the killings by the El Salvadoran military—most notably the murders of six Jesuit priests, their cook, and her daughter on November 16, 1989. In response the U.S. State Department blames the left-wing Farabundo Martí Liberation Front (FMLN) for urban bombings and assassinations of intellectuals, newspaper columnists, civilian employees of the military, former FMLN members, mayors, and government ministers and their families.

The U.S. Congress mirrors both sides in its heated debates on aid to El Salvador. On October 19, 1990, aid to El Salvador was cut by 50 percent, reflecting a frustration with the unending civil war.

| COFFEE BOYCOTT

Against this backdrop of civil war in El Salvador and disagreement with the U.S. government, activist groups have sought to draw attention to the continuing political killings and human rights abuses. Neighbor to Neighbor, a nonprofit organization critical of U.S. policy toward El Salvador, led the way in November 1989 by calling for a boycott of Salvadoran coffee imports to the United States. Nestlé Foods, Hills Brothers, and Folgers were asked to honor the boycott. After agreeing to study the issue, all three companies rejected the boycott.

Upon hearing about the boycott requests, one shareholder of Procter & Gamble, a parent company of Folgers, decided to contact the company to encourage acceptance of the boycott. What started as a polite but forceful letter to Chairman Edward Artzt soon turned into a shareholder resolution cosponsored by the great-great-grandson of one of Procter & Gamble's founders and supported by several large religious institutions, including the National Council of Churches of Christ in the U.S.A., the board of Global Ministries of the United Methodist Church, the Presbyterian Church (U.S.A.), and the Church of the Brethren.

Proponents' Arguments

The resolution's proponents called for Procter & Gamble's board of directors to adopt the following policy. "Procter & Gamble shall no longer purchase coffee from El Salvadoran suppliers until the parties of the Salvadoran conflict *fully negotiate* a peaceful settlement of the war."[1]

The proponents feel that as the leading company in the U.S. coffee business, Procter & Gamble has an unparalleled opportunity to do the right thing. Almost all factions involved in El Salvador have come to the conclusion that a negotiated settlement is the only possible alternative to endless war. By suspending purchases of Salvadoran coffee until there is a peaceful settlement, Procter & Gamble can use a powerful, nonviolent means of applying leverage and assisting the overwhelming majority of Salvadorans who pray for the negotiations to succeed.

By past actions, Procter & Gamble's management has acknowledged the morality and appropriateness of using economic leverage in this fashion. In the 1970s Folgers took the lead in the U.S. coffee industry by suspending purchases of Ugandan coffee while Idi Amin remained in power. In 1986 the company sold its South African subsidiaries and added its weight to the international pressure that has brought the apartheid regime to the bargaining table.

Opponents' Arguments

Procter & Gamble's board of directors' formal response to the shareholder resolution best represents the opposition to the boycott.

> The proposed boycott of Salvadoran coffee is opposed by a broad range of knowledgeable and respected organizations, including the Roman Catholic Bishops of El Salvador and the U.S. government. We agree with these organizations that a boycott of coffee from El Salvador will be devastating to the small farmers, growers and workers of that country, cutting off their livelihoods. These are the very people the proposers and boycotters claim they wish to help.
>
> . . . The U.S. government also opposes the boycott. John H. Sununu, White House Chief of Staff to President Bush, has written Procter & Gamble Chairman and Chief Executive, Edward L. Artzt, stating:

The Administration strongly opposes any boycott of Salvadoran coffee. This misguided attempt to cripple the Salvadoran economy will hurt the peasant farmers, small producers and other employees in the coffee industry, causing innocent people further hardship. This boycott will do nothing to advance the peace process, democracy or human rights, which are fundamental aims of this Administration.

. . . This boycott is misguided, and, if successful, could have a negative effect on our Company's coffee business and the returns which that business produces for Procter & Gamble's shareholders.[2]

The resolution was put before shareholders for a vote on October 9, 1990, at Procter & Gamble's annual meeting. After a statement of opposition by Chairman Artzt, several shareholders and religious representatives made passionate pleas for passage of the resolution. It was defeated by a margin of 2.6 percent in favor, 97.4 percent opposed.

| FUTURE SHAREHOLDER ACTIONS

As the civil war of El Salvador rages on, debate in this country over aid to El Salvador continues to grow. In January of 1991, President Bush announced that the 50 percent cut from last year's aid to El Salvador, $42.5 million, would be released to that country on March 15, 1991. In letters to the president, 116 House members and 34 senators stated that Bush had misinterpreted the conditions Congress had set before aid could be delivered. They also said that this decision could undermine the negotiating process to end the civil war.

Reminiscent of the early 1970s, when South African resolutions were being introduced to one company after another, El Salvador resolutions are being proposed on the ballots of Procter & Gamble and Philip Morris for 1991. If the strife in that country continues year after year, shareholder resolutions with companies doing business in that country surely will continue with an intensity similar to the South African resolutions.

NOTES

1. Procter & Gamble, "Notice of Annual Meeting and Proxy Statement," 1990.
2. Ibid.

SHAREHOLDER ACTIONS AND THE ENVIRONMENT

Edgar G. Crane Director, Corporate Social
Responsibility, Evangelical Lutheran Church
in America

Ariane van Buren Director, Energy & Environment
Program, Interfaith Center on Corporate
Responsibility

Andy Smith Director, Socially Responsible
Investing, American Baptist Churches

The environment will dominate the shareholder action agenda for
the foreseeable future, just as South Africa dominated the past
twenty years. This chapter presents the recent history of shareholder
actions on the environment and then surveys the proxy seasons from
1989 to 1991.

BEFORE THE VALDEZ

Shareholder action on the environment at a significant level really
began with the "second wave" of the environmental movement, if
we take as waves Earth Day 1970 and Earth Day 1990. Through the

Edgar G. Crane is the director of Corporate Social Responsibility for the Evangelical Luthern Church in America. He was formerly president of International
Development Consultants; professor of Public Affairs at Northern Illinois University; mayor of Geneva, Illinois; and director of the National Legislative Conference. He holds degrees in political science from Northwestern University
(B.A.) and the University of California at Berkeley (M.A.) as well as in public
administration from the State University of New York at Albany. He has served
on the board of the Lutheran School of Theology at Chicago.

1980s, in any year, a variety of very specific resolutions might be filed with a dozen or so different companies, particularly on energy issues: conservation, utility rates, nuclear power plant operations, and the like. Energizing a broader and more dynamic shareholder movement on the environment took a major catastrophe, one that involved no direct loss of human life: the 1989 *Exxon Valdez* oil spill off the coast of Alaska, which gave rise to the Valdez Principles.

The relative lack of shareholder attention to environmental issues until 1989 probably had two causes. First, environmental groups chose other means of influencing corporations, such as pressure by citizen groups, legislation, and regulation. Second, social investors like the churches, through the Interfaith Center on Corporate Responsiblity (ICCR), concentrated most of their attention, efforts, and resources on South Africa.

ICCR had a working issue group on energy and the environment, but it assigned no professional staff to these issues until October 1990. ICCR was emphasizing dialogue groups rather than shareholder action in related areas, such as agricultural chemicals, pesticides, and pharmaceuticals. Still, ICCR was alone in relying on shareholder action as a means of influencing corporate environmental policies and practices.

During the second half of the 1980s, ICCR members concentrated their attention on a variety of specific energy and environmental issues. These included electric power utilities and facilities—mostly nuclear—that had earned a reputation for poor health and safety practices affecting employees and potentially the broader populace. Over the years, shareholders brought such resolutions back to particular companies as they continued negotiations and sought progress reports on key issues. In some cases, companies responded by changing practices in modest ways. In others, despite years of resolutions and dialogue, the companies made no changes. Table 10-1 lists some of the first-wave resolutions.

There is a clear lineage beginning with these earlier resolutions, through the resolution seeking extensive damages for the victims of the Bhopal disaster, to the Valdez Principles. Although the future was not clear at the time, these resolutions addressing specific issues were a necessary prelude to the Principles.

TABLE 10-1

TYPICAL ENVIRONMENTAL ISSUES: THE END OF THE FIRST WAVE, 1984–88

Issue	Companies	Years
Energy conservation	Houston Industries	1984
	Philadephia Electric	1984
Least-cost energy	Philadephia Electric	1987
Pollution control	Exxon	1984
Radioactive contamination	NL Industries	1984
Life-line utility rates	Consolidated Edison	1984
Nuclear power	American Electric Power	1984
	Cincinnati Gas & Electric	1984
	Consumer's Power	1984
	Houston Industries	1984, 1985
	Union Electric	1984, 1985, 1986, 1987
	Detroit Edison	1985, 1986
	Philadephia Electric	1985, 1986, 1988
	Carolina Power & Light	1986
Nuclear power report	Carolina Power & Light	1986
	Houston Industries	1988
	Texas Utilities	1988
Nuclear decommissioning	Union Electric	1988
Nuclear power alternatives	Carolina Power & Light	1987
	Detroit Edison	1987, 1988
Nuclear power project	Texas Utilities	1987
Nuclear power	Westinghouse	1985, 1986
Acid rain	American Electric Power	1985, 1986, 1987, 1988
Mining operations	Exxon	1985, 1986, 1987
Toxic waste and pesticides	Diamond Shamrock	1985
	NL Industries	1985, 1986
	American Cyanamid	1986
Pesticide plant safety	American Cyanamid	1987
Nuclear power lobbying	Commonwealth Edison	1984
Nuclear power evacuation	Consolidated Edison	1984

| AFTER THE VALDEZ

The year 1989 was a turning point for shareholder action on the environment. The emergence of the Valdez Principles, a comprehensive set of environmental principles designed to guide corporate behavior, gave shareholders a standard to which they could hold corporations, similar to the Sullivan Principles on South Africa in the early years of that effort. (See box 10-1.)

The Valdez Principles form a comprehensive environmental ethic for corporations. They address major areas of environmental responsibility—protection of the biosphere, sustainable use of natural resources, reduction and disposal of wastes, wise use of energy, risk reduction, marketing safe products and services, damage compensation, disclosure of hazards, and production of an annual environmental report. Shareholders have introduced resolutions on the Principles since 1989. Other environmental resolutions have been offered as well.

BOX 10-1
THE VALDEZ PRINCIPLES

WHEREAS, our company has stated its commitment to protect the environment;

WHEREAS, we believe economic and ecological costs of environmental destruction far exceed costs of prevention;

WHEREAS, CERES, a broad coalition of institutional investors and environmentalists including sponsors of this proposal, announced the Valdez Principles in 1989. The Principles are intended for all types of commercial corporations and call for:

1. **Protection of the Biosphere:** Minimize and seek to eliminate release of pollutants causing damage to the air, water, or earth or its inhabitants. Safeguard habitats in rivers, lakes, wetlands, coastal zones and oceans and minimize contributing to the greenhouse effect, depletion of the ozone layer, acid rain or smog;

2. **Sustainable Use of Natural Resources:** Make sustainable use of natural resources, such as water, soils, and forests. Conserve nonrenewable natural resources through efficient use and careful planning. Protect wildlife habitat, open spaces and wilderness, while preserving biodiversity;

3. **Reduction and Disposal of Wastes:** Minimize creation of waste, especially hazardous waste, and wherever possible recycle materials. Dispose of waste through safe and responsible methods;

4. **Wise Use of Energy:** Make every effort to use environmentally safe and sustainable energy sources. Invest in improved energy efficiency and conservation in our operations. Maximize energy efficiency of products we produce or sell;

5. **Risk Reduction:** Minimize environmental health and safety risks to employees and communities in which we operate by employing safe technologies and operating procedures and by being constantly prepared for emergencies;

6. **Marketing of Safe Products and Services:** Sell products or services that minimize environmental impacts and are safe as consumers

use them. Inform consumers of environmental impacts of products or services;

7. **Damage Compensation:** Take responsibility for harm we cause to the environment by making every effort to fully restore the environment and compensate persons adversely affected;

8. **Disclosure:** Disclose to employees and the public incidents relating to operations that cause environmental harm or pose health and safety hazards. Disclose potential environmental, health or safety hazards posed by operations and take no action against employees who report conditions that create a danger to the environment or pose health and safety hazards;

9. **Environmental Directors and Managers:** Commit management resources to implement these Principles, to monitor and report on implementation, and to sustain a process to ensure that the Board and CEO are kept informed of and are fully responsible for environmental matters. Establish a committee of the board with responsibility for environmental affairs. Have one board member qualified to represent environmental interests;

10. **Assessment and Annual Audit:** Conduct and make public an annual self-evaluation of progress in implementing these Principles and in complying with all applicable laws and regulations throughout worldwide operations. Work toward timely creation of independent environmental procedures completed annually and made available to the public.

WHEREAS, we believe these Principles far exceed industry or corporate codes of environmental conduct, particularly in public perception of accountability;

RESOLVED, shareholders request that our company become a signatory to the Valdez Principles.

STATEMENT

We believe that implementing the Valdez Principles will make our company a world leader on environmental issues.

CERES Resolutions

The Valdez Principles and their originator, the CERES group, are discussed in depth in the following chapter. It is important to note here that the CERES group brought together for the first time environmental groups and social investors, with ICCR taking the lead in shareholder action, to encourage corporations to become Valdez signatories.

THE 1989 RESOLUTIONS. Nineteen eighty-nine was a test year for the Valdez Principles. The 1989 resolutions asked twenty-six companies to report on their policies and practices in relation to the principles. CERES adopted the reporting strategy out of necessity. The group had articulated the Principles, but it had not developed a system for their amplification and implementation. Asking companies to develop reports served the dual purpose of preparing companies for the kind of reporting to be required of signatories while providing CERES with a sense of what companies were *prepared* to report.

The 1989 resolutions resulted in more than fifteen reports. These encompassed a wide range of responses, including reports made as part of annual reports (Waste Management), extensive separately published reports (Amoco, Chevron, Texaco, Consolidated Paper), and company statements of their own environmental principles (Kodak, General Motors, and, later, McDonald's).

THE 1990 RESOLUTIONS. The year 1990 marked a major step forward with the filing of resolutions asking companies to become signatories to the Valdez Principles (see table 10-2). Signatory resolutions were introduced with fifty-four companies and reporting resolutions with twenty-one companies. At the same time, CERES was developing and issuing draft reporting guidelines for signatories. So, many companies were in the process of assessing the impact of, or were negotiating over, the Principles as they applied to that particular company.

A number of smaller companies became Valdez signatories (see table 10-3). At the same time, several major companies entered into extensive negotiations with CERES over the wording and implementation of the Principles, recognizing the value and necessity of the Valdez Principles and going beyond industry sector and cross-sector principles by providing for outside independent implementation and monitoring. It will be important to report progress in these efforts if at all possible, since that could open the way to much wider corporate participation.

THE 1991–92 CYCLE. Nineteen ninety-one marked the first year in which corporations could know the practical ramifications of signing the Valdez Principles. When the signatory resolutions were first filed in 1990, the "CERES Report" detailing the reporting requirements was still under development. In January 1991 this document

TABLE 10-2

CORPORATIONS WITH VALDEZ RESOLUTIONS, 1990–91

Automobiles
Chrysler
Ford
General Motors

Chemicals
American Cyanamid
ARCO Chemical
Dow Chemical
DuPont
Eastman Kodak
Kimberly-Clark
Union Carbide

Computers
AT & T
GTE
Hewlett-Packard
IBM

Electrical equipment
Cooper Industries
General Electric
Westinghouse

Financial services
American Express

Foods
McDonald's
Pepsico

Mining
Kerr-McGee
Newmont Mining

Newspapers/publishing
Gannett
Knight-Ridder
New York Times
Tribune Company
Washington Post

Oil and oil services
Amoco
Atlantic Richfield
Chevron
Exxon
Halliburton
Mobil
Occidental
Phillips Petroleum
Texaco

Paper
Champion International
  Mead
International Paper
Louisiana Pacific

Pharmaceuticals
Bristol-Myers Squibb

Pipeline
Arkla

Tobacco
Philip Morris

Transportation
Burlington Northern
Union Pacific

Utilities
American Electric
Centerior Energy
Cincinnati Gas & Electric
Commonwealth Edison
Houston Industries
Southern Company
Texas Utilities

Waste disposal
Safety-Kleen
Waste Management

Other
Armstrong World
  Industries
Corning

Sources: Coalition for Environmentally Responsible Economies and Interfaith Center on Corporate Responsibility.

was distributed to more than five hundred companies. Thus it became part of the dialogue only after most companies already had taken positions against signing the Principles.

Non-CERES Resolutions

The Valdez Principles dominated the shareholder movement on the environment. Nonetheless, from 1989 to 1991 the first-generation type of issue- or facility-oriented resolution continued to play an important role in focusing attention on specific problems. This pattern suggests that the future will include both comprehensive and specialized environmental resolutions. It also reflects an emerging

TABLE 10-3

SIGNATORIES TO THE VALDEZ PRINCIPLES

CERES's efforts to persuade companies to become signatories of the Valdez Principles have led to dialogue with more than four hundred American companies. Several major corporations are very close to signing, and we expect significant movement in 1991. Signatories to date are:

> Atlantic Recycled Paper Company, Baltimore
> Ally Capital Corporation, Sausalito, Calif.
> Aveda Corporation, Minneapolis
> The Beamery, Heiskell, Tenn.
> Bellcomb Technologies, Minneapolis
> Clivus Multrum, Lawrence, Mass.
> Co-op America, Washington, D.C.
> Crib Diaper Service, Crystal, Minn.
> Domino's Pizza Distribution Corporation, Ann Arbor, Mich.
> Earth Care Paper Company, Madison, Wisc.
> Ecoprint, Silver Spring, Md.
> Franklin Research & Development, Boston
> Harwood Lumber, Branscomb, Calif.
> Intrigue Salon, Marietta, Ga.
> Metropolitan Sewer District, Louisville, Ky.
> Smith & Hawken, Mill Valley, Calif.
> Stoneyfield Farm Yogurt, Londonderry, N.H.
> VanCity Investment Services, Vancouver, B.C.
> Walnut Acres, Penns Creek, Pa.
> World Wildlife Fund, Washington, D.C.
> Working Assets Funding Service, San Francisco

SOURCE: Coalition for Environmentally Responsible Economies.

strategy that addresses the need for both comprehensive improvement of practices and remedial action for existing problems.

PLASTIC FOAM PACKAGING. In 1989 the Evangelical Lutheran Church in America (ELCA) developed and introduced with McDonald's a resolution seeking termination of plastic foam use. ELCA withdrew the resolution in order to pursue the wider Valdez dialogue with McDonald's. In 1990 McDonald's announced that it would discontinue its plastic foam "clamshell" packaging while continuing to support its earlier initiative of plastic foam recycling.

In 1991 the emphasis has shifted to a more generic resolution on reduction of packaging materials that will be introduced with companies in the packaging industry. The strategy remains to be developed, and the specific companies remain to be identified.

CFCs. In 1989 a resolution seeking to accelerate corporate phaseout of chlorofluorocarbons (CFCs) in order to protect the endangered ozone layer of the earth's atmosphere and their replacement by environmentally safe alternatives was developed by ELCA and introduced with a number of CFC producers and users. In 1990, as international efforts continued to accelerate in this area, the resolution was substantially revised and refined to reflect wide recognition of the need for accelerated phaseout and to incorporate related chemicals. Among the companies receiving the resolution were:

Allied-Signal	Pennwalt
DuPont	Raytheon
Eastman Kodak	Texas Instruments
General Motors	Westinghouse

Results have included better reporting on initiatives under way as well as stimulation of new and improved corporate policies in some cases.

Of particular interest was the negotiation with Raytheon, cooperatively conducted by the Massachusetts Public Interest Research Group (MASSPIRG) and ELCA. As a result of agreements made in 1989 and 1990, Raytheon has revised its policies for CFC use in its electronics units and is in the process of doing so for its Amana refrigeration division.

In 1990 the ICCR environmental staff developed and introduced a resolution with the major domestic auto manufacturers, asking them to report on their policies, plans, and projects for reducing automobile fuel consumption, a major contributor of carbon dioxide to the atmosphere and thus to global warming. Meetings were held with the companies, and in-depth reports are being published. Table 10-4 lists all the specialized environmental resolutions filed from 1989 through 1991.

Strategies for the Future

The close cooperation that has emerged between environmental groups and social investors and the new professional resources now being committed to environmental shareholder action by investor groups like ICCR will produce more comprehensive environmental strategies with greater emphasis on shareholder action than in the past.

At its annual general meeting in June 1991, the ICCR considered for the first time a coherent overall strategy for shareholder action

TABLE 10-4

SPECIALIZED SHAREHOLDER RESOLUTIONS, 1989–91

Issue	Companies	Years
Nuclear power	Philadelphia Electric	1989
	Carolina Power & Light	1989
	Houston Industries	1990
Radioactive release	Union Electric	1990
Nuclear safety	General Electric	1989
Nuclear energy division	General Electric	1989, 1991
Nuclear alternatives	Detroit Edison	1989
Nuclear emissions	Union Electric	1989, 1991
Bhopal relief	Union Carbide	1989, 1990, 1991
Toxic pollution	General Electric	1989
Farmland conservation	Aetna	1990
	Travelers	1990
Environmental cleanup	Exxon	1990, 1991
Food irradiation	Borden	1990
	Castle & Cooke	1990
	A & P	1990
	Kroger	1990
	McDonald's	1990
	Ralston Purina	1990
	Super Valu Stores	1991
Uranium mining	Chevron	1990
Board of directors	Amoco	1991
	Champion International	1991
	Phillips Petroleum	1991
Carbon dioxide reduction	ARCO	1991
	Exxon	1991
Toxic chemicals	Amoco	1991

on environmental issues. This strategy features three major inter-related elements:

1. Global warming, including CFCs, auto emissions, and other initiatives now under development;
2. Environmental principles, including Valdez; and
3. Eco-justice, focusing on the impact of environmental practices on local communities, particularly poor and minority communities.

This strategic orientation should result in a much more complete implementation of the trends that had only begun to show themselves in the transition years of 1989 to 1991.

CERES AND THE VALDEZ PRINCIPLES

Joan Bavaria Cochair and CEO, Coalition for
Environmentally Responsible Economies

To understand the evolution and purpose of CERES—Coalition for
Environmentally Responsible Economies—it is necessary to revisit
a June 1988 Social Investment Forum (SIF) board retreat held in
Denver. Past and current board members participated in a facilitated
examination (a meeting led by a person trained as a mediator/group
leader) of the past, present, and future of the Forum. All present
agreed that over the years, the key issue for their social investment
clients was the environment.

Paradoxically, little was being done on the issue. That fall only
one shareholder resolution remotely connected with environmental
concerns was filed (with General Electric, concerning product
safety). Those conducting research into the environmental performance of companies were plagued with a dearth of information.
What was becoming available under federal right-to-know legislation was difficult and expensive to process and was limited to pollution quantification. Investors knew very little about how they
could, or should, contribute to the health of our plant through their
investment dollars. For that reason, the board decided that more and
better information must be forthcoming for social investors to act
decisively on environmental issues.

The year before the Denver meeting, the Forum had worked with

Joan Bavaria is Cochair of the Coalition for Environmentally Responsible Economies (CERES). A social investment pioneer, Bavaria has been active in the
movement since 1975. In 1984, she was elected the founding president of the
Social Investment Forum and is currently on the Forum's board. She now serves
as president of Franklin Research & Development Corporation, a socially responsible investment advisory firm located in Boston.

the Ford Foundation to determine why money was not flowing into community investments from investment professionals. This arrangement was seen as a model for how the Forum could help mature social investing around issues of concern to clients. The Forum would reach into the communities most intimately involved with an issue and work with them to create information exchanges and collaborative networks around which programs could be designed to directly affect solutions to problems. Around each issue a "spoke" would be built from the board of the Forum. Each spoke would become a tax-exempt—501(c)(3)—nonprofit project of the Forum and would have its own board and operating staff. The Forum would retain its tax-exempt status and its purpose, analogous to a trade association.

A committee to create the environmental "spoke" was named at the Denver retreat. That committee worked through the summer and fall to establish connections within the environmental community, to design a vision and mission statement, and to organize the first meeting. That first meeting of the environmental project of the Forum was held in Chapel Hill, North Carolina, in April 1989.

| THE VALDEZ PRINCIPLES

Prior to the meeting in Chapel Hill, a list of goals was drawn for the project. Numbering well over twenty, these goals included:

- establishing a set of environmental principles for corporations that would serve as both a baseline for performance measurement and management standards;
- beginning to procure information systematically on environmental performance;
- informing the public of the environmental impact—positive and negative—of their investments through seminars, public speaking, and writing;
- studying ways to legislate environmentally progressive investment processes; and
- finding alternative investment vehicles to assist in environmental solutions.

The first task was to establish environmental principles. The rough model was the Sullivan Principles which had isolated some of the issues for companies doing business in South Africa.

By this time, medical waste had washed up on Eastern beaches, porpoises were dying in great numbers from sudden and mysterious causes suspected to be traceable to manmade pollutants, and of course the *Exxon Valdez* had run aground in Alaska. As the group of investors and environmentalists assembled in Chapel Hill, emotions were running high around corporate environmental abuses.

In Chapel Hill an enthusiastic group kept pretty much intact the goals that had been invented by the "environmental spoke" committee of the Forum board. The Sierra Club, the National Audubon Society, the National Wildlife Federation, Lighthawk, The United Nations Environmental Program (UNEP), the Humane Society, the International Alliance for Sustainable Agriculture, the Public Interest Research Groups (PIRG), and others joined churches, research organizations, and Forum members in conceptualizing the project. The name CERES was adopted, and by early summer, work was under way on the environmental principles.

| DEVELOPMENT AND INTRODUCTION

All volunteer participants had a chance to review and contribute to the Principles. By mid-1989 several corporate environmental specialists also had seen and commented on the Principles. The coalition had expanded steadily to include public pension funds and additional environmental groups. It was decided to release the Principles to the public in early fall to take advantage of an extraordinarily high level of public interest in environmental issues. At the time of the release, CERES members did not agree as to how many companies would find the Principles easy to sign. However, on September 9, 1989, at a press conference in New York, CERES asked companies to join coalition members in a process built around the Principles to improve corporate environmental results. (For the text of the Principles, see box 10-1 in chapter 10.)

The Principles received extraordinary press coverage and drew questions from a large list of companies. Immediately CERES began to talk with companies and to work on the "1990 Guide to the Valdez Principles," which was to include answers to many of the questions that had been asked by hundreds of companies. A draft was circulated to interested companies and other organizations in early 1990.

Response to the draft criticized the rating of companies by CERES and the fee schedule. However, most companies indicated their intention to keep talking. The final version of the 1990 guide was released in April, with adjustments based on corporate feedback.

| ENVIRONMENTAL AUDIT AND PUBLIC INFORMATION

One of the most important long-term goals of CERES has been to catalyze the release of standardized information on environmental performance, using the model of the Financial Accounting Standards Board.

The tenth Valdez Principle asks for an internal audit and release of information. Although for reasons of competitive advantage and legal liability the release of all of the information in an environmental audit is impossible, it is in the best interest of the public to discern the environmental controls and results of corporate management. To give companies a guide for the release of information, CERES created the "CERES Report," the first comprehensive environmental information form, based on the Valdez Principles.

This report was circulated twice to companies for comment. Meetings were held with corporate environmentalists to talk through problems with information collection and completion of a comprehensive report. The first draft of the report was released in fall 1990, after being revised significantly as a result of feedback from companies, environmental audit specialists, toxic pollutant experts, and others. The final report was released late in the year.

Corporate Dialogue

Throughout the eighteen months since the release of the Valdez Principles, an expanding CERES has continued dialogues with companies. Shareholder resolutions filed in 1989 asking companies to disclose their compliance with the Principles numbered twenty. The average vote in favor of the resolutions was 12.5 percent—exceptionally high for a first-year resolution.

Resolutions for the 1991 annual meetings filed by CERES members and others around environmental issues numbered well over one hundred, including fifty-four resolutions around the Valdez Principles. Thirty-six stayed on ballots for the spring annual meetings. Some, however, were withdrawn by the filers because companies agreed to talk with CERES about either signing the Principles or completing the CERES Report in 1991. As this chapter is written in April 1991, some companies have held their annual meetings. The resolutions asking companies to sign the Principles are drawing a lower average favorable vote because the request is far more complex than a mere disclosure resolution. However, between 6 percent and 13 percent of the shareholders are supporting the resolutions—still considered a good showing.

The most significant thing to come out of the dialogue has been a series of earnest discussions with companies around signing the Principles and working with CERES to develop the reporting system. Months after the release of the Principles, the coalition has been able to grow and strengthen, maturing as a working group and developing much greater understanding as to the strengths and weaknesses of the Principles and of the CERES Report. It is important to keep in mind that CERES intends the Valdez Principles to be the baseline value system around which is built a process of improvement and information dissemination. That process has been working well to catalyze corporate discussion, the acceptance of the idea of "principles"—which also might be called an environmental mission statement—and the growing perception that standardized disclosure is inevitable.

Two years after CERES first met, twenty companies and other organizations have signed the Valdez Principles. A very large list of companies, some Fortune 500 and others much smaller, are working with CERES to refine the Principles and the process to overcome perceived legal and other barriers to signing.

| OTHER GOALS

CERES's agenda includes exploring ways to overcome system barriers to intelligent environmental management, such as accounting problems, short-term investment horizons, and cultural resistance. To that end, CERES will collaborate wherever possible with interested authorities. In addition, CERES will continue to explore ways to channel more investment dollars toward environmentally useful projects.

CERES will study the link between environmental degradation and poverty and how investment dollars might be used to mitigate some of those problems. The coalition has expanded in membership to include minority representatives and others working toward that end.

Watch CERES! It is a coalition that is in many ways a model for future collaboration between investors and those on the line.

INTERNATIONAL DEBT

John E. Lind Executive Director,
CANICCOR Research

Over the years, stockholder resolutions sponsored mainly by church groups have requested banks to develop policies to help prevent capital flight into their deposit accounts, to exclude from debt relief countries with severe human rights abuses, to encourage debt for development and nature conservancy swaps, and the like. This chapter places these shareholder resolutions, and others, in context.

THE DEBT CRISIS

The crisis of debt repayments by third world countries to international commercial banks began when Mexico informed its bank creditors in the summer of 1982 that it could not meet its payments. Mexican debt to commercial banks at that time was about $64 billion, of which $25 billion was owed to U.S. banks, primarily to the money center banks in New York, Chicago, and San Francisco. During the ensuing year, many other third world borrowers found themselves in similar situations.

The Burden of Debt
The debt crisis engulfed all of Latin America; some countries in Southeast Asia, particularly the Philippines; and all of sub-Saharan Africa, except South Africa. Well over half of the $384 billion debt

---

John E. Lind is the executive director of CANICCOR Research, which analyzes the social responsibility of banking institutions. This analysis resulted in the drafting of most of the basic stockholder resolutions for banks on the debt crisis and financial sanctions on South Africa over the past decade. He is now also developing a social responsibility index for mortgage lending in low-income areas domestically.

of Latin America and the Philippines was to commercial banks, but in sub-Saharan Africa the bulk of the borrowing was from governments and multilateral banks, such as the World Bank. If the oil producers, Nigeria and Gabon, are excluded, the rest of sub-Saharan Africa is so poor that its commercial bank debt amounts to only $14 billion of the $111 billion total debt.

This crisis endangered both the financial soundness of the international banks and the economic well-being of the inhabitants, especially the poor, of these countries. As Michael Camdessus, managing director of the International Monetary Fund (IMF), said recently, "too often in recent years it is the poorest segments of the population that have carried the heaviest burden of economic adjustment" arising from the debt crisis.

With that in mind, since 1984, institutional church investors have filed shareholder resolutions with the major U.S. banks. They also were concerned by the fact that the lending had often had the effect of supporting repressive military regimes that consistently violated human rights.

IMF's Effect on the Indebted Countries

The IMF was founded in 1948 to provide short-term lending to member countries with short-term liquidity problems. Its short-term lending facilities could not handle the debt crisis as a whole, but it could provide some funding. To obtain this funding, the member country had to agree to IMF proposals for the management of its economy. Thus, because the banks would not agree to reschedule their loan payments without a prior agreement between the country and the IMF, the IMF became the overseer of many economies.

IMF often required a program of stiff austerity measures that resulted in cuts in government spending, currency exchange rate reforms, and the elimination of protectionist trade barriers. This program usually resulted in a contraction of the economy, with corporate bankruptcies, increased unemployment, increased food prices, and the reduction of social provisions, such as unemployment payments. These costs were borne heavily by the poor. As a result, church leaders, such as Cardinal Arns in Brazil, spoke out against the way governments implemented these measures and highlighted the plight of the poor.

| HOW DID THIS CRISIS ARISE?

After the 1973 oil price increase the international banks had to invest the huge profits for exporters. Money needed to be lent. At times, inflation was high so that real interest rates were negative; thus it cost nothing to borrow. Prices of third world commodities also increased significantly in the mid-1970s. As a result, conditions looked good for "recycling" petrodollars back to third world oil importers. Unfortunately, oil prices stayed high and third world commodity prices dropped. Several other factors compounded these problems. Many large development projects that were funded by loans were ill-conceived and could not have made money by the time the loans were due. Corrupt regimes, such as those of Ferdinand Marcos in the Philippines, also siphoned off significant amounts. Profits, either legally or illegally made, from these projects often were invested in the first world, thus denying the third world of needed investment. And by the beginning of the 1980s benchmark interest rates, to which the interest payments on these loans were tied, started to rise rapidly, precipitating the crisis.

Who Is to Blame?

The banks are to blame for their own haste in making large loans with high returns on fees and with little regard for the economic feasibility of the projects being funded. This lack of concern with feasibility often resulted from guarantees provided for the loans by third world governments. These governments are to blame for offering the guarantees, but they often lacked expertise and took the advice of others.

The World Bank and development agencies are to blame for the misconceived idea that upon provision of large infrastructure projects, such as power generation and transportation facilities, to a less-developed country, economic progress would immediately ensue.

Corruption in the third world is to blame for the waste of funds and grandiose projects of little economic value. Finally, capital flight into the first world launched by the wealthy in the third world is to blame for depriving third world countries of the ripple effect of foreign lending. The U.S. ambassador to the Philippines, Steven Bosworth, stated in 1984 that wealthy Filipinos had sent some $10 billion in assets abroad for safety. At that time the Philippines owed $13 billion to commercial banks and had a total debt of $24 billion.

| PAYING FOR THE CRISIS

The banks have raised loan reserves and disposed of some loans at less than face value. This process costs not only the banks' stockholders but also the users of the bank, who end up paying higher fees. Third world countries have paid through austerity measures that often hurt the poorest segments of society through high food prices and unemployment. The wealthy partially escape these constraints by investing their funds in the first world. Politically the crisis has helped cause the fall of dictatorships in Argentina, Brazil, the Philippines, and finally Chile.

In the early 1980s the banks and their federal regulators played for time to build up the banks' reserves. The problem was called "short-term" and "temporary." Stockholders filed resolutions with banks asking for disclosure of information to show the magnitude of the problem. Churches already were receiving pleas from their counterparts in the third world telling of the misery that the crisis was causing the poor.

Only in October 1985 did James Baker, then secretary of the Treasury, suggest that the crisis was the result of basic structural problems; he urged more lending to solve the problem. Commercial banks were to lend another $20 billion and multilateral agencies $9 billion over three years. The banks resisted and continued to use the unending mechanism of rescheduling debts and IMF austerity measures. Church stockholders already had submitted to Bank of America for its spring 1986 annual meeting a resolution that called for bank policies to extend the length of the loans, to cut the interest rates, to write off the worst loans over a period of five years, and to add human rights constraints to this process. At this point, both investors and the Treasury were calling the debt crisis a structural problem, not a temporary one that would clear up soon.

Federal regulators were pressuring the banks to raise their loan-loss reserves for these loans. By 1987 inflation and bank growth had increased bank assets significantly, so that third world loans now amounted to less than their capital. Thus the banks had averted the danger of going bankrupt should all of these loans have to be written off. Simultaneously the banks had time to raise loan-loss reserves up to 25 percent of the face value of these loans.

Church shareholders, trying to keep one step ahead of the banks, submitted a resolution to Chase Manhattan in 1988 that requested a policy of writing off an amount of loans equal to the present reserves over a period of three years. This period would provide the bank time to raise additional loan-loss reserves while retiring a significant portion of the debt.

In March 1989 Treasury Secretary Brady proposed a plan whose emphasis was to reduce the debt rather than to raise new loans, as former secretary Baker had suggested. This plan has forced the banks to permit countries to repurchase some of their borrowings at less than face value with funds from multilateral banks and to issue long-term bonds in exchange for debt at less than face value. J. P. Morgan was the first bank to propose the latter. So far Mexico, Costa Rica, and the Philippines have been the major beneficiaries of the plan.

By 1991, loan-loss reserves equaling 50 percent to 100 percent of the face value of these loans cushioned most major banks against third world loans. For that reason, 1991 stockholder resolutions were simplified to ask for lending criteria—including economic, social, and political impact on people—and a write-off of existing loans that place an unneeded, unwanted, and unsustainable burden on people. The resolution was withdrawn from Bank of America because of an excellent policy statement developed by the bank. Thus with Bank of America, policies are in place that may avert another recurrence of this crisis. However, the working out of the present crisis will go on throughout this decade, with more stockholder resolutions seeking debt relief for less-developed countries.

RESOURCES

The annual and quarterly reports of banks describe their lending exposure and their status with the major debt-troubled countries.

Mardid, Raul L., 1990. "Over-exposed: U.S. Banks Confront the Third World Debt Crisis." Washington D.C.: Investor Responsibility Research Center.

World Bank. "Analysis and Summary Tables." Vol. 1 of *World Debt Tables 1990–91: External Debt of Developing Countries*. Washington, D.C.: World Bank.

MILITARISM

Valerie Heinonen Interfaith Center on
Corporate Responsibility

For almost twenty years, Protestant and Roman Catholic religious
investors, in calling for peace, have drawn connections among war,
preparation for war, and the companies who profit from war. Their
pioneering actions directed institutional investors to the possibilities of economic conversion, the consequences of foreign military
sales, the effects of toxic and radioactive pollution, the absurd waste
of the trillion-dollar Star Wars program, and the damage that military
spending does to the economy.

Since 1975 members of the Interfaith Center on Corporate
Responsibility (ICCR) have filed more than two hundred weapons-
related resolutions with more than fifty Department of Defense contractors on a variety of issues ranging from the B-1 bomber, the MX
missile, and the Gatling gun to nuclear and chemical warhead production and the distribution of war toys.

At their 1990 annual general meeting, ICCR members voted to
address the religious community's concerns about growing U.S. militarism as an integrated whole—the global arms race.

The Persian Gulf War further demonstrated the need for discus-

---

Valerie Heinonen, O.S.U., is director of the Program Against Militarism at the
Interfaith Center on Corporate Responsibility. Sister Valerie is an active member
of the Nuclear Weapons Facilities Network; the board of directors of INFACT–
Boycott GE; the finance committee of the Dominican Sisters of the Sick Poor;
and a peace activist who participates in strategy-planning sessions on economic
conversion, Star Wars, and U.S. military expansion abroad. In 1988, 1989, and
1990, Sister Valerie toured Asian and Pacific countries, Africa, and Europe on
international fact-finding, networking, and speaking trips examining the effects
of U.S. foreign military sales. She serves Manhattan's historic Lower East Side
as a member of New York City Community Board Number 3, the Pedro Albizu
Campos Community Center, and the Lower East Side Catholic Area Conference.

sions about high-tech conventional warfare in the nuclear context, since conventional systems may be adapted to nuclear use. The Star Wars scenario always has included nuclear warheads and nuclear reactors in space. Although Saddam Hussein was universally denounced for using chemical weapons against the Kurds, President Bush and the Department of Defense will build chemical warheads and adapt them to missiles. The Pentagon promotes foreign military sales to lower domestic unit costs. And in periods when domestic demand for weapons is flat, corporations turn to foreign markets for profits.

Global arms race issues addressed by the religious investor community now include chemical, nuclear, and Star Wars weapons production, sales of materiel and technology to foreign governments, and economic conversion and local diversification. (When ICCR members call for termination of weapons contracts, they also urge retraining of the work force and plans for alternate use of production facilities.) Distribution and promotion of war toys is also a concern for many Roman Catholic religious orders and some Protestant denominations.

| HISTORY

In 1969–71, the Vietnam War precipitated antiwar demonstrations at corporations' annual meetings. Though many of the protesters were students, investors demonstrated their concerns about corporate profits from the war through shareholder resolutions at such companies as Dow Chemical and General Electric.

By 1972, religious investors had joined the peace movement in an effort to hold corporate management accountable for its role in fueling the Vietnam War. However, in January 1972 the Corporate Information Center (CIC), one of two agencies that merged to form the Interfaith Center on Corporate Responsibility, released a study revealing that ten Protestant denominations and the National Council of Churches held sizable investments in companies supplying materiel for the Vietnam War. Each of these religious bodies was on record opposing the war as immoral and profoundly sinful. According to Frank P. White, CIC director, the report did not recommend that the churches sell defense stocks, because "selling stock obviously negates your right as a stockholder to speak to management about policies with which you disagree."

Until the 1976 proxy season, ICCR and its member organizations supported and publicized the antimilitarism shareholder resolutions filed by such organizations as Clergy and Laity Concerned (CALC). For example, General Electric was and is a contractor for all major weapons systems: the B-1 bomber, the B-2 Stealth bomber, nuclear warheads, the MX missile, the Trident submarine. At GE's 1972 annual meeting, representatives of the Sisters of Loretto and the National Council of Churches backed CALC proposals challenging the company to cease weapons production and establish a committee to study conversion from military to civilian production—to which the GE chair, F. J. Borch, responded, "I am very concerned that we may someday have another madman like Hitler unless we are in the position in this country of having a deterrent."

In the fall of 1975 ICCR members joined CALC with resolutions to General Electric on the B-1 bomber and took the lead on confronting Northrop over the revolving door between weapons contractors and Pentagon personnel.

In the years that followed, the antimilitarism program grew in importance to ICCR members, in terms of the number of companies challenged with shareholder resolutions and the diversity of issues addressed. Significant issues for the churches: economic conversion, foreign military sales, and questionable payments to foreign governments to help them retain power and the company to market its goods and services. By the fall of 1978, ICCR members had voted to hold corporate managers of nuclear warhead production facilities accountable for promoting the nuclear arms race. As part of their decision making, the churches agreed to an ongoing, regular attendance at annual shareholder meetings in order to raise these concerns and to work closely with organizations that direct attention to the nuclear warhead facilities in their neighborhoods.

| THE MILITARISM ISSUE TODAY

During the 1980s the program against militarism consistently ranked first or second among ICCR priorities. Nuclear weapons production remained the major concern. Star Wars, economic conversion, biological and chemical warfare, and foreign military sales received stronger emphasis in a given year, depending on the members' analysis of the U.S. political economy.

Foreign Military Sales
The Persian Gulf War graphically illustrates the U.S. foreign military sales dilemma. High-technology weapons were sold to the highest

bidder, regardless of customer behavior. Media focus on war technologies of both sides raised expectations for export controls. It is too soon to tell if these efforts will be effective or if desperate weapons manufacturers in this highly competitive market will continue to welcome all possible deals.

Though foreign military sales are down, more countries are manufacturing and buying weapons. Through treaties and the pursuit of aggressive national interest, the United States in particular has a military presence on the land and in the seas of other nations and is a strong economic power as well. These factors provide both a rationale for selling U.S. weapons and grounds for intervention to protect U.S. property. Many U.S. corporations, such as General Dynamics, McDonnell Douglas, and Texas Instruments, produce and coproduce components for weapons systems in overseas factories and make investments in foreign corporations, guaranteeing political and economic dependence on the United States and easier access to foreign markets for weapons.

Concerned about corporate involvement in foreign military sales, religious investors question categories of exports, service contracts, and coproduction agreements as well as commitments to provide personnel and servicing. In 1989 the leading twenty-five foreign military sales suppliers were surveyed as to foreign operations and agreements, and in 1990 shareholder resolutions were filed with Boeing and General Dynamics.

Chemical and Biological Weaponry

The horrifying specter of chemical war prompted the churches, in the fall of 1982, to survey sixty-six chemical manufacturers about how they might respond to the proposed resumption of chemical weapons production. The survey asked for corporate policy on the manufacture of nerve gas and other chemical weapons, the company's likelihood of bidding on contacts, and its current manufacture of biological or chemical weapons.

Most of the forty companies that responded knew nothing about the contracts, nor had they been invited to participate in the chemical weapons program. Of the four companies with the information, only Allied-Signal acknowledged having seen a Department of Defense advertisement. American Cyanamid, Mobil, and Union Carbide had been invited to submit bids for manufacturing chemical weapons, but each had declined.

Mobil says, "We advised the DOD that we preferred not to negotiate for any participation in their program." Union Carbide told the DOD that "the company does not intend to respond to requests for bids for . . . binary weapons systems," although in the event of national emergency, "the company would consider the national needs."

Only a handful of major corporations have chosen to bid on chemical weapons contracts. Some of these contracts are defensive—for example, gas masks and other protective gear—such as Allied-Signal's contract for detectors, which personnel carry on their bodies. Possibly recalling the publicity and political maneuvers surrounding controversial sales of chemicals and equipment to Iraq by U.S., German, and other European companies, industry officials appear reluctant to expose their companies to potential liability or consumer backlash.

In 1985, while sitting as president of the U.S. Senate, then–vice president George Bush used his tie-breaking vote to ensure approval for chemical weapons production. Currently President Bush is at once negotiating an international arms accord and promoting further production.

In a similar contradiction, the chemical industry, represented by the U.S. Chemical Manufacturers Association (CMA), is working to resolve controversial items in the Chemical Weapons Convention. The major stumbling block is how information obtained during inspections will be protected. Especially sensitive are manufacturing capacity and proprietary technical and customer information, because much of the competitive information is not patented. At the same time the CMA is cooperating in the international area, it is lobbying against U.S. legislation to tighten controls on the export of certain chemicals, some of which are dual use, to certain countries.

War in Space
Persian Gulf War combat successes of the Carter administration's Patriot missiles are being exploited by the Bush administration to demonstrate the value of the Reagan administration's Strategic Defense Initiative (SDI, or "Star Wars") research and to push for a 50 percent increase in its funding.

Once a source of national pride, the civilian space program now exists to exploit space for military advantage. The United States stands at a crossroads in its use of outer space. Since the early 1960s, space has been militarized with scores of communications, early warning, and intelligence satellites supporting Earth-based military forces. Present plans, however, call for shuttling nuclear weapons into space.

SDI will fail as a foolproof civilian shield, but the infusion of more than $21 billion since 1983 for Star Wars research and development has succeeded as a boondoggle for arms manufacturers. Full costs for the system are estimated at $500 billion to $3 trillion. As a result of SDI Office efforts, the program has consolidated itself within the bureaucracy, the weapons laboratories, and the major defense corporations. Dismantling it would be highly difficult. Religious investors continue to question companies' dependence on these kinds of contracts.

Economic Conversion and Local Diversification

The issue of peace conversion is as old as Isaiah's vision of a time when the nations of the world would "beat their swords into plowshares and their spears into pruning hooks." After decades of debate and religious support for alternative production, Congress passed the Defense Economic Adjustment, Diversification, Conversion and Stabilization Act of 1990 on a groundswell of congressional concern for economic fallout generated by the end of the cold war. The new law requires advance notice of contract cancellations and provides loans and technical assistance to companies in transition to civilian markets, but it omits planning.

Economic conversion in a company or at a plant dependent on weapons contracts means the planned transfer of productive resources to more stable diversified operations. ICCR members research corporate and local dependence on weapons production, promote development of alternative products, and educate share owners about the social and business benefits of advance planning.

Nuclear Weapons Production

All major religious denominations denounce nuclear war as unjust. Church investors believe that corporations that seek contracts to research and develop nuclear weapons systems increase the likelihood of nuclear war, strengthen U.S. first-strike posture, and ignore true human security needs. In keeping with theological and ethical principles asserting that government policies must be measured by their impact on the poor, the weak, and the oppressed, they urge that national priorities be changed to funding human health and welfare within the United States and throughout the world.

The future of the Department of Energy (DOE) nuclear weapons production system is questionable. For the first time the DOE is admitting the existence of human suffering from radioactivity and promises to release health records to researchers. The DOE budget now must assign money to the overwhelming task of cleaning and containing radioactive and other toxic wastes from production plants and their surrounding environments. At the same time, resuming or continuing production of nuclear warheads is a DOE and corporate dilemma. The reactors are old and radioactive, plutonium is unaccounted for, and states that once welcomed the facilities are now imposing environmental restrictions. Further, political and environmental problems of long-term storage of high-level waste have not been solved.

Since 1979 church investors have focused on the corporate managers of DOE facilities, raising questions of liability, health and safety, the storage and transportation of nuclear weapons and weapons materials, radioactive hazards, and damage to the environment. As new information about their past practices and errors becomes available, it is more and more difficult to understand why corporations vie to take over the management contracts. Their profits and economic viability would seem to be at risk, since the DOE plans to hold contractors liable for environmental damage caused during their tenure.

General Electric produces neutron generators for nuclear warheads at the Pinellas Plant in St. Petersburg, Florida. Work for the Manhattan Project established GE as an early participant in nuclear industry. The churches have pressured GE to terminate its contracts with DOE's Pinellas and Knolls, New York, laboratories and to stop research and development of the Star Wars orbiting nuclear generator. EG & G, manager of DOE facilities at Rocky Flats, Colorado, and Mound, Ohio, the Nevada nuclear weapons test site, and Idaho National Engineering Laboratories, has been challenged to prevent further radioactive and chemical waste damage to air, land, and water and to clean up existing waste. Among those urged to give up nuclear weapon facility contracts are:

- Allied-Signal, manager of Bendix, Kansas City, Missouri;
- AT & T, manager of Sandia Laboratories, Albuquerque, New Mexico;
- Martin Marietta, manager of Oak Ridge, Tennessee, and Paducah, Kentucky;
- Westinghouse Electric, manager of Hanford, Washington, and Savannah River, South Carolina.

Manufacturers of delivery systems have been challenged as well. Concern about the subtle nationalization of our rail system prompted MX missile resolutions to the Burlington Northern and Norfolk Southern railroads. Although railroads are common carriers, meaning that they do not bid on contracts, filers of these resolutions do believe that railroads share responsibility for the safety and welfare of the general public.

Several corporations, too, have been asked to explain the kinds of social and economic criteria they use when bidding on military contracts. Some of the considerations religious investors encourage are: long-term environmental impact, lobbying and marketing practices, and military contracts as a percentage of sales.

War Toys

ICCR members are concerned about the impact of war toys on children. Specifically, religious investors have questioned companies on the development of games and toys that produce noncooperative, sometimes violent, play and promote violence as a method of solving problems. War toys, they believe, stimulate aggressive play and prevent children from understanding that societies can solve problems by diplomatic means rather than by war.

For three years, until the downturn in the economy, when toy manufacturers ran into financial difficulties, religious investors targeted these companies through letters and demonstrations at annual toy fairs. During 1990 ICCR members focused on the leading retailers, filing shareholder resolutions and initiating dialogues with the companies and with the Toy Manufacturers Association.

RESOURCES

Church Proxy Resolutions, annual January ed. Contains texts of church-sponsored social responsibility shareholder resolutions together with numerous resolutions sponsored by nonchurch institutional investors for the current shareholder meeting season. (Available from ICCR, $18.)

The Corporate Examiner (described in chapter 20).

Government Executive, annual August ed. Ranks the top two hundred federal contractors and analyzes procurement by both defense and civilian agencies. (Available from: National Journal, Inc., 1730 M Street NW, Eleventh Floor, Washington, D.C. 20036.)

MAQUILADORA SHAREHOLDER ACTIONS

Amy L. Domini Loring, Wolcott & Coolidge

In recent years, environmental, religious, labor, women's, and Latino organizations have increasingly criticized *maquiladoras*, foreign-owned factories operating in Mexico along the U.S. border. Of the approximately two thousand *maquiladoras*, 90 percent are owned by U.S. companies. In February 1991 the Coalition for Justice in the Maquiladoras (CJM), a binational coalition of more than sixty such organizations, launched a campaign to press U.S. transnational corporations to adopt socially responsible business practices in *maquiladoras*. CJM alleges extensive environmental contamination, unsafe working conditions, and the exploitation of workers at these sites.

The coalition is urging corporations to adopt the Maquiladora Standards of Conduct. These standards require companies operating *maquiladoras* to comply with Mexican and U.S. environmental regulations; observe fundamental worker rights, including fair wages, a safe and healthy workplace, reasonable hours of work, and decent living conditions; and support community infrastructure needs, including a commitment to community economic development.

CJM asserts, for example, that the aquifer that supplies water to San Elazadio, Texas, has been so contaminated by raw sewage coming from *maquiladoras* that 35 percent of its children contract hepatitis by age eight. According to EPA and Texas Water Commission officials, much of the toxic waste generated by the *maquiladora* industry is being dumped illegally in Mexico.

Timothy Smith, executive director of the Interfaith Center on Corporate Responsibility, states, "We find a range of corporate behavior in the *maquiladoras*, from the irresponsible polluter and exploiter of labor to companies which are working to live up to standards of fairness. Though many company and plant officials proudly point to their high standards for wages, health and safety, and environment, until now most companies seem to be involved in a race to the bottom."[1]

In late 1990 religious investors sponsored shareholder resolutions asking twelve U.S. corporations to report on their facilities and plants in Mexico and the United States. Ten companies agreed to make reports or to allow inspection of facilities by coalition members. Among those companies agreeing to issue reports were Allied-Signal, AT & T, Baxter International, Ford Motor, General Motors, ITT Corporation, Johnson & Johnson, and PepsiCo.*

NOTES

1. As quoted in "Environmental, Religious and Labor Organizations Promote Corporate Social Responsibility in the Maquiladora Industry," *The Corporate Examiner*, vol. 20, no. 1 (May 1991): 1.

*For further information contact: Marcia Osgood, Coalition for Justice in the Maquiladoras, ICCR, Room 566, 475 Riverside Drive, New York, N.Y. 10115.

CHAPTER 15

RELIGIOUS INVESTORS AND THE U.S. PHARMACEUTICAL INDUSTRY

Regina Rowan Committee for Responsible
Investment, Medical Mission Sisters

Prior to the 1980s, the Catholic and Protestant religious investor groups of the Interfaith Center on Corporate Responsibility (ICCR) were seldom critical of the U.S. pharmaceutical industry. In general they shared the industry's view of itself as essential to improving the quality of life through the development and marketing of drugs that cure disease, alleviate the symptoms of disease, and in some cases save lives.

The groups observed the pharmaceutical industry as it expanded from national to international in its scope, as increasingly vast sums of money were spent on research and development to discover the new "magic pill," and as ever-greater markets were needed to generate income for these firms.

| THE CHURCHES GET INVOLVED

During this time, the religious investor groups became aware of the controversies surrounding the practices of multinational drug firms in the unregulated markets of developing countries, largely through the writings of Dr. Milton Silverman and reports from such groups as the International Organization of Consumers Unions and Health Action International.

Regina Rowan, S.C.M.M., is a member of the Medical Mission Sisters, an international group of Roman Catholic women who provide preventative and curative health care in twenty-five countries. She is executive director of the community's Committee for Responsible Investment. Sister Regina is the chair of the Pharmaceutical/International Health Issue Group of the Interfaith Center on Corporate Responsibility (ICCR).

The Bangladesh Controversy

What galvanized the religious investors to action was the pharmaceutical industry's actions against Bangladesh's enactment of the National Drug Policy and the Drug (Control) Ordinance in June 1982. The Bangladesh law listed 150 essential drugs as necessary for most therapeutic needs, and an additional 100 drugs as appropriate for use by specialists in hospitals. Drugs on these lists were considered adequate for the needs of the country and in keeping with its limited financial resources. The law's most controversial measure, however, was the removal of some 1,700 drugs from the market, drugs deemed useless, harmful, or nonessential. This measure brought protests from both multinational drug companies and local drug manufacturers. Both charged that the policy would destroy the pharmaceutical industry in Bangladesh and would damage related industries, such as packaging firms.

An executive of Pfizer, which has manufacturing units in Bangladesh, stated publicly that the policy was not beneficial for the people of Bangladesh or for Pfizer. The U.S. Pharmaceutical Manufacturers Association asked the U.S. State Department to delay implementation of the law until U.S. manufacturers had discussed it with government officials in Bangladesh. Jane Coon, U.S. ambassador to Bangladesh, arranged for a series of meetings with U.S. scientific experts. These "experts" were representatives from the Pharmaceutical Manufacturers Association, SmithKline Beckman (now SmithKline Beecham), Squibb (now Bristol-Myers Squibb), and Wyeth (now American Home Products).

Religious investors decided to stand with Bangladesh in defending its rights to implement an essential drug list, challenging corporations' actions to coerce Bangladesh to abandon this list. They did so first through an attempt to seek information on the companies' position on the essential drug list. When attempts at discussion and requests for information failed, they turned to shareholder resolutions. In the end, Bangladesh succeeded in establishing its essential drug list, and it is still in effect today. Modifications have been made to the list. The Bangladesh pharmaceutical industry has expanded. The multinational pharmaceutical industry has not withdrawn.

The debate between the pharmaceutical industry and the church investors of ICCR then moved to the broader issue of the right of any government to formulate an essential drug list. At first the industry strongly resisted the concept of essential lists. Consumer groups, ministers of health, and other institutions joined the debate.

One by one, pharmaceutical companies accepted the concept of an essential drug list for the public sector (government-funded hospitals and clinics) but not for the private sector.

As church investors began to look more closely at the pharmaceutical industry and its policies and practices in developing countries, other areas of concern quickly surfaced. These concerns were reinforced by information provided by national and international consumer groups around the world.

| DOUBLE STANDARDS FOR THE THIRD WORLD

The pharmaceutical industry has engaged in practices in developing countries not allowed or tolerated in the United States. As a result, it has been accused of using double standards of conduct, one for developed countries and another for developing countries. These practices include:

- the sale of drugs banned in the United States because the risks (side effects) from using them are considered greater than the health benefits from their use;
- the sale of therapeutically ineffective drugs;
- the sale of irrational combinations of drugs that pose health risks, are not synergistic in benefit, and can be antagonistic or therapeutically ineffective; and
- promotional activities that exaggerate or misstate the benefits or uses of a drug.

Banned Drugs
Consumers in the United States are protected by protocols that manufacturers must follow to receive Food and Drug Administration (FDA) permission to market a product. These include safety and efficacy studies. If a product, once approved by the FDA, has severe or life-threatening side effects (the risk of using it outweighs the benefits), it is removed from the market. Unfortunately, strong regulatory bodies do not exist in developing countries. Some drugs banned for use in the United States are readily available and are promoted by drug companies in these countries.

In the late 1980s Congress passed the Hatch-Kennedy Act barring the export of drugs banned in the United States except to certain developed countries that have strong regulatory agencies. (This legislation was a compromise. A more stringent version prohibited the export of banned drugs from the United States to any country.) This legislation protects developing countries from receiving drugs from the United States that are banned in the United States, but it does not protect developing countries from drugs banned here but manufactured elsewhere or from the transshipment of these products from developed countries.

For example, dipyrone, an analgesic, is banned or severely restricted for use in most industrialized countries. In developing countries, however, a number of companies, including Hoechst and Winthrop (Sterling Drugs), aggressively promote it. The most common side effect from use of dipyrone is agranulocytosis. Cardiovascular reactions such as anaphylactic shock, a life-threatening condition, are also possible from the use of intravenous dipyrone. Since alternative drugs for pain relief do exist, the continued availability of dipyrone to developing countries seems unwarranted.

Therapeutically Ineffective Drugs

Therapeutically ineffective drugs present a twofold problem in developing countries. Their use means not only that diseases or conditions are not effectively treated, but that the few financial resources available are wasted on these products. For instance, many of the "tonics" sold in these countries as vitamin supplements do not meet the nutritional needs of the population; these people would be better served by using their money for food.

In addition, a number of drugs on the markets in developing countries are in fact older therapies discarded in developed countries as ineffective and replaced with newer drugs. Most of these drugs date from the 1930s to the 1960s. After that, manufacturers had to prove therapeutic efficacy through testing before the FDA approved a drug. The FDA has grandfathered drugs put on the market before the 1960s for use without proof of therapeutic efficacy.

Irrational Combinations

It is not uncommon to find drugs that contain two or more active ingredients that do not increase therapeutic efficacy and may cause unwanted side effects. For instance, the combined use of two antibiotics that have the same spectrum of activity and do not add benefits to the treatment of an illness may lead to drug resistance to both antibiotics. A number of companies, including Pfizer, market analgesic preparations that contain both aspirin and paracetamol.

No adequate therapeutic benefit has been shown for this combination.

Promotional Activities

The pharmaceutical industry has on occasion used two types of questionable promotional activities in developing countries. One is the inappropriate promotion of a reasonably effective product. The second is the promotion of a therapeutically ineffective product. These two types of printed promotional activities can result in improper treatment of an underlying disease or condition or in side effects ranging from trivial to life threatening.

In the United States, Merck markets an antihistamine under the brand name Periactin. In developing countries it markets this same product as an appetite stimulant. The company has included in the written summary that accompanies the medicine, the statement that the product is for use as an appetite stimulant where, in the opinion of the physician, increased food intake is desirable and adequate diet is available and where an underlying disease that may be responsible for weight loss is being treated. It is an unfortunate fact that in most developing countries, the majority of the population needs to increase food intake but adequate diet is not available.

The Pharmaceutical Industry in the United States

Because of strict regulation of the pharmaceutical industry, we in the United States are faced with concerns different from many of those in developing countries. A drug banned here is removed from the market. Irrational combinations of drugs are discontinued as our medical knowledge expands. Church investors remain concerned about other issues, such as advertising abuses and the skyrocketing costs of adequate medical coverage.

The contents of prescription drug advertising to the medical profession are regulated. Drug companies, however, use other forms of advertising to create a market for their products with the general public. For example, Upjohn runs advertisements in magazines and newspapers for its remedy for male baldness, Rogaine. Marion Merrell Dow does the same with its prescription antihistamine, Seldane. These print ads carry the required drug information, usually on the back of the ad.

Magazine and newspaper articles about prescription drugs also create markets. These stories are generated by the press, not by the pharmaceutical companies, which usually have no control over what is printed. For example, articles describing Eli Lilly's Prozac as a wonder drug for the treatment of mental illness have prompted patients to ask for this drug by name.

The church investors share the concern of others in the United States over the rapidly rising costs of health care and the number of our citizens who, as a consequence, have inadequate or no health insurance coverage. Why, for example, should the price of drugs for chronic conditions regularly rise as prescriptions are refilled?

Pharmaceutical companies often argue that research and development costs make increased prices necessary. Yet these same companies continue to report healthy year-end profit margins. Profit margins are controlled in many other countries. It is not hard to believe that the United States is subsidizing other developed countries' pharmaceutical costs. Moreover, many U.S. pharmaceutical companies are less than forthright in providing details on the costs related to the development, manufacturing, and marketing of medications. This lack of disclosure adds to the concern over the prices of their drugs.

The church investors of ICCR also are concerned about U.S. companies' limited research into the treatment of those diseases that afflict 70 percent of the populations in developing countries—diseases such as malaria and schistosomiasis. At the same time, these church groups have praised Merck for its bold step in offering, at no charge, its drug invermectin, used for the treatment of onchocerciasis (river blindness), to those who need it throughout the world.

The pharmaceutical industry has the capability to improve the quality of life for all the world's citizens beyond the provision of curative medicine. How the industry will act to develop this potential remains in its hands.

RESOURCES

BOOKS AND PUBLICATIONS

BUKO Pharma-Campaign and Health Action International–Europe. 1989. *Dipyrone: A Drug No One Needs.* Netherlands: BUKO.

Chetley, Andrew. 1990. *A Healthy Business? World Health and the Pharmaceutical Industry.* P. 206. London: Zed Books.

Silverman, M., P. R. Lee, and M. Lydecker. 1982. *Prescriptions for Death: The Drugging of the Third World.* Berkeley: University of California Press.

TOBACCO SHAREHOLDER ACTIONS

Michael Crosby

This chapter outlines health hazards connected to smoking, the antismoking activities that have resulted, the effort for divestment from tobacco company stocks, and the ministry of Interfaith Center on Corporate Responsibility (ICCR)–related groups that challenges U.S. tobacco companies on their policies and practices in the United States and abroad.

| HEALTH HAZARDS OF TOBACCO

When he arrived in the New World, Christopher Columbus discovered native peoples smoking tobacco. By the middle of the sixteenth century, Spaniards cultivated tobacco commercially. By the late sixteenth century, Sir Walter Raleigh popularized tobacco in Britain. In 1613 the first commercial shipments of tobacco from Jamestown were shipped to Britain. However, as early as 1604, tobacco's health hazards were recognized—at least they were by King James I, who declared that smoking was "a custome lothsome to the eye, hatefull to the nose, harmefull to the braine, daungerous to the Lungs, and in the black stinking fume thereof, neerest resembling the horrible Stigian smoak of the pit that is bottomelesse."

Michael Crosby, O.F.M. Cap, Ph.D., is a member of the Midwest Province of the Capuchin Franciscans, a Roman Catholic Order of Brothers. He has been involved with the Interfaith Center on Corporate Responsibility (ICCR) since 1973 and heads its Tobacco Issue Group. Mike has been a pioneer among Catholics in the corporate responsibility movement. Author of *Catholic Church Investments for Corporate Social Responsibility,* he has a master's degree in economics and a doctorate in theology. He currently advises twenty-five Midwest-based members of ICCR.

Smoking grew in popularity in the United States in the eighteenth, nineteenth, and early twentieth centuries. However, an antismoking stigma has grown in the second half of the twentieth century as a result of medical data noting health hazards connected to tobacco use.

In the 1940s and early 1950s, cigarette ads portrayed various brands as more healthy than others—an implicit admission that cigarette smoking entailed health hazards. After 1953 medical research revealed increasing links between smoking and various diseases. In 1961 the Arthur D. Little Company defined Liggett & Myers's problems associated with the manufacture of a product (cigarette tobacco) that was "a) cancer causing; b) cancer promoting; c) poisonous; and d) stimulating, pleasurable and flavorful." In 1963 a "personal and confidential" Philip Morris memo warned, "The next medical attack on cigarettes will be based on the cocarcinogen idea. With the hundreds of compounds in smoke, this hypothesis will be hard to contest." In addition to nicotine, which is addictive, cigarette smoke contains hundreds of mutagens, carcinogens, and cocarcinogens; some four thousand other chemical compounds; and simple carbon monoxide.

In 1964 the surgeon general published a report linking cigarette smoking to disease. Since then, warnings from the surgeon general's office, the American Cancer Society, and the World Health Organization (WHO) have concluded that smoking is the major cause of serious health problems in the United States and other industrialized countries. In his 1982 report, then–surgeon general Dr. C. Everett Koop concluded, "Cigarette smoking is clearly identified as the chief preventable cause of death in our society." He noted a causal association between smoking and cancer of the lung, larynx, oral cavity, and esophagus and for the first time labeled smoking a "contributory factor" in the development of bladder, pancreas, and kidney cancers.

During the 1990s it is expected that of the three million people who will die from tobacco-induced disease, two million will be from developed countries. Most were smokers before the health hazards were known as fully as they are now, since, as in the case of lung cancer, the disease takes twenty to thirty years to incubate. On the basis of current smoking patterns, the date when worldwide annual mortality from tobacco will exceed ten million (of which about three million will then be in developed countries) probably lies sometime in the 2020s. Such data show a shift in the highest percentages of tobacco-related deaths from developed nations to developing nations.

In the early 1990s society became more aware of health hazards connected to "passive smoking" or environmental tobacco smoke (ETS). The Environmental Protection Agency (EPA) released data declaring secondhand cigarette smoke a known carcinogen. It is now estimated that more than 53,000 people die each year in the United States alone from ETS. A study reported in the American Heart Association's journal *Circulation* estimates that ETS has become the third leading cause of preventable deaths—after smoking and alcohol—with 37,000 heart disease–related deaths, 3,700 lung cancer–related deaths, and another 12,300 deaths due to cervical and other cancers each year. An increased association between parental smoking and bronchitis, pneumonia, and other serious childhood diseases has been documented as well. Children exposed to heavy amounts of tobacco smoke at home are more than twice as likely to develop lung cancer later in life as those who grow up in smoke-free homes.

| THE EFFECTIVENESS OF ANTISMOKING EFFORTS

Antismoking efforts at the governmental level have been highlighted by regular (and increasingly critical) reports from the surgeon general, educational campaigns warning young people, increased taxes at the federal, state, and local levels, the demand that health warnings be placed on cigarette packages and in cigarette advertising, and local legislation outlawing vending machines. In 1990 cigarette smoking was banned on all domestic flights as an increasing number of cities and municipalities created legislation banning smoking in various areas.

Litigation and Lobbying

The Tobacco Products Liability Project communicates regularly among lawyers, informing them of the progress of various legal cases brought against tobacco companies by families of victims who develop health problems from smoking. The most celebrated of these cases was *Cipollone v. Liggett Group, Inc.* In 1988 a federal jury in New Jersey found Liggett liable in the lung cancer death of Rose Cipollone and awarded $400,000 in damages to her husband. Although not establishing a precedent in other cases, the trial brought to light cigarette industry documents noting that the companies themselves had proven by the early 1960s that smoking causes lung cancer.

In 1990 the New Jersey Supreme Court ruled that warnings on cigarette packages do not protect tobacco makers from product liability lawsuits. In 1991 the Wisconsin Labor and Industry Review Commission ruled that a company was financially liable for worker's compensation to an employee who proved that smoke from her coworkers' smoking had made her sick.

Groups such as the American Heart Association and the American Cancer Society regularly publish brochures noting cigarettes' health hazards. Many states have organized groups of people working on legislation and other ways to stop smoking; among the most effective has been Groups to Alleviate Smoking in Public (GASP). Another group addressing issues of youth, Stop Teenage Addiction to Tobacco (STAT), has been instrumental in moving legislation and public opinion around the role of tobacco company support of events geared to youth. STAT was instrumental in sponsoring a boycott of RJR and Philip Morris products.

The Tobacco Divestment Effort
Spurred by the success of groups working on the South Africa issue, various groups on college campuses as well as other antismoking groups organized efforts to challenge universities and pension funds to divest their portfolios from companies with cigarette-related stocks. The main national body geared to this goal is the Tobacco Divestment Project, whose belief is that nobody should profit from tobacco addiction. The project's targets are health care insitutions, charities, and philanthropies; institutes of higher education; life and health insurers; and states and municipalities that have tobacco-related stocks in their portfolios.

Since 1990 Harvard University, Johns Hopkins University, and City University of New York have announced that they would divest their portfolios of tobacco company stocks. New England Deaconess Hospital in Boston voted to do the same. However, in 1991 the campaign to have institutional investors divest suffered a setback when executives of the California Public Employee's Retirement System rejected divestment of $300 million in tobacco-related stocks. Meanwhile other institutions, such as Stanford University, decided to study various shareholder resolutions regarding cigarette issues as an interim measure before deciding on divestment.

| THE HISTORY OF SHAREHOLDER RESOLUTIONS

In 1980, after visiting Central America, Michael Crosby, corporate responsibility agent for his Midwest Capuchin-Franciscan Province, urged his province to purchase ten shares each of Philip Morris and R. J. Reynolds in order to raise the issue of what they were doing (and not doing) in third world countries. The Capuchins filed the first shareholder resolutions based on health hazards connected to smoking with these companies the same year.

The Capuchins' Third World Resolutions
The 1980 resolution called for a report describing the companies' various markets in Africa, Asia, and Latin America, their size and share, as well as advertising and promotional activities and costs. The resolution also asked for a description of the companies' policies related to the World Health Organization's recommendation on banning the promotion of tobacco, especially in third world nations, a limitation of tar and nicotine to U.S. levels, and whether the companies would inform consumers of health hazards related to smoking in countries that did not demand such warnings. The companies opposed the resolutions, and the resolutions failed to achieve the necessary votes for refiling in the first and second years they were filed.

For several years the Province of St. Joseph was the lone shareholder voice raising the issue of cigarette sales in third world countries. Furthermore, despite efforts by the province, a member of the Interfaith Center on Corporate Responsibility (ICCR) since 1973, the issue was not voted to be an ICCR-sponsored issue until the mid-1980s. In 1987 the Capuchins were primary filers of a resolution calling on Philip Morris to prepare a report on third world activities similar to the one requested in 1980. This time the company acceded to the request, and the shareholder resolution was withdrawn. A report reflecting Philip Morris's perspective was prepared and disseminated to requesting shareholders.

The Move to Broader Health Care Issues
Given the companies' more developed strategies to deal with the shareholder resolutions, in 1988 the Capuchins and ICCR decided to move beyond specific third world issues to address the underlying issue at stake: the universal health hazards of smoking.

A resolution was drafted requesting the boards of Philip Morris and R. J. Reynolds to establish a health and smoking evaluation committee to deal with all tobacco-related business. The committee would hold hearings within a year on alleged cigarette health hazards, with testimony coming from the companies' experts and an equal number of outside experts including the surgeon general and the director general of WHO. If, following this hearing, the committee determined that "no clear refutation has been evidenced regarding the consistent medical data showing a causal connection between cigarette smoking" and various deaths, "the Committee shall vote to cause the Company to cease immediately all forms of cigarette advertising and promotion and take steps to insure the cessation of worldwide production, licensing, and sale of cigarettes by 1992."

The resolution was filed when R. J. Reynolds was in the midst of its leveraged buyout, and it became moot when the company went private. However, Philip Morris vigorously challenged the resolution at the Securities and Exchange Commission (SEC). The SEC supported the company's rationale that the resolution infringed on "ordinary business" and permitted Philip Morris to keep the resolution off the proxy statement. Neither the Capuchins nor ICCR appealed the SEC decision.

An SEC Reversal
Around this time the Tobacco Issue Group of ICCR received a great stimulus with the expertise of two antismoking experts, Dr. Gregory Connolly, health commissioner of the Commonwealth of Massachusetts, and Dr. John Slade, addictions specialist at St. Peter's Medical Center in New Jersey. In 1989 they helped Michael Crosby create two new shareholder resolutions. The first called on Philip Morris, American Brands (American Tobacco), Loews (Liggett), and Kimberly-Clark (which is involved in various stages of the cigarette production process) to amend their corporate charters to become smoke-free by the year 2000. The second resolution called for a report addressing the various ways that Philip Morris—especially with its number-one brand, Marlboro—appealed to young people.

Again the companies, especially Philip Morris and Kimberly-Clark, vigorously challenged the resolutions on "ordinary business" grounds at the SEC. The SEC staff issued a "no action" that, in effect, ruled in favor of the companies. This time the Capuchins appealed the decision through Paul Neuhauser, ICCR's attorney. Upon receiving the appeal, the staff reversed itself and notified the full SEC of its reversal. The full commission concurred, thus making ineffective for the first time the argument that such issue's could be discounted merely because they were "ordinary business."

Expanding the Targets

In 1990 the ICCR Tobacco Issue Group asked for a broader approach to the cigarette resolution, since some church groups have shunned cigarette company stocks for decades. Consequently, for those directly involved, the group produced resolutions regarding the targeting of minors and minorities and developed reports dealing with minimum standards for the labeling of warnings and compliance with the industry's code of conduct. For the first time, U.S. Tobacco received a resolution on the code. Besides the tobacco companies, other companies that serve the tobacco industry received resolutions. These included:

- Eastman Kodak—filter tows;
- Gannett—marketing;
- Kimberly-Clark—cigarette paper;
- Mobil—cellophane wrap; and
- Time Warner—marketing.

Insurance companies giving preferential rates to nonsmokers while holding cigarette stocks in their portfolios (Aetna and Travelers) were targeted as well.

The results of dialogue with insurance companies revealed levels of involvement between the insurance companies and tobacco companies not envisioned previously by the shareholders. This indicated a new thrust for future shareholder resolutions. At the same time, the increasing challenges to pension funds, and especially those related to universities and health care groups, served notice that the issue of tobacco and cigarettes was fast becoming one of the critical issues of the 1990s. Parallels were made to the way the 1960s and 1970s had laid the groundwork for the issue of South Africa to gain worldwide stature in the 1980s and 1990s; cigarettes were seen to be a main issue of the future.

RESOURCES

BOOKS AND PUBLICATIONS

Burrough, Bryan. 1990. *Barbarians at the Gates.* New York: Harper & Row.
> A fine account of one cigarette company (R. J. Reynolds) and its leveraged buyout.

Chapman, Simon. 1986. *Great Expectorations: Advertising and the Tobacco Industry.* London: Comedia.

"The World Cigarette Pandemic." July 1985. *New York State Journal of Medicine* 85.
> The entire issue addresses health hazards and smoking.

Taylor, Peter. 1985. *Tobacco, Money and Multinational Politics.* New York: New American Library.

PEOPLE AND ORGANIZATIONS

The Advocacy Institute
1730 Rhode Island Avenue
NKW No. 600
Washington, D.C. 20036-3118
Produces a series of "Action Alerts" that address various issues related to efforts to curb smoking.

Tobacco and Youth Reporter
Stop Teenage Addiction to Tobacco (STAT)
121 Lyman Street, No. 210
Springfield, Mass. 01103
Probably the best up-to-date materials available on the issue, especially related to youth.

Consumer Currents
Emmanstraat 9
2595 EG, The Hague
Netherlands
For international updates, this is the magazine arm of the International Organization of Consumers Unions.

THE IMPACT ON CORPORATIONS OF SHAREHOLDER ACTIONS

Edgar G. Crane Director, Corporate Social Responsibility, Evangelical Lutheran Church in America

Timothy Smith Executive Director, Interfaith Center on Corporate Responsibility

What impact does shareholder action actually have on corporations?

Of great importance for investors, corporations, wider stakeholders, and the general public is the substantial evidence that the answer to this question is changing—and in an encouraging direction. Shareholder action has a significant impact on corporate behavior and thinking.

Take the case of Manufacturers Hanover Bank in New York City. In 1990 and 1991 a broad coalition of church and community groups filed resolutions on the combined issues of community investment under the federal Community Reinvestment Act and South Africa bank loans. The coalition regarded the issues as related in expressing the attitude of the bank toward persons of color. Communications with the bank over a period of several years had included boardroom-style dialogue, street-level demonstrations, media involvement, and appeals to agencies of the federal government responsible for implementing the Community Reinvestment Act. Key milestones in this process were shareholder meetings and regulatory review of possible bank mergers. Toward the end, shareholders active on the South Africa bank loan issue were brought more actively into the community investment issue, with good results.

After a number of false starts, Manufacturers Hanover has announced that it is eliminating all but the last vestiges of its banking relationships with South Africa and has committed itself to a program of low- and moderate-income housing in Harlem, totaling $250 million over a five-year period. Just as important as these specific steps, channels remain open for further dialogue on issues of common concern.

This example illustrates important changes that have occurred in both shareholder and bank approaches. Both are demonstrating a growing level of sophistication and responsiveness toward each other and the larger environment within which they work.

| A PROCESS OF MATURATION

Twenty years ago, when the corporate social responsibility movement was in its infancy, shareholder rights were protected by public policy through the Securities and Exchange Commission (SEC) and state laws. However, corporations were not used to addressing the social concerns of shareholders in relation to their financial objectives. Further, corporations operated in a general political culture that relied heavily on the adversary process, one in which corporations, with the support of most shareholders, substantially outweighed socially concerned investors.

Today a generation of parties to these negotiations has become accustomed to the idea that the interests involved are not mutually exclusive but indeed often are complementary. In fact, that is what the corporate social responsibility movement has contended from the beginning.

A "maturation" process is taking place on both sides. Increasingly corporations are recognizing and affirming a constructive role for social investors, such as the churches, to raise and work through issues that must be of concern to the corporation.

Contributing Factors
These changes on both sides have created a substantial improvement in the atmosphere for shareholder negotiations and campaigns.

STAKEHOLDERS. Contributing to this change is the corporate recognition of the need to respond to the key actors in its environment—public regulatory agencies, shareholders, and the broadening corporate constituencies of "stakeholders," people and organizations on whom the activities of the corporation have a direct or indirect impact. Among those recognized as legitimate corporate stakeholders are:

shareholders	employees
holding companies	subsidiaries
the board	management
customers	suppliers
government policymakers	regulators
industry counterparts	public interest groups
neighboring communities	

Today's corporate leaders are far more accustomed to this reality than their counterparts were twenty years ago. For instance, a generation of executives has grown up in a very different environmental culture signaled by Earth Day 1970. As a result, companies generally are aspiring to be "environmental." The McDonald's fast-food chain has set the goal of reversing its former "junk" image and becoming the "Number One Environmental Company." It is doing so by developing its own unique environmental principles and entering into partnership with an outside group, the Environmental Defense Fund, to set specific improvement goals. Companies in the same industry may compete for the best environmental image. Within the chemical industry, Dow and DuPont are engaged in such a competition using the framework of a set of industry principles, the Responsible Care Program.

SOCIAL INVESTORS. Social investors have learned that a good exchange with a corporation can produce a win-win situation for the public and the corporation. In a 1990 negotiation with Chevron over the environmental management of a mining facility, new management saw the win-win potential and reversed its predecessor's adversary posture in dealing with a coalition of church and community groups.

Also, shareholders are increasingly integrating their financial and social concerns rather than dealing with one to the exclusion of the other. "We" shareholders are indeed concerned with the total condition of "our" company, just as we are with our communities.

But social investors have entered a new situation with a new set of dangers. When an adversary relationship need not be assumed, coaptation by sophisticated corporate shareholder relations strategists becomes a concern. Shareholders must know their goals more clearly and assess the possibilities in the situation more realistically.

Nonetheless, the possibility of entering into more cooperative strategies requires a willingness on both sides to develop trust levels that exceed those of the past. The challenge to the Coalition for Environmentally Responsible Economies (CERES) and the Interfaith Center on Corporate Responsibility (ICCR) to respond to corporations that have stated support of the Valdez Principles aims but are negotiating for modifications or amplifications is an example of this. Shareholder activists must find a sophisticated balance between trust and cooptation, a need they hold in common with corporate officials.

| THE BOTTOM LINE

Critics of shareholder actions often limit their criteria of success to the percentage of shares voted in favor of a resolution. The SEC presently considers that a vote of 3 percent reflects significant enough concern among shareholders that the resolution can come back for another vote the next year. Success of this magnitude enhances the interim negotiations.

Illustrative Issue Developments
Are these proxy issue "losses" actually "wins"? The evidence indicates that they are. As the South Africa issue developed its momentum through the persistence of shareholders and others, that vote climbed into the 10 to 25 percent range—unusual for a social issue. Corporations took note, and these climbing levels of support among shareholders contributed significantly to decisions to withdraw.

The environmental issue is building momentum similarly but more rapidly. Corporations are demonstrating remarkable sensitivity to this reality. Many corporations that have participated in the Valdez process—though without becoming signatories—have described the continuing impact of environmental concerns on their internal deliberations at all levels.

The tobacco issue also shows signs of taking off as it gains support from public health authorities and a wide range of portfolio owners—including major universities, such as Harvard and Johns Hopkins.

Measures of Impact
Thus, the percentage of shares voted in favor of a resolution is only one indicator of impact. As corporate stakeholder constituencies

grow, a larger and more diverse public will hold corporations accountable for the effects of their actions—beyond that measurable in a shareholder vote. This might result in greater government regulation, which most corporations want to prevent. Even if regulation is not a great risk, public goodwill in an era of consumerism and boycott consciousness is of increasing importance.

In fact, it is very likely that the greater impact is not from resolutions voted on, but from resolutions withdrawn as a result of successful negotiations. The following are some examples of the ways in which a successful negotiation on a shareholder resolution can contribute to progress in the integration of corporate financial and social considerations.

- In 1991, as a result of a lengthy and complex series of negotiations between a broad coalition and the major companies in the infant formula industry, we appear on the verge of resolving the issue of "free supplies" of infant formula in the third world. These companies and their global association, the Infant Formula Manufacturers Association, have committed themselves to the goal of terminating "free supplies" and have proposed specific implementation strategies.
- In 1989 the McDonald's plastic foam resolution was withdrawn, subject to further discussions, and in 1990 McDonald's announced that it would terminate its use.
- A number of companies cut their nonequity ties to South Africa in response to a combination of shareholder and consumer pressure.
- In 1990 BankAmerica worked with shareholders to develop a satisfactory policy on social and human rights considerations in future third world loans.
- In 1990 several strategic withdrawals of Valdez signatory resolutions opened the way to promising negotiations. Also, a new group of companies agreed to provide environmental reports.
- In 1989 negotiations between Travelers Insurance and the Land Project, under the auspices of church shareholders, led to innovative approaches to protect family farming and promote farmland conservation.
- In 1990 negotiations with Raytheon led to significant changes in its chlorofluorocarbon (CFC) policies and opened the way for possible future changes.

- In 1991, in light of its preferential insurance rates to nonsmokers, Travelers Insurance completed a review of its holdings in tobacco stocks. The insurer committed itself to limiting its tobacco stock ownership.
- In 1991 Philip Morris chose not to fight the minors and tobacco resolution at the SEC but opted instead to suggest some editorial changes that the proponents agreed to.

Obviously these victories vary widely in their immediate importance. Some represent procedural steps along the way in a larger process. Others represent achievement of an ultimate objective. Even in the latter case it is in the nature of our changing society that we and the corporations we own will face new challenges and will have to set new objectives.

| TOWARD A TYPOLOGY

The development of the corporate social responsibility movement is taking place both inside and outside corporations, as it must. In the process it is becoming as much a partnership as a contest, as much a cooperative endeavor as a conflict.

Presently it is possible to observe shareholder action and corporate response taking shape across the full spectrum of possibilities. The circumstances specific to an issue may create certain types of relationships, which may change as the parties seek to resolve their concerns.

Open Conflict

When open conflict exists, the present objectives of shareholders and the company seem to be largely contrary. Shareholders may raise the issue more as a public witness to their values and concerns than in the expectation of success. The company may respond by rejecting these concerns or by offering a limited response as a sign of good faith.

Examples of these situations are requests for companies to get out of the tobacco industry or to reduce substantially their participation in military contracting. But even here, circumstances can change. New antismoking coalitions and public policies may emerge. New demand for military technology may dampen hopes for economic conversion. Nuclear disasters may place the nuclear industry in an entirely different light.

Shareholders may continue to offer resolutions in various forms, so long as the resolutions meet the SEC's support requirements, until circumstances change. In some cases this never happens. Then the shareholder action may die or give rise to creative alternatives. Examples include challenging defense industries to state their ethical bases for accepting military contracts, and raising very specific regulatory and performance issues about a nuclear power plant.

Agreement

At the other extreme, shareholders and the company may ultimately identify an area of substantial agreement. In these cases, well-prepared shareholders can have substantial influence by working with managers who have come to hold similar views from the changing perspective of the company's interests.

The environmental area is a prime example of a convergence. In the past, withdrawal from South Africa became a similar area of convergence for many companies. In these cases the pattern increasingly becomes one of withdrawal of resolutions as partial or full agreement is reached.

Long-Range Planning

Some shareholder initiatives continue for long periods when proponents do not know what impact they eventually may have. If they succeed, the causal effect seems like that of water dripping on a rock. The breakthrough can be exhilarating for proponents and a relief for the company. This may describe the end of the infant formula campaign.

A variation is the "delayed effect," which may occur when a new board or new management acts years later. This was the case with Arco in the matter of integrating its board.

Board Coalitions and Campaigns

In some cases the impact results from the combined effects of several corporate considerations. In 1991 J. P. Morgan decided to cut correspondent banking and American depositary receipt (ADR) ties with South Africa. Among the factors the bank cited was concern about losing the business of municipalities, such as the City of Boston, that had strong antiapartheid policies.

A variant of this is an initiative that catalyzes conversations among groups of companies or industries and leads to related initiatives. The Valdez Principles have given rise to statements of principles at the corporate, industry, and business community levels.

| THE FUTURE

The impact of shareholder action on the corporate response to social issues seems likely to continue to grow. But the environment is changing.

Changes in the SEC's policies could affect shareholder actions either positively or negatively. Also, the globalization of the corporate social responsibility, social investment, consumer, and related movements could widen the impact of shareholder actions on a global economy driven by transnational corporations. Finally, as shareholder action becomes more coherently and publicly linked to broader coalitions and to other forms of action, such as divestment and boycotts, the impact of the whole effort should grow.

PART THREE

CORPORATE
SOCIAL
ACCOUNTABILITY
RESEARCH

Socially responsible investing depends on accurate information about securities issuers and investment vehicles. What distinguishes socially responsible investors from investors generally is their commitment to know in whom and in what they are investing.

Just knowing that International Widget looks like a sure thing in the highly competitive skyhook market or that it has strong fundamentals is not enough. Who's running IW? Do skyhooks have military applications? Do IW's manufacturing processes pose environmental problems?

Thus, socially responsible investors—and, more important, their advisers—need a high level of nonquantitative information about companies' relations to society and the natural environment. When screening was largely negative and limited to things like South Africa or "sin," finding information was relatively simple and applying it was simpler yet. Any broker could tell you whether a company was in alcohol, tobacco, or gambling.

As screens have become more numerous and nuanced, investors and social researchers have realized that the amount of available information on large securities issuers is vast and yet difficult to apply. And the expenses involved in research have grown exponentially—although U.S. investors still pay a small fraction of what their counterparts do in the United Kingdom, for instance.

The screens social investors apply determine the types of information they need and how the data must be structured. In their chapter on social screening, Karen Paul and Steve Lydenberg describe the different types of screening processes and their evolution. More important, they look at the various approaches to evaluating corporate social performance and comparing one company to another.

Lydenberg, this time with Lloyd Kurtz, also surveys the resources available to social investors in the principal screening areas. What should you be following? From business magazines to on-line data bases to CD-ROM, the sources of information seem to increase daily. Here is some help for the beleaguered.

One area not covered in the chapter by Lydenberg and Kurtz is research services, magazines, and newsletters published for socially responsible investors in the United States. We asked their publishers to supply us with brief descriptions of what they offer, and these will be found in the final chapters of this section.

CORPORATE SOCIAL MONITORING: TYPES, METHODS, GOALS

Karen Paul Professor of Business Environment, Florida International University

Steven D. Lydenberg Director of Research, Kinder, Lydenberg, Domini & Company

Ed. Note: *This chapter originally appeared in a slightly different form in Karen Paul, ed.,* Contemporary Issues in Business and Society in the United States and Abroad *(Lewiston, N.Y.: Edwin Mellen Press, 1991).*

Since 1980 dramatic developments have taken place in the world of corporate social accountability research. In the 1960s and 1970s academics, accountants, activists, government officials, consultants, and corporations came through differing routes and to differing degrees to grapple with these questions: What is a corporate social audit, what dimensions might be included, and how would assessment be determined? How can "social responsibility" be defined, measured, and compared? What does "ethics" mean in the business context? Academics, accountants, government officials, consultants, and corporations developed a variety of approaches to these issues, some of which faded quickly and some of which have endured.[1]

This chapter surveys one approach that has achieved some institutionalization and indeed appears to have had considerable success in influencing corporations as they attempt to understand and respond to the demands of the external society. This approach consists of the comparative "ratings" of corporate performance in areas of broad social concern, such as investment in South Africa and environmental responsibility. In the following pages, several alternative forms that this approach has taken are described, along with its successes and failures, current uses, and directions in which it may be leading.

I EVOLUTION OF RATING SYSTEMS

In the course of the 1980s, the rating system approach has evolved into a fundamentally new method for bringing essentially political impulses to bear on the actions of corporate management, and it has had an impact qualitatively different from other business ethics approaches that were developing coincidentally in the 1970s, such as the social audit. The archetype of this rating system approach is the Sullivan Principles for corporate labor and community relations in South Africa, although numerous other systems are currently active in various forms. The central significance of these systems lies in their applicability in two public forums of crucial significance to most corporations: the financial markets (important to all companies issuing stocks or bonds) and the marketplace (especially important to consumer product firms).

Social Indicators and Social Audits

In both government and business there was a movement in the 1960s to develop social indicators that would serve to supplement and in some ways to counterbalance existing economic indicators. In the federal government the short-lived War on Poverty and the other social programs of the 1960s created the need to capture some measures of social phenomena not currently captured by Census Department or economic data. An effort was mounted in the Census Department to conduct a national census of social conditions, an effort that currently results in the publication of annual population profiles. The National Science Foundation supported the Social Indicators Project, which, although discontinued in the early 1970s, left a legacy in the form of regularly issued publications in the areas of science indicators, education indicators, criminal statistics, and health indicators.[2]

In the business world a comparable effort was made in an attempt to develop a social audit, led by Abt Associates of Boston, which tried to market this type of measuring system to corporations. This system was roughly half objective and half subjective and included measures of such components as employment of minorities, contribution to philanthropic activities, and others relating to the concept of corporate social responsibility. In this approach each corporation was measured in conformance to an overall grid of desirable behaviors. The results of the audits were essentially private and individual, not particularly intended to be widely shared with external constituencies or to be used by activist groups.

These two efforts were representative of the wide interest at that time in achieving some means of measurement that would correspond to the term *social responsibility*. However, the government effort to promote social indicators and the business effort to promote the use of the social audit had rather limited success. A variety of causes contributed to this limited success. Certainly one of primary importance was the changing political climate of the 1970s after the end of the Nixon administration, when there was a retrenchment of government efforts to improve social conditions in many areas of human services. The changing economic circumstances resulting from the recession of the mid-1970s sapped the nation's capacity and perhaps its will to make new commitments to improving many of the areas that would have been measured by social indicators. The program came to represent not only unnecessary overhead at a time of cutbacks in government programs, but also had the potential for revealing information about the failures rather than the successes of the nation in dealing with problems in education, health care, housing, and other areas of human services. There was little national support from either business or government circles for the development of techniques whereby social performance could be measured and monitored in a way comparable to economic performance. To some extent the accumulation of data about social conditions within corporations was resisted because these data made corporations vulnerable to challenges from external constituencies. For example, under the antiregulatory stance of the Reagan administration, reporting the frequency of accidents in corporations was no longer mandated; hence this information could not be used for comparison between companies or for tracking the performance of any single corporation over time.

A second cause, less tangible but still crucial, was the perception of corporate decision makers that making such information public would lead to increased activism by external constituencies whose capacity to articulate specific demands would be strengthened by increased information. For example, until the implementation of the Sullivan Principles was well underway in the late 1970s, no comprehensive listing of U.S. corporate activities in South Africa existed. Regarding affirmative action, it was briefly possible to obtain under the Freedom of Information Act reports required of corporations by the Equal Employment Opportunity Commission in the mid-1970s before this information was ruled proprietary by the courts at the request of business and shut off from the public domain. The Natural Resources Defense Council's petition to the Securities and Exchange Commission (SEC) in the mid-1970s that corporations be required to report substantial details on environmental and hiring practices in 10-K filings provoked acrimonious congressional hearings and a decade-long court battle that resulted in only minimal additional reporting requirements. A trial balloon floated by Secretary of Commerce Juanita Kreps during the Carter administration suggesting greater corporate social reporting to the public also was quickly shot down.

Ratings by Social Activists

Although business and government circles were not inclined to provide support for the idea, social activists were drawn to the external monitoring systems as a means of assessing the performance of corporations.[3] The comparative rating system approach was one that was tried as early as 1970 by the Council on Economic Priorities in a series of publications that "rated" the environmental and hiring practices of a variety of U.S. corporations. But certainly the rating system that was to achieve the widest use and to provoke the greatest controversy and the most dramatic actions was the Sullivan Principles. In 1976 the Reverend Leon Sullivan and twelve U.S. multinationals announced the formulation of the Sullivan Principles to guide U.S. companies operating in South Africa and to demonstrate that they were indeed performing at an acceptable level in accomplishing some specific goals relating to the treatment of the black work force. Reverend Sullivan very quickly began monitoring the performance of companies subscribing to the principles, and he publicly announced the results of his findings. Compliance with these principles was reported with a "graded" rating system. A company's performance was on level one (the best), level two, or level three. The use of the Sullivan Principles and this monitoring system gathered a remarkable momentum starting in about 1980, and prompted debates, compromises, and actions that have been a powerful influence for many of the other similarly conceived ratings systems that have sprung up since then. The political significance of having three levels of performance was important, because these levels provided room for discussion as external groups made demands on corporations and as various constituencies mobilized. Discussions of divestment became amenable to negotiation. For example, when demands were made, often by trade unions, that cities give procurement preference to companies that had disinvested from South Africa, the demand could be negotiated so that preference would be given to companies meeting a stated level of performance.[4]

| TYPES OF RATING SYSTEMS

When rating systems are being created, a number of strategic questions should be considered.

One of the most basic relates to the target of the system. The Sullivan Principles targeted U.S. multinationals that would "voluntarily" subscribe to the principles and thereby subject themselves to external monitoring. However, other methods of determining targets are possible. One other form has been for external constituencies to target one particular company and to make social demands on it and it alone.

Another strategic question concerns the type of demand being made. It is possible to focus either on a single issue, perhaps measured in a variety of ways, or on multiple issues. When we consider these dimensions of monitoring systems together, we can see that there are four basic types of systems: single company, single issue; single company, multiple issue; multiple company, single issue; and multiple company, multiple issue.

Single-Company, Single-Issue Systems

This type of monitoring system has its origins in the boycott. Boycotts aim to have their primary effect in the marketplace. In singling out a particular company, the boycott implies a comparison between one company and all others, a comparison in which a company is portrayed as qualitatively worse than the others. Thus both boycotts and rating systems rely on relative comparisons among corporate actors. This comparison is more direct for rating systems and may be only implied in the case of boycotts. Similarly, both are oriented to actions to be expressed by external constituencies of high importance to the targeted company. This action orientation may be expressed only indirectly under most ratings systems, whereas it is likely to be central for a boycott.

Probably the most highly publicized boycott in the past two decades was that targeting Nestlé and based on objections to its marketing of infant formula in less-developed countries. After some fifteen years of lobbying, finally a resolution was reached between INFACT, the main group representing external activists, and Nestlé. This resolution depended on monitoring of Nestlé's marketing practices by an external independent commission headed by former senator Edmund Muskie. As a result, an end to the boycott was declared. This lasted until 1988, when INFACT attempted to revive the boycott, not on the basis of commission findings but rather on information coming from external sources.

The single issue forming the basis for this case of corporate social monitoring is the company's marketing of infant formula, and the single company, of course, is Nestlé. Single-issue, single-company monitoring has the potential advantage of enabling resources to be focused toward intensive measurement of the company under consideration. But, it has the problem of being so narrowly focused that more general public interest may not be forthcoming. Too, interest by the rest of the business community will not be inspired by such a narrow focus and by the relative unlikelihood that a similar effort will come to be focused on any particular company.

The degree of independence of a nominally independent monitoring body like Senator Muskie's group may be suspect. Support for such a monitoring group must come from somewhere, and the most likely source is the company itself.

Cooperation from company sources is required for even a minimal degree of assessment of their practices, but then the symbiotic nature of those doing the auditing and those being audited, without any other strong external bodies to exercise supervision and control, makes coaptation possible. Single-company, single-issue monitoring is inherently limited, but it may be extremely effective in influencing the activities of the target. The main problem is that the policy changes achieved may have a limited effect on other companies. To make an analogy from economics, the multiplier effect of changes produced is likely to be attenuated.

Single-Company, Multiple-Issue Systems

A variation on the boycott of a single company on a single issue is the boycott of a single company on multiple issues simultaneously by various groups. The most dramatic example of this approach in recent years focused on the Adolph Coors Company during the 1980s. The AFL-CIO maintained a boycott against Coors for a decade. Coors, the largest nonunion brewery, was charged with a number of practices that invaded workers' privacy, such as personal searches and drug and urine tests, and it resisted union organization vehemently. The conflict was exacerbated in 1984, when William Coors, then chairman of the company, stated that blacks lacked intellectual capacity and that one of the best things slave traders did was to drag the ancestors of today's black citizens over here in chains. Although he apologized the next day, many blacks called for a boycott of Coors products. Hispanics, gay-rights groups, environmentalists, and the National Organization for Women (NOW) all called for boycotts based on their own grievances.

The National Association for the Advancement of Colored People (NAACP), Operation PUSH, and other black groups called off their boycott after Coors agreed to a number of concessions, including awarding twenty distributorships to blacks, bringing blacks into company management, and using black advertising agencies and suppliers. A similar agreement was made with Hispanic groups. However, no concessions were made to women or to environmentalists, and union representation remained an open question.

Echoes of this approach can be heard today in the call for a boycott of grapes by the United Farm Workers Union, led by Caesar Chavez. Their campaign barely touches on union issues, but it enlists the support of environmentalists and advocates of food safety by stressing the dangers of pesticides in growing grapes. However, many different growers and distributors are involved in bringing grapes to the marketplace, and hence effective mobilization of a consumer boycott is difficult. Targeting one particular company is much easier than targeting many companies. Identification of one particular "enemy" facilitates the mobilization of external groups and can make it relatively painless for consumers to participate in a boycott, since they still can maintain access to acceptable sources of supply.

The pressure that can be brought to bear on a company by multiple constituencies organized around multiple issues can be intense, complex, and extremely difficult to manage. Concessions that are meaningful to one group may not be significant to another. A company may suffer a severely tarnished public image, considerable drain on managerial time and energy, and, ultimately, difficulties in maintaining or expanding markets. However, the external constituencies involved may experience difficulties as well. Coordination among groups of activists is hard to manage; concessions obtained by one group may be resented by another; and submission of a group's autonomy to some coordinated plan may be difficult to achieve. For these reasons, the routinization of this type of protest action into a system of corporate monitoring is rarely observed.

Multiple-Company, Single-Issue Systems

The step from single-company monitoring to a multiple-company focus is a critical change. The ramifications are far-reaching in terms of the types of systems required, the degree of organizational accommodation demanded, and the potential impact of the monitoring system. Measurement of relative performance, rather than calls to action, have become the heart of these campaigns. This form of monitoring tends to produce a call for substantial further disclosure about the issues in question and corporate plans for further action. Actions often are only implied by the raters of the companies and are left to the initiative of the "consumers" of the ratings—both the corporations themselves and their external constituencies.

The most interesting example of this type of system in action has been the Sullivan Principles, with the remarkable public debate and variety of public actions that have followed from their promulgation in 1976. The Sullivan system was based on the measurement of multiple companies, all of the signatories to the principles, on the basis of their performance on essentially a single issue—challenging apartheid in South Africa. The model was based on the assumption, often stated by U.S. companies, that they actually were providing increased employment opportunities for blacks in South Africa and hence were challenging apartheid by remaining in business there. This assertion was challenged in several critiques, and the merit of evolutionary change in a repressive system came under severe criticism.

The Sullivan system has been criticized for certain methodological problems. Nevertheless, the system of measurement and reporting it embodied was innovative in several respects. First, it compared companies on a relative basis, so that companies could be assessed in relation to one another. This approach had considerable appeal to the competitive instincts of business. Second, the results were announced to the public, so various external constituencies could use them to pressure companies toward compliance with social objectives. Third, it rated companies on a scale, with roughly three grades given to signatories.

When social activists began to use the ratings to make demands on corporations, or to make demands on other relevant bodies, such as institutional investors, to sanction corporations, the utility of having even this small range of ratings became apparent. It provided room for negotiation among those holding opposing positions.

An intermediate rating allowed concessions to be made by opposing sides. Typically activists would call for sanctions to be adopted against all companies with holdings in South Africa. They would be opposed by those who argued against sanctions against any companies on the basis of their holdings in South Africa. Then a compromise could be made whereby sanctions would be adopted against those companies scoring at an unsatisfactory level on the Sullivan Principles. The fact that there were relative ratings made negotiation possible and thereby helped to legitimate and institutionalize the use of the Sullivan Principles.

One advantage of this type of corporate social monitoring is that it provides a continuing means of assessing corporate social responsibility independent of the actions of any particular company. Another advantage is that it enables comparative judgments to be made. This process appears to tap the competitive instincts of corporations. Their energies are mobilized to achieve the goals embodied in the system. Finally, the system allows for learning to occur among the corporations included, as well as among the raters and the external groups that are using the ratings for their own intentions. In short, the degree of institutionalization inherent in a multicompany system produces considerable refinement of the monitoring process that extends to the articulation of objectives, methods of achieving goals, and the measuring process itself.

However, the resources required to implement a multicompany system are considerable. Corporate support of the process becomes almost necessary, leading to some degree of symbiosis between those doing the rating and those being rated. Coaptation becomes possible, and in fact may be inevitable, unless there are strong countervailing pressures that support the autonomy and objectivity of those doing the ratings. Even so, they will be highly dependent on company sources for data that can be used on a comparative basis.

Multiple-Company, Multiple-Issue Systems

A logical extension of the multiple-issue, single-company approach is one in which multiple companies are rated across multiple issues. Various authors and publications have adopted this approach since the mid-1980s, focusing on a variety of issues. In general these authors have taken what we would term a *Consumer Reports* approach, aimed at distinguishing the "best" from the "worst" for a particular clientele.

For example, surveys of the "best places to work" seem to have become an instant tradition since the publication of *The 100 Best Companies to Work for in America* (Addison-Wesley) in 1984. *Working Mother* and *Black Enterprise* magazines regularly publish analyses of the best companies for women and blacks to work for, differentiating among companies on issues such as benefits, profit sharing, and salaries and various aspects of corporate culture.

A more ambitious example of multiple companies rated on multiple issues is contained in two publications of the Council on Economic Priorities: *Rating America's Corporate Conscience* and *Shopping for a Better World.*[5] Both of these publications evaluate the record of consumer product companies over a broad range of social issues (South Africa involvement, military contracting, community affairs, women and minorities, environment, employee relations, and so forth).

These rating systems appear to operate on two separate levels, both of which have an implicitly political agenda. On the first level, they provide a distinct clientele with a nonfinancial means of distinguishing among companies or products. In one case this clientele is the potential or current employee in the job market; in the other, the consumer in the supermarket aisles. Providing this information gives these clienteles a factor for decision making that is different from the usual free-market "nonpolitical" overriding factor of price or salary level. (We would argue that rating systems based on quality, such as those provided by the magazine *Consumer Reports*, are a version of the price factor adjusted for product quality.)

On a second level, these systems clearly have an implicit social agenda, one in which certain corporate characteristics or actions are deemed "better" than others. By publicizing assessments of how corporations rate relative to each other on these issues, these rating systems intend to push corporate management to improve its ratings—that is, these systems are intended not only to influence consumer or employee choices but also, and of even greater importance, to directly influence corporate behavior.

The power of consumer choice to influence corporate actions should not be underestimated. The influence of an individual's deciding what brand of peanut butter to purchase on social grounds is difficult if not impossible to quantify. However, large-scale purchasers, such as municipalities or states, can exercise dramatic, demonstrable pressures. The pressure on corporations to withdraw from South Africa that the cities of New York and Los Angeles brought to bear in the mid-1980s appears, for example, to have influenced the decisions to divest taken by several companies.

In addition to consumers and employees, investors, both institutional and individual, are a third clientele for the use of the multi-issue, multicompany rating system.[6] A number of social investment advisory services have begun to publicize their own ratings of U.S. corporations—most notably, Franklin Research & Development. In addition, approximately ten mutual funds with $1.09 billion under management as of January 1990 use multiple social screens in managing their funds. These are in addition to the hundreds of billions of dollars in funds that already are being managed as South Africa–free screens.

This type of rating system requires a much greater level of professional expertise and organizational resources than simpler forms of corporate social monitoring. Thus, the institutionalization of such a system requires a predictable set of end-users who will be able and willing to support the monitoring process. This support may come from groups that aim to use the monitoring system to pressure corporations or from corporations themselves that aim to use the monitoring system to demonstrate their achievement in the dimensions measured.

One problem with this type of monitoring is that the process of institutionalization has its own characteristics. Sometimes the first generation of committed organizational leaders is replaced by functionaries less willing to take risks and less capable of arriving at creative solutions to organizational issues than their predecessors. The fact that considerable cooperation must be solicited from corporations themselves makes this type of monitoring system vulnerable to co-optation. Finally, the amount of support necessary to sustain such a system is hard to gather, especially if the monitoring system is to remain somewhat independent from corporations themselves.

However, the advantages of this type of monitoring are considerable. The fact that the evaluation process is repeated fosters organizational learning and adjustment by corporations. The professionalism required for effective comparison of multiple companies on multiple issues makes the organizers of the monitoring system a repository of information that can then be used as corporations attempt to exercise social responsibility. Activist groups can use the ratings in a variety of experimental ways to arrive at effective ways of exerting pressure on corporations.

| METHODS OF MEASURING SOCIAL PERFORMANCE

Unidimensional Versus Multidimensional Measurement

Social screens may be constructed using several dimensions of social performance, as with the consumer guide published by the Council on Economic Priorities or the format used to identify America's one hundred "best" companies. Alternatively, they may be constructed to focus on one dimension of social performance only, as in the case of the Sullivan signatories (helping to fight apartheid in South Africa) or in the case of the "Blue Angel" in Germany (environmental values). However, even in the latter, unidimensional type of monitoring, it is usual that multiple measurements are taken of various aspects by which the company is demonstrating its commitment to the basic principle in question.

Quantitative Versus Qualitative Measurement

Social screens generally employ a combination of quantitative and qualitative data to arrive at their ratings. Use of quantitative measures enables raters to have some confidence in the validity and objectivity of their ratings.

However, the particular measures used will often introduce an element of game playing into the system that may become dysfunctional. For example, in the case of the Sullivan reports, the fact that an extensive checklist was in place made companies feel obliged to give some support to many projects rather than to make substantial commitments in more limited areas. The fact that evaluation was based on the amount of spending rather than on the effectiveness of the projects undertaken led to the commitment of funds in amounts larger than could be used effectively in many of the projects supported. Since measurements were taken on an annual basis, with little concern for long-term impact, many projects were given generous support in the short run but still operated with a high level of uncertainty because of the lack of commitment for continued support.

Absolute versus Relative Measurement

In virtually all cases, those developing rating systems for U.S. corporations choose what we would call relative, rather than absolute, rating systems. An absolute rating system would be one in which corporations could be measured against a preexisting, unchanging set of standards, and in which a company's measurement against these standards would be of paramount importance.

Most of the current rating systems can be better characterized as relative in two senses. First, how the companies rate in relation to each other is more important than their conforming to an absolute, widely agreed-upon goal. Second, the standards against which they are measured change. This was true of the Sulllivan Principles, as the Reverend Leon Sullivan modified both the fundamental principles from year to year and as the monitoring committee tightened and altered the scoring system under which inclusion in each of the three categories of compliance was determined over the years.

| GOALS OF CORPORATE
SOCIAL MONITORING SYSTEMS

The crucial question here is whether these various rating systems really make a difference to either the important external constituencies of consumers or stockholders and therefore to corporations. If these systems are to be effective instruments of social change, they must be used in some way by one or both of these key external groups—consumers or investors. Ultimately, if these systems are to be a force for social change, corporate management must care enough to change the company to conform to these systems. Though the question is difficult to answer definitely, the indications are that they are having an impact on both of the key external groups as well as on the corporations themselves.

Changing Expectations of Consumers and Investors

The first issue involves the key external constituencies—consumers and investors. The mid-1980s saw a substantial number of cities, counties, and states refuse to purchase goods or services from U.S. corporations with varying degrees of involvement in South Africa. At roughly the same time, a number of cities and counties adopted similar measures banning contracts with corporations playing a role in the nuclear weapons industry. In the late 1980s few new institutions adopted such measures, perhaps because the areas where the population would be highly supportive, including many university communities, had by then taken a stand.

With consumers, the concept of integrating social concerns with shopping decisions is increasingly popular. The Council on Economic Priorities booklet *Shopping for a Better World*, for example, sold over 350,000 copies within eighteen months of its publication in mid-1988. "Affinity" credit cards—particularly those aiding specific social causes—have gained widespread acceptance. Internationally, supermarkets in Great Britain and Canada are competing to become the "greenest" through their relative abilities to stock shelves with environmentally friendly items—a movement that will, in all likelihood, spread soon to the United States.[7]

How deeply these currents now run is difficult to say. Whether they will persist is hard to predict. But the trend is certainly toward more, rather than less, consumer concern. Nor has this development gone unnoticed in the corporate world, as the rise in "cause-related marketing" within the past three or four years demonstrates.

With regard to the investors, the situation is much clearer. Fundamental changes have taken place in the investment community during the 1980s. Social investing and the responsibility of stockholders to address social issues have won major victories and prompted reforms that are unlikely to be undone. This change is most apparent among institutional investors and has been played out through two questions relating to fiduciary responsibilities. One was whether institutional investors could restrict their investment practices on social grounds, that is, South Africa, and still remain within their fiduciary obligations. The second was whether institutional investors could be expected to vote with management automatically on shareholder resolutions and still remain faithful to their fiduciary responsibilities. Both questions have been answered reasonably definitively during the course of the past ten years, the first in the affirmative, the second in the negative.

It is difficult to overstate the importance of these two developments within the investment world. The first has set the stage for tremendous growth in the assets managed under multiple screens. From a fringe activity, social investing is rapidly becoming a mainstream offering, with such traditional investment houses as Shearson Lehman Hutton and Scudder Stevens Clark marketing their newly developed socially screened products.

The second development is also of tremendous significance. It marks for the first time a trend toward the actual practice of the democratic mechanisms on which the U.S. corporate structure was founded (one share, one vote). Since 1988 the Department of Labor and the SEC have made it clear that the managers of pension funds have an affirmative obligation to vote the stock their plans hold and to do so in the best interests of their beneficiaries, independent of any pressures from corporate management.

The days of the "Wall Street Rule"—either vote with management or sell your shares—are over. In the 1980s as the Wall Street Rule crumbled, institutional investors focused their opposition to management first on South Africa and then with considerable intensity on issues of corporate governance, particularly "poison pill" measures that entrenched current management at the potential expense of shareholders.

Large institutional investors probably will not remain content to confine their activism to these two issues. After the 1989 *Exxon Valdez* disaster, institutional investors working through the shareholder resolution process were instrumental in persuading Exxon to appoint an environmental expert to its board of directors. And after the promulgation of the Valdez Principles in September 1989, controllers of both New York City and California state pension funds announced their support for the concept of environmentally responsible corporate behavior embodied in these principles. They made it clear that they would use their influence to see that the principles were adopted.

These are not developments that are likely to fade. They reflect fundamental changes in the perceptions of the rights and responsibilities of stock ownership.

Changes in Corporations
The question of whether corporations are likely to respond favorably in any way to the increasing social activism of shareholders and consumers (and the rating systems that serve as the framework

within which much of this activism takes place) is an interesting one. Instinct, cynicism, and the lessons of past experience might lead one to expect corporate resistance to being rated on social issues by independent outsiders over whom they have no predictable control. A look at the philosophical underpinnings of these rating systems, however, reveals at least one reason why corporations might prefer dialogue in these forums to alternatives.

The issues now being raised with corporate America through rating systems do not differ fundamentally from those raised in the more hectic 1960s and 1970s (civil rights and international justice, disarmament, the environment). However, the vehicles for raising them are dramatically different. One difference is in the relatively orderly procession. But another, more basic, difference is that, as opposed to calls for increased regulation or litigation, as in the past, these rating systems implicitly call for corporations to make voluntary changes.

In many ways, advocates of rating systems are proposing a "free marketplace" of social information. They implicitly believe that in a marketplace where information on the social as well as the financial records of corporations is freely available, the "efficiency" of the marketplace as expressed by consumers and investors will prompt corporate action where regulation and litigation have failed.

As a concept, the effectiveness of a free marketplace of corporate social information may appear naive. It has yet to be tested, however, and there are some indications that the free flow of social information can be as beneficial to the smooth functioning of a society and economy as is the free flow of financial information. One example of the potential effectiveness of such information can be seen in the ratings and rankings of corporate performance on toxic, hazardous, and ozone-destroying emissions that have resulted from federal disclosure requirements. Although all disclosures relate to the legal emissions of unregulated substances, numerous corporations have been prompted to make commitments to dramatic (and in some cases total) reductions in these emissions.

A further indication of the profound nature of these changes and the fundamental role that rating systems play in them is that what is happening now in the United States is not an isolated event. Although further along in the United States than in other countries, social investing has been developing rapidly in Canada and the

United Kingdom. Comparable movements are developing in Germany, France, and Belgium as well.

| CONCLUSIONS

Corporate social monitoring often supplements legal and regulatory systems, and it lends itself particularly well to political circumstances in which legal standards are difficult to enact (for example, in international affairs) or have yet to be enacted.

Within the investment community, the use of social monitoring to distinguish among investment opportunities and pressure corporate management to action has taken firm root. How extensive or effective these efforts will be remains to be seen. But the effectiveness of rating systems will be enhanced to the extent they incorporate measures that allow relative evaluations of companies on a continuing basis and permit the corporation to negotiate with key external constituencies, thereby forming a basis for social action and social change.

NOTES

1. L. J. Brooks, Jr., *Canadian Corporate Social Performance* (Hamilton, Ontario: Society of Management Accountants of Canada, 1986); and M. Dierkes, "Corporate Social Reporting and Auditing: Theory and Practice," in *Corporate Governance and Directors' Liabilities—Legal, Economic, and Sociological Analyses on Corporate Social Responsibility*, ed. Klaus J. Hopt and Gunther Teubner (Berlin/New York: Walter der Gruyter, 1984).
2. R. Rose, ed., "Symposium on Social Indicators," *Journal of Public Policy* (1990): forthcoming.
3. S. D. Lydenberg, *Minding the Corporate Conscience: Public Interest Groups and Social Accountability* (New York: Council on Economic Priorities, 1978); and J. Simon, C. W. Powers, and J. P. Gunnemann, *The Ethical Investor* (New Haven, Conn.: Yale University Press, 1972).
4. K. Paul, "Corporate Social Monitoring in South Africa: A Decade of Achievement, an Uncertain Future," *Journal of Business Ethics* 8 (1989): 463–69; and K. Paul and D. Aquila, "The Economic Impact and Political Consequences of Ethical Investing: The Case of South Africa," *Journal of Business Ethics* 7 (1988): 691–97.
5. S. D. Lydenberg, A. T. Marlin, and S. O'Brien Strub, *Rating America's Corporate Conscience* (Reading, Mass.: Addison-Wesley, 1986); and R. Will et

al., *Shopping for a Better World* (New York: Council on Economic Priorities, 1988).

6. A. L. Domini and P. D. Kinder, *Ethical Investing* (Reading, Mass.: Addison-Wesley, 1984); and J. Rockness and P. F. Williams, "A Descriptive Study of Social Responsibility Mutual Funds," *Accounting, Organizations and Society* 13 (1988): 397–411.

7. J. Elkington and J. Hailes, *The Green Consumer Guide* (London: Victor Gollancz, 1988).

CHAPTER 19

RESEARCHING SOCIAL PERFORMANCE

Steven D. Lydenberg and **Lloyd Kurtz**
Kinder, Lydenberg, Domini & Company

We at Kinder, Lydenberg, Domini & Company received a telephone call the other day from a money manager. An important client of his had heard of social investing and asked if it would be possible to incorporate social screens—particularly environmental screens—into the investing of her funds. This manager had screened two accounts for South Africa and was comfortable with the concept of social investing. But he was unsure of what an environmental screening process would entail.

Did his client know what screens she wanted to impose? Did she know with what rigor she wanted her screens applied? The answer to both questions was, "No, I don't think so, not specifically. Although I must say, she has a strong *sense* of what she wants."

| THE PROBLEMS OF APPLYING SCREENS

This conversation illustrates the challenges faced by managers running socially screened accounts. They are confronted with a diverse and sometimes confusing array of issues for which clients may wish their portfolios screened. These clients may be sophisticated and precise in their screening requirements, or they may have only a vague sense of what they have in mind.

In the first case, the manager must assess the financial implications of imposing these screens and, if necessary, present acceptable alternatives. In the second, the manager must help the client formulate screens that correspond to the intuitive feel he or she has for the issues. And in both cases, the manager must have access to adequate information to define the screens and appraise their financial implications.

Suppose a client concerned about military issues asks that all companies doing business with the Department of Defense—including those supplying toothpaste or breakfast cereals—be eliminated from his portfolio. The manager must explain that all but a small number of larger capitalization stocks would be eliminated from consideration. Similarly, a client concerned with women's issues may suggest barring companies without substantial representation of women on their boards of directors. Again, this screen would drastically curtail available investments. The manager, instead, must define a screen that can be imposed meaningfully, satisfies the client's underlying concerns, and still allows adequate freedom of investment choice.

Beyond defining the screens, the manager must be prepared to apply them to individual companies. How will he or she deal with companies' "gray" areas—where it is not immediately apparent whether a company should or should not be eliminated? Suppose a client has a military weapons screen. AMP, Inc., a manufacturer of electrical connectors, derives less than 5 percent of its revenues from sales to the military, mostly from off-the-shelf (as opposed to custom-designed) connectors. Pall Corporation, a manufacturer of proprietary filters for fluids, derives about 14 percent of sales from products for helicopters, submarines, and tanks. Should the manager eliminate one or both of these companies as a "weapons contractor"?

Research for the social investment community must be both detailed in its scope and flexible in its form, so that clients and managers can make distinctions. With the growing interest in social investing, a number of tools for social research help address these challenges. In the pages that follow, we discuss some of the basic research tools that we have found helpful. Many of the organizations and publications mentioned here are described more fully elsewhere in this book.

| BASIC RESEARCH METHODOLOGIES

In constructing the Domini 400 Social Index, we explored those issues we felt were of concern to the majority of social investors:

community involvement	nuclear power
employee relations	product safety

environment   South Africa
military contracting   women and minorities

We examined a large number of companies (more than eight hundred) because of the large investment universe we were ultimately creating. But however large or small the number of firms or issues being researched, one must conduct two types of research simultaneously. The first is the day-to-day maintenance of research files—essentially, keeping up. The second is in-depth analyses of specific companies. The two are interdependent and mutually reinforcing.

Keeping Up

The social researcher must keep up with the general business press. The *Wall Street Journal*, the *New York Times*, *Business Week*, *Fortune*, and *Forbes* mix stories of social import with financial news. Their profiles of companies can provide valuable insights into the character and quality of management.

Books by management consultants illuminate the strategies of corporate management, often pointing out companies whose vision takes in the long-term best interests of society. Ira Magaziner's *The Silent War: Inside the Global Business Battles Shaping America's Future* (Random House, 1989) or James Heskett, W. Earl Sasser, Jr., and Christopher Hart's *Service Breakthroughs: Changing the Rules of the Game* (Free Press, 1990) are two recent examples. James O'Toole's *Vanguard Management: Redesigning the Corporate Future* (Doubleday, 1985) still holds up well. Books by business writers profiling specific companies—such as Richard Preston's remarkable portrait of Nucor, *American Steel* (Simon & Schuster, 1990)—can prove invaluable.

The social investment community has a trade press of its own, providing a sense of issues of immediate importance to social investors along with detail on specific companies. *Clean Yield, Franklin's Insight, GOOD MONEY,* and DataCenter's *Corporate Responsibility Monitor* are important sources. Two recent books surveying the history and social records of a substantial number of U.S. corporations are *The Better World Investment Guide* (Prentice-Hall, 1991), by Joel Alperson and his associates, and the classic *Everybody's Business,* by Milton Moskowitz, Robert Levering, and Michael Katz (see box 19-1).

Investigative journalism can appear in as diverse sources as the

New Yorker and *Barron's*. *In These Times* (one of our favorites), the *Multinational Monitor*, and *The Nation* offer viewpoints on corporate practices often not found elsewhere. Caveat: as with any research, assertions must be verified and facts checked.

Keeping up means staying well informed about the issues of the day. Doing so provides a framework for the specialized tasks of researching individual companies and the challenges they face.

BOX 19-1
EVERYBODY'S BUSINESS 1990: A REVIEW

Peter D. Kinder Kinder, Lydenberg, Domini & Company

Ed. Note: *A version of this review appeared in the December 1990 Social Investment Forum newsletter.*

Do I pay four dollars per issue for *Forbes* to read Steve Forbes taking credit for Maggie Thatcher's economic successes or Caspar Weinberger on any subject? Hardly. I buy it because when I stand in the supermarket checkout line reading it, no one suspects that I'm getting my weekly quota of scandal. *Forbes* is the thinking person's *National Inquirer*.

But where do you go for history? Where, for instance, can you read about Conrad Hilton's marriage to Zsa Zsa Gabor and its influence on the Hilton Hotel empire? Or a coherent overview of Ford's rise and fall and resurrection?

For ten years, the answer has been easy: start with *Everybody's Business*.

Until November, the Scotch-taped remnants of my third copy of the 1980 edition sat where I didn't have to stretch to reach them. The 1990 edition of *Everybody's Business* (Doubleday Currency, $22.95) now has the place of honor.

Milton Moskowitz, Robert Levering, and Michael Katz capture the essence of each of the four hundred companies they cover in a few well-chosen words. For instance: "That the initials of the second largest company in the advertising business, WPP Group, stand for Wire & Plastic Products tells you a lot about today's industry."

The authors have a knack for finding the right quotation when they can't turn a phrase. From their profile of the Reader's Digest

Association, we learn, for example, that Thornton Wilder, the author of *Our Town*, once described *Reader's Digest* as a "magazine for bores by bores about bores."

Everybody's Business belongs on your shelf.

The Basics of Company Research

A logical starting point in any social, as well as any financial, review of a corporation is its public documents. Indispensable among these are the annual report, form 10-K, and the proxy statement, preferably for the preceding three years. Quarterly reports and form 10-Q also are helpful.

The public documents are only the starting point of the research process. They help formulate questions to be addressed in many varied contexts.

PROXY STATEMENTS. The proxy statement is an excellent place to start. It provides substantial detail on those who run the company *and* how they are compensated. In addition, if a company has profit sharing for its employees (including top officers), a savings plan, or an employee stock ownership plan, the proxy statement usually contains more detailed information than the annual report.

The proxy statement also includes shareholder resolutions being brought before the annual meeting. These resolutions sometimes address social issues of importance to the corporation. The proxy statement will contain a statement of the proponent's position and corporate management's opposition, often in substantial detail.

FORM 10-K. The SEC annual report on form 10-K is indispensable because it provides a straightforward, fairly complete description of what the company does. Usually it contains a more complete explanation of pending litigation than do the footnotes to the financial statement in the annual report, especially for environmental and employment-related cases.

ANNUAL REPORTS. The company relies on its annual report to sell itself to the investing public. The document is usually relentlessly upbeat. Consequently, it is often difficult to gather substantive information. What one often can obtain, however, is equally important—an insight into how the company wants to portray itself to the world.

The people-oriented annual reports of the Hechinger Company (a home repair retailer) and Herman Miller (an office furniture firm), for example, contrast sharply with the technology-oriented image of Tesoro Petroleum Corporation (an integrated oil and natural gas corporation), whose annual report displays photographs of oil refineries without an identifiable human shape. Further research bears out the contrast that these images project. Instinct and impressions can be useful in directing research efforts.

LITERATURE REVIEWS. A review of trade publications helps in acquiring a sense of a company's strategies and reputation within its industry. Reading *Chemical Week*, for example, supplies a sense of the environmental issues most relevant to the chemical industry. And it reports on major initiatives—or disasters.

General searches of the press (the *New York Times*, the *Wall Street Journal*, *Business Week*, and others) usually turn up significant recent controversies. Numerous on-line data bases are available—such as Newsnet, Westlaw, Lexis, Dow Jones Retrieval, Infotrac, and ADI/Inform. Their costs vary considerably. An excellent single source for much of the information these searches are likely to turn up is the DataCenter. Publications of several nonprofit organizations—such as the Council on Economic Priorities, the Interfaith Center on Corporate Responsibility, or the Investor Responsibility Research Center—cover a wide spectrum of corporate social accountability issues. In addition to these general resources, numerous issue-specific information resources are available. A number of these are discussed below.

When building and maintaining files on corporations, subscribing to the publications of local watchdog groups can be invaluable. For example, Louisiana faces some of the greatest environmental challenges in the nation. Subscribing to the newsletter of a group like the Louisiana Environmental Action Network is an excellent means of keeping in touch with local controversies. The researcher must evaluate newsletters carefully as to their usefulness and reliability as sources.

COMPANY CONTACTS. Contacting companies for publications addressing social issues can be productive. Corporate foundation reports, analyses of environmental policies and practices, or in-house newsletters that review employee relations issues are often readily available. Sending questionnaires to companies can elicit substantial information as well.

For those in the investment community, meetings with company management at presentations to analysts and money managers can provide insights into corporate management and help keep them up-to-date.

STAKEHOLDER INTERVIEWS. In social research, as in financial research, a series of interviews is helpful to complete the picture of a company. Money manager and *Forbes* columnist Kenneth Fisher, for example, recommends interviews with a company's managers, employees, suppliers, and customers for financial analyses. A similar approach can be productive in a social analysis. These conversations generally can be arranged through the firm's investor relations department.

In many cases we also have found interviews with local groups and government regulators indispensable in obtaining the full picture of a controversy. Input from the local level is always important, but for some issues it is more so than for others. In evaluating a bank's community relations, for example, it is always important to talk to local community development groups. Local newspapers are another excellent source.

| RESEARCHING SPECIFIC SOCIAL ISSUES

The issues covered below are by no means the only issues of interest to social investors, but they are in our experience the ones of most general concern.

Community Involvement
In looking at community involvement, we examine a company's record on charitable contributions, both in size and focus; involvement in public-private partnerships; and, to a lesser extent, its volunteer programs. In general, detailed and informative sources document these initiatives.

BASIC RESOURCES. The *Corporate Giving Directory* (published by the Taft Group), the *Corporate 500: The Directory of Corporate Philanthropy* (Public Management Institute), and the *National Directory of Corporate Giving* (Foundation Center) each provide basic details on company giving programs (although the *National Directory of Corporate Giving* lists only corporate foundation giving, not direct giving).

A number of excellent periodicals cover corporate giving issues. The *Chronicle of Philanthropy* lists recent grants for the corporate and noncorporate foundation world. The *Corporate Philanthropy Report* focuses exclusively on issues relating to corporate giving. The December 1990–January 1991 issue, for example, was devoted entirely to an assessment of IBM's programs. New York, Boston, San Francisco, and other large cities have foundation libraries that carry these and similar publications.

Corporations themselves often publish a foundation or community relations report. These can range from excellent (Affiliated Publications's, for example) to uninformative. The reports that list all grantees by name are particularly useful. From these one obtains a sense of the nature, as well as the dollar value, of the giving.

APPROACHES TO GIVING. Conventional corporate giving programs direct approximately 50 percent of their grants to education (primarily higher education), and 30 percent to human services (primarily United Fund drives). These grants often can appear unimaginative or self-serving. For example, in 1991 W. R. Grace & Company made a $1.5 million grant to Clemson University to endow a professorship in packaging science.

By contrast, Sara Lee Corporation and Northern States Power Company have imaginative programs that allocate a preponderance of funds to the economically disadvantaged for programs encouraging self-sufficiency. Talking with persons active in a city's nonprofit world is another excellent means of discovering which corporations are most creative in their support.

PUBLIC-PRIVATE PARTNERSHIPS. Since the early 1980s, corporations have increasingly participated in public-private partnerships. Thousands of these are now active. They range from the simplest "adopt-a-school" programs to elaborate investments in affordable housing initiatives with beneficial tax credits.

Public-private partnerships can be among the most interesting and meaningful forms of community support, although some effort is necessary to distinguish between those programs that are most meaningful and effective and those that fail to attack the roots of social problems. The National Equity Fund, sponsored by the Local Initiatives Support Corporation—and in which numerous major U.S. corporations have invested—has taken substantial steps to support affordable housing initiatives around the country and is an example of a systematic, well-executed partnership program. The Federal National Mortgage Association (Fannie Mae) is among the strongest corporate supporters of this and similar affordable housing initiatives.

VOLUNTEERISM. Corporate volunteer programs are another arena of corporate community involvement. Most companies have at least a rudimentary volunteer program. We pay close attention only to the most thorough of these programs, such as the one run by Xerox. That company has an in-house newsletter encouraging volunteerism, provides matching grants to organizations with which its volunteers work, and offers a paid sabbatical for a limited number of employees who take up to one year off to work with nonprofits.

BANKING: A SPECIAL CASE. For most corporations, community relations tell a positive rather than negative story. Banking, however, is an exception. The past two decades have seen controversies over whether banks are "redlining"—that is, accepting deposits from poorer neighborhoods but not making loans to them. Community activists and banks often paint diametrically opposed versions of the adequacy of local lending practices. It is essential to contact local groups to discover issues that have surfaced in recent years. Banks involved in acquisitions may have faced challenges and reviews under the Community Reinvestment Act (CRA), leading to press coverage of the issues. Without such challenges, local disputes may not make it into the press.

Organizations such as the Southern Finance Project or the National Association of Community Development Loan Funds are useful resources in tracking down local community development groups dealing with banks. The Chicago-based Woodstock Institute has done statistical analyses of bank lending practices in major metropolitan regions. The Center for Community Change publishes a periodical, the CRA Reporter. And a variety of thorough third-party studies of banking programs in particular cities have appeared recently (for example, Wayne State University's Center for Urban Studies' "Building the Partnership: Housing in Detroit" and Community Reinvestment Associates' "Partnership for Reinvestment: An Evaluation of the Chicago Neighborhood Lending Program"). With the recent decision by the federal government to publish evaluations of banks' community records, researching bank lending practices may become easier.

Employee Relations

Our examination of employee relations issues focuses on programs that empower employees or provide them with a sense of ownership and participation in a firm. Safety and union relations also are important issues here.

BASIC RESOURCES. *The One Hundred Best Companies to Work for in America* (Addison-Wesley, 1984), by Robert Levering, Milton Moskowitz, and Michael Katz provides an excellent starting point for any research on companies with positive work environments. Levering's book, *A Great Place to Work* (Random House, 1988) and David Levine's article in the summer 1990 issue of the *California Management Review*, "Participation, Productivity and the Firm's Environment," point out many of the characteristic programs implemented by employers who have achieved consistently positive employee relations.

Often basic information on many of the attributes praised by these authors—profit sharing, job security, an egalitarian work environment—can be found in a company's public documents. Most companies making systematic efforts in these areas document their progress—perhaps through an in-house newsletter—or have had press coverage. More than on any other issue, companies are willing to share information here.

Employee relations programs must be evaluated carefully. A company with profit sharing is not likely to generate goodwill among employees if it has not been profitable in recent years. Employee suggestion programs can be so informal and laxly executed as to promote little true sense of involvement. The thorough approach of Scanlon Plans (at Herman Miller, for example) incorporates workers more directly into the management process. Employee stock ownership plans adopted strictly as a takeover defense—and lacking in an employee empowerment component—are less effective in promoting a positive work environment than those conceived of as actively involving workers in ownership. The Center for Employee Ownership in San Francisco is a valuable resource on this issue.

UNION ISSUES. On union issues, a good starting point is the AFL-CIO's *Labor Letter* listing of boycotts. Some companies, such as Louisiana-Pacific Corporation, have been listed for many years. Various unions also have newsletters, such as the United Paperworkers International Union's *The Paperworker*, that over time provide an excellent feel for companies' relations with their unionized work force. The Bureau of National Affairs' publications on labor and employment and computerized legal data bases, such as Westlaw and Lexis, are substantial resources.

One issue on which information is easily obtained is layoffs. In our judgment, a company that has laid off more than 15 percent of its work force in a year probably is not, at least in the short run, a positive place to work. Major strikes—such as the one at the Pittston Company in the late 1980s—also are likely to leave long-lasting scars. In most cases the general press does a creditable job of covering these.

Environment

One could examine an almost infinite number of environmental issues. The nonspecialist must make choices.

On the negative side, we focus on a company's record—legal problems with regulated emissions; legal but substantial emissions of toxic chemicals, or emissions contributing to acid rain; and emissions of ozone-depleting chlorofluorocarbons. On the positive side, we look at involvement in recycling; hazardous waste-reduction programs; and support for substantial environmental initiatives sponsored by third parties.

BASIC RESOURCES. The amounts of information available are, in some cases, considerable. In other cases the information is inadequate. In addition, the evaluation of this information is challenging.

With the growth of interest in the environment among social investors, a number of groups have taken initial steps toward setting up "clearinghouses" on the environmental records of corporations—most notably the Council on Economic Priorities and the Investor Responsibility Research Center. In addition, acceptance of the Valdez Principles proposed by the Coalition for Environmentally Responsible Economies may lead to a generally accepted set of standards for corporate reporting on their environmental records (see chapters 11 and 12).

One primary source for environmental information is government records—whether at a federal or state level. The Citizens Fund has done an excellent job of compiling listings of the major legal emitters of toxic chemicals, drawing on information filed by companies under the Toxic Release Inventory requirements of the Emergency Planning and Community Right to Know Act. Similarly, local groups have compiled state-by-state listings of major emitters. But these listings have their limitations. For example, as of early 1991 environmentalists were attempting to close a large loophole in requirements that allowed companies not to report toxic chemicals they ship offsite for recycling or incineration.

REPORTS OF LITIGATION. Listings of legal actions on the state or federal level can be another helpful source. Some of the largest are reported in the national or trade press, although somewhat sporadically. Specialized newsletters, such as the Bureau of National Affairs' *Environmental Law Reporter*, are more consistently useful. It is possible to get onto the mailing lists of many state regulatory agencies that regularly report fines and settlements. Some of these are more useful than others. Legal data bases, such as Westlaw or Lexis, also are helpful. And many, but not all, companies list environmental fines or settlements of over $100,000 in their 10-K forms.

These searches can provide a useful counterpoint to what are often sunny reports from corporations on their progress in controlling pollutants. For example, the 3M company shows up high on many toxic releases lists and has paid penalties imposed by Minnesota environmental agencies—despite its clearly substantial, well-publicized efforts at hazardous waste reduction in manufacturing processes.

EVALUATION OF DATA. Often the significance of figures is far from clear in this area. The types of discharges, the circumstances under which they are being made, the nature of fines (one-time or repeated), and numerous other factors must be explored and weighed to obtain a fuller understanding of the relative performance of companies. As mentioned earlier, contacts with local environmental groups can be of substantial help. The National Toxics Campaign maintains an exhaustive list of local environmental groups around the United States.

A further problem in evaluating company records grows from the fact that accepted practices in certain industries—clear-cutting by pulp and paper companies, for example—can pose major problems for those with environmental concerns. Moreover, a company's record might be exemplary in one state and terrible in another. How does the researcher evaluate contradictory evidence for a single firm?

PRODUCTS AND SERVICES. One relatively simple question to answer is whether the company provides goods or services that contribute to the cleaning up of the environment. Groundwater Technology, for example, specializes in cleaning up contaminated groundwater and soil and has made innovative use of indigenous microbes in bioremediation. Even here, however, problems arise. Some companies with apparently similar missions—such as Waste Management, which focuses on solid and hazardous waste disposal—are the subject of substantial environmental controversies that make them unacceptable to many social investors interested in creating an environmentally sensitive portfolio.

It is helpful to examine a company's record on modernization of plant and equipment. In general, the newer the plant, the more environmentally sound it will be. America West Airlines, for example, has the youngest, and therefore most fuel-efficient and quietest, fleet in the country. Companies' efforts to reduce hazardous wastes generated in the manufacturing process can be a strong positive—Gibson Greetings's switch to water-based inks, for example. But with many companies announcing similar goals, it is difficult to distinguish those programs that are most meaningful from those that rely on numbers games.

Environmental research must be conducted with care and its results regarded with a certain skepticism.

Military Contracting

The two issues of primary concern in the category of military contracting are companies' involvement in nuclear weapons contracting and the extent of companies' dependence on weapons contracting.

BASIC RESOURCES. The most complete single source for information on a company's weapons-related prime contracting with the Department of Defense is the *Federal Prime Contracts on CD/ROM*, published annually by Eagle Eye Publishers and Nuclear Free America. Using definitions of weapons-related contracting development by U.S. Trust Company of Boston and of nuclear weapons–related contracting developed by Nuclear Free America, this data base provides detailed information on all prime contracts of over $25,000 with the Department of Defense.

Less-detailed information can be obtained at no charge from the Defense Department's public affairs office, which provides annual listings of the top one hundred prime contractors and the top five hundred contractors for research and development (R & D) work. Also available at a moderate charge through the National Technical Information Service are listings of all prime contracts of over $25,000 from the Defense Department. These microfiche have some rudimentary information about the nature of the work, but in much less detail than Nuclear Free America's data base.

One weakness of the prime contracting data bases, however, is that they do not address the complications of subcontracting work. In 1989, for example, E-systems' weapons-related prime contracts totaled 14.6 percent of sales, while military systems—including subcontracting work—accounted for 81 percent of its sales. Company documents are the only reliable source of information on subcontracting work, but they can be inadequate or confusing.

As mentioned earlier, a further problem with research into military contracting is the definition of what constitutes weapons-related work.

Nuclear Power

Involvement in the nuclear power industry is relatively simple to research and relatively free of complications.

BASIC RESOURCES. Public documents published by electric utilities list the percentage of their generating capacity derived from nuclear plants or the percentage of their fuel that is nuclear. For an occasional company (PacifiCorp, for example), the ownership position is extremely small (representing in PacifiCorp's case less than 1 percent of total capacity).

Company documents and trade magazines (such as *Power* magazine's annual directory of companies servicing electric utilities) provide a reasonably comprehensive overview of which companies are involved in the construction or design of the nuclear reactors (such as General Electric or Westinghouse) or in the nuclear fuel cycle. It might surprise some to discover that fertilizer companies, such as IMC Fertilizer Group and Freeport McMoRan, derive substantial revenues (approximately 6 percent and 2 percent, respectively, of their total revenues) from the sale of uranium oxide, a byproduct of phosphate fertilizer production, to the electric utilities industry.

In April 1991 Public Citizen published its third annual edition of *Nuclear Lemons: An Assessment of America's Worst Commercial Nuclear Power Plants*. Based on a variety of factors—including number of mishaps reported to the Nuclear Regulatory Commission (NRC), number of emergency reactor shutdowns, forced outages, and plant management performance as measured by the NRC's Systematic Assessment of Licensee Performance—Public Citizen found Carolina Power & Light Company's Brunswick 2 plant to have the worst record in the nation.

Product

Under the rubric of "product" we look at everything from involvement in alcohol, gambling, and tobacco to questionable marketing practices and fraud scandals.

SIN SCREENS. Perhaps the oldest social screens are those that exclude alcohol, tobacco, and gambling companies. Few companies are in these businesses in such a small way that the products would not be mentioned in an annual report or form 10-K. Some occasional surprises emerge. In 1989, for example, Control Data Corporation derived 5.5 percent of its sales from services to state lotteries. Kimberly-Clark has nine plants around the world devoted to manufacturing cigarette paper.

PRODUCT LIABILITY. Because of pending legal liabilities, companies must mention most major product liability cases. In 1990 Armstrong World Industries, for example, had pending litigation alleging harm to some fifty-seven thousand persons from its manufacture and sale of asbestos products. How long to "penalize" a company for discontinued products entails judgment calls. Although the cases against Armstrong are in the courts now, the company has not produced asbestos products since 1969.

MARKETING ISSUES. Mention of controversies relating to advertising and marketing rarely appears in corporate documents. Press accounts are the best source for these issues, as are certain specialized publications. The Center for Science in the Public Interest's newsletter, *Nutrition Action*, covers disputes over marketing by food companies, where health claims have been a particularly tricky issue recently. Similarly, Public Citizen Health Research Group's *Health Letter* documents advertising abuses by the pharmaceutical industry.

QUALITY. We give credit to companies that provide high-quality products at low prices, particularly to the economically disadvantaged.

Dollar General Corporation, for example, has made a policy of situating its discount outlet stores in low-income neighborhoods (and hiring its store managers from these neighborhoods as well).

We also credit companies committed to exceptionally high standards of manufacturing excellence or customer service—winners of the Malcolm Baldrige Award, for example. Since quality programs became fashionable during the 1980s (though belatedly when it came to international competition), it has become difficult to distinguish programs that go beyond industry norms. Key factors, however, are: rigorous quality programs (such as statistical process control in manufacturing) in place for several years; programs instituted companywide; long-range planning for employee improvement and education; and an obsession with customer service.

South Africa

U.S. corporate involvement in South Africa is one of the most thoroughly researched of the issues interesting social investors. In large part this wealth of information has grown up because South Africa has been since the early 1970s a focus for shareholder activism, most notably by church groups, and since the late 1970s a focus for the divestment movement, most notably among institutional investors.

BASIC RESOURCES. The Investor Responsibility Research Center (IRRC) generally is regarded as the most authoritative source of information on company involvement in South Africa, including companies with equity interests in South Africa (for example, Chevron Corporation, Texaco, and Johnson & Johnson) and those with licensing and servicing agreements for their products sold there (for example, IBM, Hewlett-Packard, and Ford). Some investors concerned with South Africa distinguish between corporations involved in "strategic" and "nonstrategic" industries, particularly with regard to licensing and distribution agreements. No single source exists for drawing the strategic-nonstrategic line. But the industries generally regarded as strategic are mining, energy, computers, and transportation.

Because church groups and major pension funds file resolutions annually with most companies with operations in South Africa, proxy statements with corporate statements supporting their continued involvement often contain detailed information. In addition, each year the Industrial Support Unit publishes its report on signatory companies to the Statement of Principles for South Africa.

U.S. corporations with employees in that country are asked to endorse these guidelines, formerly known as the Sullivan Principles, for employment practices and community relations. Those that endorse them are rated each year on compliance.

The State Department also publishes an annual listing of companies in South Africa, whether or not they have signed the Statement of Principles. The New York–based Africa Fund periodically publishes a detailed listing of companies with present and past ties to South Africa.

Women and Minorities

Researching performance on issues relating to women and minorities is difficult because the information is diffuse, emotionally charged, and largely in secondary services.

BASIC RESOURCES. An excellent starting point for research on companies making substantial progress on the hiring and promotion of women and minorities is lists of "best companies" published occasionally in magazines. Every several years *Black Enterprise* publishes its listing of best workplaces for blacks. The Chicago-based *Dollars and Sense* frequently highlights companies making substantial progress in promoting blacks. In January 1990 *Hispanic* magazine published its list of the one hundred best companies for Hispanics. The most thorough survey of the best workplaces for women has appeared annually in the October issue of *Working Mother* magazine. Baila Zeitz and Lorraine Dusky's book *The Best Companies for Women* (Simon & Schuster, 1988) provides many personal anecdotes about fifty-three firms.

Company listings of top officers and members of the board of directors can be useful, too. A few companies (Ford and Sara Lee, for example) publish in their annual reports the percentage of women and minorities in all job categories. Others (such as Bristol-Myers Squibb and General Motors Corporation) publish these figures separately. Although difficult to evaluate in themselves, these figures can be compared with industry averages (as published by the Equal Employment Opportunity Commission) to provide some perspective.

In examining listings of top officers, it is important to distinguish between the more meaningful "line" positions (including operating positions in marketing and manufacturing) from the less powerful "staff" positions (such as corporate communications or human resources). Occasionally annual reports also will list an "assistant secretary" or "assistant treasurer" among its officers; these are positions of little true responsibility.

Press accounts, listings in the 10-K forms, and searches of legal data bases are the primary sources for information about sex, racial, or age discrimination suits. For instance, many chemical and high-technology manufacturing companies have had "fetal protection" policies prohibiting women from holding jobs in which they might expose fetuses to harmful chemicals. In March 1991 the U.S. Supreme Court ruled unconstitutional such a policy at Johnson Controls. Similarly, women have often challenged the airlines' dress or weight requirements. In May 1991, Continental Airlines revoked a policy requiring women in customer service positions to wear makeup in the wake of national coverage of the firing of a ticket agent for violating the airline's grooming policy.

Other Issues
We have discussed briefly some of the research methodologies and resources we use for the issues that most concern social investors. But there are other issues investment advisers must be aware of as well. Among these are: accounting, animal rights, compensation among corporate management, international practices, and Northern Ireland.

ACCOUNTING ISSUES. Many firms in the 1980s, particularly financial institutions, abuse generally accepted accounting practices in order to inflate earnings. Monitoring who does a company's books and their "aggressiveness" on accounting issues can tell much about the client's attitudes.

In 1991 one accounting firm was bankrupted by litigation. Virtually every large public accounting firm in the United States faces lawsuits over bank or thrift audits, and one faces an investigation into loans to its managers by the thrift institutions it was auditing. Many of these issues are reported in the business press. Two groups specializing in accounting problems at publicly traded companies are Kellogg Associates and the accounting issues team at Bear Stearns.

ANIMAL RIGHTS. A substantial number of groups (People for the Ethical Treatment of Animals, Friends of Animals, and others) have publications covering current issues. Among the people most active in working directly with corporations on programs to reduce the use of live animals in product research and development is Henry Spira of Animal Rights International.

COMPENSATION OF BOARDS OF DIRECTORS AND TOP MANAGEMENT. The question of excessive compensation among corporate management is of increasing concern to institutional investors. Figures on board member and officer compensation are provided in the proxy statement and sometimes in other public corporate documents.

BOX 19-2
BOOKS ON INTERNATIONAL SRI

Peter D. Kinder Kinder, Lydenberg, Domini & Company

As Alan Miller, president of the U.K. Social Investment Forum, has patiently explained so many times, socially responsible investing (SRI) has evolved very differently in the United Kingdom and Europe. For one thing, it is newer. SRI did not get the jump start it did in the United States in the very early 1970s from the confluence of the Vietnam War, Ralph Nader's Project GM, South Africa, the civil rights movement, enactment of comprehensive state and federal environmental laws, Watergate, and the unmistakable shift rightward in national sentiments.

As an organized force, SRI came into its own in Europe only with the green movement. So shows Anne Simpson in her recent *The Greening of Global Investment* (Economist Publications, 1991, £150/ $270). Simpson, finance director of the internationally renowned Pensions Investment Research Consultants (PIRC), offers a clear overview of environmental investing with extended case studies on the corporate response. Her lengthy survey of ethical investment deserves close reading by Americans—and not just by SRI professionals. It would be a pity if a mass market publisher did not buy the rights to this invaluable book and bring it out at a reasonable price.

Alan Miller also has produced an invaluable book, considerably broader in scope than Simpson's. *Socially Responsible Investment: The Financial Impact of Screened Investment in the 1990s* (London Financial Times Business Information Service, 1991, £210/$374) is a detailed survey of who is doing what in SRI from the United Kingdom to New Zealand and from community development to portfolio investing. Miller's emphasis on the "who" of social investing makes his book especially important for the SRI professional looking for sources of information. As an introduction to the field in Europe and the United Kingdom, it is not likely to be surpassed anytime soon.

Are these books worth their price—exorbitant by American standards—to SRI professionals? They are, and they should be studied carefully. SRI professionals here have rightly avoided international investing because of its complexity. But it can be avoided no longer.

Within the year the Securities and Exchange Commission will relax reporting requirements on American depositary receipts (ADRs) to the level required in the company's country of domicile. This gesture toward rebuilding the U.S. financial markets will not encourage what had been a strong movement toward U.S. reporting requirements in the European Community. And if the relaxation achieves its goal, SRI professionals will have to deal with ADRs every day.

Very soon the need for adequate screening will force Americans to get to know the European SRI community much better. It is not too soon to start.

INTERNATIONAL PRACTICES. With international operations the norm for more and more U.S. corporations, social investors are increasingly aware of the implications of corporate actions abroad as well as at home. Until recently church groups were one of the few easily accessible sources of information on certain of these practices, most notably on the marketing of infant formula and of pesticides and drugs banned in the United States. With the development of social investing around the world, increasing information on U.S. company practices abroad will become available.

Box 19-2 briefly describes the two best surveys of social investment outside the United States.

NORTHERN IRELAND. For a number of years the Investor Responsibility Research Center (IRRC) has followed the employment practices of U.S. corporations with operations in Northern Ireland. At issue is employment discrimination on religious grounds. In some years church groups and several institutional investors have filed shareholder resolutions urging corporations to sign the MacBride Principles for fair labor practices in that part of the United Kingdom.

| CONCLUSION

As corporate social accountability research develops—and as the market for social investing expands—the task of the researcher will become easier in some ways but more difficult in others. Some factual research will be easier as independent resources develop and sources of information expand. But as has already happened with the environment, when these issues become important to the investing public, different sources—including the companies themselves—often put forth contradictory claims.

A further problem inherent in social research is the changing importance of social concerns. Unlike measurements of financial performance, which change very slowly over decades, social concerns can change rapidly. For instance, five years ago little attention was paid to warnings about the use of ozone-depleting chlorofluorocarbons (CFCs) in manufacturing processes. Today many companies are rapidly phasing out CFC use. It is to be hoped that in another five years CFCs no longer will be an issue. Similarly if allegations of health dangers from electromagnetic radiation prove well founded, electric utilities could suddenly confront an issue of major social impact and monumental complexity.

Along with methodologies for obtaining and evaluating factual data, a social researcher must develop judgment—a sensitivity to the nuances and the relative importance of issues. Issues will change, as will the companies being evaluated. A researcher's task is to be attuned to these changes and to formulate a combination of data and evaluation in ways that can be used by money managers and investors alike.

RESOURCES

Baldwin, Stuart, et al. 1980. *Pension Funds and Ethical Investment: A Study of Investment Practice and Opportunities.* New York: State of California Retirement System, Council on Economic Priorities.

Brown, Jr., Edward G. 1981. *Interim Report.* Sacramento, Calif.: Governor's Public Investment Task Force, State of California.

Campanale, Mark, and Stuart Bell. 1990. "Environmental Investment in the UK: A Survey of Recent Developments." Copenhagen: Centre for Alternative Social Analysis (CASA).

A superb study with broad implications for the United States by top re-searchers from the Merlin Research Unit and the Pensions Investment Research Consultants (PIRC). An essential work. CASA's address: Linnesgade 14, DK-1361 Copenhagen K, Denmark. Phone: (011) (45) 33 32 05 55.

Domini, Amy, and Peter Kinder. 1984. *Ethical Investing.* Reading, Mass.: Addison-Wesley.

Elkington, John, and Tom Burke. 1989. *The Green Capitalists: How Industry Can Make Money and Protect the Environment.* London: Victor Gollancz.

Gray, R. H. 1990. *The Greening of Accountancy: The Profession After Pearce,* certified research report no. 17. London: Chartered Association of Certified Accountants.

Miller, Alan. 1991. *Socially Responsible Investment: The Financial Impact of Screened Investment in the 1990s.* London: London Financial Times Business Information Service.

Millstein, Ira, and Lee Smith. June 1989. *Our Money's Worth: The Report of the Governor's Task Force on Pension Fund Investment.* Albany, N.Y.: New York State.

Minns, Richard. 1980. *Pension Funds and British Capitalism: The Ownership and Control of Shareholdings.* London: Heinemann.

Minns, Richard, et al. 1981. *The London Financial Strategy.* London: Greater London Council.

NGO Finance. A new British magazine covering nonprofits and including regular articles on social investing, *NGO Finance* is located at: Plaza Publishing Ltd., 3A Rectory Grove, London SW4 0EG. Phone: (011) (44) 71-720 0340.

Norton, Michael (ed.) 1989. *A Guide to Company Giving.* London: Directory of Social Change.

Pearce, David, et al. 1989. *Blueprint for a Green Economy.* London: International Institute for Environment and Development.

Rifkin, Jeremy, and Randy Barber. 1978. *The North Will Rise Again: Pensions, Politics and Power in the 1980s.* Boston: Beacon.

Robins, Nick. 1990. *Managing the Environment: The Greening of European Business.* London: Business International.

Schwartz, Robert J. 1985. *Socially Responsible Investment: The American Experience.* London: Greater London Council.

Simpson, Anne. 1991. *The Greening of Global Investment.* London: Economist Publications.

Ward, Sue. 1986. *Socially Responsible Investment: A Guide for Those Concerned with the Ethical and Social Implications of Their Investments.* London: Directory of Social Change.

U.S. RESEARCH SERVICES

Ed. Note: This chapter consists of descriptions of research services submitted, unless otherwise indicated, by the services. Those that chose not to submit material to us are listed in the directory in appendix B.

| COUNCIL ON ECONOMIC PRIORITIES

30 Irving Place
New York, N.Y. 10003
(212) 420-1133

The idea of a corporate social responsibility movement is relatively new, coalescing in the sixties around such concerns as the Vietnam War, civil rights unrest, and the presence of many major U.S. companies in South Africa. Americans slowly became aware of an important fact that is the basis of the movement today: the ways people make investments and use their purchasing power as consumers not only can register concern about corporate involvement in such issues, but can bring about positive change.

The History of the Council on Economic Priorities
Information was a top priority for these new pioneers. A pathfinding research organization, the Council on Economic Priorities (CEP), was founded in 1969 to answer this urgent need. As a broker with a Wall Street firm, founder Alice Tepper Marlin was asked by a Boston synagogue to put together a stock portfolio that avoided companies with involvement in the Vietnam conflict. Upon advertising the availability of the "peace portfolio," the firm received six hundred replies. Within six months Marlin established the CEP and set to work, comparing companies within an industry and rating them according to their social performance in the policy areas at the very top of the public agenda.

Efficiency In Death (CEP: 1970) identified suppliers of antipersonnel weapons in Vietnam. At least one manufacturer, Whirlpool, dropped its military contracts. *Paper Profits* (CEP: 1970) examined the pollution records of paper companies, spurring significant advances in pollution control over the next two years. *Shortchanged* (CEP: 1972) found that most women and minorities in the banking industry were relegated to low-level, poorly paid jobs. The study prompted important job advances after it was widely quoted in congressional testimony.

Over the next few years, CEP's book-length studies, reports, and newsletters gained a reputation for fairness, accuracy, and thoroughness. They were used by corporations, investors, government officials, and activists alike.

During the eighties the bloated military budget and weapons contracting (especially nuclear) were the focus of attention, culminating in *Star Wars: The Economic Fallout* (CEP: 1987), which was instrumental in significantly reducing the Star Wars budget.

That same year, the council released *Rating America's Corporate Conscience* (Addison-Wesley), a breakthrough study of the social performance of 130 consumer products and services companies. Consumers were thrilled to have at their fingertips a means to shop according to their consciences and, at the same time, to influence corporate behavior.

By the end of 1988, CEP responded to the demand for a smaller, easily portable shopping guide with *Shopping for a Better World* (CEP). Coming at a time when Americans were fed up with greed and shenanigans in the corporate arena, this pocket-size guide was an immediate success. CEP has updated it annually, adding more companies and categories and incorporating many suggestions from consumers. More than 900,000 copies of *Shopping for a Better World* had been sold by early 1991; the last two editions also have been published by Ballantine Books.

CEP's most recent addition to its "corporate conscience" series of publications is *The Better World Investment Guide* (Prentice Hall, 1991), a comprehensive sourcebook for investors and consumers. This five hundred–page compendium profiles one hundred publicly held companies—large corporations chosen for their asset size, and companies, large and small, selected because they appear in ethically screened portfolios. A special section describes how practitioners of socially conscious investing evaluate companies in such areas as South African involvement, weapons contracting, employee and community relations, and the environment. There is a brief history of the ethical investing movement, a resource section, and a chapter detailing the many investment options now available to those who wish to match their investments to their values.

In the last year, CEP has added two important new components: the Institutional Investor Research Service and the Corporate Environmental Data Clearinghouse.

CONTACT. Rosalyn Will is a coauthor of *The Better World Investment Guide* and was project director for the first pocket-size consumer guide rating companies on social issues, *Shopping for a Better World*, published in December 1988. She continues to research companies for this publication.

Corporate Environmental Data Clearinghouse

The environment tops nearly every poll as the preeminent concern of the nineties, yet there remain more questions than answers when it comes to corporate behavior toward the environment. For example: They're going to build an incinerator in my neighborhood. Should I worry, and if so, why? Am I investing in companies that produce more hazardous waste sites than dividends? Are any fast-food companies making efforts to recycle or cut down on the use of Styrofoam? Is the company I work for (or live near) taking steps to reduce toxins at the source, thus cutting down on pollution and harmful waste products?

Until recently, there was no comprehensive source where one could get this kind of information. To gather the widely scattered information into one convenient nexus, CEP established the Corporate Environmental Data Clearinghouse (CEDC).

The project, which began in April 1990, has five goals:

1. To collect the data generated on the environmental performance of the Standard & Poor's 500 companies, concentrating first on well-known consumer companies and companies in problematic industries, such as petrochemicals and paper and pulp, and on developing the ability to respond to requests for information from environmental groups, the government, the media, and concerned individuals;
2. To update the data on a continuing basis;
3. To produce company reports that make sense of the complex and varied data and that assess overall the environmental records of these companies;

4. To make the reports available for use by environmentally concerned citizens, activists, nonprofit organizations, investors, and public officials;
5. To use the data to encourage corporations to improve their environmental policies, to provide a sound basis for evaluating environmental policies, and to develop criteria by which practices affecting the environment may be judged.

As requests for information pour in, CEDC continues to expand its established network of sources among environmental groups at the national, regional, and grassroots level (currently there are more than five thousand such organizations in the United States alone). The project had provided seventy draft corporate reports to twenty groups by March 1991. A sliding fee scale ensures that all interested individuals and groups have access to clearinghouse information.

CONTACT. Jonathan Schorsch is CEDC's project director. Schorsch, a coauthor of *Shopping for a Better World* and *The Better World Investment Guide*, also authors newsletters and is a regular speaker on environmental and corporate social responsibility issues. He holds degrees in philosophy (an M.A. from the New School for Social Research in 1987) and comparative literature (a B.A. from Columbia University in 1985).

Institutional Investor Research Service

Increasingly, principles are going to be right up there with profits as key for any American corporation that wishes to remain competitive during the 1990s. The growing interest of investors and consumers in social issues such as the environment and South Africa has translated into more than $500 billion invested according to some social criteria.

The Institutional Investor Research Service (IIRS) is CEP's response to the growing demand of investors for corporate social responsibility data. Monthly IIRS reports currently inform investors of the track records of nearly two hundred publicly held companies, rating them in each of the eleven issue areas studied by CEP: the environment, South Africa, women's advancement, minority advancement, military contracts, charitable giving, animal testing, disclosure of information, community outreach, family benefits, and workplace issues. An "Alert" column highlights important company information that cannot be indicated in any of the issue areas (for example, involvement with nuclear power).

Generally companies are rated "top," "middle," or "bottom," according to the level of their social performance. In the areas of South Africa and military contracts, involvement is indicated with a simple yes or no. Where information is insufficient, this is indicated with a question mark. The ratings are absolute for some categories: giving to charity, for example, is shown as a percentage of pretax profits. For other categories, such as the environment, ratings are relative to other companies in the industry. Each monthly report consists of four sections. The first section, "Company Rating Charts," lists the most current ratings for each company in each of the issue areas. Any ratings that have changed are highlighted so that investors can spot new developments at a glance.

The second section, "Rating Changes and New Information," explains the rating changes highlighted in section one and includes any additional information pertaining to a company's social responsibility. As part of its research process, CEP reads through hundreds of journals, magazines, newsletters, and other publications. If information is found that might be of concern to social investors (even though it might not directly affect company ratings), it is included in this section.

Sections three and four explain CEP's rating criteria in depth for each issue area and provide full information concerning the abbreviated "Alert" column entries.

Research for this project is conducted in the same way as for the rest of CEP's social responsibility projects. CEP gathers its information in several ways. A detailed (and fairly lengthy) questionnaire is sent to a company requesting a description of its policies and performance in each of the issue areas rated by CEP. Though some companies do not respond, they may provide CEP with extensive information through printed materials or phone interviews with company officials.

CEP routinely contacts and receives information from institutions whose specific interests overlap with ours. These include AFL-CIO officials and trade unions and nonprofit organizations focusing on minorities, women, consumers and investors, animal welfare, workplace safety, and the environment. Council researchers also frequent business and public libraries and contact public agencies, such as the Occupational Safety and Health Administration (OSHA) and the National Labor Relations Board (NLRB). CEP consults on a regular basis with advisers who are experts in corporate social responsibility issues.

The cost of a one-year subscription to IIRS is $8,000, which is payable in soft dollars.

CONTACT. For more information and a sample report, contact Benjamin Corson, IIRS's project director. A 1987 Dartmouth graduate, Corson was project director of the 1990 *Shopping for a Better World*. He also headed up research for the 1991 America's Corporate Conscience Awards, CEP's annual recognition of outstanding company programs.

| DATACENTER

464 Nineteenth Street
Oakland, Calif. 94612
(510) 835-4692
(510) 835-3017 (fax)

Ed. Note: The philosophy guiding the almanac dictated that we allow service providers to speak for themselves. In this case, however, we felt compelled to add a few words, because from this modest description, readers might not appreciate just how remarkable the DataCenter is. And they might not realize that its people and resources are indispensable for social researchers and, therefore, for social investors. As one writer put it, exaggerating only slightly, "It's the Alexandrian Library of social research."

The DataCenter, founded in 1977, is a nonprofit, employee-managed, public-interest information and research center providing services documenting the social performance of U.S. and foreign corporations and related human rights issues. The center's search service has conducted research for major projects on corporate responsibility and socially responsible investing nationwide. Past projects have included documentation for a brokerage firm, Progressive Asset Management, *Everybody's Business Almanac*, and CEP's *Shopping for a Better World*.

The DataCenter maintains an in-house documentation center featuring 15 years of clipping files culled from some 300 news, business, labor, critical opinion, and alternative press journals, covering more than 15,000 corporate entities as well as issues related to industries, labor and employee relations, the environment, and business ethics. Patrons of the library also may browse approximately 150 shelved periodicals and newsletters, 1,500 books, and a reference collection that includes key resources documenting corporate social performance. The center's collection is supplemented with access to computer on-line commercial, private, and government information services worldwide, along with an extensive referral network, all available through the customized search service.

The DataCenter Search Service provides strategic research and document retrieval by business information specialists, tailoring each research request to meet the specific needs of the client. Projects range from a complete profile of a corporation, to documentation on a single aspect or multiple aspects of a company's operations, to information on business ethics issues. After interviewing the client and discussing project requirements, an experienced information professional searches the DataCenter's unique in-house vertical files collection and other repository holdings as well as pertinent on-line data bases and outside resouces.

| INTERFAITH CENTER ON CORPORATE RESPONSIBILITY

Room 556
475 Riverside Drive
New York, N.Y. 10115
(212) 870-2296

The history of the Interfaith Center on Corporate Responsibility, and shareholder actions sponsored by ICCR, are described in chapters 8 through 18 of this almanac.

The Corporate Examiner
Published ten times yearly ($35 for a one-year subscription), the *Corporate Examiner* is for people who know that investors with a conscience are making a difference in corporate decision making. Readers are able to read between the lines of corporate annual reports and balance sheets and see beyond share prices and dividends.

The *Corporate Examiner*

- reports "Corporate Action News";
- provides in-depth analyses of issues and trends in "Briefs";

- publishes bulletins and updates on social responsibility share-holder resolutions, the companies challenged and the issues, agreements reached with management, and the size of share-holder votes;
- reviews publications and media; and
- presents guest editorials by corporate responsibility leaders around the world.

The *Corporate Examiner* uncovers what is going on behind the scenes at corporations:

- which companies are doing business in South Africa and which have left;
- who is backing the Valdez Principles and who is considering signing;
- who is making big profits off foreign military sales and what is happening to the peace dividend; and
- who is investing in the tobacco industry and who is divesting.

The *Corporate Examiner* describes the activists:

- churches;
- giant state, municipal, and private pension funds;
- institutional investors, such as colleges, universities, unions, and foundations;
- antiapartheid, environmental, peace, health, and civil rights groups; and
- community development organizations and socially responsible investors.

The *Corporate Examiner* reveals their plans, strategies, and actions.

ICCR's Subscriber Service
The subscriber service is for investors with a conscience. It provides clients with

- five annual subscriptions to the *Corporate Examiner*;
- a copy of the year's *Church Proxy Resolutions* with texts of all social responsibility shareholder resolutions, a directory of the sponsors, and an alphabetical checklist of corporations;

- updates on the filing of resolutions and agreements reached with management; and
- regular mailing of background materials.

The minimum annual fee for this service is $350.

ICCR Associates
ICCR is a consultant to several of the most powerful pension funds in the United States, an adviser to socially responsible mutual funds, and a clearinghouse for information on alternative investments and community development. Increasingly, conscientious investors like these look to ICCR, a leading authority on corporate responsibility, for advice, products, services, and vital timely information to aid their corporate responsibility programs.

ICCR associates

- consult with ICCR staff;
- frequently join in church actions, such as shareholder resolutions, prayer vigils, and letter-writing campaigns; and
- receive all of the regular subscriber service benefits.

The minimum annual fee is $550.

Alternative Investment News Packets
The serious alternative investor receives quarterly mailings on alternative investing, community economic development, and socially responsible investing in addition to updates of ICCR's *Directory of Alternative Investments.* Cost is $50 a year.

ICCR Publications
Church Proxy Resolutions 1991 ($18) contains texts of more than three hundred church- and pension fund–sponsored social responsibility shareholder resolutions.

Corporate Responsibility Challenges, Spring 1991 ($5) is a digest of more than 375 social issue shareholder resolutions, the companies involved, the status of the resolutions, and a directory of the sponsors.

ICCR's Annual Report, July 1, 1989–June 30, 1990 (free) describes ICCR's and its members' activities, including a message from the executive director and a look at the coming year.

The Conscientious Investor's Guide to Mutual and Money Mar-

ket Funds and Investment Services, 1990 ($5) profiles those who apply social criteria to depositor and client investment decisions.

The *Directory of Alternative Investments* ($15) describes investment opportunities in worker- and cooperatively owned businesses, low- and moderate-income housing, credit unions and minority-owned banks, and development intermediaries.

The *Guide to Church Alternative Investment Funds, 1991* ($3) is an updated profile of church alternative investment funds.

CONTACT. Diane Bratcher, ICCR's director of communications, is responsible for

- publications and newsletter;
- annual report;
- public information and press and media relations;
- research reports, papers, and action alerts.

Bratcher is a member of Manhattan Community Board Number 7, a citizen advisory panel to the government of New York City representing Manhattan's Upper West Side, and secretary of the Ecumenical Employees Association, the union of employees of ICCR, and the National Council of Churches of Christ in the U.S.A.

| KINDER, LYDENBERG, DOMINI & COMPANY

Seven Dana Street
Cambridge, Mass. 02138
(617) 547-7479
(617) 354-5353 (fax)

Kinder, Lydenberg, Domini & Company (KLD) offers social research on a wide range of companies, including those in the Domini 400 Social Index and the Standard & Poor's 500 Index.

Social Investment Database
The Social Investment Database (SID) is an on-line computer service providing details on the social records of more than 800 publicly traded U.S. corporations—those on the Domini 400 Social Index and those on the Standard & Poor's 500 Index, as well as many smaller-

capitalization companies with positive social stories. The data base will grow by about 75 companies each year.

ISSUES COVERED. For each company, the SID highlights issues likely to be of most importance to social investors—the environment, military contracting, employee relations, community involvement, South Africa, and product safety, among others. The SID also contains comments on issues such as quality programs, excessive officer and board compensation, and women and minorities.

RATINGS SYSTEM. Among the SID's unique features is its keyed check-off rating system. For each issue, a key summarizes the primary reasons why social investors are likely to view recent company actions as either an area of strength or a cause for concern. The keyed data base enables users to search and sort on individual issues or combinations of issues—for example, all companies with strengths both in women and minorities and in employee relations, or all companies with negatives in employee relations and in the environment.

In addition, the SID contains text files with detailed explanations or commentary on each area of strength or concern. Users can search these text files by company name or for any word or combination of words. The data base includes verified information not included in KLD's hard copy services, described below.

SYSTEM CAPABILITY. The Social Investment Database allows users to:

- Keep up to date on questions of greatest concern within the social investment community;
- Measure the financial implications of imposing social screens. The effects of imposing a single-issue screen at increasing levels of stringency, or of imposing a combination of screens, can be assessed;
- Compare the performance of companies within a single industry across a spectrum of social issues;
- Select stocks with strong positive social histories;
- Serve a range of clients with varying social concerns;
- Maintain a general overview of the social records of a comprehensive universe of firms.

The Social Investment Database service includes:

- Two hours a week of on-line access at no charge;
- Hard copy of the text and check-off ratings for all companies;
- Two hours (annually) of consulting time at no charge.

DSI 400 Monthly Update

The *DSI 400 Monthly Update* is a seventy-page monthly publication listing the four hundred U.S. corporations in the Domini Social Index. Companies are listed alphabetically, by industry, and by market capitalization. In addition, this publication provides an indication for each company of whether there are areas for social investors that might seem of particular strength or concern. (The tables in part VIII of this almanac replicate the *Update* tables.) The *Update* is available on an annual subscription basis.

KLD Company Reviews

The KLD company reviews are one- to three-page profiles of the corporate social accountability records of publicly traded U.S. corporations. The Reviews highlight for the social investor those areas of strength or concern relevant to each company. They are available for the four hundred companies in the Domini Social Index, for the five hundred companies in the Standard & Poor's 500 Index, or for the companies in both of these indexes (approximately 650 companies). Figure 20-1 is a sample review.

KLD Consulting Services

KLD provides specialized consultation in the development of social screens tailored to clients' specific needs; the creation or reviews of portfolios in accordance with clients' social screens; and the construction of specialized socially screened benchmark portfolios.

| NUCLEAR FREE AMERICA

325 East Twenty-fifth Street
Baltimore, Md. 21218
(301) 235-3575

The Nuclear Free America (NFA) Database Project offers detailed federal government data on Department of Defense prime contracts and contractors in a variety of formats, customized to meet your

FIGURE 20-1
TANDEM COMPUTERS INCORPORATED

Ticker	Community	Employee Relations	Environment	Product	Women/ Minorities	Other	Military Contracts	Nuclear Power	South Africa
TDM		X	X	X	X				

AREAS OF STRENGTH AND AREAS OF CONCERN

No Concern =	Concern =	X	Major Concern = XX
No Strength =	Strength =	X	Major Strength = XX

Business

Tandem's primary business is the manufacture of parallel processing computers for industrial and government customers. These systems are primarily used for online financial services, communications, and distribution systems.

Employee Relations

All Tandem employees are eligible for stock options. Each year, every employee receives an option for 100 shares of Tandem stock.

The 1985 book, *The 100 Best Companies to Work for in America*, praised the firm's commitment to communication with all workers, its egalitarian work environment, and generous and innovative employee benefits. These benefits include a sabbatical policy that allows employees to take 6 weeks off (in addition to vacation time) for each 4 years of service. The firm's 1990 turnover rate, 7.2%, is well below the industry average.

Environment

The firm plans to eliminate the use of ozone-depleting chlorofluorocarbons (CFCs) from its operation by December 1992.

As of January 1992, the company had replaced 10 of its 12 CFC-based degreasers with water-based machines.

Product

Tandem makes computers that are among the most reliable in the world. The firm's 1990 research and development expenditures of $267 million (13.9% of sales) were among the highest in KLD's Computer Manufacturers industry classification.

Women and Minorities

Six of the firm's senior executives are women. Those holding operating management positions include: Roberta Henderson is Vice President—OLTP Software Development; Anne Perlman is Vice President—Marketing; Cindy Brown is Vice President—Marketing, Value Added Services, Tandem Telecommunications Systems, Inc. (TTS); and Denice Gibson is Vice President—Product Development, TTSI.

Military Commitment

According to Nuclear Free America, in fiscal year 1990, the company had $595,000 (0.03% of sales) in weapons-related prime contracts with the Department of Defense.

Source: Kinder, Lydenberg, Domini & Company.
Note: Factual material is obtained from sources that we believed to be reliable but cannot be guaranteed.

exact needs and specifications. Currently available in summary or detailed form are all data from fiscal years 1989 and 1990.

Like government microfiche and Dialog data services, NFA's data base includes a separate "record" for every prime contract action and award over $25,000. These contract data can be sorted and/or selected by any of more than fifty different fields, including prime contractor name, place of performance, and weapon name, allowing NFA to customize reports according to the client's exact needs and specifications.

In addition to this flexibility, NFA's data base has several other distinct advantages over Dialog and microfiche sources.

- Every contract record includes a field for the parent company name. The parent company designation links all of the spelling variations of a particular company as well as its prime contractor subsidiaries. Any report can thus be indexed and cross-referenced by parent company as well as prime contractor.
- Every contract record includes a field for the congressional district in which the work was done. This is in addition to fields that identify contract place of performance by city, county, and state.
- The entire data base has been researched and coded by weapon name and product or service name to create three new categories not available from other sources. The categories allow one to identify all prime contracts and contractors related to nuclear weapons (narrowly defined to include only the weapons themselves), nuclear weapons systems (broadly defined to include the weapons' launch, guidance, delivery, and deployment systems), and military systems (very broadly defined to include all conventional or nuclear weapons–related systems and services). These categories are based on definitions compiled by NFA to meet the needs of Nuclear Free Zone local authorities and socially responsible investors, and they can be further tailored by the client to match any particular definition.
- The entire data base also can be segregated according to contracts for products, services, and research and development (including research and development [R & D] and research, development, testing, and engineering [RDT & E]). This designation is based on the Federal Procurement Data Center's (FPDC) product and service codes. Breakdowns also are available by FPDC claimant code for such broad categories as construc-

tion, aircraft, shipbuilding, military, vehicles, and so on, and by standard industrial code.

Data base reports are available in ASCII, dBase, or printed formats starting at just $50 (for parent company profiles). Summary reports (giving the total of each parent company and prime contractor's Department of Defense prime contracts and/or their subtotals in any of the categories noted above) and directory reports (listing just the prime contractor and parent company names) are available starting at $300. The complete Defense Department data base (all prime contracts for all companies) is available on diskette for $1,500, and a data base of all prime contracts for all government agencies is available (in CD-ROM format only, including CD-ROM hardware) for $2,650. Nonprofit organizations are eligible for a 20 percent discount on all services.

U.S. MAGAZINES AND NEWSLETTERS

Ed. Note: *This chapter consists of descriptions of U.S. magazines and newsletters serving social investors that were submitted, unless otherwise indicated, by their publishers. Those that did not choose to submit material are included in the directory in appendix B.*

BUSINESS ETHICS: THE MAGAZINE OF SOCIALLY RESPONSIBLE BUSINESS

1107 Hazeltine Boulevard
Suite 530
Chaska, Minn. 55318
(612) 448-8864

The mission of *Business Ethics* is to promote ethical business practices and to serve that growing community of professionals striving to live and work in responsible ways. *Business Ethics* is a personal magazine written in the belief that by becoming healthier and more ethical as individuals, we can create a healthier and more ethical world. It is a magazine that celebrates integrity in business, a magazine for the new kind of businessperson coming into power today. It is for people who believe that "business" and "ethics" are words that go well together.

The people who read *Business Ethics* and the people written about in the magazine are the same: individuals trying to live lives that make sense, people hoping to leave the world better than it was when they found it.

- *Business Ethics* is solution oriented. It emphasizes the positive. Never casting stones, the magazine instead offers support in tackling difficult and complex issues—and looks at solutions other companies have developed.

- There are no exposés in this magazine. No company will ever find itself "exposed" in *Business Ethics*. But companies may find themselves acclaimed. In fact, each year in November the magazine also gives the Business Ethics Awards for ethical excellence to three outstanding companies.
- The magazine is a networking tool. *Business Ethics* offers contact names and addresses so that professionals can get in touch with one another. With high reader involvement—through features like the "Reader Roundtable," "Letters to the Editor," and "What Would You Do?"—*Business Ethics* serves as a networking tool for sharing ideas and resources.

Primary Areas of Coverage
Business Ethics has four primary areas of coverage.

1. Practical ideas—exploring socially responsible practices at other corporations; environmental office ideas, resources, tools.
2. Personal support—the ethics of wealth, bringing one's full self to work, taking time out, being an effective leader.
3. Role models—interviews, profiles of responsible business-people, case studies of ethical businesses.
4. Leading-edge thought—what the best and brightest are thinking about ethics and social responsibility.

Features
In "Musings," a regular column by editor Marjorie Kelly, you will find thoughtful essays on the human side of the business enterprise. This is a place to explore issues of human dignity and integrity. In the "Working Ideas" section each issue, you will find ideas your company can use—innovative ways that companies have helped to make the world a better place, inventive personnel policies, leading-edge strategic policies, and simple environmental programs.

"Trend Watch" tracks what is happening in business, with stories heard through the media, prospective and passed legislation, the latest technology to hit the market, and more. The "Not Business as Usual" section presents ethical perspectives on current business topics and profiles of companies implementing those perspectives—

stock ownership plans, corporate cruelty to animals, South African divestment, plant closings, and so on.

The "Ecological Office" offers readers quick tips on becoming friends of the environment. In the "Enlightened Manager" are the latest personnel policies and practical hands-on tips for implementation. In "Bookend" you will find quick-reading excerpts from some of the best books of our time—or any time: Machiavelli on power, Michael Novak on a theology of the corporation, Sissela Bok on lying.

| CLEAN YIELD

Box 1880
Greensboro Bend, Vt. 05842
(802) 533-7178
(802) 533-2907 (fax)
$85 a year for individuals and nonprofits
$100 for corporations
ISSN: 0882-3820

The *Clean Yield* is a professional stock market newsletter for investors who would like to make timely and profitable investments in publicly traded companies that pass certain social responsibility tests. Companies are screened for:

South African involvement	environmental practices
labor and community relations	weapons production
tobacco production	gambling
animal testing	nuclear power generation
corporate frankness	

Those companies that *Clean Yield* investment advisers believe are able to successfully mix financial prosperity with social responsibility are profiled and actively followed.

The *Clean Yield* newsletter has a number of regular columns. "Clear View" is an editorial piece that discusses a current social issue of importance to social investors. "Going to Market" is a discussion of the past month's economic and stock market events with a view to what is ahead. "Clean Buys" is a presentation of an industry group or a collection of stocks that currently look particularly attractive or unattractive. "Night School" is a primer in investment and social screening techniques and terms. "Managed Accounts" is a description of the stock that Clean Yield Asset Management Company, a subsidiary of the Clean Yield Group, has bought and sold for accounts.

"Clean Profiles," the heart of the newsletter, is an in-depth description of the financials, stock price, technical action, and social actions of two companies. "Company Updates" is an every-other-month discussion of eight companies previously profiled in the newsletter.

"Technical Trend," for market technicians, discusses the technical health and action of the stock market and is accompanied by a statistical table. "Clean Sweeps" is a miscellaneous collection of news items and resources of particular interest to social investors.

"The Model Portfolio" is a portfolio of social stocks that is continually tracked by the newsletter as well as by *Hulbert's Financial Digest*. Unhedged buy and sell recommendations are made regularly. The portfolio originally was constructed in March 1985 and has been tracked continually since that date. "The Model Portfolio" has significantly outperformed all of the popular market indices since its inception. "Portfolio Rap" is a companion narrative piece to "The Model Portfolio."

Biographies

Rian Fried, M.P.A. is one of the founders of the *Clean Yield*. He holds a master's degree from Harvard University and a bachelor's degree from the University of Michigan. He also writes financial and stock market columns for various newspapers, stock market digests, and national phone hot lines. Fried is a board member of a variety of civic and social service organizations.

Doug Fleer is a founder of the *Clean Yield*. He attended Colorado College and established a building-contracting company in northeastern Vermont. Fleer has been particularly active in the environmental movement. He has been a private investor for more than fourteen years.

I CO-OP AMERICA QUARTERLY (FORMERLY BUILDING ECONOMIC ALTERNATIVES)

Co-op America
2100 M Street N.W., Suite 403

Washington, D.C. 20063
(202) 872-5307
$20 a year with membership in Co-op America

Co-op America is a national membership association promoting a sustainable economy and educating businesses and consumers on how to align buying and investing habits with values of peace, cooperation, and environmental protection.

A sustainable economy, such as Co-op America promotes, requires a new vision and a new set of ideas. *Co-op America Quarterly* is dedicated to covering these emerging, hopeful alternatives to business as usual. Each issue covers a topic in depth, with special emphasis on actions that individuals can take using their economic power. The subjects covered have included: community-based health care, sustainable agriculture, new methods for measuring the GNP, national energy policy, and sustainable communities.

Regular features include "Local Self-Reliance," a column by David Morris of the Washington, D.C.–based Institute for Local Self-Reliance; "Green Consumer," a column by author Joel Makower; and profiles of socially and environmentally responsible businesses.

One of the important tools in the *Quarterly*, especially for social investment professionals, is the four- to eight-page section "Boycott Action News," the only comprehensive and regularly updated listing of consumer boycotts in the nation. In addition to announcements of new boycotts and updates on ongoing actions, it lists the target, organizer, demand, and product line for each boycott.

Editor
Cindy Mitlo is the editor of *Co-op America Quarterly*. She has been writing for Co-op America's magazine and catalog since 1986. She is also the project manager for *The Socially Responsible Financial Planning Guide*.

I CORPORATE RESPONSIBILITY MONITOR

DataCenter
464 Nineteenth Street
Oakland, Calif. 94612
(510) 835-4692
(510) 835-3017 (fax)

The DataCenter, founded in 1977, is a nonprofit, employee-managed public interest information and research center providing services documenting the social performance of U.S. and foreign corporations and related human rights issues. The center's research staff has conducted research for major projects on corporate responsibility and socially responsible investing nationwide. The DataCenter's research services are described in more detail in the preceding chapter.

The DataCenter reviews some three hundred news, business, labor, critical opinion, and alternative press journals to select articles for inclusion in the *Corporate Responsibility Monitor*. The *Monitor* is a hundred-page monthly press reprint service covering the broad range of corporate citizenship issues, including environmental impact, consumer product quality, operations worldwide, litigation, philanthropy, labor, and community relations. By tracking ongoing developments in this field, this service provides subscribers a month-by-month barometer of trends in corporate social performance reported in the previous month's press.

The *Monitor* is recommended for investor groups, specialists in corporate social performance, corporate public affairs offices, foundations, academic departments with courses in business ethics and industrial relations, as well as labor and community activists who need to keep abreast of this expanding field of interest.

| FRANKLIN'S INSIGHT: THE ADVISORY LETTER FOR CONCERNED INVESTORS

711 Atlantic Avenue, Fifth Floor
Boston, Mass. 02111
(800) 548-5684
(617) 423-6655

Franklin's Insight is a monthly investment newsletter focusing on the field of socially responsible investing. It is affiliated with Franklin Research & Development, the country's largest investment management firm specializing solely in this field. Franklin Research works with individual and institutional clients. Its minimum account size is $400,000.

Since beginning publication in early 1983, *Franklin's Insight* has evolved to offer the most complete service of any social investment newsletter. Subscribers have the option of receiving either of two services—one intended for those with a general interest in the area of corporate social responsibility and the other geared for professional and active, individual investors.

The general service, known as "Investing for a Better World," addresses the social concerns of every investor. Each edition explores a current social issue in the context of potential investments. One piece examined how to rate banks on community reinvestments. Another updated readers on the current situation in South Africa and included a list of all U.S. firms doing business in that country.

Every three months the issue is devoted to examining the recent performance of the socially screened mutual funds. Also provided monthly is the "Social Ticker" column, an update on particularly good and bad acts of corporate social responsibility. This newsletter is priced at $19.95 a year.

The professional service, while including "Investing for a Better World," goes beyond this general information and offers very specific investment advice. This information should allow both individual and institutional investors to manage their assets on a socially screened basis. Every month subscribers receive the following:

- Advice on asset allocation. How much of your money should be in stocks, bonds, cash, and alternative investments (that is, community loan funds and community-oriented bank certificates of deposit).
- A model portfolio of recommended stocks. This list of twenty stocks provides both social and financial ratings on companies that have a positive impact on society and the environment while exhibiting a potential for superior financial rewards. Since our model portfolio was established in 1985, it has outperformed the Dow Jones average by 112 percent through May 1, 1991.
- Two-page profiles on three companies that are of special interest to social investors. One page highlights the especially noteworthy social characteristics of the firm, while the other page summarizes its investment characteristics. In keeping with Franklin Research & Development's philosophy that there is a strong correlation between social and financial performance, we profile and recommend only those companies that have above-average records in the areas of employee relations, the environment, and corporate citizenship. We also do not recommend any companies involved in such avoidance issues as South Africa, defense contracting, and nuclear power. (See figure 21-1.)

- A two-page profile on the social track record of a large, controversial company. Though socially concerned investors usually will not buy stock in these companies, we do review them, since many people have inherited positions in them and they often are held in many institutional portfolios. Recently profiled firms include IBM, Eastman Kodak, and Louisiana Pacific.
- Updated recommendations on more than one hundred previously reviewed stocks. Should investors be buying, holding, or selling their positions now?
- A telephone hot line service. For those investors interested in reacting to short-term swings in the stock and bond markets, we update our economic and investment outlook twice a week in a three-minute recorded message. New information on currently recommended stocks is given particular attention.
- Quarterly, subscribers receive a fifteen-page study of a particular industry or theme. Recent examples include an overview of the recycling industry, how to analyze employee stock ownership plans for their impact on corporate financial and social performance, and a review of the alternative energy sector. Each includes an analysis of broad economic and social trends as well as specific investment advice on several companies being affected by these developments.

This complete service is available for $195.

Contact
Patrick McVeigh is a portfolio manager and investment analyst for Franklin Research & Development. He also serves as the editor of *Franklin's Insight.* He has worked with Franklin Research since its inception in 1982.

| GOOD MONEY PUBLICATIONS, INC.

Calais Stage Road
P.O. Box 363 51A
Worcester, Vt. 05682
(800) 535-3551 (orders)
(802) 223-3911 (business)
(802) 223-8949 (fax)

FIGURE 21-1
FRANKLIN'S INSIGHT EQUITY BRIEF

insight: ... Equity Brief

Franklin's

An Affiliate of
Franklin Research and Development Corporation

April 1991

H.B. Fuller

FULL — OTC
Under Valued at $43.00

Social Assessment Ratings

South Africa	Energy
3	2
Employee Relations	Product
1	3
Environment	Weapons
1	2
Citizenship	**insight's ranking**
1	1

Summary & Recommendation

Though H.B. Fuller's stock has risen by approximately 75% since we added it to our recommended list only six months ago, we still believe the investment glass is only one-half full and there is ample room for additional return. Despite the strong earnings recently recorded which have accounted for the stock's rebound, earnings per share are just back to the 1987 level and the company's return on sales remains one-half of its competitors. **One of the strongest social companies, H.B. Fuller appears on track to become one of the stronger financial firms as well. Continue to stick with this winner as we believe it will still offer superior returns over the next several years.**

Business Profile

With 1990 sales of nearly $800 million, H.B. Fuller is the world's third largest adhesives company behind Henkel of Germany and National Starch (a U.S.-based subsidiary of the British/Dutch Unilever). Fuller's sales are very diversified across industries, with the most important being packaging, automotive, graphic arts, woodworking, polymer, engineered systems, and windows. No more than 2% of sales goes to any one customer. Though the company operates in 31 countries with foreign sales accounting for 46% of total revenues, 82% of Fuller's sales come from the U.S., Germany, and Latin America. The company has ample room to grow in Europe and the Far East.

Equity Briefs are Franklin's profiles of the social and financial performance of selected companies.

Social Profile

There has never been any doubt regarding the record and commitment of Fuller's deep commitment to corporate social responsibility. This has been evidenced by the firm being selected as one of *Business Ethic's* three companies of the year in 1989 and in its receiving the prestigious Lawrence Wien Award for Corporate Social Responsibility in 1987.

The one question that has arisen over the past year is whether the recent change in management will alter this commitment. The promotion in September 1990 of Walter Kissling, the company's international manager, to the position of chief operating officer has clearly modified Fuller's culture. Chief Executive Officer Tony Andersen, whose family built the company and installed its social mission, has given up much of the day to day operations. As a result, there is clearly more emphasis on increased profitability now. Does this come at the expense of the company's social goals, though?

We have yet to see any evidence that it has and believe that Fuller's social commitment will still excel. Tony Andersen continues to oversee this goal and the Andersen family controls over 20% of the voting power of the stock. Also, there have been as many positive social developments in Fuller's international operations under Mr. Kissling as any other segment of the company.

One recent example indicates this. When Peru increased prices twentyfold on basic foodstuffs last year, H.B. Fuller stepped in to help those who could no longer afford to eat. The company opened its mess hall to the children of the community and was soon serving 1,200 meals per day. They then discovered that one of their glue-making pots idled by the recession could be used to cook food. Fuller, along with support from other firms, is now feeding 20,000 children and mothers daily.

The manner is which the company's social goals have been institutionalized gives us confidence that they will continue. Five percent of pre-tax profits are given to charites. These decisions are made by employees at each individual plant. The company has established its own Worldwide Environmental, Health and Safety Committee to bring together employees from throughout the world to proactively insure that all plants are operate at standards higher than required by local governments.

H.B. Fuller

Social Scorecard

Non-U.S. Workforce:	60%
Workforce Unionized:	5%
Social Disclosure:	Excellent
% Employee-Owned	NA
Dividend Reinvestment Plan:	Yes
Contributions (as % of pre-tax income):	5.0%
Board Members: Women:	1
Minorities:	1

Financial Profile

Though Fuller's stock has come a long way (+75%) since we added it to our recommended list six months ago, two factors comfort us in believing that it still has sizable opportunities ahead of it.

First, despite the company's amazing progress made in the past six months illustrated by the stock price's climb and earnings that have been well ahead of expectations, these financial measures are only just now approaching their 1987 levels. The company earned $2.69 per share and its stock reached $48 in 1987. So far this year, the stock has hit $44 and earnings estimates have recently been raised to $2.75.

Second, all this improvement has come during a period of weak economic growth, indicating that Fuller does not need a strong economy to continue to record excellent bottom line advances. By improving its margins Fuller should be able to grow 18-20% even if the economy continues to experience mediocre results. This is a vast improvement over the 1% earnings growth recorded over the past five years and should allow the stock's relative P/E multiple to increase by 20%.

In the company's 1990 annual report, it indicates its commitment to a 150-basis-point reduction in the ratio of SG&A to sales spread over the next three years. Such an achievement would add $0.75 to earnings (a 27% gain) over each of these years. Given that Fuller's return on sales is just about one-half of its competitors, it seems reasonable that such gains in financial performance are possible. Clearly, though, the company does not have to fully achieve this goal in order to make the stock price

move much higher. Even a 30 basis point improvement yearly would add 20% to earnings, all without an improvement in the economy.

Other positive developments for Fuller are the expected decline in raw material costs and its improving cash position. It is estimated that petrochemical raw material costs, primarily ethylene, make up 25% of the cost of sales. Ethylene prices are expected to continue to decline over the coming year. (They have declined in each of the past three months.) After having negative cash flow in 1988 and 1989, Fuller had $14 million in excess cash flow in 1990. We look for further improvement here and expect that the debt ratio will come down from 31% to 25%. At that time, as it has historically done, we believe the odds of Fuller making an acquisition are very high. Since much of Fuller's past growth has been through acquisitions, we believe that a purchase will add to earnings growth down the road.

Though the stock has moved sharply in 1991, we would continue to stick with it. Our preferred buying limit is $40 per share with a target of $50 for this year given current market conditions. We expect to be holders beyond this time frame, though, if our longer-term investment thesis works.

—Patrick McVeigh

H.B. Fuller
FULL – OTC – $33.00

2400 Energy Park, St. Paul, MN 55108
612/645-3401

EPS				
	1989A:	$1.64	52-Week Hi-Lo:	$44-21
	1990A:	$2.28	Est. Dividend:	$0.60
	1991E:	$2.75	Yield:	1.4%
	1992E:	$3.35	Book Value:	$19.93
			ROE:	11%
P/E	1990A:	18.9	Beta:	1.1
	1991E:	15.6	Mkt Cap:	$387mm
	1992E:	12.8	Debt/Cap:	31%
			1989 Rev:	$792mm
Earnings Growth:			S&P Rating:	B+
	Past 5 yrs:	12%	FY Ends	November
	Next 5 yrs:	18%	DJIA (4/8/91):	2897

(Clients and/or employees of the Franklin Companies may own this stock.)

Subscriptions to *Franklin's insight* are $195/year. Call 1-800/548-5684 (in MA 1-617/423-6655) or write to *Franklin's insight*, 711 Atlantic Avenue, Boston, MA 02111.

GOOD MONEY Publications provides publications and financial services for socially concerned investors and the financial professionals who serve them. Since 1982 GOOD MONEY Publications has published *GOOD MONEY*, the first newsletter for socially concerned investors—investors who take into account social factors in addition to financial factors when making investment decisions. GOOD MONEY also publishes the *Netback* newsletter, *GOOD MONEY's Social Funds Guide, Social Investor Strategy Reports*, and various investor handbooks. GOOD MONEY also provides custom research and portfolio social audit services; GOOD MONEY screened companies for the Vermont National Bank's Socially Responsible Banking Fund.

GOOD MONEY is not a traditional investment-advisory service. The company does not manage money and therefore has no potential conflict of interest in any of the social assessments of investments in GOOD MONEY's publications or services. GOOD MONEY does not make buy, hold, or sell recommendations. Rather, the company provides information for brokers, money managers, and individuals who seek additional resources to track the social performance of various investments. GOOD MONEY's publications provide information about the potential financial impact of making social judgments about investments and the financial performance of socially screened investments. More often than not, the impact and performance are more favorable for social investors than for investors making traditional for-profit-only investment decisions.

GOOD MONEY Newsletter

GOOD MONEY's current flagship publication is *GOOD MONEY*, a twelve-page bimonthly newsletter that reports on socially screened investments (stocks, bonds, funds, and so on). Articles emphasize positive social features and the financial performance of socially screened investments. The newsletter often contains charts and listings for such social issues as the major polluters by industry compared to companies with the best environmental records; nuclear utilities with poor operating records compared to nonnuclear utilities with good records; opportunities for investors concerned about the environment; and the companies with good records for the hiring, training, retention, and promotion of minorities and women. The newsletter also reports on the current and long-term performance of the GOOD MONEY Industrial and Utility Averages. A continuing column entitled "GOOD MONEY Pick" provides a social and financial profile of new investment opportunities for socially concerned investors. A one-year subscription of six issues is $75.

NETBACK Newsletter

Every subscriber to *GOOD MONEY* also receives, at no extra charge, *Netback*, a bimonthly networking newsletter of the social investment community. Every subscriber may have up to one hundred free words annually to make an announcement (for example, about a conference or meeting) to seek out investors for a project, to provide information about a product or service, or to present an idea about a social, economic, or political issue. To avoid any potential conflicts of interest in the social assessments of investment opportunities, GOOD MONEY does not accept advertising for any of its publications. Subscribers to *GOOD MONEY*, however, may use *Netback* to list their products or services on an equal basis with other subscribers.

GOOD MONEY's Social Funds Guide

GOOD MONEY currently publishes *GOOD MONEY's Social Funds Guide*, a comprehensive, sixty-plus-page guide to social and environmental mutual funds. The guide includes descriptions and analyses of the social screens, investor costs, and financial performance of socially screened equity, bond, and money market mutual funds. For funds with extensive social screens, charts depict the funds' mix of investments (stocks, bonds, cash, and so on) and the funds' major holdings. Each fund's holdings are analyzed for social factors as well (for example, company environmental records, links to South Africa, or nuclear weapons production). A special section of the guide analyzes the new self-styled environmental funds to note how each fund meets its environmentally sound claim. The social factors of environmental funds also are compared with those of social funds. *GOOD MONEY's Social Funds Guide*, updated annually, costs $19.95.

GOOD MONEY Social Audit Services

GOOD MONEY Publications also provides consulting, custom research, and portfolio audit services for both individual and institutional investors. Fees vary according to the client's special needs (specific social screens and investments), with estimates given to clients after the initial consultation.

Social Investor Strategy Reports

Along with GOOD MONEY's social audit services, GOOD MONEY publishes *Social Investor Strategy Reports* for investors concerned with specific social concerns, such as environmental issues, animal rights, military contractors, and women's issues. Each report analyzes the issue of concern to social investors and alternative strategies (for example, avoiding all defense contractors versus avoiding those with defense contracts worth more than 5 percent of gross sales). The social and financial implications of each strategy are analyzed. Current price is $20 per report. Available topics are provided on request.

GOOD MONEY Background and History

GOOD MONEY Publications was incorporated as the Center for Economic Revitalization (CENTER) in Vermont in 1982. CENTER's first publications were *GOOD MONEY* and *Netback*, newsletters for socially concerned investors. Soon thereafter, CENTER began publishing special handbooks and guides for social investors. These included a guide for picking the stocks of socially responsible companies; a handbook on how nonnuclear and alternative or renewable energy utilities with good environmental records provided investors with better long-term gains (in stock dividends paid plus capital gains) than nuclear utilities; and a pamphlet describing a thirty-stock GOOD MONEY Industrial Average of socially responsible companies and the GOOD MONEY Utility Average, a twenty-stock average of nonnuclear or renewable energy utilities, both of which could be tracked against the Dow Jones equivalents.

In 1985 the business initiated social audit services for both individual and institutional investors wanting their investment portfolios screened for a variety of social issues. Related to these services, CENTER published issue papers that dealt with investment strategies of social investors interested in such issues as defense contractors, South Africa, alternative energy versus nuclear energy, environmental pollution, and women's issues. Institutional clients for social audits have included St. Edmund's Society and the Vermont National Bank. In the spring of 1986, the business was reorganized and the company's name was changed to GOOD MONEY Publications.

The president and founder of GOOD MONEY is Ritchie Lowry, Ph.D. He is also professor of sociology at Boston College and former chair of the department. He is the author of many books and articles on war and the military, political power, and social problems, including *GOOD MONEY: A Guide to Profitable Social Investing for the '90s* (W. W. Norton & Company, 1991).

| LEFT BUSINESS OBSERVER

250 West Eighty-fifth Street
New York, N.Y. 10024
(212) 874-4020
$20 or $50 a year

Left Business Observer (*LBO*) is a monthly newsletter covering economics, politics, and their interactions around the world. In addition to its regular coverage of financial markets and central banks, recent articles have covered:

- The evolving North American Free Trade Area—what the U.S.–Canada free trade deal has meant for Canada so far, and what bringing Mexico into the picture might mean for its two northern neighbors.
- The military's role in the political economy, from 1945 through Vietnam to the Reagan buildup and onward to today.
- The fiscal crises of the states—why thirty-two states, scores of cities, and the federal government find themselves drowning in red ink—with alternatives to the logic of fiscal austerity.
- Sweden—social democracy in crisis?
- Why are the U.S. corporate and private sectors so deeply in debt?

Other areas of *LBO* obsession include: the World Bank, the International Monetary Fund, and the development establishment; the polarization of living standards; race, sex, and economic power; campaign finance; the media industry; financial crises (the savings and loans, the insurance business, the banks, government-sponsored enterprises, and all of the other varieties of socialism for the rich); and the shortcomings of official economic categories and statistics—all reported with a clarity, wit, and concern for the broader culture not usually associated with the dismal science.

Subscriptions

	One Year	Two Years
Individuals	$20	$35
Institutions and high-income subscribers	$50	$85

Money managers and other investment professionals are asked to subscribe at the higher rates.

Editor and Publisher

Doug Henwood got his B.A. in English from Yale in 1975 and did graduate work in English at the University of Virginia from 1976 to 1979. Besides his work at *LBO*, Henwood is a contributing editor of *The Nation* and a regular commentator on economic affairs on radio station WBAI in New York. He writes frequently for the *Village Voice*, mainly on the political economy of New York City. He also is writing a primer on Wall Street for Verso.

| RESPONSIVE INVESTING NEWS

One Liberty Square
Twelfth Floor
Boston, Mass. 02109
(617) 426-5450
(617) 422-0162 (fax)
$395 a year, twenty-six issues plus two semiannual reviews

Responsive Investing News (RIN) is a new biweekly newsletter published by Boston-based Investment Management Publications. *RIN* was established in April 1991 as an independent publication with the sole purpose of covering socially targeted investment issues. It is strictly a journalistic enterprise; *RIN*'s parent company does not sell financial services or advocate a political or social agenda.

The publication was developed by the staff of *Investment Management Weekly*, Investment Management's flagship newsletter, to meet the need for timely, accurate, and objective information about the ways in which investment capital is being used to promote social ends.

Coverage includes the full range of what traditionally is referred to as social investment issues, such as shareholder activism, environmental concerns, the promotion of local and regional economic development through the use of pension fund assets, and the growing use of minority- and women-owned businesses by institutional investors. *RIN* subscribers also receive timely reports on the increased political pressure placed on the investment process by local, state, and federal legislators and of the growing demands to use investment capital to promote political and economic change overseas.

The Staff

Editor and publisher Richard Chimberg formed Boston-based Investment Management Publications in November 1987 and began publishing *Investment Management Weekly* in January 1988. Before starting his publishing company, Chimberg was Boston bureau chief for *Trillion* magazine. Earlier he served as head of press relations for SEI's Funds Evaluation Division (now Capital Resources) and at the Merrill Lynch Consulting Group. Chimberg spent nearly two years at *Institutional Investor's Money Management Letter* as senior editor. He began his journalism career in 1978 in Washington, D.C., where he covered national and international affairs for a radio news bureau, served as a reporter on the staff of columnist Jack Anderson, and then spent two years with a newsletter company, editing energy and environmental publications.

Managing editor James Melton joined Investment Management Publications in 1988 as senior editor of *Investment Management Weekly*, a post he retains. Melton took the lead in developing the *RIN* concept. Before joining Investment Management, he covered the local business community in southeastern Michigan for *Crain's Detroit Business*, a weekly published by Crain Communications. He has a B.A. in journalism from Wayne State University.

Contributing editor Emily S. Martinez joined Investment Management in February 1991 and also serves as associate editor of *Investment Management Weekly*. She worked as news reporter and feature writer at theWaterbury, Connecticut, *Republican-American* from 1988 to 1990 and as staff writer and copy editor at the Orange, Texas, *Leader* from 1987 to 1988. Prior to coming to Investment Management Publications, Emily worked as a free-lance journalist in Boston. A Houston native, she is a 1987 graduate of the University of Houston with a degree in journalism and a minor in political science.

London correspondent Edward Russell-Walling covers social investment issues in the United Kingdom and in continental Europe for *RIN* in addition to reporting for *Investment Management Weekly*.

RIN also employs free-lance journalists, both domestic and international, to cover social investing.

I THE SOCIALLY RESPONSIBLE FINANCIAL PLANNING GUIDE

Co-op America
2100 M Street NW, Suite 403
Washington, D.C. 20063
$5

The Socially Responsible Financial Planning Guide is a beginner's handbook for planning for long-term financial security while using investments to support one's political and social values. It contains a brief introduction to the principles of social investing, simple, step-by-step directions for creating a personal financial plan, worksheets for developing a plan, and an annotated list of resources—from banks and credit unions to mutual funds and credit cards—for socially concerned investors.

The 1991 edition contains an expanded section on retirement planning; advice for evaluating your local bank against social criteria (community reinvestment, minority outreach); and an at-a-glance chart comparing the features of current social and environmental investment funds.

The *Guide* is published by Co-op America, a national membership association promoting a sustainable economy and educating businesses and consumers on how to align buying and investing habits with values of peace, cooperation, and environmental protection.

Project Director
Cindy Mitlo, editor of *Co-op America Quarterly*, has been writing for Co-op America's magazine and catalog since 1986.

I THOUGHTFUL INVESTING

P.O. Box 3546
Plant City, Fla. 33564
(813) 752-5419
$29 a year

Thoughtful Investing: Managing Money with Heart, Soul and Mind is a bimonthly newsletter created for the American Christian community. It is a publication of the Institute for Thoughtful Investing, an informal group of investment, legal, accounting, and stewardship professionals interested in applying the Judeo-Christian ethic to our handling of modern wealth. While vitally interested in the area of ethical or socially responsible investment, *Thoughtful Investing* also seeks to explore the charitable giving strategies and just economic structures that can move our handling of money into the moral and even spiritual realms.

The publication addresses four modern problems in handling resources in the spirit of ancient scriptures.

First, this is the first generation of our society that is not primarily the agricultural type of society addressed in scriptures and religious tradition. The wealth of our newly urbanized society is more and more not the land and herds viewed by our ancestors from Abraham to our parents. It is "technological wealth" merely reflected on computerized bank statements and securities statements. We at *Thoughtful Investing* feel that our ancient principles, which spoke of prudence, compassion for the poor, and ethical business practices, must be translated to speak to these new forms of wealth.

Second, our modern wealth typically separates the ownership of wealth from the management of wealth. We may "own" our certificates of deposit, mutual funds, stocks, and so on, but a manager— often distanced from those people his or her decisions affect—will decide how our money is used. While American religion has long focused on the potential conflicts in capitalism between owners and labor, the excesses of the 1980s seem to be shifting the focus toward the activities of management. We try to provide a bit of insight into how bankers, mutual fund managers, government officials, and others manage the wealth entrusted to their stewardship.

Third, *Thoughtful Investing* attempts to shed light on the common Wall Street perception that including ethical criteria, such as social screening, in the investment selection process reduces rates of return. We firmly believe that the excesses of the 1980s clearly demonstrate that it was the areas of greatest ethical concern that cost investors most dearly—either directly through capital losses or indirectly through governmental bail-out programs.

Fourth, we sense that the religious community as a whole has not made the advancements in stewardship theology necessary to deal with these new realities. While there is exciting work being done by a small group of North American stewardship theologians, the people in the pews of America actually feel a bit of apprehension at the mention of stewardship. Most perceive "stewardship" as a synonym for "fund-raising." That is a most unfortunate distortion of the powerful metaphor found in scriptures that spoke to the dangers of excessive debt, speculation, environmental destruction, greed, and so forth. The future funding needs of our moral institutions will be better met if both clergy and laity can recapture the sense that stewardship is a holistic approach to Christian life, not simply fund-raising. And stewardship in that sense is the historically proven answer to America's economic troubles.

A prominent theologian once remarked that theology is simply grasping the Bible in one hand and a newspaper in the other. *Thoughtful Investing* often relates spiritual principles to modern financial concerns. While we do our best to avoid "proof-texting," we do share our constant fascination with biblical passages, such as Deuteronomy 28:43–44, which says that foreigners will have money to lend to us and we will have none to lend to them if we lose our moral bearings!

Our theology is important to us, but it is probably of less importance to our readers. While we help them develop a basic understanding of why we all should use money in ethical, productive ways, we dedicate most of *Thoughtful Investing* to the straightforward, practical means of doing so.

We provide insight into the community development banks and credit unions; socially screened mutual funds, stocks, and bonds; money managers of the ethical investing movement; charitable giving techniques that allow one to manage capital gains and estate taxes while financing a better world; international relief activities that address human suffering in our nation and abroad; and the work of others who share our views—and sometimes those who do not! And we always try to address these topics in language the nonprofessional investor or the theologian can understand.

Overall, we try to approach a serious subject with humility and occasional humor. We believe that a true understanding of stewardship indicates that we should use all of our resources available for charity, investment, and consumption, that things might be "on earth as they are in heaven." We believe that our efforts at such stewardship are one of the clearest possible reflections of our spirituality.

Publisher

Gary Moore is the author of *The Thoughtful Christian's Guide to Investing* (Zondervan, 1991), which has been widely endorsed by top Wall Street leaders, stewardship leaders, and the financial and religious press. He is a member of the Social Investment Forum, the Council on Economic Priorities, and the Christian Stewardship Association. He is a volunteer planned giving officer for the Episcopal Church and lives with his wife and son in Plant City, Florida.

PART FOUR

THE SOCIAL

PORTFOLIO

The investment adviser or money manager responsible for a social portfolio must address both the client's financial requirements and his or her social screens and objectives. As Amy Domini points out, the portfolio management principles are the same in terms of financial objectives. Risk, return, and the client's unique circumstances dictate the constraints on the manager's strategies.

For many years an argument has raged about the compatibility of the duties imposed by law on fiduciaries with responsibility for charity or pension moneys and social investing. Bill McKeown surveys this complicated area and suggests questions fiduciaries will want answered before making investment decisions.

Measuring the performance of socially screened portfolios has been another major area of controversy. Carsten Henningsen sorts out the steps a manager should take in evaluating an individual client's portfolio. One of the key questions has been whether the general stock market indexes, like the Standard & Poor's 500, are appropriate benchmarks for measuring the performance of screened portfolios. The Domini 400 Social Index is the first U.S. index to gauge the performance of a broad market, multiscreened common stock portfolio. Lloyd Kurtz, Steve Lydenberg, and Peter Kinder describe this new measurement tool and what it has shown.

One of the first efforts to measure the effect of social screening on performance was the Boston South Africa Free (SAFE) Index. Richard Wilk recounts the history of this pioneering effort and what the index has shown. Another early effort at performance measurement was the *GOOD MONEY* averages. The editors of that newsletter describe their results. Jeff Teper takes a different approach to the performance measurement question by asking what social investment's costs are.

Most social investors will have stocks and bonds in their portfolios, either from direct investments in the market or through mutual funds. We asked three experts to discuss the aspects of stocks and bonds that social investment professionals must uniquely master: Patrick McVeigh on stocks, Diane Keefe on corporate and U.S. bonds, and Cheryl Smith on municipal bonds.

Mutual funds have played—and will continue to play—a key role in the development of social investing in the United States. We invited the fifty-five or so funds that screen on one or more social issues to submit descriptions of themselves and their performance. We were particularly interested in the philosophies that guided them and in how they expressed and implemented their screens. For ease of comparison, we divided the respondents into categories: stock and bond funds and fund families open to all investors; environmental and sector funds; money market funds; South Africa–free gold funds; and funds with restrictions on who may invest. (The names and addresses of the funds that did not respond are included in the directory of mutual funds and similar vehicles in appendix B.)

With the twentieth anniversary of the first Earth Day came a number of funds that described themselves as "environmental." Controversies immediately arose over what the term meant. Peter Camejo revisits the dispute and looks at the performance of these funds during their first years.

Stocks, bonds, and mutual funds are not the only vehicles that can appear in a social portfolio. Michael Kieschnick described the criteria an investor must consider in venture capital investment and identifies the groups in the field now. Beate Becker looks at the role of direct or community investments in social portfolios. They deserve a much more prominent role, she argues.

PRINCIPLES OF PORTFOLIO MANAGEMENT

Amy L. Domini Loring, Wolcott & Coolidge

Portfolio management is the management of assets for the benefit of an individual or institution. Portfolio management is based on the ability of the manager to achieve a client's objectives, within various restraints. Although these can be achieved through a variety of methods, all well-managed portfolios are built on an initial careful review of risk, return, and considerations unique to the client.

Wall Street professionals closely relate risk and return. The highest returns can come from successful high-risk investments. Reducing risk can reduce return but has the benefit of reducing the uncertainty of returns. Thus, the first step in portfolio management, whether the client is an individual or an institution, is to assess the level of risk a client can tolerate and the level of return the client requires.

| ASSESSING THE RISK AND THE RETURN

Turning first to the risk side of the equation, the portfolio manager must ask herself what this client's other resources are. Is this client constitutionally capable of accepting a substantial level of risk, or is he or she likely to lose sleep when the stock market drops? Is this institution more dependent on its principal's surviving than it is on its growing? These questions allow the portfolio manager to assign a client a fairly specific degree of risk tolerance.

Simultaneously the portfolio manager must assess the client's need for return. Is the need for current income high, or is there less of a demand for current income and therefore a greater ability to meet long-term objectives for asset growth? The questions crucial to assessing return objectives are: Does this client have other financial resources? How old is the client? How dependent is the client on income generated by this particular portfolio? Frequently the best way to assess the need for return is to ask the client how little they can tolerate receiving in current income from the portfolio. If, for instance, the portfolio is a trust to benefit the yet unborn grandchildren of a wealthy man, no demand for current income exists.

| CLIENT OBJECTIVES

Once risk and return levels have been assessed, the portfolio manager must sum up the client's objectives. They might be "to achieve high total return over the next eighteen years, so that at that time, high levels of income can be derived from the portfolio." Or perhaps it is "to achieve the highest possible return while generating current income of not less than 5 percent."

Once the objectives have been set, special considerations must be assessed. These include an understanding of the client's liquidity needs; how long the time horizon for the portfolio is; what taxes the client pays; what legal constraints the portfolio must operate within; and other considerations, such as social constraints. Each consideration will modify the portfolio manager's strategy for balancing risk and return to meet the client's stated needs. The portfolio manager who does not address each consideration runs the risk of failing.

Liquidity
Liquidity is an important concern. To what extent might the investor need to liquidate the portfolio and realize value? If, for instance, the investment goal is high total return until the client is ready to buy a second home in the country, the ability to sell all assets, while not immediate, is strong. Stocks, bonds, and money market accounts would provide adequate liquidity to such a client. Limited partnership interests in low-income housing would not.

If an institution has the capacity to (and wishes to be ready to) draw on up to 10 percent of its portfolio value for meeting world relief emergencies, then at least 10 percent of that portfolio ought to be kept in cash equivalents, such as a money market fund.

Timing
The timing of potential withdrawals affects liquidity. Another time-related factor is the expected duration of the portfolio. If the portfolio

is a pension fund for the benefit of employees of a corporation, then a long time horizon is in most cases appropriate to meet its objectives. On the other hand, a trust that is to be distributed to beneficiaries in two years has a considerably shorter time horizon.

Taxes

Taxes are a primary consideration in deciding how a portfolio is managed. Taxes can take away as much as 28 percent of the gain in a given stock. For most individuals it does not make sense to sell a stock merely because it will not resume its upward trend for three to six months. A non-tax-paying institution, such as a pension plan or the endowment of a school, does not pay taxes on capital gains. Managers therefore have a greater ability to sell holdings and to manage more aggressively.

Legal Considerations

Legal considerations bear on the management of a portfolio. For instance, a private trust must be managed within the standards of prudence described as the "prudent person rule." Under this standard, the acid test is whether other "prudent experts" were making similar investment decisions. Legal considerations could restrain a trustee interested in purchasing the stock of a small, start-up health food chain. Certain types of portfolios—corporate pension funds, for example—are restricted by extensive legal standards.

Special Considerations

Among the special considerations that a manager might need to make is the integration of social or ethical criteria into the investment decision-making process. For most practitioners of social investing, this means ascertaining just how a client would define social investing. Such a special consideration might be, "I want to keep 20 percent of my holdings in high-impact, direct investments in community development without giving up any liquidity." Social considerations can range from the simple to the complex.

| INVESTMENT APPROACH

Risk, return, liquidity, time, taxes, legal considerations, and special considerations combine to give the portfolio manager a clear understanding of the client's needs and of the restraints on meeting those needs. This exercise sets the framework within which the manager's specific program will be implemented.

Top-Down Management

Different managers have differing investment approaches, but the most common are "top down" and "bottom up." Top-down management can be described as starting with the economy and ending with the stock. Generally speaking, the top-down asset allocation model begins with an assessment of economic conditions, probably worldwide. From this assessment, an ideal allocation—given the client's already established objectives and constraints—can be set.

This allocation will be among such asset classes as stocks, bonds, and money market funds. The management of the bond portfolio often depends on the broad economic picture. In other words, the client's tax situation may have led to investments in municipal bonds, but the quality of those bonds and the number of years until they mature could depend on the manager's economic outlook.

On the stock side, allocations may be made among sectors of the economy. Different managers will favor different sectors, and each sector will have its own financial characteristics. For instance, natural resource firms tend to respond to commodity prices. A manager might make asset allocations here based on her view of the direction certain commodity prices are likely to take. Banks and insurance companies are sensitive to interest rates. A manager's view of the direction interest rates are likely to move would be crucial in asset allocation for these industries. Finally, the top-down manager will select the best stocks within each sector.

Bottom-Up Management

Bottom-up management generally does not take into account the economy in setting asset allocation. Rather, it is set exclusively on the basis of the client's objectives and constraints.

A manager selects particular bonds and stocks because they promise the best returns. For instance, rather than allocating 10 percent of the stock portfolio to utilities and then trying to find the best utility, the bottom-up manager would choose the best twenty stocks. If none happens to be a utility, that would not be a concern. A bottom-up approach achieves diversification by purchasing a number of stocks, not by seeking stocks in different sectors of the economy. Many individual investors take a bottom-up approach without knowing it.

| CONCLUSION

Social investors' portfolios frequently hold stocks, bonds, money market accounts, and alternative investments. Some hold art, real estate, limited partnerships, venture capital, or other less-traditional investments. But no matter what the final selections, the proper assessment of the client's objectives and constraints and the proper application of an investment methodology to meet these go a long way toward protecting the client and achieving his or her goals.

CHAPTER 23

FIDUCIARY DUTIES
AND SOCIAL INVESTMENTS

W. B. McKeown

Ed. Note: *The following discussion addresses in summary fashion legal is-*
sues regarding fiduciary responsibility that may be expected to arise when
the governing board of an institution is considering social investments. It is
not intended as, nor can it be considered, a substitute for legal advice. A
decision to make socially responsible investments should be made only after
adequate review of the facts and the applicable law—with the assistance of
legal counsel—and careful consideration, adequately documented, by the
governing board or other fiduciaries responsible. Notwithstanding this ca-
veat, many institutions may make such investments.

If an individual were to choose to invest her personal assets in a
socially screened portfolio or in community development investments, some might applaud her for being socially responsible while
others might call her foolish for mixing up economics and ethics.
No one would say the law would or should prevent her from making
these investments.

Opinion is likely to be to the contrary when "fiduciary duties"
are involved. At best, people are unsure whether fiduciaries are legally permitted to invest in a socially responsible way. Many people
think a fiduciary cannot take into account social criteria when making investment decisions.

However, the law is not as simple as that. First, investing in a
socially responsible manner may involve either greater emphasis on
investment or a greater emphasis on social responsibility. Second,
there are different types of fiduciaries, and their duties vary. Either

---

W. B. McKeown is counsel to Patterson, Belknap, Webb & Tyler in New York.
A member of the New York bar, he received his J.D. from the Columbia University School of Law. He also holds an M.Div. from Union Theological Seminary
and a B.A. from Harvard College.

the first or the second criterion may determine whether a particular fiduciary may make a particular investment.

This discussion identifies issues to consider and suggests how to go about analyzing those issues in order to determine whether or not a fiduciary, or a body of fiduciaries, may make a socially responsible investment.

I WHAT IS A SOCIALLY RESPONSIBLE INVESTMENT?

A socially responsible investment is an investment made with an intent to take into account the impact of the investment on the society in which the investment is made. Economic return may or may not be the principal goal of the investment. In fact, socially responsible investments generally should be distinguished on that basis from each other, as well as from ordinary investments. The prospective investor should first ask, What is the purpose of this socially responsible investment? Is it to make money while acting in a socially responsible way? Or is it to apply investment assets to further a social goal? Any particular social investment may offer to some degree an opportunity to achieve both, but the prospective investor should be clear at the outset as to the purpose of the investment decision.

Investing primarily for economic gain and secondarily to promote social good or to avoid social harm is one widely accepted model for socially responsible investing. A good example is applying a social responsibility screen to an investment portfolio. Another example would be placing funds in a market rate–insured bank deposit earmarked to support community development. Either would be different from a community development investment.

Community development investments are made primarily to support or encourage community development. The economic benefit to the investor is normally secondary. The same goal might be pursued by a direct grant or a program expenditure, but for a variety of reasons, some form of investment, usually a loan, is thought to be more effective or appropriate. A community development investment might be described as a grant that is to be paid back and that may produce income. Such an investment is quite different from an investment made principally for economic return. Community development investments are known as "program-related investments" to managers of private foundations. Others call them "alternative investments" or "mission-related investments."

| WHO IS A FIDUCIARY?

A fiduciary is one who is recognized under the law as occupying a position of confidence and trust, to act for others, usually with respect to property. Persons in many positions are fiduciaries, including trustees of private trusts and corporate directors.[1] Thus, fiduciary issues normally come up when one is dealing with someone else's money.

Typically the issue of socially responsible investments arises for the governing board of an institution that has some investment assets, that is, in the common meaning, some "endowment." Investment assets and endowment are discussed further later. Most such institutions fall into the broad general category of "charitable institutions." In this context, "charity" means more than improving economic conditions or the "relief of poverty" in traditional terms. Charitable purposes are public purposes, such as education, research, religion, and other activities for the public good. Thus, charitable institutions include: schools and educational entities of all types; social service organizations; private foundations (grant-making organizations, such as the Ford Foundation, that do not usually carry out programs themselves); churches; arts organizations; and entities organized to carry out functions otherwise likely to be performed by government.

Pension and similar employee benefit funds are a distinct group of institutions. Their purposes are not the public benefit, but the private economic benefit of their recipients and beneficiaries. The fiduciary standards for such funds are different from those for charities, because their purposes are different. Moreover, special regulatory schemes often apply to pension and benefit funds.

| POSING THE QUESTION

When asked to make a socially responsible investment, board members may ask, Are we permitted under the law to authorize the institution to make this investment? They commonly wonder whether the "prudent man rule" would permit the proposed investment. There is no single answer.

In order to answer this question, the governing board, with the advice of its counsel, should consider the following issues:

- What is the purpose of the proposed investment—economic return achieved in a socially responsible manner, or the use of investment assets to accomplish a social goal? Is the proposed investment at market rates and terms? How do the projected return and risk compare with the projected return and risk of other investments?
- What is the responsibility of the governing board? What type of legal entity would make the investment? What is the applicable standard of care?
- What are the purposes of the entity? Does the proposed investment decision further those purposes?
- What, if any, are the restrictions on the use of the fund proposed to be invested? Are they purpose restrictions or investment restrictions? Is the fund a legal endowment or not? Does the proposed investment fall within the purpose restrictions on the use of the fund?

The restrictions, if any, on the assets in question have an important bearing on whether fiduciaries may make a particular investment. Generally there are two types of restriction on institutional funds: purpose restrictions (for example, the fund may be used only for scholarships) and investment restrictions (for example, only income may be expended). Fiduciaries must always pay close attention to the exact terms of any gift.

State law governs on most issues. In some states, whether the institution is a not-for-profit corporation or a charitable trust may make a difference. Whether the institution is a pension fund or a charity will make a difference. If the institution is a private foundation, the effect of the private foundation rules of the Internal Revenue Code should be examined. If the assets in question belong to a pension or similar fund, special federal or state statutes and regulations are very likely to apply.

Standards of Care for Investment Decisions

Two standards of care for investment decisions are widely recognized: the "prudent man rule" and the "business judgment rule."

PRUDENT MAN RULE. The traditional "prudent man rule" was developed by the courts in the law of private trusts. The *Restatement of Trusts* defines a trustee's investment obligations as "a duty to the

beneficiary ... to make such investments and only such investments as a prudent man would make of his own property having in
view the preservation of the estate and the amount and regularity
of the income to be derived."[2] The rule has traditionally been interpreted as requiring a trustee to promote two objectives: receiving
a reasonable amount of income and preserving the trust property.[3]
The emphasis on preservation of trust property and adequate return
developed from the purpose of the private trust—the management
of a body of assets for the benefit of private persons and the eventual
distribution of that property to those persons. Traditionally, the
investment decisions of trustees of private trusts have been subject
to strict court supervision.

The purpose of a pension or similar benefit fund is like the purpose
of a trust. Accordingly, the standard of care for fiduciaries of such
funds is similar to the standard for a private trustee. Pension fiduciaries' investment decisions may not be subject to court scrutiny
as strict as that traditionally applied to trustees, since existing regulatory schemes may have altered the impact of the "prudent man
rule."

BUSINESS JUDGMENT RULE. The courts developed the "business judgment rule" in the law of business corporations. Under this rule the
governing board of such a corporation is free to use its own business
judgment as to the use of corporate assets, as long as the board acts
in what it believes to be the corporation's best interests. Under this
standard of care, in the absence of bad faith, fraud, or conflict of
interest, the courts will not question the decisions, including investment decisions, of boards of directors.

"The modern trend is to apply corporate rather than trust principles in determining the liability of the directors of charitable corporations, because their functions are virtually indistinguishable
from those of their 'pure' corporate counterparts."[4] Thus, the standard of care applicable to the board of a charitable corporation is
like that for the board of a business corporation.

Moreover, actions taken to carry out charitable purposes may not
be subject to review as readily as are actions taken for commercial
or business purposes. The New York Court of Appeals stated in
Morris v. Scribner,

As another court said so well, "[i]f the courts will not interfere with
the determination of the board of directors of a business corporation

honestly and fairly arrived at, it [sic] certainly should not do so in the case of a religious corporation, the conduct of whose temporal affairs is often actuated by considerations which cannot be measured in terms of dollars and cents."[5]

In *Morris* the organization was a church, but the principle applies to other charitable entities as well.

The Uniform Management of Institutional Funds Act is an important statutory development of the last twenty years.[6] The Uniform Act is intended to make the law in this area consistent from state to state. As of 1990 it had been adopted in thirty-four states, including California, Massachusetts, New York, and the District of Columbia. The Uniform Act states that the standard of care for investment decisions by governing boards of charitable institutions is business judgment.

> In the administration of the powers to appropriate appreciation, to make and retain investments, and to delegate investment management of institutional funds, members of a governing board shall exercise ordinary business care and prudence under the facts and circumstances prevailing at the time of the action or decision. In so doing they shall consider long and short term needs of the institution in carrying out its educational, religious, charitable, or other eleemosynary purposes, its present and anticipated financial requirements, expected total return on its investments, price level trends, and general economic conditions.[7]

Some states modified the Uniform Act language so the state statute must be reviewed. However, even if the language has been modified, the rule itself usually has not been altered.

The business judgment standard has been broadly established for charities through wide adoption of the Uniform Act. By its terms the Uniform Act applies to all organizations organized and operated for charitable purposes, whether incorporated or not.[8] Thus it applies to charitable trusts as well as charitable corporations. However, it bears repeating that the law of a particular state may treat the governing board of a charitable trust differently from the governing board of a charitable corporation.

To summarize, the traditional "prudent man rule" or some variant thereof applies to the trustee of a private trust and probably to the governing board of a pension fund, but not to the governing board of a charity, at least in those states where the Uniform Act is in effect. It also should be noted, however, that at least a few institutions may function both as pension funds and as charities. Thus, different standards would apply to the same governing board, depending on which body of assets is the subject of the proposed investment decision.

The governing board of a charity is required to be prudent, but its responsibilities are different from those of a private trustee or a pension fiduciary. The latter are to conserve assets and generate income for the support of individuals. In contrast, a charity's governing board must manage the assets of an ongoing enterprise in order to carry out its particular charitable purposes. In managing the charity, the governing board is expected to exercise its judgment to decide the appropriate uses of those assets to fulfill those purposes. Those decisions include investment decisions.

| SOCIALLY RESPONSIBLE INVESTMENTS FOR ECONOMIC GAIN

May a board of fiduciaries apply social criteria or a social screen in investing assets for economic gain? The fiduciaries should analyze the issues outlined above and consult counsel, but such investments ought to be permissible.

The primary purpose and expected effect of such an investment is an investment return, just as it is with any ordinary investment. The closer the range of risk and return is to the range of risk and return of conventional investments, the more the socially screened investment is the economic equivalent of an unscreened investment and the less there should be any issue.

As indicated earlier, different standards may govern the decisions of different fiduciaries. Fiduciaries subject to the business judgment rule (such as charity boards) should be able to decide to invest in a screened investment with a return that is less than, or a risk that is greater than, that of an unscreened investment. Accepting a lower return or a higher risk could be justified if the use of the screen, in the board's judgment, would enhance the accomplishment of the organization's purposes or would prevent the organization from making investments that were counter to its purposes. For example, the board of an organization devoted to furthering racial justice could justify, on the basis of its purposes, choosing to invest in a company with an outstanding equal employment opportunity policy, even if its dividend rate were less than that of another company without such a policy and record. Consumers Union, an organization well known for testing consumer products, has decided to invest only in government securities and not in any company, regardless of the return, in order to avoid any appearance of conflict of interest.

Even in the case of fiduciaries with the duties of or close to those of a private trustee (for example, pension boards), where the purpose of the investment is the economic benefit of individuals, the fiduciary should be able to apply a social screen. If fiduciaries determine within their reasonable judgment that either of two investments has the same potential risk and reward, then they should be able to decide between the investments based on additional social responsibility factors. That is, if two investments are economically equal but the second, in addition, avoids some social harm or promotes some social good, the fiduciaries should be able to choose the second over the first for that reason. Fiduciaries, even trustees, are not required to ignore social consequences that may follow from their investment decisions.[9]

Moreover, social responsibility judgments are not made in an economic vacuum; nor are economic judgments made in a social vacuum. The social policies of companies whose securities may be included in a portfolio affect not only the society in which they operate, but their own economic performance. For example, a company that ignores its legal responsibility to protect the environment may have lower short-term costs but longer-term risk of loss due to litigation or environmental cleanup costs. In other words, fiduciaries may conclude for economic reasons that corporate "good citizens" are better investments than corporate "bad citizens," even if investing in the "bad citizens" may, in the short term, yield a higher return to the investor.

I USING INVESTMENT ASSETS TO ACHIEVE SOCIAL GOALS

As a general rule, pension fund fiduciaries may not use investment assets of the pension funds under their management to further social goals, because they are required to pursue one purpose only: the economic benefit of plan participants and beneficiaries. Nevertheless, regulators may allow some room for pension fund fiduciaries to move in this area. However, the questions are complex and require consideration by experienced counsel. Accordingly, the discussion that follows applies only to charities.

Investment Assets

Boards of charitable institutions may misunderstand the nature of the funds under their management. Boards frequently refer to all such funds as "endowment." But not all of the institutional funds called endowment are true endowments. True endowments are funds with respect to which *the donor* has required that the principal not be consumed but be invested to produce return.

Investment assets may be board designated rather than donor designated. Funds functioning as endowment, or board-designated investment funds, are funds that the governing board rather than a donor has directed to be retained and invested. The governing board has the right at any time to change its mind and spend the principal of such funds.

The Uniform Act defines "endowment fund" as an institutional fund "not wholly expendable by the institution on a current basis under the terms of the applicable gift instrument."[10]

Section 3 of the Uniform Act also provides a rule of construction for determining when an endowment fund permits the expenditure of appreciation. In general, appreciation in an endowment fund may be expended unless the donor has stated explicitly that such appreciation is not to be expended. The fact that the donor stated that it was to be an endowment or that the principal was to be preserved would not generally prevent the expenditure of appreciation. Thus, even if a fund is a true endowment, in most states—and certainly where the Uniform Act has been adopted—a charitable institution may spend at least some of the net appreciation in the value of its endowment.

Indeed, throughout the United States, the "total return" concept has been widely adopted as an investment policy by boards of charitable institutions. "Total return" simply means spending part of appreciation as well as spending income in the traditional sense. Thus, if the total return policy is acceptable, so is spending appreciation.

Spending Versus Investing

Any fiduciary making investment decisions should realize that "if you can spend it, you can invest it." If a charitable fund is not an endowment in the sense identified above, an institution can, consistent with whatever use restrictions apply, spend 100 percent of its principal for program purposes. If the institution can do that, it also can invest 100 percent of the principal in program—that is,

community development or other socially responsible investments—*without regard* for the return or safety of the investment.
Any investment is less "risky" than an outright expenditure. That
is, if a governing board at one time chose to invest assets to support
its program, the board could later decide to expend *or* to invest part
or all of those assets to further that program.

As indicated above, even if a fund is a true endowment, an institution should be able to spend at least some of the net appreciation. For example, under its version of the Uniform Act,
Massachusetts provides a "safe harbor." Boards may authorize expenditure annually of an amount equal to up to 7 percent of the fair
market value of an endowment fund for the purposes of the fund.[11]
If an institution can spend up to 7 percent of the fair market value
of an endowment fund for community development purposes, that
institution can invest that 7 percent in community development
investments. In New York the governing board must preserve the
"historic dollar value" of an endowment fund.[12] Basically that means
preserve the original dollar value of the endowment gift, without
regard to the effects of inflation.[13] This is the same rule as that stated
in the Uniform Act.[14] Under this rule *all* appreciation in value of
the endowment gift may be expended for the purposes of the endowment. Accordingly, all appreciation may be invested for the purposes of the fund. (Whether it would be prudent to do so in a given
set of circumstances is another question.)

Under the Massachusetts rule or the New York (Uniform Act)
rule, a governing board responsible for an endowment fund created
some time ago may have considerable accumulated appreciation that
may lawfully be spent for the purposes of a fund, if the governing
board decides it is appropriate to do so. Thus, the amount of an
endowment fund available for community development investing
may be far more than appears at first glance.

As indicated above, if the fund is not an endowment but is board
designated for investing, *all* of it may be invested for community
development, consistent with the purposes of the fund and the institution.

Private Foundation Rules
Private foundations are subject to special rules under the Internal
Revenue Code (IRC). However, these should pose no problem for
"community development" or "program-related" investments.

The IRC imposes an excise tax on any "private foundation" that invests funds so as "to jeopardize the carrying out of any of its exempt purposes." However, Congress specifically provided that a program-related investment (that is, a community development investment) is not a jeopardizing investment.[15] Thus, a community development investment made by a private foundation will not cause the foundation to be subject to tax. The IRS does give examples of acceptable investments.[16] These include: low-interest or interest-free loans to needy students, high-risk investments in nonprofit low-income housing projects, and low-interest loans to small businesses owned by members of economically disadvantaged groups. In addition, although the proposal did not involve a private foundation, the Internal Revenue Service has approved an unemployment benefits trust that made investments to further social purposes. The IRS noted that such investments would "not be considered a diversion of the corpus or income from the trust's purposes even though such investments yield a rate of return lower than that in the current market."[17]

| CONCLUSION

Governing boards of charities considering socially responsible investments should carefully review their organization's investment funds to determine which, if any, are true endowments and which are not. Investment assets that are not endowments may be spent for program purposes, consistent with the purposes of the institution and the gift. Therefore, they may be invested in community development investments consistent with such purposes. Even if a fund is a true endowment, at least some part of the appreciation in value of the fund may be spent for program purposes. Accordingly, that fraction should be able to be invested in community development investments, again consistent with the purposes of the gift and the institution.

NOTES

1. See Scott (Fratcher), *The Law of Trusts*, 4th ed. §495 (1989).
2. *Restatement of Trusts* (Second), §227.
3. See Scott, *Law of Trusts*, §227.3.
4. *Stern v. Lucy Webb Hayes Nat'l Train. School for Deaconesses & Missionaries*, 381 F.Supp. 1003, 1013 (D.D.C. 1974) (construing D.C. law).

5. *Morris v. Scribner*, 69 N.Y. 2d 418, 425 (1987).
6. 7A Uniform Laws Annotated 705 (West 1985).
7. Uniform Management of Institutional Funds Act (UMIFA), §6.
8. UMIFA, §1(1).
9. See Scott, *Law of Trusts*, §227.17.
10. UMIFA, §1(3).
11. For the full statement, see section 2 of the Massachusetts Act, quoted in the annotations to UMIFA, §2.
12. New York Not-for-Profit Corporation Law, §513(c).
13. See *Estate of McKenna*, 451 N.Y.S.2d 617 (Sur. 1982).
14. UMIFA, §2.
15. IRC §4944(c).
16. Treas. reg., §53.4944-3(b).
17. Rev. rul., 70-536, 1970-2 C.B. 120.

MEASURING PERFORMANCE OF A SOCIAL PORTFOLIO

Carsten Henningsen Progressive Securities
Financial Services

Almost as certain as my morning cup of tea, I expect a phone call from Carl, one of my longtime clients, soon after I arrive at my desk on Monday. Primed with hot tips from the weekend edition of "Wall Street Week," Carl can't wait to get in on any investments touted as top performers on the program. Carl and I then spend a few minutes discussing why these hot investments may or may not be good performers for his particular portfolio.

| USING THE RIGHT BENCHMARKS

Depending on who you're talking to—or listening to—performance can be measured in vastly different ways. Many investors do not gauge performance properly because they lack the right definitions. Finding an accurate definition of performance for a particular investor or portfolio is critical for accurate measurement. Use of numbers alone leads to faulty conclusions and poor decisions.

Today most investors and portfolio managers use historical performance figures as the primary consideration in measuring performance. This quantitative approach provides useful information

Carsten Henningsen is founder and president of Progressive Securities Financial Services, a registered investment adviser specializing in socially and environmentally responsible investing. Henningsen is also a director of the Social Investment Forum and a founder of its Pacific Northwest chapter. His work has been recognized by the *Wall Street Journal, Money, USA Today,* and the Associated Press.

about the past, but measuring performance is much more than a numbers game. Qualitative characteristics, such as investment style and consistency, are also a key part of the measurement process. Both quantitative and qualitative factors must be weighed for accurate measurement.

The goal in measuring quantitative performance is to compare apples to apples, not apples to oranges. In addition, you need to know the difference between a Granny Smith and a Golden Delicious. In other words, if an equity portfolio is composed of stocks that closely resemble the Standard & Poor's 500 Index or the Domini Social Index in size or capitalization, industry type, risk, and so on, then these indices may provide the benchmark for quantitative measurement of performance.

But what if your equity portfolio contains companies smaller than those represented in the Standard & Poor's Index? Perhaps the Russell 2000 Index, which features smaller companies, is a more appropriate benchmark.

The composition of your portfolio may include asset classes other than stocks, such as bonds, cash, community development, precious metals, or even real estate. The various asset classes in your portfolio determine the asset mix, which also defines the type of apple you have.

One of my clients, Sally, has shares in Pax World Fund. Sally, who can be very excitable, recently came into my office beaming as she explained that her investment in Pax World Fund had outperformed the market by more than 10 percent during 1990. Since I was in the middle of writing this chapter, I didn't hesitate to ask Sally what she meant by "the market." She was referring to the Dow Jones Industrial Average (DJIA) Index of thirty large companies.

While Sally was correct in her statement, and I shared her excitement, I explained that she was comparing apples to oranges. Pax World Fund is a balanced mutual fund with an asset mix of cash, stocks, and bonds. One reason why Pax World Fund outperformed the DJIA Index is that Pax was only partially invested in stocks during a year when stocks, as measured by the DJIA Index, were down more than 4 percent.

Sally also has some of her individual retirement account (IRA) investment in Calvert-Ariel Growth Fund. She was not pleased to learn that this mutual fund had finished 1990 down more than 16 percent. Once again, to compare apples to apples, Sally had to understand that Calvert-Ariel Growth Fund consists of investments in smaller companies and is more likely to mirror the Russell 2000 Index, which declined more than 21 percent in 1990.

I FACTORING IN THE INVESTOR'S OBJECTIVES

Finding appropriate benchmarks or indices based on the composition of your portfolio is only part of the story. The investor's objectives or preferences also help define what type of apple or orange you are trying to measure. Each investor has different needs for income or growth, risk tolerance, and other factors. In other words, some investors care about eating well, while others care about sleeping well.

As a portfolio manager I am often called on as a consultant to measure the performance of another financial manager. Usually I am presented with a few years' worth of account statements and asked to calculate the performance. The figures that arise from these sessions are useless without knowing the investor's objectives and preferences.

The following are three steps I use to measure performance.

1. Determine the investor's objectives and preferences.
   a. Return requirements—for example, how much income or growth is needed?
   b. Social criteria—specifically, what are the investor's social criteria?
   c. Risk tolerance—for example, how much risk is appropriate or comfortable?
   d. Liquidity needs—for example, how much liquid cash should be held in reserve?
   e. Time horizon—for example, how long can the portfolio be invested?
   f. Regulatory and legal considerations—is the portfolio a personal pension, in a trust, et cetera, that may have certain regulatory or legal parameters?
   g. Tax considerations—what is the tax basis of the securities or other assets in the portfolio? What type of tax situation is the investor in?
   h. Unique needs, circumstances, and preferences—for example, does the investor have a family stock that is being held for sentimental value?

2. Analyze the portfolio composition with respect to the objectives and preferences listed above.
   a. Asset mix or allocation—what percentage of the portfolio is in equity, fixed income, cash community development, real estate, and so on?
   b. Industry allocation—for example, what percentage of the portfolio is in the auto industry versus utilities, and so on?
   c. Diversification—what percentage of the portfolio does each company represent?
   d. Risk—for example, what is the overall risk of the portfolio as determined by financial quality and volatility of the securities?
3. Compare actual performance against an index or indices that are appropriate based on the portfolio composition.

Once we have compared apples to apples and determined that the portfolio's past performance was either above or below the appropriate index or indixes, what does this tell us about our next step?

I THE VALUE OF PAST PERFORMANCE

We have all heard that past performance is no guarantee of future results. But is past performance even an indicator of the future? Past performance is seductive, because the numbers appear to promote one of the only known facts about portfolio management.

A recent study by RCB International of 144 equity portfolios in the last decade managed by 135 firms asked whether identifying above-average managers in the first half of the 1980s would have been useful in selecting an above-average manager for the second half of the decade. Of the top 20 percent of managers in the period 1980 to 1984, fewer than half were in the top 50 percent during 1985 to 1989!

Past performance records may be more helpful in understanding qualitative factors, such as investment style, consistency, and volatility, rather than indicating future quantitative performance. Of course, these qualitative factors, which are equal to, if not more important than, quantitative past performance, are difficult and time-consuming to measure.

One of the major problems with measuring quantitative performance is that many investors, especially pension plan sponsors, tend to make judgments and changes based on too short a time horizon.

Results should not be viewed as significant by the investor or manager until a reasonable period of time has elapsed—such as a market cycle for equities or an interest-rate cycle for fixed-income securities. As a general rule, an investor should look at about five years of performance.

In summary, there are many individual and institutional investors who place a great deal of emphasis on historical quantitative performance. Evaluating and measuring performance is not just a numbers game. When measuring performance it is critical to take both qualitative and quantitative factors as well as the investor's characteristics into consideration.

Coincidentally, a number of portfolio managers I interviewed for this chapter had the same conclusion, which was that in the end, performance is measured by one thing: the investor's level of satisfaction with the manager. Depending on the investor, qualitative factors, such as trust, integrity, and social responsibility, can be equally or even more important than quantitative results in measuring satisfaction.

RESOURCES

Maginn, John L., and Donald L. Tuttle. 1983. *Managing Investment Portfolios, a Dynamic Process.* Boston: Warren, Gorham & Lamont.

Interviews with portfolios managers: Brian Beitner, C.F.A., Scudder, Stevens & Clark; Melanie Burnett, C.F.A., Franklin Research & Development; Jerome Dodson, Parnassus Financial Management; Don Falvey, Franklin Management; John Harrington, Harrington Investments; Hugh Kelly, Socially Responsible Investment Group; Darrell Reeck, C.F.A., Progressive Securities Financial Services; John Schultz, Ethical Investments.

CHAPTER 25

THE DOMINI SOCIAL INDEX: A NEW BENCHMARK FOR SOCIAL INVESTORS

Lloyd Kurtz, Steven D. Lydenberg,
and **Peter D. Kinder** Kinder, Lydenberg,
Domini & Company

In March of 1988, we undertook the development of an index of common stocks that passed commonly applied social screens. Our objectives were to:

- create a market basket of primarily large capitalization issuers of common stocks that pass multiple social screens;
- establish a broad market index that managers could use to gauge the performance of screened portfolios; and
- develop historical data for evaluating the effects of social screening of portfolios.

On May 1, 1990, Kinder, Lydenberg, Domini & Company (KDL) launched the Domini 400 Social Index (DSI). The DSI is the first broad market, common stock index in the United States* designed to measure the performance of portfolios subject to multiple social constraints.

A complete evaluation of the DSI will require several years of live performance and the experience of a full market cycle. Nonetheless,

---

Lloyd Kurtz has been senior research analyst at Kinder, Lydenberg, Domini & Company since its founding in 1989. He holds a B.A. in English and psychology from Vassar College and an M.B.A. in international finance from Babson College.

*The authors wish to express their great debt to State Street Bank, and especially Lynn Symanski, for their help in formulating the DSI and their encouragement. However, the views expressed here are solely the authors'.

the results to date provide some interesting preliminary insights. In its first year (through April 30, 1991), the total return on the DSI was 19.56 percent. During the same twelve months, the total return on the Standard & Poor's 500 was 17.59 percent. In backtests from 1986, the nominal and risk-adjusted returns of the DSI also exceeded those of the S & P. The live performance and the backtests indicate a DSI tracking error of approximately 2 percent.*

Until the DSI's launch, there was no generally accepted definition of the market of securities social investors could buy. It follows that there was no means of measuring social portfolios' performance in context.

This chapter describes the construction of the DSI, its performance, our analysis of its financial characteristics, and its implications for the debate on the risk-reward characteristics of socially responsible investing.

| THE DOMINI SOCIAL INDEX SCREENS

KLD used multiple social screens to reflect the concerns of social investors. These screens have historically been applied by social investors, and they are likely to continue to be used.

Defining the market required the creation of a common social investor. Which social screens—nonfinancial criteria applied in the investment decision-making process—would this hypothetical person want, and how rigorously would he or she want them applied? The answers to those questions would define our screens and ultimately our universe of stocks.

The common social investor does not represent all social investors; nor is it a static construct. Some social investors apply only one or two screens, not the twelve we use. Others screen on issues we do not, such as animal rights. And still others apply looser or stricter screens of one type or another than we do. Social screens evolve over time. To illustrate the evolution of the DSI's screens, we have, where necessary, set out both the screen as defined in 1988

---

*Tracking error is based on the correlation of the two portfolios. The correlation statistic (r) of the DSI versus the S & P is .989. This yields an r-squared of .98, which means that 98 percent of the variance in the DSI was accounted for by changes in the S & P.

(the "stated screen")* and the screens as applied for the year ending June 30, 1991.

Primary Screens

We divide our screens into "primary" and "secondary" screens. Primary screens are primary because they came first historically and because they are the first screens we apply. These screens include:

military contracting   nuclear power
alcohol and tobacco   South Africa
gambling

These screens are purely negative. For example, most social investors do not want to hold utilities that own any nuclear generating capacity. Northern States Power would not qualify for these portfolios, even though it has a good record operating nuclear plants.

MILITARY CONTRACTING. *Stated screen:* the DSI excludes companies that derive more than 4 percent of revenues from the sale of military weapons. *Applied screen:* the DSI eliminates all companies that derive either (1) more than $10 million in sales from nuclear weapons–related contracts, (2) more than 2 percent of gross revenues from prime contracts for military weapons or weapons-related materials, or (3) more than 4 percent of gross revenues from sales that may have military weapons–related uses or origins.

This screen is intended to exclude companies that derive a substantial portion of their income from weapons-related work or from a meaningful involvement in nuclear armaments production. It does not eliminate companies contracting with the Department of Defense for nonweapons supplies—from toothpaste to fuel oil.

This screen eliminates companies that are primarily defense contractors, such as McDonnell Douglas, Grumman, and Loral. Also eliminated are large firms whose primary work is not military—and whose military sales may be less than 4 percent of total revenue—but who are among the largest contractors for nuclear weapons.

*The screens were stated at the levels described below because at an early stage of the index's development we were certain that we could conform to them. They were then incorporated in the prospectus for the Domini Social Index Trust. We have not revised the stated screen definitions in order to remain consistent with the prospectus.

International Business Machines, General Motors, and General Electric fall into this category.

Companies subcontracting substantial amounts of military work are screened out. For example, Interface, an Alabama firm specializing in computer-aided design, had no unclassified weapons-related prime contracts in 1989, but the firm did substantial subcontracting on weapons design. We eliminated it.

The DSI's weapons screen passes certain classes of companies with substantial military contracts. For instance, oil companies selling fuel to the Department of Defense can generate hundreds of millions of dollars in gross revenues. Nonetheless, we do not consider them sufficiently related to actual work on weapons to warrant exclusion.

We classify a significant number of companies as "borderline." We monitor these companies closely, both those that are eliminated and those that are included. Some examples of borderline companies will show how we apply our military weapons screen.

Raychem has virtually no prime contracts with the Department of Defense but derives around 8 percent of gross revenues from sales of electrical connectors, insulation, and communications equipment to weapons manufacturers. The volume of these sales was important in our decision to eliminate Raychem, but the fact that these products originally had been designed for weapons systems determined the matter. It must be noted that Raychem is emphasizing commercial applications of these products and is reducing its military work.

After considerable thought, we allowed in semiconductor firms, even though most semiconductor manufacturers have commercial, off-the-shelf products that end up in weapons systems. The aerospace industry can account for 10 to 20 percent of these companies' sales. But again we felt that a distinction had to be made between selling off-the-shelf components to a weapons manufacturer and actually manufacturing for weapons.

AMP manufactures electrical connectors. Approximately 5 percent of its worldwide sales end up in weapons systems. But of this amount, only half comes from connectors designed for weapons systems. Because this volume of sales fell under our 4 percent limit, because the item itself resembles a commodity product in many ways, and because the firm has a high reputation for quality and service, we decided to include it in the DSI.

In fiscal year 1989 Digital Equipment Corporation (DEC) had

weapons-related contracts totaling $20 million (.12 percent of sales). Like Hewlett-Packard, DEC asserts that its military sales consist of off-the-shelf computers not tailored to military specifications. However, DEC has long sold computers to Raytheon for use in weapons systems. While it is very much on the borderline of the DSI's military screen, DEC's strong performance in employee relations, community involvement, the environment, and women and minorities convinced us to include the firm.

Zurn Industries designs small power plants and manufactures waste-water equipment—both products with environmental positives. In 1987 Zurn announced that it intended to seek military markets for its clutches and crankshaft lines. It won a contract to develop specialized components for the Osprey vertical takeoff and landing aircraft. In 1990 Zurn announced that it had ended active pursuit of these markets, although it would honor past commitments. With the fate of the Osprey still in doubt, Zurn's long-term involvement in this market is difficult to project, but it will not be more than 4 percent of sales in the foreseeable future. On that basis, we added Zurn to the DSI in May 1991.

ALCOHOL AND TOBACCO. *Stated screen:* the DSI excludes companies that derive more than 4 percent of gross revenues from the manufacture of tobacco products or alcoholic beverages. *Applied screen:* the DSI excludes companies that derive any revenues from the manufacture of tobacco products or alcoholic beverages.

Most companies involved in these two highly profitable businesses derive well over 4 percent of sales from these products. While tobacco firms, such as Philip Morris and American Brands, are diversifying their product lines, their revenues remain overwhelmingly tied to tobacco. Of the one thousand largest U.S. companies in market capitalization, there is no company whose participation in one of these businesses might be considered insignificant.

Historically social investors in the United States have applied their tobacco and alcohol screens to manufacturers but not retailers. Following this precedent allows the DSI to include retail stores for which sales of tobacco products or alcoholic beverages might account for over 4 percent of sales—as is the case with Walgreens, for example.* We would exclude a retail firm that depended totally on

---

*It is worth noting that some U.K. unit investment trusts do eliminate tobacco vendors. We do not see a movement in that direction in the United States.

alcohol or tobacco sales, although we have not encountered that situation.

The DSI's screen does not expressly cover subcontractors. Kimberly-Clark has nine factories around the world that make cigarette paper. Calgon Carbon sells activated carbon to cigarette manufacturers for filters. Shorewood Packaging makes packaging for cigarettes. Are these firms involved in the manufacture of tobacco products? We have included both Calgon Carbon and Shorewood Packaging on the DSI because these products are not specific to the manufacture of tobacco products. Kimberly-Clark's commitment to manufacturing cigarette papers probably crosses the border into manufacturing. However, we did not have to consider Kimberly-Clark's tobacco activities, because its equity interests in South Africa had already disqualified it.

GAMBLING. *Stated screen:* the DSI excludes companies that derive more than 4 percent of gross revenues from gambling enterprises. *Applied screen:* the DSI excludes companies that derive any revenues from gambling enterprises or more than 4 percent of gross revenues from gambling equipment, paraphernalia, or services.

As with tobacco and alcohol, gambling does not attract dabblers. Firms running casinos, such as Promus or Hilton Hotels, derive well over 4 percent of revenues—and an even larger percentage of profits—from their gambling enterprises. We also excluded Control Data because it provides computer services to state lotteries. In 1989 that business accounted for 5.5 percent of the company's sales.

NUCLEAR POWER. *Stated screen:* the DSI excludes companies that operate or own directly more than 4 percent interest in a nuclear power plant or that derive more than 4 percent of gross revenues from sales to the nuclear power industry. *Applied screen:* the DSI excludes companies that either (1) operate nuclear power plants, (2) own directly an interest in a nuclear power plant, (3) derive any income from the nuclear fuel cycle, or (4) derive more than 4 percent of gross revenues from sales to the nuclear power industry.

We have excluded all electric utilities taking any power from nuclear fission—other than purchases from a grid—from the DSI. PacifiCorp's interest in a nuclear plant entitles it to less than 1 percent of its total capacity. Although this is well below our stated threshold, we did not include the firm in the DSI.

In this country, utilities have not placed new orders for nuclear power plants since the mid-1970s, and few are under construction. However, we exclude companies that are involved in the sale of nuclear power plants abroad, such as Westinghouse. We also eliminate companies that mine or refine uranium for the nuclear power industry. For example, IMC Fertilizer extracts uranium oxide from the wastes it generates in phosphate fertilizer production.

One borderline company is Ionics, a water purification company—and a favorite of many environmental investors. A subsidiary does specialized welding on the containment vessels for the reactors of nuclear power plants and nuclear-powered submarines. These contracts—well under 4 percent of revenues, although the company will not give more precise figures—are below our threshold. This work does not involve the nuclear fuel cycle but does affect the reactors. Were it not for the environmental positives of the rest of Ionics' business, it would not be in the DSI.

SOUTH AFRICA. The DSI excludes companies that have operations in South Africa or, through licensing or sales arrangement, are widely perceived to aid in the enforcement of the apartheid system.

Hundreds of billions of dollars in assets in the pension funds of public and private institutions now operate under South Africa restrictions. These restrictions range from disallowing only companies with operations in South Africa that have not signed the Statement of Principles (formerly the Sullivan Principles), which eliminates a handful of firms, to disallowing all firms with any formal sales or distribution agreements with South Africa, which eliminates more than one hundred of the S & P 500.

The DSI's screen falls in the middle of this spectrum. We exclude all companies with equity interests in South Africa, as well as firms (such as Hewlett-Packard and Ford) that have withdrawn from South Africa but maintain service or sales agreements in industries crucial to the central government. We also eliminated three banks—Citibank, Chase Manhattan, and Manufacturers Hanover—whose policies on outstanding loans to South Africa appear to support the government. However, the screen admits companies that have withdrawn but maintain sales agreements strictly for health or consumer products, such as Merck and Coca-Cola.

Secondary Screens
Our secondary screens (so called because they are applied after the purely exclusionary primary screens) track corporate responses to

the demands of today's society. It is in these areas that the future of social investing and of the corporate social responsibility movement lie. The secondary screens are:

environment	corporate citizenship
product quality and attitude	employee relations
toward consumers	women and minorities

Unlike our primary screens, our secondary screens rarely—*very* rarely—yield yes-or-no answers. The secondary screens demand qualitative evaluations of what a company is doing to make society better and to preserve the environment. They have both positive and negative applications, and therefore the screening process in these areas is more complicated—as are the screens themselves.

ENVIRONMENTAL PERFORMANCE. The DSI seeks to include companies that have taken notably positive environmental initiatives. It excludes companies whose environmental performance falls below generally accepted standards.*

Environmental screening can take a "best of the industry" approach that includes companies that in absolute terms would not pass. Usually investment managers favor this approach to avoid eliminating whole industries, such as chemicals, from an investment universe. However, this method is not acceptable among social investors with environmental concerns. Therefore, we have taken an absolute approach. For this section, we have chosen several issues that illustrate our environmental screening.

None of these choices was easy. We started from the premise that the typical social investor was not likely to exclude all environmentally sensitive companies. From that point, we chose those companies that lacked overwhelming environmental negatives and had a history of positive initiatives.

The marketing or use of environmentally benign fuels is one

---

*By "generally accepted standards," we do not necessarily mean regulatory standards. Many firms in the United States are in strict regulatory compliance but still emit substantial amounts of toxic chemicals that could harm human health. For example, according to Citizens Fund research based on 1989 Environmental Protection Agency (EPA) data, 3M Corporation legally released sixty-seven million pounds of toxic chemicals known to cause or suspected of causing birth defects. (It should be noted that 3M has made considerable efforts to reduce hazardous wastes in its production processes.)

positive for which we screen. Natural gas has clear advantages over coal or oil, although it has some drawbacks. Consequently, the DSI includes a number of natural gas distribution, exploration, and production firms. We particularly sought natural gas companies with positives in other social areas. The Chicago-based distribution company Peoples Energy, for example, has a notable record of promoting minorities and supporting minority-owned businesses.

Companies making substantial use of recycled materials as a primary source of raw materials for their manufacturing processes have been included, as have companies whose primary business involves cleaning up of the environment. Wellman is a fabric and fiber company whose principal raw material is recycled plastic soda bottles. Nucor is a minimill steel company that uses scrap for its primary raw material. Groundwater Technology specializes in the remediation of contaminated groundwater. However, simply being in the "cleanup" business does not qualify a company. Neither Waste Management nor Browning-Ferris is in the DSI.

We look for companies whose top management has taken an aggressively positive environmental stance. The chief executive officer of TJ International, a building products company headquartered in Boise, Idaho, has spoken out on a number of environmental issues, criticizing the practices of other forest products companies.

We exclude companies with major environmental problems. We eliminated companies with recent environmental disasters, such as Exxon, or those facing huge cleanups of hazardous wastes, such as Panhandle Eastern, with its $700 million estimated bill for remediation of PCB contamination at its Texas Eastern subsidiary. We also screened out the largest emitters of potentially carcinogenic chemicals, although these emissions are legal under current law. The large chemical companies, such as American Cyanamid and DuPont, are high on these lists.

Environmental screening always poses the question, How far do we go? Without much difficulty, one could construct an environmental screen that would eliminate not just industries, such as chemicals and forest products, but all extraction and processing companies—mining, metal refining, oil exploration, forest products, chemicals, and specialty chemicals.

The DSI takes a middle course. It holds none of the major international oil companies (for example, Exxon, Mobil, Chevron, and Texaco) and none of the major commodity chemical firms (such as DuPont, Dow Chemical, Monsanto, and Rohm and Haas). We included natural gas exploration companies (for example, Anadarko Petroleum, Apache, Enron, and Consolidated Natural Gas) and a handful of domestic oils.

Atlantic Richfield, which is in the DSI, has a history of environmental controversies in Alaska, where it is, among other things, one of the primary owners of the Alaska pipeline. ARCO is very much on the borderline for inclusion in the DSI. If not for the company's strong record on employee relations, women and minorities, and community involvement and its history of commitment to social ideals, we would have excluded it. Amoco presents similar positives and negatives, although its recent environmental negatives stand out less glaringly than ARCO's.*

Specialty chemical companies are smaller than the commodity chemical firms and face lesser environmental challenges—in part because they simply are less involved in the dirty business of transforming raw materials into chemical products. These firms also are generally not involved in the agricultural chemicals business, which entails substantial environmental risks. Some, such as Betz Labs and Calgon Carbon, specialize in products used in cleaning up the environment. But here, too, we find companies on the borderline. Take ARCO Chemical: in July 1990 an explosion killed seventeen workers at its Channelview, Texas, plant. The firm also faces environmental problems typical of its industry. Yet its history indicates a relatively high level of commitment to community and to the environment, which argued in its favor.

Similarly difficult choices arise in the pulp and paper industry. We have excluded for environmental and other reasons most of the largest companies (such as International Paper, Louisiana-Pacific, and Georgia-Pacific). But we have retained Consolidated Papers, with its history of positive union relations, and Scott Paper, because of its current initiatives with labor and its well-thought-out community programs.

PRODUCT QUALITY AND ATTITUDE TOWARD CONSUMERS. The DSI evaluates the quality of a company's products and its attitudes with regard to consumer issues. There are many definitions of quality (one business school professor we know has collected more than a dozen). The DSI's screens focus primarily on two: a high ratio of

---

*Despite its good record recently, the unsatisfactory and insensitive resolution of the *Amoco Cadiz* spill in 1978 remains deeply troubling.

value to cost, and the continuous improvement paradigm introduced by W. Edwards Deming.

As a general rule, social investors require that a corporation should strive for excellence in its products and services and pay close attention to the needs of its customers. For that reason, we seek companies that provide basic products or services at reasonable prices to the economically disadvantaged. Dollar General is a low-margin department store chain dedicated to serving low- and moderate-income households. Federal National Mortgage Association, formerly a federal agency and now a private corporation, provides liquidity in the home mortgage market with an emphasis on affordable housing for low-income families.

We look for firms that have long-standing product quality programs in the manufacturing and customer service areas, accompanied by a commitment from top management to the continuous training of employees. Winners of the Malcolm Baldrige Award (for example, Federal Express, which defined the overnight delivery service) have demonstrated the seriousness of their commitments. Some smaller firms (such as Huffy Corporation, which makes bicycles) have broad-ranging quality programs in place as well. Since so many companies claim excellence in quality, however, distinguishing one program from another can be difficult.

Our product screen excludes companies that are the subject of major product liability cases, particularly those alleging life-threatening consequences. Pfizer faces substantial damage claims over an allegedly faulty heart valve it manufactured. Beverley Enterprises, operator of a nationwide chain of nursing homes, has settled regulators' charges of poor patient care in several states. Former manufacturers of asbestos-based products, including W. R. Grace and Owens-Corning Fiberglas, must resolve tens of thousands of cases seeking hundreds of millions of dollars in damages. We excluded these companies even though they have not marketed asbestos products for years.

Companies with liabilities resulting from a single event are examples of borderline companies in the product area. For example, Delta Air Lines faces potential liabilities from the deaths of passengers in a 1988 crash. American Stores is resolving millions of dollars' worth of claims resulting from the 1985 sales of salmonella-contaminated milk by one of its chains. We monitor companies like these for indications that these events might result from practices within the firms. But under this screen, we tend to exclude companies with liabilities resulting from ongoing practices rather than from isolated events.

We do not often exclude companies solely on the basis of questionable marketing practices, although this is an issue we monitor closely. The marketing issue that we view most seriously—and the one that has received the greatest attention within the social investment world—relates to marketing practices for infant formula sales in developing nations.

CORPORATE CITIZENSHIP. The DSI considers a company's corporate citizenship, which includes the company's record of philanthropic activities and its interactions with the communities it affects.

We include companies that make notably generous or innovative contributions to the communities in which they operate. Because social investors, among others, have followed charitable giving and community involvement for some time, the information necessary to identify excellent programs is readily available. We look for companies with outstanding records in three areas.

First, we look for generosity in giving cash, which we define as contributing more than 1.5 percent of pretax earnings. Minneapolis is a city whose culture has promoted generous giving among corporations headquartered there. They range from large firms, such as Dayton Hudson, to smaller companies, such as Graco, both of which have taken a prominent role in promoting giving in the corporate world.

Second, we look for corporations that take an innovative approach to their giving. ARCO has emphasized support for women, minorities, and the economically disadvantaged. A committee with employees drawn from all levels of the company allocates Polaroid's giving, with a large number of smaller grants going to community organizations.

Third, we look for companies that have participated in public-private partnerships, particularly those addressing the problems of affordable housing and homelessness. In Chicago, Amoco has taken a leading role in the Local Initiative Support Corporation's Chicago Equity Fund and in supporting the South Shore Bank and other neighborhood development organizations. We also have included companies that have chosen to site plants in inner-city neighborhoods. During the early 1980s in Boston, both Wang and Digital Equipment built facilities in such neighborhoods.

We have excluded few companies explicitly because of poor corporate citizenship. Cases exceptional enough to be cause for concern are usually clear-cut. We would exclude companies with major community disasters from which unresolved repercussions still can be felt—such as the Bhopal disaster for which Union Carbide's Indian subsidiary was responsible. We also look closely at those rare situations where basic relations between a city and a corporation have deteriorated dramatically. Bethlehem Steel and the city of Lackawanna, New York, for example, have a recent history of exceptionally poor relations.

Wal-Mart, which is in the DSI, is a borderline company. Its policy of siting highly competitive outlets in small towns can cause the deterioration of the town's base of small enterprises. Academic studies disagree on the magnitude of the effect, but Wal-Mart does change the economies of the small towns near which it locates.[1] In some ways these effects are balanced by the benefits Wal-Mart provides, especially a broader range of goods at lower prices.

The banking industry is particularly difficult to evaluate. Banks' obligations to the communities they serve are greater than those of corporations in other industries. Careful research at a local level is necessary to determine the nature and effectiveness of these commitments. We have excluded from the DSI banks whose community lending practices have been questioned by federal agencies.

EMPLOYEE RELATIONS. The DSI takes into account a company's relations with its employees. This screen includes a company's record on labor matters; its commitment to workplace safety; its commitment to equal employment opportunity; the breadth, quality, and innovativeness of its employee benefits programs; and its commitment to provide employees with a meaningful participation in company profits, either through stock purchase or profit-sharing plans.

We have included companies with cash profit-sharing policies, such as J. P. Morgan, Longs Drugs, Commerce Clearing House, and New England Business Services. Some companies in financial difficulties have granted less-meaningful cash profit-sharing plans to workers in exchange for wage concessions, while others have made profit sharing a part of retirement plans. We are less enthusiastic about these types of arrangements.

We also include companies—such as Herman Miller, the office furniture firm, and Apogee Enterprises, the construction products firm—that encourage employee involvement through Scanlon-type productivity improvement plans that share cash gains with workers, or through sharing of financial information and decision making with employees down the line. We tend not to give much credit to suggestion programs and quality circles that are not systematic in their approach to worker involvement.

Because of substantial corporate tax advantages and management's desire to make hostile takeovers more difficult, employee stock ownership plans (ESOPs) have become almost commonplace within the past five years. We look for ESOPs established in conjunction with other employee empowerment programs with the clear intention of creating ownership (including voting rights), in contrast to those set up to make top management secure from takeovers.

We include companies that have strong labor records and exclude those with a long history of poor relations with organized labor, particularly those in heavily unionized industries. For the most part, we have eliminated corporations with the most dramatically bad relations—such as Louisiana-Pacific, Brown & Sharpe, and Pittston. In 1991 the dispute between unions at Nordstrom's posed difficulties for us. The company's actions alienated the firm's unionized work force. If Nordstrom's had not had a long history of positive employee relations, and no substantial recent changes in management or management style, we might well have removed it from the DSI. Given these past positives, however, we have chosen to monitor the situation, hoping that a positive resolution will emerge.

WOMEN AND MINORITIES. We include companies that have made notable progress in the promotion of women and minorities. Among the DSI companies with exceptional records are Xerox, which is one of a few large corporations to have an African-American in the line of potential succession to chief executive officer, and Golden West Financial, the West Coast savings and loan. Among smaller companies on the DSI that have women serving as chief executive officers are Lillian Vernon, the mail-order catalog company, and Spec's Music, the music and video retail chain in Florida.

We have implemented our women and minorities screen as an affirmative one. We have not excluded companies that have failed to promote women and minorities to top management or to boards of directors. We have, however, excluded companies (for example,

USX and Andrew Corporation, the electronics company) that have a recent record of substantial fines or settlements in affirmative action cases.

COMPANY SELECTION

Once the screens were in place, choosing companies for the index began. This process can best be thought of in terms of the three stages:

1. Application of screens to the Standard & Poor's 500;
2. Identification of smaller-capitalization companies with superior social responsibility records;
3. Selection of large-capitalization companies with strong social records in underrepresented industries.

The Standard & Poor's 500

The S & P 500 represents the market of stocks traded on U.S. exchanges from which most investors—institutions and individuals—buy. In particular, the S & P is generally thought of as representing the market available to institutions, organizations that manage funds on behalf of others and are therefore, by law, subject to fiduciary obligations. These institutions include pension funds, insurance companies, college endowments, and the like. While the S & P *represents* the institutional market, it does not define it. Most institutions have universes several times larger than the S & P.*

We decided to keep on the DSI any S & P company that did not fail any of our screens. Because of their inherent capacity to influence the social investment movement, we wanted large institutions and the major wire houses to use our index.

We had suspected that the S & P was not an appropriate benchmark for a social portfolio. And indeed, 243 of the 500 failed at least one of our screens. We kept the remaining 257, even though many of them were simply neutral.

As table 25-1 indicates, the DSI includes seven of the S & P's top twenty companies, beginning with number five, Wal-Mart. The thirteen that failed our screens did so for different reasons: Exxon, en-

*The principles guiding the construction of the S & P 500 are discussed later.

TABLE 25-1

TOP TWENTY FIRMS, MARKET CAPITALIZATION
April 30, 1991

S & P 500	DSI 400
Exxon	Wal-Mart Stores
General Electric	Merck & Company
Philip Morris	Coca-Cola Company
IBM	Procter & Gamble
Wal-Mart Stores	Amoco Corporation
Royal Dutch Petroleum	BellSouth Corporation
Merck & Company	Pepsico
AT & T	Atlantic Richfield
Bristol-Myers Squibb	Bell Atlantic
Coca-Cola Company	American International Group
Johnson & Johnson	Ameritech
Procter & Gamble	Pacific Telesis
EI duPont de Nemours	Southwestern Bell
Mobil Corporation	Walt Disney
Chevron Corporation	US West Communications
Amoco Corporation	Sears Roebuck
GTE Corporation	Federal National Mortgage Association
BellSouth Corporation	McDonald's
Pepsico	American Express
Eli Lilly & Company	Microsoft

vironment and employee relations; IBM, weapons; GE, weapons; Philip Morris, tobacco; Royal Dutch, environment; and so forth.

Smaller Companies
After the S & P companies, we sought companies with the strongest social positives—Johnson Products, Isco, Ben & Jerry's, and the like. The forty companies in this category appear mainly among the smallest in the DSI and affect performance negligibly.

Remainder
For our last one hundred stocks, we looked for large capitalization companies in underrepresented industries. These companies not only could not fail any of our screens, they also had to have an outstanding record in at least one area we screened.

Composition of the DSI Market Basket
We attempted to develop a portfolio diversified across all of the industries open to social investors and to weight industry groups

according to their importance to the social investment market. The social screening and selection process created an index with capitalization characteristics that are substantially different from those of the S & P. As already noted, the screens eliminated a number of the largest firms. See table 25-1.

We sought to address imbalances in industry distribution by identifying acceptable substitute companies. For example, to compensate for underrepresentation in pharmaceuticals (most drug companies have equity interests in South Africa), KLD added companies from the health care industry. Similarly, we added specialty chemical companies to the DSI to compensate for the exclusion of the large commodity chemical firms.

In spite of these efforts, several industry segments (particularly oil companies and electric utilities) are underrepresented in the DSI relative to the S & P 500. These are listed in table 25-2. Conversely, several industries are overrepresented relative to the S & P. The screens favored firms whose business franchises depend on public goodwill, such as retail stores. The screens also favored banks and telephone companies, which are regulated and therefore benefit economically from good citizenship records. The industries that are most overrepresented in the DSI are listed in table 25-3.

In addition to the industry rebalancing process, KLD also assessed candidate firms' financial health. KLD excluded companies deemed likely to face bankruptcy within three years. We made this determination based on bond ratings, financial strength assessments from inde-

---

TABLE 25-2

**UNDERWEIGHTED INDUSTRIES IN THE DSI 400
(RELATIVE TO THE S & P)
As a Percent of Portfolio Market Value**

International oil	−4.49%
Electric utilities	−3.88
Drugs, medicine	−2.78
Aerospace	−2.03
Producers of goods	−1.72
Tobacco	−1.64
Foreign petroleum reserves	−1.52
Motor vehicles	−1.27
Chemicals	−1.21
Liquor	−1.15

SOURCE: Barra Portfolio Optimization, March 28, 1991.

TABLE 25-3

OVERWEIGHTED INDUSTRIES IN THE DSI 400
(RELATIVE TO THE S & P)
As a Percent of Portfolio Market Value

Nonfood retail	6.45%
Insurance (excluding life)	2.55
Services	2.25
Banks	2.11
Beverages	1.82
Miscellaneous finance	1.59
Publishing	1.40
Hotels, restaurants	1.21
Apparel, textiles	1.08
Life insurance	1.00

SOURCE: Barra Portfolio Optimization, March 28, 1991.

pendent rating agencies, and Altman's Z-score model.* We also excluded companies whose stock was trading at less than $5 per share.

Comparative Financial Characteristics

In general the DSI's financial characteristics closely resemble those of the S & P. (See table 25-4.)

As of October 31, 1991, the DSI's weighted-average market capitalization was less than the S & P 500's: $13.7 billion versus $20.4 billion.† By comparison, the S & P Midcap Index had a weighted-average market capitalization of $1.5 billion.

The DSI has a historical beta of 1.07 when compared with the S & P 500. Beta is a measurement of the volatility of portfolio performance relative to the market (which the S & P represents in this instance). A higher beta means that a portfolio is likely to outperform when the market is going up and underperform when the market is going down.

The stocks in the DSI have a lower dividend yield than those in the S & P. Thus, DSI stocks must appreciate in price at a greater

*We used the model introduced in Altman, "Financial Ratios, Discriminant Analysis and the Prediction of Corporate Bankruptcy," *Journal of Finance*, September 1968. Altman has developed models with better predictive power, but this one has the virtue of using only inputs that are available from the subject's public financial statements.

†This is a market-weighted average capitalization, which some analysts have criticized as double-counting. The median capitalization of the DSI is approximately half that of the S & P.

TABLE 25-4

COMPARATIVE FINANCIAL CHARACTERISTICS

	DSI 400	*S & P 500*
Average cap	$12,124mm	$19,277mm
Asset growth*	11.78%	11.51%
Earnings growth*	16.35%	15.91%
P/E ratio	19.43%	18.95%
Yield	2.45%	3.1%
Dividend payout*	37.63%	46.73%
Price/book ratio	2.36	2.17
Return on equity*	21.3%	19.39%
Beta*	1.07	1.00
%NYSE	89.82%	96.73%
%NASDAQ	8.71%	2.78%
%other	1.47%	0.49%

SOURCE: Kinder, Lydenberg, Domini & Co., October 31, 1991.

* Trailing five-year averages.

rate than those in the S & P if the DSI's total return is to match or exceed the S & P's, since the S & P stocks pay higher dividends.

The DSI's slightly higher debt-equity ratio enables it to achieve a higher return on equity than the S & P, despite roughly equal underlying earning power.

| FINANCIAL PERFORMANCE OF THE DSI

The DSI went live on May 1, 1990. In the following pages we first examine its one-year performance. We then couple that with back-testing to suggest what the index's performance might be under a broader spectrum of market conditions.

First-Year Performance

In June 1990 we performed an analysis of the likely sensitivity of the DSI to political and economic events. Based on that study, we developed a worst-case scenario for the DSI, which included:

- A recession, which would hurt retail firms;
- Rising oil prices, which would help big oil companies;
- A war, which would benefit weapons manufacturers;
- A financial crisis, which would hurt banks and insurance companies.

All of these things happened in the DSI's first twelve months. At the end of those twelve months, however, the DSI had outperformed the S & P. (See figure 25-1.)

The DSI's first year (May 1, 1990, through April 30, 1991) saw a sharp market downturn—from July, when the Dow Jones Industrial Average (DJIA) touched 3000, to October, when it bottomed at just below 2400. And it saw an equally sharp rise—to 3000 in April 1991 after the war with Iraq. The S & P showed a similar pattern, although it was off more for 1990 than the DJIA.

In July 1990 the DSI underperformed the S & P by 2.33 percent, the greatest monthly disparity of the year between the two indexes. The S & P's performance was attributable to the sharp rise in the stocks of international oil companies, an industry in which the DSI is underrepresented. By contrast, in March 1991 the DSI outperformed the S & P by 2.15 percent. The DSI benefited from the generally strong performance of smaller capitalization stocks versus larger capitalization stocks at that time.

As figure 25-1 shows, the DSI outperformed the S & P in up markets and underperformed in down markets. This pattern is consistent with the DSI's higher beta.

The Backtests

State Street Asset Management* has conducted backtests on the DSI covering the period from January 1, 1986, through April 30, 1990. The results of these backtests can be combined with the DSI's live results to provide a better picture of the DSI's probable performance across a broad spectrum of market conditions (see figure 25-2). Backtests are great predictors of the past and cannot be regarded as portents of future performance.

AGAINST THE S & P. The results of the backtest are consistent with the live performance of the DSI versus the S & P. In bull markets the DSI outperformed the S & P 500. In the 1987 crash, it underperformed. This pattern persisted even when the up or down movement of the two indexes was relatively small. Figure 25-3 illustrates this effect by plotting relative returns against a ninety-degree line.

*State Street Bank & Trust, of which State Street Asset Management is a subsidiary, is the portfolio manager of the Domini Social Index Trust, a tracking fund based on the DSI. Three other independent analyses of the index produced results that did not vary significantly from State Street's.

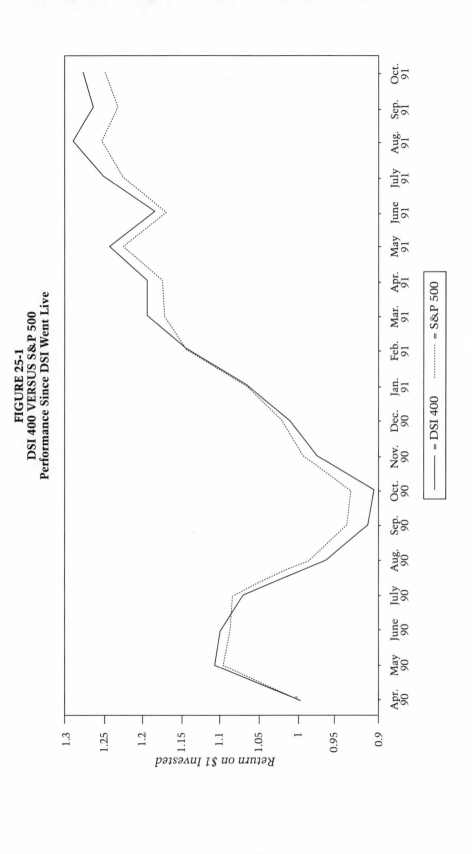

FIGURE 25-1
DSI 400 VERSUS S&P 500
Performance Since DSI Went Live

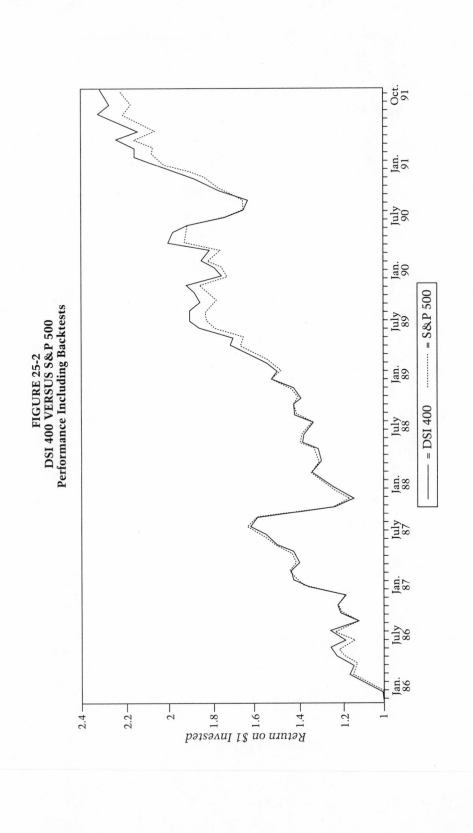

FIGURE 25-2
DSI 400 VERSUS S&P 500
Performance Including Backtests

—— = DSI 400   ········· = S&P 500

Return on $1 Invested

On the right-hand side of the chart (positive returns for the S & P), the DSI results are mostly above the ninety-degree line, indicating better performance. On the left-hand side (negative returns for the S & P), the DSI results generally fall below the ninety-degree line, indicating underperformance.

The backtesting also indicated that the DSI outperformed the S & P 500 on a risk-adjusted basis. Investment theorists argue that returns should be adjusted for the amount of risk (usually defined as the volatility of the investment) assumed by the investor. A portfolio with greater risk should compensate the investor by offering greater returns.

RISK-REWARD CHARACTERISTICS. Table 25-5 shows that the DSI had both higher rewards (geometric average of returns*) and higher risks (standard deviation of returns and beta). An investor in the DSI would have been sufficiently rewarded for this additional risk. There are two simple measures for making this determination: the Sharpe measure and the Treynor measure.

The Sharpe measure uses standard deviation as a measure of risk. The standard deviation measures the variability of returns for each investment, without attempting to relate the two portfolios. The model is expressed as:

$$S = \frac{Ri - RFR}{Vi}$$

where . . .

S is the Sharpe value
Ri is the return on the portfolio
RFR is the risk-free rate
Vi is the standard deviation of returns for the portfolio[2]

*The alternative measure would be the arithmetic mean—the average of monthly returns. Investment theorists prefer the geometric measure because the arithmetic mean tends to overstate returns. For example, if a $100 investment were to appreciate by 30 percent, then depreciate by 30 percent, it would be worth only $91 ($100 + $30 − $39), but the arithmetic mean return would be 0 percent. The geometric mean for the same investment would be −4.6 percent.

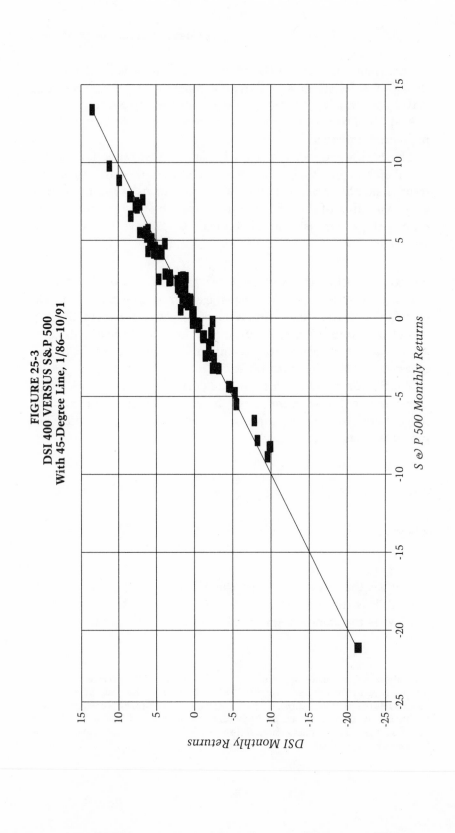

FIGURE 25-3
DSI 400 VERSUS S&P 500
With 45-Degree Line, 1/86–10/91

S & P 500 Monthly Returns

DSI Monthly Returns

The Treynor measure is identical to the Sharpe, except that it uses beta as the risk measure. As noted earlier, beta in this context is the degree to which the DSI varies *relative* to the S & P:*

$$T = \frac{Ri - RFR}{Bi}$$

where . . .

T is the Treynor value
Ri is the return on the portfolio
RFR is the risk-free rate
Bi is the beta of the portfolio

TABLE 25-5

COMPARATIVE RISK-REWARD CHARACTERISTICS

	DSI 400	S & P 500	T-Bills
Geometric mean	1.191%	1.127%	0.597%
Standard deviation	5.48%	5.12%	0.10%
Beta	1.066	1.00	

SOURCE: Kinder, Lydenburg, Domini & Co., October 31, 1991.

Both formulas estimate the ratio of risky return to the level of risk incurred. As table 25-6 shows, the DSI scored slightly higher than the S & P using both measures. Although the DSI has been

TABLE 25-6

COMPARATIVE RISK-ADJUSTED RETURNS

	DSI 400	S & P 500
Sharpe	0.11	0.10
Treynor	0.56	0.53

SOURCE: Kinder, Lydenberg, Domini & Co., October 31, 1991.

*Based on a regression of the DSI returns against the S & P 500 returns. The 1.06 figure is the slope of the regression line for the December 21, 1985–April 30, 1991 time period. The beta cited here is different from State Street's beta discussed earlier because the calculation is based on a different period.

more risky than the S & P 500, the total return on the DSI would have adequately compensated an investor for accepting that risk.

Expected Returns from the DSI and S & P

The financial data reported by State Street indicate that the DSI's expected return is higher than the S & P's and that the DSI's superior earning power (as expressed by return on equity) compensates for the additional risk assumed by the investor. We arrived at this conclusion using the following analysis.

EXPECTED RETURN VERSUS S & P. We used a transformation of the well-known perpetuity dividend discount model to estimate expected returns.* This model is specified as:

$$P = \frac{D1}{k-g}$$

where . . .

P is the valuation of the security or index
D1 is the expected dividend for the next twelve-month period
k is the required rate of return
g is the expected growth rate of dividends to perpetuity

The model can be transformed to solve for the required rate of return. The resulting equation uses the dividend yield and expected growth rate of dividends to give an expected rate of return:

$$k = \frac{D1}{P} + g$$

That is, the expected return is equal to the expected dividend yield for the next twelve months plus the expected growth rate of dividends.

We calculated g (the growth rate of dividends) by multiplying return on equity by earnings retention rate (see table 25-7).[3] We then used the dividend yield data for the DSI and S & P to calculate the rates of return implied by their current prices and expected growth

*This is the best-known approach, but any model that relates earning power and earnings retention rates will give similar results.

TABLE 25-7

COMPARATIVE EXPECTED GROWTH RATES

	DSI 400	S & P 500
Return on equity	21.30%	19.39%
Earnings retention	62.37%	53.27%
Expected growth	13.28%	10.33%
(ROE × retention)		

SOURCE: Kinder, Lydenberg, Domini & Co., October 31, 1991.

TABLE 25-8

COMPARATIVE REQUIRED RATES OF RETURN

	DSI 400	S & P 500
D1/P*	2.45%	3.1%
Dividend growth (g)	13.28%	10.33%
Expected return (k)	15.73%	13.43%

*Absent twelve-month dividend forecasts for both indexes, we use current dividend yield as a proxy for D1/P.

rates (see table 25-8). We found that according to this simple analysis, investors might expect to earn a higher rate of return (k) from the DSI than they do from the S & P (15.7 percent versus 13.4 percent).

ADJUSTED RETURNS USING BETAS. An investment theorist may argue that what matters are the relative risk-adjusted returns of the two portfolios. This is difficult to calculate from an expectations stand-point, because there is no widely accepted procedure for quantifying expected risk. We used the highest beta of the DSI's historical range (1.07) to obtain what we believe to be a conservative estimate of future risk.

If one accepts the premise that the DSI is not likely to become more volatile in relation to the S & P 500 than it has been in the past, then its expected risk-adjusted return, using the Treynor formula introduced above, is higher (see table 25-9). These results are consistent with both the DSI's twelve-month record and the State Street backtests.

CONCLUSION. The analysis in this section is not a forecast of the DSI's results. It is simply a mathematical procedure designed to estimate the return implied by the market's pricing of the DSI.

TABLE 25-9

COMPARATIVE REQUIRED RISK-ADJUSTED RETURNS

	DSI 400	*S & P 500*
Expected return (k)	15.73%	13.43%
Estimated T-bill rate	8.00%	8.00%
Expected beta	1.07	1.00
Expected Treynor score	.072	.054

Despite the positives of its first twelve months, the DSI remains vulnerable to a slowdown in retail spending, and its relative performance will suffer if oil and defense industry stocks turn in superior results. Its higher historical beta also means that it is likely to underperform in a bear market.

Time will tell.

| OTHER BENCHMARKS FOR SOCIALLY SCREENED PORTFOLIOS

The Domini Social Index is unique in the number of screens it applies and in its attempt to measure performance in the broad market. However, it is not the first attempt to gauge the effect of social screens on U.S. portfolios.* Most of these efforts start with the S & P 500.

Construction of the S & P 500

The S & P 500 can be thought of as a model portfolio whose purpose is "to portray the pattern of common stock price movement."[4] Its building blocks are indexes for industry groups.

> Component stocks are chosen solely with the aim of achieving a distribution by broad industry groupings that approximates the distribution of these groupings in the New York Stock Exchange common stock population, taken as the assumed model for the composition of the total market.[5]

Standard & Poor's regards the industry groupings making up the five hundred as, themselves, indexes. It therefore avoids "construc-

---

*Nor is it the first put forward by a firm in the social investment industry. That honor goes to the GOOD MONEY indexes, described in chapter 27. However, since their referents are the Dow Jones averages, they are not discussed here.

tion of a group index in which the movements of a single, dominant stock would effectively determine the movements of the group index."[6] For this reason, the S & P does not include the top five hundred companies in market capitalization; some industry groups consist mainly of smaller capitalization companies.

The Ex-Indexes
Some researchers have attempted to gauge the effects of social screens by applying a negative screen to the S & P 500 and calculating the performance of the remaining stocks. In some instances the resulting universe is called an "index," as with the Boston South Africa Free (SAFE) Index. In others it is referred to as a "portfolio," as with the Prudential Securities Social Investment Research Service's "Sin"-Free Portfolio. In neither case is there any attempt to replace the stocks eliminated by the screen with stocks of a similar quality and market capitalization and, where possible, from the same industry group.

PRUDENTIAL SECURITIES SOCIAL INVESTMENT RESEARCH SERVICE MODEL PORTFOLIOS. The most recent entrant in the ex-index group is Prudential Securities. In April 1991 its Social Investment Research Service (SIRS) began publishing a series of model portfolios: South Africa–Free; South Africa Ex-Non-Signatories of Statement of Principles; "Sin"-Free; Tobacco-Free;[7] Ex Top 100 Defense Contractors; and Ex Top 500 Defense Contractors.[8]

All of the Prudential portfolios underperformed the S & P for the five quarters ending March 31, 1991, and only the two ex-defense portfolios outperformed for the preceding four quarters.[9]

Prudential acknowledges that its "benchmark portfolios have more risk than typical screened portfolios," essentially because Prudential does not replace companies screened out to reduce any risk exposure introduced by the screening. Although the language is murky, Prudential seems to claim that risk increases when screens, such as South Africa, apply across several industry categories.[10] (The same criticism would apply to all of the DSI's secondary screens.)

Prudential offers a solution: SIRS provides techniques to "modify" socially responsible investors' screens to reduce the number of eliminated companies. One example Prudential uses would apply 1 percent of Department of Defense weapons contracts as a screen. This screen would eliminate only eighteen companies on the S & P and twenty-two on the Top 500 Contractors.[11] In contrast, the DSI's military screen, which is by design middle of the road, eliminates fifty-two S & P companies. And the DSI's screen has been criticized as too lax.

The difficulty with Prudential's "solution" is that the "problem" has not been shown to exist.

Increased risk is a problem only if the investor is not compensated for accepting that risk. As we have seen, socially responsible investors can reasonably expect a competitive risk-reward ratio. Further, Prudential did nothing to improve the diversification of its portfolios after applying its screens, despite the fact that academic studies have shown a poorly diversified portfolio will be less efficient than a well-diversified portfolio. Prudential has proven only that it can construct inefficient portfolios.

| THE DEBATE OVER SOCIALLY RESPONSIBLE INVESTING

The Prudential portfolios are nothing more than props in the debate over socially responsible investing. It is worth visiting this debate, for it puts into context not only Prudential's arguments but also the purpose of the Domini Social Index. There are three main theoretical objections to socially responsible investing: it limits return, it reduces opportunities for bargain hunting, and there is no place for ethics in investing.

Limiting an Investment Universe Hurts Return

"If you limit your investment universe, you will limit your return." That is the oldest and most consistently used argument against socially responsible investing.[12] Efficient market theorists make the same argument against active asset management.[13] Mathematically, a theoretician can always demonstrate greater risk-adjusted returns by increasing diversification until an "optimal risky portfolio" is reached. One conclusion of modern portfolio theory, then, is that reducing the size of the investment universe will hurt risk-adjusted returns.

Anomalies in markets can, however, allow investors to achieve superior results by focusing on certain types of stocks at certain times. One of the most important anomalies is the size effect, which has been a subject of intense academic discussion for many years.

Smaller capitalization stocks behave differently from larger capitalization issues. Some studies indicate that over the long term (thirty to fifty years), smaller stocks have outperformed larger ones.[14]

However, commentators disagree on whether this outperformance offsets the transaction costs and higher risk associated with smaller stocks. Some argue that when all factors are considered, smaller stocks actually have underperformed the larger issues in the past thirty years.*

For social investors this issue is important, because *all* socially screened universes accept some size risk. As we have seen with the DSI, the largest capitalization stocks tend to be most affected by social screens. Social investors can reduce their industry risk through substitution, but short of applying less-stringent screens, they cannot reduce size risk. There is only one Exxon.

The practical effect of size risk in social portfolios has yet to be established. For instance, the WM Company, a consultant in the United Kingdom, hires managers for portfolios of 126 charities with an aggregate market value of £3.7 billion. Approximately 20 percent of these portfolios have social constraints. In its 1989 annual report, WM assessed its experience with ethical investing:

> Ethical constraints in their own right seem to have little impact on the performance of the constrained universe other than through the small company/large company effect. The performance of actual funds indicates that other factors, such as stock selection, can more than offset these constraints.
>
> At an extreme level of constraint, where a significant number of large companies are excluded, a very large fund may find difficulties with liquidity, but in practice this is unlikely to arise.[15]

LIMITING A UNIVERSE REDUCES THE BARGAIN HUNTER'S OPPORTUNI-
TIES. The second argument against social investing is that it limits the bargain hunter's opportunities. John Train cites the willingness to look at any stock, regardless of qualitative objections, as one of the keys to the outstanding success of Peter Lynch, the former manager of Fidelity's Magellan Fund.

> Lynch says that he has an edge because a lot of the people he competes with are looking for reasons not to buy: the company is unionized; GE will come out with a new product that will kill them; or whatever.

---

*David Dreman has pointed out that the return on the Value Line Index (a small to medium capitalization index) was less than one-quarter that of the S & P 500 for the December 1961 to December 1990 time period (Dreman, "Megacycles," *Forbes*, April 1, 1991).

There is a whole list of biases that scare most investors away from studying the situation at all.[16]

Social screens, the argument goes, add to the list of biases and hurt the manager's ability to identify good opportunities in stocks.

Theoretically this argument is the converse of the first. It might be advanced by stock pickers who believe that markets are not efficient and, therefore, superior profits can be earned by identifying bargain stocks. Thus, if all of the bargains are in the liquor industry and you do not buy liquor companies, your investment results will suffer.

However, the main bias of social screens is against the largest companies. The largest-capitalization companies are, under most market conditions, the most efficiently priced securities and, therefore, offer the fewest targets for bargain hunters.* The DSI's screens eliminate a much lower percentage of smaller stocks—the universe where the most effective stock pickers tend to operate.

A protean stock picker with one of the best long-term investment records (on both a nominal and risk-adjusted basis), John Templeton, has endorsed socially responsible investing: "Investment mutual funds avoiding various companies because of ethics do perform a service to certain people and their growth should be encouraged."[17] Templeton's funds have never bought alcohol, tobacco, or gambling stocks.

ETHICS HAVE NO PLACE IN INVESTING. The third argument against social investing is that concerned investors should follow the example of Alfred Nobel: make millions on munitions so that they can be munificent to the masses.[18] According to this argument, the professional investor cannot be sentimental. He or she should look *only* at financial results and projections when making investment decisions.

This argument is naive. Most market participants use qualitative information in making investment decisions. A recent academic study quantified the effect of qualitative information by showing a positive relationship between a high ranking in *Fortune* magazine's annual "Most Admired Companies" survey and a firm's stock mar-

*Both Lynch and Warren Buffett have acknowledged that their jobs became much more difficult as the size of their funds grew. Buffett explicitly lowered his return goals for Berkshire Hathaway because it had grown so large.

ket performance.* It is interesting to note that the five companies with the highest scores on the 1991 *Fortune* most-admired list— Merck, Rubbermaid, Procter & Gamble, Wal-Mart, and Pepsico— are on the DSI.

Warren Buffett, one of the most successful and respected American investors, says he applies nonfinancial standards to his investments, particularly long-term holdings. "We do not wish to join with managers who lack admirable qualities," he says, "no matter how attractive the prospects of their business. We have never succeeded in making a good deal with a bad person."[†]

Most social investors and many conventional investors think this way. For them, social research can be a process for systematically addressing the qualitative factors in their investment analysis. Sophisticated managers understand that responsible public behavior can appeal to those investors. When investors have significant buying power, they can affect the firm's stock price and therefore its cost of capital. In this way, responsible public behavior can become a source of competitive advantage for the firm.

| A PROGRAM FOR FURTHER STUDIES

Like any investment approach, socially responsible investing entails risk. The task of investment managers working with socially constrained accounts is to achieve returns commensurate with the risk accepted. We believe that the DSI describes a universe where managers can achieve that objective.

---

*Eugene Szwajkowski and Raymond E. Figlewicz, "Risk and Reputation: A Market-based Analysis" (unpublished paper, University of Notre Dame and Kent State University, 1991). The authors used the *Fortune* "most-admired corporations" as a predictor of the residual of a standard Capital Asset Pricing Model (CAPM) regression and found a statistically significant relationship. In subsequent work the authors found that the bottom quartile—the least-admired firms—have significantly different price patterns from the rest of the market.

†Berkshire Hathaway Corporation, *Annual Report*, 1989. It is hard to know how serious Buffett is when he talks about socially responsible behavior. In B. Burrough and H. Helyar's *Barbarians at the Gate* (New York: HarperCollins, 1990), he is quoted as saying, "I like the cigarette business. It costs a penny to make. Sell it for a dollar." He immediately added that he did not want to own a cigarette business because, in the authors' words, "owning a tobacco company, with its social baggage and all that Death Merchant business, wasn't a burden Buffett felt he was ready to bear." Buffett certainly is not a social investor in any conventional sense. He has been a major trader of RJR bonds and also owned Washington Public Power Supply (WPPS) bonds that financed construction of nuclear reactors.

Like ours, several studies have found positive correlations between stock market returns and socially responsible behavior of
companies.[19] Other studies have raised questions about the costs of
social screens. Richard Wilk of PanAgora Asset Management has
found that the South Africa Free (SAFE) Index created by the Boston
Company "underperformed the S & P in each of the last five years,"
though it outperformed earlier in the decade.[20] Jeffrey A. Teper of
Colonial Consulting uses historical returns from socially responsible
mutual funds to argue that "there has been a consistent cost to social
investing."[21] Sociologist Samuel Mueller of the University of Akron
argues that investors in ethical mutual funds historically have given
up approximately 1 percent per annum in returns.*

Much work remains to be done before the risk-reward relationship
of socially responsible investing can be accurately quantified. We
suggest that future studies should:

- Compare investment vehicles with similar objectives, that is,
  socially responsible growth funds should be compared with unscreened growth funds;
- Distinguish between different types of social screening, for example, tobacco-free, South Africa–free, multiple screens, and
  so on;
- Use multiple methods of assessing risk.

Some time must pass before we have live data covering an entire
market cycle that should supply many answers. Until then, the
Domini Social Index will offer the best guide to the effects of social
screening on performance. For now we can only concur with the
WM Company: "In general the message seems to be that constraints
do not damage your wealth."[22]

---

*Professor Mueller's thesis, simply put, is that in order to demonstrate their com-
mitment to the causes on which they screen, social investors should lose money.
The underperformance of social mutual funds does not represent a sufficient sacrifice
in Mueller's view and therefore, using a term coined by the Christian martyr Dietrich
Bonhoeffer, amounts to "cheap grace." "Investors in ethical mutual funds sacrifice
about 100 basis points of return per year; Bonhoeffer's sacrifice was his life," says
Mueller.

NOTES

1. "Merchants Mobilize to Battle Wal-Mart in a Small Community," *Wall Street Journal*, June 5, 1991; "To Wal-Mart or Not to Wal-Mart," *Economist*, March 17, 1990.

2. Frank Reilly, *Investments and Portfolio Management* (New York: Dryden, 1988). Readers of Reilly's book will recognize our indebtedness to his approach throughout this article.

3. As recommended by Reilly, ibid.

4. The description in this section is based on that contained in *Stocks in the Standard & Poor's 500*, December 31, 1990, p. i.

5. Ibid.

6. Ibid.

7. Suzanne G. Harvey and Susan J. Levine, "What Is the Cost of Good Intentions? A New Prudential Securities Service," *Prudential Securities Strategy Weekly*, April 3, 1991, pp. 12ff.

8. Suzanne G. Harvey and Susan J. Levine, "Another Benchmark Portfolio for Social Investors—Ex Defense Contractors," *Prudential Securities Strategy Weekly*, April 17, 1991, pp. 13ff, and "Social Investors Draw a Bead on Weapons Makers," *idem*, May 15, 1991, pp. 10ff.

9. Harvey and Levine, "Another Benchmark," p. 18.

10. Harvey and Levine, "Social Investors Draw a Bead," p. 13.

11. Ibid.

12. See, for example, Sheldon Jacobs, ed., *The Handbook for No-Load Fund Investors*, 11th ed. (Hastings-on-Hudson, N.Y.: No-Load Fund Investor, 1991), p. 86. Jacobs also cites for this proposition Samuel A. Mueller, "The Opportunity Cost of Discipleship: Ethical Mutual Funds and Their Returns," a paper presented at the thirteenth annual conference of the Network for the Study of Implicit Religion, Denton Hall, Ilkley, England, May 13, 1990. The paper is to be reprinted in *Sociological Analysis* 52 (March 1991).

13. *Cf.* Mueller, "Opportunity Cost of Discipleship."

14. For a discussion of the long-term rewards of holding smaller stocks, see Ibbotson Associates, *Stocks, Bonds, Bills, and Inflation* (Chicago: Ibbotson, 1989). The firm found that the smallest stocks on the New York Stock Exchange returned 12.3 percent (geometric mean) for the sixty-three years ending in 1989, a 2.1 percent annual advantage over the larger issues. See also Rolf Banz, "The Relationship Between Returns and Market Value of Common Stocks," *Journal of Financial Economics* 9 (1981).

15. The WM Company, *1989 Annual Review Charity Fund Service*, p. 4.

16. John Train, *The New Money Masters* (New York: Harper & Row, 1989).

17. Norman Berryessa and Eric Kirzner, *Global Investing the Templeton Way* (Homewood, Ill.: Dow Jones-Irwin, 1988).

18. Jacobs, *Handbook for No-Load Fund Investors*, p. 86.

19. See the survey compiled by A. A. Ullman, "Data in Search of a Theory: A Critical Examination of the Relationships Among Social Performance, Social

Disclosure, and Economic Performance of U.S. Firms," *Academy of Management Review* 10.

20. Mr. Wilk's "The Boston South Africa Free (SAFE) Index," may be found in chapter 26 of this almanac.

21. Jeffrey A. Teper, "The Cost of Social Criteria," *Pensions and Investments,* May 13, 1991. See also Mr. Teper's "Evaluating the Cost of Socially Responsible Investing" in chapter 28 of this almanac.

22. The WM Company, *1989 Annual Review,* p. 4.

THE BOSTON SOUTH AFRICA FREE (SAFE) INDEX

Richard T. Wilk Senior Manager, U.S. Equities,
PanAgora Asset Management

The process of creating an investment portfolio incorporates a series of decisions made by the investment manager and the client. Each decision changes the risk-return balance of the portfolio and therefore affects the likely range of future returns. By altering the universe of available investments, the decision to implement a socially responsible investment policy can materially change portfolio structure.

Organizations that consider adopting a socially responsible investment policy often find themselves in a debate over implementation costs. For organizations with an existing portfolio, there is a one-time transactions cost to restructure the holdings to conform to the new guidelines. This one-time cost depends on a number of factors, including the size of the portfolio, the percent of the portfolio that must be replaced, the liquidity of the stocks being replaced, the trading techniques that will be used to accomplish the transition, and the time horizon available to complete the task. The variability of these costs makes it difficult to generalize. An analysis of transaction costs must address the unique characteristics of each fund.

Restricting potential investments has an additional, ongoing ef-

Richard T. Wilk is a Senior Manager, U.S. equities at PanAgora Asset Management, formerly the Structured Investment Products Group of The Boston Company. Wilk joined The Boston Company in 1980. Previously he was an independent consultant and worked for the Computer Research Center of the National Bureau of Economic Research. Wilk is a chartered financial analyst and a member of the Boston Security Analysts Society. He currently manages several portfolios for institutions using social guidelines.

fect on returns. History shows that this impact can be either positive or negative, depending on the time period measured. Studies have found that South Africa divestment had a positive impact on portfolio returns in the first half of the 1980s,[1] while our work found that the opposite was true in the latter half of the decade. We created the Boston South Africa Free Equity (SAFE) Index to measure the ongoing impact on equity portfolio returns from divesting companies doing business in the Republic of South Africa. The SAFE Index can help fiduciaries separate the divestment policy's effect on returns from the contribution provided by each manager's stock selection skills.

I THE STANDARD AND POOR'S 500 INDEX

The choice of an appropriate benchmark is a key factor in measuring the effectiveness of an investment strategy. Returns of common stock portfolios often are compared to broad market yardsticks, such as the Standard and Poor's (S & P) 500 Index. The S & P 500 represents a broad industry spectrum and enjoys wide acceptance in the investment community as a performance benchmark. The five hundred component stocks selected by the Standard and Poor's Corporation represent approximately 75 percent of the value of all stocks on the New York Stock Exchange. The index also includes some of the larger companies traded over the counter and on the American Stock Exchange.

The S & P 500 is a market value–weighted index. The market value or capitalization for each stock is computed by multiplying its current price by the number of common shares outstanding in that issue. For example, a stock selling for $50 a share with ten million shares outstanding has a market value of $500 million. Each stock's weight in the index is in proportion to its market value. A stock's weight in the index is computed by dividing its market value by the sum of the market values for all five hundred companies. The S & P 500 has an aggregate market value of approximately $2.4 trillion. The four largest stocks—Exxon, Philip Morris, IBM, and General Electric—currently account for over 10 percent of the S & P 500's capitalization. By contrast, the one hundred smallest S & P 500 stocks together represent only about 2 percent of the index's value.

The wide acceptance of the S & P 500 as an investment benchmark has contributed to the popularity of index funds since the early

1970s. Historically the S & P 500 index has been a difficult benchmark for investment managers to outperform consistently over time.[2] Index funds are designed to match the total returns of a stated benchmark, such as the S & P 500. Typically, lower fees are charged for index fund management than for active management. Today over $250 billion and over 18 percent of all tax-exempt U.S. equity assets are managed using index funds.

Index funds are not limited to the S & P 500 but have been created for a variety of published indexes in several asset classes. This concept can be combined with a divestment policy to build a portfolio that replicates a custom index of eligible securities. The Boston SAFE Index approximates the returns of an index based on the South Africa–free S & P 500 universe.

| CONSTRUCTION OF THE BOSTON SAFE INDEX

The Boston SAFE Index is based on the universe of stocks in the S & P 500 Index, excluding those companies having either a direct investment or employees in the Republic of South Africa. Banks with loans outstanding to the South African public and private sectors also are excluded from the index. The remaining eligible stocks are market value weighted, following the construction of the S & P 500. Quarterly total returns that include dividends are reported in table 26-1.

The primary sources of information for building our index are the Standard and Poor's Corporation and the Investor Responsibility Research Center (IRRC). Most of the clients for whom we manage divested portfolios subscribe to IRRC's South Africa review service and use IRRC's publications to determine the set of permitted investments. The quality and popularity of IRRC's South Africa services have made their lists a de facto standard among large fund sponsors.

| CUSTOM BENCHMARKS

In recent years more attention has been paid to the use of alternative benchmarks that provide a more meaningful evaluation of investment programs. In many cases it is more appropriate to compare a portfolio's performance to a custom index, sometimes called a "normal portfolio," rather than to a broad market index.

Investment managers are often hired with a mandate to follow a

TABLE 26-1

BOSTON SAFE INDEX
Total Returns, 1986 to 1990

	Boston SAFE Index	S & P 500 Index
1986		
1st quarter	+ 16.99	+ 14.07
2d quarter	+ 15.71	+ 5.95
3d quarter	+ 5.44	− 6.97
4th quarter	− 7.50	+ 5.40
Annual	+ 16.85	+ 18.50
1987		
1st quarter	+ 19.42	+ 21.32
2d quarter	+ 3.95	+ 4.94
3d quarter	+ 6.26	+ 6.58
4th quarter	− 22.60	− 22.55
Annual	+ 2.10	+ 5.09
1988		
1st quarter	+ 5.29	+ 5.70
2d quarter	+ 6.99	+ 6.50
3d quarter	+ 0.52	+ 0.38
4th quarter	+ 2.69	+ 3.11
Annual	+ 16.28	+ 16.51
1989		
1st quarter	+ 6.62	+ 7.01
2d quarter	+ 9.80	+ 8.81
3d quarter	+ 10.53	+ 10.61
4th quarter	+ 1.40	+ 2.06
Annual	+ 31.21	+ 31.44
1990		
1st quarter	− 2.88	− 3.01
2d quarter	+ 5.90	+ 6.29
3d quarter	− 14.88	− 13.74
4th quarter	+ 8.93	+ 8.96
Annual	− 3.74	− 3.10

SOURCES: PanAgora Asset Management and Standard and Poor's Corporation.

specific *style*. For example, the Frank Russell Company classifies equity managers into four style categories: price driven, earnings growth driven, market oriented, and small capitalization. The nature of manager styles often constrains the manager to select stocks from a subuniverse of the overall market. The manager's skill lies in the ability to add value by identifying issues within the subuniverse that will outperform their peers. It is common for individual styles to be in or out of favor over certain time periods. When a style is out of favor, the subuniverse of stocks (normal portfolio) underperforms the overall equity market. A custom index is helpful in this context to measure the manager's skill in picking stocks within the subuniverse. The construction of a normal portfolio is usually a collaborative effort between the investment manager, the client, and the sponsor's consultant.

The combination of divestment with style investing adds an additional level of complexity to the analysis of performance. The style's performance relative to the overall market has to be measured as well as the divestment effect. Divestment does not affect all styles equally. For example, a small capitalization growth manager may be able to identify easily a number of substitutes for each restricted stock and therefore be relatively unaffected by divestment. On the other hand, a large capitalization value manager may find that a large portion of the eligible universe is restricted, thereby forcing a significant change in portfolio structure. The Boston SAFE Index is an effective benchmark in measuring broadly diversified investment styles that base their universe on the S & P 500 Index. In other cases a custom benchmark that matches the manager's available set of opportunities may be a more appropriate yardstick.

| 1985 to 1990: A CHANGING ENVIRONMENT

In 1985, Douglas Love analyzed the characteristics of S & P 500 companies with direct investment in South Africa.[3] Love found that the affected companies were predominantly large capitalization firms with strong industry concentrations. Twenty-seven of the fifty largest S & P stocks were excluded by divestment, representing 58 percent of that group's market value. Only 89 of the remaining 450 stocks were affected. Over 90 percent of the market value of several industries, including drugs, international oil, and business machines, were restricted. Other industries, such as utilities, defense-related industries, and retailers, were relatively free from South Africa ties.

Faced with protests from shareholders and social activists as well as a deteriorating economic climate in the Republic of South Africa, many companies decided to end or reduce their presence there. As the IRRC reports:

The number of U.S. companies ending their direct investment in South Africa accelerated rapidly beginning in 1985, and peaked in

1987. Seven U.S. companies sold or closed down their operations in 1984, 40 followed in 1985, another 53 disinvested in 1986, followed by 56 in 1987. The pace of disinvestment dropped significantly in 1988, with only 29 withdrawals, followed by 19 in 1989, and 10 in 1990.[4]

This disinvestment trend has had a major impact on the SAFE Index and social investing in general. Table 26-2 lists the largest companies ending their direct investment in South Africa over the past five years. Figures 26-1 and 26-2 show the dramatic changes in the size of the restricted portion of the S & P 500. In 1986 the 122 companies doing business in South Africa represented almost 46 percent of the S & P's value. By the end of 1990 the 48 companies retaining a South Africa presence accounted for only 18 percent of the S & P's value.

Tables 26-3 and 26-4 compare the characteristics of the SAFE Index with the S & P 500, both in 1986 and today. In 1986 the average capitalization of companies in the SAFE Index was significantly below that of the S & P 500. Disinvestment has narrowed the capitalization gap between the indexes. The SAFE Index's per-

---

TABLE 26-2

**LARGEST COMPANIES ENDING THEIR
DIRECT INVESTMENT IN SOUTH AFRICA, 1986 to 1990**

	Withdraw Date	Market Value ($billion)
General Electric	April 1986	$33
Coca-Cola	November 1986	15
General Motors	December 1986	21
Exxon	December 1986	51
IBM	March 1987	73
Eastman Kodak	June 1987	15
Merck	March 1988	22
Ford Motor	April 1988	20
Dow Chemical	June 1988	17
Boeing	January 1989	9
Hewlett-Packard	January 1989	13
Mobil	July 1989	26
American Home Products	September 1989	17
Tenneco	April 1990	8

SOURCES: IRRC and PanAgora Asset Management.

FIGURE 26-1
BOSTON SAFE INDEX
Percent of S&P 500 Value Excluded

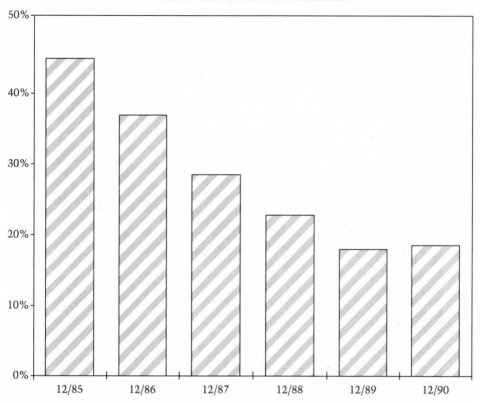

centage in health care issues has remained 5 percent below the S & P 500's weight—2 percent versus 7 percent in 1986 and 5 percent versus 10 percent in 1990. In 1986 the SAFE Index was underweighted relative to the S & P 500 in energy and technology and overweighted in consumer services and utilities. These differences exist in today's index but are much smaller.

Performance
Figure 26-3 shows that the SAFE Index underperformed the S & P 500 in each of the last five years. Much of the performance difference

FIGURE 26-2
BOSTON SAFE INDEX
Number of S&P 500 Stocks Excluded

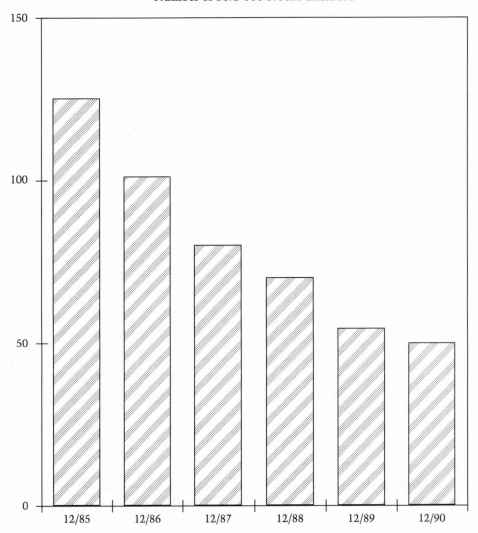

can be explained by the outperformance of the largest S & P stocks relative to the smaller capitalization groups. The strong performance of drug stocks over this period represented the greatest challenge to managers of divested portfolios. Not only did drug stocks perform well, but there were few alternatives, because most of this group is restricted.

TABLE 26-3

THE BOSTON SAFE INDEX, 1986
Characteristics   Table 1

Sector distribution	S & P 500	Boston SAFE Index
Finance	8%	10%
Health	7%	2%
Consumer nondurables	11%	11%
Consumer services	11%	19%
Consumer durables	4%	3%
Energy	11%	6%
Transportation	3%	5%
Technology	12%	6%
Basic industries	8%	9%
Capital goods	10%	10%
Utilities	13%	20%
Value criteria		
P/E	12.1×	12.3×
Yield	3.6%	3.5%
Growth criteria		
Sustainable growth	9.8%	10.0%
Dividend growth (last 5 years)	7.1%	8.4%
EPS growth (last 5 years)	9.2%	10.3%
Risk criteria		
Market beta	1.00	1.02
S & P 500 equity quality		
(A+, A, A−, B+, etc.)	A	A
Capitalization (mean in $billions)	$13.1	$ 5.3

SOURCES: The Boston Company and Standard & Poor's (definition of S & P stock index).

The worst relative year for divested funds was 1987, a volatile year in which the S & P 500 rose 39 percent during the first eight months, then fell 30 percent over the next three months. Figure 26-4 shows that the 50 largest S & P stocks as a group peformed far better than the remaining 450. This trend is not surprising. During times of uncertainty and volatility, there is often a flight to quality. The largest stocks are viewed as a safe harbor from economic turmoil. This group contains most of the market value of issues restricted by divestment.

Future Trends
The activists for South Africa disinvestment have achieved impressive results. Many of the companies withdrawing from South Africa

TABLE 26-4

**THE BOSTON SAFE INDEX: PORTFOLIO CHARACTERISTICS
AS OF NOVEMBER 30, 1990**
Characteristics   Table 1

Sector distribution	S & P 500	Boston SAFE Index
Finance	7%	8%
Health	10%	5%
Consumer nondurables	15%	15%
Consumer services	11%	13%
Consumer durables	3%	3%
Energy	14%	12%
Transportation	2%	2%
Technology	8%	9%
Basic industries	7%	6%
Capital goods	8%	9%
Utilities	15%	19%
Value criteria		
P/E	12.4×	12.1×
Yield	3.8%	3.9%
Growth criteria		
Sustainable growth	10.2%	10.2%
Dividend growth (last 5 years)	12.6%	11.8%
EPS growth (last 5 years)	16.2%	16.0%
Risk criteria		
Market beta	1.00	1.00
S & P 500 equity quality		
(A+, A, A−, B+, etc.)	A	A
Capitalization (mean in $billions)	$17.2	$16.9

SOURCES: The Boston Company and Standard & Poor's (definition S & P stock index).

have cited shareholder resolutions and the influence of public opinion as contributing to their decision. The level of U.S. direct investment in South Africa has declined significantly in the past five years. The good news for fund sponsors and investment managers is that South Africa divestment has a much smaller impact on portfolios today than it did in the past. Divested portfolios are now much closer in structure to their nondivested counterparts.

NOTES

1. A. Domini and P. Kinder, *Ethical Investing* (Reading, Mass.: Addison-Wesley, 1984), pp. xii–xiii. See also R. Arnott and R. Boling, "Divestiture Risks Can Be Reduced With Planning, Eye to the Issues," *Pension and Investment Age,*

FIGURE 26-3
BOSTON SAFE INDEX
Calendar Year Total Return

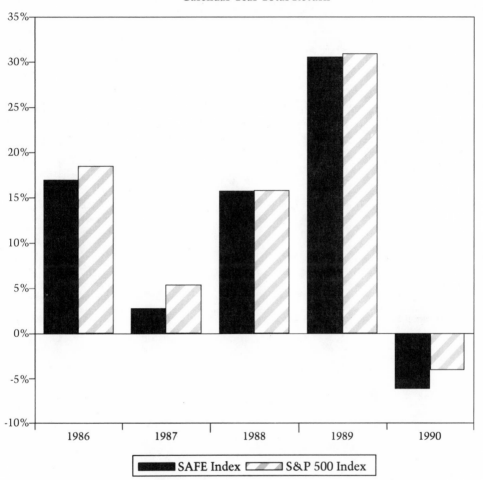

August 5, 1985. Arnott and Boling note that the higher returns are accompanied by an increase in extra market risk.

2. SEI Corporation, a major pension consulting firm, reports that the median equity manager underperformed the S & P 500 by 0.7 percent annually in the five-year period ending December 1990. The S & P 500 outperformed the median equity manager in four of the past five years.

3. Douglas A. Love, "On South Africa," *Financial Analysts Journal*, May–June 1985.

4. Alison Cooper, *U.S. Business in South Africa* (Washington, D.C.: Investors Responsibility Research Center, 1991), p. 9.

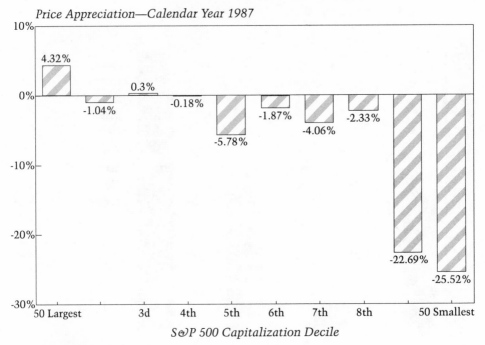

FIGURE 26-4
S&P 500 INDEX
Relative Performance by Capitalization

Price Appreciation—Calendar Year 1987

S&P 500 Capitalization Decile

Source: Salomon Brothers.

GOOD MONEY'S STOCK AVERAGES

Ritchie Lowry and **Steven Heim**
GOOD MONEY Publications, Inc.

In 1982 Ritchie Lowry started GOOD MONEY Publications to provide information for socially and ethically concerned investors. For about four years before then he had been tracking a utilities and industrials stock average composed of socially responsive companies. For comparison with the Dow equivalents, he went back to the end of 1976, the last big market bottom at that time.

| THE AVERAGES

The GOOD MONEY Utilities Average (GMUA) is nuclear-free and specifically targets companies developing alternative or renewable energy sources, such as Magma Power with its development of geothermal energy; Southwestern Public Service with its state-of-the art pollution controls; Otter Tail Power with its diversification into renewable energy technologies; and Hawaiian Electric Industries with its renewable energy program.

In contrast, for the GOOD MONEY Industrial Average (GMIA), there were many socially acceptable companies available. When Lowry first designed the stock averages, he tried to find acceptable companies in the same industries that appeared on the Dow Jones Industrial Average. For example, at that time Atlantic Richfield stood out in the petroleum industry, especially in terms of the environment and employee relations. Since then ARCO's record has not been good, and it has been dropped from the GMIA. Finding an acceptable best-of-the-industry company was sometimes impossible. For that reason, no aerospace company appears on the GMIA, although there are several on the Dow. GOOD MONEY feels that its average well represents the American economy and can be fairly compared with the Dow, making it a true test of whether or not investors lose money through socially responsible investing.

FIGURE 27-1
GOOD MONEY Utility Average Versus Dow Jones
Utility Average, 1977 to 1991

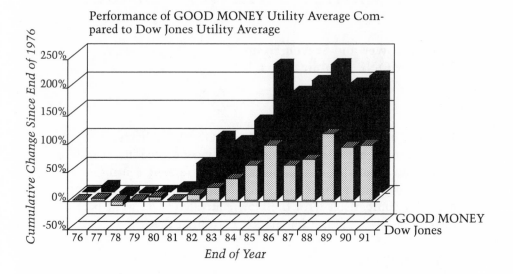

Performance of GOOD MONEY Utility Average Compared to Dow Jones Utility Average

Cumulative Change Since End of 1976

End of Year

| COMPANY SELECTION

Lowry also attempted to construct a transportation average. Unfortunately, an insufficient number of transportation companies could pass social screening that included good employee relations, good safety records, or good records for community service. GOOD MONEY is still looking for twenty good transportation companies in order to design an average that could be tracked against the Dow equivalent.

From time to time, companies are replaced on the GMIA for the same reasons they are replaced on the Dow: the company is merged with another one or it goes private. Esquire and Levi Strauss used to be on the GMIA. Esquire was purchased by Gulf & Western (now Paramount)—not a responsive company—and Levi Strauss went private. The divisor for the thirty-stock average is adjusted so that the stock of the replacement company will not influence the actual value of the total average.

A company also is replaced if it runs into serious social problems. Waste Management was on the GMIA until it ran into several toxic waste dumping problems. However, no change is ever made for fi-

FIGURE 27–2
GOOD MONEY Industrial Average Versus Dow Jones
Average 1977 to 1991

Performance of GOOD MONEY Industrial Average compared to Dow Jones Industrial Average

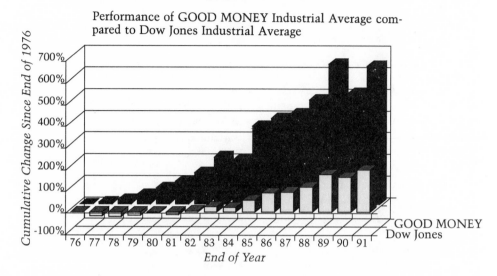

nancial performance reasons. Thus, the GMIA is a true test of whether or not investors lose money through socially responsible investing.

Two cautions: First, it is important to recognize that, like the Dow averages, the GMIA and GMUA are merely indexes. They are not recommendations to buy, hold, or sell. They are designed to test the Wall Street myth that social investing causes investors to realize lower gains over time.

Second, the GOOD MONEY averages are not selected because they meet every social criterion imaginable. There is no such thing as perfection in the corporate world. For instance, Johnson & Johnson appears on the GMIA because of its more than one-hundred-year commitment to safe and quality products and its involvement in community affairs. However, the company does do business in South Africa. Nevertheless, the manufacture and selling of pharmaceuticals and health care products in South Africa has at best a tenuous relationship to apartheid.

Though there are companies on the GMIA and GMUA that would not meet all of the criteria used by socially concerned investors, they are selected because of some outstanding social program or action. These companies are the "try-harders." They try to respond to basic social issues rather than always using profit as the only basis for decision making.

GOOD MONEY INDUSTRIAL AVERAGE COMPANIES (APRIL 1992)

Ametek
Blockbuster Entertainment
Consolidated Papers
Cross, A. T.
Cummins Engine
Dayton Hudson
Digital Equipment
First Virginia Banks
FlightSafety International
Fuller, H. B.
Hartmarx
Hershey Foods
Johnson & Johnson
Maytag Corporation
McDonald's
Melville Corporation
Merck & Company
Miller, Herman
Minnesota Mining & Manufacturing
Pitney Bowes
Polaroid
Procter & Gamble
Rouse Company
Student Loan Marketing Association
Stride Rite
US West
Volvo AB
Washington Post
Worthington Industries
Zurn Industries

GOOD MONEY UTILITY AVERAGE COMPANIES (APRIL 1992)

Cilcorp Inc.
Citizens Utilities
Consolidated Natural Gas
Hawaiian Electric
Idaho Power Company
Kansas Power & Light
LG & E Energy
Magma Power
Montana Power
Oklahoma Gas & Electric
Otter Tail Power
Southwest Gas
Southwest Public Service
United Water Resources
UtiliCorp United

FIGURE 27-3
**GOOD MONEY Stock Averages Versus Dow Jones Stock
Averages, 1977 to 1991**

Performance of GOOD MONEY Stock Averages Compared to
Dow Jones Stock Averages

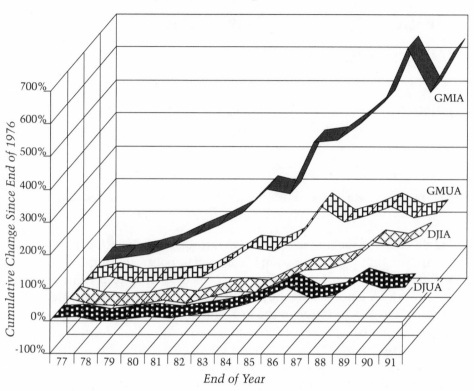

EVALUATING THE COST OF SOCIALLY RESPONSIBLE INVESTING

Jeffrey A. Teper Senior Vice President,
Colonial Consulting Corporation

Ed. Note: *This chapter was previously published in similar form in* Pensions and Investments.

As the scope of socially responsible investing grows, investors need to analyze thoroughly the complex financial, political, moral, and social issues involved. The purpose of this chapter is to present a framework for determining the financial cost of socially responsible criteria. It is left to the investor to evaluate the perceived benefits of the criteria in light of this cost information.

Social responsibility is no excuse for financial irresponsibility. Fiduciaries, financial staff, portfolio managers, consultants, and constituents (for example, a university's students, a pension plan's participants) all must be aware of the expected costs of the social responsibility program under consideration. This knowledge is vital when deciding whether to adopt, continue, expand, or contract social criteria, because advocates of such a program must show that the moral and social benefits outweigh the associated financial costs. Although they may seem small, these costs cannot be ignored, because the nature of compounded interest will magnify them over time.

Jeffrey A. Teper is a senior vice president of Colonial Consulting Corporation, an investment consulting firm specializing in advising large not-for-profit organizations. Teper received a B.S. from New York University's Stern School of Business and an M.B.A. from the Harvard Graduate School of Business Administration. He currently advises the firm's clients on issues including asset allocation, spending policy, manager selection, and performance evaluation.

Even those institutions that are committed to social criteria must be aware of their program's cost so that they can determine what changes should be made to other policies, specifically asset allocation and spending levels, in order to protect their real asset value for the future.

RESEARCH BACKGROUND

Colonial Consulting Corporation conducted the research for this chapter. The firm provides investment consulting services to large institutional investors, primarily not-for-profit organizations (endowments, foundations, and religious organizations), many of which employ some social criteria.

The investment world in general, and socially responsible investing in particularly, is highly dynamic. Past data and definitions become obsolete quickly. Nevertheless, Colonial Consulting has adopted a conservative approach to measuring the cost of social criteria based on recent performance history. This methodology, in contrast to one that attempts to forecast cost reductions, is appropriate for institutions that are susceptible to the emotional appeal of social responsibility but are strained financially even without the added cost.

THE SOCIALLY RESPONSIBLE INVESTOR'S DECISIONS

Until recently, socially responsible investors were primarily religious organizations that adopted sin-free portfolios and universities, the most common users of South Africa–free criteria. Sin-free programs typically eliminated alcohol, gambling, and tobacco stocks but sometimes restricted defense and birth control manufacturers. During the last five years, there has been a strong movement toward expanding the scope of social criteria. This expansion has brought new guidelines, which include evaluating companies according to their records on environmental, employment, community, and product safety issues. Recently social investing has evolved beyond simply screening out bad stocks to adding companies with good records to a portfolio. As the options become more complex, so does the task of measuring the cost of social criteria versus an unrestricted portfolio.

Investors also have difficult choices in implementing these criteria. For example, Hilton has a small portion of its business in hotels with casinos. Is it a gambling stock or a hotel stock? Even more difficult is evaluating the case of Johnson & Johnson. While the company does business in South Africa, it is highly regarded for its handling of the Tylenol tampering. Does the company's moral leadership outweigh its presence in South Africa? These kinds of difficult decisions can make the difference between a restricted list with a few dozen stocks and one with a few hundred. Clearly such decisions have a significant impact on determining the cost of the criteria.

Similarly, the investment vehicles used to implement the criteria also affect the cost. Investors can adopt more traditional products, such as index funds, and active managers whose portfolios are screened to eliminate the restricted companies. They can go a step further and substitute secondary companies and statistically optimize the portfolio to reduce the impact of biases in the client's criteria, such as a reduced exposure to companies with international earnings. Alternatively, investors can choose from products specially designed for social responsibility, including a number of mutual funds (for example, Calvert), investment managers (such as Franklin Research), and even a social index fund (Domini Social Index Trust). It is important to note that while the investment strategy, process, and optimization used may well reduce the investor's cost, it is not prudent to assume that these costs will be "managed away" without hard evidence.

Measuring the Cost in Reduced Risk-Adjusted Returns

When measuring the cost of socially responsible investing, it is critical to use risk-adjusted returns, because the biases of many social criteria are likely to increase portfolio volatility. Risk-adjusted returns are determined by using regression analysis to increase or decrease the returns depending on their risk relative to a specified benchmark. In this analysis the benchmark is the Standard & Poor's (S & P) 500 Index, a commonly used proxy for the stock market.

There are five primary reasons why socially responsible portfolios may have lower risk-adjusted returns than unrestricted portfolios:

1. Lower security returns—if better performers are on a restricted list and poorer performers are either overweighted or subsequently added to the portfolio.
2. Higher security risk—if large companies are replaced by smaller, more volatile companies.

3. Lower portfolio diversification—if the criteria force the portfolio to be underweighted in major industries or sectors.
4. Divestment transaction cost—the one-time cost of eliminating nonqualifying stocks and adding or reweighting others.
5. Opportunity cost of eliminating an asset class—for example, not investing in international equities because it may be too difficult to monitor social responsibility.

The following analysis represents evidence for the cost of several social criteria. It will focus on the first three reasons for lower risk-adjusted returns because they are ongoing and can be generalized enough to be meaningful. The studies look at simple compounded

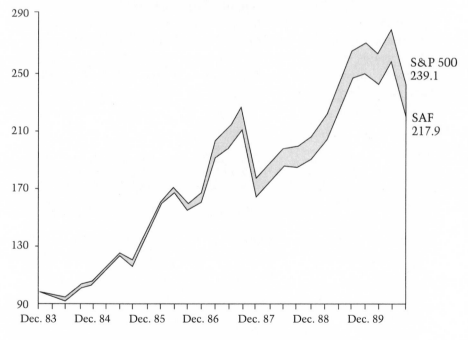

FIGURE 28-1
SOUTH AFRICA-FREE INVESTING
South Africa–Free Index Versus S&P 500 —12/83–9/90

Risk-Adjusted Annual Cost: 1.7%

Annual Under-Performance: 7 of 7 years

Source: The Boston Company and PanAgora Asset Management.

total return, consistency of costs, and the risk-adjusted returns discussed above.

The South Africa–free portfolio (see figure 28-1) was the first policy evaluated. It underperformed the S & P 500 each of the seven years examined (including the first nine months of 1990), providing a risk-adjusted annual cost of 1.7 percent. This result is particularly important because it represents the most commonly used social criterion. It also is significant for investors considering other policies, because it shows the highly consistent cost of using what is currently a restricted list of sixty to seventy stocks. This demonstrates that while eliminating 10 to 20 percent of the companies from a universe may seem a small concession, it is not, particularly if the criteria are biased against large companies and sectors of the market.

The second policy evaluated was sin-free portfolios. This analysis shows how the subsets of a policy impact its overall cost. Table 28-1 shows that core sin stocks (alcohol, gambling, tobacco) and birth control manufacturers' stocks significantly outperformed the S & P 500 during the 1980s, while defense stocks underperformed during the same time frame. While this may not always occur, it certainly demonstrates the potential cost of missing key sectors. Figure 28-2 shows the impact of these sectors on actual investment managers. The graph compares the performance of nine portfolios managed

TABLE 28-1

SIN-FREE INVESTING: PERFORMANCE OF STOCKS
Price Change of Sin Stocks Versus S & P 500—12/79–12/89

	Cumulative Price Change	Annualized Price Change	Annualized Difference from S & P 500
S & P 500	217.7%	8.1%	
Alcohol, gambling, and tobacco stocks	566.4%	18.9%	+ 10.8%
Major defense contractor stocks	169.8%	5.4%	− 2.7%
Birth control manufacturer stocks	401.1%	14.9%	+ 6.8%

SOURCE: Merrill Lynch Asset Management.

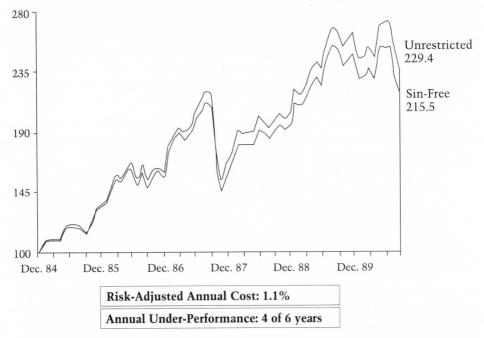

FIGURE 28-2
SIN-FREE INVESTING: PERFORMANCE OF MANAGERS
Sin-Free Versus Unrestricted Portfolios—12/84–9/90

Risk-Adjusted Annual Cost: 1.1%

Annual Under-Performance: 4 of 6 years

Source: Colonial Consulting Corporation.
Note: Both sin-free and unrestricted portfolios include the same managers. Sin stocks
are tobacco, alcohol, and gambling.

with sin-free criteria restricting from twenty-five to seventy-five
stocks with unrestricted portfolios managed by the same nine firms.
While the cost was neither as consistent nor as expensive as in the
South Africa–free case, the sin-free restricted lists were generally
shorter and there was some opportunity for compensation by active
management, which did not exist in the South Africa–free example.

The final category of policy examined was broad social guidelines,
which include both positive and negative criteria. It is difficult to
measure this category because of the wide range of social definitions
and the relatively short time frame that applicable investment vehicles have been in existence.

Figure 28-3 compares the Domini Social Index (the most thorough
of the social benchmarks and one that actually may be invested in)
and the S & P 500. Figure 28-4 compares an average of twelve major
socially oriented mutual funds and investment managers with the

FIGURE 28-3
BROAD SOCIAL GUIDELINES: SOCIAL INDEX
Domini 400 Social Index Versus S&P 500—12/85–9/90

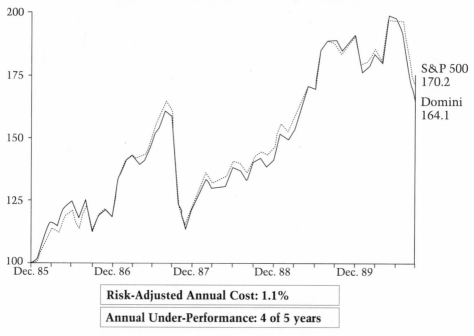

Risk-Adjusted Annual Cost: 1.1%

Annual Under-Performance: 4 of 5 years

SOURCE: Kinder, Lydenberg, Domini & Company and State Street Bank and Trust.
NOTE: Backtested performance through April 1990; actual performance since.

S & P 500. In both instances the results were in line with the other analyses—a consistent cost to social criteria and risk-adjusted returns reduced by more than 1 percent on an annualized basis. Ironically, the active managers performed worse than the social index—despite the opportunity to compensate for biases and add the skill of portfolio managers. This provides strong evidence for not assuming that active management can eliminate the cost of socially responsible criteria.

| MEASURING THE COST IN REDUCED SPENDING AND ASSET GROWTH

While reduced risk-adjusted returns are a useful measure for comparing alternative policies, financially responsible investors should eventually translate the reduced returns into dollars. A dollar cost figure is more tangible for an institution debating whether it can afford the criteria under consideration.

This process involves five steps:

1. Define the asset allocation and spending policies for a given time frame;
2. Lower the equity returns for the impact of social responsibility (the above analysis shows that 1 percent is reasonable) using an appropriate benchmark, such as the S & P 500, as a base;
3. Calculate the portfolio's adjusted return based on its asset allocation and the new equity return;
4. Track spending and asset growth using the adjusted total return for a long enough period of time to capture the effect of compounded interest;

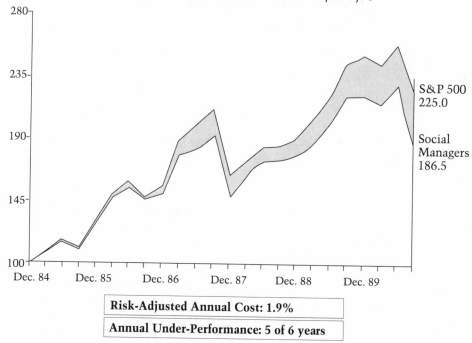

FIGURE 28-4
BROAD SOCIAL GUIDELINES: SOCIAL MANAGERS
Social Manager Universe Versus S&P 500—12/84–9/90

Risk-Adjusted Annual Cost: 1.9%

Annual Under-Performance: 5 of 6 years

SOURCE: Colonial Consulting Corporation for socially responsible manager composites and CDA Investment Technologies for socially responsible mutual funds.

FIGURE 28-5
POTENTIAL COST IN REDUCED SPENDING AND ASSETS
Hypothetical Cost of Social Investing—12/79–9/90

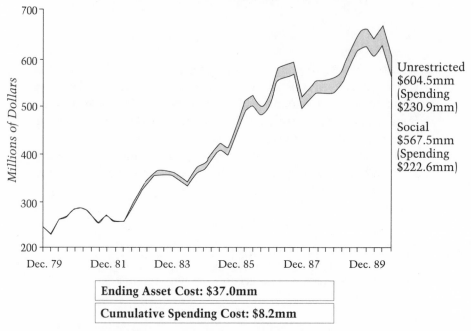

NOTE: Assumptions: $250 million initial assets, 5 percent annual spending, 60 percent stocks and 40 percent bonds asset allocation, 1 percent annual cost of social investing for stocks.

5. Compare the spending and ending asset values using socially responsible returns to those figures using the unrestricted returns.

Figure 28-5 shows the projected dollar cost for a large representative institution with a 60 percent equity allocation, 5 percent annual spending rate, and 1 percent assumed cost of socially responsible investing for ten and three-quarters years. This analysis demonstrates that while 1 percent may seem a small price, the cost accumulates quickly. When viewed in light of the budget crunches faced by many institutions, social criteria may force the institution to compromise its activities. Consequently, it becomes necessary to compare the perceived benefit of socially responsible investment policies to the direct social benefit of the investment pool (for example, providing for retirement, educating students) that may have to be curtailed.

| CONCLUSION

The evidence presented demonstrates that there has been a consistent cost to socially responsible investing. While this cost varies with the policies and vehicles chosen, conservative investors can assume roughly a 1 percent annualized reduction in equity returns if they adopt restrictive criteria. This may well be less than the perceived social and moral benefit for some investors, but it does not excuse any investor from measuring the costs both historically and prospectively.

While this cost may decrease as more companies become socially responsible and active managers attempt to compensate for the cost in the interim, currently, financially responsible investors do not have sufficient evidence to assume that either is true. Therefore, investors must assume some cost for socially responsible investing, and if they choose to adopt it, they must reevaluate their investment goals and policies with the cost of socially responsible investing in mind.

STOCKS

Patrick McVeigh Franklin Research &
Development Corporation

Would you marry just for money?—Warren Buffett

Though widely recognized as one of the most successful investors of all time, Warren Buffett is not usually thought of as a socially responsible investor. Yet his opening question cuts to the core of a socially responsible approach to investing in stocks. His query implies a long-term commitment and the existence of important variables beyond financial gain.

In an era when the average turnover in mutual funds is above 100 percent (signifying that the average period of ownership of a stock is less than one year) and a person with a long-term view is someone who can plan beyond lunch, a typical social investor's approach to equity investing may seem out of place.

RIGHTS AND RESPONSIBILITIES OF OWNERSHIP

A socially responsible approach accepts the basic tenet of stock ownership—that stocks are a share of ownership in a business. By buying one hundred shares of Xerox Corporation, you are becoming an owner not just of the stock, but also of the company. Ownership carries with it certain rights and responsibilities. These rights include:

Patrick McVeigh is a portfolio manager, research analyst, and vice president at Franklin Research & Development Corporation, a Boston-based registered investment advisory firm that specializes in socially responsible investing. He is also the editor of *Franklin's Insight*, an investment newsletter focusing on socially responsible investing. He holds a B.S. degree in economics from the University of Santa Clara.

- The right to vote for corporate directors and on proxy issues, usually one vote per share owned;
- The right to financial disclosure in the form of quarterly income statements and balance sheets and an annually audited financial report;
- The right to participate in profits in the form of dividends to the extent of your proportionate ownership;
- The right to enter shareholder resolutions if you have owned $1,000 of the company's stock for at least one year.

With the benefits of ownership also come many responsibilities. For social investors interested in knowing that their money is working to create a better world, these responsibilities include:

- The responsibility to ensure that the company operates in an ethical manner;
- The responsibility to ensure that employees are treated fairly and that women and minorities are represented throughout the company;
- The responsibility to ensure that protection of the environment goes beyond the minimum restrictions demanded by law;
- The responsibility to ensure that domestic and overseas host communities are not exploited and that they participate in the success of the firm;
- The responsibility to ensure that a quality product or service is offered at a fair price.

These responsibilities rarely concern those who expect to keep stocks less than a year. There is a direct correlation between an investor's time frame and his or her degree of concern about the responsibilities of share ownership.

| THE EVILS OF SHORT-TERM EMPHASIS

The importance of an investor's time frame on an individual company's performance and overall economic performance was all too clear in the 1980s. Money managers were once judged on their three- to five-year performance results. In the past decade they were judged on their quarterly, and sometimes daily, performance. It mattered little whether these results were derived from improved earnings by companies in their portfolios or from premiums that accompanied the frenzy of buybacks and spinoffs, mergers and acquisitions, and leveraged buyouts and recapitalizations induced by corporate raiders.

The emphasis on short-term performance that arose in the 1980s translated into expectations that corporate chief executive officers would act the same way. Companies were forced to shorten their investment time frames and to adopt tactics that led to immediate increases in their stock price, no matter what the long-term implications. For example, General Motors chose to buy back stock in the late 1980s rather than conserve resources to fight foreign competition. As auto sales plummeted in 1991, General Motors cut its dividend and sold a new issue of preferred stock in order to rearm itself—belatedly—in its fight to maintain market share.

Where investors once viewed themselves as taking part in and benefiting from the building of stronger companies, the investment decision has gradually been separated from the economic decision. Where corporations and investment bankers once worked hand in hand, now they are often at odds. "If you bare your soul to these people, you're a fool," declares Andrew C. Sigler, chief executive officer of Champion International. "We consider investment banks to be amoral."

| RISK-FREE DECISION MAKING

This rise in amoral posturing has become so prevalent that it has earned its own descriptive phrase from academics: "risk-free decision making." The growth of restructurings, buyouts, megamergers, and options trading reflects behavior of people who act as if their decisions are risk-free—as if they are not responsible for the consequences of their decisions. This attitude has arisen as people have lost the ability to perceive themselves as part of a larger, unified body of individuals to which each contributes, either to the good or the detriment of the whole. Each act or decision is seen as independent, with no implications for affecting others.

Socially responsible investors reject the view that investment decisions are amoral. They assert that ethical and moral considerations are key to making better financial decisions. As Warren Buffett's words suggest, investing in stocks is about more than just the prospects for an immediate financial return and "marrying just for money." A core belief of social investing is that positive records on important ethical factors, such as employee relations, environmental protection, product quality, and community support, are necessary to create a lasting "marriage" and successful long-term investment.

| CORRELATION BETWEEN
SOCIAL AND FINANCIAL PERFORMANCE

Several studies have supported the contention that there is a positive correlation between social and financial performance.

- In a study published in the *Academy of Management Journal* (March 1984), Philip Cochran and Robert Wood report finding a definite correlation between corporate social ratings and three measures of economic performance.
- The National Center for Employee Ownership found that firms with employee stock ownership plans (ESOPs) that allowed for relatively high degrees of employee input into job-level decision making grew 8 to 11 percent faster with the ESOP than they would have without one.
- A recent study by David Lewin at the Columbia School of Business found that employee morale was three times higher in companies with a strong degree of community involvement than in companies that were not involved.
- In a study by Franklin Research & Development, firms included in the book *The 100 Best Companies to Work for in America* (Addison-Wesley, 1984) outperformed the Standard and Poor's (S & P) 500 Index by 367 percent over a ten-year period.

Environmental Considerations

The importance of treating social and financial variables as interchangeable is perhaps best observed by examining the current interest in environmental issues. In light of the rapidly increasing environmental liabilities facing most firms, investors must research this issue if they are to make a sound investment.

According to analysts at the investment firm of Smith Barney, "the size of Corporate America's toxic-waste cleanup liability has been placed at anywhere from $100 billion to $700 billion, the latter number being around 13 percent of the U.S.'s nominal GNP." The size of this problem is immense and growing bigger rapidly. Two years ago the Environmental Protection Agency (EPA) estimated the average cost of cleaning up a Superfund site to be approximately $11 million. It recently revised this estimate to $25 million.

Despite the size of this problem for corporate America, you will not find the potential costs reflected on financial statements. My firm's recent survey of the annual reports and 10-K filings of the

S & P 500 for environmental disclosure yielded mostly accounting boilerplate. The companies maintain that they anticipate "no material adverse effect" from federal environmental legislation. In contrast, Moody's Investors Services (the leading agency rating the financial strength of corporations) recently warned that "substantial costs for environmental compliance and cleanup may alter the credit profiles of some industries" and that new "green" legislation "may lead to repeats of the bankruptcies of Manville Corporation and Eagle-Picher Industries, which were forced into bankruptcy by a tide of asbestos litigation."

ENVIRONMENTAL RESEARCH RESOURCES. At Franklin Research & Development, we recognize the importance of environmental issues and take special care to analyze them completely before making an investment. Though the task may seem daunting to the average investor, a number of resources make it manageable.

- From the EPA, one can receive a free yearly listing of the National Priorities List, which provides a ranking of the worst Superfund sites in the country and the corporations involved with them.
- The Environmental Research Foundation (Washington, D.C.) makes available a data base that includes all civil lawsuits filed by the EPA since 1972. It is available at no cost.
- The Toxic Release Inventory is another free data base. Created by recent legislation, it has information on the emissions of 309 chemicals spewed forth by more than 19,000 manufacturing companies. (A free report on how to use this data base, "The Citizen's Toxic Waste Audit Manual," is available from Greenpeace.)

All of this information is reviewed by our firm, together with interviews with environmental groups and the companies in question. (Similar low-cost or free resources are available to help research other important social issues, such as employee and community relations.)

The Hidden Research Factor

Within this context of recognizing how important social research is to making a profitable investment, it is interesting to note how social research is a hidden addition to the work of many noted investors.

Barton Biggs, chief investment strategist at Morgan Stanley, has written that he believes that "every professional investor should filter investment ideas through an ecology screen." Noted economist and successful investor John Maynard Keynes contended that investment decisions "cannot depend on strict mathematical expectations" but must look at social issues as well. Benjamin Graham, certainly the most famous investor of all time, wrote in *Security Analysis: Principles and Techniques*, "The typical analysis of a security will treat the qualitative factors in a superficial or summary fashion and devote most of its space to the figures. The qualitative factors . . . are exceedingly important, but they are also exceedingly difficult to deal with intelligently."

The goal of Franklin Research & Development and others in the social investment field is to show how these qualitative, or social, issues can be dealt with intelligently. The overall investment philosophy utilized at this firm is that no company is invested in unless it has both positive social and financial track records and outlooks. We do not invest in firms that have an "average" or "acceptable" record, but only in those companies that stand out for their superior employee relations, environmental, product quality, and community profiles. Our investment premise is that companies that embrace broad-based corporate responsibility have the vision, values, and integrity that help them outperform those with narrow social concerns. Over the past six years, from January 1, 1984, to March 31, 1991, this has resulted in an average annual gain of 17.6 percent in the stocks in which we have invested.

| STYLES OF SOCIAL INVESTING

Within the social investment umbrella, many different financial styles can be used in investing in stocks. While these styles have numerous names, from "growth" to "value" to "contrarian" to "core," they can be summarized into two camps: investors who prefer to deal with "what is," and those who like to look at "what if."

"What Is" Investors

"What is" investors, also known as "value" or "contrarian" investors, ignore the future and try to value a company on what is presently known about it. They look to invest in existing businesses at prices that are below the intrinsic value of the company. A good socially responsible example of such an approach is given by the

Parnassus mutual fund. This fund buys stock in companies that are selling at low historical prices, usually because the company or its industry has run into some problem. Parnassus applies its in-depth social screens to these companies in order to determine which have the best chance for overcoming their problems. The fund looks for firms with good management, a high-quality product, positive employee relations, and a good reputation with consumers.

"What If" Investors

"What if" investors, also known as "growth" investors, look toward the future and try to value the company on what its potential is. These investors believe that, fundamentally, stock prices are driven by earnings. They seek to identify companies with above-average growth prospects for which they would have to pay average prices. Social issues play an important role in helping to predict the likelihood of future growth.

Franklin Research & Development uses the what-if style. More specifically, we look for a catalyst that will cause a company's growth rate to increase in the near future and that has not yet shown up in the company's price. This catalyst is often a new product or a societal trend. The following are some examples of catalysts that have led us to invest in companies.

- Growing environmental concerns have increased the growth rate for baking soda, the primary product of Church & Dwight. Baking soda can be used to lower the level of lead in drinking water and reduce sulphur dioxide emissions from power plants.
- New employee involvement and environmental programs are causing Cabot Corporation, a specialty chemical company, to change from being a high-cost, low-quality manufacturer to becoming the low-cost, high-quality supplier in its industry.

Despite the particular financial style, social investing is proving to be a more effective and integrated type of investing.

| THE ANSWER

And what of Warren Buffett's question about marrying for money? "It is a mistake under most circumstances, and insanity if one is already rich," says Buffett. Not considering social criteria when investing in stocks would provide the same outcome.

BASICS OF BONDS

Diane Keefe

To advise clients about socially responsible bond investments, one must understand the risks and opportunities in the bond market and the key factors that affect bond investors. An adviser must first define clients' tolerance for the three forms of risk common to all bonds:

- liquidity risk;
- credit risk; and
- interest rate risk.

An adviser should inform investors how their portfolios are currently weighted by industry and by maturity. The adviser then can make sales or purchases to adjust the client's portfolio to meet the client's stated objectives and risk tolerances.

This chapter begins with an examination of the concept of "risk" in the bond markets. It then looks at who and what constitute these markets. It closes with an extensive discussion of the types of corporate bonds social investors may choose from. This chapter treats only three types of bonds: Treasuries, agencies, and corporates. Municipals are discussed in the next chapter.

Diane Keefe is a bond analyst and institutional salesperson in New York City. Her work has included municipal investment banking and taxable bond sales. She is president of the board of directors of Co-op America, a Washington, D.C.– based membership organization that promotes social responsibility in business. Keefe's government service included employment with the Environmental Protection Agency and the state governments of Connecticut and Massachusetts in positions related to air and water pollution control and hazardous and nuclear waste disposal. She holds an M.B.A. in finance from Columbia University and a B.A. in political economy from Wellesley College.

| THE CONCEPT OF RISK

The *risk* associated with a bond portfolio or a single bond investment is the possibility that a bond price will decrease or that interest payments will be delayed or suspended. In government agency and investment-grade corporate bonds, the effect of interest rate changes is the dominant risk factor, while in high-yield bonds, credit and liquidity risks dominate.

Liquidity Risk

Liquidity risk, the degree of difficulty in buying and selling bonds, is a function of issue size, credit quality, and quantity for sale. One measure of liquidity risk is the spread between dealers' bid and ask quotes. A spread of one-fourth to one-half point is associated with ample liquidity, while a 2 to 3 percent spread suggests less liquidity.

Bond investment strategies are implemented most easily by institutional investors, since the market making is done over the counter (OTC). Individual investors are better served by purchasing bonds that trade on the major exchanges with listed prices. (The ticker symbols are listed in the Quotron book.) For exchange-listed bonds, the liquidity for odd lots (under $250,000 in par amount) is maintained. In the OTC issue it frequently is difficult to buy less than $100,000 to $250,000 in par amount ($100 of price for every $100 of face value).

Electronic data bases, such as the Bloomberg System, provide essential bond prices and analytical data that are required for any significant amount of bond investing. Social investors should not have to decrease liquidity or pay onerous transaction costs to realign their portfolios to reflect their social concerns.

Credit Risk

Credit risk measures the probability that (1) the bondholder will receive scheduled interest payments and/or principal at maturity, or (2) the bond issuer will not experience a decline in financial condition reflected in lower profitability (that is, the ratio of earnings to shareholder's equity), lower asset turnover (the ratio of earnings to assets), or higher leverage (the ratio of assets to equity). A deterioration in one or more of these measures can lead to the investment community's disenchantment with a particular issue or a credit rating agency downgrade, which in turn puts selling pressure on the bonds and leads to price declines for the bonds in the secondary market.

MONITORING THE RISK. The most commonly monitored ratings are those provided by Moody's and Standard & Poor's (S & P). As table 30-1 shows, bonds are rated from strongest to weakest. These ratings have real meaning. For example, the three-year (1987 to 1989) median pretax interest coverage on AAA industrial long-term debt was 12.02; on BBB, 3.62; on CCC, 0.75. *Standard & Poor's Credit Week* reports the key ratios for bonds.

TABLE 30-1
COMPARISON OF MOODY'S AND STANDARD & POOR'S BOND RATINGS

Moody's	S & P	Moody's	S & P
Aaa	AAA	B1	B+
Aa	AA	B2	B
A1	A+	B3	B−
A2	A	Caa1	CCC+
A3	A−	Caa2	CCC
Baa1	BBB+	Caa3	CCC−
Baa2	BBB	Ca1	CC+
Baa3	BBB−	Ca2	CC
Ba1	BB+	Ca3	CC−
Ba2	BB	C	C
Ba3	BB−	D	D

Whether the social investor is a high–net worth individual or a fiduciary for an institution, he or she should plan to spend a substantial amount of time on financial analysis to manage credit risk. Important analytical factors include:

- The company's business fundamentals—its competitive position, its cyclicality, and so on;
- Near-term debt maturities;
- Cash flow on debt ratios, including:

$$\frac{\text{Earnings before interest and taxes (EBIT)}}{\text{Interest expense}}$$

This equation measures cash available to pay debt before borrowing costs and tax rates are considered.

$$\frac{\text{EBIT} + \text{depreciation and amortization (EBITDA)}}{\text{Interest expense}}$$

This equation measures cash available to pay debt, recognizing that depreciation and amortization of intangible assets (such as goodwill) are expenses deducted for financial reporting purposes that do not require a cash outflow and therefore provide a cash cushion for payments due on bonds.

$$\frac{\text{EBITDA} - \text{Capital expenditures} - \text{Maturities of debt}}{\text{Interest expense}}$$

This equation measures cash available to pay debt, considering that capital expenditures often put a drain on corporate resources.

In each instance, the higher the number the equation produces, the better.

If the time and resources are not available to allocate to credit research, invest only in bonds rated A or better to avoid losses that may result from weakened credit quality if bonds are sold in the secondary market before maturity.

Interest Rate Risk

Interest rate risk considers how much a bond's price rises when interest rates fall and how much it declines when interest rates rise. Investors should strike a balance between lower yields offered on short-maturity bonds and the interest rate risk of longer-maturity bonds. If an investor sells an intermediate or long-term bond before its stated maturity, when prevailing interest rates are higher than when the bond was issued, he or she will likely realize a loss on the investment. On the other hand, an investor with a ten- to twenty-year investment horizon may sacrifice significant profit opportunities by avoiding bonds with long maturities.

The Treasury bond market is the benchmark against which interest rates on corporate bonds in the United States are measured. The assumption that underlies the Treasury benchmark is that the taxing power and currency printing capability of the U.S. government guarantee payment of principal and interest on Treasury bonds. Therefore, Treasury bond investors are compensated only for the time value of their money, not for any credit risk. Normally bonds with longer maturities command higher yields to compensate long-term investors for expected inflation. Yields on new corporate and agency issues will increase when Treasury note and bond yields rise. Then all bond investors, whether in corporate, mortgage-backed, asset-backed, or municipal issues, will require a higher yield.

TOTAL RETURN AND YIELD. The two components of total return, commonly known as *yield*, are interest payments and price (depreciation or appreciation). Just as in the stock market, investors are concerned with the holding period return:

$$\frac{\text{Bond price (end)} - \text{Price (beginning)} + \text{Interest payments}}{\text{Bond price (beginning)}}$$

If an investment is determined to be risky (that is, the bond price is expected to fluctuate a great deal during the holding period), the investor must expect a higher return to compensate for the risk. *Realized yield* is the actual total return received by the investor who holds a bond for a defined period.

The interest payments due on a bond are fixed at issuance for the vast majority of bonds. Exceptions include: *floating rate notes*, whose payments change in line with changes in the *London interbank offered rate* (LIBOR); *reset bonds*, whose coupon payments are adjusted periodically based on a formula defined at issuance; *step-up bonds*, whose coupon increases on a specified date; and *adjustable-rate mortgage securities* (ARMS), based on the formulas defined in the underlying adjustable-rate mortgage pools.

The total return on a bond adjusts to market forces by a price decrease when interest rates rise or a price increase when interest rates fall. Prices of fixed-rate bonds decline as interest rates on Treasury bonds rise, because new issues can be purchased at higher yields to maturity than fixed-rate bonds issued when interest rates were lower. In contrast, reset, adjustable, and floating-rate bonds can increase in price or have price stability when prevailing interest rates rise, because their interest payments will be adjusted to higher rates.

Yield to maturity is the interest rate that will make the present value of the cash flows of a fixed-rate bond held to maturity equal to the price. Yield to maturity equals realized yield only when interest can be reinvested at the *purchase yield* (that is, the annual percentage return defined at the time of bond issuance). This happens when interest rates remain constant. Investors who want to lock in a yield to maturity can buy a zero coupon bond. If it is held to maturity the investor will realize the yield to maturity as defined by the purchase yield.

CALL RISK. *Call* and *refund* are methods that issuers use to retire debt prior to maturity. When a bond is called, all investors in that issue are paid a final interest payment and the price set for the principal outstanding. No further interest payments are required. A refunding occurs when a corporation calls a higher-interest bond and pays the bondholders with the proceeds from a new, lower-interest issue. Generally bond calls hurt investors by forcing them to tender their bonds and reinvest the proceeds at a lower interest rate. A rare scenario in which a bond call is positive for the investor may occur when credit quality of the issuer has improved and prevailing interest rates are higher or stable. Then a *premium call price* (a price above par) might be paid to the bondholder. Call provisions and current call prices are noted in Moody's and S & P bond manuals (published monthly) and can be found in Bloomberg and other electronic data bases.

The risk that a bond will be called or refunded before maturity by the issuer is a function of three variables:

- prevailing interest rates;
- the coupon payment percentage; and
- credit quality of the issuer.

Improvement in the issuer's credit quality can increase the risk of a call, because the issuer's costs of funds from alternative sources declines. These sources of funds include internally generated cash, bank loans, and refinancing in the capital markets.

Yield to the worst call must be considered whenever a bond recommended for purchase has call or refunding provisions. Institutional investors emphasize call risks more than individual investors do, because institutions are subject to accounting and regulatory conventions that encourage them to match bond investments more closely with intermediate and long-term liabilities. Once a bond is called, the investor must find a replacement of a similar *credit quality* and a more certain maturity so that the institution can meet liabilities with the cash flow from the replacement bond.

A way to avoid unexpected calls is to buy only *noncallable issues*. The market attaches an extra value to these issues, so the investor will pay a higher price for not taking the risk. Conversely, the investor will pay a lower price for taking the risk in purchasing a *callable bond*, a bond with call features. Investors should not shy away from callable bonds priced at a premium to par if they are compensated adequately in yield premium for the call risk.

Diversification

Often institutional portfolios are so large that, to maintain portfolio diversification, they are constrained from buying many bonds of the same issuer. Individual investors should be just as vigilant as institutions in matching investments to projected liabilities. Typically individuals will not exhaust the choices the capital markets have to offer in order to replace called bonds and maintain a well-diversified socially screened portfolio.

The investor who chooses from ten to twenty bonds representing different industries whose cyclicality is diversified can avoid some measure of the risk associated with concentration in one industry or sector. The *high-grade corporate bond market*, defined as those companies with ratings of BBB− and Baa3 or better by the rating agencies (Moody's, Standard & Poor's, Duff & Phelps, and Fitch) can be categorized by issuer type into four major sectors:

1. industrials;
2. utilities and telephones;
3. banks and finance; and
4. Yankees (bonds issued in the United States by foreign entities, government or corporate, that pay in U.S. dollars).

An investor can enhance the performance of bond portfolios by constantly monitoring the *spreads between sectors*, the risk premium required to invest in each sector as expressed in basis points of yield over the *Treasury yield curve*, the interest rates on Treasuries from three months to thirty-year maturity drawn on a graph, with time on the horizontal axis and yield on the vertical axis. Once an investor masters sector relationships (for example, once it is determined that prices of industrials are generally cheaper than utilities or vice versa), he or she must analyze individual bonds within each sector to determine credit quality. Then he or she can buy or sell bonds to adjust portfolios to risk tolerances, profit objectives, and social responsibility concerns. For example, a risk-averse investor may not want to buy all of the bonds in the least expensive sector if he or she finds too much risk or not enough social responsibility in the companies in that sector.

| U.S. GOVERNMENT ISSUES

Treasuries (U.S. Treasury bonds) provide the greatest liquidity among all domestically issued bonds. The interest they pay is exempt from state and local—though not federal—taxes. But by investing in them, the investor supports the federal government's spending plans, including its high priority on military expenditures and its continued deficit spending. Agencies offer social investors a number of alternatives with tax advantages similar to Treasuries.

Treasuries

U.S. Treasuries traditionally have represented the lowest credit risk of any U.S. issued bond, since the government, unlike corporate issuers, can print currency to repay its debts on maturity. Recently many financial pundits impugned this presumption of safety. Most notably, Jim Grant, in his widely read newsletter, *Grant's Interest Rate Observer*, posits that the United States may be undermining its credit quality and thus the value of its currency.[1] Increasingly, bonds are traded globally based on the relative value of one currency versus another, one corporation versus another, or one structure of principal and interest payments versus another. Therefore the United States is no longer "safe" but is just as subject to investors' perceptions of risk and return as other issuers of debt.

Of particular concern is the magnitude of the United States' net overseas indebtedness—about $850 billion at the end of 1990. Grant observes, "This puts the debt-to-export ratio at over 200 percent, which is high. Ratios of Brazil, Argentina et al., in the crisis year of 1982 clustered in the 240 to 280 percent range." International lending agencies have imposed harsh economic policies on countries with similar ratios who have defaulted on their interest payments. The United States has far greater borrowing capacity than the less-developed world, but the difficulty of servicing a debt this size "with exports as meager as ours is nearly hopeless," Grant concludes.[2]

In a future crisis, less indebted powers may require higher interest rates on U.S. Treasury securities to compensate them for lending to a country in financial distress. Nevertheless, through mid-1991, borrowing to finance record U.S. budget deficits had been well received. Domestic investors put funds in Treasuries instead of higher-risk bank deposits, money market instruments, and stocks. In recent years both stock and bond markets have changed frequently and rapidly. If the U.S. government's financial strength deteriorates, investors will invest elsewhere.

Agencies
Several *agencies* (corporations established by acts of Congress but generally owned by private shareholders) issue bonds. These issues vary in quality, and only a few are backed by the full faith and credit of the federal government.

MORTGAGE-BACKED SECURITIES AND GINNIE MAE. *Mortgage-backed securities* are AAA rated. They support the liquidity of the secondary market in mortgage loans. They pay bondholders monthly based on the cash flows from pools of mortgages created by financial intermediaries, such as banks and thrifts. These are a reasonable alternative to Treasuries for social investors who need top credit quality and strong liquidity.

The Government National Mortgage Association (GNMA or "Ginnie Mae") is backed by the full faith and credit of the U.S. government and guarantees timely payment of principal and interest, even if the underlying mortgages in a Ginnie Mae pool go into foreclosure. (Fannie Mae and Freddie Mae, described below, also offer timely payment of interest, but the latter guarantees only eventual payment of principal.)[3]

Mortgage-backed securities provide yield spreads that are 60 to 180 basis points more than Treasuries. The longer the maturity or the higher the interest coupon, the larger the *spread,* the difference in yield between mortgage-backed securities and a specified Treasury issue. For example, if the seven-year Treasury yield is 8 percent and a Ginnie Mae yields 9 percent, the spread is 1 percent or 100 basis points. (A *basis point* is 1/100th of a percent.) The extra yield goes to investors because of the uncertainty as to the timing of principal and interest payments, since underlying mortgages can be prepaid when homes are sold or mortgages refinanced. That cash flow is passed through to the mortgage-backed securities investors. When mortgage-backed securities are purchased at a *discount* (a price less than $100 per $100 face amount of bond), mortgage prepayments will increase total return. Since interest and principal payments will be made to the investor more rapidly than expected, it is analogous to owning a bond with a shorter maturity. This presents a further complication in that prepayments must be reinvested when prevailing interest rates are lower.

AGENCIES WHOSE INTEREST IS NOT GUARANTEED. Federally sponsored agency securities other than Ginnie Mae yield more than Treasuries but do not have as much liquidity. These federally sponsored agencies are privately owned, publicly chartered entities for which there are no explicit or implicit federal guarantees. Since the federally sponsored agencies borrow less in both issue size and frequency of new issues in the financial markets than the U.S. Treasury ($500 million per issue versus $8 billion to $10 billion per auction), agencies have less liquidity, because broker dealers devote fewer resources to trading agency securities. Therefore, investors require a higher return in agencies.[4]

There is a market perception of "moral obligation" to cover federal agency defaults. Some of these perceived obligations are currently being debated in the deficit-conscious Congress. These agencies include:

- Federal Home Loan Bank (FHLB, $138.2 billion);
- Federal Farm Credit Bank (FFCB, $800 million);
- Financing Corporation (FICO, $8.2 billion);
- Resolution Funding Corporation (REFCORP, $4.5 billion);
- Student Loan Marketing Association (SLMA or "Sally Mae," $27.6 billion);[5]
- Federal Home Loan Mortgage Corporation (FHLMC or "Freddie Mae," $27 billion); and
- Federal National Mortgage Association (FNMA or "Fannie Mae," $115 billion).

Federal agencies including the Small Business Administration, Department of Housing and Urban Development (HUD), and U.S. Agency for International Development (AID) issue fixed-income securities, but their smaller issue sizes and limited liquidity make them more appropriate for institutional investors.

Federal Farm Credit System issues bonds in short-term (up to nine months) and intermediate (up to ten years) maturities. The proceeds fund agricultural loans to farmers. FHLB bonds are not guaranteed by the U.S. government, although the FHLB has a $4 billion line of credit in place at the Treasury. The bonds issued are one- to ten-year maturities. FICO began issuing thirty-year noncallable bonds in October 1987, the principal of which is collateralized by zero-coupon Treasury bonds. REFCORP bonds have the same collateralization, but only $30 billion of these are authorized. FICO and REFCORP bonds are exempt from state and local taxes, as are most federally sponsored agencies.[6]

FANNIE MAE AND FREDDIE MAE. Fannie Mae and Freddie Mae were established to maintain a secondary mortgage market. They are owned by private stockholders but have credit lines of $4 billion (Fannie Mae) and $2.25 billion (Freddie Mae) with the U.S. Treasury. Total agency debt is approximately $375 billion, while the Treasury market is over $1.9 trillion.

Freddie Mae issues *collateralized mortgage obligations* (CMOs), bonds that were created to increase the predictability of payments and to make interest payments semiannual or quarterly rather than monthly. Investors can purchase CMOs with two- to fifteen-year average lives. They are priced according to the type of underlying mortgage-backed securities collateral, the average life of the underlying mortgages, and other variables. The actual average life of a CMO may vary dramatically from the assumed average life. An investor may end up with a fifteen-year investment when the original estimated average life was ten years, for example. Beware: CMOs offered at large spreads to benchmark Treasuries have unpredictable payment streams.

As residential loan delinquencies have increased recently, the lack of a government guarantee on Fannie Mae and Freddie Mae has received more publicity. Still, spreads on Fannie Mae issues remain relatively low, approximately thirty-five basis points above the Treasury yield curve. For example, if the ten-year Treasury has an 8.10 percent yield, the Fannie Mae would yield 8.45 percent. For social investors the benefits of supporting home ownership in the United States may provide enough intrinsic value to compensate them for investing in mortgage-backed securities, CMOs, and federal agency bonds instead of Treasuries.

INVESTMENT CONSIDERATIONS. Social investors who are watchful can take advantage of trading opportunities caused by inefficiencies in the federal agency market, because certain maturity ranges are in great demand while others remain cheaper to buy. An investor can buy the cheap maturities and "ride down the yield curve" into a preferred maturity range before selling.[7]

Agencies should appeal to any social investor in favor of *peace conversion*—the movement to encourage more government support for civilian economic development instead of military programs. We do not have much say about where our income taxes go, but we do have a choice as to where we invest.

I CORPORATE BONDS

The same screening issues apply to corporate debt as they do to stocks. An adviser must determine which social issues are important to the investor. By screening their portfolios, social investors forgo some profit opportunities while avoiding some pitfalls of investing in some risky enterprises. This suggests that investors must make some trade-offs. The following section looks at some examples of these trade-offs.

Caveat: I am writing this chapter in March 1991. Price, yield, and spread relationships are constantly changing. So, my observations about the corporate bond market illustrate only general principles applicable in other market contexts.

A useful tool here is a "rich-cheap" analysis. The table at the end of this chapter lists specific corporate bonds, their ratings, maturities, and call features; this table allows comparisons of their prices and spreads in the March 1991 market environment in order to see which corporate bonds offer the most attractive combination of risk and reward. These companies were picked for their socially progressive characteristics vis-à-vis their competitors in their industries, if not on an absolute basis. Their bonds were then compared to other bonds of similar credit quality to determine whether they have a low spread to Treasuries (and therefore were "rich") or a high spread to Treasuries (and therefore were "cheap"). Large spreads to Treasuries mean that prices will be lower and yields higher for these bonds than for others with similar ratings and maturities.

Utilities and Yankees
Certain utility bonds and Yankee bonds have spreads comparable to Treasuries for similar credit quality and call risk. The yields to maturity required to compensate investors to own utilities or Yankees are in some cases only ten basis points (one tenth of 1 percent) apart. Social investors who want to sell utility bonds because they are not satisfied with the environmental risks of high-sulfur coal or nuclear energy can sell them and buy Yankee bonds, including the

debt issues of Canadian provinces, Sweden, or other sovereign governments that are denominated in U.S. dollars.

The telephone bond market, composed largely of AA- and AAA-rated companies, is priced at lower yields relative to other sectors in the bond market (specifically utilities, Yankees, and industrials), because investors perceive the industry as recession resistant. In addition, some of the telephone companies may experience growth and profitability associated with investments in cellular communications systems. Social investors may consider swapping Treasury bonds for those of telephone companies to increase yield. In order to maintain credit quality in telephone company investments, avoid companies in large urban areas. Commercial customers are bypassing the telephone companies by installing their own telecommunications systems. This could lead to significant declines in earnings in the future. Also, avoid companies with substantial investments in nontelecommunications-related businesses. Utilities that try to diversify often fail in business lines with which they have no prior experience.

Credit Providers

Asset-backed securities are created by credit providers from pools of car loans, credit card receivables, boat loans, and other loans with credit enhancements, such as bank lines of credit, so that ratings rise to the AA or AAA level. They typically have five-year maturities and average lives of from one to three years. They provide an acceptable alternative to short-term Treasury securities, if they are held to maturity. Since they are not as liquid as Treasury bonds, they are offered at cheaper prices, higher spreads to the Treasury yield curve. Their pricing is sometimes cheaper than that offered for equal or lower credit quality corporate bonds. So they can provide an attractive investment opportunity to socially responsible investors with a two- to four-year time horizon.

As a sector, banks have the highest average spreads to Treasuries. This spread, I believe, results from the perceived risk associated with continued capital adequacy problems and depressed earnings in the money center banks and in many regional banks arising from their exposure on commercial and residential real estate loans. Nonetheless, with extensive research into loan-loss reserves, quality of management, cost containment measures, and acquisition plans, investors can profit from this sector. Security Pacific, Fleet/Norstar,

First Chicago, and Wells Fargo have been long-standing favorites of social investors.

The differences between banks' portfolios, acquisition strategies, management, and geographic location may determine required return and perceived risk. For example, Security Pacific's ten-year bonds now yield 11 percent, while First Chicago's yield 10 percent. If social investors want to increase yield, the bank bond market has opportunities for those with a high tolerance for risk and a lengthy time horizon. For example, in the last year the bonds of some New England–based banks displayed price volatility comparable to high-yield bonds with 10 to 20 percent price changes in a matter of weeks. To invest in bank bonds, you must have "patient money" and be prepared to lose a significant proportion of your investment if your research is wrong.

Event Risk
In 1988 to 1989 leveraged buyouts led investors to consider the debt of industrial companies more risky than bank debt. This event risk caused the bonds of threatened companies to experience the high yields and limited liquidity associated with junk bonds. Now leveraged buyouts are out of favor, and that threat has all but disappeared. Investors require only about fifty basis points (half of 1 percent) more to invest in a high-grade industrial bond than a comparable quality utility bond. Consumer finance bonds lie closer to the riskier end of the spectrum because of recession-related concerns about increased consumer and business loan delinquencies.

Socially conscious investors may seek to rid themselves of the risk of a sudden, unpredictable loss of revenues and consequent financial crisis caused by a nuclear accident—a probability that institutional investors discount more than the environmentalist community does. Kansas Power & Light, a favorite issue of the Clean Yield Group, has an Aa3/AA-rated 9⅞ percent bond due March 1, 2000, with a yield to maturity seventy-five basis points over the ten-year Treasury. Another nonnuclear utility is Hawaiian Electric Company, but its bonds are relatively expensive as they are top quality and in short supply. Hydro-Quebec also provides a clean energy substitute to fossil fuel and nuclear utility investments in the United States, but it is highly controversial on other environmental grounds.

An alternative to BBB bonds issued by nuclear and high-sulfur coal utilities is United Telecommunications, which derives its income from U.S. Sprint and several local telephone companies. In March 1991 its Baa3/BBB-rated 9¾ percent bonds due April 1, 2000, were offered at a spread of 150 basis points above the ten-year Treasury. The market perceives United Telecommunications bonds as more risky than BBB-rated electric utilities, since the company's capital expenditures for U.S. Sprint are expected to drain cash over the next couple of years. However, the firm's longer-term prospects are strong. Its local telephone companies would provide a solid base of revenues in an economic downturn, while U.S. Sprint continues to expand its long-distance business. Its bonds appear relatively cheap over a two- to ten-year time horizon.

Another alternative that looks attractive compared to other BBB-rated utilities is Long Island Lighting Company (LILCO). This company is recovering from the financial tumult created by mothballing its Shoreham nuclear plant. If all goes according to plan, LILCO eventually will refinance high-cost debt issued when it was in worse financial shape. As interest rates fall, LILCO's high-coupon bonds have a higher probability of getting taken out of the market by call or refund, assuming that LILCO's credit quality improves. Investors could sell utilities that have had environmentally problematic power plants and buy LILCO at a significantly higher spread to Treasuries.

Retail and Consumer Durables
The bonds of many retailers are favorites of social investors. Some of the strongest performers are Dayton Hudson, Nordstrom, Dillard, Kmart, Wal-Mart, and Walgreens. However, retailers face stiff competition. Sluggish consumer demand has forced many of them to discount, thereby narrowing profit margins. It is important to analyze a company's leverage, capital expenditures, and growth prospects before investing heavily in this sector. See table 30-2 at the end of this chapter, which resulted from a 1991 "rich-cheap" analysis.[8]

If their managers do not actively research new areas in which to invest, socially responsible investment portfolios tend to be biased toward retail and consumer durable–related companies. It is possible to choose such a portfolio while maintaining diversification, but certain assumptions are inevitable. For example, the autos pose a dilemma for social investors. Their manufacturing operations have significant defense contracts and environmental problems. But some investors who screen on these questions might consider the debt of their financial subsidiaries, General Motors Acceptance Corporation

(GMAC), Ford Motor Credit, or Chrysler Finance. These subsidiaries are in consumer and business finance, not car manufacturing. Their bonds expose investors to more financial services industry (interest-rate) risk rather than auto industry cyclicality, but when auto sales improve, the subsidiaries often improve as well. The finance subsidiaries depend on access to the financial markets for relatively inexpensive corporate borrowing. They then lend to consumers at higher rates. If the parent auto company weakens, the financial subsidiaries' borrowing costs increase, weakening their performance.

Alcohol and Tobacco
Alcohol manufacturers and tobacco companies are priced "rich" (that is, with a lower yield compared to other bonds of similar credit rating) because of the high profit margins on their products. Most social investors can sell these issues and gain significantly in realized yield by investing in mortgage-backed securities or other corporate bonds. Alternatives to alcohol or tobacco company issues might include large issuers whose consumer products do not pose public health concerns, for example, Archer-Daniels-Midland and Maytag.

Heavy Industrials and Commodities
It has been difficult to find heavy industrial companies and primary commodity producers with positive social profiles. Some social investors take a best-in-the-sector approach in order to maintain widely diversified portfolios. Both Franklin Research & Development and the Domini Social Index have identified Amoco and Atlantic Richfield as having better-than-average social records relative to other oil companies. Their bonds have high credit quality (A rated or better) and are widely available across the maturity range (from two to thirty years) at spreads between 60 and 105 basis points above the Treasury yield curve.

Paper
Among the paper companies, social investors have preferred Weyerhaeuser because of its attempts to reduce pollution. Their bonds trade at 125 basis points over the four-year Treasury and 175 basis points over the fifteen-year Treasury. Other paper companies trade at 120 basis points to 295 basis points off the Treasury yield curve, based on leverage and the cyclicality of paper companies' cash flow. In a recession, demand for paper products declines dramatically. Purchased just before an economic recovery, these bonds outperform

less-cyclical companies, but a prolonged recession would do some harm to their prices.

Health Care

A somewhat neglected company is Kaiser Permanente, the largest health maintenance organization in the United States. Many investors shun the health care industry because increased government regulation aimed at cost control squeezes profit margins. However, Kaiser Permanente grows as employers seek to limit costs. It provides many preventive medical services at lower cost per employee than traditional medical treatments. Kaiser Permanente should benefit, too, as employers make provisions for employee health benefits in response to new accounting regulations.

Airlines

In the tumultuous airline industry, Delta is one of the survivors. It has a reputation as one of the more humanitarian employers in the industry.[9] If oil prices stay down and passenger traffic picks up after the Persian Gulf War, the conservatively capitalized Delta should gain both market share and profitability. In contrast, Eastern and Continental played a high-stakes game coupling labor conflicts with high leverage and collapsed under their debt burdens. A more energy efficient choice within the transportation sector is Conrail. Its 9¾ percent due June 1, 2000, is rated A3/A to yield 120 basis points over the ten-year Treasury.

Food Retailers

Grocery stores are largely ignored by investors who confine themselves to *investment grade bonds* (Baa3, BBB-, or higher ratings). Great Atlantic & Pacific Company (A & P) is the only supermarket chain company that is rated investment grade. Stop & Shop, Safeway, Vons, Kroger, Big Bear, Cullum, and Ralph's all went through highly leveraged transactions, and their debt has since been labeled *junk bonds* (bonds with a lesser rating than Baa3 or BBB). However, these chains distribute most of the food in U.S. urban centers. For that reason, they have a more recession-resistant business than do many investment-grade companies.

Corporate debt rated BB has higher debt ratios or more cyclicality to its business and therefore has greater financial risk. However, higher yields compensate investors for the higher risk. In the wake of the bankruptcy of Drexel, Burnham, Lambert and the subsequent bankruptcies of many companies that issued junk bonds, many investors have refused to buy junk bonds. However, to neglect an entire $200 billion subsector—grocery chains—may mean missed profit opportunities.

Social investors seeking higher yield and relatively stable prices would be well advised to allow their advisers to include high-quality, below-investment-grade issues such as these in their portfolios. Table 30-2 charts other high-yield issues that have socially responsible product lines. Although they have not been screened for employment practices and so forth, these companies deserve attention, because some of them provide equitylike returns.

NOTES

1. *Grant's Interest Rate Observer*, February 15, 1991, p. 3.
2. Ibid.
3. F. J. Fabozzi and J. M. Pollack, eds., *The Handbook of Fixed Income Securities*, 3d ed. (Homewood, Ill.: Dow Jones-Irwin, 1991), p. 564.
4. Ibid., p. 211.
5. Ibid., p. 209.
6. Ibid.
7. Ibid., p. 220.
8. Evan Mann, Dillon Read Taxable Fixed Income Research.
9. S. Lydenberg et al., *Rating America's Corporate Conscience* (Reading, Mass.: Addison-Wesley, 1986) p. 251.

TABLE 30-2

CORPORATE BOND RICH/CHEAP ANALYSIS

(INTEREST RATE VOLATILITY 12.00 PERCENT)

Prices as of 3/15/91, Settlement as of 3/22/91 (Prices Subject to Change)

Security	Coupon	Maturity	Call Price Date or Prepay Rate*	Spread	Quality†	Price	Yield to Maturity	Option Adj.‡ Yield	Option Adj.‡ Spread
					VERY CHEAP				
SHAWMUT NATL	9.850	6/1/99		10yr note 1623bp	:B2/BB− 13.0	49.51261	24.320	24.320	1,645bp
BNK OF BOST	9.500	8/15/97		7yr note 1009bp	B1/BB+ 12.5	68.27898	18.050	18.050	1,023bp
CHEM BNK	9.750	6/15/99		10yr note 521bp	Ba2/BBB 10.5	82.51857	13.300	13.300	534bp
CHEM BNK	10.125	11/1/0		10yr note 500bp	Ba2/BBB 10.5	84.02043	13.090	13.090	508bp
GR WEST BNK	10.500	5/30/0	100.0 2/26/99CP	10yr note 375bp	Baa1/A- 7.5	92.32940	11.840	11.934	407bp
GR WEST BNK	10.250	6/15/0	100.0 3/15/99C	10yr note 375bp	Baa1/A- 7.5	91.17864	11.840	11.813	381bp
SEAR ROE CO	6.000	5/1/0	100.0 5/1/82C	10yr note 160bp	A2/A 6.0	77.99131	9.690	9.682	162bp
SEAR ROE CO	7.000	11/15/1	100.0 11/15/81C	10yr note 160bp	A2/A 6.0	82.35839	9.690	9.668	157bp
	9.122			525bp	8.9		13.325	13.332	536bp
					CHEAP				
SECURITY PAC	7.875	1/20/97	100.0 1/20/92C	7yr note 309bp	A3/A 6.5	86.59502	11.050	11.041	324bp
SECURITY PAC	11.500	11/15/0		10yr note 321bp	Baa1/A- 7.5	101.12404	11.300	11.300	328bp
MERRIL LNCH	9.250	11/15/94		4yr note 180bp	A2/A 6.0	99.82639	9.300	9.300	191bp
HOUSEHLD FIN	9.250	10/1/93		3yr note 180bp	Baa1/A+ 6.5	100.50490	9.020	9.020	193bp
SEAR ROE CO	9.250	8/1/97		7yr note 130bp	A2/A 6.0	99.93156	9.260	9.260	140bp
HOUSEHLD FIN	8.750	6/1/93		2yr note 180bp	A3/A+ 6.0	99.93867	8.770	8.770	176bp
XEROX CRD	10.125	4/15/99	100.0 4/15/96C	7yr note 195bp	A2/A 6.0	100.82642	9.910C	9.714	181bp
SEAR ROE CO	9.350	5/15/93		2yr note 130bp	A2/A 6.0	102.06590	8.270	8.270	127bp
DELTA AIRL	9.875	5/15/0		10yr note 140bp	A3/A 6.5	102.29578	9.490	9.490	146bp
XEROX CORP	9.625	9/1/97		7yr note 125bp	A2/A 6.0	101.97204	9.210	9.210	134bp
AMR CORP	9.750	3/15/0		10yr note 155bp	Baa1/A- 7.5	100.64691	9.640	9.640	162bp
PENNEY JC CO	6.000	5/1/6	100.0 5/1/81C	10yr note 145bp	A1/A+ 5.0	71.95858	9.540	9.518	130bp
MAY DEPT	9.600	6/15/95		5yr note 110bp	A2/A 6.0	102.71480	8.810	8.810	128bp
MAY DEPT	9.875	6/15/0		10yr note 125bp	A2/A 6.0	103.23362	9.340	9.340	131bp
SEAR ROE CO	8.550	8/1/96		5yr note 125bp	A2/A 6.0	98.26605	8.960	8.960	122bp

Issuer	Coupon	Price	Call	Maturity	Term	Spread	Rating	Yrs	Price	Yield	Yield	Spread
XEROX CORP	9.200	100.0	7/15/96C	7/15/99	10yr note	130bp	A2/A	6.0	98.89551	9.390	9.176	125bp
DAYTON HUDSN	9.875			7/1/20	30yr bond	145bp	A3/A	6.5	101.27137	9.740	9.740	149bp
NEWFOUNDLAND	9.875			6/1/20	30yr bond	140bp	Baa1/A-	7.5	101.76096	9.690	9.690	143bp
DAYTON HUDSN	10.000			12/1/0	10yr note	115bp	A3/AA-	5.5	104.77114	9.240	9.240	119bp
XEROX CORP	9.750			3/15/0	10yr note	120bp	A2/A	6.0	102.75679	9.290	9.290	127bp
DAYTON HUDSN	9.625			2/1/8	30yr bond	135bp	A3/A	6.5	99.85330	9.640	9.640	143bp
DAYTON HUDSN	10.000			1/1/11	30yr bond	140bp	A3/A	6.5	102.67746	9.690	9.690	144bp
MAY DEPT	10.250			1/1/21	30yr bond	135bp	A2/A	6.0	105.91444	9.640	9.640	139bp
FINLAND	9.500			11/1/94	4yr note	50bp	Aa1/AAA	1.5	104.60624	8.000	8.000	62bp
SWEDEN	8.125	100.0	11/1/93C	11/1/96	5yr note	80bp	Aa1/AAA	1.5	98/29643	8.510	8.253	62bp
FINLAND	7.600			12/15/93	3yr note	50bp	Aa1/AAA	1.5	99.69168	7.720	7.720	57bp
UN TELECOM	9.750			4/1/0	10yr note	105bp	Baa3/BBB	9.5	103.68965	9.140	9.140	111bp
SO CENT TEL	8.250	105.0	11/1/90C	11/1/15	30yr bond	85bp	Aaa/AAA	1.0	91.32654	9.140	8.789	64bp
SO CENT TEL	9.625	106.1	3/1/91C	3/1/19	30yr bond	115bp	Aaa/AAA	1.0	101.79948	9.440	8.451	53bp
SO BELL TEL	8.625	104.7	9/1/91C	9/1/26	30yr bond	94bp	Aaa/AAA	1.0	93.70303	9.230	8.755	61bp
	9.289					139bp		5.4		9.302	9.221	139bp

NEAR AVERAGE

Issuer	Coupon	Price	Call	Maturity	Term	Spread	Rating	Yrs	Price	Yield	Yield	Spread
POC GAM SrA	9.360			1/1/21	30yr bond	74bp	Aa1/AA+	2.0	103.34861	9.030	9.030	76bp
AETNA LIFE	8.000	104.0	1/15/97CS	1/15/17	30yr bond	90bp	Aa1/AAA	1.5	88.30347	9.190	8.916	73bp
HOUSEHLD FIN	8.400			8/3/94	3yr note	180bp	A3/A+	6.0	98.21662	9.020	9.020	171bp
MORGAN JP	8.875			8/1/94	4yr note	80bp	Aa2/AA+	2.5	101.63741	8.300	8.300	99bp
CHUBB CAP	8.625			1/15/95	4yr note	70bp	Aaa/AA+	1.5	101.34798	8.200	8.200	76bp
FST CHICAGO	9.000			6/15/99	10yr note	244bp	Baa1/A-	7.5	91.68510	10.530	10.530	254bp
SECURITY PAC	9.750			5/15/99	10yr note	244/bp	Baa1/A-	7.5	95.77693	10.530	10.530	255bp
XEROX CORP	8.625	101.7	11/1/90CS	1/15/95	10yr note	90bp	A2/A	6.0	97.82824	8.990	8.358	69bp
KNIGHT-RIDD	9.875			4/15/9	30yr bond	100bp	A1/AA-	4.5	105.06342	9.290	9.290	105bp
HOUSEHLD FIN	9.625			7/15/0	10yr note	174bp	Baa1/A	7.0	98.74081	9.830	9.830	180bp
MAYTAG CO	9.750			5/15/2	10yr note	130bp	A2/A-	6.5	102.43208	9.390	9.390	130bp
WEYERHAEUSER	9.250			11/15/95	5yr note	85bp	A1/A+	5.0	102.58038	8.560	8.560	94bp
WHIRLPOOL	9.500			6/15/0	10yr note	105bp	A2/A+	5.5	102.18619	9.140	9.140	110bp
KMART	8.375	106.7	1/15/91CS	1/15/17	30yr bond	130bp	A1/A	5.5	88.43649	9.590	9.329	116bp
MCDONALD'S	8.875	107.2	8/7/90C	8/1/19	30yr bond	105bp	Aa2/AA	3.0	95.37490	9.340	8.850	73bp
WESTVACO	10.125	105.1	6/1/0CS	6/1/19	30yr bond	150bp	A1/A	5.5	103.16199	9.790	9.263	113bp
HYDRO-QUEBEC	9.375			4/15/30	30yr bond	100bp	Aa3/AA-	4.0	100.87668	9.290	9.290	102bp

TABLE 30-2

CORPORATE BOND RICH/CHEAP ANALYSIS

(INTEREST RATE VOLATILITY 12.00 PERCENT)

Prices as of 3/15/91, Settlement as of 3/22/91 (Prices Subject to Change)

Security	Coupon	Maturity	Call Price Date or Prepay Rate*	Spread	Quality†	Price	Yield to Maturity	Option Adj.‡ Yield	Option Adj.‡ Spread
PROC GAM CO	8.125	1/15/17	105.4 1/15/91CS	80bp 30yr bond	Aa1/AA+ 2.0	90.43287	9.090	8.741	57bp
HYDRO-QUEBEC	9.500	11/15/30		100bp 30yr bond	Aa3/AA- 4.0	102.17627	9.290	9.290	102bp
DAYTON HUDSN	9.750	7/1/2		125bp 10yr note	A3/A 6.5	102.79385	9.340	9.340	124bp
HYDRO QUEBEC	8.500	12/1/29		100bp 30yr bond	Aa3/AA- 4.0	91.72674	9.290	9.290	102bp
CONRAIL	9.750	6/1/0		115bp 10yr note	A3/A 6.5	103.08731	9.240	9.240	121bp
HYDRO QUEBEC	8.250	1/15/27		100bp 30yr bond	Aa3/AA- 4.0	89.21647	9.290	9.290	102bp
QUEBEC PROV	9.125	3/1/0		80bp 10yr note	Aa3/AA- 4.0	101.41877	8.890	8.890	86bp
JAPAN FIN	9.250	9/21/98		50bp 7yr note	Aaa/AAA 1.0	104.32029	8.460	8.460	49bp
NEWFOUNDLAND	9.000	6/1/19	100.0 6/1/4P	110bp 10yr note	Baa1/A- 7.5	98.55152	9.190P	9.468	125bp
ONTARIO HYDR	9.250	5/1/95		50bp 4yr note	AAA/AAA 1.0	104.28912	8.000	8.000	49bp
WILLIAMS CO	10.250	7/15/20		175bp 30yr bond	Baa3/BBB 9.5	101.94397	10.040	10.040	179bp
PROC GAM CO	8.500	8/10/9		55bp 30yr bond	Aa1/AA+ 2.0	96.92164	8.840	8.840	58bp
PENNZOIL CO	10.125	11/15/9		130bp 30yr bond	A3/A- 7.0	104.58140	9.590	9.590	135bp
SO BELL TEL	8.250	4/15/16	104.7 4/15/90C	80bp 30yr bond	Aaa/AAA 1.0	91.74440	9.090	8.699	56bp
AMOCO	8.375	6/15/5	103.0 6/15/90CS	50bp 10yr note	Aaa/AAA 1.0	98.23142	8.590	7.825	-6bp
KAN PWR LT	8.875	3/1/0		65bp 10yr note	Aa3/AA- 4.0	100.81606	8.740	8.740	71bp
PROC GAM CO	8.625	4/1/16	106.4 4/1/90CS	85bp 30yr bond	Aa1/AA+ 2.0	94.96273	9.887	8.618	50bp
SO BELL TEL	8.750	11/1/24	104.6 11/1/91C	93bp 30yr bond	Aaa/AAA 1.0	95.13203	9.220	8.645	54bp
QUEBEC PROV	9.375	4/1/99		70bp 10yr note	Aa3/AA- 4.0	103.31346	8.790	8.790	80bp
QUEBEC PROV	8.625	12/1/26		95bp 30yr bond	Aa3/AA- 4.0	93.58597	9.240	9.240	97bp
N BRUNS	9.750	5/15/20		100bp 30yr bond	A1/A+ 5.0	104.57753	9.290	9.290	103bp
DAYTON HUDSN	9.875	6/1/17	108.4 6/1/90CS	160bp 30yr bond	A3/A 6.5	99.83221	9.890	9.239	117bp
WHIRLPOOL	9.100	2/1/8		100bp 30yr bond	A2/A+ 5.5	98.37637	9.290	9.290	107bp
TRANSAMER FN	8.750	10/1/99	100.0 10/1/94P	130bp 4yr note	A2/A+ 5.5	99.84673	8.800P	9.123	157bp
INTL BNK REC	9.875	10/1/97		40bp 7yr note	Aaa/AAA 1.0	107.49728	8.360	8.360	48bp
WESTVACO	10.250	7/1/18	109.2 7/1/90CS	155bp 30yr bond	A1/A 5.5	103.83286	9.840	8.932	96bp

Name	Coupon	Maturity	Price	Call	Type	Spread	Rating	Yrs	Price	Yield	Yield	Spread
WESTVACO	9.650	3/1/2			10yr note	100bp	A1/A	5.5	103.82044	9.090	9.090	100bp
GEN FOODS	7.000	6/15/11	100.0	6/23/81C	30yr bond	120bp	A2/A	6.0	77.76253	9.490	9.427	116bp
BANC ONE CO	9.875	3/1/9			30yr bond	120bp	A2/AA-	5.0	103.27650	9.490	9.490	126bp
NOVA SCOT	9.500	2/1/19			30yr bond	110bp	A2/A-	6.5	101.05852	9.390	9.390	113bp
NOVA SCOT	9.250	3/1/20			30yr bond	110bp	A2/A-	6.5	98.60292	9.390	9.390	113bp
TOKYO METRO	9.250	10/11/90			7yr note	48bp	Aaa/AAA	1.0	104.44786	8.440	8.440	47bp
ALBERTA PROV	9.250	12/23/94			4yr note	40bp	Aa1/AA +	2.0	104.30074	7.900	7.900	48bp
PENNEY JC CO	9.000	7/1/16	104.0	7/1/90CS	30yr bond	125bp	A1/A+	5.0	94.85056	9.540	8.991	90bp
LONG ISL LT	8.750	2/15/97			5yr note	120bp	Baa3/BBB-	10.0	99.26684	8.910	8.910	110bp
DENMARK KING	7.750	12/15/96			5yr note	65bp	Aa1/AA	2.5	96.54883	8.360	8.360	56bp
BNKRS TR NY	9.200	7/15/99			10yr note	139bp	A2/AA-	5.0	98.38906	9.480	9.480	148bp
SUN CO	9.375	6/1/16	100.0	6/1/6CS	30yr bond	125bp	A2/A	6.0	98.40990	9.540	9.294	109bp
NOVA SCOT	9.375	7/15/2			10yr note	100bp	A2/A-	6.5	101.96421	9.090	9.090	99bp
MELLON BANK	8.875	9/1/98	100.0	9/1/93C	10yr note	250bp	Baa2/BBB +	8.5	91.30767	10.590	10.550	262bp
INTER AM DEV	9.450	9/15/98			7yr note	45bp	Aaa/AAA	1.0	105.68526	8.410	8.410	45bp
EURO INV VNK	8.875	3/1/1			10yr note	47bp	Aaa/AAA	1.0	102.07104	8.560	8.560	48bp
ARCO CHEM	9.350	11/1/19	108.9	11/1/90C	30yr bond	135bp	A2/A	6.0	97.17645	9.640	9.138	104bp
ARCO CHEM	10.250	11/1/10	100.0	4/1/94C	30yr bond	105bp	A2/A	6.0	108.09799	9.340	9.340	108bp
COCO-COLA CO	7.875	4/1/97			7yr note	70bp	A2/AA-	5.0	96.37037	8.660	8.533	77bp
SCOTT PAPER	9.750	10/1/97			7yr note	110bp	A3/BBB +	7.5	103.33878	9.060	9.060	118bp
PEPSICO INC	8.100	11/15/92			2yr note	50bp	A1/A	5.5	100.94424	7.470	7.470	74bp
SO CENT TEL	7.375	11/1/7	102.5	11/1/90C	10yr note	70bp	Aaa/AAA	1.0	87.74601	8.790	8.617	44bp
ARCHER-DAN-M	7.000	5/15/11	100.0	5/15/81C	30yr bond	75bp	Aa2/AA-	3.5	81.21794	9.040	8.937	68bp
SECURITY PAC	8.350	8/15/94			4yr note	200bp	A3/A	6.5	96.71058	9.500	9.500	218bp
CSX CORP	9.500	8/1/0			10yr note	125bp	A3/BBB	8.0	100.96206	9.340	9.340	130bp
CAP CIT/ABC	8.875	12/15/0			10yr note	80bp	A1/A+	5.0	99.87966	8.890	8.890	83bp
ALBERTA PROV	9.250	4/1/0			10yr note	47bp	Aa1/AA +	2.0	104.27302	8.560	8.560	53bp
SASKATCHEWAN	9.125	2/15/21			30yr bond	100bp	A2/A	6.0	98.32466	9.290	9.290	102bp
MANITOBA	9.250	4/1/20			30yr bond	90bp	A1/A+	5.0	100.59981	9.190	9.190	92bp
SECURITY PAC	8.750	9/15/94			4yr note	200bp	A3/A	6.5	97.81685	9.500	9.500	215bp
INTER-AM DEV	8.500	3/15/11			30yr bond	55bp	Aaa/AAA	1.0	96.83342	8.840	8.840	55bp
INTL BNK REC	9.250	7/15/17			30yr bond	56bp	Aaa/AAA	1.0	104.03353	8.850	8.850	57bp
SO BELL TEL	4.375	4/1/1	101.3	4/1/90C	10yr note	45bp	Aaa/AAA	1.0	72.31660	8.540	8.536	40bp
MANITOBA	8.800	1/15/20			30yr bond	90bp	A1/A+	5.0	96.05191	9.190	9.190	92bp
AMOCO	8.625	12/15/16	104.3	12/15/96CS	30yr bond	60bp	Aaa/AAA	1.0	97.31376	8.890	8.356	21bp
WEYERHAEUSER	8.375	2/15/7			10yr note	100bp	A1/A +	5.0	94.03336	9.090	9.090	88bp

TABLE 30-2

CORPORATE BOND RICH/CHEAP ANALYSIS

(INTEREST RATE VOLATILITY 12.00 PERCENT)

Prices as of 3/15/91, Settlement as of 3/22/91 (Prices Subject to Change)

Security	Coupon	Maturity	Call Price Date or Prepay Rate*		Spread	Quality†		Price	Yield to Maturity	Option Adj.‡	
										Yield	Spread
SO BELL TEL	7.600	9/1/8	103.1	9/1/90C	10yr note	70bp	Aaa/AAA	1.0	89.47310	8.790	8.565	40bp
INTL BNK REC	8.250	9/1/16			30yr bond	55bp	Aaa/AAA	1.0	94.05561	8.840	8.840	55bp
ARCO CHEM	9.800	2/1/20			30yr bond	105bp	A2/A	6.0	104.54897	9.340	9.340	108bp
WAL-MART STR	9.100	7/15/0			10yr note	50bp	Aa3/AA	3.5	103.20233	8.590	8.590	54bp
MCDONALD'S	9.750	5/1/19	106.6	5/1/90C	30yr bond	115bp	Aa2/AA	3.0	103.01904	8.440	8.165	40bp
AMOCO	7.875	8/1/7	103.6	8/1/90CS	10yr note	40bp	Aaa/AAA	1.0	94.59853	8.490	8.071	-2bp
INTL BNK REC	8.875	3/1/26			30yr bond	56bp	Aaa/AAA	1.0	100.25894	8.850	8.850	57bp
MCDONALD'S	8.875	3/1/16	106.1	3/1/91CS	30yr bond	90bp	Aa2/AA	3.0	96.92667	9.190	8.584	49bp
BANC ONE CO	10.000	8/15/10			30yr bond	109bp	A2/AA-	5.0	105.47438	9.380	9.380	113bp
MANITOBA	9.500	9/15/98			7yr note	70bp	A1/A+	5.0	104.55158	8.660	8.660	70bp
ATL RICHFLD	9.250	2/15/93			2yr note	50bp	A1/A+	5.0	103.08139	7.470	7.470	58bp
COCA-COLA EN	8.350	6/20/95			5yr note	45bp	A2/AA-	5.0	100.64938	8.160	8.160	62bp
CONS NAT GAS	8.750	10/1/19	103.8	10/1/99CS	30yr bond	85bp	Aa2/AA-	3.5	96.06175	9.140	8.689	54bp
GOLDEN WEST	10.250	5/15/97			7yr note	210bp	Baa1/A-	7.5	100.82941	10.060	10.060	224bp
ALUM CO AMER	7.000	11/15/96	100.0	11/18/81C	5yr note	90bp	A2/A	6.0	92.90198	8.610	8.565	80bp
CSX CORP	9.000	8/15/6			10yr note	135bp	A3/BBB	8.0	96.44848	9.440	9.440	125bp
XEROX CRD	9.250	3/15/93			2yr note	130bp	A2/A+	5.5	101.75363	8.270	8.270	132bp
SCOTT PAPER	8.875	3/1/98			7yr note	100bp	A3/BBB+	7.5	99.55763	8.960	8.960	102bp
BNKAMERICA	9.700	8/1/0			10yr note	180bp	A3/A-	7.0	98.83362	9.890	9.890	186bp
BNKRS TR NY	8.000	3/15/97			7yr note	119bp	A2/AA-	5.0	94.78871	9.150	9.150	132bp
SUNTRUST BNK	8.875	2/1/98			7yr note	120bp	A1/A+	5.0	98.55190	9.160	9.160	123bp
BNKRS TR NY	10.200	3/15/99	100.0	3/15/94C	5yr note	200bp	A2/AA-	5.0	102.67402	9.710	8.907	126bp
SUNTRUST BNK	8.375	3/1/96			7yr note	80bp	A1/A+	5.0	98.47293	8.760	8.760	107bp
	8.960					102bp		4.5		9.078	8.963	98bp
							RICH					
ONTARIO	9.375	11/30/8	103.3	11/30/93C	10yr note	105bp	Aaa/AAA	1.0	101.99130	9.140	8.361	34bp
GERBER PROD	9.000	10/15/6			10yr note	90bp	A2/A+	5.5	100.07185	8.990	8.990	79bp

	Coupon	Maturity	Call Price	Call/Option*	Spread	Type	Rating†	Weight	Price	Yield	Yield‡	Spread
ATL RICHFLD	9.875	3/1/16			75bp	30yr bond	A1/A+	5.0	108.20745	9.040	9.040	77bp
CAP CIT/ABC	8.750	3/15/16	106.1	3/15/91CS	100bp	30yr bond	A1/A+	5.0	94.78509	9.290	8.808	69bp
AIR PROD CHE	8.500	4/1/6	100.0	4/1/4C	84bp	10yr note	A1/A+	5.0	96.47615	8.930	8.858	68bp
ONTARIO	8.750	1/5/8	103.5	1/5/93C	80bp	10yr note	Aaa/AAA	1.0	98.76764	8.890	8.298	25bp
ATL RICHFLD	9.125	3/1/11			70bp	30yr bond	A1/A+	5.0	101.23138	9.190	9.190	71bp
SCOTT PAPER	10.000	3/15/5			110bp	10yr note	A3/BBB+	7.5	106.30006	8.790	8.790	103bp
ATL RICHFLD	10.875	7/15/5			70bp	10yr note	A1/A+	5.0	116.76883	8.760	8.760	63bp
GR A&P TEA	9.125	1/15/98			80bp	7yr note	A3/A-	7.0	101.82071	8.090	7.145	84bp
COCA-COLA CO	7.750	2/15/96	100.0	1/15/91C	38bp	5yr note	Aa2/AA	3.0	98.63487			6bp
	9.193				82bp		4.6			8.918	8.666	62bp

	Coupon	Maturity	Call Price	Call/Option*	Spread	Type	Rating†	Weight	Price	Yield	Yield‡	Spread
MCI COMMUN	10.000	4/1/11	110.0	4/1/91CS	150bp	30yr bond	Baa2/BBB-	9.5	101.82295	9.790	9.137	106bp
NOVA SCOT	9.625	1/1/95			25bp	4yr note	A2/A-	6.5	106.01404	7.750	7.750	33bp
	9.813				87bp		8.0			8.762	8.438	69bp

SOURCE: Diane Keefe.

* Shows first option only. C = callable bond, P = putable bond, S = sinking fund bond.

† Moody's/S & P followed by an average of their rating scores. For Moody's Aaa has a weight of 1.0, Aa1 has a weight of 2.0, Aa2 has a weight of 3.0, and so on. For S & P AAA has a weight of 1.0, AA+ has a weight of 2.0, AA has a weight of 2.0, and so on.

‡ Adjusted for call risk.

MUNICIPAL BONDS

Cheryl Smith U.S. Trust Company, Boston

Municipal bonds are debt obligations of cities, counties, states, and government entities below the federal level, such as state housing authorities and turnpike authorities. In general these bonds pay a fixed coupon rate on a semiannual basis and repay principal on a stated maturity date. When municipal bonds are issued, an indenture is prepared. The indenture contains a legal opinion concerning the tax-exempt nature of the obligation as well as useful information about the issuer and the purpose of the issue.

As fixed-income obligations, municipal bonds are suitable for portfolios where a high level of current income is required or where the relative stability of market value for debt instruments over equities is desired. They also may be useful for diversification, particularly for individuals in high-marginal tax brackets.

Like any fixed-income instrument, municipal bonds are subject to interest rate risk. Like corporate bonds, they are subject to credit risk, the risk that the issuer will not repay the principal and interest in a timely fashion (or at all). Municipal bonds also are subject to political risk, the risk that the privileged tax-exempt status that they enjoy may be changed by legislative acts.

Cheryl Smith, C.F.A., Ph.D., is portfolio manager, research analyst, and economist at U.S. Trust Company, Boston. She holds Ph.D., M. Phil., and M.A. degrees in economics from Yale University and a B.S. in foreign service from Georgetown University. She holds the chartered financial analyst designation from the Association for Investment Management and Research and is a member of the Boston Security Analysts Society and the Boston chapter of the Social Investment Forum.

| TAXABILITY

Municipal bonds enjoy a privileged position with regard to taxability. The federal government does not tax the interest income from municipal bonds. The states also may exempt income from taxation. Some states tax income from all issuers; some tax only income from out-of-state issuers; and some exempt all municipal bonds from taxation.

Exemption-After-Tax Current Yield

This tax advantage provides a powerful reason to invest in municipal bonds for taxpayers in a high-marginal tax bracket, as the effective after-tax current yield (the coupon, or interest payment rate on the bond, divided by the price) is much higher than that on a comparable taxable bond. The following formula provides the effective after-tax yield on a municipal bond, assuming that the bond is exempt only from federal income tax:

$$\text{Effective after-tax current yield} = \frac{\text{Tax exempt current yield}}{(1 - \text{federal tax rate})}$$

For example, if the coupon on the municipal bond was 6.5 percent, the price was 99.5 percent, and the individual was in the 28-percent marginal tax bracket, the effective after-tax current yield would be $(^{6.5}/_{99.5})$ divided by $(1 - .28)$, or 9.07 percent. That is, to achieve a comparable level of after-tax income, a taxable bond would have to provide a 9.07-percent current yield.

Only the coupon income is tax exempt, however, and bonds that are purchased at a discount receive part of their return in the form of capital gains, which is taxed at the same rate as for a taxable bond. However, bonds purchased at a premium do not generate a capital loss, because the premium most be amortized, or written down, over the life of the bond.

Political and Economic Risk

Because of their special tax treatment, municipal bonds are subject to political risk in that the regulations on the taxation of interest income, which holders may take advantage of, are subject to revision. Such changes can greatly affect prices in the municipal market relative to other fixed-income markets. For example, the 1986 tax reform act reduced the attractiveness of municipal bonds for banks and insurance companies. In 1987 these holders left the municipal bond market, depressing bond prices considerably. The 1986 act also created the alternative minimum tax, which changed the tax treatment of some special purpose and industrial development bonds for certain high-income individuals. This tax requires a complex calculation of how much tax an individual is paying relative to their income. If the percentage is too low, these bonds are taxable. If the individual is paying a sufficient level of tax, the bonds retain a tax-exempt status.

Investors should remember to diversify municipal bond holdings by geographic region as well as by maturity and by issuer. Investors in a state with high tax rates, which provides favorable tax treatment only to in-state municipal bonds, will find it appealing to concentrate their purchases in issues from that state. However, geographic concentration exposes the portfolio to a higher risk of economic deterioration in that region. Municipal bonds are subject to economic risk in that they are the obligations of state and local entities. When the economy of a region deteriorates, the actual and perceived safety of the principal and interest payments may deteriorate.

| BONDS AND THEIR MARKETS

Municipal bonds come in different types, and issues vary in size. Their market is quite different from other fixed-income vehicles.

Types of Bonds

A municipal bond may be issued as a general obligation, which is backed by the general taxing powers of the issuer. This gives the bondholder the protection of a variety of tax revenues and sources. A second major type of municipal bond is the revenue bond, which is backed by the revenues from a specified source. Examples of this type of bond would be education, hospital, pollution control, power, transportation, water and sewer, and single-family mortgage revenue bonds. A third type of bond, which is taxed differently since the 1986 tax reform act, are industrial development bonds. These bonds are issued by municipalities for commercial and industrial purposes and are secured by revenues from particular companies that use the facilities. As noted earlier, they may be subject to the alternative minimum tax.

Size of Issues

Municipal issues vary greatly in size, from a few million dollars for smaller issuers to billion-dollar issues for such states as California, Massachusetts, or New York. Some states have set up municipal bond banks to help smaller issuers save costs by banding together.

Unlike corporate, federal agency, and Treasury bonds, which generally are issued with a single maturity date, municipal bonds usually are issued with a *serial structure*. That is, the issue is divided into a series of bonds, each due on the same date over several years, and with different coupons and yields, with a final-term bond. Serial structure has liquidity implications, since there may be only a few million dollars in bonds of a particular issue for each year.

The Market

The market for municipal bonds differs considerably from those for Treasuries or agencies. The market is thin to nonexistent in particular issues, except for a few actively traded large issues.

There is an active market for *selling* bonds, through the *Blue List* or through the J. J. Kenny Wire. However, anyone purchasing bonds in sizes below one hundred bonds should plan to hold the bonds to maturity, as trading costs are very high for sizes below this and the spread (the difference between the dealer's bid and asking price) can vary between as low as a quarter point on round lots of actively traded issues to as much as 4 percent on odd lots of inactive issues.

The market for *purchasing* municipal bonds is active at the time of issue, but thereafter it is inactive. Someone wishing to purchase a specific issue may find it difficult to do so. Often one is better served by looking at dealer inventory or at available offerings through the *Blue List*. Because of the higher trading costs, diversification by maturity or spreading out the final maturity dates of bonds held in a portfolio may be a more desirable strategy for a smaller municipal bond portfolio than trying to predict interest rates and positioning the portfolio accordingly.

Because many states tax in-state and out-of-state issues differently, there may be persistent differences in yield levels from state to state. States with high tax rates and preferential treatment for in-state bonds, such as New York, California, and Pennsylvania, have lower relative yields, because New York bonds are in high demand by New York investors.

Like corporate bonds, municipal bonds may be callable. This means that the issuer may, under conditions detailed in the indenture, repay the bondholder early. Investors should check for call provisions before purchasing bonds, especially if the bond has an above-market coupon or if interest rates are expected to decline.

Credit Risk

Like corporate bonds, municipal bonds are subject to credit risk. During the Depression many municipalities defaulted on their bonds. While all of the bonds were eventually repaid, investors lost interest and suffered from delays in payment. After New York City's fiscal crisis and the default of the Washington Public Power System (WPPS), popularly known as "Whoops," credit quality has again moved to a prominent position.

Ratings

Moody's and Standard and Poor's rate municipal bonds, although they use somewhat different criteria for their ratings. An issuer may have a split rating, with one agency rating the bonds more favorably than the other. Their rating systems are similar to those used for corporate bonds. Moody's considers bonds rated Aaa, Aa, A, and Baa as of investment grade, and Standard and Poor's AAA, AA, A, and BBB. AAA and Aaa, respectively, are the highest ratings, indicating a very small degree of risk. Such a rating indicates that the issuing entity could survive an economic period similar to the Depression without being likely to default on either principal or interest. The lowest investment grade rating, Baa or BBB, respectively, indicates an adequate capacity to repay principal and interest, but it also means that the issuer is more sensitive to changes in economic conditions.

Since applying for a rating costs money, some municipalities elect to be rated by only one agency. The rating agencies look at four basic categories of information for each issuer:

1. the issuer's overall socioeconomic condition;
2. the debt structure and burden of the entity;
3. the political situation and the ability of the entity to form and maintain sound budgeting policies; and
4. the amount and availability of taxes and revenues available to fund the payments for the obligation.

Moody's pays more attention to the debt burden and the budgetary operations of the issuer, while Standard and Poor's pays more attention to the general economic condition of the issuer.

Insured Bonds

Some municipal bonds are insured, with several companies providing guarantees of timely payment of interest and principal. These insured bonds receive an AAA or Aaa rating. The scope of insured issuance is rising; 25 percent of new long-term municipal issues were insured in 1989.

In general the market evaluates insured bonds as somewhere between the rating of the uninsured bond and the stated AAA or Aaa rating of the insured bond. That is, the yield on an insured AAA bond would be expected to be higher than that on a bond that had an AAA rating on its own merits. The yield would be lower than the yield required to sell the uninsured bond, thus providing an incentive for issuers to purchase insurance and save on issuing costs.

The vast majority of municipal bond insurance is provided by three companies: Municipal Bond Investors Assurance Corporation (MBIA), AMBAC Indemnity Corporation, and Financial Guaranty Insurance Company (FGIC). The ownership of the bond insurers may be an issue for some social investors. One third of MBIA's stock is publicly held, and the remainder is owned by Aetna, Fireman's Fund, CIGNA, and Community Loan Funds (CLF). AMBAC is owned by Citibank. FGIC is owned by General Electric Capital Corporation.

I SOCIAL ISSUES TO CONSIDER

Many of the screening issues that apply to equities or to corporate bonds also are relevant to municipal bonds. Basic information about the issuer and the use of the proceeds can be obtained from the indenture accompanying the issue of the bond.

Environment

Investors should consider the purpose of the issue and the proposed use of the proceeds.

The social quality of the bond may depend not only on the stated purpose but on the location of the investment. For example, issues that fund sewers may be viewed differently if one's purpose is to expand development in the Arizona desert and the other's purpose is to rehabilitate systems in downtown Detroit.

Whether resource recovery bonds are viewed positively might depend on the technology used or might be avoided altogether. Public power revenue bonds may be for a single issuer or for a group of public or private investor-owned utilities. These should be investigated for the source of the energy and for the operating plant's environmental record in the same way that an electric utility stock would be screened. Industrial revenue bonds that finance solid waste disposal require consideration of the method of disposal being used, the alternatives to that method, and the company's environmental record.

Energy

Some municipal bonds support nuclear power plants. Sometimes this is not obvious, and information must be obtained from the indenture.

Employee Relations

One issue to consider is whether the bond issue will help finance job creation—for example, by financing infrastructure investment. The type of jobs created should be considered as well.

The type of jobs to be created is also an issue for private-purpose bonds. Is the bond financing the movement of a company from one place to another with no net job creation? For those with union screens, whether the new state has a right-to-work law is an issue, especially if the company is transferring production facilities from a unionized plant. Another issue to consider is whether the municipality is offering reduced regulatory enforcement in order to attract business.

Product

What will the bond revenues be used for? Funds may be designated simply for general municipal purposes. Or they may be designated for hospitals, roads, bridges, and schools. Some investors prefer one social purpose over others.

Within types of purposes, there are differences among the entities receiving the revenues. For example, on hospital bonds, one might want to consider community involvement by looking at the hospital's indigent care accounts receivable write-off as a percentage of revenue (it averages between 3 and 4 percent). For an educational facilities bond, what are the demographic characteristics of the institution? Does the bond issue support the expansion of a well-endowed, well-funded institution, or does it support a community college or an urban university? Single and multifamily housing bonds can be examined for affordability issues. For airport revenue bonds, the issues of community impact, noise impact, and the development of feeder and secondary impact should be considered.

Corporate Citizenship

For municipal bonds, this area overlaps somewhat with employee relations in terms of attracting new business to an area. Is the municipality involved in predatory economic development, offering substantial tax and other concessions to businesses to attract production away from other locations? Another issue is whether the local community is involved in the planning process for new industrial development.

Weapons and South Africa

For industrial revenue bonds, using the same procedures as for a stock, the company's record on South Africa and whether it produces weapons or is a major military contractor can be examined.

RESOURCES

BOOKS AND PUBLICATIONS

The Blue List of Current Municipal and Corporate Offerings, Blue List Publishing Company, 65 Broadway, New York, N.Y. 10006. (212) 770-4300.

Annual subscription: $635-$810. Daily listing of municipal bonds offered for sale by hundreds of brokers; useful for establishing market price ranges as well as for locating bonds.

The Bond Buyer, One State Street Plaza, New York, N.Y. 10004. (800) 221-1804.

The trade publication of the municipal bond industry. Daily source on municipal market news, including information on planned and new issues and the results of competitive and negotiated sales.

Munifacts is an on-line computer screen service that provides news on all new issues, pricing, calendar. Most up-to-date source of information on municipal bonds. Also provides information on economic releases.

F. J. Fabozzi and I. M. Pollack, eds., *The Handbook of Fixed Income Securities*, 2d ed. (Homewood, Ill.: Dow Jones-Irwin, 1987).

The authoritative source on fixed-income investments. Chapters by Feldstein and Fabozzi (pp. 291–328), Feldstein (pp. 540–66), and Feldstein and Fabozzi (pp. 567–78) cover the general characteristics of municipal bonds and analyzing the credit quality of municipal bonds. The chapter on tax considerations for municipal bonds is outdated.

Moody's Bond Record, Moody's Investor Service, 99 Church Street, New York, N.Y. 10007.

Contains basic information on bond issues for corporates, convertible bonds, government issues, and municipal bonds. Lists municipal bond ratings.

Moody's Municipal and Government Manual, published annually by Moody's Investors Service, 99 Church Street, New York, N.Y. 10007. (212) 553-0300.

Very valuable information source on outstanding bond issues. Contains information about demographics, debt burden, tax revenues, purposes of issues, issue size, call provisions and sinking funds, and Moody's ratings. Also available as a subscription service, updated weekly.

Muniweek—News for Tax-Exempt Issuers, Lawyers, and Finance Professionals, published weekly by The Bond Buyer, One State Street Plaza, New York, N.Y. 10004.

A weekly compilation rather than *The Bond Buyer*'s daily news. Subscription: $525 annually.

Standard & Poor's, *Municipal Bond Book, Notes, Commercial Paper, and IRBs*, published bimonthly by Standard & Poor's Corporation, 25 Broadway, New York, N.Y. 10004. (212) 208-1146.

Provides issuer CUSIP, current and five-year rating history, final maturity of the issue, some minimal financial and issuer information, and brief comment on each bond. Back of issue contains rating rationales for major issuers. Subscription: $889 a year.

U.S. STOCK AND BOND FUNDS
AND FUND FAMILIES
OPEN TO ALL INVESTORS

Ed. Note: *Some fifty-five mutual funds say they screen on issues social investors pay attention to. These range from South Africa to the environment.
This chapter describes U.S. stock and bond funds and fund families that are
open to all investors. Later chapters examine funds with financial or screening niches.*

*We asked the funds to describe themselves and their screens. Those that
did not respond are included in the directory in appendix B.*

| CALVERT SOCIAL INVESTMENT FUND
MONEY MARKET PORTFOLIO
MANAGED GROWTH PORTFOLIO
EQUITY PORTFOLIO
BOND PORTFOLIO

Calvert Group
4550 Montgomery Avenue
Bethesda, Md. 20814
(800) 362-2748
(301) 951-4820

Calvert Group serves more than 180,000 investors. Since its beginning in 1976, Calvert's assets under management have risen to over
$3.4 billion. Six of Calvert's twenty-one investment options, rep-
resenting more than $1 billion, are socially and environmentally
responsible mutual funds. Calvert offers the nation's first and by far
the largest family of socially sensitive mutual funds.

Calvert Social Investment Fund's basic investment approach
stems from the belief that companies that make a positive contribution to society are the most likely to prosper. The fund consists

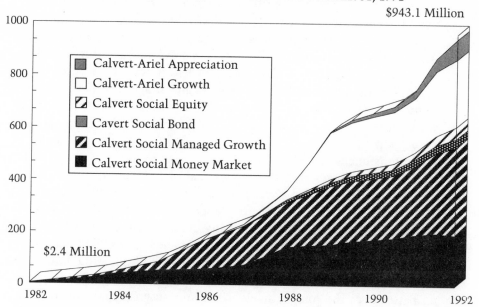

FIGURE 32-1
CALVERT GROUP SOCIALLY RESPONSIBLE FUND
GROWTH IN ASSETS THROUGH OCTOBER 31, 1991

Source: The Calvert Group.

of four separate funds: Money Market Portfolio, Managed Growth Portfolio, Equity Portfolio, and Bond Portfolio.

Calvert Group's family of socially and environmentally responsible funds includes two other funds: Calvert-Ariel Growth Fund (closed to new investors as of April 30, 1990) and Calvert Ariel Appreciation Fund. (See pages 400–404.)

Fee Structure

Minimum initial investment is $1,000; subsequent investments: $250. There are no restrictions on investors. Other services:

- automatic reinvestment of dividends and capital gains distributions at no charge;
- automatic investment and withdrawal services;
- automatic deposit of income from one Calvert fund to another;
- same-day electronic transfers;
- twenty-four-hour quotation service;
- telecommunications device for the hearing impaired.

Investment Objectives and Philosophy

Calvert Social Investment Fund (CSIF) is the first and largest family of socially and environmentally responsible mutual funds. CSIF entered the social investment arena in 1982 as the first mutual fund to take a human rights stand and include divestment from South Africa in its social criteria. The fund has developed an enlightened and practical approach that provides investors with both solid financial returns and an opportunity to encourage positive social change. Investors can achieve a variety of investment objectives within the CSIF family of four portfolios (actually four separate funds) and easily move from fund to fund when investment goals or circumstances change.

The fund believes that the overall goal of every company, organization, and individual should be long-term, sustainable profitability for the benefit of the entire planet. Investment philosophy is based on the view that every company must carefully consider the full impact of its decisions on all stakeholders. Those companies that understand the fact that today's social and environmental issues are likely to become tomorrow's economic problems are likely to do better over the long term. It is a commonsense approach that tends to reduce risk and portfolio volatility while investing in companies likely to outperform their competitors over time.

Stressing financial criteria and performance first, CSIF fund managers invest broadly diversified portfolios. The fund's conservative approach emphasizes diversification and the downside protection it provides. All companies considered for investment must pass all of the fund's basic financial and social criteria.

MONEY MARKET PORTFOLIO. CSIF Money Market Portfolio is designed for current income from safe, liquid (cash-equivalent) investments. This portfolio provides investors with a convenient cash-management vehicle, market rates of interest, and free check writing or wire transfer services. The Money Market Portfolio invests in the following instruments: commercial paper, bankers acceptances, repurchase agreements, certificates of deposits, government agency obligations. All securities mature in less than one year.

MANAGED GROWTH PORTFOLIO (BALANCED). CSIF Managed Growth Portfolio seeks long-term growth of capital while investing in enterprises making a significant contribution to society. Fund managers use a top-down scenario forecasting approach that seeks attractive investment opportunities in a diversified portfolio of stocks and bonds while maintaining a high degree of performance consistency and low portfolio volatility.

EQUITY PORTFOLIO. CSIF Equity Portfolio seeks to provide growth of capital while investing in the equity securities of enterprises making a significant contribution to society. The Equity Portfolio selects stocks based on the quality of the investment and the company's social impact. Fund managers seek out companies with the following characteristics relative to their market segments: superior profitability, growing faster than the market, selling at or below average prices, low risk, and average or below average volatility.

BOND PORTFOLIO. The Bond Portfolio seeks to provide high current income while investing in the fixed-income securities (bonds) of enterprises making a significant contribution to society. Its performance has consistently ranked in the top ten for its category of bond funds. The portfolio's holdings are predominantly U.S. government agency securities and corporate bonds (BBB or better).

Social Criteria
Once CSIF managers have identified financially attractive companies, they are screened according to explicit social criteria. The fund's criteria are generally recognized as the most comprehensive and stringent in the social investment community. If a company does not meet any one of the basic criteria, it is ineligible for investment purposes.

For Calvert Social Investment Fund, social screening is a dynamic process. The fund continually works to improve the social screening process, reflecting evolution in shareholder concerns, emerging social issues, and the availability of new research resources. An advisory council of committed experts in a variety of fields meets regularly to debate, discuss, and make policy recommendations to the fund's board of trustees and investment advisers.

Performance standards have been developed to evaluate a company's track record on corporate responsibility. Several broad areas of social concern are examined: environmental impact, product safety and desirability, workplace issues, and international operations.

Summarized below are the basic criteria that all companies must satisfy. Calvert Social Investment Fund works to invest in compa-

FIGURE 32-2
SOCIAL INVESTMENT SCREENING
The Calvert Group Funds

	Calvert-Ariel Appreciation Fund	Calvert-Ariel Growth Fund	Calvert Social Investment Fund			
			Money Market Portfolio	Managed Growth Portfolio	Equity Portfolio	Bond Portfolio
South Africa (−)	●	●	●	●	●	●
Weapons Systems (−)	●	●	●	●	●	●
Nuclear Power (−)	●	●	●	●	●	●
Alcohol/ Tobacco (−)	○	○	●	●	●	●
Gambling (−)			●	●	●	●
Polluters (−)	●	○	●	●	●	●
Environmental (+) Improvement	●	○	●	●	●	●
Management/ (+) Labor	○	○	●	●	●	●
Consumer (+) Protection	○	○	●	●	●	●
Equal (+) Opportunity	○	○	●	●	●	●
Repressive (+) Regimes			●	●	●	●
Women's (+) Issues			●	●	●	●
Sexual (+) Orientation			●	●	●	●
Animal (+) Testing			●	●	●	●
Alternative (+) Energy			●	●	●	●

(−) Avoidance Criteria   ● Active/Direct Screens
(+) Positive Criteria   ○ Passive/Indirect Screens

SOURCE: The Calvert Group.

nies with these attributes to support their innovations and to promote them as models worth emulating. It is understood that these are ideal standards of behavior that few, if any, organizations totally satisfy. As a matter of practice, evaluation of a particular organization in the context of these ideals involves subjective judgment by the fund's investment advisers.

ENVIRONMENT. CSIF's minimum environmental standard requires that companies comply with federal, state, and local environmental regulations and maintain at least an average record in their industries for pollution control and waste management. The fund does not invest in nuclear power plant operators, owners, or contractors, because current nuclear power technology is neither environmentally nor economically viable. Beyond these basic criteria, the fund directs investments toward companies that:

- have developed new products or processes that will help sustain or enhance the environment;
- have initiated innovative pollution control programs;
- have made progress in reducing waste at the source or recycling waste where possible;
- have adopted technologies to conserve energy;
- take responsibility for monitoring third-party waste haulers;
- have implemented emergency-response systems for potential accidents resulting from operations;
- conduct audits of their own environmental performance.

PRODUCTS. Companies in CSIF portfolios must produce safe and useful products and services in accordance with federal consumer product safety guidelines. Fund managers exclude companies guilty of negligence in the production of goods and services. Believing that tobacco and alcohol contribute to a variety of economic and health problems, including cancer, producers of alcoholic beverages and tobacco products are avoided. The fund seeks to include companies that:

- produce or market goods and services that enhance the quality of life for consumers;
- maintain quality control and customer satisfaction;
- respond promptly to correct problems with product safety;
- are honest in their advertising and labeling here and abroad.

Fund managers require companies using animals in product safety testing to demonstrate progress in reducing the number of animals used in such tests. Companies also must set standards for the humane treatment of animals, support research on alternatives to animal testing, and provide a viable rationale for using animals at all.

WORKPLACE. Companies eligible for CSIF portfolios provide safe and healthy work environments and promote healthy development of all employees. CSIF avoids companies that show a pattern of violating fair labor practices, occupational safety and health regulations, and equal opportunity standards concerning pay, promotion, and tenure with regard to race, religion, gender, age, sexual preference, HIV/AIDS status, or disability. The fund also rejects firms that are the object of serious National Labor Relations Board actions or are on the AFL-CIO boycott list. Fund managers favor companies that:

- are innovative with respect to employee ownership or participation in management;
- actively hire and promote minorities and women;
- compensate their workers fairly;
- enjoy good union-management relations;
- provide programs and benefits that support workers and their families.

WEAPONS CONTRACTING. Excessive production and deployment of destructive weapons are the greatest threat to the survival of life on our planet. CSIF will not invest in companies significantly involved in weapons production. Specifically, we avoid the top one hundred weapons contractors, companies whose weapons contracts exceed 10 percent of their sales, or manufacturers of components designed primarily for nuclear weapons systems.

INTERNATIONAL OPERATIONS. CSIF expects companies to be responsible for corporate citizens abroad as well as at home. Fund managers pay particular attention to the activities of corporations in countries that have records of political repression and basic human rights violations, such as South Africa.

Because South Africa's legislated racism is the target of an international campaign, the fund prohibits investment in any company with direct or indirect ties (through licensing, franchise, or trademark agreements) in that country. Financial institutions may be included in CSIF portfolios only if they have no outstanding loans to South Africa or they have a policy prohibiting future lending to its public or private sectors, and if they have ended correspondent banking ties to South Africa.

For multinational operations outside of South Africa, fund managers examine corporate behavior rather than the political activity of host governments, which may be prone to change. Multinationals are held accountable on the same issues that apply domestically: respect for the environment, product safety and fairness to workers, and no involvement in repressive acts or weapons contracting.

Fund Adviser

Calvert Asset Management Company
4550 Montgomery Avenue
Bethesda, Md. 20814
(301) 951-4800

Fund Subadviser

U.S. Trust Company
Asset Management Division
40 Court Street
Boston, Mass. 02108
(617) 726-7271

Primary Portfolio Managers

MONEY MARKET PORTFOLIO. Colleen M. Trosko has been with the Calvert Group since June 1986 and has been a member of the Portfolio Investment Department of Calvert Asset Management Company since January 1987. She has managed the Money Market Portfolio since March 1988. Trosko graduated from Radford University in 1986 with a B.S. in finance.

MANAGED GROWTH PORTFOLIO AND EQUITY PORTFOLIO. Domenic Colasacco is executive vice president, U.S. Trust Company of Boston. He is chairman of U.S. Trust's Executive Policy Committee and has been chief investment officer since 1974. He has managed the CSIF Managed Growth Portfolio since 1984 and the Equity Portfolio since its inception. Colasacco is a chartered financial analyst and a member of the Boston Security Analysts Society. He earned B.S. and B.M.S.A. degrees from Babson College.

BOND PORTFOLIO. Lawrence Litvak is a senior vice president of U.S. Trust Asset Management Division and has been the primary manager of the Bond Portfolio since its inception. He is responsible for the first practical application of portfolio risk models to socially screened investment portfolios. Litvak earned a B.A. in economics from Stanford University, a master's degree in public policy from Harvard University's Kennedy School of Government, and is a chartered financial analyst.

Contact
Seven J. Schueth is vice president of Socially Responsible Investing of the Calvert Group. Schueth coordinates marketing, serves as

FIGURE 32-3
CALVERT SOCIALLY SCREENED EQUITY FUNDS
VERSUS
S&P 500 AND NASDAQ/OTC MARKET INDEXES
SEPTEMBER 30, 1991

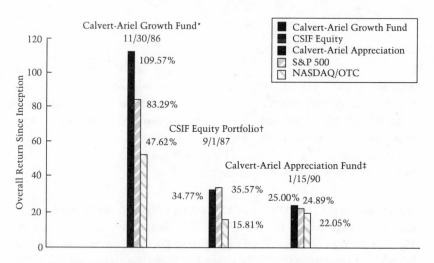

*Calvert-Ariel Growth Fund: Inception 11/6/86 compared with S & P 500 and NASDAQ/OTC. Indexes from 11/30/86.
†Calvert Social Investment Fund Equity Portfolio: Inception 9/1/87.
‡Calvert-Ariel Appreciation Fund: Inception 1/15/90 compared with S & P 500 and NASDAQ/OTC. Indexes from 12/31/89.

SOURCE: The Calvert Group.

TABLE 32-1

CALVERT SOCIAL INVESTMENT FUND PERFORMANCE DATA

The performance figures are overall return, which do not reflect deduction of the fund's applicable sales charges. They are provided for comparison purposes with the Lipper averages and market indexes, which also do not reflect any sales charges.

Money Market Portfolio*

1982	1983	1984	1985	1986	1987	1988	1989	1990
9.93†	9.31	10.21	7.77	6.16	6.02	7.07	8.79	7.69

*CSIF Money Market Portfolio should be compared to Donoghue's Domestic Prime Average.

†Inception of the Money Market Portfolio was October 1982. Performance is from October 21 through December 31, 1982.

Managed Growth Portfolio*

1982	1983	1984	1985	1986	1987	1988	1989	1990
4.80†	11.29	6.79	26.91	18.14	4.98	10.73	18.72	1.77

*CSIF Managed Growth Portfolio should be compared to the Lipper Balanced Fund Average.

†Inception of the Money Market Portfolio was October 1982. Performance is from October 21 through December 31, 1982.

Equity Portfolio*

1987	1988	1989	1990
−14.10†	14.76	27.45	−4.88

*CSIF Equity Portfolio should be compared to the Lipper General Equity Fund Average, the S & P 500, and the NASDAQ/OTC index. The Equity Portfolio has outperformed all three of these market indexes since its inception.

†Inception of Equity Portfolio was August 1987. Performance for 1987 is from August 28 through December 31, 1987.

Bond Portfolio*

1987	1988	1989	1990
3.82†	8.02	13.55	8.30

*CSIF Bond Portfolio should be compared to the Lipper BBB Corporate Bond Fund Average and the Shearson Lehman Government–Corporate Bond Average.

†Inception of the Bond Portfolio was August 1987. Performance for 1987 is from August 28 through December 31, 1987.

spokesman for Calvert Group's family of socially and environmentally responsible mutual funds, and serves on the board of directors of the Social Investment Forum. His background includes twelve years of experience in sales and management in the investment and financial services industry and three years in the nonprofit sector as director of development for the University of Pennsylvania's Wharton School.

| CALVERT-ARIEL GROWTH FUND
CALVERT-ARIEL APPRECIATION FUND
CALVERT-ARIEL FUNDS

4550 Montgomery Avenue
Bethesda, Md. 20814
(800) 362-2748
(301) 951-4820

Fee Structure

Minimum initial investment is $2,000. Subsequent investments: $250. There are no restrictions on investors, but Calvert-Ariel Growth Fund was closed to new investors as of April 30, 1990. Other services:

- automatic reinvestment of dividends and capital gains distributions at no charge;
- automatic investment and withdrawal services;
- automatic deposit of income from one Calvert fund to another;
- same-day electronic transfers;
- twenty-four-hour quotation service;
- telecommunications device for the hearing impaired.

Investment Objectives and Philosophy

The Calvert-Ariel funds seek long-term capital appreciation by investing in smaller companies demonstrating excellent long-term growth potential. These companies can be purchased at attractive prices relative to their expected earnings growth. This potential enables the funds to seek substantial gains during up markets, while the value aspect helps provide downside protection.

The investment philosophy revolves around the search for earnings consistency and does not trade or time the market for short-term gains. Investing strictly for long-term capital appreciation, fund managers expect that as a company grows, an investment in the company will grow as well.

CALVERT-ARIEL GROWTH FUND. Calvert-Ariel Growth Fund seeks long-term capital appreciation by investing in companies whose market capitalization falls between $50 million and $200 million and that demonstrate excellent long-term growth potential.

The fund looks for companies that have been overlooked or misunderstood by institutional and individual investors. Through extensive in-house research, Ariel Capital Management strives to identify companies in secure market segments with solid products and services that are expected to prosper.

CALVERT-ARIEL APPRECIATION FUND. Calvert-Ariel Appreciation Fund was created to offer investors the opportunity to participate in today's dynamic growth stocks while minimizing the risk potential normally associated with such investments. Fund managers look for sound investments that can not only keep pace with inflation but outperform it.

Designed to enhance tomorrow's goals today, the fund favors investment in undervalued companies demonstrating excellent growth potential. In addition, the fund seeks to achieve above-average returns as compared to those realized by similar equity products heavily invested in highly capitalized blue chip corporations. The fund searches for companies whose market capitalization falls into the $200 million to $3 billion range.

The fund does not trade or time the market for quick gains. Rather, it invests for long-term capital appreciation in securities which are undervalued relative to the market as a whole. This investment approach is designed to maximize growth while guarding against substantial risk.

Social Criteria
The Calvert-Ariel funds actively seek to invest in companies that provide excellent opportunity for financial return and also meet certain social criteria.

The funds will not invest in companies engaged in the manufacture of weapons systems, the production of nuclear energy, or the manufacture of equipment to produce nuclear energy. The inherent instability of nuclear power and defense-dependent industries reinforces the premise that a commonsense social policy goes hand in hand with a prudent fiscal policy. Additionally, neither fund will invest in companies directly engaged in business in South Africa.

The fund's investment advisers believe that there are long-term benefits inherent in an investment philosophy that demonstrates concern for human rights, economic priorities, and international relations.

CALVERT-ARIEL APPRECIATION FUND. In addition to the screening criteria, the Calvert-Ariel Appreciation Fund actively seeks to invest in companies that achieve excellence in both financial return and environmental soundness, selecting issuers that take positive steps toward preserving our environment and avoiding companies with poor environmental records. Each potential investment is carefully screened for possible environmental violations by Franklin Research & Development (Boston), which also provides ongoing environmen-

---

TABLE 32-2

CALVERT ARIEL PERFORMANCE DATA

The performance figures below are overall return, which do not reflect deductions of the fund's applicable sales charges. They are provided for comparison purposes with the Lipper averages and market indexes, which also do not reflect any sales charges.

Calvert-Ariel Growth Fund*

1986	1987	1988	1989	1990
2.04[+]	11.40	39.93	25.11	−16.08

*Calvert-Ariel Growth Fund is measured against the S & P 500, the NASDAQ/OTC index, and the Lipper General Equity Average. It has outperformed all of these market indexes since its inception.

[+]Inception of Calvert-Ariel Growth Fund was November 1986. Performance for 1986 is for the period from November 6 through December 31, 1986.

Calvert-Ariel Appreciation Fund*

1990
−1.18%[+]

*Calvert-Ariel Appreciation Fund is measured against the S & P 500, the NASDAQ/OTC index, and the Lipper General Equity Average. It has outperformed these market indexes since its inception.

[+]Inception of the Calvert-Ariel Appreciation Fund was from January 15, 1990. Performance for 1990 is for the period from January 15 through December 31, 1990.

tal monitoring for all issues selected for inclusion in the portfolio. The fund's investment advisers feel that concern for the environment now reduces the risk of future litigation and the consequent impact that may have on earnings.

Fund Adviser
Ariel Capital Management
307 North Michigan Avenue
Chicago, Ill. 60601
(312) 726-0140

Primary Portfolio Managers

CALVERT-ARIEL GROWTH FUND. John W. Rogers, Jr., is chairman, president, and founder (in January 1983) of Ariel Capital Management, the largest minority-owned money-management firm in the United States. The success of the Calvert-Ariel Growth Fund has brought Rogers significant media attention. *Sylvia Porter's Personal Finance* named him 1988 Portfolio Manager of the Year. He has appeared on "Wall Street Week" and "The Nightly Business Report" and has been profiled or interviewed by such publications as *Barron's*, *Fortune*, the *New York Times*, and *Money*.

CALVERT-ARIEL APPRECIATION FUND. Eric T. McKissack is senior vice president and director of research for Ariel Capital Management and primary portfolio manager for Calvert-Ariel Appreciation Fund. McKissack earned a B.S. in management and architecture from Massachusetts Institute of Technology and an M.B.A. from the University of California at Berkeley. Prior to joining Ariel Capital Management, he served as an investment officer with the First National Bank of Chicago. He is a chartered financial analyst.

Contact
Steven J. Schueth, vice president of Socially Responsible Investing of the Calvert Group, coordinates marketing and serves as spokesman for Calvert Group's family of socially and environmentally responsible mutual funds. He also serves on the board of directors of the Social Investment Forum. Schueth's background includes twelve years of experience in sales and management in the investment and financial services industry and three years in the nonprofit

sector as director of development for the University of Pennsylvania's Wharton School.

| DOMINI SOCIAL INDEX TRUST

Six St. James Avenue
Boston, Mass. 02116
(800) 762-6814

Fee Structure and Restrictions on Potential Investors
The fund has no load. It has a .25-percent 12b-1 fee. Its operating ratio is .75 percent. Minimum initial investment is $1,000, except for an individual retirement account (IRA), where it is $250. The fund is open to all investors. Annual dividends are reinvested at net asset value (that is, without a sales charge).

Investment Objective and Philosophy
The investment objective of the fund is to provide its shareholders with long-term total return (reflecting both dividend and price performance of the fund), which corresponds to the total return performance of the Domini Social Index (DSI).

The fund seeks to achieve its investment objective by investing all of its assets into the stocks comprising the DSI, a common stock index developed and maintained by Kinder, Lydenberg, Domini & Company (KLD). The fund is not managed in the traditional investment sense, since changes in the composition of its securities holdings are made in order to track the changes in the composition of securities included in the index.

Social Screens
The Domini Social Index is an index of four hundred companies that meet certain social criteria. The index's criteria, which are described in chapter 25, are also the fund's criteria. The index's screens may be more strict than those stated in the fund's prospectus, which states:

> The primary criteria exclude companies which, based on data available to the Advisor, derive more than 4% of their gross revenues from the manufacture of tobacco products or alcoholic beverages; derive more than 4% of gross revenues from gambling enterprises; own directly

more than a 4% interest in or operate nuclear power plants or derive more than 4% of gross revenues from sales to the nuclear power industry; or have operations in South Africa or, through licensing or sales arrangements, are widely perceived to aid in the enforcement of the apartheid system. In evaluating stocks for inclusion in the Index, the Advisor will also consider other secondary criteria such as the quality of a company's products and its attitudes with regard to consumer issues; its environmental performance, particularly in taking positive initiatives in environmental matters; the company's corporate citizenship; and its employee relations. Corporate citizenship includes the company's record of philanthropic activities, its interaction with the communities it affects, and the presence of women and minorities on its Board of Directors. Employee relations includes a company's record with regard to labor matters, its commitment to workplace safety and to equal employment opportunity (reflected, for example, in the number of women and minorities in executive positions), the breadth, quality and innovation of its employee benefit programs, and its commitment to provide employees with a meaningful participation in company profits either through stock purchase or profit sharing plans.

Advisers and Subadvisers
State Street Bank & Trust Company is the portfolio investment manager. Kinder, Lydenberg, Domini & Company is the portfolio investment adviser. This firm has sole responsibility for maintaining the Domini Social Index and its composition.

Performance Data
The fund opened May 30, 1991.

| DREYFUS THIRD CENTURY FUND

The Dreyfus Corporation
200 Park Avenue
New York, N.Y. 10166
(212) 922-6000
(212) 238-4512 (fax)

Fee Structure and Restrictions
Minimum investment is $2,500 initially, $100 for subsequent investments. This fund has no load. Management fee is 0.75 percent; redemption fee: none.

Philosophy and Screens

Goal: growth.

Founded in 1972 by Howard Stein, Dreyfus's chairman and CEO, the Third Century Fund is a common stock fund primarily serving socially minded individual and institutional investors concerned with protection of the environment, consumer protection and product safety, equal employment opportunity, and occupational health and safety. Companies with any direct investment in South Africa or owning another company with a 10 percent or more equity interest in South Africa are barred from consideration. Also, because of the product safety screen, companies manufacturing tobacco products are automatically excluded.

Tiffany Capital Advisors, a minority-controlled firm, serves as subadviser to the fund and selects potential stocks based on their financial attributes. Then, before a security is purchased, the Dreyfus social responsibility research staff evaluates each company's record in the areas listed above. In examining companies, Dreyfus analysts employ a variety of sources: data bases, such as NEXIS and LEXIS; government records; business and trade publications, such as those of the Council on Economic Priorities; and the Domini Social Index; and reports of watchdog groups, including the Citizens Fund, the National Wildlife Federation, and the National Resources and Defense Council. The fund is also a member of the Social Investment Forum.

If the initial search does not reveal any negative patterns of con-

TABLE 32-3

THE DREYFUS THIRD CENTURY FUND PERFORMANCE

Since Inception	10 Years	5 Years	1 Year	1Q '91	1990	1989	1988	1987	1986
841.7%	179.1%	79.7%	21.0%	19.8%	3.6%	17.3%	8.2%	2.5%	4.8%

1985	1984	1983	1982	1981	1980	1979	1978	1977	1976
30.2%	1.4%	19.8%	4.6%	−11.1%	42.0%	59.9%	10.2%	13.2%	23.6%

1975	1974	1973	1972
54.8%	−29.4%	−12.4%	−0.3%*

SOURCE: Lipper Analytical Services.
*Figures indicate fund performance since inception.

duct in any of the screened areas, the company is then approved for purchase. Dreyfus augments its research with questionnaires and interviews with company management willing to provide a comprehensive understanding of the company's philosophy and its records in the special areas of interest to the fund. At any point in this process, the directors of the fund may oblige the managers to divest any holding it deems unfit.

As of June 30, 1991, the Third Century Fund's assets were $260 million and its top five holdings were Astra A Free (health care), Microsoft (microcomputer software), General Motors Class E (business systems), Wal-Mart Stores (discount houses), and SYSCO Corporation (food distributors), and Coca-Cola (soft drinks).

Contact
Diane M. Coffey, vice president.

| FIDELITY SOCIAL PRINCIPLES FUND

Fidelity Bank
Charitable/Corporate Funds Management
1700 Market Street, Ninth Floor
Philadelphia, Pa. 19103
(215) 496-1963

Fee Structure and Restrictions on Potential Investors
Trust customers of Fidelity Bank are eligible investors for the Social Principles Fund. There is no minimum level for initial or subsequent investments and no charges on dividend reinvestments.

Investment Objective and Philosophy
The objective of the Fidelity Social Principles Fund is to seek an acceptable total rate of return on investment while applying social and ethical principles to the investment process. The primary objective of the fund is growth of capital and the secondary objective is growth of income. The fund is an equity fund, with the turnover less than average when compared to other endowment equity funds. The Investment Policy Committee of Fidelity Bank determines the cash balance in the fund. Market timing is not a factor in the investment style of the Social Principles Fund.

Social Screens

SOUTH AFRICA. Companies are ineligible if they have direct equity investments in South Africa or if they maintain any indirect, non-equity investments (licensing, trademarks, and so on).

MILITARY. Eligible companies do not manufacture military or weapons-related products as a primary source of income. If a company derives 10 percent or more of its total income from military manufacturing, it is not eligible for investment.

GAMBLING, LIQUOR, AND TOBACCO. Companies whose primary source of income is derived from the gambling, liquor, or tobacco industries are ineligible. If a company derives 10 percent or more of its total income from any of these three industries, it is not eligible for investment.

NORTHERN IRELAND. Only companies that demonstrate fair employment practices in operations within Northern Ireland are eligible.

PROACTIVE INVESTMENT. Up to 10 percent of the fund may be invested in proactive, socially focused firms. This will reward firms that have a socially positive influence through their products and services (for instance, plastic recycling) or exert a positive influence on the community (such as a firm's community outreach program).

Contact
David P. Harrison, vice president, serves as head of the Charitable/Corporate Funds Management Unit of First Fidelity Bancorporation, with over $1.3 billion under management. Harrison joined the bank in 1966 and has worked as an investment research analyst and per-

TABLE 32-4

FIDELITY SOCIAL PRINCIPLES FUND PERFORMANCE DATA
Annual Performance Data on Total Return Basis

1988*	1989	1990
5.00%	18.97%	−6.77%

NOTE: The performance of the FSPF should be compared to the S & P 500.
*Fund inception: June 1, 1988.

sonal portfolio manager. Currently he is the fund manager of the Social Principles Fund and the Charitable Equity Fund.

| LINCOLN NATIONAL SOCIAL AWARENESS FUND

Lincoln National Life Insurance Company
1300 South Clinton Street
Box 2340
Fort Wayne, Ind. 46801
(800) 348-1212

The Lincoln National Social Awareness Fund is one of eight variable funding options available through the Multi Fund, Separate Account C Variable Annuity.

Fee Structures and Restrictions on Investors

PERIODIC PAYMENT CONTRACTS

Tax-deferred annuity (TDA)	$200 annually ($10 per payment desired)
Deferred compensation	$260 annually ($10 per payment desired)
Simplified employee pension plan (SEPP)	
Keogh Plans (HR-10)	
Individual retirement account (IRA)	
Nonqualified	$600 annually (not less than $25 per payment)
Lump sum payments	$5,000 initial, $1,000 subsequent

Multi Fund Variable Annuity Charges

On the Multi Fund Variable Annuity, a maximum annual charge of 1.482 percent will be made against the variable assets of the contract to cover investment management expenses and mortality and expense guarantees. This charge is assessed daily in the unit value calculations.

The 1.482-percent maximum represents the following charges:

1. Charge for investment management expense:
   .48 percent of the first $200 million of net assets in each fund; plus
   40 percent of the next $200 million of net assets in each fund; plus
   .30 percent of net assets over $400 million in each fund.

2. Charge for mortality and expense guarantees: 1.002 percent of all variable net assets.

Also, during the accumulation period, an administrative maintenance fee of $25 will be deducted from each contract owner's payment contract at the end of each contract year and at the time of surrender. The $25 fee does not apply to a single or flexible contract with deposits over $10,000.

Multi Fund is a lifetime money-management program available to all individuals and institutions, depending on market. It combines tax advantages, savings and investment choices, and flexibility through the eight investment options.

Investment Objective and Philosophy

Assets in the fund are invested in common stocks that are selected in accordance with the fund's social criteria. The primary criterion is to not invest in companies that operate in South Africa. The investment objective is long-term capital appreciation.

Social Screens

As a matter of fundamental policy, the fund will not purchase securities issued by companies organized under South African law. Nor will it invest in companies listed in section one of the directory *U.S. Business in South Africa 1991* or section one of the directory *International Business in South Africa 1990*, both published by the Investor Responsibility Research Center (IRRC), Washington, D.C., as updated from time to time. This policy may not be changed without shareholder approval.

The fund will not invest in or hold securities of companies that, in the determination of the adviser or subadviser, are engaged in activity that has a substantial negative impact on one or more of the following:

- the protection of the environment;
- the proper use of natural resources;
- the health and safety of their workers;
- the protection of consumers;
- the purity of their products;

- the availability of equal employment to their job applicants and employees.

These criteria are not fundamental and may be changed by the board of directors of the fund without shareholder approval.

Adviser
Lincoln National Investment Management Company
1300 South Clinton Street
Box 1110
Fort Wayne, Ind. 46801
(219) 455-4978

Subadviser
Modern Portfolio Theory Associates
630 Fifth Avenue
New York, N.Y. 10111
(212) 247-5858

TABLE 32-5

LINCOLN NATIONAL SOCIAL AWARENESS FUND PERFORMANCE DATA

1988	1989	1990	Inception to 12/31/90*
+4.22%	+30.18%	−5.30%	+24.48%

NOTE: The figures in this table are net of recurring expenses.
*Introduced to the Multi Fund Variable Annuity on May 2, 1988.

Lincoln National Life

Lincoln National Life (LNL), with assets worth more than $18 billion, is a subsidiary of Lincoln National Corporation, an insurance holding company based in Fort Wayne, Indiana. With assets exceeding $27 billion, Lincoln National Corporation is the country's seventh-largest holding company whose subsidiaries are engaged primarily in insurance investment management. Today LNL serves more than 375,000 annuity participants and more than 7,000 corporate clients.

| MUIR CALIFORNIA TAX-FREE BOND FUND

One Sansone Street
Suite 810
San Francisco, Calif. 94104
(415) 616-8500
(800) 648-3448

Fees and Restrictions

The minimum investment is $2,500, with the minimum subsequent investment being $100. The expense ratio is limited to no more than one hundred basis points. There is no 12b-1 plan. The maximum sales charge is 4.5 percent, declining to zero for investments of $1 million or more. There is no sales charge on dividend reinvestment. The fund is available to all investors, but it is appropriate only for those paying personal or corporate income tax to the State of California.

Objective

Our investment objective is to provide a high level of current income exempt from both federal and California state personal income tax. We plan to create a national tax-free fund as well. We seek to achieve this objective by concentrating our investments in securities that we believe will provide social, environmental, and economic benefits. The fund is intended to operate with very low turnover.

Social Screens

We invest primarily in tax-exempt securities in the following three areas:

1. Education—we invest in securities that finance such projects as the construction of public and private education facilities, including schools; vocational training; libraries; and child care. We also will invest in securities used to provide student loans.

2. Environment—we invest in securities that finance projects like the acquisition and development of parks, the preservation of ancient forests and wildlife habitats, the creation of public transit, the development of recycling facilities, the conservation of energy and the development of renewable energy sources, and the construction of water treatment facilities.

3. Housing—we invest in securities that provide funds for the construction, development, or purchase of affordable housing. To the extent possible, we concentrate our investment on low-income housing.

While we do not intend to concentrate on any other categories, we may invest a portion of our assets in other types of securities that we believe are positive. For example, we may invest in securities that finance a hospice for AIDS patients, a community health clinic primarily serving patients without health insurance, or a cogeneration facility.

We do not invest in securities that provide funding for projects and programs that our board of trustees has determined not to have a positive social and economic impact. For example, we do not acquire securities that finance the construction or the maintenance of correctional facilities, highways, parking garages, toxic waste dumps, dams or other water utilization facilities, golf courses, country clubs, power transmission, or utilities relying on nuclear power.

Managers
The fund's investment manager is Sand County Securities, L.P. (One Sansone Street, Suite 810, San Francisco, Calif. 94104. [800] 648-3448). The president and chief executive officer of the trust is Michael Hall Kieschnick. The vice president for marketing and social research is Christina Desser, former executive director of Earth Day 1990. The vice president for investor relations is Keith Goodlett, former manager of customer services and sales at Working Assets Money Fund. The fund's investment adviser is GMG/Seneca Capital Management (909 Montgomery Street, Suite 600, San Francisco, Calif. 94109. [415] 677-1600). The managing partner is Gail Seneca, former senior vice president in charge of fixed-income investment at Wells Fargo Bank.

Performance Data
The fund began operations on June 1, 1991.

Contact
Michael Kieschnick is the president of the Muir California Tax Free Bond Fund. He is also president of Sand County Ventures, a venture capital firm focusing on opportunities in environmental and human services. Kieschnick is also the chairman of Working Assets Fund-

ing Service, which runs a donation-linked VISA program and long-distance telephone service with more than 150,000 customers. In 1983 he helped found Working Assets Money Fund, the largest socially responsible money market fund, and served on its board of trustees until 1988. Earlier he served as the economic adviser to the governor of California and as an economist for the Environmental Protection Agency (EPA).

Kieschnick also serves on the boards of the Tides Foundation, the California League of Conservation Voters, Feeling Better Health Daycare, PureHarvest, and Zofcom. For six years he was a visiting lecturer at the Graduate School of Public Policy, University of California at Berkeley, teaching a graduate seminar on financial innovation. He holds a Ph.D. in public policy (1982) from Harvard as well as undergraduate degrees in biology and economics from Stanford. With Julia Parzen, he is the coauthor of a forthcoming book on development banking entitled *Credit Where It Is Due*.

| THE PARNASSUS FUND

244 California Street
San Francisco, Calif. 94111
(415) 362-3505
(800) 999-3505

Fee Structure

The minimum investment is $2,000, or $1,000 for IRA and SEP-IRA accounts. Subsequent investment minimum is $100. Maximum sales charge is 3.5 percent. There is no sales charge on reinvesting dividends or for redeeming shares. There are no 12b-1 charges. The fund is open to all kinds of investors—individuals, institutions, investment clubs, and retirement plans.

Investment Objectives and Philosophy

The Parnassus Fund is a long-term growth fund that invests in equities. We use a "contrarian" investment philosophy where we look for companies that have fallen out of favor with Wall Street. We use valuation ratios to compare the price of a firm's stock to its book value, sales per share, earnings, and cash flow to determine if the stock is undervalued. We also examine the company's financial health.

Once a company meets the undervalued tests, we look closely at its management to see if it has the necessary spark to bounce back from adversity. In evaluating management, we look at the quality of the company's products, the manner in which it treats its employees, and whether or not the company acts in an environmentally responsible manner.

Thus, companies that have both a positive social profile and an undervalued stock price are considered for inclusion in the Parnassus Fund's portfolio. In addition, we do not invest in companies that have operations in South Africa, manufacture weapons, generate nuclear power, produce alcohol or tobacco, or are involved with gambling.

Social Screens

SOUTH AFRICA. The fund does not invest in firms with operations in South Africa. South Africa has always been an important social question that we have considered, but in our first few years in operation, we did invest in firms that had a minor presence in South Africa. In 1987, following the lead of the Reverend Leon Sullivan and the South African trade unions, we changed our policy to avoid investing in firms with any operations in South Africa. We look askance on licensing agreements, although a licensing agreement does not automatically disqualify a company from consideration.

WEAPONS. With regard to weapons, the fund does not invest in companies that manufacture weapons, such as Rockwell and General Electric. However, a contract with the Department of Defense does not disqualify a company automatically. If the product being sold to the Department of Defense is the same product available to the civilian public (a Coleman lantern, a laptop computer, food, a computer chip), that is all right. We recognize that a certain amount of military spending is necessary for our security, but we very clearly do not want to be in the weapons business and do not want to own the stock of companies whose business depends on large government contracts and ever-increasing levels of military spending.

ALCOHOL AND TOBACCO. We also do not want to invest in the alcohol and tobacco industries. We feel uncomfortable with making money as people smoke and drink more, and we do not want to lose money as people smoke and drink less. Gambling and the gaming industry are approached in the same manner.

ENVIRONMENT. We look at a potential company's environmental record very closely. If a company has a long record of EPA fines or citations, we will not invest in that firm. We also check to see if a company has made improvements in its environmental behavior; we would consider a company that has had a violation but has made good-faith efforts to clean up its mess and has maintained a clean record since then. We believe that when a company's top management realizes that environmentally responsible behavior makes economic sense, it is probably well managed in other areas as well.

WORKPLACE RELATIONS. Workplace relations is another crucial area in which we evaluate a company. We look for firms that give its workers latitude for decision making, fair compensation, recognition for work done well, room for promotion, and a stake in the company's future through stock ownership. Union-management relations are important as well, and a company with a history of bad relations with its unions will not be considered.

CORPORATE CULTURE. A company's overall corporate culture is very important to the Parnassus Fund. We look at the composition of a firm's board of directors to see if it includes women and minorities (which tends to reveal the degree of fair treatment and opportunities for women and minorities within the company as a whole). A company that has a history of or is noted for unfair treatment of women and minorities will not be considered. We also determine whether or not a company behaves responsibly and is sensitive to the communities in which it operates. We look favorably on a company that gives a generous amount of its pretax profits to charitable causes.

We believe that the ultimate responsibility for corporate social responsibility lies in a company's top management and that firms led in a responsible manner not only will make a positive contribution to the social fabric of our society, but also will earn money in the long run, rewarding both employees and shareholders.

Adviser

The adviser is Parnassus Financial Management, Jerome L. Dodson, president. In addition to managing the Parnassus Fund, Parnassus Financial Management also manages private portfolios using the same criteria as for the fund. Minimum portfolio size is $500,000.

TABLE 32-6

THE PARNASSUS FUND PERFORMANCE DATA
Total Return Figures in Percentages

1985	1986	1987	1988	1989	1990	1991*
18.5	2.47	−6.8	42.4	2.78	−22.0	33.8

NOTE: Benchmarks against which we should be compared include the Lipper Growth Fund Average and the Russell 2000.

*Through March 31, 1991.

Officers

Jerome L. Dodson, president and portfolio manager, has an M.B.A. from Harvard University. He is president of Continental Savings & Loan and a cofounder of Working Assets Money Fund. Dodson lives in San Francisco with his wife and two children.

Howard Fong, vice president and chief financial officer, earned a B.A. degree from San Francisco State University. He is chief financial officer of Continental Savings & Loan, and he lives in San Francisco with his wife.

David Pogran is vice president and director of research. He has an M.B.A. from the University of California at Berkeley. He lives in Oakland with his wife.

| THE PIONEER GROUP

60 State Street
Boston, Mass. 02109
(617) 742-7825

PIONEER FUND (FOUNDED FEBRUARY 10, 1928)

Fee Structure and Restrictions on Investors

Maximum load: 8.5 percent; decreases with volume purchases, beginning at $10,000.

Minimum initial investment: $50.

Subsequent investments: $50.

Open to all investors.

Quarterly dividends are reinvested at net asset value (NAV) (that is, without sales charge).

Investment Objective and Philosophy

As a growth and income equity fund, the Pioneer Fund seeks reasonable income and growth of capital predominantly from dividend-paying stocks of established companies. The fund pursues a "value-investing" philosophy, generally seeking companies with good management, solid balance sheets, and low price-earnings ratios whose true value is higher than its share price as determined by fundamental analysis performed by Pioneer's team of securities analysts. The orientation of the fund is toward long-term investing, with low portfolio turnover. The fund does not use market timing and is substantially fully invested at all times.

Social Screens

The fund does not invest in a firm whose principal business is in alcohol, gambling, or tobacco. The fund also does not currently invest in firms headquartered in South Africa, but this is predominantly a business risk screen.

TABLE 32-7

PIONEER FUND PERFORMANCE RESULTS SINCE JANUARY 1, 1970
Dividends Reinvested, Maximum Sales Charge Included

Date	Value	Percentage of Change	Cum Change
12/31/70	9,239	−7.61%	−7.61%
12/31/71	10,483	13.46	4.83
12/31/72	12,086	15.29	20.86
12/31/73	11,688	−3.29	16.88
12/31/74	9,497	−18.75	−5.03
12/31/75	13,191	38.90	31.91
12/31/76	18,053	36.86	80.53
12/31/77	18,714	3.66	87.14
12/31/78	21,021	12.33	110.21
12/31/79	26,881	27.88	168.81
12/31/80	35,127	30.68	251.27
12/31/81	34,072	−3.00	240.72
12/31/82	38,667	13.49	286.67
12/31/83	48,304	24.92	383.04
12/31/84	47,891	−0.86	378.91
12/31/85	60,357	26.03	503.57
12/31/86	67,293	11.49	572.93
12/31/87	70,956	5.44	609.56
12/31/88	83,961	18.33	739.61
12/31/89	103,599	23.39	935.99
12/31/90	92,702	−10.52	827.02
TOTAL	92,702	827.02	

NOTE: This table provides performance information, which is calculated at net asset value and at maximum offering price.

Advisers and Subadvisers
Pioneering Management Company, a subsidiary of the Pioneer Group, manages the fund.

PIONEER II (FOUNDED OCTOBER 1, 1969)

Fee Structure and Restrictions on Investors
Maximum load: 8.5 percent; decreases with volume purchases, beginning at $10,000.

Minimum initial investment: $50.

Subsequent investments: $50.

Open to all investors. Semiannual dividends are reinvested at net asset value.

Investment Objective and Philosophy
As a growth and income equity fund, Pioneer II seeks reasonable income and growth of capital predominantly from dividend-paying stocks of established companies. The fund pursues a "value-investing" philosophy, generally seeking companies with good management, solid balance sheets, and low price-earnings ratios whose true value is higher than its share price as determined by fundamental analysis performed by Pioneer's team of securities analysts. The orientation of the fund is toward long-term investing, with low portfolio turnover. The fund has no market timing and is substantially fully invested at all times. Generally 10 to 25 percent of investments are in international equities.

Social Screens
The fund does not invest in a firm whose principal business is in alcohol, gambling, or tobacco. The fund also does not currently invest in firms headquartered in South Africa, but this is predominantly a business risk screen.

Advisers and Subadvisers
Pioneering Management Company, a subsidiary of the Pioneer Group, manages the fund.

TABLE 32-8

PIONEER II PERFORMANCE RESULTS SINCE JANUARY 1, 1970
Dividends Reinvested, Maximum Sales Charge Included

Date	Value	Percentage of Change	Cum Change
12/31/70	8,502	−14.98%	−14.98%
12/31/71	10,600	24.68	6.00
12/31/72	12,853	21.25	28.53
12/31/73	11,750	−8.58	17.50
12/31/74	9,159	−22.05	−8.41
12/31/75	13,736	49.97	37.36
12/31/76	22,123	61.06	121.23
12/31/77	27,321	23.50	173.21
12/31/78	31,285	14.51	212.85
12/31/79	41,424	32.41	314.24
12/31/80	53,234	28.51	432.34
12/31/81	57,815	8.61	478.15
12/31/82	71,157	23.08	611.57
12/31/83	92,557	30.07	825.57
12/31/84	89,593	−3.20	795.93
12/31/85	117,735	31.41	1,077.35
12/31/86	132,421	12.47	1,224.21
12/31/87	131,966	−0.34	1,219.66
12/31/88	160,692	21.77	1,506.92
12/31/89	196,382	22.21	1,863.82
12/31/90	172,762	−12.03	1,627.62
TOTAL	172,762	1,627.62	

NOTE: This table provides performance information, which is calculated at net asset value and at maximum offering price.

PIONEER III (FOUNDED NOVEMBER 19, 1982)

Fee Structure and Restrictions on Potential Investors

Maximum load: 8.5 percent; decreases with volume purchases, beginning at $10,000.

Minimum initial investment: $1,000.

Minimum subsequent investment: $50.

Open to all investors.

Semiannual dividends are reinvested at net asset value.

Investment Objectives and Philosophy

As a growth and income equity fund, Pioneer III seeks reasonable income and growth of capital predominantly from dividend-paying stocks of established companies. The fund pursues a "value-investing" philosophy, generally seeking companies with good management, solid balance sheets, and low price-earnings ratios whose true value is higher than its share price as determined by fundamental analysis performed by Pioneer's team of securities analysts. The orientation of the fund is toward long-term investing, with low portfolio turnover. The fund has no market timing and is substantially fully invested at all times. It is restricted to small and medium-sized companies, that is, companies with market capitalization of under $750 million at the time of purchase.

Social Screens

The fund does not invest in a firm whose principal business is in alcohol, gambling, or tobacco. The fund also does not currently invest in firms headquartered in South Africa, but this is predominantly a business risk screen.

Advisers and Subadvisers

Pioneering Management Company, a subsidiary of the Pioneer Group, manages the fund.

TABLE 32-9

PIONEER III PERFORMANCE RESULTS SINCE NOVEMBER 19, 1982
Dividends Reinvested, Maximum Sales Charge Included

Date	Value	Percentage of Change	Cum Change
12/31/82	9,149	−8.51%	−8.51%
12/31/83	11,884	29.89	18.84
12/31/84	12,452	4.78	24.52
12/31/85	15,448	24.06	54.48
12/31/86	17,178	11.20	71.78
12/31/87	15,820	−7.91	58.20
12/31/88	20,564	29.99	105.64
12/31/89	24,772	20.46	147.72
12/31/90	21,563	−12.95	115.63
TOTAL	21,563	115.63	

NOTE: This table provides performance information, which is calculated at net asset value and at maximum offering price.

I PIONEER CAPITAL GROWTH FUND (FOUNDED JULY 25, 1990)

Fee Structure and Restrictions on Potential Investors

Maximum load: 5.75 percent; decreases with volume purchases, beginning at $50,000.

Fee: .25 percent 12b-1.

Minimum initial investment: $1,000.

Minimum subsequent investment: $50.

Open to all investors.

Annual dividends are reinvested at net asset value.

Investment Objectives and Philosophy

The objective of this fund is growth of capital, derived from stocks of established companies. The fund pursues a "value-investing" philosophy, generally seeking companies with good management, solid balance sheets, and low price-earnings ratios whose true value is higher than its share price as determined by fundamental analysis performed by Pioneer's team of securities analysts. The orientation of the fund is toward long-term investing, with low portfolio turnover. The fund has no market timing and is substantially fully invested at all times.

Social Screens

The fund does not invest in a firm whose principal business is in alcohol, gambling, or tobacco. The fund also does not currently invest in firms headquartered in South Africa, but this is predominantly a business risk screen.

Advisers and Subadvisers

Pioneering Management Company, a subsidiary of the Pioneer Group, manages the fund.

PIONEER EQUITY-INCOME FUND (FOUNDED JULY 25, 1990)

Fee Structure and Restrictions on Potential Investors

Maximum load: 5.75 percent; decreases with volume purchases, beginning at $50,000.

Fee: .25 percent 12b-1.

TABLE 32-10

PIONEER CAPITAL GROWTH FUND PERFORMANCE RESULTS
SINCE JULY 25, 1990
Dividends Reinvested, Maximum Sales Charge Included

Date	Value	*Percentage of Change*	*Cum Change*
12/31/90	7,693	−23.07%	−23.07%
TOTAL	7,693	−23.07	

NOTE: This table provides performance information, which is calculated at net asset value and at maximum offering price.

Minimum initial investment: $1,000.
Minimum subsequent investment: $50.
Quarterly dividends are reinvested at net asset value.

Investment Objectives and Philosophy

Current income with growth of capital is the objective of this fund, which seeks to exceed the dividend rate of the S & P 500. Its goals include reasonable income and growth of capital, predominantly from dividend-paying stocks of established companies. The fund pursues a "value-investing" philosophy, generally seeking companies with good management, solid balance sheets, and low price-earnings ratios whose true value is higher than its share price as determined by fundamental analysis performed by Pioneer's team of securities analysts. The orientation of the fund is toward long-term investing, with low portfolio turnover. The fund has no market timing and is substantially fully invested at all times.

Social Screens

The fund does not invest in a firm whose principal business is in alcohol, gambling, or tobacco. The fund also does not currently invest in firms headquartered in South Africa, but this is predominantly a business risk screen.

Advisers and Subadvisers

Pioneering Management Company, a subsidiary of the Pioneer Group, manages the fund.

TABLE 32-11

PIONEER EQUITY-INCOME FUND PERFORMANCE RESULTS SINCE JULY 25, 1990
Dividends Reinvested, Maximum Sales Charge Included

		Percentage of	
Date	Value	Change	Cum Change
12/31/90	8,567	− 14.33%	− 14.33%
TOTAL	8,567	− 14.33	

NOTE: This table provides performance information, which is calculated at net asset value and at maximum offering price.

PIONEER GOLD SHARES (FOUNDED JULY 25, 1990)

Fee Structure and Restrictions on Potential Investors
Maximum load: 5.75 percent; decreases with volume purchases, beginning at $50,000.

Fee: .25 percent 12b-1.

Minimum initial investment: $1,000.

Minimum subsequent investment: $50.

Open to all investors.

Annual dividends are reinvested at net asset value.

Investment Objectives and Philosophy
This fund concentrates on the growth of capital through investment in gold mining, processing, or refining companies and gold ore. Bullion should not exceed 10 percent of assets. A significant portion of Pioneer Gold Shares' assets will typically be international securities. This fund pursues a "value-investing" philosophy.

Social Screens
The fund does not expect to invest in firms headquartered in South Africa until significant changes occur in the current political and economical conditions there.

Advisers and Subadvisers
Pioneering Management Company, a subsidiary of the Pioneer Group, manages the fund.

TABLE 32-12

PIONEER GOLD SHARES PERFORMANCE RESULTS SINCE JULY 25, 1990
Dividends Reinvested, Maximum Sales Charge Included

Date	Value	Percentage of Change	Cum Change
12/31/90	8,014	−19.86%	−19.86%
TOTAL	8,014	−19.86	

NOTE: This table provides performance information, which is calculated at net asset value and at maximum offering price.

PIONEER BOND FUND (FOUNDED OCTOBER 31, 1978)

Fee Structure and Restrictions on Potential Investors
Maximum load: 4.5 percent; decreases with volume purchases, beginning at $100,000.
Fee: .25 percent 12b-1.
Minimum initial investment: $1,000.
Minimum subsequent investment: $50.
Open to all investors.
Monthly dividends are reinvested at net asset value.

Investment Objectives and Philosophy
The Pioneer Bond Fund's objective: current income from high-quality corporate and U.S. government bonds, with prudent regard for capital preservation. Eighty-five percent of the portfolio must be in the top three investment grades (A or better); all purchases are in the top four grades. The portfolio is managed for total return. There are no options and no futures. The fund employs a cyclical analysis in analyzing business credit cycles to monitor interest rates and select fixed-income securities for the portfolio.

Social Screens
This fund does not invest in the debt of a firm whose principal business is in alcohol, gambling, or tobacco. The fund currently adheres to the first two Sullivan Principles.

Advisers and Subadvisers
Pioneering Management Company, a subsidiary of the Pioneer Group, manages the fund.

TABLE 32-13

PIONEER BOND FUND PERFORMANCE RESULTS SINCE OCTOBER 31, 1978
Dividends Reinvested, Maximum Sales Charge Included

Date	Value	Percentage of Change	Cum Change
12/31/78	9,637	−3.63%	−3.63%
12/31/79	9,818	1.88	−1.82
12/31/80	9,822	0.04	−1.78
12/31/81	10,394	5.82	3.94
12/31/82	13,635	31.18	36.35
12/31/83	14,902	9.29	49.02
12/31/84	16,656	11.77	66.56
12/31/85	19,990	20.02	99.90
12/31/86	22,157	10.84	121.57
12/31/87	22,752	2.69	127.52
12/31/88	24,501	7.69	145.01
12/31/89	27,349	11.62	173.49
12/31/90	29,347	7.31	193.47
TOTAL	29,347	193.47	

NOTE: This table provides performance information, which is calculated at net asset value and at maximum offering price.

PIONEER MUNICIPAL BOND FUND (FOUNDED OCTOBER 22, 1986)

Fee Structure and Restrictions on Potential Investors
Maximum load: 4.5 percent; decreases with volume purchases, beginning at $100,000.

Fee: .25 percent 12b-1.

Minimum initial investment: $1,000.

Minimum subsequent investment: $50.

Open to all investors.

Monthly dividends are reinvested at net asset value.

Investment Objectives and Philosophy
The objective of this fund is current income from a high-quality portfolio of municipal securities with due regard to the preservation of capital and investment risk. Eighty-five percent must be municipal bonds rated A or better. Investments are limited to the top four grades or their equivalents. The average stated maturity is currently expected to be greater than fifteen years.

TABLE 32-14

PIONEER MUNICIPAL BOND FUND PERFORMANCE RESULTS
SINCE OCTOBER 22, 1986
Dividends Reinvested, Maximum Sales Charge Included

Date	Value	Percentage of Change	Cum Change
12/31/86	9,561	−4.39%	−4.39%
12/31/87	9,187	−3.91	−8.13
12/31/88	10,361	12.78	3.61
12/31/89	11,374	9.78	13.74
12/31/90	12,104	6.42	21.04
TOTAL	12,104	21.04	

NOTE: This table provides performance information, which is calculated at net asset value and at maximum offering price.

Social Screens
The fund does not invest in the debt of municipal entities connected to alcohol, gambling, or tobacco.

Advisers and Subadvisers
Pioneering Management Company, a subsidiary of the Pioneer Group, manages the fund.

PIONEER CASH RESERVES FUND (FOUNDED JUNE 22, 1987)

Fee Structure and Restrictions on Potential Investors
Load: none.
Fee: .15 percent 12b-1.
Minimum initial investment: $1,000.
Minimum subsequent investment: $100.
Open to all investors.
Daily dividends.

Investment Objectives and Philosophy
This fund's objective is high current income, with preservation of capital and convenient liquidity from a portfolio of high-quality, short-term money market securities. Investments include U.S. government and agency securities, bank obligations, such as the cer-

tificates of deposit of domestic banks, and high-grade commercial paper.

Social Screens
The fund does not invest in the debt of a firm whose principal business is in alcohol, gambling, or tobacco. The fund also does not currently invest in firms headquartered in South Africa, although this is predominantly a business risk screen.

Advisers and Subadvisers
Pioneering Management Company, a subsidiary of the Pioneer Group, manages the fund.

TABLE 32-15

PIONEER CASH RESERVES PERFORMANCE RESULTS SINCE JUNE 22, 1987
Dividends Reinvested, Maximum Sales Charge Included

Date	Value	Percentage of Change	Cum Change
12/31/87	10,348	3.48%	3.48%
12/31/88	11,077	7.04	10.77
12/31/89	12,052	8.80	20.52
12/31/90	12,985	7.74	29.85
TOTAL	12,985	29.85	

NOTE: This table provides performance information, which is calculated at net asset value and at maximum offering price.

| PIONEER TAX-FREE MONEY FUND (FOUNDED APRIL 11, 1988)

Fee Structure and Restrictions on Potential Investors
Load: none.
Fee: .15 percent 12b-1.
Minimum initial investment: $1,000.
Minimum subsequent investment: $100.
Open to all investors.
Daily dividends.

Investment Objectives and Philosophy
The fund's objective is high tax-free current income, with preservation of capital and convenient liquidity from portfolio of high-

quality, short-term money market securities. Investments are limited to short-term municipal obligations in order to provide income that is free from federal income taxes.

Social Screens
The fund does not invest in the debt of municipal entities connected to alcohol, gambling, or tobacco.

Advisers and Subadvisers
Pioneering Management Company, a subsidiary of the Pioneer Group, manages the fund.

TABLE 32-16

PIONEER TAX-FREE MONEY FUND PERFORMANCE RESULTS SINCE APRIL 11, 1988
Dividends Reinvested, Maximum Sales Charge Included

Date	Value	Percentage of Change	Cum Change
12/31/88	10,371	3.71%	3.71%
12/31/89	11,000	6.06	10.00
12/31/90	11,602	5.47	16.02
TOTAL	11,602	16.02	

NOTE: This table provides performance information, which is calculated at net asset value and at maximum offering price.

I PIONEER EUROPE FUND (FOUNDED APRIL 2, 1991)

Fee Structure and Restrictions on Potential Investors
Maximum load: 5.75 percent; decreases with volume purchases, beginning at $50,000.
Fee: .25 percent 12b-1.
Minimum initial investment: $1,000.
Minimum subsequent investment: $50.
Open to all investors.
Annual dividends are reinvested at net asset value.

Investment Objective and Philosophy
This growth fund seeks long-term growth of capital by investing in a diversified portfolio of European stocks. Normally at least 70 percent of assets are divided among six European subadvisers in the

United Kingdom, Germany, France, the Netherlands, Spain, and Italy. Each of these six subadvisers invests its portion of the assets in equity securities of its country. Pioneer does the asset allocation among the six subadvisers and invests the remaining assets in equities of other European countries. The network of subadvisers gives the fund the benefit of their deep and specialized knowledge of the local markets. Each subadviser is free to select the stock he or she believes represents the best growth opportunities; each has a long history of fundamental research and smaller company analysis.

Pioneer pursues a "value-investing" philosophy. Its orientation is long-term investing. The fund has no market timing and is substantially fully invested at all times.

Social Screens
The fund does not invest in a firm whose principle business is in alcohol, gambling, or tobacco.

Advisers and Subadvisers
Pioneering Management Company, a subsidiary of the Pioneer Group, manages the fund.

European subadvisers: Edinburgh-Wilmington International Capital Management/Edinburgh Fund Managers (United Kingdom); Schroder Munchmeyer Hengst Capital GmbH (Germany); BGP Advisory Investment, S.A./Banque de Gestion Privee (France); Mees & Hope Fund Management B.V. (Netherlands); Gestemar Gestion, S.A. (Spain); Euromobiliare S.p.A. (Italy).

Performance Data
None.

Contact
For literature or more information on any of the Pioneer funds and their socially conscious policies, please call Pioneer's regional marketing specialists at (800) 622-9876.

| RIGHTIME SOCIAL AWARENESS FUND

The Forst Pavilion, Suite 1000
Wyncote, Pa. 19095-1596
(215) 887-8111
(800) 242-1421

Sales Charges

| | SALES CHARGE AS A PERCENTAGE OF: | | |
| | Offering | Amount | Dealer's |
Amount of Purchase	Price	Invested	Commission
Less than $50,000	4.75	4.99	4.25
$50,000 but under $99,999	3.75	3.90	3.35
$100,000 but under $499,999	2.75	2.83	2.45
$500,000 but under $999,999	1.75	1.80	1.55
$1,000,000 but under $3,000,000	.75	.76	.65

Purchase Information	Initial	Subsequent
Minimum amount	$2,000	$100
Individual IRA minimum	waived	waived
Keogh minimum	$2,000	$100
Phone purchases minimum	N/A	$1,000
Wire purchases minimum	$2,000	$100
ACH/EFI wires	N/A	N/A

The deadline for purchases: 5:00 P.M. EST, which is also the deadline for switches to other funds.

Funds that can be switched into by phone are: Rightime Fund, Rightime Blue Chip, Rightime Growth, Rightime Money Market, and Rightime Government Securities Fund. There is no limit to the number of switches per year, no minimum, and no charge. The fund is open to all investors in all states except New Hampshire.

Redemption Information

	yes	no	minimum
Redemption by phone via wire	X		none
Redemption by phone via ACM/EFT transfers	N/A		
Letter redemption: without signature guarantee	X		less than $5,000
Letter redemption: with signature guarantee	X		greater than $5,000
Check writing redemption	X	net	

Annual Maintenance Fees for Tax Qualified Plans:	$10
Annual expense ratio	2.57 percent
Annual 12-b1 fee	0.90 percent
Redemption fee	none
Deferred sales charge	none

Investment Objective

The Rightime Social Awareness Fund seeks to invest in securities of companies with prospects for above-average capital growth that, in the opinion of the fund's adviser, show evidence in the conduct of their business (relative to other companies in the same industry) of contributing to the enhancement of the quality of human life.

Investment Strategy

The fund offers the opportunity to invest in a socially responsible way at reduced market risk. Rightime Econometrics, the fund's investment adviser, attempts to actively manage stock market risk through the use of a systematic quantitative investment technique called market timing. This technique attempts to move fund assets into equity securities during favorable market conditions and move fund assets into cash equivalents during adverse market conditions. During periods of favorable market conditions, the fund will invest in securities that meet both its financial and social criteria.

Social Screens

The fund seeks to invest in companies that:

- do not operate in South Africa or have equity interests in companies that operate in South Africa;
- are committed to sound environmental practices;
- have high-quality employee relations;
- do not engage in nuclear energy production;
- do not receive substantial revenue from tobacco, alcohol, or weapons production;
- display superior community citizenship through innovative leadership and charity.

The fund's goal is to identify those profitable enterprises that merit financial support because of their overall superior social performance. The adviser uses well-known industry sources to build its social responsibility data base, such as: Arthur D. Little; Kinder, Lydenberg, Domini & Company; Investor Responsibility Research Center; Franklin Research & Development Corporation; and Interfaith Center on Corporate Responsibility.

Fund Statistics

Assets: $5.5 million
Number of shareholders: 657
Number of shares outstanding: 240,637

PORTFOLIO COMPOSITION

	Percentage of
All Funds	*Total Net Assets*
Cash and equivalents	6
Stocks	94
Bonds (nonconvertible)	
Preferreds (nonconvertible)	
Convertible securities	
TOTAL	100

Portfolio Highlights

Total market value of common stock	$5.1 million
Largest equity holding	Manor Care
Value	$.3 million
Number of individual securities	40
Fund leverages: no	
Fund sells short: no	

DISTRIBUTIONS

Income distribution date:	none
Frequency of income distribution:	annually
Capital gains date:	none
Frequency of distribution of capital gains:	annually
Record date:	December 27, 1990
Ex-dividend date:	December 28, 1990
Reinvestment date:	December 28, 1990
Income:	.40 percent
Capital gains:	
Reinvestment price	$22.71

MONTH-END NET ASSET VALUES

Date	*NAV*
October 31, 1990	$22.29
November 30, 1990	$22.63
December 31, 1990	$22.84

PERFORMANCE

March 1990:	−0.32
April 1990:	1.00
May 1990:	2.82
June 1990:	−3.71
July 1990:	−3.57
August 1990:	−2.04
September 1990:	0.38

October 1990: −5.67
November 1990: 1.53
December 1990: 2.71
January 1991:   2.93
February 1991: 6.85

Portfolio Managers
David J. Rights and Anthony W. Soslow are the portfolio managers
of the Rightime Social Awareness Fund. Rights is the president of
the fund and its adviser, Rightime Econometrics. Rights founded
Rightime Econometrics in 1979 and now has more than twenty years
of investment experience. Rights graduated from Lehigh University
in 1967, earning a B.S. degree in electrical engineering. Soslow is a
portfolio manager for the fund and other clients of the investment
adviser. Soslow joined Rightime in 1986 and is a C.F.A. He graduated
from the University of Pennsylvania in 1987, earning a B.S. degree.

CHAPTER 33

U.S. ENVIRONMENTAL AND SECTOR FUNDS

Ed. Note: *This chapter consists of descriptions of U.S. environmental and environmental sector mutual funds submitted, unless otherwise indicated, by the funds. Those funds that did not submit material to us are listed in the directory in appendix B.*

| ALLIANCE GLOBAL ENVIRONMENT FUND

1345 Avenue of the Americas
New York, N.Y. 10105
(800) 247-4154

A nondiversified, closed-end management company, its shares are listed (as AEF) on the New York Stock Exchange.

Investment Objective and Philosophy
The fund's investment objective is long-term capital appreciation through investment in equity securities of companies expected to benefit from advances or improvements in products, processes, or services intended to foster the protection of the environment. Under normal circumstances the fund invests at least 65 percent of its total assets in equity securities of environmental companies.

The fund will invest in two categories of eligible companies: "environmental companies" and "beneficiary companies." The fund may invest up to 25 percent of its total assets in securities that are not readily marketable.

Social Screens
Not applicable.

Advisers and Subadvisers
Alliance Capital Management L.P. is the fund's investment manager and administrator.

TABLE 33-1

ALLIANCE GLOBAL ENVIRONMENT FUND PERFORMANCE DATA

Statistics as of December 31, 1990
Assets: $88.8 million
Total return (since inception): −5.48%
NAV: $12.85
Market price: $11.00
Discount: 14.40%
Total returns as of February 28, 1991 (at NAV) year to date: 9.88%
Total returns since inception: 4.45%
NAV: $14.12
Market price: $12.625
Premium (discount): (10.59)
Assets: $97.6 million

Statistics as of October 31, 1990 (fiscal year end)
Ratio of expenses to average net assets: 1.72% plus
Portfolio turnover rate: 4%
1990 distributions: $.335
Ex-dividend date: December 21, 1990

Contacts

Elaine Goldberg Harris is vice president of Alliance Capital Management and comanager of the Alliance Global Environment Fund. Prior to joining Alliance in 1988, Harris was an equity portfolio manager at Fidelity in Boston. She holds an undergraduate degree from Tufts University and an M.B.A. from the Wharton Business School. Investment experience: eight years.

Joseph C. Williams is vice president of Alliance Capital Management L.P., vice president of the Austria Fund, and comanager of Alliance Global Environment Fund. Prior to joining Alliance, Williams was manager of the North American and Japanese equity portfolios for the Mercantile Investment Trust, managed by Robert Fleming & Company in London. He specialized in investments in small capitalization, high-growth American companies. He also was responsible for managing foreign exchange exposure. From 1970 to 1975 Williams was the research analyst for Halgarten & Company in London and a sales representative for Smith Barney International in London. Williams is a cum laude graduate of Yale University and a graduate of the Harvard School of Business Administration. He is a chartered financial analyst with twenty years of investment experience.

I ENVIRONMENTALLY RESPONSIBLE MUTUAL FUND

Green Century Capital Management
29 Temple Place
Boston, Mass. 02111-1305
(617) 482-0800
(800) 93-GREEN

The Public Interest Research Groups (PIRGs), the country's fastest-growing network of grassroots environmental and consumer protection organizations, expect to launch their new family of no-load environmentally responsible mutual funds in late winter, 1991–92. All profits of the investment adviser company will be channeled back into environmental advocacy programs. This unique partnership of for-profit and not-for-profit entities will facilitate a powerful synergy of capital working to promote positive environmental change.

The funds will be administered by Green Century Capital Management, the investment adviser company responsible for developing the funds. Court Street Capital, a wholly owned subsidiary of U.S.T. Corporation, will be the portfolio manager and will be responsible for investment decisions.

Initially the family will include a balanced fund and a money market fund. The goal of these funds is to, wherever possible, invest their portfolios in companies doing something positive for the environment and to avoid investing in companies with a negative environmental record.

I KEMPER ENVIRONMENTAL SERVICES FUND

Kemper Financial Services
120 South LaSalle
Chicago, Ill. 60603

Fee Structure, Restrictions
The minimum investment is $1,000. There is no minimum on subsequent investments and no charge on dividend reinvestments. There are no restrictions on who may invest in the fund.

Investment Objective
The objective of this fund is to provide long-term capital appreciation. The fund pursues its objectives by investing primarily in a

portfolio of equity securities of issuers that are principally engaged in environmentally related service activities.

Social Screens
None.

Portfolio Manager
Frank Korth joined Kemper Financial Services in 1990 as first vice president and portfolio manager of Kemper Enrivonmental Services Fund.

Before coming to Kemper, Korth worked at Value Line in New York as manager of the Value Line Fund as well as several large pension funds. He was also chairman of Value Line's investment committee. Previously he was a senior vice president and market strategist for Shearson Lehman Brothers. During much of the 1970s he was a market analyst and director of quantitative products for Dean Witter Reynolds.

A graduate of the University of Minnesota at Mankato, Korth received his bachelor of arts in mathematics in 1968, followed by his masters of business in finance from Baruch College of City University of New York in 1976. In 1982 he completed his doctorate of finance studies at CUNY. Korth is also a chartered financial analyst.

TABLE 33-2

**KEMPER ENVIRONMENTAL SERVICES FUND
PERFORMANCE DATA**

Total return basis per year	N/A
Fund's inception	May 18, 1990
Total return as of year end 1990	−12.85%
Total return year to date (February 28, 1991)	+15.44%

NOTE: Figures are not adjusted for sales charge.

I MERRILL LYNCH EQUITY INCOME FUND (CONCEPT SERIES) ECO LOGICAL TRUST 1990

Merrill Lynch Pierce, Fenner & Smith
Unit Investment Trusts
Box 9051
Princeton, N.J. 08543-9051
(609) 282-8500

Fee Structure

The minimum initial investment is one hundred units, which is approximately $1,000. For retirement accounts, minimums are lowered to twenty-five units, approximately $250. Subsequent investments are not subject to any minimums. There is no reinvestment feature on the fund. The sales charge is a one-time fee of 4 percent. Investments in the fund generally are made by retail clients, but sales charges are reduced for quantity purchases.

Investment Objective and Philosophy

We are structured as a unit investment trust, which differs from a mutual fund. The major difference between the two structures is that our unit trust has a defined portfolio and we are able to change the portfolio only under limited circumstances.

Our philosophy for the Eco Logical Trust is to invest in companies positively committed to the environment. These companies were run through internal financial and market screens to determine suitability. Since the trust is a buy and hold vehicle, we must be particularly critical of the companies' fundamentals (credit quality, growth prospects for the holding period, market, and regulatory concerns).

The stocks for this portfolio were selected because the issuers are engaged in industries that are expected to expand in response to public opinion and legislative regulation relating to the environment or that are considered environmentally responsible and are well placed to capitalize on the growing public demand for environmentally sound products and services.

We will buy and hold the securities for the five-year life of the fund. We review our holdings regularly and will direct the sale of a security only if holding it would be detrimental to the unit holder. These circumstances may include dividend cuts, deteriorating financial conditions, or business climate, but no security will be sold to take advantage of market movement.

By adhering to these strict initial screenings and review criteria, we hope to provide investors with a convenient, cost-effective way to participate in the growth potential of environmentally responsible companies.

Advisers and Subadvisers

Progressive Asset Management, Oakland, California
Council on Economic Priorities, New York

DataCenter, Oakland, California
Kinder, Lydenberg, Domini & Company, Cambridge, Massachusetts

Biography
Merrill Lynch's Unit Investment Trust Department and our co-sponsors have sponsored over $83 billion of unit investment trusts over the past twenty years. We offer trusts that allow investors to participate in municipal, corporate, international, and government bond markets. We offer equity funds for investments in the S & P 500, utility stocks, and other timely equity concepts, including the Eco Logical Trust (see page 446). We maintain a staff of investment professionals dedicated exclusively to selecting and then monitoring securities for these funds.

I SCHIELD PROGRESSIVE ENVIRONMENTAL FUND

Schield Management Company
390 Union Boulevard, Suite 410
Denver, Colo. 80228
(800) 275-2382
(303) 985-9999
(800) 826-6412 (nightly net asset value update)
(415) 952-2030 (fund manager)

Fee Structure and Restrictions on Investors
Shares may be purchased at the public offering price, which includes a sales load of 4.5 percent. The sales load decreases incrementally for larger purchases. Break points are noted in the prospectus. Shares also may be purchased in exchange for common stock and other securities that meet the fund's investment objective. The minimum for this type of purchase is $10,000. Investors may purchase shares at net asset value (NAV) and without the sales load if the investment

TABLE 33-3
_____

ECO LOGICAL TRUST PERFORMANCE DATA

Inception (April 17, 1990) to March 28, 1991:   16.14%
First quarter 1991 (January 1 to March 29):   14.95%

NOTE: Figures represent the total return, including dividends but not including sales charge.

represents proceeds from the redemption within the past sixty days of shares of another mutual fund, where the initial purchase of such shares included a sales load.

Shares of the fund may be purchased by individuals, institutions, or basically any person or group. A bona fide group or association and its members may be treated as a single purchaser and obtain quantity sales charge discounts. The group must meet certain conditions, which are described in the prospectus.

Shareholders of common stock of Schield Management Company (NASDAQ symbol: SMCC) may purchase shares at NAV.

Minimum initial investment is $1,000 for a standard account and $250 for a qualified retirement account. Subsequent investments can be a minimum of $100 for each share purchase of $50 under our automatic payment plan. Dividends are reinvested automatically unless the shareholder requested that they be distributed.

Investment Objective and Philosophy
The fund seeks capital growth by investing principally in companies engaged in contributing to a cleaner and healthier environment. Up to 25 percent of its assets may be invested in the securities of foreign issuers traded in the U.S. markets.

Social Screen
Our social screen is executed by a nonaffiliated party. Investors may request a description of the screens employed from Progressive Asset Management at (415) 834-3722.

The screen primarily focuses on the environmental policies and practices of the companies. However, other considerations for social screen criteria are at the discretion of Progressive Asset Management. The distributor of the fund donates 5 percent of its marketing fees to environmental organizations.

Advisers and Subadvisers
The fund adviser is Progressive Ventures, a subsidiary of Schield Management Company, Denver, Colorado.

Performance Data
The fund became available for investment to the public in 1990. The actual effective date was February 5, 1990.

For 1990, Schield Progressive Environmental Fund achieved a percentage change in NAV of 4.12 percent. The total return included a cash distribution of 12.6 cents per share. For 1991, the fund has a percentage change in NAV of 32.66 percent through March 1, 1991 (the time of this writing).

The fund was the leading fund in the environmental sector for 1990 and is currently (March 2, 1991) the leading fund in its sector for 1991, according to Lipper Analytical Services.

Fund Manager

Glenn S. Cutler is chief operating officer and senior executive vice president at Schield Management Company; portfolio manager of the Schield Progressive Environmental Fund; publisher and editor of *Market Fax*, a nightly fax investment advisory service; publisher and editor of *Market Mania*, a monthly investment advisory newsletter; and a member of the Social Investment Forum. He is also a source for and subject of articles in many leading publications, including: *Barron's, Forbes, Money, Business Week, Wall Street Journal, Investor's Daily, USA Today, San Francisco Chronicle, Miami Herald, New York Times*, and *Denver Post*.

YEAR ONE: THE PROENVIRONMENTAL FUNDS OUTPERFORM WALL STREET

Peter Camejo President,
Progressive Asset Management

Eleven "environmental" mutual funds faced off in 1990.

Eight of these funds included major polluters in their portfolios. They used "environment" to mean the environmental services sector of the economy, investing in companies that provide such services as solid waste management, recycling, pollution control, and hazardous waste treatment, regardless of the companies' own environmental records.

The other three funds used "environment" to mean more than just a sector of the economy. They defined themselves as proenvironmental—excluding major polluters from their portfolios and investing in companies that actually are helping the environment. Conventional wisdom tells us that the three funds that cared about the environment would not be able to compete.

| THE RESULTS

For years the argument against socially responsible investing has been that it lowers the universe of choices and therefore must lower performance. The eight environmental funds that did not screen their investments on the basis of environmental responsibility could invest in any company they wanted.

The eight were all backed by the securities experts of major investment firms: Fidelity, Oppenheimer, Alliance, Kemper, Merrill Lynch, and John Hancock. The three green funds were initiated by unknowns. The Schield Progressive Environmental Fund was managed by Glenn Cutler and owned by Schield Securities. The Global

Environmental Fund was started by John Earhart and Jeffrey Leonard, two environmentalists active for years in the World Wildlife Fund. The Eco Logical Trust 1990 was proposed by Progressive Asset Management to Merrill Lynch.

The results for year one: the three proenvironmental funds came in first, second, and third.

Not only did the proenvironmental funds outperform their competitors, they also outperformed all of the major indexes for the year—the S & P 500, the Dow Jones Industrial Average, and perhaps most important, the Environmental Composite Index of environmental stocks. All three funds edged into positive territory for the year despite significant declines in the Dow Jones Industrial Average and other indexes. The drop in the Environmental Composite Index was most dramatic, losing 19.1 percent for the year. None of the eight managed to end the year up and only one matched the Dow Jones performance, down 4.5 percent.

One would think that articles on this striking development would have been seen in one business section after another. In fact, exactly the opposite took place. Progressive Asset Management issued a press release announcing these interesting first-year results, but evidently not a single daily newspaper covered this story.

If the results had been the opposite, with the three mutual funds that cared about the environment coming in last, certainly there would have been more than one humorous essay on the price for caring.

| PROGRESSIVE ASSET MANAGEMENT VERSUS WALL STREET

The first-year result of these environmental mutual funds bring to culmination a period during which Progressive Asset Management, with the support of the socially responsible investment community, challenged the major Wall Street firms on the issue of environmental investing.

The story of this battle began with the *Exxon Valdez* oil spill. The enormous public outcry pricked up many ears on Wall Street. A Merrill Lynch report to its brokers in early 1989 noted, "The huge oil spill in Alaska's Prince William Sound may prove to be more than just an ecological disaster. . . ." The report argued that the outcry would result in new government intervention that would lead to further growth of the environmental sector. Hence, interest in the environmental sector as a separate investment category started to grow. Several firms began preparations to launch sector mutual funds in this area.

At Merrill Lynch it was Stan Craig of the Unit Trust Department who initially recognized the marketing potential of environmental sector investing. His department was the first out the door with an environmental sector fund, the Environmental Technical Trust. The sales results were spectacular for an equity unit trust, and in a few days the fund reached its target size. He launched a second trust, which also did well.

Craig's marketing success made other firms speed up their plans for launching environmental sector funds. As 1989 ended, approximately half a dozen funds had been launched, with more on their way.

Naturally, the public did not differentiate between a fund that invested just in the environmental sector and a fund that was proenvironmental. The word *environment* could be interpreted two different ways. It could mean picking stocks out of a universe of about three hundred listed environmental services companies (the list is run in each issue of *Waste Tech News*) or it could mean excluding major polluters and selecting the stocks of companies that truly are helping to solve environmental problems—firms that are proenvironmental.

Blowing the Whistle

As 1990 began, the *San Francisco Bay Guardian*, a large-circulation alternative weekly, asked Progressive Asset Management to do a study on the development of these environmental sector funds.

The study showed that not a single "environmental" fund used any criteria to judge their investments' actual impact on the environment. Nor did any of these funds make clear in their prospectuses or sales literature that it could invest in:

- companies that had been cited repeatedly for pollution violations;
- firms found guilty of felonies in relation to pollution violations; or
- corporations found guilty of other acts disapproved of by large segments of the investing public.

Without exception, the sector funds included firms with dozens of pollution violations. None excluded corporations with major criminal convictions, or with significant involvement in the nuclear power industry, or with connections in South Africa.

Most of the funds took advantage of the confusion and remained silent. The Freedom Environmental Fund of the John Hancock Insurance Company did something worse: it advertised itself as being "socially responsible" and claimed concern with helping the environment in order to promote the fund's sales. The Freedom Environmental Fund had no criteria whatsoever regarding the environmental records of the firms in which it invested, and it still has no such criteria. To the contrary, the fund's managers purchased additional stock of a company held in the fund on at least one occasion when its stock declined after being found guilty of a serious pollution violation by a New York court. That company was Browning-Ferris Industries.

The *Bay Guardian* ran Progressive Asset Management's report on its front page. Some major dailies picked up this story and ran small articles. A month later, the *Wall Street Journal* covered the story in an article that basically tried to defend the polluters. The *New York Times* remained silent.

One investor in the Freedom Environmental Fund, Ruth Dyke, protested to the Securities and Exchange Commission (SEC) that a fund should not be allowed to advertise itself as being for the environment when in fact it uses no environmental criteria and makes no environmental study when it invests. The SEC, however, remained silent. It took no steps to prevent false advertising in the sale of these funds.

The Eco Logical Trust 1990
Just before the *Bay Guardian* report appeared, one major Wall Street firm responded favorably to criticism sent to it by Progressive Asset Management. This was none other than Merrill Lynch. Stan Craig, who had been the first to see the financial potential of environmental sector investing, recognized the validity of Progessive Asset Management's position.

Merrill Lynch had been very careful with its advertising. Nonetheless, Craig saw that people would assume that an environmental fund used proenvironmental screening criteria. It would be difficult for investors to differentiate the common usage of the term *environmental*, meaning "proenvironmental," from the technical usage, meaning "companies in the environmental sector regardless of environmental record." More important, Craig saw that making environmental funds proenvironmental was "the right thing to do."

Craig retained Progressive Asset Management to assist in the creation of a new unit trust that would be environmental in the broader sense—that is, proenvironmental. He wanted this new fund to look for companies that were making important contributions to help solve environmental problems and that could be expected to do well financially as well.

Craig suggested that several organizations oriented toward socially responsible investment work together, sharing information and analyses to make sure that the list of stocks selected could be considered authentically proenvironmental. Progressive Asset Management coordinated research with three other organizations: the DataCenter in Oakland, California; Kinder, Lydenberg, Domini & Company in Cambridge, Massachusetts; and the Council of Economic Priorities in New York.

The Eco Logical Trust 1990 was launched just prior to Earth Day. The fund included in its prospectus that it would donate part of the fees earned by Merrill Lynch to the Environmental Federation of America, a coalition of twenty-seven national environmental organizations formed to provide national coordination for environmental fund-raising and workplace giving programs. Other major brokerages, including Prudential, Dean Witter, Shearson, and Paine Webber, joined in selling the trust.

Unfortunately, by the time the Eco Logical Trust was begun, this investment field was crowded. Hundreds of millions of dollars had been raised for environmental sector funds. Few investors found out that a fund of a quite different nature had appeared, so the amount of money received by the Eco Logical Trust 1990 was lower than the amount raised by some of the other major firms' environmental sector funds.

However, before a full year passed, the Eco Logical Trust had become Merrill Lynch's second-best-performing equity unit trust. Even more spectacularly, the Eco Logical Trust had outperformed the other two Merrill Lynch environmental sector funds by a substantial margin, even though the final choice of stocks had been made by the same people. The only difference was that Progressive Asset Management and the other three socially responsible investment organizations had restricted the selection universe to one hundred proenvironmental companies, from which Merrill Lynch ultimately selected the twenty-nine companies included in the trust.

The Schield Progressive Environmental Fund

Simultaneously with the work being done with Merrill Lynch, Progressive Asset Management participated in launching another proenvironmental investment project, the Schield Progressive Environmental Fund. This fund's financial performance has consistently been first among environmental and environmental sector funds. See box 34-1.

BOX 34-1

ENVIRONMENTAL SERVICES SECTOR MUTUAL FUNDS 1990 FINANCIAL RESULTS

In a survey of the 1990 financial performance of all of the environmental services sector mutual funds, Progressive Asset Management found that the three funds screened to exclude major polluters, the Schield Progressive Environmental Fund, the Global Environmental Fund, and the Eco Logical Trust 1990 came in first, second, and third.

The environmentally screened funds not only outperformed all of the non-screened environmental funds, they also bettered the Dow Jones Industrial Average and all of the other major securities indexes.

Fund or Index	1990 Results
1. Schield Progressive Environmental Fund	+ 1.6%
2. Global Environmental Fund	+0.1%
3. Eco Logical Trust 1990 (Merrill Lynch)	+0.1% UIT
4. Fidelity Select Environmental	−4.2%
5. Oppenheimer Global Environmental Fund	−5.0%
6. New Alternatives	−10.7%
7. Freedom Environmental Fund	−11.8%
8. Alliance Global Fund	−12.2%
9. Kemper Environmental Fund	−13.4%
10. SFT Environmental Fund	−14.7%
11. Enviro-Tech TR Ser 1 (Merrill Lynch)	−14.7% UIT

12. Enviro-Tech TR Ser 2 (Merrill Lynch)	−18.2% UIT
Environmental Composite Index	−19.1%
OTC Environmental Stocks	−26.1%
Major Environmental Stocks	−10.1%
Dow Jones	−4.5%
S & P 500	−7.0%

Some of these funds began in the first half of 1990, so the figures reflect a partial year. The listed figures do not include dividends paid during the year. For instance, if dividends were included, the Schield Progressive Environmental Fund would be up 4% for the year.

UIT means Unit Investment Trust. The pro-environmental Eco Logical Trust 1990 dramatically outperformed its sister Unit Investment Trusts. All three were prepared by the Merrill Lynch Unit Trust Department.

New Alternatives, an alternative energy mutual fund which also excludes polluters and is sometimes included in environmental sector lists, came in sixth for the year.

The environmental indexes are taken from The Environmental Investing News, published by Robert Mitchell Associates, Newton, Mass.

The above information is based on sources believed to be reliable but its accuracy cannot be guaranteed. This table is not an offer to sell nor a solicitation of an offer to buy any of these mutual funds. Mutual funds are sold by prospectus.

Market newsletter editor Glenn Cutler initiated this fund. Cutler wanted his fund to be proenvironmental. He not only felt that this was the best stance to take from a social and ethical point of view, but he also thought that this strategy would be more successful in terms of long-term financial performance and marketing. He designed a team concept for operating the fund. Robert Kruger, Progressive Asset Management's vice president for portfolio management, joined the advisory board and took charge of monitoring the fund to make sure that the companies included in it were environmentally responsible.

Once in operation, Cutler and the other members of the team began evaluating and selecting stock. Cutler demonstrated his stock selection skill almost immediately when for the second quarter of 1990, the Schield Progressive Environmental Fund had the best financial performance of all the mutual funds in the United States, according to Lipper Analytical Services. For the first time, a socially responsible fund had been the top fund in the country. And for the first time, a fund in its first quarter led all other mutual funds.

Later in 1990, all of the stocks in the environmental sector dropped dramatically. The Schield Progressive Environmental Fund also declined, but it stayed in first place in its group. With the surge in the stock market in 1991, it resumed its stellar performance, closing out its first year up 36 percent. According to Lipper, for the first quarter of 1991, the Schield Progressive Environmental Fund ranked nineteenth for financial performance out of the more than eighteen hundred mutual funds in the United States.

A Third Proenvironmental Fund

The third proenvironmental fund, the Global Environmental Fund, was established around the same time as the Eco Logical Trust 1990 and the Schield Progressive Environmental Fund.

The Global Environmental Fund was set up as a limited partnership aimed at institutional investors. Run by Jeff Leonard and John Earhart, two dedicated environmentalists, the fund has performed exceptionally well. It outperformed all of its Wall Street competitors, using a less-aggressive philosophy than that of the Schield Progressive Environmental Fund. Its financial performance is comparable to that of the Eco Logical Trust.

| DRAWING SOME CONCLUSIONS

Nineteen ninety, the year of the environmental sector funds, has offered the first head-on contest between the socially and environmentally responsible type of investments and the type of investments that apply to environmental or social standards because of a fear that use of these standards would lower financial performance.

The conclusion that should be drawn from 1990 is not that proenvironmental investing will always financially outperform investments that use no criteria of environmental responsibility. The 1990 comparisons are not scientific. It is difficult to measure the role of chance and the role of temporary factors, such as the impact of the relatively small amount of assets included in the proenvironmental funds. The victory of the proenvironmental funds does indicate, however, that the widely held belief that social and environmental funds underperform financially because they involve an opportunity cost due to their reduced investment universe may well be incorrect.

The financial impact of social criteria varies greatly with the criteria involved. Given relatively equal skill in stock selection, divestment from South Africa (for instance) should improve financial performance, because it will lower the level of capitalization of a portfolio. Traditionally lower-capitalization portfolios outperform higher-capitalization portfolios.

The reverse occurred in the 1980s because of the drop in the dollar. The largest corporations tend to have the most extensive international investments. As the dollar dropped, their financial performance was better than the corporations with less international exposure. Most of the firms remaining in South Africa tended to be high-capitalization firms with substantial foreign involvement. This peculiar circumstance skewed the results against socially responsible portfolios that excluded companies in South Africa.

Based on these results, investment firms have claimed a scientific validity for the assertion that there is a 1-percent opportunity cost to socially responsible investing. The fact is that no scientific studies can show either a positive or negative impact or prove a cause-and-effect relationship. The empirical evidence is not convincing either way. Nor have careful studies been completed in relation to environmentally responsible investing.

But in this case application of environmental criteria should, in fact, tend to help performance. Recent literature seems to point in that direction. All investment strategies limit the investment universe. The problem is to limit the universe in a way that highlights the investments that will perform well financially. Michael Silverstein's book *The Environmental Factor* (Dearborn, 1990) documents how evaluation of environmentally positive behavior has become a factor in most, if not all, investments. Environmental risk is now recognized as a financial factor by most industries, including the environmental services industry.

As we have seen, the results from year one indicate that limiting the universe for environmental funds to those companies that are not major polluters seems to have enhanced financial performance. The environmentally responsible funds outperformed the nonscreened funds.

To the degree that any extrapolating is done, the evidence seems to indicate that there is no opportunity cost for environmentally responsible investing. If anything, there is an opportunity benefit. The results for year two and subsequent years will tell, but so far, proenvironmental investors are well ahead.

U.S. MONEY MARKET FUNDS

Ed. Note: This chapter consists of descriptions of U.S. money market mutual funds submitted, unless otherwise indicated, by the funds. Those funds that did not choose to submit material are listed in the directory in appendix B.

| CALVERT SOCIAL INVESTMENT FUND
CALVERT MONEY MARKET PORTFOLIO

1715 Eighteenth Street NW
Washington, D.C. 20009
(800) 368-2748
(301) 951-4820

For a full description, see "The Calvert Group" in chapter 32.

| THE PIONEER GROUP
PIONEER MONEY MARKET TRUST: CASH RESERVES
PIONEER MONEY MARKET TRUST: TAX FREE MONEY

60 State Street
Boston, Mass. 02109
(800) 225-6292
(617) 742-7825

For a full description, see "The Pioneer Group" in chapter 32.

| WORKING ASSETS MONEY FUND

230 California Street
San Francisco, Calif. 94111
(800) 533-3863 (8:30 A.M. to 5 P.M. PST)
(415) 989-3200

Fee Structure and Restrictions on Potential Investors

Working Assets Money Fund is the nation's largest socially responsible money market fund. The minimum initial investment is
$1,000. The minimum for subsequent investments is $100, unless
the investor establishes an automatic monthly investment plan,
which has a minimum of $50 a month.

Working Assets Money Fund is a no-load fund. There are no sales
charges on new investments or dividend reinvestments. Fund operating expenses are outlined in the prospectus. The fund offers
unlimited check writing at no charge for checks written for $250 or
more. There is a $0.30 fee on checks written for less than $250. The
fund also offers electronic fund transfers to or from your local bank
account at no charge. However, same-day federal funds wires are
subject to bank charges. The fund is open to individuals and institutions nationwide. Foreign investors may invest in the fund, but
investments must be in U.S. dollars drawn on a U.S. bank.

Investment Objective and Philosophy

Working Assets Money Fund is a money market mutual fund. We
seek as high a level of current income as possible while maintaining
liquidity and safety of capital and at the same time concerning ourselves with the social and economic impact of our investments. We
seek to achieve these goals by investing in a portfolio that consists
of short-term debt securities meeting high-quality investment standards as well as certain social criteria. We seek safety by maintaining
a diversified portfolio and investing in obligations that in the judgment of our adviser present minimal credit risks.

Social Screens

Working Assets Money Fund has been a leader in developing and
implementing social investment criteria. The fourteen social screens
outlined in our prospectus are among the broadest and strictest in
the social investing industry.

ENVIRONMENT AND NUCLEAR POWER. We seek out enterprises that are
in compliance with Environmental Protection Agency (EPA) regulations. We also look for firms involved in alternative energy or
energy conservation. In screening potential investments, we first
eliminate companies that supply nuclear equipment or own nuclear
power plants. Next we review EPA and Justice Department reports
to determine whether a company has a pattern of violating air, water,

toxics, or hazardous waste regulations. We also examine each company's environment inside its plants by reviewing its compliance with Occupational Safety and Health Administration regulations. Finally, we contact the companies and environmental groups for additional information.

HUMAN RIGHTS: THE STRUGGLE AGAINST APARTHEID. We avoid investing in companies that do business in South Africa or help finance the country in any way. In response to the antiapartheid movement's 1987 Guidelines for Divestment, we strengthened our screens to include all indirect ties to South Africa, such as franchise, licensing, or management agreements, as well as ties by parent or subsidiary companies. We applaud recent reforms in South Africa but remain in solidarity with the antiapartheid movement in calling for continued sanctions until apartheid is completely replaced by a nonracial, democratic system.

TOWARD A PEACE ECONOMY. We avoid investing in firms that manufacture or distribute weapons as a principal business activity. First, we rule out the top one hundred defense contractors. Second, we eliminate any other companies that do research or development on the Strategic Defense Initiative, or Star Wars. Then we attempt to determine if the company has any other contracts with the Defense Department or has any foreign military sales.

We also screen our government securities, because we do not want to finance wasteful military spending even indirectly through Treasury bills. Instead we invest in federal agency debt for family farming, small business, housing, and higher education as well as state-sponsored community development programs. Similarly, we invest in financial institutions with strong records on housing and community investment and seek out firms that are creative and generous in their charitable contributions, particularly with respect to investment in their own communities.

EMPLOYEE RELATIONS: PROMOTING A JUST WORKPLACE. We seek to invest in companies that bargain fairly with their employees and have policies that promote the welfare of their workers. At the same time, we do not knowingly invest in companies that:

1. consistently violate regulations of the National Labor Relations Act;

2. appear on the national AFL-CIO "Do Not Patronize" list;
3. have a record of hiring "union-busting" consultants; or
4. have fewer than half of their employees in the United States, unless a majority of their eligible U.S. employees are represented by organized labor.

We seek out firms that promote the economic advancement of women and minorities. At the same time, we do not knowingly invest in companies that discriminate on the basis of race, religion, age, disability, or sexual orientation, or that consistently violate regulations of the U.S. Equal Employment Opportunity Commission.

Advisers and Subadvisers
The fund adviser and distributor is:

Working Assets Capital Management
230 California Street
San Francisco, Calif. 94111
(415) 989-3200

Contact
Investors should contact the sales manager.

TABLE 35-1

1983	1984	1985	1986	1987	1988	1989	1990
9.40%*	10.00%	7.50%	6.08%	5.86%	6.68%	8.46%	7.45%

*Annualized return from inception, September 20, 1983.

NOTE: This table presents an annual yield history for the fund since its inception. Performance may be measured against IBC/Donoghue's annualized compound yield averages for taxable prime money market funds.

SOUTH AFRICA–
FREE GOLD FUNDS

Ed. Note: This chapter consists of descriptions of South Africa–free gold funds submitted, unless otherwise indicated, by the funds. Those who did not choose to submit material are listed in the directory in appendix B.

MONITREND MUTUAL FUND—GOLD SERIES

Kensington Capital Management
Nine Quintard Avenue
Old Greenwich, Conn. 06870
(203) 637-3522

Fee Structure
(See table 36-1.)

Deferred sales load: nil
Redemption fee: nil
Exchange fee: nil

TABLE 36-1

MONITREND MUTUAL FUND—GOLD SERIES FEE STRUCTURE

Amount of Purchase	Sales Charge as a Percentage of Offering Price	Sales Charge as a Percentage of Amount Invested	Commissions as a Percentage of Offering Price
Less than $100,000	3.50%	3.63%	3.00%
$100,000 to $249,999	3.00	3.09	2.75
$250,000 to $499,999	2.50	2.56	2.25
$500,000 to $999,999	2.00	2.04	1.75
$1,000,000 or more	1.50	1.52	1.25

ANNUAL FUND OPERATING EXPENSES
(AS A PERCENT OF AVERAGE NET ASSETS)

Management fees	1.00 percent
12b-1 fees	1.00 percent
Other expenses	0.50 percent
Total fund operating expenses	2.50 percent

MINIMUM INVESTMENT. The minimum investment is $1,000 ($100 for retirement plans). A preauthorized check plan may be opened with a minimum of $250. The minimum subsequent investment for all accounts is $50.

EXCHANGE PRIVILEGES. Shares of the fund may be exchanged for shares of other Monitrend funds as well as funds distributed by Pallas Financial Corporation at no cost.

DIVIDEND REINVESTMENT. Dividends are reinvested automatically unless payment is requested.

VOLUME DISCOUNTS. Share acquisition costs may be saved with single purchases of certain amounts or purchases spread over a period of thirteen months under a letter of intent.

Investment Objective
The Monitrend Gold Fund seeks long-term capital growth by investing in shares of companies involved in the gold industry. It also seeks to preserve capital by employing hedging strategies when gold is in a down trend without limiting the upside potential for value appreciation in the event of a major rally in the price of gold.

Social Screens
The Monitrend Gold Fund does not invest in the shares of companies that operate in South Africa.

Investment Committee
As members of the American Stock Exchange Inc., the investment committee of Kensington Capital Management Inc., comprising of Johann A. de Villiers and Doron Linz, have actively traded stocks and options for their own accounts since the mid-1980s. Trading

TABLE 36-2

MONITREND MUTUAL FUND—GOLD SERIES
PERFORMANCE DATA

	1988	1989	1990	1991 (First Quarter)
Monitrend Gold	−8.8%	14.9%	−8.6%	−2.87%
Lipper Gold Index	−15.7%	31.0%	−14.1%	−4.30%

strategies were based on a fundamental analysis, a "fair-value" option pricing model and a technical analysis system based on trend analysis. The trading strategies ensured consistent returns during some of the most volatile markets in recorded history.

Prior to becoming members of the American Stock Exchange, de Villiers was managing director of an international mining company and Linz was a controller of a textile importer.

Subadviser

Monitrend Investment Management
272 Closter Dock Road
Closter, N.J. 07624
(201) 767-5400

Distributor

Pallas Financial Corporation
2325 Crestmoor Road, Suite P200
Nashville, Tenn. 37215
(615) 298-1000

I **PIONEER GROUP**
PIONEER GROWTH TRUST: GOLD SHARES

60 State Street
Boston, Mass. 02109
(800) 225-6292
(617) 742-7825

For a full description, see "The Pioneer Group" in chapter 32.

CHAPTER 37

U.S. MUTUAL FUNDS WITH RESTRICTIONS ON POTENTIAL INVESTORS

Ed. Note: This chapter consists of descriptions of U.S. mutual funds that have restrictions on who may invest in them. The descriptions were submitted, unless otherwise indicated, by the funds. Those funds that chose not to submit material are listed in the directory in appendix B.

CHRISTIAN BROTHERS INVESTMENT SERVICES

675 Third Avenue, Thirty-first Floor
New York, N.Y. 10017-5704
(800) 592-8890 (national WATS)
(212) 490-0800
(212) 490-6092 (fax)

Christian Brothers Investment Services (CBIS) was founded in 1981 to serve the needs of Catholic religious investors. It is owned by the Brothers of the Christian Schools and its profits go to support their educational ministries.

CBIS offers a wide range of programs and services. Currently we serve more than 750 organizations, whose combined assets total over $600 million.

Adviser to All CBIS Funds
Christian Brothers Investment Services
903 Commerce Drive, Suite 327
Oak Brook, Ill. 60521-8830

CATHOLIC UNITED INVESTMENT TRUST BALANCED FUND

Catholic United Investment Trust (CUIT) was established under a trust agreement dated February 18, 1983, for religious, charitable, and educational purposes. The Balanced Fund was established by the trustees on September 27, 1983. CBIS began managing funds for the Balanced Fund in January 1984.

Fee Structure and Restrictions on Potential Investors

The Balanced Fund requires a minimum initial investment of $25,000. Subsequent investments of at least $1,000 may be made. The net investment income and net capital gains of the Balanced Fund may be reinvested in additional trust units or may be distributed at no additional charge. There is a management fee of 1 percent per year.

The Catholic United Investment Trust Agreement stipulates that only member or subsidiary organizations meeting the following criteria are eligible:

- listed in the *Official Catholic Directory*;
- exempt from federal income tax under the provisions of section 501(c)(3) of the Internal Revenue Code of 1954; and
- not a private foundation as defined in section 509(a) of the IRS code.

Investment Objectives and Philosophy

The CUIT Balanced Fund is a conservative long-term growth- and income-oriented fund whose objective in capital appreciation and current income through investments in high-quality equity, fixed-income, and investment-grade corporate securities.

The Balanced Fund offers the investor an opportunity to participate in the growth of market advances through high-quality stocks. Through the income earned from high-quality bonds, it also seeks to provide some stability in market downturns. The CUIT Balanced Fund offers management diversification as well, as its assets are divided between two subadvisers.

The Balanced Fund uses a value-oriented approach to investing. CBIS believes that value can be achieved by identifying those companies with strong fundamentals that are low in price relative to the market. In seeking value, CBIS believes that it is possible to achieve higher returns while maintaining a lower-risk exposure. Both Duff & Phelps and Dodge & Cox, as subadvisers, strive to execute this value-oriented philosophy in the day-to-day management of the fund.

Social Screens

One of the areas in which CBIS has distinguished itself is in the field of socially responsible investing. It is our belief that Catholic organizations must participate with care in the capital markets. They must see to it that investments are comparable with their mission.

In addition, CBIS strongly feels that as owners, there is a responsibility to participate in the companies in which one invests. CBIS has an eight-part strategy that we employ on behalf of our participants:

CORPORATE DIALOGUE. Through corporate dialogue, we assist corporations in the creation of socially responsible practices or to remind them of previous commitments.

SHAREHOLDER RESOLUTIONS. When dialogue fails to produce the desired effect, we sponsor resolutions backed by the shares of those participants and mutual funds under our advisement that empower us to act in their behalf.

PROXY VOTING. We vote on resolutions at annual shareholder meetings or by proxy on behalf of any participants who empower us to do so.

PRINCIPLED PURCHASING: LABOR DIGNITY AND EQUALITY. We take affirmative action, through research and dialogue, to provide equal employment opportunities, comparable-worth wages, safe working conditions, and the use of transnational labor. We withhold votes for boards noninclusive of women and minorities in conjunction with written communication objecting to this lack of inclusion. We sponsor resolutions for greater inclusiveness of women and minorities among directors and senior management.

INTERNATIONAL PURCHASING. We will make no new purchases of securities issued by any company with direct investment (assets or employees) in South Africa until apartheid is ended. We conduct research and dialogue on international debt held by U.S. banks. We support human rights progress—for example, coffee companies in El Salvador. We sponsor resolutions on:

- South Africa—the complete withdrawal from South Africa, cutting all ties to the apartheid economy, and urging relocation in sub-Saharan Africa;
- Northern Ireland—abiding by the MacBride Principles;
- *Maquiladora* factories along the U.S.-Mexican border—calling for fair wages, safe working conditions, and an unpolluted living environment.

MILITARISM. We will make no new purchases of securities issued by the twenty-five firms identified by CBIS for their prominence in overall weapons manufacturing, manufacturing of weapons of mass destruction, or exportation of weapons.

ENVIRONMENT. We conduct research and dialogue with companies to:

- sign the Valdez Principles (standardizing environmental reports), including a commitment to an independent audit;
- protect the atmosphere, fresh water sources, ocean, and coastal resources;
- stop deforestation and desertification;
- conserve biological diversity;
- work toward the safe management of hazardous and toxic wastes.

We sponsor resolutions to report to shareholders on the Valdez Principles—reactions, compliance, objections, and signatory intent.

BIOETHICS. We will make no purchases of securities issued by firms that market products or services designed to aid the cessation of human life. We conduct research and dialogue for:

- the safe management and prudent application of biotechnology;
- global marketing of infant formula and other medical products within the guidelines of the World Health Organization.

We will vote proxies to support the minimization of minors' access to tobacco and the advertising of harmful products in poor and minority communities.

TABLE 37-1

CUIT BALANCED FUND ANNUAL PERFORMANCE DATA
Data on a Total Return Basis (Net of Fees)

1984	1985	1986	1987	1988	1989	1990
−.45%	31.90%	13.50%	−1.90%	8.80%	17.80%	1.40%

NOTE: Benchmark: Lipper Balanced Fund Index.
Please note that past performance is not necessarily indicative of future results.
The offering and sale of securities is made exclusively through CBIS Financial Services.

Subadvisers

Duff & Phelps Investment Management Company
710 Ohio Savings Plaza
Cleveland, Ohio 44114-3189

Dodge & Cox
One Sansome Street
San Francisco, Calif. 94104

CATHOLIC UNITED INVESTMENT TRUST GROWTH FUND

The CUIT Growth Fund was established by action of the trustees on October 2, 1990. CBIS began managing funds for the Growth Fund in December 1990.

Fee Structure and Restrictions on Potential Investors

The Growth Fund requires a minimum initial investment of $25,000. Subsequent investments of at least $1,000 may be made. The net investment income and net capital gains of the Growth Fund may be reinvested in additional trust units of the Growth Fund or distributed on a monthly basis at no charge.

There is an annual management fee of 1.25 percent.

The Catholic United Investment Trust Agreement stipulates that only member organizations or subsidiary organizations meeting the following criteria are eligible:

- listed in the *Official Catholic Directory;*
- exempt from federal income tax under the provisions of section 501(c)(3) of the Internal Revenue Code of 1954; and
- not a private foundation as defined in section 509(a) of the IRS code.

Investment Objectives and Philosophy

The CUIT Growth Fund is an all-equity fund whose objective is to achieve long-term capital appreciation by investing in a broadly diversified portfolio of equity securities of well-known, established companies believed to have above-average market appreciation potential.

Historically investing in equities of this type has resulted in higher total returns on average. But doing so means the ability to tolerate a high degree of price fluctuations caused by market volatility. The Growth Fund is an aggressive vehicle for those willing to accept a moderate to high degree of risk. It should be part of a well-diversified investment strategy and should not be an organization's sole investment program.

The Growth Fund is an actively managed portfolio. CBIS believes in identifying those companies with strong fundamentals that are low in price relative to the market. Nicholas-Applegate Capital Management, in execution of this philosophy, targets companies that are marked by earnings acceleration, sustainable growth, and positive relative price momentum.

Social Screens

See the description of the CUIT Balanced Fund social screens, pages 459–62.

Subadviser

Nicholas-Applegate Capital Management
501 West Broadway, Suite 2000
San Diego, Calif. 92101

TABLE 37-2

CUIT GROWTH FUND PERFORMANCE DATA

January 1991	9.6%
February 1991	9.6%

NOTE: Figures are net of fees. Benchmark: Lipper Growth Fund Index.

Please note that past performance is not necessarily indicative of future results. The offering and sale of securities is made exclusively through CBIS Financial Services.

| CBIS CERTIFICATES OF DEPOSIT PROGRAM

Fee Structure and Restrictions on Potential Investors

The certificate of deposit (CD) program requires a low minimum investment of $1,000. There are no fees assessed directly to CD investors; CBIS Financial Services is compensated by banks participating in the program.

Only member organizations or subsidiary organizations of the Roman Catholic Church may invest in this program.

Investment Objectives and Philosophy

The CD is an income-oriented investment vehicle whose objective is to provide income and fixed-term investing of funds. CDs offer conservative institutional investors the ability to invest short- and intermediate-term funds in FDIC/SAIF-insured CDs with maturities that range from six months to five years.

CBIS has access to over more than 160 bank and savings and loan institutions across the country. We select CDs that reflect geographic preference and find competitive rates. CBIS applies financial screens to participating banks to make sure they meet our criteria in terms of their community and lending activities. In order to protect the investor's assets, CBIS will not purchase more than the insured limit at any one bank or savings and loan.

Social Screens

Where CBIS has the freedom to choose the institutions providing the CDs and provided that these choices do not conflict with our fiduciary responsibilities, we will give preference to those financial institutions that:

1. Have a positive orientation or creative approach toward CBIS's socially responsible investing issues. An institution must:
   - have a positive record of community reinvestment practices;
   - have a positive affirmative action and equal employment opportunity record; and
   - be owned by corporations satisfying the CBIS Purchasing Principles.

2. Have no ties to the economy of South Africa as long as apartheid exists there. A financial services institution will be con-

sidered to have severed ties to South Africa when it, for example:

- has no outstanding loans to South Africa;
- has established a policy precluding investments, loans, credits (including trade credits), and related services to entities in which South Africa capital holds at least a 10 percent interest;
- does not provide financing for joint ventures and partnerships with such entities;
- does not participate in financing the transactions of entities in which South Africa capital holds an interest of 10 percent or more; and
- does not provide South African entities with correspondence banking services or other routine transactions, such as sight letters of credit, clean and documentary collections, and incoming or outgoing transfers.

3. Have similarly severed ties with any government with an established history of repression of its constituents.

I RELIGIOUS COMMUNITIES TRUST COLLEGE FUND

The Religious Communities Trust (RCT) was established under a trust agreement dated May 18, 1976, to help Roman Catholic organizations invest their funds with integrity and security. CBIS began managing funds for the RCT College Fund in August 1985.

Fee Structure and Restrictions on Potential Investors

There is no minimum deposit or balance requirement. There is a management fee of .5 percent per year.

TABLE 37-3

CBIS PROGRAM PERFORMANCE DATA

	1989	*1990*
1 year	8.8%	8.2%
2.5 years	—	8.4%

NOTE: The CD program was established in 1989.
Please note that past performance is not necessarily indicative of future results. The offering and sale of securities is made exclusively through CBIS Financial Services.

The College Fund is restricted to Catholic colleges and universities. The RCT Trust Agreement stipulates that only member or subsidiary organizations meeting the following criteria are eligible:

- listed in the *Official Catholic Directory*;
- exempt from federal income tax under the provisions of section 501(c)(3) of the Internal Revenue Code of 1954; and
- not a private foundation as defined in section 509(a) of the IRS code.

Investment Objectives and Philosophy
The RCT College Fund is an income-oriented fund whose objective is to provide total cash flow management and short-term investment for Catholic colleges and universities. The College Fund is ideal for obtaining high money market rates of return and zero-balance checkwriting capabilities. It is an easy way for Catholic colleges and universities to maximize earnings on operating funds without sacrificing the features needed to manage cash flow.

The College Fund adheres to the following philosophy:

- Preserve capital: the investment process is one that requires that all assets are liquid and investments are made only on an overnight basis.
- Earn a competitive rate of return: CBIS has negotiated a favorable interest rate that generally is available only to corporations or institutions with large cash flows.
- Invest all funds ethically: the institutions with which we deal in this program have met our criteria with regard to their corporate activity.

Social Screens
See the description of social screens for CDs, page 465.

RELIGIOUS COMMUNITIES TRUST INTERMEDIATE BOND FUND

CBIS began managing funds for the RCT Intermediate Bond Fund in January 1985.

Fee Structure and Restrictions on Potential Investors
There is no minimum deposit or balance requirement. Participants have the option to take income or reinvest their dividends at no

TABLE 37-4

**RELIGIOUS COMMUNITIES TRUST COLLEGE FUND
PERFORMANCE DATA**

1986	1987	1988	1989	1990
6.4%	6.2%	7.2%	9.1%	7.9%

NOTE: Performance data is on a total return basis (net of fees) for each year. Benchmark: Bank Money Market Deposit Average, Donoghue Money Market Fund, and Donoghue Government Money Market Fund Average.

Please note that past performance is not necessarily indicative of future results. The offering and sale of securities is made exclusively through CBIS Financial Services.

additional charge. There is a management fee of .5 percent per year.

The RCT Trust Agreement stipulates that only member or subsidiary organizations meeting the following criteria are eligible:

- listed in the *Official Catholic Directory*;
- exempt from federal income tax under the provisions of section 501(c)(3) of the Internal Revenue Code of 1954; and
- not a private foundation as defined in section 509(a) of the IRS code.

Investment Objectives and Philosophy

The RCT Intermediate Bond Fund is an income-oriented fund whose objective is to provide income for non–cash flow funds. It was designed for the religious investor seeking a greater degree of price stability than is offered by longer-term bond funds. It invests only in the highest-quality fixed-income instruments. The fund has an average maturity of between one and ten years.

The RCT Intermediate Bond Fund is an actively managed fixed-income portfolio. CBIS believes that through this active management, it is possible to achieve higher returns while maintaining a lower risk exposure. The emphasis is on intermediate-term, high-quality securities with an average maturity that does not exceed ten years (on average it is much less). We do not feel that the higher rates available at the lower end of the market are commensurate with the incremental credit risk often incurred.

Social Screens

See the discussion of social screens for the Catholic United Investment Trust Balanced Fund, pages 459–462.

TABLE 37-5

RCT INTERMEDIATE BOND FUND PERFORMANCE DATA

1985	1986	1987	1988	1989	1990
15.1%	10.9%	3.1%	5.1%	11.0%	8.6%

NOTE: Performance data is on a total return basis for each year. Benchmarks: Shearson/Lehman Intermediate (1–3) Index and a money market fund.

Please note that past performance is not necessarily indicative of future results. The offering and sale of securities is made exclusively through CBIS Financial Services.

Subadviser

Duff & Phelps Investment Management Company
710 Ohio Savings Plaza
Cleveland, Ohio 44114-3189

RELIGIOUS COMMUNITIES TRUST MONEY MARKET FUND

CBIS began managing funds for the RCT Money Market Fund in January 1985.

Fee Structure and Restrictions on Potential Investors

There is no minimum deposit or balance requirement. There is a management fee of .5 percent per year.

The RCT Trust Agreement stipulates that only member or subsidiary organizations meeting the following criteria are eligible:

- listed in the *Official Catholic Directory*;
- exempt from federal income tax under the provisions of section 501(c)(3) of the Internal Revenue Code of 1954; and
- not a private foundation as defined in section 509(a) of the IRS code.

Investment Objective and Philosophy

The RCT Money Market Fund is an income-oriented fund whose objective is to provide Roman Catholic organizations with an effective way to manage their operating cash flow. The fund is flexible enough, so no matter how small or complex the cash management needs are, it generally can handle them. It offers competitive money market rates with full check-writing ability, all in one package.

The RCT Money Market Fund adheres to the following philosophy:

- Preserve capital: the investment process is one that requires that all assets are liquid and investments are made only on an overnight basis.
- Earn a competitive rate of return: CBIS has negotiated a favorable interest rate that generally is available only to corporations or institutions with large cash flows.
- Invest all funds ethically: the institutions with which we deal in this program have met our criteria with regard to their corporate activity.

Social Screens
See the description of social screens for the CBIS CD Program, pages 465–66.

TABLE 37-6

RCT MONEY MARKET FUND PERFORMANCE DATA

1985	1986	1987	1988	1989	1990
7.8%	6.1%	5.9%	7.1%	9.0%	7.8%

NOTE: Peformance data is on a total return basis for each year. Benchmarks: bank money market deposit accounts, Donoghue Money Market Fund, and Donoghue Government Money Market Fund Average.

Please note that past performance is not necessarily indicative of future results. The offering and sale of securities is made exclusively through CBIS Financial Services.

| MAS POOLED TRUST FUND SELECT PORTFOLIOS SOUTH AFRICA–FREE INVESTMENT SERVICES

Miller, Anderson & Sherrerd
One Tower Bridge
West Conshohocken, Pa. 19428
(215) 940-5000

Fee Structure and Restrictions on Potential Investors
The MAS Pooled Trust Fund was established to allow institutional clients investing a minimum of $4 million to utilize the full range of investment management services at Miller, Anderson & Sherrerd (MA & S).

Social Screens

MA & S has been managing portfolios for clients with South Africa restrictions since 1982. Today they represent a significant percentage of all of our assets under management.

We work in conjunction with the Investor Responsibility Research Center (IRRC) to establish the guidelines for the Select portfolios of the MAS Pooled Trust Fund. The IRRC is an independent, not-for-profit corporation that conducts research and publishes impartial reports on contemporary social and public policy issues and the impact of those issues on major corporations and institutional investors.

Advisers

The investment adviser to the MAS Pooled Trust Fund, Miller, Anderson & Sherrerd, is a partnership formed in 1969. MA & S provides investment counseling services to employee benefit plans, endowment funds, foundations, and other institutional investors.

SELECT EQUITY PORTFOLIO

Fee Schedule

Fees are deducted from unit values at the following annualized rates:

Investment management fee: 0.500 percent

Total expenses: 0.610 percent

Total expense ratios include investment management, administrative, and custody fees, which are based on net assets of the trust and have been estimated at an annual rate as of December 31, 1990. Investment management and administrative fees are accrued daily and are deducted from each portfolio's daily net asset value (NAV). They are paid out of this accrual quarterly and fund clients are not billed for fees.

Investment Objective and Philosophy

Our objective as an equity manager is to achieve long-term investment results that are above average in both total return and consistency as compared with the performance of the broad market averages and other investment managers. Our equity investment philosophy has an underlying premise that believes that common stock prices change more frequently and by a greater magnitude than the underlying earnings power. We believe that successful equity investing requires ongoing, rigorous comparisons of investment alternatives. The objective is to buy the most future earnings power at the lowest possible price. We have developed useful, well-defined quality standards and a valuation methodology that provides a basis for avoiding overvalued securities and serves as insulation against the inaccuracy of forecasts. Our philosophy can best be described as applying a disciplined analytical process to the task of identifying stocks that sell below some definable concept of value.

The Select Equity Portfolio has the same investment objective as its traditional counterpart, with the investment restriction that it will not invest in any companies listed by the IRRC as having direct investments or employees in South Africa.

SELECT FIXED INCOME PORTFOLIO

Fee Schedule
Fees are deducted from unit values at the following annualized rates:

> Investment management fee: 0.375 percent
>
> Total expenses: 0.470 percent

Total expense ratios include investment management, administrative, and custody fees, which are based on net assets of the trust and have been estimated at an annual rate as of December 31, 1990. Investment management and administrative fees are accrued daily and are deducted from each portfolio's daily NAV. They are paid out of this accrual quarterly; fund clients are not billed for fees.

Investment Objective and Philosophy
Our objective is to achieve a positive real return, reduce overall portfolio risk, and generate favorable investment performance relative to other fixed-income managers and the broad market indexes. We believe that we can add value through active management. This is achieved by making judgments about the future direction of interest rates and by making value decisions that drive portfolio composition. While the fixed-income market is fairly efficient, it is possible through analysis of new and/or complicated securities to reveal opportunity in the marketplace.

Our basic philosophy is value investing. We purchase securities that we believe are relatively cheap and hold them until relative

TABLE 37-7

MAS POOLED TRUST FUND—SELECT EQUITY PORTFOLIO
Performance Data

Year	Quarter	Quarterly Return	Wealth Index	Rolling 4 Quarter	Rolling 2 Year	Annualized Since Inception
			1			
1988	2/26–3/31	4.00%	1.040			
	2	7.24	1.115			
	3	(1.25)	1.101			
	4	1.57	1.119			
1989	1	7.15	1.199	15.25%		18.04%
	2	7.30	1.286	15.31		20.62
	3	11.50	1.434	30.20		25.41
	4	(1.75)	1.409	25.95		20.46
1990	1	(2.13)	1.379	15.05	15.15%	16.60
	2	9.21	1.506	17.10	16.20	19.10
	3	(14.37)	1.290	(10.07)	8.21	10.31
	4	10.08	1.420	0.75	12.65	13.12
1991	1	17.06	1.662	20.50	17.74	17.85

NOTE: MAS Pooled Trust Fund returns are net of management, administrative, and custody fees. Returns represent past performance and the investment return and principal value of an investment will fluctuate so that an investor's shares, when redeemed, may be worth either more or less than their original cost.

Inception for the MAS Pooled Trust Fund—Select Equity Portfolio: February 26, 1988.

The Select portfolios of the MAS Pooled Trust Fund are managed via the same investment philosophy as their nonrestricted counterparts but do not invest in companies doing business or having employees in South Africa.

values change or until we identify other securities that we consider to be better values. We have a long-term perspective and are willing to purchase a core portfolio that represents the best values in the market, even if that value may not be recognized in the near future.

The Select Fixed Income Portfolio has the same investment objective as its traditional counterpart, with the restriction that it will not invest in any companies listed by the IRRC as having direct investments or employees in South Africa.

SELECT VALUE PORTFOLIO

Fee Structure and Restrictions on Potential Investors

The MAS Pooled Trust Fund was established to allow institutional clients investing a minimum of $4 million to utilize MA & S's full

TABLE 37-8

MAS POOLED TRUST FUND—SELECT FIXED INCOME PORTFOLIO
Performance Data

Year	Quarter	Quarterly Return	Wealth Index	Rolling 4 Quarter	Rolling 2 Year	Annualized Since Inception
			1			
1987	4	5.69%	1.057			
1988	1	3.79	1.097			
	2	0.90	1.107			
	3	1.83	1.127	12.72%		12.72%
	4	1.41	1.143	8.15		11.29
1989	1	1.38	1.159	5.64		10.33
	2	6.22	1.231	11.21		12.61
	3	(0.06)	1.230	9.14	10.91%	10.91
	4	3.34	1.271	11.22	9.67	11.26
1990	1	(1.73)	1.249	7.80	6.71	9.31
	2	3.74	1.296	5.29	8.21	9.89
	3	(1.37)	1.278	3.90	6.49	8.52
	4	6.61	1.363	7.19	9.18	9.99
1991	1	3.79	1.414	13.22	10.47	10.41

NOTE: MAS Pooled Trust Fund returns are net of management, administrative, and custody fees. Returns represent past performance and the investment return and principal value of an investment will fluctuate so that an investor's shares, when redeemed, may be worth either more or less than their original cost.

Inception for the MAS Pooled Trust Fund—Select Fixed Income Portfolio: September 30, 1987.

The Select portfolios of the MAS Pooled Trust Fund are managed via the same investment philosophy as their nonrestricted counterparts but do not invest in companies doing business or having employees in South Africa.

range of investment management services. See the fee schedule for the Select Fixed Income Portfolio (page 472).

Investment Objective and Philosophy

Our equity investment philosophy is best described as applying a disciplined analytical process to the task of identifying stocks that sell below some definable concept of value. Superior returns are unlikely to be attained by owning popular stocks. We try to benefit from the fact that the prices of stocks move more frequently, and in greater magnitude, than do the fundamentals of companies. The Value Portfolio seeks to exploit the opportunities existing in the equity market through the use of a systematic, disciplined valuation process. The approach taken in constructing the Value Portfolio is to focus our search on stocks that are cheap in an absolute sense. Stocks are ranked within a consistently applied valuation process. The portfolio is constructed from the most attractive stocks as ranked by this process. A high percentage of the securities selected are in the lowest Price/Earnings quintile. The other securities included are cheap by some measure of value, such as price-cash flow or dividend yield.

The Select Value Portfolio has the same investment objective as its traditional counterpart, with the restriction that it will not invest in any companies listed by the IRRC as having direct investments or employees in South Africa.

SELECT BALANCED PORTFOLIO

Fee Schedule
Fees are deducted from unit values at the following annualized rates:

Investment management fee: 0.450 percent

Total expenses: 0.554 percent

Total expense ratios include investment management, administrative, and custody fees, which are based on net assets of the trust and have been estimated at an annual rate as of December 31, 1990. Investment management and administrative fees are accrued daily and are deducted from each portfolio's daily NAV. They are paid out of this accrual quarterly and fund clients are not billed for fees.

Fees for the Balanced Investment Program are based on the current equity–fixed income ratio, which is presently 60:40. The actual fees and total expense ratios will vary as the asset allocation changes.

Investment Objective and Philosophy
Our investment objective is to achieve an above-average return over a full market cycle with a greater degree of consistency than the broad market averages and other investment managers. We believe that successful balanced account management requires an effective approach to both equity and fixed-income investing, plus the application of a consistent, disciplined process of asset allocation.

Balanced accounts are divided into equity and fixed-income portions, each of which is managed separately. Equity management

TABLE 37-9

MAS POOLED TRUST FUND—SELECT VALUE PORTFOLIO
Performance Data

Year	Quarter	Quarterly Return	Wealth Index	Rolling 4 Quarter	Rolling 2 Year	Annualized Since Inception
			1			
1987	11/24–12/31	0.47%	1.005			
1988	1	11.39	1.119			
	2	6.99	1.197			
	3	(0.26)	1.194			
	4	1.60	1.213	20.77%		19.23%
1989	1	7.73	1.307	16.80		21.95
	2	6.31	1.390	16.05		22.83
	3	8.93	1.514	26.74		25.12
	4	(5.29)	1.434	18.15	19.45%	18.71
1990	1	(3.52)	1.383	5.81	11.17	14.80
	2	2.75	1.421	2.27	8.94	14.47
	3	(16.24)	1.190	(21.36)	(0.17)	6.31
	4	10.92	1.320	(7.91)	4.31	9.38
1991	1	18.33	1.562	12.95	9.32	14.25

NOTE: MAS Pooled Trust Fund returns are net of management, administrative, and custody fees. Returns represent past performance and the investment return and principal value of an investment will fluctuate so that an investor's shares, when redeemed, may be worth either more or less than their original cost.

Inception for the MAS Pooled Trust Fund—Select Value Portfolio: November 24, 1987.

The Select portfolios of the MAS Pooled Trust Fund are managed via the same investment philosophy as their nonrestricted counterparts but do not invest in companies doing business or having employees in South Africa.

combines strategic investing with a systematic, disciplined process of stock selection. Fixed-income management combines an intermediate maturity orientation with value investing. The allocation decision between the equity and fixed-income portions is based on our appraisal of the relative attractiveness and risks that exist for those types of securities. We use a systematic approach to allocating assets among sectors. Three key influences in our asset allocation process are liquidity, valuation, and investor sentiment. In considering risk, we focus more on the probability of a permanent loss of capital, measured in real terms, than we do on volatility of return.

The Select Balanced Program has the same investment objective as its traditional counterpart, with the restriction that it will not invest in any companies listed by the IRRC as having direct investments or employees in South Africa.

TABLE 37-10

MAS POOLED TRUST FUND—SELECT BALANCED PROGRAM
Performance Data

Year	Quarter	Quarterly Return	Wealth Index	Rolling 4 Quarter	Rolling 2 Year	Annualized Since Inception
			1			
1988	2	4.69%	1.047			
	3	(0.05)	1.046			
	4	1.51	1.062			
1989	1	4.87	1.114	11.37%		11.37%
	2	6.72	1.189	13.54		14.82
	3	7.73	1.280	22.38		17.92
	4	(0.21)	1.278	20.31		15.04
1990	1	(2.01)	1.252	12.43	11.90%	11.90
	2	7.38	1.345	13.12	13.33	14.06
	3	(9.90)	1.211	(5.39)	7.60	7.98
	4	8.69	1.317	3.05	11.35	10.53
1991	1	11.81	1.472	17.58	14.97	13.76

NOTE: MAS Pooled Trust Fund returns are net of management, administrative, and custody fees. Returns represent past performance and the investment return and principal value of an investment will fluctuate so that an investor's shares, when redeemed, may be worth either more or less than their original cost.

Inception for the MAS Pooled Trust Fund—Select Balanced Investment Program: March 31, 1988.

The Select portfolios of the MAS Pooled Trust Fund are managed via the same investment philosophy as their nonrestricted counterparts but do not invest in companies doing business or having employees in South Africa.

Contact

Glenn E. Becker of Client Services, MAS, has a B.S. degree (1971) and an M.B.A. (1974) from Drexel University. Before coming to MA & S in 1988, he was senior vice president and director of marketing and client relations (1987–88) and vice president and portfolio manager/securities analyst (1975–86) at Provident Capital Management; and trust officer, employee benefits at Girard Bank (1970–75). Becker is a certified employee benefit specialist; a former member of the Philmont Christian Academy school board; secretary of the board of trustees and a member of the Administrative Board, Jarrettown Methodist Church; and a member of Financial Analysts of Philadelphia.

I STATE STREET BANK & TRUST COMPANY

Asset Management Division
225 Franklin Street, Third Floor
Boston, Mass. 02110
(617) 786-3000

Through common trust funds, State Street Bank & Trust's Asset Management Division offers institutional investors a variety of specialized socially screened index funds. As the manager of the Domini Social Index Trust, the bank also is able to offer common trust funds that are indexed to this more broadly based index. (For more information on the Domini Social Index, see chapter 25.)

Contact
Lynn Symanski.

SOCIAL VENTURE CAPITAL

Michael Hall Kieschnick President,
Sand County Ventures

The United States has thrived on the principles of entrepreneurship and individual and collective risk taking. In many ways the nation's development has sprung from the willingness of investors and entrepreneurs to assume the risks inherent in new business development. The imagination, boldness, and energy of entrepreneurs, combined with the involvement and persistence of experienced venture capital investors, have created new industries and new technologies.

| THE NATURE OF VENTURE CAPITAL

Venture capital is that form of capital that typically purchases equity investments in privately held companies, holding it for long periods

---

Michael Kieschnick is the president of Sand County Ventures, a venture capital firm focusing on opportunities in environmental and human services. The firm is the general partner for the Sand County Venture Fund, the nation's first socially responsible venture capital fund.

Kieschnick is also the president of the Muir California Tax-Free Bond Fund, which is described in chapter 32. In 1983 he helped found Working Assets Money Fund, the largest socially responsible money market fund, and served on its board of trustees until 1988. He serves as the chairman of Working Assets Funding Service, which runs a donation-linked VISA program and long-distance telephone service. He also serves on the boards of the Tides Foundation, the California League of Conservation Voters, Feeling Better Health Daycare, PureHarvest, and Zofcom.

For six years he was a visiting lecturer at the Graduate School of Public Policy, University of California at Berkeley, teaching a graduate seminar on financial innovation. He holds a Ph.D. in public policy (1982) from Harvard as well as undergraduate degrees in biology and economics from Stanford. With Julia Parzen, he is the coauthor of a forthcoming book on development banking entitled *Credit Where It Is Due.*

of time in the hope that the stock can be sold later for a substantial gain.

The venture capital market is both diverse and dispersed geographically. This "market" is not a single place like the New York Stock Exchange. Rather, it is a complicated series of personal relationship reflected in previous investments and Rolodexes. Hence, the market comes together around particular venture funds seeking to raise investment capital or particular transactions in which a young company sells stock in return for cash.

Sources of venture financing include venture capital funds as well as wealthy individuals seeking to make direct investments in particular companies. Investors tend to vary widely in their capacity and willingness to take risks. Some are willing to back unproven ideas, while others prefer established companies. Some may be willing to be relatively passive, while others seek effective control of a young company.

The professional venture capital industry, consisting largely of limited partnerships organized by individual general partners, has grown dramatically since the late 1970s. Then it consisted of a pool of roughly $3 billion; today it exceeds $30 billion. At the same time, the informal market for venture capital, consisting of wealthy individuals, has grown as well. Some evidence indicates that this informal market puts something on the order of $10 billion a year into thousands of enterprises.

| SOCIAL VENTURE CAPITAL

Social venture capital applies disciplines developed in the venture capital industry to building companies that make money by providing solutions to major public concerns. A successful social venture investment requires both financial success (as measured by rate of return on investment) and social success (for example, an environmental problem reduced or eliminated or a human need met). Thus, a social venture capital investment usually involves the purchase of stock or convertible debt in a young company. Outside investors typically have significant board representation and seek to add value to the company beyond that represented by their cash.

In a grand sense, traditional venture capital also seeks to invest in companies that meet human needs, in that success depends on the existence of a market for their product or service. Perhaps the difference between traditional and social venture capital investments can be illustrated by comparing an investment in Williams Clarissa (a purveyor of perfumes and cosmetics for children) with one in Bright Horizons (a provider of affordable day care at work sites), or an investment in a new garbage hauler and landfill operator with one in a recycler of wine bottles. The perfume purveyor and the garbage company have markets, but they do not solve social concerns. The day-care provider and the recycler meet basic human needs or reduce the impact on commercial activity on the environment.

Social Venture Capital Funds

Three venture funds describe themselves as social venture capital funds. In order of their creation, they are: the Sand County Fund (1988), Calvert Social Venture Partners (1989), and HFG Expansion Fund (1990).

SAND COUNTY VENTURE FUND. The Sand County Venture Fund is a venture capital–limited partnership located in San Francisco and founded by Michael Kieschnick, the author of this chapter. The fund restricts its investments to California companies and focuses on environmental companies that reduce, substitute for, or eliminate harmful waste, as well as human service companies. As of March 20, 1991, the fund had made four investments:

- Feeling Better Health Daycare (Sunnyvale, California), which provides day care for mildly ill children.
- National Water Management (San Jose, California), which uses a patented ozonization process to purify water in industrial cooling towers without the use of harmful chemicals and with dramatic water savings.
- Pure Harvest (Napa, California), which has developed methods of growing row crops without the use of pesticides or herbicides and is bringing to the retail food market rice products grown without chemicals.
- Zofcom (Palo Alto, California), which serves the quadriplegic population with rehabilitation devices.

CALVERT SOCIAL VENTURE PARTNERS. Calvert Social Venture Partners is also a venture-limited partnership. Located in Bethesda, Maryland, it is managed by the Silby Guffey Company, started by Wayne Silby and John Guffey, founders of the Calvert Investment Group. The managing partner is John May. The fund focuses on investments in the Mid-Atlantic states with an emphasis on companies that solve environmental and social problems. As of March 20, 1991, the fund had made five investments:

- Shaman Pharmaceuticals (San Carlos, California), a pharmaceuticals company developing new drugs from naturally derived sources. It seeks to combine knowledge of traditional medicines with advanced chemistry to provide an alternative drug discovery route.
- Espro (Columbia, Maryland), a biological pesticides company currently focusing on the use of viruses to combat insects.
- Ecological Systems (Washington, D.C.), a company with rights to a water purification process utilizing algae developed at the Smithsonian Institution.
- Katrina, Inc. (Hagerstown, Maryland), has developed a revolutionary on-line process-sorting and control instrument that should allow for higher-quality prepackaged food.
- Tiregator (Dallas, Texas), a vertically integrated tire recycling company currently operating two tire collection centers and a crumb rubber production facility.

HFG EXPANSION FUND. The HFG Expansion Fund is a venture-limited partnership located in Cambridge, Massachusetts, and managed by the Alterra Group. The Alterra Group is managed by Artemis Joukowsky and William Ware. The fund focuses on companies that already have sales from products or services and that address fundamental human concerns in the areas of energy, the environment, and natural food products. As of March 1, 1991, the fund had made investments in three companies:

- Seventh Generation (Burlington, Vermont), the leading environmental catalog company, distributing environmentally sound consumer products through direct-mail marketing.
- Pronatec (Portland, Maine), a natural foods company selling a raw cane sugar to food manufacturers and consumers.
- Aquafuture (Amherst, Massachusetts), an organic fish-farming company.

IN THE FUNDS' FUTURE. This kind of investing requires an enormous amount of time devoted to hand holding, searching for additional managers, helping with sales, and contributing to key choices. All three social venture capital funds are actively involved in the management and strategic planning for the companies in their portfolios. In some cases a fund may even serve temporarily as chief executive officer while an appropriate leader is found.

While the funds are making exciting investments, it is too early to tell how they will perform. Only the Sand County Venture Fund has committed most of its capital to investments. In all cases the companies receiving capital will need several years to prove themselves. An iron rule of venture capital is that the bad investments show up early and the good investments take a long time to become apparent. Perhaps by 1993, we will be able to evaluate the possibility of good financial and social returns.

How Risky Is Venture Capital Investment?
The risks of investing in a single company are very high. While generalizations provide little guidance for a particular investment, the odds of a particular start-up company succeeding to the point of self-sustaining revenues are surely less than 50 percent, unless the management team has built a similar business previously.

Given this level of risk, diversification is critical. Diversification can be achieved in two ways: by investing in a venture fund that itself invests in many companies, or by investing directly in a number of companies, which simulates a venture fund. Diversification is discussed in more detail later.

Only wealthy individuals or institutions can afford to take the risks inherent in venture capital. An individual investor also must be someone who can lose the entire investment without losing sleep or changing his or her life-style. This rule serves both the investor, who generally has relatively little day-to-day control, and the entrepreneur, who should not be diverted by worries about nervous investors.

The Rewards of Venture Capital Investing
The financial rewards of venture capital investment can be substantial, but as noted, the losses can be total. Most venture capital funds seek to achieve annual returns of at least 20 percent. To achieve such returns, they look for companies that can grow very rapidly, providing returns on a successful investment of 40 percent or more. Funds need high returns on their successes to compensate for their inevitable losses. Toward the end of the 1980s, returns on

venture capital investing were well below these targets, reflecting both the huge influx of money into the industry and the weakness of the market for initial public offerings.

The goal of social venture investing is to make a difference. In contrast to mutual fund investments, where it is difficult to influence a company, a private investment in a young company can bring into being a company that otherwise would not eliminate the use of pesticides, or provide affordable child care, or purify water without chemicals. Therefore, the difference the investor can make is tangible.

| VENTURE OPPORTUNITIES

Individual investors can find opportunities in several ways.

They can contact any of the social venture capital funds listed in the directory in appendix B. While it is unlikely that they will be raising capital at the point of contact, they may in the future. But the funds will know if any new social venture funds are in organization or are now raising capital.

In addition, portfolio managers frequently are approached by individual companies seeking to raise capital. Registered representatives and portfolio managers usually are reluctant to do anything with the business plans they receive, because of the possibility of personal liability if they pass it on to someone who ultimately does invest. Nonetheless, it is not uncommon for a portfolio manager to pass on a business offering to a client's accountant or lawyer for further review or, if both the company seeking capital and the client are well known to the portfolio manager, to arrange a direct introduction without further personal involvement.

In general, lawyers or accountants can be sources of investment opportunities. The best sources are practitioners whose firms represent a large number of young companies.

Questions to Ask Before Making an Investment

It is very difficult to tell whether a company has a reasonable business plan and whether the financial terms of the deal are attractive. Here are three critical questions to explore before making an investment. An investor uncomfortable with the answer to any one of them would be foolish to consider making the investment.

1. Has the management team had success in a prior undertaking, not necessarily in business but in some significant area akin

to a start-up? For example, have they created a nonprofit organization and built it to a substantial size with significant impact? Have they had a position in a public agency where they came into a troubled situation and solved a major problem? This is hardly to imply that entrepreneurs without prior success cannot succeed; it's only that the odds are much longer.

2. Who will represent your interests on the board of directors? Management does not represent shareholder interests, and a broker seeking capital in return for a fee does not represent your interests, either. Only if the board will include someone who has invested a significant amount on the same terms available to you and who plans to be active on the board should you consider writing a check.

3. Are the risks of the deal spelled out clearly and in the front of the offering? Some entrepreneurs see writing down a list of risks as a necessary evil required to keep lawyers happy. They try to make the list short and place it after the cheery section on anticipated profits. The best entrepreneurs see risks as challenges to be named and discussed, and they develop responses that make sense. Look for risks in the front. If they are not there, stop reading.

None of these questions is about the product or its costs, or about the method of sales. Such questions are critical, too, but they are not worth exploring if you are not comfortable with the answers to the three questions preceding. The most comprehensive, if exhausting, treatment of how to do due diligence on private companies can be found in David Gladstone's book *Venture Capital Investing: The Complete Handbook for Investing in Small Private Businesses for Outstanding Profits.*

| LIQUIDITY

Lack of liquidity is probably the key difference between venture investing and stock market investing. Once you invest, you must be prepared to be an investor for a number of years without recourse to sale by dialing a telephone. If success is difficult to achieve for young companies, liquidity is even harder for private venture capital investors.

Exit Strategy

Very early in discussions with a company, the investor should ask how he or she will get out of the investment. If no thoughtful answer is forthcoming, the investor would do as well to write a check to a favorite charity. If you never receive your capital back, even the most financially successful company is good only for party conversation.

What might a thoughtful answer be? Perhaps the stock purchase agreement has a put, a repurchase requirement after, say, five years at a predetermined price. Perhaps the entrepreneur indicates a willingness to sell the company to a larger company for cash or liquid stock. (This probably is helpful only if outside shareholders have a majority interest.) Perhaps the stock purchase agreement contains a "take me along" provision that prevents the founders from selling any of their stock unless the investors can sell a proportionate amount.

A danger sign might be an answer indicating an intention to go public—sell shares in a public offering—within a year. The vagaries of the market's reception to initial public offerings of any kind is notorious. Another is a promise to pay high dividends. Since the company has to pay corporate income tax and the shareholders' personal taxes on dividends, why extract money from the corporation—unless the business has no use for it?

Diversification

Given the importance of diversification, should an individual ever make an investment in a single private company? Yes, but only under two circumstances: first, if the investor has some great expertise in an area such that he or she can have great insight into the likelihood of success. Alternatively, an investor building a portfolio of individual companies has to make the first investment sometime. However, the dollar amount invested in the first company should take into account a prior decision to invest some target amount in a portfolio of at least five companies.

A reasonable private portfolio might consist of five companies. In deciding how much to invest in any individual company, one must begin by deciding how much to invest in private companies as a group. No rule of thumb works for everybody, but an upper limit might be 10 percent. On average, then, an individual company should have no more than 2 percent of the investor's net worth.

The dirty little secret of private company investing is that in most cases, companies need to raise money more than once. Usually this is part of the business plan, but sometimes it happens because circumstances are worse than expected. All too often those raising money for their company are simply silent on the need for additional capital, hoping to get the largest possible check out of an interested investor. Perhaps the worst situation for a private investor to be in is to receive a request from a company for more capital but be unable to make any more investments. Then the terms for the capital infusion will be set by the new investors, who quite justifiably have no interest in protecting earlier investors.

For this reason, an investor should decide how much to invest in a single company (not a single offering), and then invest no more than half of that at first. The worst that can happen is that business goes better than expected and the investor regrets having invested more. Applying this principle to the 2 percent per company rule of thumb provides a 1 percent of net worth standard for an additional investment.

| GETTING STARTED: A CHECKLIST

An investor should enter the venture capital market carefully but hopefully. By carefully taking a number of steps, the possibilities of financial rewards and making a difference to society can be greatly enhanced.

1. Set an upper limit on the amount of the portfolio that should be available for venture investments.
2. Decide whether diversification should be achieved through a venture fund investment or by creating one's own portfolio.
3. Create a "deal flow" by talking with brokers, existing venture funds, portfolio advisers, business lawyers, accountants, and well-known social entrepreneurs.
4. As deals begin to arrive, ask the key initial questions discussed earlier. Say no to most of them quickly.
5. For those that look promising, keep asking questions and find out who else is investing—never invest in a hurry (the company always needs the money quickly but then keeps it for years).
6. Have a lawyer who is used to private investing review the documentation. In venture capital investing, God surely lurks in the details.

7. Finally, having found a good investment, write the check and be as supportive as possible as the entrepreneur tries to make a difference.

RESOURCES

Fischer, Donald E., ed. 1989. *Investing in Venture Capital*. Charlottesville, Va.: Institute of Chartered Financial Analysts.

An excellent introduction to the venture capital market, with most examples relevant to institutional investors.

Gladstone, David J. 1987. *Venture Capital Investing: The Complete Handbook for Investing in Small Private Businesses for Outstanding Profits*. Englewood Cliffs, N.J.: Prentice-Hall.

Morris, Jane, et al., eds. 1990. *Pratt's Guide to Venture Capital Sources*. Needham, Mass.: Venture Economics.

An annual listing of professional venture capital firms, along with a series of essays on key topics in venture capital.

CHAPTER 39

THE ROLE OF DIRECT INVESTMENTS IN SOCIAL PORTFOLIOS

Beate Klein Becker

Socially responsible investing has enjoyed increasing popularity in recent years. Broadly defined as any investment or investment strategy that takes into account an investor's social and financial objectives, social investment activities include voting shareholder proxies on social issues, screening investment securities for their social performance, and investing directly in projects that have an explicit social purpose.

The vast majority of socially oriented portfolios are invested in government or corporate securities widely traded on public markets. Although the issuers of these securities may have positive social attributes, the delivery of a socially beneficial product or the remedy of a social ill is rarely their principal purpose. These objectives are more characteristic of direct social investments, which usually represent a very small portion of the typical social portfolio.

DIRECT INVESTMENTS DEFINED

Direct social investments defy standardization and are as varied in form as they are in name. Known as alternative investments, community development investments, program-related investments, and targeted investments, a direct social investment can be a private

---

Beate Klein Becker was a social research analyst and portfolio manager at U.S. Trust Company in Boston before directing the 100 Rooms Campaign, a $2 million private loan initiative that finances single-room occupancy housing in Boston. She is now a consultant on direct social investments. A former vice president of the Social Investment Forum, she coauthored the membership survey on community development investments on which this chapter is based.

placement in a social venture capital fund, a deposit in a community development bank that lends to capital-deprived communities, or a non-interest-bearing loan to a revolving loan fund that finances microenterprise businesses. Direct social investments usually capitalize projects whose financing needs are not met by traditional market mechanisms because they fail (or are perceived to fail) conventional measures of risk and return.

These social-purpose investments seek to create affordable housing, finance small businesses and cooperatives, support community land trusts, and foster income, employment, and ownership opportunities for lower-income peoples. Many direct investments challenge societal norms regarding the control and distribution of wealth and seek to create alternatives to those norms.

As with socially screened stocks and bonds, the attractiveness of a direct investment is measured in terms of both its financial and social attributes. However, where the return on capital market investments accrues as a financial gain to the private investor, direct social investments aim to deliver a positive financial return to the investor as well as a beneficial social return to the public. The calculation of the "total return" on a direct social investment can take into account not only the income and capital appreciation of the asset but also its tangible return to society.

Limitations on Direct Investments
Most securities associated with portfolio investing are registered with the Securities and Exchange Commission and traded in public securities markets. The existence of a vast market of buyers and sellers ensures that these securities are highly liquid, well researched, readily priced, and efficiently administered. However, the expense of registration limits this market to large securities issuers and effectively precludes participation by small securities issuers.

In contrast to capital market assets that dominate both social and conventional investment portfolios, direct investments are usually small investments. They typically cannot be sold on public exchanges but are "privately placed" with investors. Although private placement spares the expense of registration, the absence of a public market means that direct investments are less liquid than publicly traded securities, more difficult to price, and more cumbersome administratively.

Direct social investments are not unique in this respect. All private placements, regardless of social purpose, are subject to these limitations. Because direct social investments are typically smaller than traditional private placements, however, they suffer these woes disproportionately.

| SOCIALLY RESPONSIBLE INVESTING PROFESSIONALS AND DIRECT SOCIAL INVESTMENTS

Many community development advocates believe that even after taking into account the inherent limitations of private placements, the market for direct social investments falls short of its potential. Despite an increase in the number, variety, and sophistication of direct social investment vehicles, they continue to capture only a tiny fraction of funds committed to social portfolios.

The Social Investment Forum Study

This belief was substantiated in a 1989 study of social investment practitioners' attitudes and experience with community development investments. The study surveyed members of the Social Investment Forum (SIF), a national association of individuals and organizations active in socially responsible investing.* SIF members include financial professionals who advise clients on the socially responsible placement of capital, venture capitalists and development lending institutions that provide capital and technical support to projects, and individual and institutional investors.

COMMITMENT OF ASSETS. The survey attempted to quantify the extent to which socially managed portfolios include direct social investments. The study showed that although many of the SIF brokers, financial advisers and planners, investment managers, and mutual funds possess the interest and capability necessary to do direct investing, the proportion of assets committed to these investments is very small indeed. SIF member financial professionals reported that the median exposure to direct social investments amounted to one tenth of 1 percent (.1 percent) of their firms' social assets. Nearly half of the financial professionals surveyed said their clients had no investments in community development projects. Of those who had

*The Social Investment Survey on Alternative Investments (Social Investment Survey, 430 First Avenue North, Suite 290, Minneapolis, Minn. 55401). The survey was one of a series of studies sponsored by the Ford Foundation in an effort to gain a better understanding of the range of investor experience with social purpose investing.

some exposure, the median allocation to direct social investments was 3 percent of their firms' socially managed assets.

MOTIVATION FOR INVESTING. The study also sought to determine social investors' motivation for placing their assets in direct community investments. Among individual investors, the personal and emotional appeal of community investments is particularly important in attracting and retaining capital. Unlike capital market investments, to which the investor has little direct connection, community investments result in tangible projects with a direct social impact. The sense that one can use one's capital to effect social change is one of the most powerful appeals of community investing.

Institutional investors are more reluctant than individuals to engage in direct social investments and more likely to cite concerns over an investment's level of risk, rate of return, and liquidity. The institutions most likely to make community investments are foundations and religious organizations whose social mission can be more fully realized through their investment programs. Institutions with a less explicit social mission often are reluctant to commit funds to projects not clearly in the best financial interests of the beneficiaries.

PERCEPTIONS OF LOWER RETURN AND HIGHER RISK. The survey identified a number of obstacles that impede widespread acceptance of direct social investments. One problem is the popular perception that social investing requires financial concessions from the investor. Even investors committed to social investing often expect lower returns and greater risks, though many types of social investing do not exact a financial penalty. Survey respondents mentioned numerous cases of investments with conventional financial qualities that were deemed risky, excessively difficult, or of dubious financial quality once they were identified as "social" or "community oriented." This prejudice against social investments extends to investment vehicles as diverse as socially screened mutual funds to affordable housing projects.

Survey respondents agreed that the most significant deterrent to direct social investments is the level of risk that investors associate with community investing. By contrast, a below market rate of return does not pose as much of a problem to investors. In other words, SIF members prefer to invest in relatively secure investments that offered below market rates as opposed to riskier projects that offered a much higher, risk-adjusted market rate of return. The tolerance for below-market rates of return seems to be higher for individual investors who, according to SIF financial advisers, often establish an arbitrary, acceptable rate of return that bears little relationship to the risk of the investment. By contrast, institutional investors are more concerned about relative rates of risk and return and require market rates on their investments.

DUE DILIGENCE AND LIQUIDITY. Another major deterrent to broad participation in direct social investing is the lack of historical and comparative information about the performance of different community development investments. Investors and financial professionals alike attested to difficulty in conducting the detailed project assessment, or due diligence, required on many of these investments. Similarly, lack of liquidity posed a significant problem for social investors.

Expanding the Market

Some of the obstacles confronting direct social investments are perceptual rather than actual. Direct social investments often are perceived as a single type of investment, when in fact there is a multitude of direct investment options, each of which needs to be evaluated on the merits of unique financial characteristics. Direct investments in small businesses and new ventures are riskier than housing loans, and consequently they experience a much higher failure rate. But this is true for nonsocial as well as social investments and is not necessarily a function of the social nature of the investment.

CHANGING PERCEPTIONS. Community development proponents often question the different standards by which risk is measured in alternative and conventional investments. They maintain that, like beauty, risk is too often in the eye of the beholder. Development banks and revolving loan funds in particular compare the low historical loan-loss rates on affordable housing against the poor performance of the luxury condominium and commercial loans made by their counterparts in the banking industry. A comparison of default rates on conventional real estate investments against investments in low-income housing would help dispel the perception of extraordinary risk associated with alternative investments.

Similarly, examination of many direct social investments reveals investment vehicles that meet conventional market measures of return and liquidity. Community development banks and credit unions offer market rate demand and term deposits as liquid as their nonsocial counterparts.

It can be expected that direct investments would be more attractive to investors if they were less risky, more liquid, better researched, more lucrative, and acceptable for recommendation by financial services firms. In short, the ideal alternative investments would behave like conventional capital market securities, but finance socially beneficial projects.

"DO WELL ENOUGH WHILE DOING GOOD." The market for direct social investments exists precisely because there are many worthy social investments that do not fulfill conventional investment requirements. Were these projects to conform to conventional standards of scale, risk and return, and liquidity, they would be able to meet their financing needs through conventional capital markets' mechanisms. But because direct social investments are alternative in both investment form and social content, they must be treated differently than standard investments.

"Doing well by doing good" accurately describes the return that investors can expect from some social investments, but is not an appropriate aphorism for all investments. Many alternative investments offer investors the opportunity to "do well enough while doing good." Still others appeal to investors for whom simply doing good is sufficient investment incentive.

| CHANGING HEARTS AND MINDS

The return on many alternative investments cannot be measured solely in financial terms. Growth of the direct social investment market depends on redefining the concept of an acceptable return on investment so that it includes the social return of an investment. Factoring the social impact of an investment into the return equation would do much to "level the playing field" between investments, by increasing the return on social investments and diminishing the return on the many conventional assets whose negative social impacts are hidden costs borne by society.

One suggestion for expanding the market for alternative investment concentrates on improving the quality of the vehicles by which investors can place funds with these projects. This assumes that sufficient demand for alternative investments exists but is being thwarted by the lack of smooth financial intermediation.

A different analysis suggests expanding the alternative investment market by developing demand. Under this scenario, effort should be directed toward increasing demand for alternative investments and letting the private market develop the means to satisfy that demand.

The Lessons of South Africa

The South Africa divestment movement illustrates how market mechanisms respond to client demand. In the early stages of the divestment campaign, one of the most frequently cited obstacles to divestment was the absence of portfolio managers capable of managing a South Africa–free portfolio. Investment managers were unwilling to manage such portfolios because of lack of information about companies' South African activities, the difficulty of monitoring changes in company behavior, inexperience with divested portfolios, and fears about the effect of divestment on the portfolios' performance.

It was not until investment managers were threatened with the loss of significant institutional clients that they began offering South Africa–free investment services. With the South Africa–free market now valued at hundreds of billions of dollars, it is the rare financial manager who is not capable of managing a South Africa–free portfolio.

Incentives for Institutional Participation

There are many legitimate reasons why financial institutions do not offer direct social investment services. Were a sizable demand for this service to develop, however, this situation probably would change. Individual investors and religious organizations are currently the largest investors in community development investment vehicles, but growth of the market depends on the participation of large institutional investors. Institutions engaged in alternative investments often treat their financial resources as one means to directly or indirectly further their mission and make a significant social contribution. A union that commits a portion of its assets to an economic development project employing its members; a tax-exempt educational institution that makes a "payment in lieu of taxes" in the form of an investment in local development efforts; a bank that makes below-market rate development loans as part of a linked-deposit agreement; a foundation that purchases a building to house a grantee organization—all are examples of alternative investments consistent with each organization's function. In addition, the government can play a role in supporting alternative corporations, through tax credits, linked development deposits, and permanent capital grants.

The benefit of such institutional investing lies not only in its direct dollar value investment but in its multiplier effect on society. Each investment develops a performance history, creates expertise and track records, and builds credibility, thereby laying a foundation upon which other institutions can build. It is the corporation informing its shareholders of its investment, the financial institution notifying its clients, and the foundation reporting to other foundations that set an example, encourage like action, and eventually transform the novel into the norm.

PART FIVE

COMMUNITY

DEVELOPMENT

INVESTING

No area of social investing can be as rewarding as community development investing. Here the investment takes the form of a loan that, depending on the vehicle, may be at market rate or below. Not only does the investor have an opportunity for a decent return, but he or she often can see the tangible results of the investment—low-income housing, family farms, and the like.

As Dan Leibsohn shows, low-income communities need capital of several types. No single source, whether it be banks, loan funds, or nonprofits, can do the job alone. An additional source of funds, as Carol O'Cleireacain urges, should be public pension funds. (In this context, chapter 23—Bill McKeown's essay on fiduciary responsibilities—should be revisited.)

Of the sources of community capital, none comes to mind ahead of community development banks. Joan Shapiro tells us why, and how the model can be adapted in the future. David Berge describes how a variation of the community development bank can be put to work within a traditional bank. Another type of financial institution that can have a dramatic effect is the community development credit union. Cliff Rosenthal shows how people pooling their money can better themselves.

Community development loan funds have a justified reputation for versatility and repayment. Martin Trimble, Mark Pinsky, and Greg Ramm outline the reasons for their growth. Community land trusts, Greg Ramm relates, have proven their worth as vehicles for creating and preserving low- and moderate-income housing stock. Because they are democratically organized, they also have considerable community-building potential.

Microlending programs supply tiny sums of money and peer group support to people who want to start small businesses. As Jeff Ashe points out, these programs have had dramatic effects in the third world and are now coming to the United States. Gabriela Romanow describes how a compensating deposit program can work to fund microlending programs.

MEETING CAPITAL NEEDS IN LOW-INCOME COMMUNITIES

Daniel M. Leibsohn President,
Low Income Housing Fund

Low-income communities need many kinds of capital in order to survive and flourish. No single institution can supply all of these capital needs; instead they require several different kinds of financial institutions. A short list of the kinds of capital needed would include:

- debt and equity;
- short term, medium term, long term;
- small size, medium size, large size;
- early, middle, end stages of development;
- low, medium, and high risk;
- secured by real estate, secured by other assets, unsecured;
- working capital, expansion, start-up;
- standardized and flexible; and
- market rate and below market rate.

Moreover, different kinds of capital are needed by many different kinds of users—consumer, housing, and business capital is needed by individuals, families, businesses, nonprofit organizations, and service organizations. They need capital to construct, rehabilitate, acquire, and refinance housing; to purchase education, necessaries (such as furniture, cars), and consumer items; to begin or expand businesses; and to construct, purchase, or rehabilitate community facilities, such as day-care centers, offices, and health care centers.

Community groups, nonprofit developers, and the public sector tend to discuss capital needs in terms of conventional lenders—primarily commercial banks and savings and loans, but also insurance companies—and how they should assist community development efforts in low-income communities. Such discussions assume that conventional lenders should be responsible for satisfying most or all of the debt capital requirements.

And in fact, many conventional lenders are deeply involved with community lending. In the area of affordable housing, they are demonstrating for other conventional lenders new programs and approaches, the use of flexible underwriting and pricing, and the ways to take on new risk safely. These leaders are showing the need to step outside traditional lending boundaries and traditional concepts in order to generate successful community development lending practices. Indeed, conventional lenders have a fairly long and very successful track record for this type of lending in housing. However, these efforts need to be increased substantially in housing and expanded dramatically in business and community development lending.

But conventional lenders can go only so far. They are regulated institutions that use their depositors' publicly insured funds, and there are limits to the risks and costs that they can withstand without threatening their institutions. For the most part they are just not equipped to address certain kinds of high-risk, high-transaction-cost lending.

Some lenders do make these loans. For example, Wells Fargo Bank has supplied unsecured lines of credit to experienced nonprofit developers, and several others have joined a microbusiness pool in West Hollywood with limited public guarantees—generally areas that are difficult for lenders. Experienced conventional lenders acting cautiously can do this kind of lending, but it is complicated, time consuming, and often risky.

Other kinds of lenders are better able than conventional lenders to take on these risks and costs. In the United States today, an infrastructure of nontraditional financial institutions is developing in a very unsystematic, ad hoc manner. Where they exist, these lenders—mostly community-based nonprofits or public sector agencies—are successfully taking on some of the most difficult lending situations in poor communities. They tend to be sensitive to local needs and very democratic in character, and therefore are uniquely suited for this kind of lending.

These nontraditional institutions take many forms, including:

- community loan funds (CLFs)
- community development credit unions (CDCUs)
- development banks

- microbusiness funds
- community development loan funds (CDLFs)
- hybrids, such as the Low Income Housing Fund
- public sector loan funds

The institutions range from local to national. Many combine some form of technical assistance with their lending. They generally operate in the riskiest markets with low-paid, relatively inexperienced staffs and inadequate capital.

Nontraditional institutions fill gaps conventional lenders cannot. They complement conventional lending, both intentionally and unintentionally. They make conventional lenders more effective; in turn, conventional lending could make these institutions more effective. For example, nontraditional financial institutions in low-income communities may undertake the following types of lending:

- predevelopment and other gap financing in a project's early stages that allow the development to reach the stage where it is bankable;
- cushioning conventional loans with junior financing above certain loan-to-value (LTV) ratio limits (for example, loans over 75 percent LTV);
- seasoning loans to demonstrate their safety so that conventional institutions can purchase them;
- loans that allow developers to gain experience and a track record so they can proceed to conventional lenders afterward;
- demonstrating the effectiveness of new lending approaches and underwriting so that conventional institutions can become comfortable with the new programs;
- high-transaction-cost loans—loans that are too small and/or too complicated generate high costs because of the time involved;
- high LTV land loans and land banking loans;
- start-up and microbusiness loans;
- unsecured loans;
- high-risk loans, in general, for such reasons as lack of financial strength, lack of takeout, difficult neighborhood, specialized use, mixed use, scattered sites, nontraditional income steam, and so on.

Nontraditional lenders have addressed these needs while achieving an excellent track record of very low loan losses and defaults despite the perceived and real risk.

The development of these new institutions is in an early stage. As a result, there are many issues that need to be addressed in order to strengthen their capacity to provide capital in poor communities. First, there is, for the most part, an inadequate analysis of the kinds of capital needed. Second, there is no real analysis of what kinds of institutions can provide this capital and what the division of labor is between nontraditional and conventional institutions. Third, the nontraditional institutions are developing in an ad hoc way. And fourth, there·is very little connection between the nontraditional and conventional sectors. As a result, capital needs in these communities are being met very inefficiently and inadequately.

This analysis therefore suggests several general approaches to increasing the effectiveness of finding capital for low-income communities:

- Analyze the kinds of capital needed in a community.
- Analyze the kinds of institutions that can provide different kinds of capital.
- Systematically develop the necessary nontraditional financial institutions.
- Coordinate with conventional lenders and develop joint programs and approaches. For example, nontraditional lenders can establish a pool of conventional lenders to make interim or permanent loans in which the nonprofit undertakes most of the administration and underwriting in order to reduce the lenders' costs, and the lenders pool their funds in order to increase underwriting oversight while reducing risks. The Low Income Housing Fund has established two of these pools and is working on two others.
- Create more complete partnerships by including nontraditional lenders, foundations, and religious institutions in addition to conventional lenders, the public sector, and community representatives. For example, foundations can play a major role in building the capacity of nontraditional lenders and, perhaps, in establishing guarantees where needed. The Marin Community Foundation has created a guarantee program and is exploring the establishment of a pool with conventional lenders.

These steps can greatly enhance the movement of capital to areas of greatest need.

BOX 40-1
WOODSTOCK INSTITUTE

407 South Dearborn, Suite 550
Chicago, Ill. 60605
(312) 427-8070

The Woodstock Institute is a not-for-profit organization that works to explore and promote forms of investment in disadvantaged communities that contribute to economic opportunity, community capacity, equity formation, and the creation of economically and racially diverse communities. The institute's primary work includes the design, implementation, and evaluation of reinvestment programs that increase private investment in modest-income urban and rural communities to produce affordable housing and jobs. The reinvestment program development work is supported by an extensive and ongoing applied research and policy development agenda.

Description of Services
The institute works in a technical assistance capacity with nonprofit organizations and in a consulting capacity with financial institutions, philanthropic organizations, and government agencies.

Community organizations wishing to increase investment in housing, business, and industry can obtain a design of reinvestment programs and community building institutions; assistance in reinvestment management so as to allow new investment to take place without displacement; an assessment of community credit needs and financial institution performance; training of staff and leadership about the role of reinvestment; and an evaluation of reinvestment programs.

Financial institutions wishing to improve community lending performance for better service to their communities can contact the institute for help with identification of unmet community credit needs; an analysis of existing loan markets; an analysis of existing loan products and recommendations of how they can be targeted more effectively; the design of new products and services for community development that meet the institutions' standards of risk and income;

the identification of opportunities to work more closely with important community institutions and organizations to improve lending performance; and the evaluation of community lending programs.

Philanthropic organizations wishing to target their giving and investment more effectively so as to support neighborhood efforts and encourage private investment may consult Woodstock Institute for the design of targeted giving programs; the identification of social investment opportunities; and program design.

Government agencies that wish to carefully target their scarce resources so as to best leverage private investment may utilize the institute's services of public deposit program design; evaluation of reinvestment programs; research and policy analysis; and staff training on community reinvestment.

Current Focus

Woodstock Institute is currently involved in a three-part program that focuses on:

- building greater understanding of reinvestment and disinvestment in today's environment;
- creating incentives for reinvestment in disadvantaged communities; and
- forging new community building credit models.

Specific projects are outlined in the following pages.

BUILDING UNDERSTANDING OF REINVESTMENT AND DISINVESTMENT TODAY. The Invisible Lenders: An Analysis of Mortgage Banker Lending is a project that examines census tract loan origination data to determine mortgage banker lending patterns in the Chicago metropolitan area and in one metropolitan area in Michigan.

Demographic data is being used to determine the effect of such market factors as income and housing prices on the lending patterns. Data analysis uses statistical tools to compute credit flows at the census tract level between communities within each metropolitan area. Data research is supplemented with interviews of realtors, lenders, and community organizations.

SURVEY OF CHURCH CREDIT NEEDS. A new organization, Inspired Partnerships, has been formed to assist churches in Chicago to provide space and support for community-based activities. Inspired Partnerships asked Woodstock Institute to research the credit needs and available resources for churches interested in becoming a community resource. Interviews of denominations, local congregations, banks, and potential resources, along with a mail survey to local congregations, contribute to the understanding of unmet credit needs and will help to open a new resource for community building in disadvantaged communities.

CREATING INCENTIVES FOR REINVESTMENT. Public deposits offer a substantial opportunity for encouraging reinvestment in disadvantaged communities. Building from past research conducted by Woodstock Institute, the institute will publish two papers in 1992. The first will describe the state of the art of public deposits and the second will describe public policy and program design recommendations.

FORGING DEVELOPMENT-BUILDING CREDIT MODELS. Woodstock Institute formed and staffed the Chicago Credit Union Network, a group of fifteen low-income and community development credit unions. The institute provides technical assistance to members of the network and is negotiating with the Illinois Credit Union League for special status.

Woodstock Institute is assisting one church-based credit union, the Cosmopolitan Community Church Credit Union, convert its charter from a church-based credit union to a community development credit union. Following the charter change, the institute will help market the credit union and expand its membership base and service area.

In the late 1960s and early 1970s, the federal Office of Economic Opportunity (OEO) provided staff and funding to create more than four hundred community credit unions in low-income areas across the country. All but forty or fifty of those credit unions have closed. Woodstock Institute has been gathering information and interviewing people involved in the OEO effort. A report on the history of these credit unions will be published to expand the understanding of the elements necessary to ensure that current community development credit unions avoid the mistakes of the past.

COMMUNITY DEVELOPMENT FINANCIAL INSTITUTIONS. Woodstock Institute has gathered information on various types of community development lenders. Case studies describing four of these lenders are being published in 1991. These include community development credit unions, community loan funds, development banks, and microloan funds.

Contact
Jean Pogge, president of Woodstock Institute, joined the institute in January 1982. Pogge brings to Woodstock Institute a depth of experience in the private sector, highly developed management skills, and leadership experience in a variety of community organizations.

An active member and leader of several community organizations in the past, Pogge is currently on the boards of CANDO Community Development Corporation (CANDO CDC), the Women Employed Institute, and the North Side Community Federal Credit Union, and she is a member of the Regional Partnership. She also served on the transitional team for the treasurer for the State of Illinois and the Cook County Citizens Budget Review Committee and is a member of the Federal Home Loan Bank advisory council.

RESOURCES

BOOKS AND OTHER PUBLICATIONS
BY THE WOODSTOCK INSTITUTE, CHICAGO

Choca, M., and J. Pogge. 1989. *Tools for Lenders: A Guide to Successful Community Reinvestment.*
> $150. Additional copies $50 each.

Flax-Hatch, D. 1989. *A Community Guide to the Insurance Industry.*
> For-profit organizations: $16. Government agencies and university or non-profit organizations: $8.

Flax-Hatch, D., and K. Tholin. 1991. *Banking in the Public's Interest: Promoting Community Development with the Public Deposits of Cities and States.*
> For-profit organizations: $16. Government agencies and university or non-profit organizations: $8.

Hoyt, J., and Choca, M. 1989. *A Model State Insurance CRA.*
> For-profit organizations: $16. Government agencies and university or non-profit organizations: $8.

———. 1989. *The Silent Partner: The Insurance Industry's Potential for Community Reinvestment.*
> For-profit organizations: $16. Government agencies and university or non-profit organizations: $8.

Pogge, J., and D. Flax-Hatch. 1987. *The Bankers of Today, the Banks of Tomorrow: The Financial Services Industry and Its Role in Community Reinvestment.*
> For-profit organizations: $16. Government agencies and university or non-profit organizations: $8.

Pogge, J., and V. McLenighan. 1991. *The Business of Self-Sufficiency: Micro Credit Programs in the United States.*
> For-profit organizations: $16. Government agencies and university or non-profit organizations: $8.

Stevens, J., and K. Tholin. 1991. *Lender of First Resort: Community Development Loan Funds.*

For-profit organizations: $16. Government agencies and university or non-profit organizations: $8.

Tholin, K. 1989. *Putting It All Together: The Birth of the Austin/West Garfield Federal Credit Union.*

For-profit organizations: $16. Government agencies and university or non-profit organizations: $8.

Tholin, K., and J. Pogge. 1991. *Banking Services for the Poor: Community Development Credit Unions.*

For-profit organizations: $16. Government agencies and university or non-profit organizations: $8.

Woodstock Staff. 1991. *Banking on Communities: Development Banking in the United States.*

For-profit organizations: $16. Government agencies and university or non-profit organizations: $8.

PENSION FUNDS
AND SOCIAL INVESTMENT

Carol O'Cleireacain Commissioner,
New York City Department of Finance

American workers have more than two trillion dollars in their pension funds. They own about one quarter of all the corporate shares on the New York Stock Exchange and account for almost half of daily trading activity. Having tripled in size in the 1980s, these funds are bigger now, in dollars and power, than even those of us close to them imagined ten years ago.

Growth in the labor force and growth in earnings alone would have guaranteed a growing pool of pension fund savings. But, in addition, the past decade's booming capital markets (and the wonders of compound interest) generated spectacular growth. On average, pension funds returned 12 to 15 percent per year in the 1980s; annual inflation averaged about 5 percent.

The markets that brought phenomenal pension fund growth also brought the rise of corporate raiders and hostile takeovers and their defenses—greenmail, golden parachutes, and poison pills, to name a few. Leveraged buyouts by corporate management brought arguments over the appropriate value of corporate shares. Junk bonds blurred the line between equity and debt and changed the risk-return trade-off for stocks, bonds, and subordinated debt.

Further, the disastrous macroeconomic policy of the first Reagan

Dr. Carol O'Cleireacain is commissioner of the New York City Department of Finance. She serves as chair of the New York City Employees Retirement System (NYCERS) and the Teachers Retirement System (TRS) and is a trustee of both the New York City police and fire pension funds. O'Cleireacain is a member of the editorial board of *Dissent* magazine. This chapter originally appeared in the winter 1991 issue of *Dissent*.

term raised both interest rates and the value of the dollar. The resulting loss of manufacturing jobs and agricultural exports produced a rusted-out, boarded-up American heartland. The dramatic shift of federal government spending toward the military crippled any local government response to these events. As the "1990 Report of the Joint Economic Committee of the U.S. Congress" puts it, "The most damaging legacy of the 1980's is the weakening of the public sector."

Organized workers recognized that their money was part of the corporate restructuring game, which often cost them jobs and always cost them wages, and insisted that their unions focus on ways that their pension funds could help them survive. Public officials eyed this growing pool of off-budget money that might be used to meet rising public needs. Corporate treasurers raided their funds for help in fighting takeovers or achieving leveraged buyouts.

The economy of the 1980s led pension fund activism in two distinct directions. One was toward shareholder rights and corporate governance. The other was toward the strategic placement of pension fund capital in sectors of the economy that appeared to suffer from a capital shortage.

| CORPORATE GOVERNANCE

Pension funds were forced to recognize that the traditional split in American corporations between ownership and management left them unprotected in the casino market of the 1980s. They could not count on management to represent their interests. Indeed, in many takover battles the shareholders were neither warned nor consulted. On top of their theoretical ownership responsibility, which pension funds had ceded to corporate management, came the very practical issue of protecting the value of their assets in takeover fights and choosing the proper value for shares.

In the 1980s public pension funds emerged into the forefront of the shareholder rights movement. It is not hard to understand why. Pension funds cannot leave the market; they have huge dollars to invest and reinvest annually; in effect, they *are* the market. They have the ability to think and act long term. Using the power of shareholder voting, especially in combination with other investors, pension funds have a tool for achieving fund growth.

Public pension funds, in addition, have trustees who are public officials and who easily can transfer the principles of electoral democracy to corporate democracy. Hence the special fondness of public pension funds for supporting proxies calling for confidential voting (secret ballots), one share, one vote, and not counting abstentions when determining the majority.

Public funds, of course, do not have to worry about whether their shareholder activism will come home to roost in their own boardrooms. Corporate funds do. Corporate fund trustees, usually corporate treasurers, have been reluctant to participate in the movement for independent directors or the implementation of democratic standards at corporate boards, lest their own boards be the next targets. This fear has provided strong impetus for public funds' placing confidential voting in corporate proxy fights at the top of the "Shareholder Bill of Rights." There is a firm belief that if corporate pension funds were able to have the secrecy of the voting booth rather than the public roll call, the corporate democracy movement would win many more votes.

However, corporate democracy is different from issues of corporate financial restructuring, raiders, and takeovers. On these issues there has been far less unanimity among institutional investors. The three largest public pension systems—in California, New York State, and New York City—voted on different sides when Carl Icahn bid for Texaco and Harold Simmons attempted to replace the board of Lockheed. The trustees of the larger public funds recognized earlier than private trustees that proxy voting is a necessary component of fiduciary responsibility, but that recognition has not brought with it a unanimity of position on various proxy votes. It is the act of voting that is deemed to be important. There is not yet a "right" or a "wrong" way to vote on corporate restructuring. That is the area of fiduciary judgment that will not disappear; one should not anticipate large pension funds moving in lockstep. Reasonable trustees may reasonably differ, as long as they engage in detailed and intelligent decision making.

| ECONOMICALLY TARGETED INVESTING

As the budget deficit has constrained the federal government's ability to meet investment needs, the creative use of public pension assets to meet those needs has become a potent political issue. The "economically targeted investing" (ETI) of pension funds to achieve a market rate of return and, in addition, a benefit (social or economic) to the public at large is the new terminology replacing "social investing." A recent survey financed by the Ford Foundation documents more than $7 billion in ETI by public employee pension funds around the country. More than half of the large public funds (especially state funds) have ETI programs. New York (state and city) funds constitute about 10 percent of ETI nationally.

ETI programs are directed primarily toward filling gaps in private capital markets, largely the housing market, small business loans, and venture capital. Pension funds require a financial investment that is marketable, safe (either federally guaranteed or publicly insured), of appropriate size for the large amounts of cash flowing into the system, and with administration and oversight of the investment done by independent professionals outside the board of trustees. The pension fund investment yields a market rate of return (measured by the opportunity cost, controlling for risk, duration, and liquidity). Although individual ETIs may have a subsidy component, that subsidy comes from the involvement of an accompanying public program. For the pension fund to accept a rate of return that is below the market, thus subsidizing the venture, is seen as a violation of fiduciary responsibility.

A security backed by the full faith and credit of the U.S. government is the most risk-free asset a pension fund can hold, so ETI programs try to leverage federal guarantees or federal insurance—for example, New York City's funds buy Ginnie Mae securities backed by mortgages issued in what are otherwise redlined neighborhoods. In Boston and in New York, building trades' pension funds have invested in federally insured certificates of deposit at financial institutions, rolling them over for a designated period of time, to free up funds for construction lending by those institutions on favorable terms to local developers. This technique has leveraged capital to build housing and provide jobs for members.

There are those who argue that markets are perfect and "capital gaps" to not exist. By definition, then, if, through ETI, a pension fund invests in a venture, or a neighborhood, or an industry that has not been receiving investment, it must be because the fund is getting a riskier investment for the same rate of return or a below market rate of return for average risk. That appears to be an ideological rather than an experience-based position.

Those who work with housing, small business, or venture capital lending know that standard rules of thumb as to return and risk have closed out access to capital for certain borrowers. Often financial institutions find it easier to continue in the same patterns than to seek new ones. Pension fund trustees have discovered that there is a shortage of financial intermediaries willing to find and package deals that would make pension fund capital available to borrowers and also be profitable business.

For example, the New York City police fund set out to invest in small businesses in New York City. Its managers looked to the most obvious place: securities backed by Small Business Administration (SBA) loans. They were shocked to find that the banks in the financial capital of the world did not use SBA loan programs. The staff of the pension fund trustees had to bring in SBA experts to city banks to teach them the details and rules and how to do the paperwork. As a result there are now large New York City banks that will make these loans to small businesses, and the police fund is committed to purchasing $50 million worth of securities backed by these loans. This is just one case of a clear market imperfection that was eliminated by the supplier of capital—the pension fund—training the financial intermediary (the bank) to play its necessary role in the market so that the borrowers (small businesses) could be served.

| CONCLUSION

As long as pension funds represent the major form of savings for a growing generation of Americans, the use to which those savings are put will be an important issue. The funds are too large, their need for diversified investment too real, their share ownership too major, their ability to fill gaps in selected parts of the capital markets too visible to ignore. Whether politicians or others want to tax pension funds to help get rid of the deficit, have them finance their own needs (bridges, roads, or buyouts), use them to keep hometown industries like Colt alive, or place environmentalists and others on corporate boards, we must not lose sight of the overriding issue: who has control over the workers' money and in whose interest do they exercise it?

COMMUNITY DEVELOPMENT BANKS

Joan Shapiro Senior Vice President,
South Shore Bank of Chicago

A "community development bank" is a regulated financial institution whose business is the permanent, long-term economic development of low- and moderate-income communities and that targets loan resources to residents of its primary service area—the people living, working, and doing business in this marketplace.

| THE NATURE OF DEVELOPMENT BANKING

Likewise, "development banking" is a for-profit enterprise organized to accelerate local economic activity and to stimulate market forces where they have stalled or ceased to function. In pursuit of these development goals, the development bank must generate reasonable returns (generally moderate or deferred) for shareholders, competitive returns for depositors, and lasting benefits for residents of the communities in which it operates.

Joan Shapiro is senior vice president of both the South Shore Bank of Chicago and its holding company, Shorebank Corporation. She joined the corporation in 1976 and in 1981 took over management of Development Deposits^sm, the bank's socially responsible investing deposit portfolio held by socially concerned individuals and institutions from all fifty states. Under her management, the portfolio has grown from $20 million to over $100 million. On the founding board of the Social Investment Forum, Shapiro was president for two years and continues to serve as a director. She is an adviser to the Council on Economic Priorities and the Center for Economic Conversion, a director of the National Association of Community Development Loan Funds, a trustee of the Parnassus Income Fund, and a governor of the International House of the University of Chicago.

Like commercial banks, development banks are permitted to make loans in three basic categories: business, real estate, and consumer (or personal). Given their community and development orientation, however, they tend to spend more time with borrowers, providing more technical assistance and ongoing monitoring than do conventional commercial banks. They also strive to consider more flexible and creative underwriting to make credit work. Loans with government guarantees, such as those offered by the Small Business Administration and the Federal Housing Administration, are often used to reduce risk and provide liquidity (that is, sell loans on the secondary market); and loans for multifamily purchase and rehabilitation, education, and lines of credit to community organizations are widely used to meet the bank's community development purposes.[1]

South Shore Bank focuses on such loans. In addition, "development lending" at South Shore means:

- targeting loan dollars to specific geographic areas to generate maximum development impact;
- investing at least 50 percent of its loan portfolio in development loans, defined as market rate credits that generate long-term benefits to the community; and
- seeking out borrowers (many of whom are first-time or less-sophisticated bank borrowers) who demonstrate the capacity, ingenuity, and energy to succeed in the marketplace.

| DEVELOPMENT BANKING: HISTORY AND THEORY

Despite recent scandals and unprecedented losses in the banking and savings and loan industry, socially responsible banking is not a contradiction in terms. Rather, this notion is at the heart of America's banking system: banks are chartered to serve the credit needs of their local communities.

A 1971 interpretation, by the board of governors of the Federal Reserve System, of the Bank Holding Company amendments Congress had passed the year before broadened that mandate when it observed that "bank holding companies possess a unique combination of financial and managerial resources making them particularly suited for a meaningful and substantial role in remedying [the nation's] social ills." The Community Reinvestment Act (CRA) of 1977, strengthened in 1989, reinforced the original charter purposes, affirming banks' and savings institutions' continuing obligation to meet local credit needs and requiring them to make public their annual loan production numbers as well as their CRA ratings.

South Shore Bank

Development banking started at the corner of Seventy-first and Jeffery in Chicago when, in August 1973, a small group of investors bought a failing bank in a failing neighborhood to test an untested idea: Could the South Shore Bank of Chicago, a regulated bank chartered in 1939, use its commercial banking powers to renew distressed urban neighborhoods? And if it could do so in one struggling minority neighborhood, couldn't other banks apply the approach in comparable communities, effectively using the hard dollars of America to rebuild our cities?

BOX 42-1
ELK HORN BANK & TRUST COMPANY

Box 258
Arkadelphia, Ark. 71923-0248

Southern Development Bancorporation is a privately owned and capitalized development bank in Arkansas patterned after Shorebank Corporation. Arkansas is one of America's poorest states. Designed to undertake a broad program of rural economic development rather than earn a substantial return on equity, Southern contributes excess earnings to its tax-exempt affiliate to support job creating and microenterprise activities for low- and moderate-income people (addressing both the unacceptably high rate of unemployment and the low rate of job formation in rural Arkansas). Through Elk Horn Bank and its other for-profit subsidiary, Southern Venture, Southern Development Bancorporation is organized to finance and develop support mechanisms for businesses with credit needs of between $500 and $1,000,000.

Southern was created at the initiative of the Winthrop Rockefeller Foundation (WRF). Its objective is to accelerate the rate of economic activity among low-income rural residents in a multicounty region of Arkansas. It also intends to become a model for other privately owned banks by demonstrating the rural development and job-creating potential of bank holding companies. If successful, it will expand

---

throughout the state and disseminate its acquired knowledge and/or establish operations in other states. While a financially independent corporation, Southern maintains a consulting contract with Shorebank Corporation for oversight and management.

The three-year planning, organizing, and capitalization process between WRF and Shorebank culminated in May 1988 with Southern's acquisition of the $55 million asset-based Elk Horn Bank & Trust Company, a regulated commercial bank located in Arkadelphia, a town of ten thousand people sixty-five miles southwest of Little Rock. Like Shorebank, Southern is an integrated development banking business operating through coordinated bank and nonbank, for-profit and nonprofit entities. While serving a similar function as Shorebank's nonprofit affiliate, the Neighborhood Institute, Southern's nonprofit, Arkansas Enterprise Group, is designed to respond to the needs of a multicounty, rural development agenda encompassing a venture capital company, marketing and information support, and a group lending program. Like South Shore Bank, Elk Horn Bank offers Development Deposits to fund its development lending programs.

A decade and a half later, David Osborne described the results of that bold experiment:

Picture a black urban community of 80,000 in which crime, drug abuse, and unemployment have reached such levels that landlords are deserting their buildings rather than trying to sell them. Now picture the same neighborhood 15 years later, with $160 million in new investments, 350 large apartment buildings rehabilitated, and property values rising five to seven percent a year. Hundreds of businesses have started, and thousands of people have received remedial education, job training, and job placement. The community is stable, crime is down, and the crack epidemic hasn't taken root. Yet none of this has been accomplished through gentrification. The community is still 99 percent black. Rents are still fairly low. People on welfare can still afford to move in.[2]

Most bankers predicted that South Shore would fail, but the bank has been profitable every year since 1975. In the seventeen years ending December 31, 1990, the bank had grown fivefold, its repayment rate on more than $160 million of development loans had exceeded 98 percent, and it had provided over $270 million in capital for community development.

Today Shorebank Corporation, the regulated, parent holding company of the $190 million asset-based South Shore Bank, operates in Illinois and Arkansas as well as other parts of the country and abroad.* (See box 42-1.) Shorebank's approach and track record are the foundation for the nascent development banking movement in this country.

Community Banking as a Business Solution

Almost two decades of development banking at South Shore Bank began, in the late 1960s, with management's search for a *business* solution to neighborhood decline and disinvestment. Neither government nor nonprofit organizations had been successful in addressing this problem. The answer would have to be in the private sector—in a business that was self-sustaining and independently capitalized, and where the discipline of the profit motive would temper development zeal. Somehow they would have to create a bank that would:

- reinvest in its neighborhood according to prudent underwriting standards;
- be tough but fair with borrowers;
- meet rigorous examination guidelines; and
- still renew the area without gentrifying it.

According to Ronald Grzywinski, Shorebank's chairman, rebuilding community confidence was a principal objective. But that could happen only if Shorebank succeeded in getting market forces functioning again. The "invisible hand" worked alone in wealthy areas; in the South Shore it would need significant help. "Indeed," says Grzywinski, "we had to orchestrate a massive, focused combination of capital, credit, talent, and enterprise in order to restore the normal forces of investment and entrepreneurialism."[3]

THE SHOREBANK MODEL. As conceived by Shorebank, the neighborhood bank was the core institution of a broad-based, privately capitalized and managed bank holding company organized as a for-profit

---

*Shorebank began consulting with the Grameen Bank in Bangladesh in 1983. In October 1990 it entered into a relationship with the Polish-American Enterprise Fund to help reestablish private banking in Poland for the first time since the 1930s. This includes creating small business loan programs at eight state banks, training Polish bankers, and helping to organize and manage new banks in which Shorebank will have an ownership position.

neighborhood development corporation. Yet while access to credit and prudent development lending were key to sustained economic development, a bank and credit alone could not revive entire city neighborhoods or overcome the economic and social barriers found in distressed communities. Thus, the 1972 Shorebank model was designed with nonbank subsidiaries to diversify the renewal process and to facilitate the wholesale release of local talent and energy for neighborhood redevelopment. It included:

- a real estate development company, City Lands Corporation, to buy and renovate residential and commercial properties;
- a venture capital company, the Neighborhood Fund, to make debt and equity investments in minority-owned businesses; and
- a nonprofit organization, the Neighborhood Institute (TNI), to operate housing, education, and jobs programs.

A development consulting firm (Shorebank Advisory Service) was added in 1988. This integrated approach is what distinguishes South Shore Bank from most other banks and development banking programs here and abroad.

BOX 42-2
COMMUNITY CAPITAL BANK

111 Livingston Street
Brooklyn, N.Y. 11201
(718) 802-1212

Community Capital Bank is a new commercial bank approved by the New York Federal Reserve Bank in 1990. Its official opening, celebrated after five years of organizing and planning, was January 8, 1991.

In its offering prospectus, Community Capital describes its purpose: "to specialize in lending for community development while operating a safe and profitable bank. The Bank's lending focus is designed to improve capital access for low and moderate income communities of New York City, thus helping to revitalize those neighborhoods." Further, it identifies its lending priorities as "affordable housing developers, both not-for-profit and for-profit," and "small businesses, especially small manufacturers and service businesses which employ

---

lower income people or which provide products and services that benefit the community, such as health care." In its prospectus and much of its marketing material, Community Capital generously cites South Shore Bank as its model in development banking.

The bank offers standard consumer banking services and FDIC-insured, market rate deposit products to fund its lending activities. Like South Shore and Elk Horn, Community Capital will raise deposits locally and nationally, marketing them as social investment products. While hoping to add nonbank development subsidiaries some time in the future, initial operations comprise the one regulated commercial bank. Community Capital raised $6 million in common stock, capitalizing the institution with investments from institutions and individuals primarily in the New York and New England areas.

FOUR FUNDAMENTAL CONCEPTS. Three writers have looked closely at Shorebank. In 1988 Richard Taub, a sociology professor at the University of Chicago, published a history of Shorebank Corporation, *Community Capitalism*,[4] in which he describes Shorebank's operation as a development bank holding company and its impact on one community. David Osborne describes Shorebank's unique approach as a "permanent, specialized development finance institution."[5] In his series on how to fix the ailing economy, William Greider calls for a national network of public sector banks as the key to true financial reform and cites South Shore Bank as the one such bank that already exists. Along with "dozens of community-development loan funds [that] operate around the country . . . South Shore's founders were smart enough to figure out that credit and banking are the key to social progress."[6] These writers affirm four concepts fundamental to development banking theory. First, financial institutions have responsibilities to the public—as beneficiaries of public policy, as fiduciaries of depositors' savings, as managers of the billions of dollars that flow through our economy daily, and as decision makers about where and how those funds are allocated. Second, within legislated guidelines banks have an enormous, inherent capacity to innovate and to produce, within the disciplines of the marketplace, sustained, measurable, lasting benefits to those normally excluded from the conventional banking system. Third, credit can be organized and used as a poverty alleviation strategy; it is a powerful tool to create equity and ownership of residents in their communities. And fourth, community development banking and neighborhood renewal requires "patient" capital and is inconsistent with short-term profit maximization.

Funding for Development Banking: Insured Bank Deposits

In most poor neighborhoods, residents' savings flow out of their banks to loans in wealthier parts of the city, state, country, and even other countries. South Shore's innovation was to reverse that outflow, thereby providing the bank with a predictable, steady source of lendable funds. Thus, like all banks, South Shore takes in deposits and makes loans. Different from most others, South Shore converts those deposits into credit for development.

Development Deposits[sm], the bank's social investment portfolio, are FDIC-insured deposits that support development lending in geographically defined areas. Introduced in 1974, they represent the first program of its kind established by any bank to finance economic development through a regulated depository institution. They are also one of the nation's earliest social investment products.

By definition, Development Deposits[sm] come from outside the bank's primary service area. They are placed by individual and institutional investors around the country who share two investment objectives: they care about, and want to know, what their bank does with their money, and they seek a positive social investment option rather than a negative screen. At the same time, Development Deposits[sm] are ordinary bank deposits in terms of what people buy—certificates of deposit (CDs); money market accounts; checking, negotiable order of withdrawal (NOW), and savings accounts; individual retirement accounts (IRAs); and automatic teller machine (ATM) access. They also receive market rates of interest.

Customized programs, such as the Rehab CD, the TNI Community Renewal CD, Industrial Cooperative Association's Community Jobs CD, and ACCION CDs, give investors the opportunity to receive a below market rate of interest in order to support a particular social concern, be it job creation, education, affordable housing, small business lending, employee ownership, or minority economic development.

As of April 1, 1991, Development Deposits[sm] stood at $94 million, representing just over 50 percent of the bank's total liabilities. They are held by social investors in all fifty states and in thirteen countries. Development Deposits[sm] will be used to support Shorebank development initiatives as it expands to other parts of the United States and abroad.

NOTES

1. See "Capital and Communities: A Community Guide to Financial Institutions" (Washington, D.C.: Community Information Exchange, 1990), for an introduction to various forms of community and other development finance.
2. David Osborne, "A Poverty Program That Works," *New Republic*, May 8, 1989, pp. 22, 25.
3. Ronald Grzywinski, "The New Old-Fashioned Banking," *Harvard Business Review*, May–June 1991, pp. 88–98. The "we" included the three other members of Shorebank's management team, Milton Davis, Mary Houghton, and James Fletcher. Davis, Grzywinski, and Houghton started at Shorebank in 1972, Fletcher in 1978. Along with a few other colleagues, they all developed the Shorebank strategy twenty years ago.
4. Richard P. Taub, *Community Capitalism: Building Strategies and Economic Redevelopment* (Boston: Harvard Business School Press, 1988), p. 57.
5. David Osborne, *Laboratories of Democracy, a New Breed of Governors Creates Models for National Growth* (Boston: Harvard Business School Press, 1988), p. 305.
6. William Greider, "The Economy: How to Fix It," pt. 2, *Rolling Stone*, February 7, 1991, p. 35.

ONE BANK'S COMMUNITY DEVELOPMENT BANKING PROGRAM

David Berge Director, Vermont National Bank,
Socially Responsible Banking Fund

Vermont National Bank's Socially Responsible Banking (SRB) Fund was started in 1989 to offer the individual depositor and money manager a unique investment option, one that can meet both their financial goals and their social goals.

By designating deposits (currently over $48 million) for use in the areas of affordable housing, environmental and conservation projects, agriculture, education, and small business development, the SRB Fund satisfies many of the requirements of today's socially responsible investor. The SRB Fund currently has more than six hundred loans for more than $31 million to projects in these areas. Vermont National Bank, through the SRB Fund, carefully reviews loan requests using both financial and social criteria.

| DEPOSITS

The Socially Responsible Banking Fund is administered by Vermont National Bank, a full-service bank headquartered in Brattleboro, Vermont. All depositors are covered by FDIC insurance up to $100,000. Minimum opening deposits in the SRB Fund are $500 ($1,000 for money market accounts). SRB Fund accounts earn the same rate of

---

David Berge is the director of the Vermont National Bank Socially Responsible Banking Fund. In 1990, Berge left the Institute for Community Economics in Springfield, Mass., where he was senior loan officer, for Vermont National. Before joining ICE, Berge worked with a number of nonprofit organizations in the areas of small business development, alternative secondary markets, and community investment.

return as the bank's regular accounts. The following accounts are available to all investors:

- Savings
- Checking
- Certificate of deposit (CD)
- Money market
- Premier money market
- Individual retirement (IRA)
- Simplified employee pension plans (SEPs)
- NOW
- Sweep
- Richer Life
- Premier banking
- College Opportunity Fund

The SRB Fund publishes a newsletter highlighting specific projects supported by the fund and other socially responsible investment activities nationwide. Financial reports showing the amounts loaned out in each category as well as deposit activity also are sent to depositors.

| LOAN PROGRAMS

The following are brief descriptions of the SRB Fund's loan programs.

Affordable Housing

Purpose: to provide low- and moderate-income families access to credit in an attempt to secure affordable housing. To provide creative financing to community groups, nonprofit developers, and private-public partnerships to assure that housing is available to more families.

Eligible projects include, but are not limited to:

- single-family homes for low- and moderate-income families;
- community land trust properties;
- limited-equity cooperatives and condominiums;
- transitional housing and shelters;
- affordable elderly housing;
- affordable rental housing; and
- mobile and manufactured homes.

Priorities: special emphasis on housing organizations and projects that provide permanently affordable housing.

Environmental and Conservation Projects

Purpose: to finance the acquisition of land for conservation purposes. To provide financing to individuals and enterprises that have a positive impact on the environment.

Priorities: to assist projects that promote responsible use of the land and provide permanent assurance of those responsible uses (such as the gift or sale of development easements in conjunction with the project, or use restrictions on agricultural land). Special emphasis is on enterprises that provide innovative models for environmental companies.

BOX 43-1

IMPLEMENTING A COMMUNITY DEVELOPMENT BANKING PROGRAM

Elizabeth K. Glenshaw Loring, Wolcott & Coolidge

A community development banking program (CDBP) works within the conventional structure of a bank to provide loans for local community and economic development. A CDBP earmarks deposit and loan dollars for community-based projects for those people who systematically have been unable to gain access to credit.

THE SECONDARY MARKET AND DEREGULATION

The secondary market has become a driving force under which a bank does business. The bank sells its loans to this market to renew funds and to reduce the risk of exposure between short-term deposits and long-term loans. Unfortunately, only loans that meet rigorous statistical criteria are saleable. This process has slowly eliminated making loans to individuals or businesses that do not fit the standards of the secondary market.

After becoming deregulated, banks focused on making profits rather than on meeting the need to provide an economic service to the community at large. As a result, not only did banks invest in speculative ventures because of their promise of a high return, but a gap developed between the bank's core depositors and its loan recipients. With a

---

CDBP, banking returns to the business of making loans to the people who deposit their money there.

Provided that a bank creates a clearly defined mission statement for its CDBP, develops a set of lending principles, and writes an achievable implementation plan, a CDBP represents an easy way for any bank to address the needs of its community.

PLANNING AND IMPLEMENTATION

Development of the mission statement, lending principles, and an implementation plan require that a bank undergo a demanding organizational evolution.

Support from senior management—including the bank's president and board of directors—is crucial to the success of a CDBP. The board of directors and the president must develop a mission statement. The creation of a mission statement based on the executives' input ensures that the bank will accept the structural changes that must occur in order to assimilate a CDBP into the current bank framework. The president must sell the CDBP program as an integral piece in the commercial banking structure. Reluctant members of senior management often can be convinced to accept a CDBP within the conventional banking structure once it is shown that the program meets the requirements of the Community Reinvestment Act (CRA).

Once its mission has been established, a CDBP must build a definition, or set of principles, under which to govern itself. These principles answer such questions as, What kind of criteria does the bank need to follow to lend the money? and, What mechanism will the bank use to gather the deposits to make these loans?

Deposit Gathering

Creating a deposit-gathering mechanism for CDBPs is a relatively straightforward process. The bank must track the funds separately from the conventional bank deposit, provide some reporting for those deposits, and monitor the outcome of the loans made with these deposits. Diligent record keeping attracts the socially responsible depositors, for it allows them to know exactly where their money has been used.

Lending

The lending portion of a CDBP has been more difficult to execute. CDBPs have found that the hiring of a specialized community-based lender has been the most workable solution to building the structural framework for a community development lending program.

The intricacies of community development lending and its perceived risks have often been the stumbling block for many banks interested in setting up a CDBP. The conventional bank lender without training does not have the expertise to successfully loan money to community development projects. The structural framework for community development projects requires packaging that is not currently taught to banking lenders.

Most conventional loan proposals fit into an application form. They meet well-established criteria acceptable to the secondary market, but they also are decidedly oriented away from the person. A hands-on, specifically personal approach is what makes a CDBP successful. Although debt to equity, cash flow, income ratios, credit quality, collateral, and so forth are important, a community-based lender relies on these figures for each project only on a project-to-project basis.

PROJECT-SPECIFIC APPROACH. Using a project-specific approach—where varying combinations of cash, character, capacity, collateral, and credit are considered independent of other projects—helps the lender loan to a project versus loaning a type of loan to a project.

Case-by-case lending also prevents the current lending faux pas where only statistically acceptable loans are made, which furthers the systematic divestment in a community by emphasizing numbers rather than restoration of a community's surroundings. In time, hopefully, both the banks with CDBPs, as they see the successes of this type of lending, and the recipients, as they feel change in their communities, will close the gap between people and banking.

Banks started because people recognized that by pooling their funds and lending those funds out to constituents in their community, all would benefit and ultimately would help their community grow. Through the efforts of CDBPs, we may again see banking as a business more closely aligned to the needs of the community.

Elizabeth K. Glenshaw works for the trust firm Loring, Wolcott & Coolidge as an associate trustee. Prior to joining Loring, Wolcott & Coolidge, she founded the Socially Responsible Banking Fund in Brattleboro, Vermont. Glenshaw currently sits on SRB's advisory board as the vice chair; the board of Co-op America; the board of the Vermont Community Loan Fund; and the board of the Social Investment Forum. She received her B.A. in psychology and sociology from Marlboro College in 1981.

Agriculture

Purpose: to provide financing for organizations, individuals, and projects that provide ownership opportunities for family farms and agricultural enterprises in Vermont.

Priorities: to provide financing for projects developed by or in conjunction with nonprofits or other agencies providing assistance to new, young, or low-income farm families. To provide financing for land acquisition, equipment, or working capital for projects providing innovative, sustainable, and environmentally sound models of family farming or agricultural enterprise.

Education

Purpose: to provide financing to individuals and Vermont educational institutions.

Priorities: to assist educational institutions providing high-quality, innovative organizational or curriculum development models. Special emphasis is on individuals providing day-care services, educational consulting services (such as curriculum development), or alternative education options, or organizations or programs providing benefits to low-income students or students with special needs.

Small Business

Purpose: to assist small businesses starting up, operating, or expanding in Vermont, or organizations providing financing to those businesses.

Priorities: special emphasis is on women- and minority-owned businesses, rural businesses, and businesses working in the other four SRB lending areas. There is also a special emphasis on businesses that provide new or creative models of ownership or operation or provide jobs, training, educational benefits, or a product or service that benefits low-income members of the community.

| FUND GUIDELINES

The guidelines of the SRB Fund are maintained by Vermont National Bank, assisted by an advisory board of community representatives.

Any cash balances in the fund are held in investments targeted toward companies that make positive contributions to the environment, their communities, and their employees.

Investment Guidelines

In a world of limited resources, we choose to do business with those who, in our view, will use funds from the SRB Fund to do the most good.

We seek to lend to or invest in companies that make positive contributions to our natural environment, use or develop appropriate energy technologies, contribute significantly to the communities in which they operate, and treat their employees well. We will not lend to or invest in companies that have negative records in these areas or that derive income from the manufacture of alcoholic beverages, tobacco products, or the sale of military weapons or weapons systems. Nor will we lend to or invest in companies that maintain more than minimal contact with South Africa.

THE ENVIRONMENT. We seek to lend to and invest in companies that make positive contributions to the effort to preserve our natural environment for future generations and that work to remedy past mistakes—whether or not of their own making. We give high marks to a company that takes a positive approach to programs to clean up its operations or that has designed a new operation to avoid problems in the first place.

We acknowledge that considerable controversy continues on how to evaluate environmental performance. Nonetheless, commonly accepted standards of environmental responsibility do exist, and we will not consider lending to or investing in any company that fails to meet them.

ENERGY. We seek to lend to and invest in companies that display a high degree of sensitivity to environmental concerns relating to energy consumption and production, that pursue energy conservation and renewable energy sources, and that recognize the need for stable energy supplies.

Among the extractors of fuel, we seek companies that minimize the effects of their operations on the environment and the communities in which they operate. Among the transporters of fuel, we identify the companies that pay most attention to safety. Among the generators of electricity, we look for companies that closely attend to the back end of the fuel cycle—what happens after the fuel is converted into energy—and that emphasize energy conservation and cogeneration. Among the transmission companies, we look for sensitivity to environmental and scenic concerns and for a strong awareness of safety issues.

EMPLOYEE RELATIONS. We seek to lend to and invest in companies that deal fairly with their employees—union and nonunion alike—and provide them with reasonable compensation and benefits. We prefer companies with positive employee relations records over those with merely neutral performance.

In investing, we consider the availability of benefits, such as retirement plans, profit sharing plans, and employee stock purchase plans open to all employees. We note employee ownership of stock and the inclusion of women and minorities in top management. When data are available, we also consider programs for workers with special needs, child care, elder care, handicap access, safe working conditions, relations with organized labor and unionized employees, and a broad range of other issues. We also consider whether managers and officers are rewarded disproportionately. Where a company is deficient—but not derelict—in one area, we may balance positive factors against the deficiency.

PRODUCT. We do not lend to or invest in any company that derives income from military weapons or weapons-related businesses, from the manufacture of alcoholic beverages, or from the manufacture of tobacco products.

In addition, we do not invest in any company that manufactures or derives income from gambling or gambling-related products or services. Nor do we lend to any company or organization that manufactures or derives income that is primarily from gambling or gambling-related products or services.

SOUTH AFRICA. We do not lend to or invest in companies with operations in South Africa, equity interests in companies doing business in South Africa, or sale or licensing agreements that make strategic equipment available to that nation's military and police.

COMMUNITY DEVELOPMENT CREDIT UNIONS

Clifford N. Rosenthal Executive Director,
National Federation of Community Development
Credit Unions

Credit unions are nonprofit, tax-exempt financial cooperatives.* Since they are member-owned and democratically controlled (one member, one vote, regardless of the amount of one's deposits), they are inherently "user-friendly," proconsumer institutions. All surplus is either returned to members as dividends on shares (interest on savings accounts) or retained as reserves. The bulk of a credit union's deposits—usually 60 to 90 percent—is invested in loans to members. The balance is invested in government securities, certificates of deposits (CDs), or other nonspeculative instruments. Credit unions have no international loan exposure, they do not finance leveraged buyouts, and in fact, they tend to maintain only a small portion of their portfolios in commercial loans. By historical mission and statute, credit unions are bound to loan only for "provident and

---

*The following description applies, except where noted, to federally insured credit unions, which represent approximately 90 percent of all credit unions in the United States. The credit unions closed during the Rhode Island crisis of early 1991 were all state-chartered, privately insured institutions subject to a regulatory system quite different from that of federally insured credit unions. Social investors are encouraged to determine the insurance status of any credit union considered for deposits.

Clifford Rosenthal joined the National Federation of Community Development Credit Unions in 1980 and became its executive director in 1983. He has worked in paid and unpaid capacities with low-income cooperatives for more than twenty years. A member of the Federal Reserve's Consumer Advisory Council since 1989, he also serves on the advisory boards of Community Capital Bank and Chemical Community Development Corporation, both in New York City.

productive purposes," which translates into portfolios dominated by consumer and, to a lesser degree, mortgage loans.

Despite the consumerist bent of credit unions, they do not typically attract the interest of social investors. In fact, the majority of credit unions are permitted to serve only a limited, well-defined "field of membership," which may include, for example, employees of an enterprise, members of a profession, members of a particular church, and so on.

However, one segment of the credit union movement—community development credit unions (CDCUs)—has attracted substantial attention and support from social investors. CDCUs are credit unions chartered specifically to serve low-income communities—the only depository institutions with such a mission. Their legal structure is identical to that of other credit unions, with one exception: in 1970 Congress granted credit unions serving predominantly low-income communities the right to raise deposits from "nonmember" sources, such as foundations, churches, banks, and corporations. These deposits are insured on the same basis as member deposits—as of January 1991, up to $100,000 per depositor per institution. Nonmember depositors may neither vote nor borrow from a credit union, thus assuring that the credit union members always maintain control of the institution.

CDCUs appeal to social investors for a number of reasons. They are self-help institutions, owned by the poor and operated for their own benefit. CDCUs fill the growing gaps in the banking system created by the "upscaling" and consolidation of commercial banks. CDCUs are reinvestment institutions par excellence. Not only do they recycle member deposits or loans within the community (as opposed to banks, which typically drain and export capital from low-income areas), but they engage outside capital from nonmembers in the revitalization of economically depressed inner-city and rural areas. About two thirds of CDCUs are urban, while one third are rural. There are more than three hundred credit unions serving predominantly low-income communities in thirty-five states, the District of Columbia, Puerto Rico, and American Samoa. Most CDCUs serve predominantly minority communities, especially African-American, Hispanic, Native American, and Asian-American. Finally, unlike other credit unions, CDCUs stress economic and community development lending—for affordable housing, small businesses, minority- and women-owned businesses, cooperatives, nonprofits, and the like.

I HISTORY OF CDCUs

Some CDCUs trace their roots back half a century. Many were formed during the civil rights and antipoverty movements of the 1960s. During the last fifteen years, a number of CDCUs were organized as a response to redlining or bank branch closings. The number of CDCUs has declined in recent years, paralleling a trend that has affected all financial institutions—despite the growing need for banking services in many low-income communities. However, the achievements of individual CDCUs have far exceeded all but the most extravagant dreams of the CDCU movement progenitors. The largest CDCUs have built deposit bases in excess of $20 million and have established outstanding records in community lending. First American Credit Union (Window Rock, Arizona) serves more than eleven thousand members of the Navajo and other tribes headquartered in Arizona and has made more than $60 million in loans. Self-Help Credit Union (Durham, North Carolina) operates as a statewide "development bank" financing minority businesses, child-care centers, affordable and special-needs housing, and worker cooperatives. Santa Cruz Community Credit Union (California) has created hundreds of manufacturing, farming, and retail jobs and has a loan-loss rate considerably below 1 percent.

As early as 1970, CDCUs could solicit nonmember deposits from philanthropic and other sources. However, little money came in until the early 1980s, when the social investment movement began to accelerate and expand. Nonmember deposits in CDCUs have grown sharply since 1985, but they still probably account for no more than $50 million out of a total deposit base of about $400 million. While the relative amount remains small, these social deposits are critically important to CDCUs. Because nonmember deposits are usually of substantial size and often bear a below market interest rate, they help very small depositors and low-income borrowers, thereby enabling CDCUs to serve a market that cannot be served profitably by any other financial institution.

The CDCU movement suffered a significant setback in 1988, when it was discovered that the Franklin Community Federal Credit Union in Omaha, Nebraska, had fraudulently solicited deposits. All depositors were paid off up to $100,000 by its insurer, the National Credit Union Administration (NCUA), whose fund is backed by the full faith and credit of the U.S. government. However, the NCUA quickly moved to promulgate regulations in December 1988 to limit the amount of nonmember deposits that could be accepted by any low-income credit union.* This limit—20 percent of a CDCU's deposit base, unless it obtains a waiver permitting a higher figure—has impaired the ability of some of the poorest, smallest credit unions to raise outside funds.

BOX 44-1

NATIONAL FEDERATION OF COMMUNITY DEVELOPMENT CREDIT UNIONS

59 John Street, Eighth Floor
New York, N.Y. 10038
(212) 513-7191

The National Federation of Community Development Credit Unions was established in 1974 to serve and represent financial cooperatives in low-income communities.

The federation is the national advocate for the community development credit union (CDCU) movement on regulatory and policy issues affecting low-income credit unions. It has waged a successful battle to create and maintain a $6 million federal Revolving Loan Fund, which provides CDCUs with low-cost capital. In January 1990 the federation's executive director was appointed to the Consumer Advisory Council of the Federal Reserve system.

Apart from the public-sector advocacy, the federation has raised more than $4 million in low-cost deposits from the private sector, particularly foundations, churches, and banks through its Capitalization Program for CDCUs.

The federation provides training and management support to CDCUs. In addition, since 1985 it has assisted nearly a dozen groups in organizing new credit unions in low-income communities, particularly in response to branch closings and "upscaling" by commercial banks.

The federation publishes newsletters (the *CDCU Report* and *Community Finance*) and conducts research on the CDCU movement. In 1986 it published a report to the White House entitled *An Analysis of the Role of Credit Unions in Capital Formation and Investment in Low- and Moderate-Income Communities*. In 1991 it published

---

*The National Credit Union Administration did not allege improprieties at other CDCUs prior to the regulation, nor has it since uncovered other instances of fraud.

| INVESTING IN CDCUs

There are two ways to invest in community development credit unions: by making direct deposits in individual credit unions or by investing through an intermediary—the National Federation of CDCUs (see box 44-1).

Direct Deposits

A social investor may make an insured nonmember deposit of up to $100,000 in any low-income credit union in the country, if:

1. the credit union is officially designated as "limited income" by the NCUA; and
2. the credit union is either under its 20 percent nonmember deposit quota or has a waiver allowing it to exceed that limit.*

Rates should be negotiated prior to making a deposit. However, investors should understand that no credit union can legally *guarantee* a particular dividend rate on a savings deposit, since the yield will be determined by a credit union's available earnings. A mature CDCU with a solid financial track record over several years can generally offer a projected dividend rate with a reasonable degree of confidence.

Some CDCUs offer only passbook or statement savings accounts; others may offer individual retirement accounts (IRAs) and Keogh accounts, share draft (checking) accounts, and share certificates (comparable to certificates of deposit) of varying maturities. The highest rates—which may be fully competitive with banks and thrifts—are generally found at larger CDCUs ($3 million or more

---

*The National Federation of CDCUs encourages investors to request written confirmation of these two facts from a credit union prior to making a nonmember deposit.

in assets). Smaller credit unions and those serving the poorest communities may offer dividend rates substantially below market (3 to 4 percent). Investors should bear in mind that a credit union generally must pass on its cost of funds to its borrowers. All other factors being equal, a higher rate paid to an investor translates into a higher loan rate for the low-income community.

The majority of CDCUs are computerized and issue statements at least quarterly. However, some retain a semiannual dividend period. Although there are some three hundred CDCUs across the country, these are not evenly distributed, and an investor cannot necessarily count on finding one in the area of his or her choice. Finally, not all CDCUs are interested in receiving nonmember deposits. Some prefer to rely solely on their own community resources, while others cannot offer competitive rates.

The Capitalization Program for CDCUs

Since 1983 the National Federation of CDCUs has offered another means of investing in low-income credit unions: the Capitalization Program for CDCUs. Social investors make loans to the federation (a 501[c][3] organization) at below market rates. The federation reinvests the funds as deposits in local CDCUs according to the geographic, social, or sectoral interests of the investors. This approach offers investors the possibility of developing a diversified portfolio without the administrative burden that otherwise would be required. The federation analyzes and monitors the financial and regulatory status of the CDCUs in which it places deposits.

Investors are cautioned that loans to the federation are not insured. However, the federation uses the proceeds to make federally insured deposits in credit unions and assigns these deposits as collateral for the loans. Thus, it offers a high degree of safety. There is no fee for the federation's services. However, it passes along a small spread (averaging 125 basis points) to the credit unions in which it makes deposits. Depending on the requirements of investors, the federation makes interest payments as frequently as quarterly. Investors receive their interest payments regardless of whether credit unions make their dividend payments to the federation. The federation has not missed an interest or principal payment since the Capitalization Program was started in 1983.

Loans to the Capitalization Program have come from foundations, banks, religious organizations, and other social investors at rates from 0 to 5.5 percent. Loan sizes have ranged from $30,000 to $1 million. Terms are generally from three to five years. Because of the need to tailor loan agreements to investor needs, the federation believes that the Capitalization Program is generally more suitable for institutional than for individual investors. As of early 1991 the federation had approximately $4 million under management. Its largest investors included the Ford Foundation and the John D. and Catherine T. MacArthur Foundation.

RESOURCES

PUBLICATIONS OF THE NATIONAL FEDERATION OF COMMUNITY DEVELOPMENT CREDIT UNIONS

Community Development Credit Union Report.

This quarterly newsletter (eight to twelve pages) of the National Federation of Community Development Credit Unions includes reporting and analysis of credit union and banking issues, news of social investment activity, innovative credit union programs, and profiles of individual CDCUs. Subscriptions: $27 yearly. (Community organizations, $18; individuals, $12.)

Community Finance.

This newsletter of the Community Financial Network reports on credit unions serving low-income communities in New York State, reinvestment and housing issues, and the banking scene. Subscriptions: $12.

People's Credit: A Study of the Lending of the Lower East Side People's Federal Credit Union, 1986–89.

People's Credit is the case study of a credit union formed to replace the last bank branch serving a low-income neighborhood of fifty-five thousand people on New York City's Lower East Side. It is the only study to include an analysis of the complete loan portfolio of a low-income credit union during its initial years of operation. The seventy-two-page work, which includes thirty statistical tables, analyzes the demographics and banking histories of the credit union's borrowers as well as the policies, practices, and portfolio of the Lower East Side People's FCU. Extensive interviews with low-income borrowers form about half of the report. Single copies, $7.50; six or more copies, $6 each.

"Report to the White House": An Analysis of the Role of Credit Unions in Capital Formation and Investment in Low- and Moderate-Income Communities.

This is the most comprehensive study of credit unions serving low-income communities in the deregulated banking environment of the 1980s. It contains more than one hundred pages of statistics, case studies, and policy recommendations about CDCUs. The report was presented to the Low-Income Opportunity Group of the White House Office of Policy Development in December 1986.

CHAPTER 45

COMMUNITY DEVELOPMENT LOAN FUNDS: CAPITAL FOR ECONOMIC, SOCIAL, AND POLITICAL JUSTICE

Martin Paul Trimble, Mark A. Pinsky, and **Greg Ramm**

Community development loan funds (CDLFs) are financial intermediaries that borrow capital and lend it in lower-income communities to support nonprofit rental housing, community-based businesses, home ownership, microenterprises, and community development generally. CDLFs also provide technical assistance to borrowers to ensure that they develop the necessary skills and resources to achieve and sustain economic self-sufficiency.

CDLFs are a proven vehicle for economic and social justice. Since the first loan fund began operating in 1969, they have made more than three thousand loans nationwide totaling $88 million. As a result, hundreds of communities have seen returns on investments

---

Martin Paul Trimble is the executive director of the National Association of Community Development Loan Funds (NACDLF), a position that he has held since July 1989.

Mark A. Pinsky, a free-lance writer and former executive director of the Democracy Project, edits *Community Investment Monitor*, NACDLF's quarterly newsletter.

Greg Ramm is executive director of the Institute of Community Economics, an NACDLF member fund located in Springfield, Massachusetts. From 1986 to 1989 he coordinated NACDLF's programs.

of time and hard work—most notably the creation of eleven thousand affordable housing units and thirty-five hundred jobs. Equally important, these communities have developed democratic methods of decision making and gained control over institutions essential to a stable and prosperous community life, housing, businesses, social services, and financial intermediaries.

Each CDLF is unique in the types of community development projects it finances, the geographical area it serves, and the sources and size of its capital pool. All CDLFs that belong to the National Association of Community Development Loan Funds (NACDLF), however, share a deep concern about the growing economic polarization of American society and a commitment to democratic access to capital. NACDLF is described in box 45-1.

| OPERATION

CDLFs are chartered as nonprofit organizations, staffed by paid and volunteer financial and community development specialists and operated with minimal overhead costs. Most NACDLF member funds evolved out of ongoing community organizing efforts and reflect their communities' diversity.

All CDLFs balance the needs and concerns of borrowers and lenders. At the same time, each loan fund structures itself in the way that best meets the needs of its community. Thus, each is unique and able to adapt to changing requirements.

BOX 45-1
NATIONAL ASSOCIATION OF
COMMUNITY DEVELOPMENT LOAN FUNDS

924 Cherry Street
Philadelphia, Pa. 19107
(215) 923-4754
(215) 923-4764 (fax)

The National Association of Community Development Loan Funds (NACDLF) represents forty local, regional, and national nonprofit loan funds managing more than $70 million in capital. The member funds act as financial intermediaries, channeling investment capital into housing, small business, and community economic development projects denied access to traditional capital sources. Associate members include other financial intermediaries, community development practitioners, investment firms, and individuals or organizations that share NACDLF's purpose.

NACDLF performance standards and its member-fund review program are key to the association's financial and social integrity. NACDLF maintains strict criteria for accounting, financial planning and management, and loan supervision. Selected fund managers and loan officers conduct reviews to assess each fund's management and lending practices as well as how loans are used to advance the shared commitment to economic and social justice—the common thread linking NACDLF member funds.

NACDLF member loan funds have an excellent performance record. From 1987 to 1990, the loss rate on loans among NACDLF member funds was 1.3 percent—substantially lower than that of many federally regulated commercial lending institutions. Through their public-spirited lending, CDLFs are proving that:

- lower-income people and communities are creditworthy;
- successful efforts to overcome chronic poverty depend on democratic control over economic resources and access to credit so that the poor can pursue their own self-development initiatives; and
- conventional notions about risk, security, and profit in lending must be reexamined when serving borrowers with little credit history, development experience, or collateral.

NACDLF provides a broad range of evaluation, financial service, advocacy, and educational functions for its member funds. NACDLF

- operates a Central Fund, currently capitalized at $2.5 million, to enhance the lending work of its members. NACDLF mobilizes capital from national and international lenders to redistribute to its member funds;
- provides technical assistance to member funds, including an annual training conference to provide intensive education in lending and management;
- conducts a rigorous evaluation and review program to ensure the financial stability of member funds, to identify necessary improvements in lending and management, and to strengthen lender security;
- acts as an advocate for member funds as well as for socially responsible investing generally, at the national, state, and local levels;
- maintains a resource library available to member funds and others seeking information on socially responsible investment opportunities and CDLF management;
- serves as a primary clearinghouse about financial management, reg-

ulatory affairs, and loan activity for members, lenders, borrowers, and others;

- provides media relations support and technical assistance to member funds and assists the national media;
- conducts an expanding research and policy development program seeking innovative ways to direct available private capital to worthy community development projects;
- publishes a directory of members and associates providing summary descriptions of all funds as well as a quarterly newsletter.

CDLFs assist communities in identifying areas for effective use of capital. They work with borrowers to establish sound financial plans and assist housing and business ventures in a wide range of technical areas for the term of the loan. CDLFs also assist past and potential borrowers in overall community development.

CDLFs apply the lessons of creative community organizing, helping borrowers develop plans that are appropriate and specific to individual communities. Because they know their communities well, loan funds design loans to match available capital to community needs in ways that traditional lenders cannot. Their ongoing involvement with the communities helps ensure that loans are monitored closely and that appropriate technical assistance is provided.

Accountability

CDLFs follow fundamental principles of sound finance and lending, including rigorous lending requirements, external review of individual loan fund practices, and emerging performance standards for responsible financial management. Unlike most other lending institutions, however, CDLFs are governed by the constituencies they serve—lenders, borrowers, and community development practitioners.

Security

CDLFs provide many layers of lender protection:

- They know and work closely with their borrowers.
- Loans are underwritten rigorously.
- Most loans are collateralized.
- Loan risks often are spread among lenders on a pro rata basis.
- Loans are monitored closely and technical assistance is available to most borrowers.

- If all else fails, loss reserves are maintained by an increasing number of loan funds.

Investments are neither insured nor guaranteed. As with all investments, risk exists.

I LENDERS

NACDLF member funds raise capital from both individuals and institutions.

Individuals account for 27 percent of the loans to NACDLF members. Religious groups, foundations, banks, and insurance companies are the leading institutional lenders. Investments from private for-profit and not-for-profit corporations, universities, and socially responsible mutual funds are increasing. The acceptance of CDLFs by traditional capital sources implies a steadily increasing flow of capital to meet community needs.

Lenders usually place their funds at rates from 0 percent to just below money market levels. CDLFs accept loans on a variety of terms. Some funds require a one-year minimum commitment, and all prefer longer-term loans.

The growth in capital lent to CDLFs has been dramatic. Since July 1986 twenty-three NACDLF member funds managed $19 million. By December 1990 forty member funds were managing $73 million.

I BORROWERS

Capital made available through CDLFs is loaned in response to the needs of lower-income communities, and according to criteria requested by lenders and set by loan funds, within the guidelines of NACDLF's principles, which are:

- to provide capital for basic housing, employment, democratic social structures, and other human needs that traditional markets either cannot or do not meet;
- to enable low-income people to meet their own needs;
- to give people and organizations who have been excluded from standard credit markets access to affordable capital;
- to renew and sustain the social and economic health of communities;

- to support organizations and institutions that are community centered *and* democratically controlled.

Recipients of the more than twenty-one hundred loans made since 1969, when the first fund began lending, include:

- community land trusts;
- limited-equity housing cooperatives;
- nonprofit housing developers;
- worker-, consumer-, and nonprofit-owned businesses;
- nonprofit service providers;
- microbusinesses operated by lower-income people.

Loans have ranged from $500 to $350,000. Many have leveraged much larger sums from commercial lenders, state agencies, housing finance authorities, and other sources. As the lender of last resort in many cases, CDLFs often help lower-income borrowers escape a credit catch-22—the borrower cannot get conventional financing without a solid credit history and cannot develop a credit history without a first loan. In addition, CDLF start-up loans have created new borrowers for the conventional credit markets that would not, or could not, serve them in the past.

Social Investment and Community Development
CDLFs are part of the socially responsible investing (SRI) movement. Over the past four decades, the SRI movement in America has helped fund organizing and educational efforts for civil rights, labor rights, peace, environmental protection, and social justice. Strategies ranging from shareholder resolutions opposing corporate weapons production to the powerful South Africa divestment campaign are examples of how SRI has influenced corporate and public thinking.

CDLFs focus on the root causes of poverty and social injustice—unequal distribution of wealth and exclusion of the poor from credit markets. By helping socially responsible investors direct capital to impoverished communities seeking self-sufficiency, CDLFs enable people in these communities to develop affordable housing and community-controlled businesses.

Poverty results less from a lack of individual capabilities (as often thought) than from the unequal ownership and control of land and housing, businesses, and financial institutions. A structure of economic dependence drains resources from lower-income communities. CDLFs challenge and overcome this inequality by providing credit and technical assistance to communities and by training community residents to organize and to operate their own development projects.

CDLFs also educate those with capital about the causes of poverty. In this way, the loan funds encourage socially responsible investments among individual, religious, and traditional financial lenders.

Finally, CDLFs work to strengthen and support organizations that share their commitment to economic and social justice. For this reason, loan funds place a high priority on lending to community land trusts, housing cooperatives, microenterprises run by lower-income people, as well as community-owned and worker-owned businesses. These organizations are community based, community centered, and community controlled. They democratize access, participation, and ownership. They address both immediate needs and the root causes of economic distress. And they build a stronger economic base in and for their communities.

CHAPTER 46

COMMUNITY LAND TRUSTS AND SOCIALLY RESPONSIBLE INVESTING

Greg Ramm Executive Director, Institute for
Community Economics

The community land trust (CLT) represents one of the most innovative methods for extending secure housing and affordable home ownership to people with low and moderate incomes. Improving on conventional home ownership opportunity programs, CLTs also serve the surrounding community's long-term interest by creating a new stock of housing that remains permanently affordable without requiring repeated infusions of scarce public subsidies.

During the 1980s community land trusts emerged with a growing nonprofit housing development sector as some of the most cost-effective providers of affordable housing. Designed by the Institute for Community Economics (described on pages 549–51), the CLT approach draws ancient land stewardship traditions together with modern real estate practices to create a contemporary form of alternative home ownership that blends the best features of public and private ownership.

More than one hundred land trusts in twenty-three states are

Greg Ramm is the executive director of the Institute of Community Economics (ICE). He has worked at ICE for six years, for most of that time as assistant director, providing technical assistance to community loan funds throughout the United States. He served as coordinator of the National Association of Community Development Loan Funds (NACDLF) during its first three years while it was under ICE management. Ramm currently serves on the board of the Social Investment Forum and on the Community Advisory Board of Vermont National Bank's Socially Responsible Investment Fund. Before coming to ICE, he spent three years in the Peace Corps, teaching high school math and physics in rural Zaire. He earned a bachelor's degree in computer science from Dartmouth College in 1981.

currently in operation. Major cities with CLTs in varying stages of development include New York, Atlanta, Dallas, Boston, and Philadelphia. Among smaller cities with CLTs are Trenton, New Jersey; Burlington, Vermont; Syracuse, New York; Durham, North Carolina; and Norwich, Connecticut. Nearly one third of all CLTs operate in small towns and rural areas.

Although the oldest CLTs have little more than a decade of experience, land trust development is gaining momentum. The number of CLTs has more than tripled since 1987. In a little more than ten years, grassroots community land trusts have collectively built, renovated, and preserved permanently several thousand units of affordable housing.

Community land trusts are uniquely tied to the socially responsible investing movement. Their early development and ongoing expansion both derive from investments extended by socially committed individuals and religious institutions, often working through nonprofit community investment intermediaries. Social investors have been involved in some of the earliest CLT efforts and continue to play an important role in providing low-cost capital to create effective and lasting solutions to the affordable housing crisis.

| HOW COMMUNITY LAND TRUSTS WORK

A community land trust is a democratically structured nonprofit corporation with an open membership and an elected board. It is organized to acquire land and remove it from the speculative market, much like a conservation trust. The purpose of most community land trusts, however, is to make land permanently accessible to community residents in need of affordable housing.

Individuals, families, cooperatives, and other organizations may lease land from a CLT for housing and other purposes using long-term (ninety-nine-year) renewable leases. All lessees are members of the CLT and are represented on its board. While leaseholders do not own the land they use, they may own their homes or housing units. The CLT retains an option to purchase the building, should the owner decide to sell, for the amount of the owner's investment and improvements, usually adjusted for inflation and depreciation. Homeowners are thus guaranteed a fair equity for their investments and their successors can purchase the homes at a fair price.

A fundamental feature of the CLT is its ability to strike a fair balance between individual and community interests in property.

The CLT concept is rooted in the understanding that property value is created both by individual owners and by the surrounding community in the form of commercial and public investments. Its guiding principle is that housing can be kept affordable by treating the land beneath it, not as a commodity, but as a community resource.

Like most affordable housing developers, CLTs use public investment to lower initial housing costs, reducing the price lower-income home buyers must pay. The CLT land lease, however, limits land trust homeowners from reaping windfall profits at resale. In addition, it prevents absentee ownership. The result is that the value of the community's investment stays with the land and can be recycled indefinitely to benefit future residents.

Management
Committees of the CLT selected by the board help with the work of managing the organization, assembling acquisition financing, creating lease agreements, selecting tenants, and coordinating volunteers, renovation, and maintenance. The required mix of board skills and representation is drawn from the membership using a formula of thirds: one third of board seats are reserved for CLT residents, another third for members of the community at large, and the final third are made up of community members with needed skills in law, accounting, real estate, nonprofit development, government, and so forth. Democratic representation on CLT boards maintains the community's interest in long-term affordability and locally controlled development. Most CLTs hire staff to coordinate development and serve the elected board.

Housing Approach
CLTs can be organized in both urban and rural communities with vastly different conditions and needs. In some cases they are initiated by individuals acting on their concern about local housing and land-use trends. In others, coalitions of housing, social justice, and community groups have joined with nonprofit developers and local governments to bring ongoing housing and land preservation efforts under the umbrella of a CLT framework. CLTs can be readily adapted to specific community needs while providing a galvanizing focus for a community organizing for economic justice.

The CLT can serve as a structural, economic, and political link between many kinds of development without compromising the independence or the distinctive features of any one. Any CLT has the capacity to develop cooperatives, condominiums, single-family housing, multiple rental units, and elderly housing within a neighborhood or over a geographic area. CLTs also can serve other land-use purposes, such as preserving open space and farmland and creating commercial facilities.

CLTs also meet a wide variety of housing needs for people with a broad range of incomes. People with very low incomes and assisted incomes participate in creating low-cost rental housing. Low-income families can find ownership and security in multifamily limited-equity cooperatives on CLT land. And people with moderate incomes who have been priced out of the housing market are discovering affordable single-family home ownership opportunities with CLTs.

| INVESTMENT VEHICLES

Individual investors and religious organizations sometimes make direct loans to CLTs to finance housing purchase, renovation, or construction costs. In these cases loans usually are made to nearby land trusts with whom the investor is familiar and can evaluate the loan's security and the CLT's progress at close range. Typically such loans are secured by the collateral value of the CLT land and housing.

Most individual investors prefer to lend to CLTs through qualified financial intermediaries, such as community loan funds (CLFs), whose staff evaluate CLT loan proposals and provide technical assistance when problems arise. Nonprofit loan funds also maintain loss reserves and spread investment risk among a pool of lenders.

HOW INVESTORS CAN PARTICIPATE. The Institute for Community Economics (ICE) Revolving Loan Fund (described in box 46-1) is one of the few national nonprofit financial intermediaries that enable socially concerned individuals to participate in financing CLTs. Its origins provide the first case in point.

In 1979 ICE received a call from a long-time associate, a Cincinnati minister, urgently seeking housing for a single mother and eight children facing eviction. ICE hastily brokered a $15,000 loan from one of its individual supporters to provide the down payment on a home, securing housing just in time.

That single loan launched two organizations: ICE's Revolving Loan Fund and the Community Land Co-operative of Cincinnati (CLCC), now one of the oldest community land trusts. CLCC has

BOX 46-1
INSTITUTE FOR COMMUNITY ECONOMICS

57 School Street
Springfield, Mass. 01105-1331
(413) 746-8660

The Institute for Community Economics (ICE), founded in 1967, is a national nonprofit organization.

MISSION AND INNOVATIONS

ICE's mission is to assist communities in developing the practical tools, skills, and local institutions for regaining control over their land, housing, capital, and other resources, and for insuring their appropriate use and economically just allocation. Its twenty-four staff members provide technical assistance and low-cost financing to community-based economic development groups that work to produce and preserve permanently affordable housing, jobs, and social services in communities where they are most needed. ICE also provides general information and educational materials on land, housing, and community investment issues to interested individuals.

ICE's two primary contributions to the community development field are the community land trust (CLT) and the community loan fund (CLF). These nonprofit community development institutions are designed to provide opportunities for people from all walks of life—including those with investment resources—to participate directly in community efforts to create urgently needed affordable housing, jobs, and services. Most of ICE's technical assistance efforts are aimed at assisting local communities in developing CLTs and loan funds.

The CLT is the institute's principal approach to creating permanently affordable housing, an approach to community development that ICE works to organize with local coalitions—religious groups, nonprofit developers, local public officials, and concerned citizens. Designed by ICE in 1967, the CLT is emerging rapidly among the most innovative and cost-effective methods of permanently preserving access to affordable housing and land for people with low and moderate incomes.

ICE serves as the principal provider of technical assistance to developing CLTs and currently coordinates a national network of more than one hundred community land trusts. These nonprofits operate in both urban and rural communities in twenty-three states. Most CLTs focus on developing and preserving affordable housing, though some also preserve farmland and commercial space to create affordable business opportunities.

REVOLVING LOAN FUND

ICE established its own national Revolving Loan Fund in 1979, to bridge the gap between community groups in need of low-cost capital and socially concerned investors wishing to participate in development efforts meeting urgent social needs. The fund often provides the critical financial catalyst that community land trusts and other community organizations need for their first projects—money that enables them to develop a track record and leverage conventional financing. It also is designed to help community development groups overcome credit barriers and expand, while encouraging banks and other conventional financial institutions by positive example to fulfill their community investment responsibilities.

Loans to the Fund

The fund accepts loans from both individual and institutional lenders and directs low-cost loans primarily to CLTs and other nonprofit community groups producing affordable housing. Of its nearly five hundred lenders, more than 80 percent are individuals. Other lenders include religious institutions, foundations, and other corporations.

The minimum amount lenders may place is $1,000 for at least one year. Average loans are placed for periods of two to five years and earn 5 percent interest (lenders may propose their own terms and interest rates; the fund's rates currently range from 0 to 6 percent).

Loans by the Fund

Borrowers must meet the fund's performance criteria and provide collateral for security. The fund is not insured, but it maintains a loan-loss reserve, provides technical assistance to borrowers, and holds a strong, ten-year track record of successful loan repayment.

Beginning with a single $15,000 loan, the fund has grown to a current portfolio of nearly $10 million, placing it among the largest funds of its kind in the United States. Since 1979 the ICE Revolving Loan Fund has placed over $18 million in 260 loans to innovative projects in 26 states. All lenders have been repaid at loan termination and the fund has written off only $11,000, a .06 percent loss rate. One of the oldest and largest funds of its kind in the United States, ICE's Revolving Loan Fund remains a pioneer of the growing community investment field.

COMMUNITY LOAN FUND MODEL

Guided by its own Revolving Loan Fund experience, ICE developed the community loan fund model to help replicate similar institutions regionally and in local communities. (See chapter 45, "Community Development Loan Funds.") Since 1983 ICE has provided start-up technical assistance to local and regional funds in the United States and Canada.

In 1986 the National Association of Community Development Loan Funds (NACDLF) incorporated with ICE's assistance. ICE provided staffing and management for the association during its first three years. Today the NACDLF is a fully independent nonprofit located in Philadelphia. Its forty member funds collectively manage more than $60 million in loan capital.

PUBLICATIONS

ICE publishes a quarterly newsletter, *Community Economics*, which provides news and information about the community land trust and community investment movements. ICE's resource list of publications includes the *Community Land Trust Handbook* (228 pages), the *Community Loan Fund Manual* (375 pages), the *Community Land Trust Legal Manual*, a CLT video, and other technical and general information resources. Contact ICE for free introductory information on the Revolving Loan Fund or community land trusts.

---

since gone on to develop thirty-eight units of housing with the low-income residents of Cincinnati's West End, using donations and financing provided solely by socially concerned investors. Other lenders include the Cornerstone Loan Fund—a Cincinnati-based intermediary—and the Dominican Sisters of the Sick Poor.

Amy Domini, coauthor of *Ethical Investing* and former treasurer of the Interfaith Center on Corporate Responsibility (ICCR) sums up the combined social and financial rewards of lending through community loan fund: "There is virtually no other type of investment that gives people the type of involvement and commitment where they can drive by a building and say—'I helped make that happen.' At the same time, investors have the security of knowing that their money is being managed by professionals who are skilled in evaluating financially sound projects that banks too often overlook."

SOME ICE PROJECTS. ICE's Revolving Loan Fund has grown to become a national nonprofit lending intermediary and is the largest CLF to provide financing for CLTs. Many of the forty member organizations of the National Association of Community Development Loan Funds (NACDLF) also direct social investor capital to CLTs. (See chapter 45, "Community Development Loan Funds.") The CLTs financed by the Revolving Loan Fund exemplify their surge:

The Rehab in Action to Improve Neighborhoods (RAIN) Community Land Trust is located on New York City's Lower East Side. With the help of the Lower East Side Catholic Area Conference, lower-income residents organized as homesteaders in 1981 to convert abandoned city-owned buildings into limited-equity cooperatives. ICE's Revolving Loan Fund made an early $35,000 loan that enabled the homesteaders to rent dumpsters and tools to empty and clean the vacant buildings.

The homesteaders successfully pressed recalcitrant city officials to grant them title to thirteen buildings, and they have sunk thousands of hours of "sweat equity" into building renovations, thereby lowering total costs by up to $15,000 per unit. In 1987 the homesteaders organized RAIN as a CLT to federate their scattered-site cooperatives into a single organization.

More than 150 units of housing are currently under construction, with over $7 million in public grants and loans from city, state, and federal housing programs. ICE's fund made an additional loan of $75,000 to help complete construction on two of RAIN's buildings. The RAIN Community Land Trust ground lease adds an extra layer of legal protection as well, ensuring that the buildings created with community labor and public investment will continue providing affordable housing for future generations.

The Rose City Community Land Trust for Housing is Connecticut's first CLT. Launched in a Norwich soup kitchen in 1986 at the initiative of a group of low-income residents displaced by downtown gentrification, Rose City focuses most of its efforts on renovating existing single-family and multifamily buildings for rental to very low-income people. Rose City has preserved eleven properties, providing housing for sixty people. One third of Rose City residents earn less than 25 percent of the area median income. Half fall below 50 percent of the median.

The trick for the land trust is scraping together funding sources and matching buildings with people. Rose City has received more than $200,000 in low-cost financing from ICE's Revolving Loan Fund. Other sources of financing include federal Community Development Block Grant funds, federal section 8 rental certificates, and state housing programs. To build community and cut rehab costs, each land trust resident is required to put "sweat equity" into a Rose City building. Forty prospective residents are now working on projects while waiting for a housing match.

Rose City is also the first nonprofit to receive property under

Connecticut's Surplus State Properties Program. Initiated in 1988, the program had inventoried thirty-eight surplus properties by mid-1991 and conveyed three to nonprofits, two of them to Rose City.

In contrast to Rose City, ICE's social investors played only a very small part in the success of the Burlington Community Land Trust in Burlington, Vermont. Launched in 1984 with a $200,000 seed grant from the city of Burlington, the Burlington CLT has developed more than one hundred units of housing, including transitional housing for women, multifamily co-ops, and moderately priced single-family homes. In 1987 the Burlington CLT was one of fifteen U.S. nonprofits recognized for innovative housing efforts by the United Nations during its International Year of Shelter for the Homeless. The Burlington CLT has secured an impressive array of financing, including a $1 million investment commitment from the city's employee pension fund and a $3 million line of credit from the Bank of Vermont for affordable CLT mortgage financing for potential homeowners.

ICE's fund has placed loans totaling more than $500,000 to provide acquisition financing for five dairy farms in southeastern Wisconsin. The Wisconsin Farmland Conservancy (WIFC) in Menomonie developed a CLT in 1987 as part of a strategy for creating affordable farming opportunities for younger or foreclosed farmers and for preserving the family farm system. Its strategy includes conservation-oriented farming methods, equipment sharing, establishment of informal networks of mutual support for WIFC farmers, and prevention of agricultural land loss.

Lenders to ICE's Revolving Loan Fund are contributing to a ground-breaking experiment in farmland preservation. They maintain 597 acres of farmland in permanent trust and increase the organizational strength of the farmland conservancy.

State and Federal CLT Investments

While financing from social investors has played a crucial role in catalyzing the development of CLTs, up-front commitments of state and federal resources are also clearly needed to bring down initial housing costs to affordable levels. For the most part, the private real estate market has not proven capable of creating and financing affordable housing on its own.

Long-term trends have opened a housing "affordability gap" that persists through both boom and bust market cycles. Research by the National Association of Homebuilders indicates that the costs of land and financing (mortgage interest rates) for single-family homes have been rising at twice the rate of other home building costs during the past forty years. Since 1975, wages have stagnated. The result is a wide gap between the wages of working people and the high prices of land and housing in their communities.

The impact of successful local CLTs is beginning to percolate upward. In 1987 legislatures in Connecticut and Vermont were the first to approve state funding programs specifically designed to re-direct state housing dollars to CLTs and other nonprofit developers of permanently affordable housing. Since then, Connecticut's Land Trust/Land Bank program has provided over $30 million to local projects. Vermont's Housing and Conservation Trust Fund has made available more than $20 million in state funding. In 1989 a $5 million bond issue for land trusts and permanently affordable housing was approved in Maine. And currently the Minnesota state legislature is considering a CLT funding bill.

To increase the participation of banks and state housing finance agencies in providing permanent mortgage financing for moderate-income housing on CLT land, ICE is working with local land trusts to win the backing of a major federal mortgage insurer, the Federal Housing Administration (FHA). In 1990 ICE and a Connecticut CLT negotiated modifications in the CLT's ground lease and gained FHA approval of the land trust lease as an insurable mortgage instrument.

The model lease already has been replicated in several Connect-icut land trust projects, securing lower-interest housing finance agency mortgages and the more flexible FHA insurance underwriting standards. This precedent has the potential to vastly broaden access to financing for moderate-income housing from mortgage lenders across the country that use FHA insurance. During the federal government's decade-long retreat from housing, CLTs made cost-effective use of scarce public resources, demonstrating in the process that both public dollars and farsighted housing policies are needed to create lasting solutions. But more of both are needed.

| TOWARD A LONG-TERM STRATEGY

At the beginning of the last decade, a report issued by the National Association of Homebuilders warned:

> Unless current trends are reversed soon, a housing crisis of unknown proportions could engulf this nation, pitting one generation of Amer-

icans against another, and further pushing from the mainstream of American society those who are being denied decent affordable housing—the young, the elderly and the poor.

This tragic prophecy continues to unfold in the 1990s. The federal government remains strapped by continuing budget deficits and mounting debt. Many state governments, buffeted by recession, are cutting housing budgets.

Federally subsidized mortgages on more than 340,000 units of low-cost rental housing built during the Great Society era are eligible for prepayment during the 1990s, freeing private owners to convert their units to market rate housing. Though Congress stepped in to require options for tenant buyouts in 1990, federal funding for such purchases has not been appropriated and remains uncertain. Nonetheless, a recent Massachusetts Institute of Technology study projects 9.4 million low-income rental units available in the year 2003 for 17.2 million income-eligible families, leaving a deficit of 7.8 million affordable housing units.

The Elements

This crisis in housing—with its combination of disinvestment and gentrification and the confluence of growing needs, declining production, and government budget deficits—presents unique challenges. To respond effectively, a housing program for the 1990s and beyond must have three strategic objectives:

1. providing decent affordable housing to those who need it most, with the essential benefits of home ownership where possible;
2. ensuring long-term affordability by controlling transfer costs, protecting the gains made today from being lost to the market tomorrow;
3. building an economic base in low-income communities, enabling residents to reinvest the fruits of their labor and benefit from their own economic development efforts.

Traditional housing programs and economic growth assumptions fail to meet these requirements. In different parts of the nation, economic upswings and downturns have caught a growing segment of the population in a housing squeeze. Neither the cooling of the Northeast real estate boom nor signs of recovery in the economically depressed oil-producing states substantially change the housing prospects of low-income families. In regions with rapidly escalating land and housing values, middle-income Americans as well as the poor are increasingly locked out of the home ownership market. They pay a growing portion of their income in rent and fall farther behind.

THE ROLE OF COMMUNITY LAND TRUSTS. The housing contributions of community land trusts and other nonprofit developers of permanently affordable housing represent only a small drop in an ocean of housing needs. Yet their innovative community-based solutions, founded on the simple proposition that affordable housing can and should stay permanently affordable, hold the promise of lasting gains for communities working to create secure housing for all of their residents.

CLTs and other community-based housing organizations will continue to gain momentum, slowly pushing state and federal housing policies, as small tugboats turn an ocean liner, in the direction of spending public resources only on permanent housing solutions. ICE technical assistance director Chuck Collins puts it this way: "We need more public/private partnerships like the land trust, which don't give away the public's equity stake every few years."

CLTs add a needed step on the housing ladder between rental housing and full-equity home ownership. They also strike a fair balance between competing public and private interests in housing, meeting immediate individual needs while conserving resources to create a community-controlled framework that can guide sustainable economic development that is appropriate to local conditions and needs.

On a small scale, CLTs demonstrate the practical makings of a new social contract in housing, one that in the 1990s may form the underpinnings of broader housing reform efforts combining fiscal conservatism and social justice. It is a movement that social investors can be proud to be part of, and proud to have joined "on the ground floor."

RESOURCES

PUBLICATIONS

Davis, J. 1991. *Contested Ground: Collective Action and the Urban Neighborhood.* Ithaca, N.Y.: Cornell University Press. 332 pp.

An analysis of community-based organizing and its relation to property ownership interests, this case study centers on the West End neighborhood of Cincinnati and the Community Land Cooperative of Cincinnati, the oldest existing community land trust.

Geisler, C., and F. Popper, eds. 1984. *Land Reform American Style*. Totowa, N.J.: Rowman & Allanheld. 338 pp.

This volume consists of eighteen essays on the history of land reform movements in North America. Current initiatives in agriculture and in rural and urban communities are discussed.

Institute for Community Economics. *Community Economics*. 16 pp.

This is the quarterly newsletter of the Institute for Community Economics. It provides news and updates on community land trusts and community loan funds and profiles local organizations. Articles on related nonprofit and local, state, and federal policy and program initiatives in housing and community investment fields are included.

————. 1982. *The Community Land Trust Handbook*. 228 pp. Emmaus, Pa.: Rodale Press.

This basic sourcebook of the origins and development of community land trust describes the CLT organizing process and includes case studies.

————. 1987. *The Community Loan Fund Manual*. Springfield, Mass.: Institute for Community Economics.

A basic sourcebook for organizing a community loan fund, this book includes detailed case studies.

Institute for Policy Studies Working Group on Housing. 1989. *The Right to Housing: A Blueprint for Housing the Nation*. 68 pp. Oakland, Calif.: Community Economics.

This brief primer outlining origins of the housing crisis proposes a program of federal initiatives designed to preserve existing affordable housing and create new limited-equity "social-sector" housing on a scale sufficient to meet the need.

National Association of Community Development Loan Funds. 1989. *Directory of Members and Associates*. 53 pp. Philadelphia: NACDLF.

One-page descriptions of each of the forty member loan funds of the NACDLF and example loans are provided. The introduction briefly describes the community development lending process.

ORGANIZATIONS

Institute for Community Economics
57 School Street
Springfield, Mass. 01105-1331
(413) 746-8660
Best single source of technical assistance and general information on community land trusts.

National Association of Community Development Loan Funds
924 Cherry Street
Philadelphia, Pa. 19107
(215) 923-4754
Information source on community loan funds, for investors interested in placing loans through nonprofit intermediaries to community land trust projects.

CHAPTER 47

MICROLENDING PROGRAMS

Jeffrey Ashe Director, Working Capital

This essay describes microlending. Microlending projects extend credit to the lowest rung of the entrepreneurial class. In developing countries these businesses can be as simple as selling oranges on a street corner, or managing a one-acre farm, or producing school uniforms on a treadle sewing machine. In North America microlending projects assist the full- and part-time self-employed, especially those with home-based "tabletop" businesses. There may be as many as a billion "microbusinesses" in the world, and they generate the livelihood for the great bulk of the world's population.

Well-designed and well-managed microlending projects reaching this "informal" economy can be cost-effective, large scale, and even profitable. The results have been very encouraging. The poor pay back their loans at a rate far higher than the rich, and the impact of very small loans on these microentrepreneurs translates directly into increased income, which is used for improved nutrition, housing, and health care. Basic needs, then, are taken care of through enterprise rather than handouts.

The ground-breaking methodology required for efficiently reaching these businesses devolves the decisions bankers usually make to the microentrepreneurs themselves. Deciding who should receive

Jeffrey Ashe has designed, evaluated, and administered microlending programs throughout Latin America, Asia, and Africa for the last twelve years, first as senior associate director of ACCION International and later as a consultant. In this country he assisted in the start-up of programs in Arkansas, North Carolina, South Dakota, and Ontario. He is currently director of Working Capital, a microlending program for Vermont, New Hampshire, and western Massachusetts, and consults to other programs. He has published widely in the microlending field.

loans, pressuring for loan repayment, and in some cases even managing local mobilized savings that are loaned back to the community are delegated to peer lending groups. In these projects loan officers act more as catalysts of an emerging group process than checkers of documents and credit ratings.

| THE IMPORTANCE OF THE INFORMAL SECTOR

The backbone of the economy of the developing world is the myriad of self-initiated, informal economic activities of the poor. In cities, the streets and back alleys teem with market vendors, food sellers, cobblers, and mechanics. In the villages, most struggle to supplement their meager income from farming with trading, crafts, and food processing. For the foreseeable future, microenterprises such as these will generate most of the income for the third world poor—especially women, those displaced by war and famine, and the landless. These intelligent, practical, and skilled entrepreneurs have managed to provide for their families through their own initiative despite the crushing obstacles of lack of affordable credit (the rates charged by moneylenders range from 20 percent a month to 10 or even 20 percent per day), exploitation, and government harassment.

The loans required to significantly change the profitability of these businesses may seem ridiculously small to us—$50 to perhaps a few hundred dollars often make the difference. A market vendor from Bogota, Colombia, provides a concrete example. Before she received a loan from an ACCION International project (see box 47-1), she went hat in hand to the middleman every morning to buy on credit the vegetables she would sell that day. In exchange she received the worst produce at the highest prices. When she joined the program, all of that changed. With her first $50 loan, she bought her produce for cash and increased her profits 20 percent. With her next loan, she increased the variety of the vegetables she sold, and with the third loan, she built a stand with an umbrella to display her produce and to protect herself from the sun. Within a year her profits had more than doubled.

This woman is typical of the some forty thousand microbusinesses assisted by ACCION International. ACCION delivers its services through a network of forty-five nonprofit intermediaries in thirteen Latin American countries and the United States.

BOX 47-1
ACCION INTERNATIONAL

130 Prospect Street
Cambridge, Mass. 02139
(617) 492-4930
(617) 876-9509 (fax)

THE BRIDGE FUNDS

ACCION International is a private nonprofit organization that was founded in 1961 to reduce poverty in the Americas. ACCION provides credit and business assistance to the self-employed poor of Latin America.

From Mexico to Chile, between one third and two thirds of those in the labor force cannot get jobs in the mainstream economy. Millions start their own little businesses, or microenterprises, in order to survive. These businesses are considered "informal" because they are not registered with governments or counted in national statistics. Yet an estimated 50 percent of all economic activity in the developing world takes place in this sector.

Since 1973 ACCION has concentrated its development efforts on assisting the self-employed poor of the informal sector. ACCION has proven that incomes can be dramatically increased and jobs can be efficiently created with the simple inputs of credit and basic business training. Over the last five years ACCION, working through local affiliate organizations in thirteen countries of the Americas, has lent $100 million in loans to 100,000 microenterprises. The loans averaged $300. Loan clients enjoy an average increase in income of 30 percent in one year. And a new job is created or strengthened with every $900 loaned.

> In a large outdoor market in Guatemala City, Maria del Carmen Hernandez sells shoes. She received a loan from ACCION for $100. She paid it back on time and with interest, and received a larger loan. Two years and eight loans later, Maria del Carmen says that the loans have changed her life. "Before," she explains, "my only source of credit was from loan sharks, who charged 25 percent per day. With the ACCION loans at 2.5 percent per month, I have been able to pay all of my debts, get out from under the loan sharks, and increase the size of my business."

The size of the informal sector and its demand for fair-rate credit led ACCION to develop a creative means to raise money for the revolving loan funds of its affiliates. The small credit needs of microenterprises, their lack of credit history or collateral, and their marginalization in the formal sector severely limit microentrepreneurs to access bank credit. ACCION decided to create a guarantee mechanism that would enable banks to open their doors to this otherwise ineligible population.

Because of the difficulties of obtaining donated or concessionary funds, ACCION needed to access local bank resources for its target population. To meet this need, ACCION International in 1984 designed the Bridge Fund. Through the *compensating deposit* mechanism, individuals and institutions in the United States could lend money to ACCION. ACCION would use the money to guarantee credit extended by Latin American banks to microentrepreneurs. (Compensating deposit programs are described in chapter 48.)

The Bridge Fund "credit chain" works as follows: loans to ACCION are used to purchase certificates of deposit, government agency bonds, and other socially screened low-risk financial instruments in the United States. These U.S. deposits are then used as collateral for the issuance of guarantees, in the form of standby letters of credit, by the U.S. bank in favor of banks in Latin America. Based on these letters of credit, the Latin American banks lend to ACCION's affiliate organizations, which in turn use the funds to lend to the microentrepreneurs.

The compensating deposit mechanism enables Bridge Fund lenders to significantly leverage their money. On average, ACCION guarantees only 55 percent of the credit extended by local banks, with a maximum guarantee of 90 percent. Funds also are leveraged at the microenterprise program level, since ACCION's revolving loan funds turn over an average of 3.5 times per year. So that for every dollar in the Bridge Fund, an average of $6.50 is lent each year to the self-employed poor.

As an institution, ACCION projects significant growth in the next ten years. ACCION will increase its number and size of programs in Latin America, the Caribbean, and, increasingly, North America. In order to reach hundreds of thousands of clients, ACCION will count on expanding resources in the Bridge Fund. ACCION also will explore new mechanisms for obtaining funds for local affiliates that use Bridge Fund guarantees but do not involve banks. Possible future uses for Bridge Fund loans include providing guarantees so that ACCION affiliates can access blocked currencies (multinational corporations often hold resources in local currencies that, because of host country laws and regulations, cannot be repatriated) and for the issuance of bonds and certificates of deposit at the local level.

For information on how to make a loan to the Bridge Fund, see chapter 48.

Microenterprises and microentrepreneurs are not only a developing world phenomena. In the United States, 8.5 percent of the labor force receives part or all of its income from self-employment, and the net increase in the number of self-employed is close to 500,000 businesses a year. There are 8.4 million businesses with gross receipts of less than $25,000. A total of 9.35 million businesses have no employees.

Ironically, the owners of the smallest businesses in this country face virtually the same problems getting a business loan as do their third world counterparts. Of a group of seven businesses in Bellows Falls, Vermont, I recently trained as part of the Working Capital project I direct, four had been denied business credit by banks and the other three had not even bothered asking. We financed them all. Who were they? An animal trainer; a firewood seller; a jeweler; a distributor of high-tech cloth diapers; a taxi cab operator; a woodworker; and a flea market operator. They are typical of the more than 110,000 self-employed businesspeople in the hard-hit towns and rural areas of Vermont, New Hampshire, and western Massachusetts where Working Capital is beginning to provide credit services.

So far, all of those participating in the project have made good use of their initial $500 test loans. They can expect their line of credit to expand in steps to $5,000 per business if their payments on the smaller loans are exemplary. Six New England banks provide the funds.

| THE IMPORTANCE OF MICROLENDING

Hundreds of millions of microentrepreneurs in the developing world and several million in this country and Canada could use loans for their businesses. But this demand for capital means little if there is no effective way to deliver credit services to them. The development of efficient programs that assist these smallest entrepreneurial initiatives has been one of the most significant innovations in the area of community economic development of the last ten years. Table 47-1 lists several international microlending programs.

Most of the programs use one variation or another of "peer group lending," where groups ranging from four to thirty business-owning members are provided access to a rapidly increasing line of credit, with future loans contingent on repaying the previous ones. Peer group pressure keeps loan repayment high. The best known of these programs is the Grameen Bank of Bangladesh, which is currently lending to more than 800,000 virtually landless, mostly illiterate villagers, 85 percent of whom are women. Loan repayment is over 98 percent on loans that average less than $70. The interest charged to borrowers covers operational costs (although international donors provide capital to the bank at below market rates). Similar programs are underway in other Asian countries, in Latin America, and in Africa. Most of them reach a few hundred to a few thousand borrowers, although a handful are assisting more than 100,000 businesses.

In this country and Canada, more than twenty projects have adopted the peer group model, although the objectives and the specific form of these programs vary widely. These North American projects are too new to have produced the kind of results that have been seen in the developing country programs, and most are still feeling their way as they adapt third world methodologies to North America. See table 47-2 for a list of American programs.

The Impact of Microenterprise Projects

As I designed and evaluated peer group projects in Africa, Asia, and Latin America, I have been struck by the ways they transform the communities they serve. At the most obvious level, the income of those involved with the projects often increases 30 to 75 percent. And new jobs are created at one tenth to one twentieth the cost of investment in larger enterprises. This new income is used most commonly to improve housing, diet, health care, and education, especially when women receive loans. These chronic problems of poverty, then, are dealt with through self-sustaining entrepreneurship that leads to increased income and opportunities rather than more handouts. Increased income from the businesses that have received loans, in turn, stimulates other businesses in the community. The rickshaw puller can afford to buy more food, which means more income for the market vendor, who buys more from the farmers, who can now afford to be transported by the rickshaw puller, and so on.

On a personal level, participation in these projects translates directly into increased aspirations, self-esteem, and skills, since often for the first time in their lives, poor people can see a way to get out of poverty—or at least a way to mitigate its impact. Another out-

TABLE 47-1

INTERNATIONAL MICROLENDING PROGRAMS

ACCION International	Pioneer in microlending since 1974. Working with 40,000 businesses in 13 Latin American countries.
CARE	Extensive network of projects, especially in Africa and Asia.
CARE Canada	Microcredit programs in Africa and Asia.
FINCA	Pioneered the innovative Village Bank methodology. Extensive work in Latin America, especially Central America.
Freedom From Hunger	Fast-growing projects in Africa and Latin America. Major innovator in developing programs that start with a microenterprise program and then incorporate health and nutritional education.
Opportunity International	Microenterprise projects in Asia and Latin America.
Save the Children	Microenterprise programs around the world.
Technoserve	Develops larger-scale cooperative ventures incorporating many poor entrepreneurs, mainly in Africa and Latin America.
Trickle Up Program	Innovative program providing $50 grants for business start-ups. Operates in 90 countries.

NOTE: This by no means exhaustive list covers some of the major players in the microlending field. But new programs are being started continually. The community investment directory in the back of the almanac contains addresses and phone numbers for all of the programs listed here.

come is better-organized communities that take on issues ranging from exploitation by landlords to participation in local politics, to starting new schools, to improving the status of women.

These psychological and organizational outcomes are at least as important as increased income and employment. They occur virtually automatically as a consequence of the business owners working in a group and helping one another. Since these groups meet year after year, whatever process of change has been started continues over time and builds in intensity and sophistication. The groups I interviewed that started three years earlier addressed community and business issues on an entirely different level than new groups.

I expect that peer group projects will create a similar dynamic for positive change in this country, because entrepreneurs at the lowest level here face the same problems as their counterparts in Bangladesh or Bolivia: lack of encouragement, information, and capital. This process of change is already beginning to emerge in Athol, Massachusetts, where Working Capital has been active for only a few months. Participants comment on how much less isolated they feel, information and advice pass freely, and the rudiments of a "mini–chamber of commerce" are beginning to form.

Why These Projects Can Work so Well

Peer group lending projects work so well because they deal with all three of these components—encouragement, information, and capital—all at once.

- Encouragement—loans are provided through a peer group that meets frequently and becomes a source of support for the borrowers.
- Information—contacts, knowledge, and linkages are provided among borrowers and some (limited) technical assistance is provided outside the group.
- Capital—the loans provide the resources that businesses need to grow.

The power of combining all three of these elements in a single program can best be understood by reflecting a moment on the enormous progress made by recently arrived Koreans in Manhattan. Korean entrepreneurs are in constant contact with their friends and relatives who are also entrepreneurs. Their businesses are tied together into an interlocking, synergistic network that creates wealth. The Korean community provides the capital businesses need to get started and grow. A dollar entering the community is exchanged fourteen times before it leaves. By contrast, in most minority and Native American communities, a dollar entering often leaves before it is exchanged even once. There is virtually no wealth-generating multiplier effect.

Peer group lending programs create the base for a structure that builds in the kinds of advantages enjoyed by Korean entrepreneurs. The peer group provides encouragement, contacts, knowledge, and linkages, and the program provides access to credit.

TABLE 47-2

NORTH AMERICAN MICROLENDING PROGRAMS

First People's Fund	Links Canadian banks with reserve managed loan funds throughout Canada. Cost-effective model. Based on peer group lending methodology.
Good Faith Fund	A program of Southern Development Bancorporation, which is affiliated with the South Shore Bank of Chicago. One of the first programs in the United States to adopt the Grameen Bank methodology.
Lakota Fund	Sioux Indians. Combines a microenterprise program with an intensive social education program.
Neighborhood Reinvestment	Start-up of peer group projects in Philadelphia, Pasadena, and elsewhere.
Women's Enterprise Development Corporation	One of the oldest projects in North America. Excellent track record in dealing with women on public assistance. Provides loans to individual businesses.
Women's Self Employment Program	Deals with the smallest-scale women-owned enterprises in Chicago.
Working Capital	Provides credit to self-employed in western Massachusetts, Vermont, and New Hampshire. Loan fund provided by six New England banks. Major concern with scale and cost-effectiveness. Provides a "turnkey" package of services to eleven local development agencies that implement the project in their service areas. Loans start out at $500 and build to $5,000. Entire loan repayment to date: 100%.

NOTE: This by no means exhaustive list covers some of the major players in the microlending field. But new programs are being started continually. The community investment directory in the back of the almanac contains addresses and phone numbers for all of the programs listed here.

| HOW SOCIALLY RESPONSIBLE INVESTORS CAN BECOME INVOLVED

Microlending programs may be appropriate for investors who want to place part of their resources in investments that could be of major importance in dealing with some of the most intractable problems of our nation and the developing world. Investors should see themselves as participating in an initiative that encourages entrepreneurship among those once denied this opportunity. Their investments create a structure of mutual support, community involvement, and wealth that will help transform disadvantaged communities.

Investors can get involved in several ways, ranging from passive to active.

1. Investments in loan-loss reserve funds—investors can place their money at risk in a fund that will provide a loan-loss reserve to encourage the participation of banks in these programs. Investors receive the normal rate that they would from a certificate of deposit. Their money is protected by an up-front guarantee provided by the implementing agency and the participating borrowers. If this first line of defense is exhausted, the investors' money is at risk. ACCION International's Bridge Fund provides this defense for the programs it works with. There have been no losses to the fund, which currently has $4.5 million in deposits.

2. Investments in loan funds for borrowers at below market interest rates—an investment in a loan fund at below market rates significantly reduces the amount of grant funding required for programs to cover their operational costs or makes it possible to reduce the interest rate charged to borrowers. For example, Working Capital is looking for below market investments in a loan fund that will match the contribution of the banks dollar for dollar. Projections show that the additional 3 percent spread received by the program will reduce the need for grant funding by $272,000 over six years. It also will generate a $97,000 surplus as the loan portfolio grows to close to $11 million and serve more than two thousand businesses. Virtually any microcredit program would welcome this kind of investment.

3. Donations to programs that are assisting the informal sector—programs always need additional resources to invest. Con-

tributions can be invested in either the organizations carrying out the various programs or specific businesses, communities, or "village banks." The donor "adopts" a number of the businesses of the poor in a community, so bootstrap entrepreneurship rather than welfare deals with the problems of poverty.

4. Long-term investments in programs with the expectation of recouping this investment through the profits generated—as an example of that strategy, ACCION and the Calmeadow Foundation are actively seeking private investors to create a private bank for the informal sector in Bolivia. The bank's initial customers will be the ten thousand borrowers already participating in an ACCION-sponsored program.

This list is hardly definitive. A group of investors might explore ways they could collaborate with microloan practitioners in this country. They might even want to launch a microcredit program combining a vision of serving the disadvantaged with some of the management techniques of the private sector. The active participation of socially motivated private investors may be able to greatly expand the number of business owners being reached.

RESOURCES

ACCION International. "An Operational Guide for Micro-Enterprise Projects."
    The ACCION methodology is presented in an easy-to-follow format. Also available in Spanish. ACCION International, 130 Prospect Street, Cambridge, Mass. 02139.
Ashe, Jeffrey, and Christopher Cosslett. "Credit for the Poor," United Nations Development Programme.
    This step-by-step guide for setting up a microenterprise program is available from: United Nations Publications, Room DC2-0853, New York, N.Y. 10017. (Sales number: E.89.III.B.6.)
"Training Resources for Small Enterprise Development—From the Community of SEEP Agencies."
    This is an evaluation of a large range of training materials for microenterprise projects, including videos, manuals, computer programs, and so on. SEEP, c/o PACT, 777 United Nations Plaza, New York, N.Y. 10017.

COMPENSATING DEPOSIT PROGRAMS: HOW ONE PROGRAM WORKS

Gabriela Romanow ACCION International

Two compensating deposit programs are in operation today: ACCION International's Bridge Fund and the Industrial Cooperative Association (ICA) Revolving Loan Fund. This chapter describes how ACCION International operates. The unique aspect of ACCION's program is its mission of reducing poverty among the self-employed poor in communities throughout the Americas. ACCION itself is described in chapter 47.

Through ACCION's Bridge Fund, interested parties make loans to ACCION that are pooled with other Bridge Fund monies in a trust account under ACCION's name at Citibank. These funds never leave the United States but, rather, are used as collateral. Based on the funds lodged in the trust account, the commercial bank in the United States issues a guarantee in the form of a standby letter of credit in favor of a local bank in Latin America. With the letter of credit guarantee, the local bank makes resources available to ACCION's local affiliates for lending to microentrepreneurs.

MAKING A LOAN TO THE FUND

In order to make a loan to ACCION, the lender requests a loan agreement from ACCION's Bridge Fund Department. ACCION sends the loan agreement along with simple instructions as to how to fill it out. The lender then writes a check to ACCION for a minimum of $10,000 (this amount may change over the next few years). The term of the loan is a minimum of eighteen months; longer terms are encouraged. He or she sends the check and the signed loan agreement to ACCION.

ACCION then signs the loan agreement as well as a promissory note, retaining the original loan agreement and a copy of the promissory note. The lender receives a copy of the loan agreement and the original promissory note, evidence of ACCION's legal obligation. ACCION pays a maximum of 5 percent interest on loans. A lender may write any amount up to 5 percent into the loan agreement. ACCION makes interest payments semiannually, on June 30 and December 31. Any earnings of the Bridge Fund above and beyond the interest payments to lenders help defray ACCION's costs of operating the fund.

Once a lender sends the check to ACCION, the lender does not have to do anything more. ACCION automatically sends interest payments and keeps lenders informed of Bridge Fund operations through two semiannual updates. In addition, lenders receive a quarterly bulletin from ACCION describing program activities as well as an annual report with audited financial statements.

At least two months before a loan reaches maturity, ACCION sends the lender a letter accompanied by a simple form to be filled out if the lender wishes to renew the loan. Otherwise the loan is repaid at the agreed maturity date.

| HOW THE MONEYS ARE APPLIED

When the loan is received, ACCION deposits the check into the Bridge Fund trust account at Citibank. ACCION chose Citibank as its depository institution because of the bank's excellent investment management team; extensive branch and correspondent bank network throughout the Americas; effectiveness and cost efficiency in issuing international letters of credit; and willingness to work within a framework of socially responsible investment criteria.

The portfolio manager pools the proceeds of Bridge Fund loans and channels them into socially screened vehicles chosen by ACCION (with the advice of Kinder, Lydenberg, Domini & Company) in accordance with ACCION's conservative investment parameters. These vehicles may include certificates of deposit and time deposits fully insured by FDIC at such banks as the South Shore Bank of Chicago and Community Capital Bank in Brooklyn; commercial paper rated at least A-1 by Standard & Poor's or Prime-1 by Moody's Investor Service; and obligations issued or guaranteed by the United States or an agency or instrumentality thereof.

OBTAINING A BRIDGE FUND GUARANTEE

In Latin America and, increasingly, in the United States, affiliate programs request Bridge Fund guarantees when they need resources for their revolving loan funds. ACCION carries out an extensive financial review of each affiliate and of the banks that will make the loans to the affiliate. Based on this review, ACCION determines whether the affiliate is eligible to participate in the Bridge Fund and, if so, the dollar amount of Bridge Fund monies it will commit to a given program.

ACCION bases its decision on the financial condition and performance of the affiliate and the local bank; the affiliate's compliance with terms spelled out in the agreement between ACCION and the affiliate, and comparative need (among affiliate programs). ACCION currently works in fourteen countries; the Bridge Fund is operating in eight.

Upon a request by ACCION, and based on Bridge Fund collateral, the U.S. bank issues a letter of credit in favor of the local bank working with the ACCION affiliate. When the local bank receives the letter of credit, it disburses funds to the affiliate in accordance with a prior arrangement. The financing generally is structured as a revolving line of credit with a maturity of one year and usually is refinanced.

At present ACCION guarantees an average of 55 percent of the credit extended by the local bank and will negotiate no more than a 90 percent guarantee. In this way, funds are significantly leveraged at the program level.

PROVISION FOR LOSSES

Bridge Fund monies have two principal layers of protection. Each affiliate maintains a loan-loss reserve of between 2 and 5 percent locally, based on the program's historical loan-loss record and estimated future losses. ACCION's programs overall maintain a 98 percent payback rate.

In addition, ACCION itself has a loan-loss reserve in dollars totaling 5 percent of the amount of outstanding letters of credit. The Public Welfare Foundation, the Charles Stewart Mott Foundation, and other private foundations, corporations, and individuals have funded this reserve. ACCION holds the loan-loss reserve in units of up to $100,000 in FDIC-insured institutions that are nationally recognized by the socially responsible investment community.

To date, the Bridge Fund has experienced no losses. But if losses were ever to be so great as to exhaust the affiliates' and ACCION's loan-loss reserves, Bridge Fund lenders would absorb the losses on a pro rata basis. Therefore, lenders with $10,000 in the Bridge Fund would lose one tenth of what a lender with $100,000 would lose. The only exception to this rule applies to the Ford Foundation. In March 1991 ACCION received a program-related investment of $2 million from the Ford Foundation for the Bridge Fund. The loan agreement governing the program-related investment stipulates that Ford Foundation losses will be limited to $100,000. But, in addition, the agreement states that affiliate programs using guarantees from proceeds of the Ford Foundation loan must maintain, locally, a higher loan-loss reserve of 5 percent.*

---

*For further information, contact the Bridge Fund, ACCION International, 130 Prospect Street, Cambridge, Mass. 02139 (617/492-4930).

CHAPTER 49

INSTITUTIONALLY ORIENTED PROGRAMS

A few of the community development programs are designed specifically to appeal particularly to the institutional investor. As large intermediaries offering both financial and technical assistance, these funds frequently are crucial to the development of affordable housing in cities across America.

The New York–based Local Initiatives Support Corporation (LISC) was created in 1980, largely with funding from the Ford Foundation. Its mandate is to raise funds for "locally created, locally executed" community development projects. LISC has been tremendously successful in raising funds for this important work and has emerged as a strong participant nationally in development projects.

Institutionally oriented programs fill an important need. The access to capital that will commit to a program for ten or fifteen years is beyond the reach of many of the grassroots community development efforts. These institutional funds, along with the Central Fund at the National Association of Community Development Loan Funds (see chapter 45) have an important role to play in taking community development the next step.

CONSUMER AND

EMPLOYMENT

ISSUES AFFECTING

SOCIAL INVESTING

Based on her interviews with prospective clients, one well-regarded socially responsible investment money manager believes that product quality and consumer issues will dominate social investing in the 1990s. A top social researcher predicts that the emerging issues will relate to social welfare, particularly health and retirement benefits. This unit looks at what some experts think are the coming issues.

For some years, Richard Freierman and Steve Bennett have watched the interplay between business and environmental concerns. They argue that after many false starts, consumers are bringing their environmental concerns into their purchasing decisions. Longtime editor of the *Boycott News*, Todd Putnam would agree, though the environment is only one cause whose advocates he sees bringing effective pressure to bear on corporations.

And, what about the savings and loan–banking crisis? Have we seen the end of it? Not according to Tom Schlesinger. He sees more crises to come, particularly in the interplay between the banks and the environment.

The relationship between employees and their employers appears likely to reemerge in the nineties, after being in eclipse for more than twenty years. Diane Bratcher discusses a new campaign to encourage workers to protect the rights of gays and lesbians in the work force. How companies treat these employees reveals much about their attitudes toward workers generally.

Employee ownership was a radical concept twenty years ago. Today, thanks to its usefulness as an antitakeover device, it hardly occasions comment. Corey Rosen has great hopes for employee ownership where workers have a real voice in their companies. David Sand sees organized labor playing a greater role in the governance of corporations through the shares its pension funds own. He expects labor to take a more aggressive role in the 1990s.

GREEN CONSUMING

Richard Freierman and Steven J. Bennett
Bennett Information Group

On August 15, 1989, Wal-Mart ran a full-page ad in the *Wall Street Journal* encouraging manufacturers to join forces with them in creating products that will not harm the environment. The headline read: WE'RE LOOKING FOR QUALITY PRODUCTS THAT ARE GUARANTEED NOT TO LAST: WE'RE CHALLENGING OUR MANUFACTURING PARTNERS TO IMPROVE THEIR PRODUCTS, TO HELP PREVENT LASTING ENVIRONMENTAL PROBLEMS.

Earlier that year, the giant discounter had conducted a survey and discovered that a large percentage of its customers, who hailed from the ranks of the rural lower and middle class, were willing to pay a premium for environmentally sound goods. This result surprised many trend analyzers, most of whom had assumed that the environment was largely the concern of affluent, urban professionals.

Shortly after the Wal-Mart ad appeared, "green products" became one of the hottest topics in the media. In England *The Green Consumer* became a runaway best-seller. In the United States a mail-order company, Seventh Generation, located in Colchester, Vermont, made headlines with its extensive offerings of environ-

---

Richard Freierman and *Steven J. Bennett*, respectively, are the managing and executive directors of the Bennett Information Group, a research consortium that studies business and environmental issues. The group has published *The Green Pages* (Random House, 1990), a guide to nine hundred environmentally safe products, and *Save the Earth at Work!* (Bob Adams, 1990), which teaches employees and business owners how to create environmentally safe and responsible workplaces. Bennett is also the author of *Ecopreneuring* (John Wiley, 1991), a complete guide for environmental entrepreneurs. Bennett and Freierman are the coauthors of *Green Inc.* (John Wiley, 1992), which describes how major corporations can build cultures that foster positive environmental thinking and action.

mentally sound products. And by Earth Day 1990, the twentieth anniversary of the first such event, supermarkets throughout the nation began highlighting green products. Consumer product makers began trumpeting the environmental soundness of goods ranging from deodorants made without ozone-destroying chlorofluorocarbons (CFCs) to trash bags designed to degrade in landfills. Today, Fortune 500 companies and cottage enterprises alike are introducing new green products every week that vie for shelf space with traditional products.

| ANATOMY OF A GREEN PRODUCT

Green products are the environmentally safe counterparts of the traditional products purchased for use in the kitchen, laundry, nursery, bathroom, workshop, and other areas of the home. They do not contain substances that are harmful to the users and, when disposed of, they do not cause environmental damage. For example, many traditional personal-care products contain small amounts of formaldehyde, a known carcinogen. Green personal-care products are formaldehyde-free and do not contain artificial coloring, dyes, or other substances deemed unnecessary. In addition, green products contain no petroleum-based ingredients. Instead they use vegetable-based substances whose production does not pose the pollution problems associated with oil drilling, transport, and refining.

Green paper products (napkins, coffee filters, paper towels, toilet paper, and other products) are not only made from recycled paper, but they are unbleached as well. Conventional paper-making processes entail chlorine bleaching, a byproduct of which is the release of dioxin, the same highly toxic substance found in the herbicide Agent Orange. Unbleached and oxygen-bleached papers are free from potential dioxin contamination. More important, their manufacture does not contribute to dioxin pollution from the paper mills.

In the food aisle, green products are pesticide-free, dye-free, and preservative-free. Not only are foods healthier without pesticides, but reduced demand for foodstuffs grown with pesticides will lead to lower levels of chemical runoff into waterways.

In addition to environmentally safe formulations, green products are wrapped in minimal packaging and use recycled and recyclable materials where possible. When plastics are called for, they tend to be the recyclable PET and HDPE varieties, with close attention paid to the overall amount of packaging required. Finally, cellophane—

a truly biodegradable material—is being used increasingly instead of clear plastic wrap.

Ecomarketing

The growing demand for green products has not gone unnoticed by marketeers at large corporations. In 1989 the late Malcolm Forbes summed up the situation like this: "If 90% of your customers paid you to package 'green,' wouldn't you be awfully stupid not to?" Forbes posed the question after citing a Gallup poll that revealed:

- 92 percent of men and 96 percent of women would make a special effort to buy products from companies trying to protect the environment;
- 96 percent of men and 94 percent of women would be willing to give up some convenience, such as disposability, in return for environmentally safer products or packing;
- 87 percent of men and 90 percent of women would be willing to pay more for products or packaging made environmentally safer.

Studies that examine the habits and practices of green consumers more closely provide a glimpse of just how complicated the issues of green products can be. A 1990 survey conducted by the Roper Organization and cited in *American Demographics* divided the country in terms of environmental attitudes and behaviors: True-Blue Greens, Greenback Greens; Sprouts; Grousers; and Basic Browns. Although the truly committed environmental consumers (True-Blue Greens and Greenback Greens) make up less than 25 percent of the American public, they include in their ranks some of the most affluent and well-educated consumers. In addition, women outnumber men by more than 50 percent in these two groups. Surprisingly, 43 percent of the True-Blue Greens described themselves as politically conservative (that was the highest percentage cited by any group).

| GREEN MARKETING AND THE LAW

Many environmentalists view with caution the discovery that a large percentage of the public is eager to purchase green products. The demand for green products has led to a spate of dubious claims and the misuse of the words *green, environmentally friendly,* and *biodegradable.* The term *biodegradable* in particular has raised the hackles of lawmakers, especially when applied to plastics. Biodegradable plastics do not decompose under the conditions existing in most landfills, and many environmentalists consider them to be marketing scams. After several state attorneys general filed suit against them, Mobil Oil Company ceased using the term *degradable* to describe its Hefty trash bag line.

Some lawmakers have aggressively pursued companies that use misleading labeling. For example, Hubert Humphrey III, attorney general of Minnesota, has joined a ten-state task force to study the misuse of environmental labeling. As an example of the problems with environmental marketing, consider Consort hair spray, made by Alberto-Culver. For a time the product was labeled "ozone friendly," because it was made without ozone-destroying CFCs. To the layperson, the fact that the product does not contain CFCs sounds good. In fact, CFCs have been banned by law since 1978, so the company was merely complying with regulations. Worse, the substitutes used contain volatile organic compounds (VOCs), which are major contributors to ground-level smog. Alberto-Culver has removed the ozone-friendly claim from the product.

Sometimes the task of debunking a green marketing claim can be more complicated—for example, a new Heinz ketchup bottle claimed to be made from recyclable plastic. If, however, as the Natural Resources Defense Council points out, the nearest plastic recycling facility is hundreds of miles away, that ketchup bottle is headed for the nearest landfill. According to Heinz's vice president for consumer products, David Ruder, the company will work to initiate plastic recycling programs where there are none. In addition, he claims that the label will help educate consumers about how to recycle plastics.

The terms *recycled* or *recyclable* are widely abused because of vague regulations. The U.S. Environmental Protection Agency (EPA) has deemed that inclusion of mill scraps, converter scraps (from processes such as making envelopes), and sawdust could all be used to meet criteria for the label "recycled." While it certainly is preferable to use these materials for making new paper rather than simply discarding them, the fact is that they have *always been recycled.* The use of these scraps does nothing to reduce the amount of so-called postconsumer waste being sent to landfills. Fortunately, many manufacturers and distributors of paper products are now guaranteeing minimum percentages of true postconsumer waste in their products.

It remains to be seen whether the skepticism from consumers about green claims will result in more responsible practices by manufacturers. Senator Frank Lautenberg of New Jersey has filed legislation that would require the EPA to establish standards and definitions for environmental claims. And a group of marketers representing such companies as Procter & Gamble, Lever Brothers, and Kraft General Foods is petitioning the Federal Trade Commission to adopt a national green standard. There is likely to be animated debate as industry, federal, and state representatives submit their own guidelines for environmental advertising and packaging copy.

RESOURCES

BOOKS AND PUBLICATIONS

A number of books have been written that describe the nature and selection of green products. The most informative include:

Elkington, John, Julia Hailes, and Joel Makower. 1990. *The Green Consumer.* New York: Penguin.
　　The American version of the best-selling English book credited with helping to launch the green products movement in Europe contains useful information about the need for green products and how nongreen products can damage the fragile environment.
Bennett Information Group. 1990. *The Green Pages.* New York: Random House.
　　This is the first applied green products book. It presents more than nine hundred green products and describes their environmentally positive qualities (formulation, packaging, and so on). The first part is designed to enable consumers to make specific purchasing decisions at their local supermarket or natural foods store. The second part lists products found in mail-order catalogs. Addresses and telephone numbers for each catalog are provided.

PEOPLE AND GROUPS
Environmental Defense Fund
257 Park Avenue South
New York, N.Y. 10010
(212) 505-2100

Greenpeace
1436 U Street NW
Washington, D.C. 20009
(202) 462-1177

Natural Resources Defense Council
40 West Twentieth Street
New York, N.Y. 10011
(212) 727-2700

The Environmental Defense Fund, Greenpeace, and NRDC have been extremely active in researching and challenging industry claims of environmental friendliness. All three organizations have taken strong advocacy positions in the green products arena and have issued studies and position papers on the subject.

Green Seal
30 Irving Place, Ninth Floor
New York, N.Y. 10003
(212) 533-SEAL
Founded in 1990, Green Seal assesses the environmental desirability of products from manufacturing through disposal. The group has developed criteria for a broad range of consumer products.

Marketing Intelligence Service
33 Academy Street
Naples, N.Y. 14512
(716) 374-6326
Marketing Intelligence Service is a research firm that tracks new product introductions from numerous sectors of the economy. Its on-line data base includes products deemed green by their manufacturers. In addition to conducting custom data base searches, Marketing Intelligence Service publishes special reports on product trends.

Seventh Generation
Colchester, Vt. 05446-1672
(802) 655-6777
The premier mail-order source of green products, Seventh Generation, offers items ranging from canvas shopping bags and environmentally safe cleaners to energy-efficient lightbulbs and rechargeable batteries. The company's catalogs are also excellent sources of information about a variety of environmental issues.

BOYCOTTS:
VOTING WITH YOUR DOLLARS

Todd Putnam *National Boycott News*

Each dollar spent amounts to a vote in favor of a corporation, its policies and practices.

While the term *boycott* has been with us only since 1880, the concept is as ancient as it is simple. The principle behind the boycott is familiar to most: if you disapprove of something, don't support it. Boycotting, broadly defined, is the withholding of economic, social, or political participation as a means of protesting or forcing the alteration of various policies or practices deemed unjust or unfair by the boycotter. Today, however, the term usually is used to describe an organized collective effort by individual consumers to effect changes in the policies or activities of particular businesses or governments by refusing to purchase products or services.

| BOYCOTT STRATEGY: CHANGING WITH THE TIMES

Perhaps the best-known American boycott was called in 1773 by American colonists who refused to buy tea to protest taxes imposed by the British government. But it was not until Irish tenants decided to ostracize—socially and economically—a particularly ruthless rent collector, Charles Boycott, that this classic strategy finally was named. In 1920 Mohandas Gandhi called for a boycott of British linen to protest the repressive nature of British colonialism in India. The success of that boycott led Gandhi to launch a boycott ten years later against British salt to protest Britain's continued refusal to allow India's independence.

Also during the first half of this century, boycotts had taken hold in the United States. Labor unions used the boycott to force businesses to recognize the unionization of workers. American Jewish groups called for boycotts of German products to protest that country's anti-Semitic policies. In 1955 a boycott led to the integration of the public bus system in Montgomery, Alabama. That success led to the widespread use of the tactic by the civil rights movement in its efforts to integrate other businesses. Since then, the consumer boycott has been used to protest everything from human rights abuses and wars to environmental destruction and the testing of products on animals.

The 1980s: A Sea Change

Until recently, the primary goal of the consumer boycott had been to cause a loss in the target's sales as a direct result of the redirection of boycotters' spending. The objective was to enlist as many boycotters as possible and thereby increase the cost to the corporation.

In the 1980s American business underwent enormous changes. The corporate world was swept by a whirlwind of mergers, takeovers, and buyouts. Since then, an ever-decreasing number of conglomerates controlled more and more businesses and product lines. At the same time, the mood of the country seemed to shift away from the social progress of the sixties and seventies toward cynicism and personal enrichment.

These changes amounted to a triple whammy for boycotters. Not only were companies bigger and more powerful than ever, but deregulation allowed them to act with greater impunity and irresponsibility toward the environment, workers, consumers, and people in the third world. To top it off, Americans appeared less interested than before in dealing with social problems.

So how, in the 1980s, did boycotters go about trying to get a less-sympathetic public to boycott companies with seemingly endless lists of products to be avoided? A look at how corporations were going about marketing their products to the public provides the answer.

From a Numbers Game to an Image Game

The American market has become heavily saturated with consumer products, so it is increasingly difficult for companies to get an edge on their competition. In many cases competing products are so similar that few differences stand out. For these reasons, among others, more and more companies use image advertising to create market differentiation. By associating products with a highly crafted image, such advertisements presumably wear down the critical and analytical thought processes of the viewer. This approach sells products by selling an image. Boycotters, realizing the value of these images, saw a new way to reach the American consumer—and, more important, the company.

By projecting their own images of corporations, boycotters hoped to undermine the corporation's public face and affect its ability to market products. To undermine a corporate image, boycotters would plant a new one in the consumer's mind. Suddenly "grapes: nature's snack" became "poisoned grapes." Folgers' "deep, dark, rich" coffee was associated with blood spilled by Salvadoran death squads. Starkist tuna became a symbol of "dolphin killers" (see box 51-1).

With image campaigns, it was no longer essential that the boycott "sign on" consumers. Whether or not consumers knowingly joined the boycott campaign, the buying habits of many would be affected. Perhaps more important, the carefully crafted multimillion-dollar company image could be badly damaged, possibly for years to come. The goal was no longer to affect profits directly; it was to affect profits indirectly by damaging the company's image.

Many boycotters are using the new image tactic, but most have not completely abandoned the tried-and-true numbers game. Many campaigns continue to use the consumer petitions and the boycott pledge card strategies of past boycott successes. Nevertheless, the question arises whether, if the power of the boycott lies in an image campaign, direct consumer boycotts will become obsolete? This is unlikely. The success of a boycott is still best measured in terms of public support. Large numbers of consumers will always be needed to get the boycott message to others. By gearing image campaigns to consumer participation, boycotters are also more likely to be in touch with the public. An image campaign, no matter how slick or expensive, will not overly concern boycott targets if they do not perceive public support for it. If boycotts stray too far from the individual consumer, the public's acceptance of them will not last. Excessive dependence on image campaigns runs the risk of turning boycotts into empty rituals in the eyes of the public.

Many consumers are no longer standing by the sidelines to have their shopping habits changed by some boycott's image campaign. Today's consumers actively seek out ways to effect change. The nation's increasing social, environmental, and economic problems compel the public to look for new ways to bring about change.

This trend toward increased individual responsibility may be a response to the "selfishness" of the 1980s. The green consumer movement is the most recent newcomer. It joins the ranks of a burgeoning boycott movement, increased shareholder activism, and the expanding field of socially responsible investment.

1990: The Year of the Boycott

In 1989, when the *Exxon Valdez* spilled eleven million gallons of oil into Alaskan waters, Americans became outraged. Within days, much of that outrage was channeled into grassroots boycotts. Many of these people were inexperienced in confronting large corporations over environmental issues. Expectations were unrealistic. Despite the failure of these actions to achieve their stated aims, they did help the American public rediscover the boycott.

On April 12, 1990, Heinz Corporation—the central target of a nationwide boycott—announced that it and its subsidiary, Starkist, would no longer purchase tuna caught using fishing techniques that harm dolphins. In less than two years, a boycott by consumers succeeded in doing what decades of federal legislation had failed to do. The message to consumers was clear and the impact was immediate. A new national boycott was called almost every other week. The *Wall Street Journal* dubbed 1990 "the year of the boycott." For the first time in years, much of the public felt that it could influence change through individual actions.

| BOYCOTTING: THE PSYCHOLOGY OF EMPOWERMENT

People discovered empowerment in their pockets and purses. And, in turn, that empowerment spawned an increased interest in social and environmental problems. Just as a sense of individual responsibility cannot exist without a feeling of individual empowerment, lack of empowerment is not conducive to learning about problems.

Boycotts are excellent educational tools because they provide the five essential components that make education most relevant and information most useful:

1. knowledge (of a problem);
2. a line of action (a way to act on that knowledge);
3. a larger framework (that makes the action effective);
4. a sense of individual empowerment; and
5. a sense of individual responsibility.

In the 1970s Watergate, Vietnam, the Church Commission Report, and the Iran hostage crisis left the American public feeling disempowered. Americans felt betrayed by the institutions they had trusted. Having lost faith, many began to feel cynical about their ability to influence change. People began to shed the social responsibilities of a more idealistic time. Shedding was easy; for decades government had gradually been relieving individuals of any sense of personal responsibility for social problems. The public viewed these problems as both the fault of and the responsibility of the government.

But with the continuing corruption of the federal government, the public began to look for new ways to exert its influence. More and more it has turned to economic power as a means of wielding political power.

I DO BOYCOTTS REALLY WORK?

How effective are boycotts? Theoretically, if the question is whether boycotts can damage company profits, boycotts can be extremely effective. Because boycotts are direct actions, no politicians compromise the consumer's influence. The direct nature of boycotting means that the effects of consumer action are immediate, usually more so than attempts to resolve issues through legislation. Boycotts are easier to participate in than demonstrations, marches, or civil disobedience. A boycott should succeed if the demands made by the boycott have the support of the public—theoretically.

Perhaps the greatest problem for boycott initiators is convincing consumers that boycotts work. Many people are under the impression that they do not. The media usually does not report boycotts when they are called. Many people assume that the absence of reporting on boycotts is a reflection of their ineffectiveness. When reporting changes in corporate policy, the media often fail to mention the boycotts that pushed for those changes. For example, most media failed to credit boycotts for the policy changes by Heinz regarding tuna and McDonald's on its Styrofoam containers.

Another stumbling block to translating a boycott's theoretical effectiveness is convincing the targeted company of the boycott's effectiveness. Too many variables influence profits for a targeted company to know how much the boycott is affecting sales. Dips in a company's sales may be due to its current ad campaign, the ad campaigns of its competitors, the cost and quality of its products, changing consumer tastes, or other trends. But even companies suffering miserably from a boycott may stubbornly hold out. Eastern

Airlines died at least in part because of a boycott aimed at defeating Frank Lorenzo's attempt to bust Eastern's unions.

Boycotting's Hidden Successes

To imply that a boycott is effective only if it succeeds in achieving its stated goals is misleading. For example, boycotts may be effective in ways that tend to be overlooked. Boycotts educate consumers about the political and economic system and the influence corporations have in that system. And boycotts can empower and lead people to take a second look at whom and what they support with their consumer dollars.

Boycotts also can affect corporations in ways other than hurting profit margins or denting corporate images. Boycotts may succeed in making corporations more cautious and responsible in future decisions and activities. Boycotts may even lead corporations to increase community involvement and charitable giving in response to adverse publicity. Boycotts also can cost companies management time. Boycotts can lead companies to cut prices to maintain market share, devise more promotions for products, and increase advertising. Employee morale also may suffer during a boycott, and the corporation may find it difficult to recruit top employees.

One of the most remarkable aspects of a successful boycott is its ability to affect businesses that are not targeted. When a boycott succeeds in forcing a targeted business to change, potential targets may institute similar changes. For example, after its successful seven-year boycott against the Campbell Soup Company in support of union recognition for tomato workers, Heinz, another major purchaser of tomatoes harvested by migrant laborers, contacted the Farm Labor Organizing Committee to open a dialogue. Similarly, when Starkist surrendered to tuna boycotters' demands on April 12, 1990, only hours later Chicken of the Sea and Bumble Bee followed with announcements that they also would switch to dolphin-safe tuna. This domino effect allows boycotts to reform an offending practice in an entire industry through the successful boycott of a single offender.

An even more striking example of this domino effect is the growing success of the movement that aims to end the use of animals in cosmetics testing. During the past few years more than fifteen major cosmetics and toiletries companies have announced that they no longer will test their products on animals. It began with the successful boycott of Revlon, followed by Avon, Benetton, and Mary Kay. Other companies quickly got the message.

Assessing Boycott Success

Boycotts, until recently, have largely been ignored by the economic and academic communities. However, the few preliminary studies indicate that boycotts can be remarkably effective in altering corporate and governmental policies. The studies also indicate that some types of boycotts are more effective than others.

Michigan State psychology professor Monroe Friedman has divided boycotts into four categories based on the degree of effort put forward by the boycott initiators. Not surprisingly, initial results strongly indicate that those actions backed by the greatest effort have the greatest chance of success. It may be assumed that of the estimated 50 percent of boycotts that achieve their primary goals, a high percentage fall under Friedman's classification of "action taken" boycotts, as opposed to boycotts of lesser efforts—those that are "action organized," "action requested," and "action considered."

Certain elements of action-taken boycotts have a strong influence on their success. These include:

- the size of the organization calling the boycott;
- the amount of organizational networking done by the boycotting organization;
- the types of products or services targeted by the boycott;
- the level of media coverage; and
- the issue or dispute over which the boycott was initiated.

Other issues have less bearing on a boycott's success:

- the level of response by the boycott target;
- the type of concern represented in the boycott (environment, civil liberties, labor, and so forth); and
- the length of the boycott.

The figure of 50 percent for boycotts that do not succeed is somewhat deceiving. These failures typically are among boycotts classified as action considered, requested, or organized. Boycotts considered may be best described as threats. Many groups may threaten to launch a boycott, but only a few have the resources to carry through with their threats. One organization that has made effective use of threats is the American Family Association (AFA). AFA targets sponsors of television programs that it believes undermine traditional family and conservative American values. AFA's threats are effective only because it has proven capable of following through on them. For instance, the group convinced Domino's Pizza, Ralston Purina, and General Mills to end sponsorship of "Saturday Night Live" because of its alleged anti-Christian bias and sexual content.

Groups that announce a boycott but do not organize the action at a higher level (Friedman's action-requested boycott) fare no better than if they simply had threatened one. Companies do not appear concerned with boycotts lacking organized efforts. Often an organization will call a boycott just to draw the attention of the media and the public to a particular issue. In 1984 the National Coalition on Television Violence called a boycott of Mattel toys and the United Farm Workers called a boycott of Chiquita bananas. But little was done after the initial announcements. Both groups admit that the boycotts are largely inactive, but they say they are continuing.

Organized actions are, according to Friedman's classification, boycotts that never go beyond the organizing level—the most critical phase of a boycott. Success at this level determines whether a boycott can move on to the next level, action taken. Here organizers decide how the boycott will be promoted and who will be its initial audience. These decisions determine whether the boycott will proceed to the action-taken level. As a tactical matter, some groups never take a boycott beyond the organizing phase. Media Watch, for example, monitors the media for images that degrade and dehumanize women. It calls so many boycotts that it would have difficulty organizing and promoting each of them. Rather, the group's newsletter announces a boycott, such as that of corporate advertisers in *Sports Illustrated*'s swimsuits edition, and includes preprinted postcards that Media Watch readers may sign and send to the offending companies. At that point the boycott usually is added to the group's printed list. Some of the group's boycotts have succeeded. The majority, however, have failed to achieve their stated goals, although they make companies more cautious in future advertising decisions.

| CURRENT TRENDS IN BOYCOTTING

Boycotting appears most influenced by changes in federal legislation and the media. Where legislation and regulation lag, boycotts help pick up the slack. The number of labor-oriented boycotts doubled after former president Ronald Reagan was elected to office, presumably due to that administration's poor enforcement of federal labor laws. Boycotts targeting apartheid rose in 1986 and 1987 after the media brought the issue to the attention of the public and Congress failed to impose comprehensive sanctions. Peace-oriented boycotts grew in the early 1980s in response to the nuclear weapons buildup and the growing nuclear-freeze movement. Boycotts focusing on abortion started in the early 1980s. Boycotts aimed at the media grew in the 1980s in response to the growing domination of sex-and-violence programming. Civil rights–oriented boycotts increased during the late 1980s in response to a perceived backsliding in social attitudes toward racism.

Although environmental boycotts attracted the least attention among the readers of the *National Boycott News* when it first began in 1985, today environmental boycotts rank as the leading concern of that publication's readers. Save for some other tragedy of mass proportions, the environmental crisis is likely to dominate the boycott scene well into the next decade.

One recent trend in boycotting is the use of full-page newspaper ads, usually in the *New York Times* or one of several progressive magazines. Rainforest Action Network used full-page ads accusing Burger King of supporting tropical rain forest destruction by purchasing some of its beef from Costa Rica. Earth Island Institute used ads to publicize its boycott of Heinz and tuna (see box 51-1). Several groups placed ads attacking Exxon following its oil spill in Alaska. Corporations often respond to boycotts with ads of their own. When Earth Island Institute used a full-page ad in the *New York Times* to accuse Bumble Bee of killing dolphins after it had pledged not to, the company took out a full-page ad to state its case. Burger King ended a month-long boycott by the American Family Association by taking out full-page ads across the country stating that the company supported family values in television programming.

For years, when most companies were targeted for a boycott, they barely blinked. Many companies refused to even acknowledge they were being boycotted. Today the word *boycott* sends many companies scrambling. Some have even sued those who spread word of the boycott. When the cruelty-free and politically progressive Carmé beauty-products company was bought out by an animal research firm, International Research and Development Corporation, several boycotters who opposed the takeover were slapped with lawsuits in an apparent attempt to silence critics. Other companies hire public relations firms to devise media campaigns that will undercut a boycott's efforts. For example, Nestlé's public relations firm, Ogilvy & Mather, recommended that the company provide church youth groups and children's groups with funding as a way to improve its image regarding children. Other companies, like McDonald's and Heinz, have engaged in behind-the-scenes negotiations with boycotters in order to resolve their disputes quickly.

To a lesser degree, there also has been a recent trend toward "secondary" boycotts—actions aimed not at the offending party but at some entity that has influence with the offending organization. For example, in 1991, when the Dallas City Council resisted attempts to achieve greater ethnic balance on the council by redistricting, local African-American leaders responded with a boycott of the city's convention industry. Dallas is the country's second-largest convention site. The boycotters hoped that by applying pressure to the convention industry, businesses and workers that depend on the industry might pressure the city council to withdraw its objection to the proposed redistricting.

Boycotting as a Stepping Stone
One of the most important functions of the boycott is a stepping-stone to start the consumer on the path toward broader ethical purchasing habits. After boycotts empower, educate, and activate, consumers are ready to move on. When they come to realize that corporations view each purchase as an endorsement of their business practices, every purchase begins to take on social, environmental, and even political ramifications. As a result, many consumers now go out of their way to purchase the products of companies with the most responsible business practices.

This form of consumer activism has been dubbed "buycotting" by some, "girlcotting" by others, and, more recently, "procotting." The idea behind the "procott" is that if we want change, we help promote it by encouraging those who are already doing something about it, not by reinforcing the status quo. Rather than asking consumers *not* to put their money where their ethics are *not*, "procotts" take the less awkward and more proactive stance of asking consumers to put their money where their morals are.

More and more consumers are taking the boycott path, realizing that if they want ethical products and an ethical society, they must begin to reward companies for responsible behavior. In a highly competitive society, even multibillion-dollar giants will not last long without the support of consumers. Past consumer movements have had to demand affordability, quality, and safety in products. Once consumers begin to demand ethics, companies will comply.

Consumers are beginning to realize that they actually can restore ethics to their own lives through the economy. The values (or the lack thereof) in our businesses are mirrored in our society—in our work, our entertainment, our art, our government, our educational system, our foreign policy, and our crime rates. Being an ethical consumer is nothing more or less than investing in a better future.

BOX 51-1
EARTH ISLAND INSTITUTE'S SAVE THE DOLPHINS PROJECT

Deborah S. Flagg
Earth Island Institute

The goal of the Save the Dolphins Project is to eliminate the injury and death of dolphins caused by the international tuna fishing industry. Preservation of marine ecosystems is contingent on prohibiting the two most destructive fishing technologies: purse seining on dolphins and drift-net fishing. Our campaign seeks to end the use of these fishing methods, ensure consumer confidence in the dolphin-safe labeling of products, and establish a verifiable international monitoring program.

FISHING TECHNOLOGY

The development and widespread use of two fishing technologies pose an unprecedented threat to world marine biodiversity. Open-ocean drift nets and the setting of purse seine nets on schools of dolphins in the eastern tropical Pacific (ETP) are both indiscriminate and eco-logically unsustainable. The deployment of thousands of miles of drift nets, sometimes terms "walls of death," over the past few years by Japanese, Taiwanese, and South Korean fleets has decimated marine ecosystems in the North and South Pacific, Atlantic, and Indian oceans. The casualties include seabirds, sharks, dolphins, and sea tur-tle populations as well as target and nontarget fish species. The use of drift nets is estimated to kill more than fifty thousand dolphins every year.

For reasons still unknown, yellowfin tuna form mixed schools with dolphins in the ETP, a seven million square mile area of ocean stretching from southern California south to Chile. The use of purse seines and set nets on dolphins, practiced in the ETP, entails encircling dolphin schools and yellowfin tuna together in the mile-long nets. Drawn in like purse strings, the nets are tightened with cables and are hauled aboard by powerful winches. Being air-breathing mammals like us, the dolphins often become entangled in the nets and drowned, or they are maimed or crushed in the gears of the winches. Dolphins are intentionally trapped by this tragic method as a way of catching the yellowfin tuna that swim below. Over one hundred vessels in the ETP, both U.S. and foreign fleets, participate in the slaughter every year. Seven million dolphins have been killed in the last thirty years as a direct consequence of this fishery. Each year more than 100,000 dolphins are killed in the ETP purse-seine fishery for less than 5 percent of the world's tuna harvest.

CORPORATE POLICIES

The first phase of Earth Island Institute's program to save the dolphins has focused on alerting the public and policymakers about the tuna-dolphin issue. Much progress was made in these areas as we developed a dolphin-safe standard for tuna, pressured tuna companies to adopt dolphin-safe corporate policies, and won court-ordered embargoes on countries whose tuna industries continually harm and kill dolphins.

Earth Island Institute's Save the Dolphin Project is now developing a global monitoring program to close all markets to dolphin-unsafe tuna.

Through our educational efforts about this tragedy, there is now growing consumer demand for dolphin-safe tuna around the world. Earth Island has established a strict dolphin-safe standard required for any company to properly consider itself dolphin-safe. The following criteria have been accepted internationally.

1. Documentation must be provided verifying that no tuna products purchased, processed, trans-shipped, or sold by the company are caught in purse-seine nets in association with dolphins or by use of drift nets of any length.
2. Purchases from the eastern tropical Pacific must include a certificate from a U.S. government or an observer from the InterAmerican Tropical Tuna Commission observer attesting that no dolphins were encircled during the entire fishing trip.
3. The policy must be applied worldwide and include related companies, including all parent, subsidiary, and sister companies.
4. The policy must cover all products containing tuna purchased, processed, trans-shipped, or sold, including those

products not intended for human consumption, such as pet food.

5. Companies must agree to support federal legislation to set a uniform standard for the use of the "dolphin-safe" label.

6. The policy must be implemented pursuant to a fully verifiable procurement program that includes on-site inspection, access to records, and the requirement of certificates from suppliers that they do not process or sell dolphin-unsafe products.

In April 1990, as a result of a consumer campaign led by Earth Island Institute, the H. J. Heinz Company—owner of Starkist, the largest tuna company in the world—decided to cease all purchase, processing, and sale worldwide of fish products caught by methods harmful to dolphins.

The public's awareness of the tuna-dolphin issue contributed to the success of the Heinz corporate dolphin-safe policy conversion. Through boycotting all canned tuna products and participating in a nationwide letter-writing campaign, consumers pressured Heinz to set the dolphin-safe standard and thus save the lives of many dolphins. Restaurants and schools stopped serving tuna on their menus in efforts to convince the tuna industry to go dolphin-safe. By adopting a complete dolphin-safe policy, Heinz has set an industry standard that is now being met by other U.S. and foreign-based tuna companies. Companies that have adopted this standard now require that all products provided to them are caught by methods safe for dolphins. By ensuring the fulfillment of these claims, we can save the lives of many dolphins.

CONGRESSIONAL ACTION

During the final days of the 101st Congress, the Dolphin Protection Consumer Information Act of 1990, introduced by Congresswoman Barbara Boxer of California, was signed into law. This bill establishes federal criteria for the use of "dolphin-safe" labels, prohibits false and misleading labels, and establishes a framework for monitoring and enforcing these label requirements. This law has set a precedent for the general concept of ecolabeling. Earth Island Institute staff are carefully monitoring the enforcement of this bill to ensure company compliance and guarantee consumer confidence in the dolphin-safe label.

Another important stipulation of the Dolphin Protection Consumer Information Act is that a U.S. import ban was placed on the import of tuna products caught by use of open-ocean drift nets, effective July 1, 1992.

An immediate and dramatic implication for marine conservation resulting from our campaign activities is that the number of dolphins killed as a result of the U.S. tuna fleet has been reduced from the past levels of twenty thousand per year to less than five thousand in 1990, and the mortality figure will drop further in 1991. Currently there are only two U.S. vessels setting nets on dolphins. U.S. tuna fishers no longer can find domestic markets for tuna caught by setting nets on dolphin. Instead they are resorting to alternative fishing techniques or moving to areas where dolphins do not associate with tuna.

In the international markets, a court-ordered U.S. import embargo has been placed on all tuna caught by Mexico—the country killing dolphins at the highest rate—and a similar import ban is expected on tuna from Venezuela and Vanuatu. Other countries that export tuna to the United States also must prohibit importation of tuna from Mexico or face an embargo of all of their own tuna into the United States. Recently Ecuador and Panama, whose tuna fleets have a history of killing dolphins, adopted policies prohibiting fishing methods harmful to dolphins. These countries must maintain a 100 percent observer program ensuring that their vessels do not set nets on dolphins. The effect of these developments is that the total foreign killing of dolphins is dropping as well.

THE NEXT STEP

Establishment of a global monitoring program is critical to ensuring that all facilities in which tuna is purchased, processed, or sold are accepting only certified dolphin-safe tuna. We are developing monitoring programs in Thailand, Malaysia, Fiji, the Philippines, and Indonesia to inspect the canning and off-loading facilities. Thailand, the largest tuna-processing nation in the world, is key to the success of the worldwide dolphin-safe policy, since it exports more than $400 million of tuna to the United States every year and is also a major supplier to Europe. We are establishing a monitoring office in Thailand to keep track of their purchasing and processing operations through examining purchase records and certificates from each vessel bringing in loads of tuna.

At the same time, we are stepping up our efforts to convert major supermarket chains to purchase and sell only dolphin-safe tuna products. This demand will set yet another precedent, forcing other supermarkets to follow suit and participate in this dolphin-saving program. And we are continuing our litigation to require full enforcement of the Marine Mammal Protection Act.

Earth Island Institute's Save the Dolphins Project will not rest until the world's oceans are safe for dolphins. Much progress was made in 1990, but the battle is far from over.

THE BANKING INDUSTRY

Tom Schlesinger Director,
Southern Finance Project

Not since the 1930s have financial institutions, particularly commercial banks, been in such turmoil. Economic downturns, driven
by real estate busts, led to tighter regional credit conditions in New
England and the Southwest. When the national economy fell into
recession during the second half of 1990, many analysts identified
the chief culprit as the financial follies of the roaring eighties, an
era when households, businesses, and government units paid record-
high real interest rates to incur unprecedented amounts of debt,
much of which served questionably productive purposes epitomized
by leveraged buyout mania.

The excesses of the 1980s produced the due bills of the 1990s—
a taxpayer bailout of the savings and loan industry that may ultimately exceed $1.5 trillion and the growing likelihood of a similar
rescue by the guarantee systems that underpin banks, insurance
companies, and pension funds.

These public costs and the general erosion of confidence in the
financial system should, by all rights, lead to a healthy debate over
the role of banks and other financial intermediaries in our economy.
After all, government bailouts and deposit insurance constitute only
part of the extraordinary matrix of public protections afforded these
intermediaries. The time is ripe for a far-reaching discussion of how
to reformulate the public obligations of financial institutions within
the context of changes in industry structure, regulatory framework,
and the international marketplace.

Unfortunately, neither political institutions nor the media have
provided a forum for a discussion of the social contract between our

---

Tom Schlesinger is the director of the Southern Finance Project, an independent
research center that monitors financial markets and policy issues.

nation and its financial institutions. Instead a much narrower series of debates has arisen over capital standards, geographic and product restrictions on commercial banks, deposit insurance ceilings, and the duties and structure of regulatory agencies.

What is missing from these debates is a grounding in how banks and other financial institutions actually affect—or should affect— our real economy and America's social fabric. These are precisely the issues that citizen organizations and activists have raised over a number of years. This chapter describes issues that most concern organizations and activists.

| COMMUNITY REINVESTMENT

The federal Community Reinvestment Act (CRA) of 1977 mandates that banks and other regulated depositories provide credit and other banking services to all parts of the communities they serve, including poor and moderate-income segments. Despite this law, studies by community groups, newspapers, and independent researchers show that redlining—the practice of discriminatory lending—persists in many banking markets.

The 1989 savings and loan bailout law ostensibly strengthened the CRA by requiring the primary regulator of a bank to disclose to the public the grades lenders receive in their CRA examinations. However, the savings and loan bailout itself has undermined this advance. By providing acquirers with franchises at fire sale prices, federal regulators have largely displaced the private market for bank mergers and acquisitions.

Unlike market mergers and acquisitions, which give activists a chance to challenge the community reinvestment record of merging institutions, the government deals are conducted behind closed doors and announced as a fait accompli. In contrast, for parties who feel that the bank has failed to meet its obligations under the act, the CRA provides a means to challenge before a federal regulator what a bank proposes to do: merge, open or close a branch, and the like. If the parties prove their case, the regulator can refuse to approve the bank's proposal.

CRA challenges continue to provide grassroots campaigns with the single most widely used device to educate citizens and reform banking practices. In the past two years, banks, regulators, and elected officials have demonstrated a new sensitivity to the importance of community reinvestment concerns, and grassroots groups have struck a number of impressive targeted lending agreements with banks and savings and loans.

While government bailouts of financial firms have impeded CRA challenges, they also have helped clarify the private responsibilities required by government assistance. In the spring of 1991, for example, the mayor of Boston and community groups insisted that bidders for the failed Bank of New England make a commitment to neighborhood reinvestment. For the first time such an effort involved groups literally from coast to coast, because banks on both coasts—Bank of America on the west, Bank of Boston and Fleet/Norstar on the east—were bidding. Unfortunately, the successful bid of Fleet/Norstar and Kohlberg Kravis promised less in terms of CRA than the others.

| IMPACT ON MANAGEMENT DECISIONS

As financiers of corporate raids, buyouts, and other forms of ownership change, banks increasingly find themselves in a position to make life-or-death decisions for distressed firms—and their stakeholders—sagging under debt service burdens.

Increasingly labor unions and other stakeholder groups find themselves directly negotiating with, or attempting to pressure, debt holders to restructure loans in order to forestall or minimize job loss, plant closings, and other destructive impacts. The Amalgamated Clothing and Textile Workers Union (ACTWU) pressured NCNB and Security Pacific to restructure debt at the troubled Healthtex Corporation when the apparel manufacturer faced failure in 1990.

Box 52-1
SOUTHERN FINANCE PROJECT

329 Rensselaer
Charlotte, N.C. 28203
(704) 372-7072

Founded in 1986, Southern Finance Project (SFP) is an independent, nonprofit research center that monitors financial markets and policy issues on a regional and national basis. SFP works primarily with grassroots organizations, labor unions, policymakers, and journalists.

SFP research focuses on depository institutions and the insurance industry. To a lesser degree it also scrutinizes pension funds and the securities industry. In recent years much of the project's research program has been organized around investigations into the savings and loan crisis and bailout; public guarantees for private insurers; and financial industry impacts on the natural environment.

RESEARCH

SFP has prepared detailed, in-depth analyses of financial industry firms for clients, such as the United Food and Commercial Workers Union, the United Mine Workers, ACORN, and a number of local community reinvestment coalitions. SFP also has compiled background analyses of some financial companies for socially responsible investment firms.

A Regular Series of Research Publications

SFP publishes a series that covers diverse topics. In the past two years SFP reports have analyzed Resolution Trust Corporation sales of insolvent thrifts; the case for and against banks branching on a nationwide basis; the condition of state guaranty funds for property/casualty and life/health insurers; and the actual incidence of lender liability at Superfund sites.

SFP responds to a variety of policymaker requests for information and analysis on matters of current interest. Users of such research have included the North Carolina Rural Economic Development Center, the Antitrust Subcommittee of the Senate Judiciary Committee, and the Texas Department of Agriculture.

OUTREACH

The project maintains regular contact with press outlets and frequently is asked to work with reporters on in-depth stories. For example, SFP was a primary consultant and provided part of the research for the Atlanta *Journal-Constitution*'s Pulitzer Prize–winning 1988 series on mortgage discrimination. SFP research is widely cited in such publications as *Business Week, Wall Street Journal,* and *National Journal.* SFP staffers also contribute articles and op-ed columns to a number of major periodicals and appear frequently on broadcast programs dealing with financial issues.

Conferences, Briefings, and Workshops

SFP staffers participate as speakers and panelists in a broad range of public meetings, and SFP sponsors and organizes occasional conferences. For example, SFP and the Texas Center for Policy Studies cosponsored a major Earth Day 1990 symposium on the financial industry and the environment at the LBJ School of Public Affairs.

Education and Policy Development
In addition to conducting classes and seminars on financial topics, SFP is preparing a curriculum for use by public schoolteachers on financial deregulation and the eruption of problems among savings and loans and banks. SFP also produces a wide-ranging series of policy proposals for use by constituency groups with which it works.

SFP maintains an extensive set of hard copy and computerized data files that it makes available to various user groups. It also acts as a sponsor for research projects by academicians, students, and independent scholars.

| IMPACT ON THE NATURAL ENVIRONMENT

Banking's relationship to the leading environmental issues of the day is direct and increasingly controversial.

In 1990 and 1991, environmental and public interest groups had to withstand a lobbying drive by the banking industry to exempt lenders from liability for toxic waste under the federal Superfund laws. Court interpretations of these laws have stimulated lenders to play an important role in preventing or minimizing toxic messes by making environmental audits a routine part of the underwriting process.

Lenders have complained that Superfund liabilities might bankrupt their industry and squeeze the supply of credit to small businesses. Some federal courts have held that banks that play a role, either by managing or owning, in a Superfund site are liable for remediation. This policy issue demonstrates the important role that financial intermediation plays in determining the fate of our natural environment.

The problem extends much further than toxic wastes. Consider the case of Pacific Lumber Company (PALCO). PALCO was an exemplary forest products company because of its sustainable forestry practices in its Humboldt County, California, operations. In 1985 Charles Hurwitz's Maxxam Inc. took over PALCO. The company began cutting redwoods at more than double its previous rate in order to generate income to service Maxxam's immense junk bond debt. Workplace health and safety standards also suffered. So did PALCO's pension plan. Maxxam terminated it and replaced it with an Executive Life plan. First Executive, the discredited insurer's parent, had bought some of the junk bonds that financed the PALCO takeover.

The only bright spot in this sorry saga is that California, with the public blessing of Governor Pete Wilson, is trying to engineer a debt-for-nature swap with the Resolution Trust Corporation (RTC), the federal government's receiver for the assets of failed financial institutions. The RTC's large junk bond portfolio contains PALCO debt that could give California title—if RTC agrees—to thousands of acres of redwoods. Tree huggers and loggers agree: Humboldt County's economic base will disappear if Maxxam continues logging at current rates.

| THIRD WORLD LENDING

Concern remains strong among religious, environmental, labor, and other groups over the effects of private and multilateral banks' project lending in the third world. A leading concern among environmentalists is World Bank financing for road building and agricultural colonization in Brazil's rain forest. Over the past decade, most large U.S. banks have reduced their exposure in less-developed countries, but several still play a prominent role in determining the models of development in those countries—and therefore the local consequences for environmental health, indigenous cultures, and relations between citizens and their governments.

U.S.-based banks have cut back their operations in South Africa. Nonetheless, activists continue to challenge their role in trade finance and currency exchange as well as major bank stockholdings in boycotted companies, such as Royal Dutch Shell, that supply the country's apartheid regime.

| BASIC SERVICES AND FEES

As they have for more than a decade, consumer, community, and public-interest organizations continue to press banks to moderate service charges and to provide basic banking services in all of their markets. For example, consumer groups want banks to cash government checks for anyone in their market area, not just for their own customers. Such services would benefit primarily the poor and the elderly, many of whom do not have bank accounts or extensive identification. Challenges by community and public interest groups will continue as service fees rise and become an increasingly large portion of banking industry income and as banks continue to close branches and "demarket" customers in poor, moderate-income, rural, and minority communities.

| LABOR PRACTICES

As the industry consolidates, employment in banking is becoming increasingly insecure—and poorly paid.

A handful of banks have unionized work forces. Late in 1990 the United Food and Commercial Workers Union won a twelve-year battle to gain a contract for its members at Seafirst, a BankAmerica subsidiary that is the largest bank holding company in Washington and the first major bank in the United States to be organized. Unions and labor-community coalitions also have challenged the direct and indirect contributions of banks to the mistreatment of service workers—particularly janitors—and challenged the hiring of nonunion construction firms for various bank-financed projects.

| PUBLIC POLICY AND THE POLITICAL PROCESS

Finally, a growing number of organizations and activists have challenged the domination and distortion of public policymaking by industry political action committees (PACs) and lobbying muscle. A broad spectrum of civic, religious, labor, farm, and consumer groups called the Financial Democracy Campaign has called attention to regulatory and legislative preferences given such banks as NCNB that both cost taxpayers dearly and skew competitive forces in the financial marketplace to the detriment of investors, borrowers, and savers.

RESOURCES

PEOPLE AND ORGANIZATIONS

Virtually all of the organizations listed here produce valuable resource materials on banking and financial industry topics.

ACORN
739 Eighth Street SE
Washington, D.C. 20003
(202) 547-9292

ACORN is a national organization of low-income citizens. It has extensive experience in antiredlining campaigns.

Amalgamated Clothing & Textile Workers Union
1808 Swann Street NW
Washington, D.C. 20009
(202) 745-1710

This is one of the most active unions in keeping banks accountable for the impacts of corporate ownership changes, activities in South Africa, and credit distribution patterns.

BankWatch
215 Pennsylvania Avenue SE
Washington, D.C. 20003
(202) 546-4996

BankWatch is a Nader-associated entity that monitors banking issues.

Center for Community Change
1000 Wisconsin Avenue NW
Washington, D.C. 20007
(202) 342-0567

The center is an excellent source of technical assistance for groups interested in community reinvestment.

Consumer Federation of America
1424 Sixteenth Street NW, Suite 604
Washington, D.C. 20036
(202) 387-6121

The Consumer Federation of America produces surveys on banking fees.

Financial Democracy Campaign
2009 Chapel Hill Road
Durham, N.C. 27702
(919) 419-1841

This is a broad citizen alliance seeking banking reform legislation and equitable taxation for financial industry bailouts.

Chuck Finn
Hubert H. Humphrey Institute
University of Minnesota
Minneapolis, Minn. 55411
(612) 625-8302

The institute is an excellent source of research and research methodology on urban reinvestment patterns.

Justice for Janitors
Service Employees International Union
1313 L Street NW
Washington, D.C. 20005
(202) 898-1505

Justice for Janitors is a union-led campaign for improved wages and working conditions for janitorial workers at banks and bank-financed properties in cities across the country.

National Training and Information Center
810 North Milwaukee
Chicago, Ill. 60622-4103
(312) 243-3035

The center is a reliable source of organizer training and data on community reinvestment.

Public Advocates
1535 Mission Street
San Francisco, Calif. 94103
(415) 431-7430

Public Advocates provides legal and tactical assistance to groups seeking to end redlining.

Anne Shlay
Institute for Public Policy Studies
Temple University
Philadelphia, Pa. 19122
(215) 787-5156

Here is an excellent source of research and research methodology on urban reinvestment patterns.

Southern Finance Project
329 Rensselaer
Charlotte, N.C. 28203
(704) 372-7072

Southern Finance conducts industrywide studies and firm-specific investigations of banks, savings and loans, insurance companies, and other financial industry actors, as well as specialty research on Resolution Trust Corporation and financial industry impacts on environment.

Texas Center for Policy Studies
1300 East Twenty-eighth Street
Austin, Tex. 78722
(512) 474-0811

This is the best single source of information on the environmental consequences of savings and loan bailouts.

Woodstock Institute
407 South Dearborn, Suite 550
Chicago, Ill. 60605
(312) 427-8070

Woodstock is an excellent source of research and research methodology on urban reinvestment patterns. See box 40-1.

CHAPTER 53

CORPORATE RESPONSIBILITY AND GAY AND LESBIAN RIGHTS

Diane Bratcher Director of Communications,
Interfaith Center on Corporate Responsibility

Though a number of cities and states have laws barring employment discrimination against lesbians and gay men, few companies have policies against such discrimination, and even fewer have implementation programs.

Jennie Merovic, an activist and an individual investor; Diane Bratcher, director of communications for the Interfaith Center on Corporate Responsibility (ICCR); Donn Mitchell, an Episcopal seminarian; and others are developing a corporate responsibility campaign to press corporations to adopt regulations barring discrimination against lesbians and gay men. At this point the project is conducting research on the status of lesbian and gay antidiscrimination policies and building a nationwide network of actively concerned individual and institutional investors.

Donn Mitchell's early research shows that more than thirty million Americans are protected by state and local laws and regulations that bar employment discrimination based on sexual preference, orientation, or affinity. These rules generally have some sort of enforcement mechanism, typically in some form of legal redress. However, short of a formal complaint to a government agency or a lawsuit, there is no way to encourage private corporations to comply,

---

Diane Bratcher, director of communications for the Interfaith Center on Corporate Responsibility, is a member of Manhattan Community Board No. 7, a citizen advisory panel to the government of New York City, representing Manhattan's Upper West Side. She is also secretary of the Ecumenical Employees Association, the union of employees of ICCR, and the National Council of Churches of Christ in the U.S.A.

to calculate how many corporations are in compliance, or to evaluate how a particular corporation is complying.

By encouraging individuals and institutions involved in the corporate responsibility movement to put lesbian and gay employment rights on their agendas and by encouraging lesbians and gay men to add corporate social responsibility tactics to their strategic repertoire, we will give corporations powerful incentive to adopt and implement nondiscrimination policies for lesbians and gay men.

| EARLY RESEARCH

Currently we are in the research phase, and we are discovering how many corporations have nondiscrimination policies and how they implement those policies. We also are developing a method to evaluate corporate policy and practice.

Through ICCR and with foundation support, Mitchell queried ninety-five major corporations on their policies and willingness to provide personnel education and training to eliminate prejudice against lesbians and gay men. He will follow up with companies that responded incompletely or unsatisfactorily as well as with those that did not respond at all. He also plans initial inquiries to new corporations.

It should be noted that some companies already have positive policies on gay and lesbian rights. These include:

Digital Equipment	Lotus Development
Sears Roebuck	Apple Computer
Shawmut Bank	US West

These companies have shown a strong commitment to diversity and pluralism in their work force. Their human resources programs include sensitivity to sexual orientation.

| WHAT CAN THIS CAMPAIGN DO?

The campaign can press corporations to adopt antidiscrimination policies—whether or not they are required by law—and become sensitive to the needs and assets of their gay and lesbian employees. In so doing, the campaign can contribute to a climate in which lesbians and gay men can be out at work and have the same employment rights as straight people.

Outreach and Education

At a May 1990 meeting in New York City, lesbians and gay men, representing pension funds, foundations, lesbian and gay community organizations, socially responsible investment advisers and companies, and churches, met to chart a campaign. They identified five groups to mobilize:

- pension funds—public, private, and unions;
- religious groups;
- the academic community, including faculty, students, and employees;
- philanthropic and civic organizations, such as foundations, charities, associations, and community groups;
- individuals, both investors and consumers.

Through meetings, discussions, articles, and educational events, each of the groups at the May 1990 meeting have begun internal discussions and planning and have taken responsibility for a phase of the campaign, including contacting companies and further outreach.

Box 53-1
PHILANTHROFUND FOUNDATION

607 Marquette Avenue, Suite 101
Minneapolis, Minn. 55402-1709
(612) 891-6150

The Philanthrofund Foundation, a nonprofit corporation, is a permanent endowment fund that provides support to organizations and individuals that seek to serve the needs and enhance the quality of the gay and lesbian community. The Philanthrofund Investment Survey is for the investor who is concerned that his or her investments will be in companies or mutual funds that are sensitive to the issues concerning the gay and lesbian community.

Philanthrofund begins with mutual funds that promote themselves as "social investments" and with stocks that are recommended by one of several "socially responsible" newsletters. These organizations are then sent surveys as to their employment and hiring policies regarding gays and lesbians as well as other issues of concern to the gay

---

and lesbian community. The responses to these surveys are then made available to subscribers and to the member organizations of the National Network of Gay and Lesbian Foundations.

The Philanthrofund Investment Survey makes no recommendations about the investment worthiness of any instrument; it only passes on information provided by the surveyed organizations.

The survey is still in its formation, and subscription rates and frequency of publication are yet to be determined.

LESBIANS AND GAY MEN. Lesbians and gay men are individual investors, pension holders, taxpayers, and church members. They must be educated about their rights and power as investors and be mobilized in this campaign so that their pension funds and religious institutions will protect their future and their community. Mitchell, Merovic, and Bratcher have begun writing and speaking to community groups about corporate and investor responsibility. They have been very warmly received. Now that specific strategies and target companies have emerged, lesbians and gay men—through their pension funds, schools, political leaders, community groups, and religious institutions—will be making demands of companies and stockholders.

THE CHURCHES. Many lesbians and gay men have been working to sensitize churches and religious institutions to gay and lesbian issues. Success here will be no small feat. Most religious institutions consider homosexuality sinful, and only a few will ordain lesbians and gay men. Nonetheless, lesbians and gay men are organizing support for the campaign among lesbian and gay committees, caucuses, and organizations within churches and other communities of faith.

PENSION FUNDS. Public pension funds are particularly important to the campaign, because they are governed by people who must be concerned about a company's financial bottom line as well as its impact on society and the environment. For this reason, public pension funds have been particularly influential in the corporate responsibility movement, especially with regard to South Africa and the environment.

Equal Employment for All Lesbians and Gay Men

Aside from the arguments about morality and consistency, in practical terms the employment rights of lesbians and gay men now depend on their staying in a protected jurisdiction. But if one must stay in San Francisco to be protected from discrimination, then he or she does not have equal employment opportunity. Suppose you work for Chevron in San Francisco and are offered a great promotion to run a division in Peoria. If you move to Peoria, you have no legally protected right not to be discriminated against on account of sexual preference.

Companies also transfer people to protected jurisdictions from other parts of the country. If antidiscrimination policies and personnel training are not companywide, people moving to a protected jurisdiction may not be aware of or sensitive to the rights of lesbians and gay men.

Just as failure to protect the rights of lesbians and gay men amounts to selective enforcement of civil rights laws, so, too, is enforcement of those laws and policies only in certain locales or in certain policy areas. It might be argued that selective enforcement is itself discrimination.

Pension Funds Should Not Invest in Companies That Discriminate

State and municipal governments are investors, primarily through pension funds. A city or state that prohibits discrimination against employees and residents should not invest in ways that may support gay discrimination.

Pension funds, legally defined as employees' deferred wages, are an important though unexplored aspect of employment policy. The campaign will urge companies in a protected jurisdiction to apply antidiscrimination policies to its management of employees' pension funds. After all, jurisdictions that have laws barring employment discrimination against lesbians and gay men should not invest their employees' deferred wages in a way that supports or profits from discrimination. Their employees' pensions should not support companies that may discriminate, even outside jurisdictional boundaries, whether those areas are legally protected or not. The logic behind pension fund concern about U.S. corporate involvement in South Africa is similar. The deferred wages and investment dollars of employees and residents should not support apartheid in South Africa, even though the jurisdiction itself does not have apartheid.

Investors: Ask Questions, Press for Change

Imagine how responsive a corporation might be if an official of a giant municipal pension fund wrote asking whether a company has an equal employment opportunity policy that prohibits discrimination against lesbians and gay men. When the City of San Francisco objected to an antigay internal advertising campaign recently, General Motors canceled the offensive campaign, apologized to the lesbian and gay community, and adopted an antidiscrimination policy. Imagine how receptive a company would be to a pension fund official who has ideas about training and affirmative action. Investors have power.

While big pension funds have considerable clout, companies also are concerned about the opinions of smaller investors. The campaign will mobilize investors, big and small.

Initially investors should ask the companies in their portfolios the same questions about their policies on discrimination against lesbians and gay men—the same questions we have been asking—and share the results with us and similarly concerned institutions. By asking these questions, individuals and institutions will express a consistent commitment to the rights of lesbians and gay men and put companies on notice that the owners of their companies believe they should have these policies and take seriously how they comply with and implement antidiscrimination laws.

Once a fairly substantial body of information about company policies and practices has been established, the campaign will shift to promoting adoption and implementation of policies or to changing policies and initiating remedial action.

Linking Up With a Nationwide Campaign

In a second phase of the campaign, we will be in a position to press companies to adopt and implement appropriate policies and/or take remedial actions. The campaign will target companies with records of discrimination against lesbians and gay men, companies with inadequate policies or implementation, and companies with no policy.

In this phase the campaign will use a variety of tactics, planned according to the company, the willingness of investors to act, and the potential for the effectiveness of the strategy. Tactics may include letter or postcard campaigns, shareholder resolutions, dialogue, avoidance investing, affirmative investing, and, if necessary, divestment or consumer boycotts and selective purchasing restrictions for institutional customers.

Simultaneously, outreach and education will continue to get new individual and institutional investors involved in supporting our shareholder resolutions, expressing their opinions to companies, and asking questions of companies.

The potential is unlimited. Nationwide fair employment for lesbians and gay men can be achieved.

EMPLOYEE OWNERSHIP
AND THE SOCIAL INVESTOR

Corey Rosen Executive Director, National Center
for Employee Ownership

According to the Federal Reserve, just 1 percent of the population
holds 60 percent of the privately held stock (stock not held by mutual
funds, pensions, and other institutions) in U.S. corporations. The
Forbes 400, the wealthiest four hundred families in the United
States, have assets totaling over $200 billion. If these families le-
veraged their assets at ten to one, they could buy half of all of the
stock in U.S. companies.

By contrast, the Federal Reserve reported that the median financial assets of a family at retirement in 1983, other than home equity,
were just $11,000. A household in the top one half of one percent
of the population owns an average of five hundred times the wealth
of a household in the "bottom" 90 percent.

Capitalism has done a terrific job of generating wealth; the problem
is that it has done a lousy job of distributing it. To some, the answer
has been to do away with capitalism, but socialism's dismal economic
record has left it few ardent adherents. To supporters of employee stock
ownership plans (ESOPs), the answer is: create more capitalists.

| WHAT ARE ESOPs?

Creating an ESOP is surprisingly simple. A company sets up a trust
fund, creating an ESOP. The trust fund borrows money to buy com-

Corey Rosen is cofounder and executive director of the National Center for Em-
ployee Ownership, a private, nonprofit membership and information organization.
He is the coeditor of *Understanding Employee Ownership* (Cornell University
Industrial and Labor Relations Press, 1991) and two other books on the subject.

pany stock. It may buy outstanding stock—stock held by share-holders, treasury stock, or newly issued shares. The company makes tax-deductible contributions to the trust, which uses the money to repay the loan. As the loan is repaid, the trust releases shares from a "suspense account" and allocates them to accounts for individual employees. Employees receive their shares when they leave the company.

Thanks to a variety of tax incentives and a growing perception that ESOPs can help improve corporate performance, ESOPs, which first appeared in 1974, now cover more than eleven million employees in more than ten thousand companies. ESOPs and similar plans hold about $120 billion in stock, or about 3 percent of all of the stock in U.S. companies. Eighty-five percent of these plans and 60 percent of the employees are in privately held companies (companies whose stock is not publicly traded), where ESOPs are often set up to provide for business continuity, add an employee benefit, or promote greater identification with the firm. However, the 15 percent of the ESOPs that are in public companies are of most concern to social investors, and these are the focus of this chapter.

BOX 54-1
THE NATIONAL CENTER FOR
EMPLOYEE OWNERSHIP

2201 Broadway, Suite 801
Oakland, Calif. 94612
(415) 272-9461

The National Center for Employee Ownership is a private, nonprofit information, research, and membership organization. Founded in 1981 by Corey Rosen and Karen Young, who remain its directors, the center is supported entirely by the work that it does, rather than by foundation, government, or major contribution support. The center currently has seventeen hundred members from employee ownership companies, companies considering employee ownership, professionals in the field, public officials, unions, academics, and other interested people.

The center does not lobby or consult. Instead it focuses on providing accurate and objective information about employee ownership through a number of forums. Its bimonthly newsletter is a detailed report on legislation, research, case studies, and ideas on making employee ownership work well. It publishes fourteen monographs on various aspects of employee ownership, ranging from an introductory reader to a model plan to a primer on managing an employee ownership company. It also publishes a series of research papers and a quarterly professional journal, the *Journal of Employee Ownership Law and Finance*. Its staff also has written or edited four textbooks on employee ownership published by various outside publishers, the most recent of which is *Understanding Employee Ownership* (Cornell University Industrial and Labor Relations Press, 1991).

In addition to its publication series, the center holds more than twenty-five meetings each year, including an annual conference, meetings "just for employee owners," introductory workshops for businesses considering employee ownership, a union symposium, and regional meetings. It has started to establish a series of networks of employee-ownership companies that want to meet with one another on a regular basis to discuss common concerns.

Recently the center has started to focus on international developments in employee ownership, working with governments, businesses, union groups, and people interested in this idea. There has been particular interest in eastern Europe, in the Soviet Union, and in English-speaking countries.

Finally, the center maintains an active data base on employee ownership companies, which it uses to do its own research as well as to work with others interested in doing research in this field. The center has seven full-time staff people and an annual budget of approximately $450,000.

Evaluating ESOPs

How should social investors evaluate ESOP companies? The dramatic growth in ESOPs has not been without its critics. Some charge that ESOPs benefit mostly management; others say they have little impact on corporate performance; still others contend that they harm other stockholders by making companies less open to takeovers. For social investors, these are important concerns. If ESOPs do not really benefit employees, then ESOP companies should not qualify as social investments. If ESOPs have no positive effect on corporate performance or if they hurt shareholders by keeping raiders at bay, then ESOP companies do not qualify as very good investments.

Extensive research at the National Center for Employee Ownership (NCEO; see box 54-1) and elsewhere has produced clear guidelines for evaluating ESOPs in public companies.

- Does the ESOP really make employees better off? In private companies employees usually do not give anything up for an ESOP; in public companies they usually do. Most public companies want their new ESOPs to be "shareholder neutral" (that is, at no extra cost to the shareholder), but some of these ESOPs are more favorable to employees than others.
- Do employees own enough of the company to block a takeover? To some social investors, employee ownership that can block an acquisition is a lousy idea. Others believe that employees should have this kind of say about their work lives.
- Does the company try to create a culture of ownership in which employees have significant opportunities to affect decisions impacting their jobs or their company? The research is conclusive: companies that combine employee ownership with participative management programs perform substantially better than those that do not.

| THE RUSH TO ESOPs IN PUBLIC COMPANIES

Until 1988 public companies never borrowed more than $1 billion in any year to fund their plans. In 1988 they borrowed about twice that. In 1989 they borrowed $24 billion and in 1990, about $8 billion. Why this rush to ESOPs?

Tax Incentives
Federal tax incentives passed in 1987 made ESOPs an attractive way to restructure employee benefits. In a typical scenario, a company that has been making matching cash or stock contributions to an employee savings plan (the employee puts up a dollar, the company fifty cents, for instance) replaces its match with an ESOP. The company borrows money through the plan to buy back outstanding shares or buys treasury shares. It then either puts these shares in an ESOP or retires them and replaces them with preferred shares. The company can deduct both principal and interest on the loan; dividends paid on the stock to repay the loan are deductible as well.

As the loan is repaid, stock is released from the ESOP suspense account to provide a match for employee savings contributions. If the value of their stock exceeds the company matching requirement for what portion of their pay employees have earmarked to go into their savings plan, employees get a windfall; if the value of the shares is less than the match requirement, the company usually makes up the difference. Say employees put up $10 million and the company agrees to match at 50 percent. If the shares released from the suspense account go up in value faster than anticipated, this match might be $6 million, not $5 million.

This somewhat complex transaction has the result of lowering the company's cost of funds needed to provide a match. As long as the share price goes up faster than this reduced cost of funds, then the company comes out ahead. If the shares do worse, the shareholders end up losing.

The Polaroid Ruling

The second major catalyst came in February 1989. A Delaware judge ruled in favor of an ESOP Polaroid had set up to prevent a hostile takeover by Shamrock Holdings. Under Delaware law—half of all major U.S. companies are incorporated in Delaware—an acquirer cannot enter into a business combination with a target for three years unless at least 85 percent of the "disinterested" shareholders agree to the takeover. Are ESOP participants disinterested? The Delaware court said yes, provided that the participants could direct the voting or tendering of the shares (hence the liberal provisions on these issues in public companies). However, the court also ruled that an ESOP was not adverse to the interests of other stockholders if it was "shareholder neutral." That holding discouraged public companies from setting up plans that increase employee benefits by any significant amount.

According to a 1989 NCEO survey and a separate survey by University of Michigan scholars, almost half of the major ESOPs set up in public companies in 1989 were in firms that had been mentioned as takeover targets. Now many other public companies that were not targets felt free to set up ESOPs, because they no longer feared that proposing an ESOP would make them more vulnerable to a takeover, as some lawyers had argued.

Research by Joseph Blasi and Douglas Kruse at Rutgers indicates that now more than one thousand public companies are at least 4 percent employee owned, including at least 25 percent of the largest one thousand companies. A 1990 A. T. Kearney survey of *Business Week* 1,000 companies showed that half said they had an ESOP, with a median ownership of 7.9 percent.

I FINANCIAL EFFECTS ON EMPLOYEES

One of the criteria a social investor might use in evaluating an ESOP is whether it really benefits employees financially. In private companies the answer is clear: ESOPs almost always represent a significant financial improvement over what employees otherwise would have had. The NCEO calculates that an employee making $20,000 a year will accumulate in a typical ESOP $31,000 in stock over ten years and $83,000 over twenty years. In public companies the answer is not so clear.

Three Studies

In a 1989 study the NCEO found that about half of the ESOPs in large public firms increased employee benefits, usually by increasing the size of the company's match to an employee savings plan by about 20 percent. Companies could justify this as still "shareholder neutral" by arguing that they were just passing on some of the additional tax benefits.

A study by economists Susan Chaplinsky and Greg Niehaus in the same year came to similar conclusions: 48 percent of the surveyed public firms increased compensation as a result of the ESOP, 40 percent showed no change, and 6 percent decreased employee compensation. Economist Michael Conte, in another 1989 study, found that public company ESOP participants received an annual average of 12 percent of pay in ESOP contributions and stock growth, compared to just 3 percent of pay for pension plan participants. Overall compensation of ESOP participants, however, was about the same as non-ESOP participants, a fact that could be explained by the sampling differences of ESOP and non-ESOP firms.

These data indicate that employees generally come out whole or somewhat better off as a result of public company ESOPs. While ESOPs are riskier, this element can be overstated. ESOPs are almost always just one of an employee's deferred compensation programs in public companies. Many public companies use less-risky preferred shares in their plans, while others have "make-whole" provisions that guarantee a floor price for the shares. While some ESOP participants will suffer from the added risk, most will not.

There are horror stories, of course. Harcourt Brace Jovanovich and Carter Hawley Hale beefed up their plans to prevent takeovers. Then employees saw their stock plummet to a small fraction of its value when the companies suffered business reversals. The ESOP itself did not cause the problems, but the added debt taken on to buy back shares and a failure to meet business targets did. But for most employees, an ESOP is at least somewhat good news.

ESOPs and Corporate Control

By law, employees must be able to vote all of the shares allocated to them in public companies. As disinterested shareholders in publicly traded firms, employees also can direct the ESOP trustee to tender their allocated shares. The ESOP trustee votes and tenders unallocated shares in the same proportion as allocated ones. Smaller, publicly traded ESOP companies are probably much less likely to go beyond the legal requirements, allowing employee control only of allocated shares. Management, not employees, would direct the trustee's voting and tendering of unallocated shares.

NCEO data indicate that the median percentage ownership in public companies is about 9 percent. At least 12 percent of the public company ESOPs own more than 20 percent of the shares, and 37 percent of the ESOPs own 25 percent or more. (See table 54-1.) These are impressive amounts, but employees have not yet used their ownership position in an active way. We know only of the public companies that have employees elected to their boards (for instance, Oremet, Weirton, and Polaroid). Two of these, Oremet and Weirton, are majority employee owned. In only one case, Pacific Enterprises, have employees initiated an attempt to elect a board member when management was opposed (management won, although barely).

EFFECTS ON RAIDERS. The most significant control that employees have exercised is in hostile takeover situations. Although few of these have actually come to a vote, as at Lockheed and Carter Hawley Hale, the threat of a large employee block has discouraged many raiders. Management and raiders alike assume that employees will oppose takeovers. Although there is little data on this so far, the assumption seems reasonable. Ironically, then, the liberal voting and tendering provisions and the large blocks of stock held by ESOPs may serve to *bolster* management control, not limit it. It may also, of course, allow management to feel freer to focus on long-term concerns rather than short-term demands for profits.

Nonetheless, employees do own enough stock to make a difference if someone were to organize them around particular issues. That has happened very rarely, but substantial employee holdings in companies are relatively recent phenomena. We may see this more

TABLE 54-1

PUBLIC COMPANIES WITH 25 PERCENT OR GREATER ESOP OWNERSHIP

Company	Percentage of ESOP Ownership
Anadac	30%
Applied Power	26
Avondale Industries	54
CBI Industries	27
Carter Hawley Hale	40
Century Telephone	39
Craftmatic	30
DST Systems	30
Diablo Petroleum	30
E-Systems	25
FMC Corporation	32
Graham Corporation	62
Granite Construction	44
J. C. Nichols	30
J. C. Penney	25
Jeffries Group	30
KMS	30
Kerr Glass	26
Kroger Company	35
Lowe's Companies	30
Merrill Lynch	25
Old Stone Bank	37
Olin Corporation	25
Oremet	80
Oregon Steel	40
Phillips Petroleum	25
RLI	25
Ruddick Corporation	44
STV Engineers	30
Stone & Webster	26
Swank Inc.	33
Termiflex	25
Tyson Foods	25
U.S. Sugar	47
USG	26
Weirton Steel	77

NOTE: This list is incomplete, but we believe it includes most of the companies that fit this category. Ownership percentages are based on the most recent published data but are subject to change. In some cases the percentages are only estimates. In all cases the percentages should be regarded as general indicators rather than firm numbers.

frequently in the future. At the very least these holdings will prompt management to take employee interests more seriously.

| EMPLOYEE INVOLVEMENT AND CORPORATE PERFORMANCE

The relationship between employee ownership and corporate performance is clear: if employees have both a financially significant ownership stake and an opportunity to have input in decisions affecting their jobs, the companies will, other things being equal, perform better. According to an NCEO study, participative employee ownership companies grow 8 to 11 percent per year faster than they would have without these programs. A General Accounting Office study found that these firms have a productivity growth rate 52 percent per year higher than they would have had without participation and ownership. (In other words, if their productivity growth rate had been 3 percent per year, it would be 4.5 percent with a combination of ownership and participation.)

The Nature of Participation

By "participation" we mean such practices as quality circles, employee advisory committees, employee participation groups, ad hoc employee problem-solving teams, and other structures designed to provide regular, meaningful opportunities for employees to have input in decisions affecting their work. The popularity of these practices has been increasing among American companies, although they are still not very common.

Hundreds of studies have failed to reveal a consistent relationship between participation alone and performance. For one thing, 80 percent of the participation programs in large companies do not last four years. Both employees and management lose interest. For another, these programs are often so narrowly focused or so limited in the number of people involved that their impact is necessarily small.

By contrast, according to one recent Michigan State survey, 40 percent of the ESOP companies have some substantial employee involvement program, and the percentage of companies having various kinds of participation plans increased from 50 to 100 percent after the ESOP was established. That is, if the incidence of a particular kind of participation program was 20 percent before an ESOP, it would be 30 to 40 percent afterward. Even more remarkable, we have yet to find an ESOP company that has terminated its participation program. Apparently ownership provides both a financial reason for employees to get and stay involved in the programs and a kind of cultural glue that helps change people's expectations about the role of employees in their companies.

IN PUBLICLY TRADED COMPANIES. These general findings apply to all ESOP firms. Publicly traded companies appear to trail far behind privately held companies in adopting participative management approaches. Michael Conte found that among publicly traded companies, ESOP firms were no more likely to have employee involvement programs than non-ESOP firms. An explanation for this may be that privately held companies pioneered ESOPs and have had time to learn more about how they work best. Even in these firms, participation did not become common until the late 1980s. For the most part, publicly traded companies are new to substantial employee ownership, and they, too, may move slowly toward an "ownership culture."

Herman Miller and Polaroid are two companies that have embraced the notion of participation. Herman Miller, of course, is a well-established favorite of social investors. Through an ESOP-like plan, employees own close to 20 percent of the company. They also participate in a gain-sharing program. Employees are organized into work teams, where employee ideas and information are actively solicited. Managers are judged as much on their ability to be participative as their technical skills. At Polaroid, employees own about 20 percent of the company, thanks to a 1989 ESOP. Just after starting the plan, Polaroid initiated a "total quality" program in which employees are divided into teams to help elicit input about how to improve the performance of their particular areas.

The assumption behind the approach of Herman Miller, Polaroid, and the other participative firms is that ownership provides a financial motivation to be involved, while participation provides the structure to channel motivation into the sharing of ideas and information. The guiding principle is that employees are a major resource that most companies ignore.

Effect on Share Prices

Comprehensive data now exists on the market's reaction to the announcement of an ESOP. In companies that have not been mentioned as takeover targets, stock prices typically decline—about 2 percent more than would be expected over a two-day period. Where there is no threat of a takeover, share prices increase 2.4 percent over what would be expected, perhaps because shareholders see the ESOP as an indicator of an impending battle.

Long term, ESOPs increase yield in the first year but decrease it over time. One-year total returns almost doubled in the year after adoption, from 18 percent to 35 percent (these figures include share prices and dividends). After the first year, dividend yield dropped from an average of 4.6 percent preadoption to 2.8 percent postadoption, while capital gains dropped from 13.3 percent preadoption to 12.6 percent postadoption.

Economists Michael Conte and Steven Isenberg have concluded from these data that ESOPs increased return during the first year by adding another buyer to the market and increasing trading volume. After the first year, and therefore after the ESOP had made its major purchases, returns declined to reflect decreased risk for shareholders. Because the ESOP is a large potential buyer, shareholders may be less concerned that prices will decline because not enough people will want to buy.

These studies look at ESOPs simply as financial tools, and that, it appears, is how the market evaluates them. At this point that view probably is appropriate. Few publicly traded companies make much effort to use them as more than that.

| AN ESOP SCREEN

Social investors have many screens, of course, and not all of them are consistent. Most, however, probably would favor a more equitable distribution of wealth and greater influence for employees in companies. Research indicates that companies favor these goals as well. But most publicly traded companies fail to pursue one or both of these goals.

Still, some public companies do meet these criteria and are in businesses social investors do not avoid. Avery Dennison (office products), Donaldson (environmental control and other products), Proctor & Gamble, Standard Brands (paints), and Weirton Steel come to mind.

Investors looking for firms like these should look first at the percentage of ownership held by the ESOP. While there is no strict dividing line, ownership under 10 percent generally means that employees are not getting more than 3 or 4 percent of their pay in an ESOP—probably not enough to make them very aware of, or interested in, being an owner. In companies with more than this percentage, investors should check annual reports and other public materials for signs of a participative management orientation. Most companies that have this orientation are quite proud of it and go to some lengths to let people know about it.

The NCEO maintains lists of publicly traded employee ownership companies and tries to identify which are participative. It also keeps newspaper clippings on these companies, which may provide further clues.

Employee ownership is in a very early stage in publicly traded firms. NCEO believes that the number of such firms will continue to grow and that existing companies will further expand their employee ownership base. While the universe of companies from which social investors might choose is small now, it should expand in the future, providing another valuable set of criteria for concerned investors.

RESOURCES

BOOKS AND PUBLICATIONS

Blasi, Joseph, and Douglas Kruse. 1991. *The New Owners.* New York: Harper Collins.

Chang, Saeyoung. 1990. "Employee Stock Ownership Plans and Shareholder Wealth." *Financial Management* 19 (1): 48–68.

Chaplinsky, Susan, and Greg Niehaus. 1990. "The Tax and Distributional Effects of Leveraged ESOPs." *Financial Management* 19 (1): 29–38.

Conte, Michael. 1989. "Employee Stock Ownership Plans in Public Companies." *Journal of Employee Ownership Law and Finance* 1 (1): 89–138.

Curtis, Jack. 1989. "ESOPs as a Takeover Defense Strategy." *Journal of Employee Ownership Law and Finance* 1 (1): 49–62.

Durso, Gianna. 1989. "Using ESOPs in Public Companies." *Journal of Employee Ownership Law and Finance* 1 (1): 75–88.

Rosen, Corey, and Karen Young, eds. 1991. *Understanding Employee Ownership.* Ithaca, N.Y.: Cornell University Industrial and Labor Relations Press.

Young, Karen, ed. 1990. *The Expanding Role of Employee Ownership in Public Companies.* Greenwich, Conn.: Quorum Books.

NATIONAL CENTER FOR EMPLOYEE OWNERSHIP PUBLICATIONS

Journal of Employee Ownership Law and Finance.
    The *Journal* is a publication of the NCEO. Single issues are available for $25 to members and $35 to nonmembers.

NCEO. "List of ESOPs in Public Companies."

Approximately eight hundred companies are included in this list, which is updated regularly. $50 to members, $100 to nonmembers.

Rosen, Corey, and Karen Young, eds. *Employee Ownership Reader.*

Employee Ownership Reader provides a basic introduction to the field. $15 to members, $25 to nonmembers.

NORTHEAST OHIO EMPLOYEE OWNERSHIP CENTER PUBLICATIONS

Bado, J., ed. *The Case for Ownership: Ohio Case Studies.*

Detailed case studies of five successful Ohio employee-owned firms (20 pp., $5).

Bado, J., and John Logue. *Hard Hats and Hard Decisions: The Evolving Union Role in Employee-Owned Firms.*

A discussion of the role of the union in theory and in practice in employee-owned firms (25 pp., $5).

Bell, Daniel, and Mark Keating. *The Lending Environment for ESOP Companies: The Ohio Bank Study.*

A primer for loan officers and company finance officers (28 pp., $5).

Ivancic, Catherine, and John Logue. *Democratizing the American Corporation: Illusions and Realities of Employee Participation and Ownership.*

A survey of the development of employee participation and ownership in the United States (25 pp., $5).

———. *Employee Ownership and the States: Legislation, Implementation and Models.*

State legislation designed to encourage employee ownership and its implementation (63 pp., $5.95).

Logue, John, and Cassandra Rogers. *Employee Stock Ownership Plans in Ohio: Impact on Company Performance and Employment.*

(38 pp., $5.95.)

PEOPLE AND GROUPS

ESOP Association
1100 Seventeenth Street, Suite 1207
Washington, D.C. 20036
(202) 293-2971

ICOF Consultants Ltd.
318 Summer Lane
Birmingham B19 3RL
    United Kingdom
(011) 44 21 3590188
(011) 44 21 3596357 (fax)
Contact: Leon Boros

Industrial Cooperative Association
58 Day Street, Suite 200
Somerville, Mass. 02144
(617) 629-2700

National Center for Employee
    Ownership
2201 Broadway, Suite 807
Oakland, Calif. 94612-3024
(415) 272-9461
(415) 272-9510 (fax)

New York Center for Employee
Ownership and Participation
1515 Broadway, Fifty-second Floor
New York, N.Y. 10036
(212) 930-0108

Northeast Ohio Employee Ownership Center
Kent State University
Kent, Ohio 44242
(216) 672-3028

Northeast Ohio Employee Owner-
ship Center
Kent Popular Press
Box 905
Kent, Ohio 44240
(for publications)

LABOR ISSUES

David F. Sand Managing Director,
Commonwealth Capital Partners

At a pivotal moment in the 1937 sit-down strike at General Motors, an injunction against the strike was overturned when labor organizers obtained the GM shareholders list and discovered the judge's ownership of several thousand shares of GM stock. Despite this early lesson in the potential power of financial information as a tool for labor, it would be many decades before organized labor began to weave social and financial issues into its portfolio of tactics.

| ORIGINS OF THE CORPORATE CAMPAIGN

By the late 1970s the J. P. Stevens Company had earned the title of America's worst labor law violator. Rather than allow the Amalgamated Clothing & Textile Workers Union to organize the firm, the company shut down any plant that voted to unionize. Working conditions were atrocious, wages low, and benefits practically non-existent. The company would slug it out with the unions in the courts, knowing that it would be found guilty of labor law violations and fined again and again. The leadership of the Amalgamated, spearheaded by its president, Jack Sheinkman, devised a bold plan for pressuring Stevens to recognize the union. In addition to traditional organizing efforts at the factory gates, the union would seek to reach

---

David F. Sand has more than ten years' experience in the field of socially responsible investment. He has been a portfolio manager and research analyst and currently is managing director of Commonwealth Capital Partners, an investment banking firm that specializes in the allocation of investments for housing, jobs, and the environment. A graduate of Princeton University, Sand has a master's degree in public administration from the Kennedy School at Harvard. He lives in Cambridge, Massachusetts.

the company in corporate boardrooms, on Wall Street, and in the minds of consumers. Organizer Ray Rogers helped the Amalgamated launch the first "corporate campaign" using the now-familiar tactics of identifying interlocking corporate directors, putting together stock ownership profiles to target major shareholders, and launching a consumer boycott. The cry "Don't sleep with J. P. Stevens" was used to get consumers *and* investors to change their buying habits. Long successful at stonewalling the union in the factory, J. P. Stevens found itself unprepared for an assault on its corporate board and pressure by the financial community.

At the same time as the campaign against Stevens was bringing national attention to powerful organizing tactics that labor had previously failed to exploit, unions were alerted to the enormous potential possessed by the growth and size of their pension fund assets. Randy Barber and Jeremy Rifkin's *The North Will Rise Again*, which came out in 1978, remains the seminal work for people advocating the use of pension funds for economic purposes in addition to the generation of retirement benefits. Business guru Peter Drucker had sounded an early signal about the growing importance of pension fund ownership of corporate stocks and bonds. But it was Barber and Rifkin who forced union leaders and strategists to recognize that while their political power had diminished, their economic importance was ascending. In an ironic twist—as unimaginable to theorists from Adam Smith to Karl Marx as to labor leaders like John Lewis and George Meany—workers had come to *own* much of the outstanding stock of American corporations. What to do with ownership remains an open question.

The success of the corporate campaign to organize J. P. Stevens and the debates about pension trustees' fiduciary responsibilities ushered in the modern era of union use of economic and investment tactics as part of union organizing and confrontations with corporate power. Throughout the 1980s union experiences with corporate campaigns spread and union leaders became better informed and more active in seeing how their pension assets were invested. The Industrial Union Department of the AFL-CIO started a corporate campaign program office in 1985 that assists unions in developing techniques for the application of financial pressure on antiunion companies. Major efforts in recent years have included campaigns against Litton Industries, Phelps Dodge, and General Dynamics. Over the last decade several major unions, including the Carpenters', Glass Workers', Rubber Workers', and Service Employees' unions, have joined.the Textile Workers' in setting up their own special projects departments to run corporate campaigns.

| LABOR ISSUES FOR INVESTMENT PROFESSIONALS

Social investment professionals face a number of choices in deciding what options about labor issue screening they should offer to clients. Like many social issues, the definitions of "good" and "bad" are in the mind of the beholder when applied to the labor records of companies. Once in a while a company will emerge with a labor record so heinous that it becomes a consensus choice for exclusion from portfolios screened for labor issues, but usually there is no consensus. People should not be discouraged by this murkiness, because worker issues are emerging as one of the pivotal social battlegrounds for the 1990s.

Anyone attempting to screen companies on the basis of union membership will quickly find that many multinational firms have some subsidiaries that are organized and others that are not. One union may have good relations with a subsidiary of the same corporation that a different union is fighting bitterly. A company may have a good record with its organized workers in the United States even as it invests huge sums in outsourcing future manufacturing to low-wage countries. There is an official national "boycott list" maintained by the AFL-CIO, but jurisdictional disputes tend to keep the list short and the companies on it are small and often not publicly held. Reading the *AFL-CIO News* is a good way to track how these issues bubble up at the national level.

An investment manager has to follow a variety of trends in labor issues. It is difficult to get current and accurate information on any of these, but with some digging one can at least monitor:

- company experiences with the National Labor Relations Board. NLRB sanctions for company violations of laws protecting workers' right to organize are an indication of antiunion bias;
- work stoppages due to authorized or unauthorized strikes;
- violations of Occupational Safety and Health Administration or Environmental Protection Agency regulations;
- trends in a company's employment levels in the United States and worldwide;
- the extent of worker ownership, profit sharing, and representation in corporate decision making;

- benefit levels, especially changes in workers' health care coverage;
- funding levels for vested pension benefits and any experiences with plan reversions or recaptures;
- the use of union labor in major company-sponsored construction projects;
- a company's stance as a public citizen, including lobbying efforts on such issues as minimum wage and labor law and charitable contributions to proworker or antiworker causes.

One excellent source for following some of these topics is *Labor and Investments,* a quarterly publication of the AFL-CIO's Industrial Union Department.

| PROXY VOTING

Unions have been part of the recent surge in interest in proxy voting. In its now famous "Avon Letter," the Labor Department, which has primary oversight responsibility for the private pension industry, including union funds, declared that the voting of proxies is a "plan asset" and consequently is part of a trustee's fiduciary obligation to consider how shares are voted. Historically, union trustees—like their corporate counterparts—have not involved themselves in proxy voting. In February 1991, recognizing that unions no longer could leave proxy voting to fund managers, the AFL-CIO issued "Model Proxy Voting Guidelines," which includes discussions of such issues as corporate governance, poison pills, independent directors, South Africa, the MacBride Principles on business in Northern Ireland, and the Valdez Principles on the environment. By urging pension funds to exercise their voices in corporate affairs, organized labor recognizes the reality that unions' power in the marketplace must be added to their power in the workplace.

Union involvement in investment issues now also includes an occasional role for pension funds as direct investors in job-saving or -creating enterprises. Labor's experience with direct investment has been mixed as union pension funds have been investors of last resort in difficult situations, such as airline bailouts. Better economic and social results have come from direct investments in housing and mortgages where union investors have provided prudent capital for jobs *and* worthy social goals.

While unions have been slow to grasp the portent of their economic power, they will continue to expand the scope of worker and social issues applied to the investment of their pension funds. As Amalgamated president Jack Sheinkman put it recently, "We can't afford to just operate on the pavement; we have to be in the Board room."

RESOURCES

AFL-CIO News.

Issued every two weeks, the *AFL-CIO News* is a good buy at $10 a year. (AFL-CIO News, 815 Sixteenth Street NW, Room 209, Washington, D.C. 20006.)

Bulletin of the Department of International Affairs, AFL-CIO.

The Bulletin offers a good way to follow organized labors' views on international issues. It is published monthly by the AFL-CIO (815 Sixteenth Street NW, Washington, D.C. 20006).

Drucker, Peter F. 1976. *The Unseen Revolution: How Pension Fund Socialism Came to America.* New York: Harper & Row.

Labor and Investments.

This quarterly publication of the AFL-CIO's Industrial Union Department (815 Sixteenth Street NW, Washington, D.C. 20006) is the only authoritative publication that regularly tracks issues pertaining to unions and pension fund investment. Subscriptions are $40 per year.

Pensions and Investments.

This biweekly publication by Crain Communications (740 Rush Street, Chicago, Ill. 60611-2590) frequently covers issues of investing and labor. A one-year subscription is $135.

Rifkin, Jeremy, and Randy Barber. 1978. *The North Will Rise Again: Pensions, Politics and Power in the 1980s.* Boston: Beacon Press.

The ground-breaking work on the economic power of union pension funds.

SOCIAL INVESTING

OUTSIDE THE

UNITED STATES

Social investing is alive and well in Canada, northern Europe and the United Kingdom, Australia, and New Zealand. But the movement is at very different stages in these areas, and the screens that social investors deem important can vary significantly from those used in the United States. Especially in screening, we in the United States have much to learn.

We also must make an effort to get to know social investment professionals abroad, because the regulatory strictures that have kept us out of one another's markets are crumbling. If the Securities and Exchange Commission has its way, our markets will soon be open to many foreign issuers, possibly as early as December 1992. We will have to learn a lot about companies rooted in other cultures, and the best source for that information will be socially responsible investing professionals in their home countries.

To our north, Canada has an active social investment community. Marc de Sousa-Shields describes its history and its aspirations. Michael Downie looks at the several socially screened mutual funds that have appeared over the last few years.

Alan Miller not only wrote much of what appears in the eight chapters on the United Kingdom, he also pointed us to the sources for the rest of the material. Only the United States—a country four times the size of the United Kingdom—has a larger social investment community, though it is at least arguable that on a per capita basis, more assets are invested subject to constraints in the United Kingdom. We asked the U.K. mutual funds and service providers to submit descriptions of their activities, just as we did with their U.S. counterparts. Again we emphasized philosophy and screening. Their submissions are most revealing.

Alison MacDonald surveys Europe as it prepares for the introduction of cross-border sales of financial instruments, especially mutual funds. She notes the activities of banks, especially in Germany, in social investing and identifies several of the important research sources.

SOCIAL INVESTMENT IN CANADA

Marc de Sousa-Shields Coordinator,
Social Investment Organization

Social investing is a more recent phenomenon in Canada than it is in the United States. Nonetheless, Canada has a vibrant professional organization, the Social Investment Organization, and a growing number of investment vehicles it is publicizing.

| SOME HISTORY

The first organized forum for social investment in Canada was the Taskforce on the Churches and Corporate Responsibility (TCCR), a Toronto-based coalition of church investors founded in 1975. The TCCR's mandate was (and is) to undertake, as shareholders, research and action relating to the social and environmental impact of Canadian corporations.

Canadian Network for Ethical Investing
The TCCR was the only social investment organization in Canada until the formation of the Canadian Network for Ethical Investing (CNEI). The CNEI was the brainchild of a Victoria, British Columbia, stockbroker, Larry Trunkey. Trunkey was responsible for the first real development of social investing in Canada. In a cross-country tour during 1986 and 1987, Trunkey managed to attract the attention of most major newspapers and television stations. For three years,

Marc de Sousa-Shields, currently the coordinator of the Social Investment Organization, has two degrees specializing in regional and community economic development. Prior to joining the SIO, he did consulting research for unions, social activist organizations, and alternative trading companies.

until it disbanded, the CNEI functioned as the voice for ethically minded investors in Canada.

The Ethical Fund's Appearance

At the same time CNEI was active, other developments increased the profile of social investment. In the mid-1980s Canadians were introduced to several multicriteria ethical mutual funds. These funds applied several ethical screens, including environmental, labor, sin, and human relations screens. The Ethical Growth Fund offered by Vancouver City Savings Credit Union and the Investors Syndicate's Summa Fund were available to both individual and institutional investors. Two others introduced at about the same time, CEDAR Balanced Fund and Crown Life's Crown Commitment Fund, were aimed at institutional investors. All of the funds applied negative ethical screens—screens that avoided investment in companies that did not pass ethical criteria. (The funds are described in chapter 57.)

The Parallel Summit

In 1988 the annual G7 economic summit was held in Toronto, the financial heart of Canada. Worried that the agenda of socially concerned economists and social investors would not be represented at the G7 meetings, a group of church activist and alternative think-tank groups organized a "parallel" conference to debate innovative, socially responsible means of solving world economic problems.

The parallel conference demonstrated the need for continued work and more networking among Canadian social investors. In 1989 a similar coalition led by the economic think-tank Caledon Contemporaries organized the first Canadian National Conference on Social Investment. This conference attracted more than three hundred participants from across the country and demonstrated a growing interest in social investment. From that conference, a continuation committee was formed to establish a formal organization to encourage social investment in Canada.

Thus, the combination of the CNEI, the new funds, and the continued work of TCCR led to developments in the late 1980s that precipitated the formation of Canada's first incorporated nonprofit social investment information clearinghouse: the Social Investment Organization (SIO).

| THE SOCIAL INVESTMENT ORGANIZATION

Led by noted experts in the field of social investments such as Eugene Ellmen (author of *A Canadian Guide to Profitable Social Investment*), Ted Brown (a manager at progressive Toronto Credit Union), Stuart Coles and Don Warne (both United Church ministers), and Carolyn Langdon (a women's rights activist), the Social Investment Organization was incorporated in the spring of 1990.

Today the SIO represents some 120 professional and another 250 institutional and individual investors. These members participate in official SIO activities and take an active role in policy development.

SIO Mandate

The mandate of the SIO is to collect and disseminate information that promotes investment opportunities that benefit society. More specifically, the SIO is to promote investment that encourages the elimination of discrimination based on color, gender, sexual orientation, religion, class, or ethnic background; the advancement of sustainable development; the improvement of workplace and labor relations; access to fair housing and health care; the cessation of the international arms race; and the construction of fair global trade and monetary policies.

To achieve these goals, the SIO works to foster cooperation, mutual assistance, and the exchange of information among individuals and institutions active or interested in the field of social investment. Essentially the SIO is an information clearinghouse and networking facilitator.

The SIO is currently in the process of instituting a professional members network to generate more supply-side interest in social investments. A recent conference hosted by the SIO showed that Canadian social investment needs a mechanism to allow the proven demand for various social investment opportunities to hook up with capital, especially leading-edge venture projects in the environmental technologies industries and cooperative sectors.

BOX 56-1
ETHICSCAN CANADA*

Box 165
Postal Station S
Toronto, Ontario M5M 4L7
(416) 783-6776

EthicScan prepares independent research reports on the social performance of fifteen hundred Canadian companies. These reports include
the *Corporate Ethics Monitor*, comparative assessments of individual
companies and industry groups, and reviews of leading-edge management themes, such as codes of ethics, environmental audits, flexible
benefits, and new-wave management techniques.

Our one-of-a-kind fax and telephone query service provides data on
environmental, hiring and promotion, job creation, strikes and lock-
outs, military-related production, involvement in overseas economies,
and dozens of other performance themes for Canadian companies.

Our Canadian Clearing-house for Consumer and Corporate Ethics
provides such services as seminars, books, and speakers on subjects
including enhancing ethical management, assessing social responsibility, monitoring ethical trends, and related topics.

EthicScan also will publish a unique Canadian consumer publication in 1992, called *Shopping for a Better Canada*. It will be a "green"
life-style guide with shopping information linked to the performance
of companies behind those products.

---

*Submitted by EthicScan.

Publications and Research

To serve members' information needs, the SIO publishes a quarterly
newsletter that provides general information about advances and
events in social investment nationally and internationally. Besides
its newsletter, SIO publishes a series of short guides focusing on
aspects of social investment. The first, *A Short Guide to Social
Investment*, was published in the fall of 1990.

A Short Guide to Socially Responsible RRSP followed. RRSPs are
registered retirement savings plans, an official tax shelter in which
Canadian taxpayers can invest up to 18 percent of their taxable
income tax-free. The purpose of the funds are threefold: (1) to provide
a tax break for the average Canadian; (2) to promote retirement
savings, thus reducing dependence on state-run pension plans; and

(3) to promote investment in Canadian business (only 10 percent of an RRSP can be held in foreign investments). The RRSP guide was particularly successful in providing Canadians with information on how to make an important investment vehicle socially responsible.

Other installments in the SIO guide series will be: *Ethical Investing and Ethical Mutual Funds; Socially Responsible Savings and Deposits;* and *Alternative Investing.* The completion of the guide series will culminate in a larger publication in 1992, *A Canadian Guide to Socially Responsible Investment.*

The SIO periodically researches social investment–related topics. Two recent publications are: *Social Investment Initiatives and Rural Economic Development* and *Social Investment Initiatives and International Development: A Case for Community Social Service Groups and Micro-enterprise Loans.*

In 1990 the SIO focused on developing the consumer aspects of social investment. This activity has increased the levels of social investment. A 1991 survey of SIO members indicated that the average size of its members' social investment portfolios is between $10,000 and $20,000. Another survey of nine social and environmental mutual funds in Canada showed investments in excess of $150 million. These investments, in combination with several labor funds and deposits in Canadian credit unions (considered a form of socially responsible banking) put Canadian social investment assets at well over $150 billion.

Information Network and Seminars
The SIO also offers an information network service. For a small fee the SIO will assess information from its considerable data base to provide members and nonmembers information on a range of investment activities. The SIO data base offers updates on the financial and social investment field and a newspaper clipping service. Beginning in December 1991 the SIO publishes the data base annually in the form of a directory.

Finally, the SIO has developed a series of seminars introducing individual and institutional investors' possibilities. Its seminars encourage participants to seek help from social investment professionals in integrating ethical criteria into their financial decision-making process.

The SIO hopes to become the center of the social investment world in Canada. By providing information and networking services to members and interested parties, the SIO will help to increase the size and the quality of social investment in Canada.

RESOURCES

Social Investment Organization
366 Adelaide Street East, Suite 447
Toronto, Ontario M5A 3X9
(416) 360-6047

CANADIAN MUTUAL FUNDS

Michael Downie Nuala Beck & Associates

Social investment in Canada started with the first credit unions or *caisse populaires*—a cooperative savings and lending association formed by a group with common interests. Members pooled their money to help smooth the cyclical nature of financing a farm operation. To this day credit unions offer members the chance to invest their money in an institution where loans are made to other members, many of whom would not qualify at the local branch of one of Canada's chartered banks. It was a credit union, the Vancouver City Savings Credit Union, that in 1986 kicked off the first ethical mutual fund in Canada, the Ethical Growth Fund.

Ethical investing has not grown as fast in Canada as it has in other countries because of the perception Canadians have of themselves. In the United States, big business has earned the reputation of not acting in the public's best interests. I do not suggest for a moment that Canadian businesses are inherently more humane; rather, there is a perception among Canadians that they operate on a more human scale.

Michael Downie is an economist with Nuala Beck & Associates in Toronto. He received a B.Sc. in life sciences at Queen's University and is presently completing an M.B.A. at York University. Downie has previously worked as a medical researcher at McGill University and as a marketing researcher in biotechnology at York University. His present areas of research include patterns of employment in knowledge-intensive industries and the economic implications of the environmental movement on corporate Canada. He is the author of "The Changing Urban Landscape" and "The New Knowledge Economy of the 1990's," both published by Nuala Beck & Associates.

| CANADIANS' PERCEPTIONS AND CANADIAN REALITIES

We Canadians have felt that we have little impact on the world, even through the operations of our companies and institutions abroad. However, the South African divestment drive of the last decade made people realize that Canadian companies and institutions were involved in regimes that abused human rights—and that a public outcry could affect such questionable business dealings.

In the same vein is Canadians' astonishment when they realize the destruction being carried out on what has always seemed an infinite wilderness. Clear-cut logging and acid lakes in northern Ontario are partially hidden by the vast dimensions of these areas. Likewise, as most Canadians view Canada as a neutral, peace-keeping nation, it comes as a big surprise to learn that Canadian businesses produce military products and deliver services.

Another reason for social investment's slow growth is that it tends to be of greater concern to urbanites, who are more likely to feel the social ills of society. City dwellers witness firsthand a level of crime, pollution, and poverty that does not exist to the same degree in rural areas. Canadians have become more centralized around the three major urban centers. Between those centers are vast tracts of land whose inhabitants may still question the need for social investing.

So it seems that our perceptions tend to lag behind the reality of where this nation stands. Our traditional views of Canada and Canadian business have suggested that there may not be much need for social investing. Nevertheless, as we become more aware of the impact Canadian business has on the environment, developing nations, and the military, we will see growth in the number and net asset size of ethical mutual funds.

| THE GROWTH OF MUTUAL FUNDS IN CANADA

Today more than $100 million is invested in ethical funds across Canada. The focus of the different funds covers most social concerns of society. Some funds focus on one issue, such as the protection of the environment, while other funds try to screen investments away from a broad range of social ills. To the credit of their managers, a few of the ethical mutual funds have been among the top-performing funds over the last three years. This has helped to convince the public that investing in ethical mutual funds means investing in companies with long-term strategies that may outperform the market.

Managing ethical funds in Canada is, by most accounts, quite different than managing ethical funds in the United States or in Europe. One of the challenges of creating and administering an ethical fund is the creation of the screen. Few businesses provide advice and information on creating the desired social screen. Most ethical funds use a combination of different information sources to create their social screen.

Ethical mutual funds face an extra challenge in obtaining consistent information about the activities of Canadian companies. In Canada companies are not required to disclose as much information as in the United States. There is no Canadian equivalent of the Securities and Exchange Commission's form 10-K, so as a result, it is harder to obtain uniform, consistent information on companies. However, Canadian firms listed on American stock exchanges are required to publish 10-K forms, which usually are available in Canada.

Problems of Diversification

One of the challenges facing ethical funds in Canada is how to maintain the required diversification of investments when there are limitations in the number of public companies to invest in.

Over 80 percent of the volume on the Toronto Stock Exchange, Canada's largest, involves only thirty-five companies. This skew suggests the limitations in maintaining portfolio diversification. However, Canada has four exchanges, and by substituting several smaller firms for the larger firms that happen to fail a screen, it is possible to maintain portfolio diversification. There may be an added benefit to this scenario, if ethical mutual funds decide to invest in small companies that require equity capital.

Within the ethical mutual funds, a few public companies make up a sizeable portion of each. This suggests that there may be a shortage of socially acceptable firms within certain industries. The natural-resource sector still represents a large proportion of the Canadian economy. This limits the potential for completely screening resource sectors from ethical funds while maintaining portfolio diversification. And if a particular firm is taking real strides toward improving their social performance, several funds do invest in companies in industries that have not historically been regarded as socially responsible.

While it may be hard to maintain portfolio diversification as a result of screening natural-resource sectors, Canadian funds that screen military associations do not have to exclude as many firms as do U.S. funds. There is less military spending per GNP in Canada, and as a result, fewer firms are involved in supplying the military.

The problem with maintaining portfolio diversification while applying environmental screens may be more a function of the small size of the Canadian high-tech and research industries, many of which are inherently, environmentally benign. The computer hardware and software industries are proportionately smaller in Canada. Ethical funds that invest in foreign firms tend to invest in U.S. technology stocks.

For the most part the ethical mutual funds have not taken a very active role in influencing companies' social performance. When asked if the fund would inform a company if it failed to pass a screen, four out of five said they would not. Only two of the mutual funds will advise the company that it is being dropped from a portfolio. None of the funds reported that it would initiate or support shareholder actions. They reason that once a company passed their screens, they would have no need to influence the company's actions.

It will become a big challenge in the future for ethical mutual funds to differentiate between companies in terms of social commitment. Over the last year many natural-resource companies have begun to focus their energies on changing their image as a destroyer of Canadian wilderness. To a certain degree resource firms have learned to play the public relations game. In the future social screens will have to dig a little deeper than a policy statement or an annual report to determine who has been naughty and who has been nice.

Tax Status of the RRSP Funds and Unitholders

Each fund is considered to be a "mutual fund trust" by the Income Tax Act (Canada); accordingly the funds are taxable only on the investment income and capital gains not allocated to unitholders. Unitholders are taxed on the investment income and capital gains allocated to them. Dividends from taxable Canadian companies are grossed up at the present rate of 25 percent, while unitholders are entitled to a dividend tax credit on the grossed-up amount.

If the trustee does not allocate all capital gains to the unitholders, the remainder is subject to income tax, which will be refunded to the funds when the issued units are redeemed. Of allocated capital gains, 75 percent is taxable and qualifies for the cumulative capital gains exemption. If units are registered retirement savings plans (RRSPs) or registered retirement investment funds (RRIFs), allocated income and capital gains are exempt from income tax until such time as they are withdrawn and do not qualify for any of the tax advantages related to dividends of Canadian corporations and capital gains.

Unitholders may deduct from their taxable income the contributions made to their RRSP or to their spouse's plan, up to the limits allowed under applicable income tax legislation. The contribution limits for an RRSP for 1990:

1. If the unitholder is a member of a registered pension plan (RPP), or if his or her employer contributes on the employee's behalf to a deferred profit-sharing plan (DPSP), 20 percent of earned income less the unitholder's contributions to his or her RPP; or
2. In all other cases, 20 percent of earned income, to a maximum of $11,500.

| CANADIAN MUTUAL FUNDS

Ed. Note: *Unless otherwise noted, the descriptions of the funds in this section were prepared by Michael Downie.*

DESJARDINS ENVIRONMENTAL FUND

Fonds Desjardins Environment
One Complex Desjardins
Box 34
Montreal, Quebec H5B 1E4
(418) 835-4403

Let us start with the baby of Canadian ethical mutual funds, the Montreal-based Desjardins Environment Fund. This fund was established September 10, 1990, and at the end of 1990, the total asset value was listed at $6 million. The trustee of the fund is Desjardins Trust, formerly known as Fiducie du Quebec.

Fund Objectives
The fund's stated investment objectives and practices are "to provide unitholders with a reasonable income return and long-term capital

appreciation. However, the Fund's portfolio consists primarily of shares of environmentally conscious Canadian corporations, more specifically corporations which, . . . through their operations and orientation, make a significant contribution to safeguarding and improving the environment."

This fund is the first of its kind in Quebec and is available only to residents.

Research

The Desjardins Environmental Fund's research is handled by an independent environmental committee, news media, and contracted watchdogs. The fund asks prospective companies to fill out a questionnaire. The research is centered on checking out a company's record and policies of change. The fund's managers believe that some of the industries known traditionally as degraders of the environment provide necessary services. As an example, the fund invests in upstream oil and gas and utilities firms. Jean Morissette, vice president of marketing, comments that "some companies have commitments to the environment even though they are in polluting industries, so we also look at company policies to improve the situation."

Comment

The Desjardins publicity material states that it will not invest in companies that do not strive to improve their environmental performances. It seems that the Desjardins management will be attempting to codify or formalize the selection process. It is left more to the judgment of the independent committee whether or not a company is striving to improve or is following its environmental policies to the letter. It seems that the fund will take the company policy at its word until something should occur and be reported that casts doubt on the stated company line.

INVESTORS SUMMA FUND LTD.

I. G. Investment Management Ltd.
280 Broadway Avenue
Winnipeg, Manitoba R3C 3B6
(204) 956-8536

The second largest of the Canadian mutual funds, the Summa Fund, is sponsored by the Investors Syndicate Limited and managed by I. G. Investment Management Ltd., a subsidiary of Investors Syndicate Limited. The Summa Fund is a mutual fund company. The fund is designed for individuals, RRSPs, RPPs, DPSPs, group RRSPs, and RRIFs.

Fund Objectives

The Summa Fund's publicity material states that the fund refrains from investing in corporations whose primary activities, in the informed opinion of the manager, include:

- the manufacture and distribution of alcohol and tobacco products;
- gambling and gambling-related projects;
- the manufacture of critical weapons systems; or
- the production, importation, or distribution of pornographic material.

The fund also will endeavor to exclude from the fund's portfolio any corporations:

- that have failed to adopt and administer effective pollution control and environmental protection policies; or
- whose practices openly or passively support the acts of repressive regimes.

The aforementioned criteria are applied by the investment department's research and by independent researchers. Investment criteria may be reviewed and changed as a result of client feedback. Any changes would require shareholder approval at the fund's annual meeting.

Fund Performance

As of December 31, 1990, the net assets in the fund totaled $47 million. The fund had approximately fourteen thousand shareholders. The return on investment was 14.4 percent in 1989, down from 17 percent in 1988.

The five largest investments as a percentage of total fund assets are:

- BCE Inc. (telecommunications services)
- Bank of Montreal (Canadian chartered bank)

- CIBC (Canadian chartered bank)
- Toronto-Dominion Bank (Canadian chartered bank)
- Bank of Nova Scotia (Canadian chartered bank)

American corporations held in the fund include Warner-Lambert Company, Intel Corporation, and Tandem Computers.

Comment

Of all Canadian ethical investment funds, the Summa Fund incorporates the least number of evaluation criteria. The fund has put particular emphasis on financial services and consumer-related companies based in Canada. The fund has taken a position in a number of technology stocks in the U.S. market, probably in computer and electronics firms that do not supply the military.

ETHICAL GROWTH FUND

Vancouver City Savings Credit Union
515 West Tenth Avenue
Vancouver, British Columbia V5Z 4A8
(604) 877-7613

The Ethical Growth Fund is the largest ethical fund in Canada. The fund is an open-end trust sponsored by Vancouver City Savings Credit Union. Its investment manager is Connor, Clark & Lunn Investment Management. The fund is designed for individuals, RRSPs, RPPs, DPSPs, group RRSPs, and RRIFs.

Fund Objectives and Criteria

The investment objective is to manage the fund prudently as a common share equity fund in order to maximize capital return on the funds invested, all within the framework of the investment policies. The following investment criteria must be met in order for a company to be held by the fund:

- either registered in or has a head office in Canada;
- encourages progressive industrial relations with staff and employees;
- regularly conducts business in countries that provide racial equality;

- main business is the provision of products and services for civilians (nonmilitary);
- energy corporations' or utilities' major source of revenue is from nonnuclear forms of energy;
- strives to comply with environmental regulations established by governments and government agencies and is committed to implementing environmentally conscious practices; and
- does not derive a significant portion of its income from tobacco.

These criteria are applied by the investment adviser, trustee, and fund administrators. Investment objectives and policies may be amended only at a meeting at which a majority of unitholders are represented.

Fund Performance

For the period ending in March 1990, the Ethical Growth Fund was Canada's top equity mutual fund as measured over the prior three years. For the period, its compound annual rate of return was 10.1 percent, while the average rate of all equity funds was −0.9 percent. As of December 31, 1990, the total assets of the fund were approximately $48 million. The fund had approximately fifty-five hundred shareholders.

The five largest investments as a percentage of total fund assets are:

- BCE (telecommunications), 3.47 percent
- Power Corporation (financial holding company), 2.31 percent
- CIBC (Canadian chartered bank), 2.30 percent
- Placer Dome (gold and metal mining), 2.23 percent
- Finning Ltd. (industrial products), 2.17 percent

Comment

As one of Canada's top-performing mutual funds, the Ethical Growth Fund has been instrumental in attracting investors who once believed that ethical funds would underperform. The Ethical Growth Fund has been expanding the scope of the criteria incorporated in the screen. Returns have declined somewhat since the addition of tobacco and environmental criteria to the fund. However, the decline may be due less to the screen than to the lackluster performance of the Canadian stock markets during most of 1990.

ENVIRONMENTAL INVESTMENT CANADIAN FUND
ENVIRONMENTAL INVESTMENT INTERNATIONAL FUND

EIF Fund Management Ltd.
225 Brunswick Avenue
Toronto, Ontario M5S 2M6
(416) 978-7014

The Canadian Fund and the International Fund are open-end trusts. The sponsor, EIF Fund Management, is a supporter of Energy Probe Research Foundation, a registered charity. The investment manager of the two funds is McLaren Investment Management. The funds are designed for individuals, and the Canadian Fund also is designed for RRSPs, RRIFs, and DPSPs.

Fund Objectives and Criteria

The funds' investment objectives are to achieve maximum growth of capital consistent with reasonable security and income. The Canadian Fund will invest only in Canadian securities. The International Fund will invest only in securities of Canadian and American issuers that are traded on a stock exchange or that trade regularly in a public trading company.

The funds also will promote the causes of the Energy Probe Research Foundation, which are to:

- educate Canadians about the benefits of conservation and renewable energy;
- help Canada to secure long-term energy self-sufficiency with the fewest disruptive effects and with the greatest societal environmental and economic benefits;
- promote the democratic process by encouraging individual responsibility and accountability;
- provide business, government, and the public with information on energy and energy-related issues; and
- help Canada contribute to global harmony and prosperity.

The criteria for both funds are applied by Energy Probe Foundation, incorporating findings from trade journals, government records, and news media.

Fund Performance

As of January 31, 1991, the simple rate of return, including dividends, for the Canadian Fund was −34 percent on the year. The average return for Canadian equity funds was −7.2 percent. For the same period the International Fund showed a simple rate of return of −10.8 percent, while the average return for International equity funds was −7.3 percent. Both funds are relatively small—the Canadian Fund has a total asset value of $700,000, with three hundred shareholders. The International Fund has total asset value of $600,000, with three hundred shareholders.

The five largest investments as a percentage of total fund assets for the Environmental Investment Canadian Fund are:

- Treasury bills, 14.2 percent
- Woodward's (department stores), 13.8 percent
- Air Canada (transportation), 12.2 percent
- Noma Industries (electrical products), 9.4 percent
- National Business Systems (business machines), 9.3 percent

The five largest investments as a percentage of total fund assets for the Environmental Investment International Fund are:

- British Water Utilities, 30.9 percent
- Dow Jones, 8.4 percent
- Maytag (home appliances), 7.9 percent
- Viceroy Homes (home construction), 7.7 percent
- Pacific Western Airlines (transportation), 7.5 percent

Comment

The Canadian Fund and the International Fund had a tough time finding good investments in 1990, and their rates of return reflect this. An investor looking for an average return may be turned off by the funds' holdings in poorly performing industries, such as construction and merchandising. Both funds, however, apply a wide range of evaluation criteria, and their environmental and energy criteria rule out entire industries.

CROWN COMMITMENT FUND

Crown Life Investment Management
160 Bloor Street East, Tenth Floor
Toronto, Ontario M4W 1B9
(416) 928-5102

The Crown Commitment Fund is sponsored by Crown Life. The fund manager is Beutel, Goodman & Company, an investment counseling firm, partially owned by Crown Life or its parent, Crownx.

Fund Objectives
The Crown Commitment Fund is a pooled-equity fund investing in securities of Canadian companies traded on Canadian markets. Its publicity material states that the fund is designed to allow pension plan sponsors, trustees, and participants in group RRSPs to make socially responsible investments. Units of the fund are eligible investments for RRSPs, RPPs, and deferred profit-sharing plans.

Philosophy
The Crown Commitment Fund will invest only in securities of companies that demonstrate social, moral, and ethical responsibility. All potential investments are evaluated according to five criteria:

1. corporate citizenship;
2. progressive employee relations;
3. weapons manufacturing;
4. South African trade; and
5. environmental sensitivity.

Potential investments will be evaluated and classified in one of three categories: suitable, marginal, and not acceptable. Suitable investments will be eligible for purchase by the fund assuming that they meet the managers' other security selection requirements. Securities classified as marginal may be considered for purchase if management of the subject company is clearly moving the company toward the suitable category.

Fund Performance
As of March 31, 1991, the net assets in the fund totaled $5.7 million. The return on investment for the year ending March 31, 1991, was 3 percent; for the year ending March 31, 1990, the return on investment was 4.6 percent; and for March 31, 1989, it was 9.7 percent.

The five largest investments as a percentage of total fund assets are:

• Northern Telecom (telecommunications), 6.7 percent
• Royal Bank (Canadian chartered bank), 6.7 percent

- BCE (telecommunications), 6.3 percent
- Toronto Dominion Bank (Canadian chartered bank), 6 percent
- Empire Life Company A (insurance), 5.5 percent

| THE CANADIAN, ETHICAL, DYNAMIC AND RESPONSIBLE BALANCED FUND*

CEDAR Investment Services Ltd.
902, Kapilano 100, Park Royal
West Vancouver, British Columbia V7T 1A2
(604) 926-7358
(604) 925-2120 (fax)

Fee Structure
The fund is available to Canadian institutional investors and non-profit organizations and is registered pension plan (RPP) eligible. Minimum subscription is $250,000 (Canadian). Initial fees range between .1 percent and .8 percent, based on subscription amount. The quarterly administrative fee covers the services of the manager, custodian, and investment counsel.

Investment Objectives and Philosophy
The primary investment objective of this fund is to preserve capital. The secondary aim is to obtain the maximum rates of return, consistent with minimum real risk, as distinct from volatility.

Within a balanced portfolio, the asset mix decision can have the largest impact on return and risk. In the equity section our investment managers focus on traditional value and control portfolio risk using state-of-the-art optimization techniques. The fixed-income style is based on their top-down economic view, which employs interest rate anticipation as the main source of added value.

Disciplined security selection is based on social responsibility as well as financial performance.

Social Criteria
The manager will evaluate the following social responsibility criteria:

- International—the extent and nature of investment in, or trade with, countries whose governments are oppressive;

*Submitted by the CEDAR Balanced Fund.

- Military—the extent of involvement in the production, distribution, and sale of weapons and other life-threatening products;
- Nuclear energy—the extent of participation in the development, production, and sale of nuclear energy;
- The environment—the extent of environmentally unsound practices in the areas of resource extraction and use, the generation of waste residuals (including emissions and postconsumer waste), and the protection of ecosystem integrity, including endangered species;
- Community relations—the extent of insensitivity to the community;
- Ethical standards—the extent of involvement in illegal or unethical activities;
- Employee relations—the extent of disregard for the principles of equality, dignity, health, and safety of workers; and
- Consumer products—the extent of involvement in the production, distribution, and sale of products that are harmful to consumers.

Responsibility Criteria
In addition, preference will be given to corporations that:

- develop and use renewable energy sources;
- follow responsible environmental practices;
- are sensitive in their community and employee relations;
- employ superior product design.

Investment Counsel
Dustan Wachell Institutional Capital Management
Bentall One
505 Burrard Street, Suite 1850
Vancouver, British Columbia V7X 1M6
(604) 683-4554

Advisers
The fund has a National Advisory Board, whose members act in their personal capacities.

Contact
Crawford E. Laing, F.C.I.A., F.F.A., A.I.A., A.S.A., F.C.A., is president of Crawford E. Laing Ltd. and CEDAR Investment Services Ltd. Laing

TABLE 57-1

CEDAR BALANCED FUND HISTORICAL PERFORMANCE RECORD

| | DATE AS AT: | | | |
	1 Year	2 Years	3 Years	4 Years
December 31, 1991	10.16%	11.29%	10.78%	9.90%
January 31, 1991	13.20	10.18	10.13	9.98
February 28, 1991	13.12	11.11	10.03	10.05

NOTE: The CEDAR Balanced Fund was founded in 1986.
　　Benchmarks for Canadian balanced fund performance include COMSTAT Diversified Universe Median and SEI Median.

qualified as an actuary in Scotland in 1952. He has owned his own consulting actuary business since 1970 and has advised corporations, governments, and unions on pensions and employee benefits as well as acted as a consultant to workers compensation boards. Having been involved in investments since the early years of his career, Laing assists clients in the selection of investment managers and monitors their performance on behalf of pension funds and other clients.

TABLE 57-2

THE CEDAR BALANCED FUND HISTORY OF UNIT VALUE

	1987	1988	12-Month Increase	1989	12-Month Increase	1990	12-Month Increase	1991	12-Month Increase
January 1	$100.000	$ 99.327	7.30%	$102.614	9.78%	$104.578	12.43%	$102.984	10.16%
January 31	100.666	102.075	9.54	105.681	10.02	102.732	7.24	103.962	13.20
February 28	101.226	103.176	10.11	104.764	7.90	103.652	9.14	104.817	13.12
March 31	101.804	103.766	10.11	105.238	7.77	104.751	9.80	105.615	12.78
April 30	102.349	103.825	9.59	106.391	8.89	105.798	9.70	106.524	12.63
May 31	102.972	104.259	9.38	110.119	12.24	107.067	7.26	107.383	12.19
June 30	103.782	105.877	10.21	112.224	12.64	108.269	6.43	108.136	11.72
July 31	103.138	105.926	10.95	116.501	16.88	109.515	3.70	109.016	11.35
August 31	103.307	104.916	9.71	115.116	16.60	110.707	6.09	109.816	10.96
September 30	103.030	106.917	12.10	113.611	12.92	111.782	8.54	110.671	10.75
October 31	106.237	110.063	11.92	114.803	10.84	112.994	8.58	111.451	10.33
November 30	105.322	108.528	11.32	114.158	11.78	114.088	10.25		
December 31	107.301	109.045	9.78	115.364	12.43	115.200	10.16		
Year-end Dividend	7.974	6.431		10.786		12.216			
Ex-Dividend Value	99.327	102.614		104.578		102.984			

NOTE: The CEDAR Balanced Fund was founded in 1986.
Benchmarks for Canadian balanced fund performance include COMSTAT Diversified Universe Median and SEI Median.

SOCIAL INVESTMENT
IN THE UNITED KINGDOM

Alan Miller Financial Platforms Ltd.

Money has traditionally been a tool of exchange. In recent years it has in the United Kingdom become a tool for change—social and economic change.

| SOCIALLY RESPONSIBLE INVESTMENT IN THE UNITED KINGDOM

Socially responsible investment (SRI) in the United Kingdom can be traced back to Victorian England to both social reformers who advocated "5 percent philanthropy"—the provision of affordable housing for the poor while still providing a reasonable investment return—and the early Quaker company pension funds that had restrictions on investments in armaments.

Postwar history and a significant American influence provide the key to the modern-day phenomenon of SRI in the United Kingdom. Children born in the postwar baby boom grew up in a time of unprecedented change, both political (with the cold war between East and West and the resultant arms race) and social.

In America, concerns over social issues crystallized in the 1960s

---

Alan Miller is director of Financial Platforms Ltd. He has spent more than ten years in the U.K. financial services industry, specializing in social investments. He has written extensively on socially responsible investing in the United Kingdom. In May 1991 the London Financial Times Business Information Service published his *Socially Responsible Investment: The Financial Impact of Screened Investment in the 1990s.* A leading advocate of social investing in the United Kingdom, he is the founding chairman of the U.K. Social Investment Forum.

youth culture and the growth of the peace movement. In the 1970s there was vociferous resistance to involvement in the Vietnam War, with draft resisting and shareholder action against companies involved in the war. Through the struggle, attention also was drawn to wider issues, such as investment in countries where human rights were denied, equal opportunities for both women and ethnic groups, and pollution and environmental concerns.

It was, however, the issue of divestment from South Africa that became a focal point for socially concerned investors in the 1970s and, through legislation, became an action point, particularly in the United States, in the 1980s. Peace, civil rights, antinuclear and environmental pressure groups (largely precipitated by the Bhopal and Chernobyl accidents) also helped to fan the flames of social investing.

| INVESTMENT ALTERNATIVES

For many years wealthy individuals in the United Kingdom have been able to match their investments with their social conscience, and indeed, many social and religious bodies have done so. In June 1984 the launch of the Stewardship Fund extended ethical investment, as SRI is more commonly known in the United Kingdom, to the smaller investor. The Stewardship Fund is a unit trust, the most popular form of individual investment in the United Kingdom. The fund's launch had as much to do with the Quaker origins of the parent insurance company as with any commercial judgment. Nonetheless, it was the first ethical unit trust.

Types of Funds

Since 1984 more than twenty socially responsible investment alternatives have been started, many as unit trusts, although there are also bond funds (life assurance vehicles that resemble unit trusts but are taxed differently), pension funds (retirement plans), and personal equity plans (PEPs, a statutory scheme designed to encourage small investors to invest in equities). A number of funds also are offered as life insurance bond funds. U.K. bond funds are similar in approach to unit trusts, but different taxation rules apply, making them attractive particularly to higher-rate taxpayers and those who wish to receive a high level of income. Usually the bond uses the unit trust equivalent as the underlying investment vehicle, but two bond funds (the Ethical Investment Fund and the Homeowners Green Chip Fund) invest directly in equities.

Many ethical unit trusts can be linked to various types of retirement plans, but two specialist pension funds for substantial investments are available as well.

Screening

Most of the ethical trusts seek first to avoid particular issues, then look for positive qualities in those ethically acceptable companies that remain.

Environmental funds primarily seek environmentally conscious companies while maintaining negative social screens that tend to be less restrictive than ethical funds. A number of environmental sector funds have appeared, most of them in the wake of the explosive "green consumerism." Some of these funds do not apply any social assessment to their investment and may invest in socially unacceptable companies, simply because of the environmental nature of their products. Table 58-1 charts the screens applied by the major U.K. funds.

Many SRI funds conduct their social screening themselves, although screening organizations, such as Ethical Investment Research Information Service (EIRIS), offer social research commercially. An advisory committee is an important ingredient in a socially screened fund, as it helps establish and maintain the ethical standards of the fund and provides an additional resource for the fund manager.

Performance

In its first year of operation, not only did the Friends Provident Stewardship Fund outperform the Financial Times All-Share Index, but it consistently outperformed by a significant margin all of the Friends Provident's nonscreened funds. The Medical Investments Health Fund was the top trust in its sector (international growth) for the calendar year 1990 (and was the top trust over two years to end 1990), and it was the top of *all* unit trusts in the year to end February 1991—the first time ever that a U.K. ethical fund topped the list.

I INSTITUTIONAL INVESTMENTS

Local authority (local government) pension fund investments, like their U.S. counterparts, form the major part of the institutional

TABLE 58-1

SOCIAL CRITERIA APPLIED BY U.K. FUNDS

Areas of Avoidance	FUND NAME							
	AL	AC	AM	CL	EN	FE	FI	FR
Advertising standards								
Alcohol	•	•	•			•		
Animals:								
Cosmetics	•		•					
Medical research			•					
Fur								
General					•			•
Armaments	•	•	•	•	•	•		•
Banks								
CFC production				•				
Gambling	•		•	•		•		•
Nuclear processing/power	•			•				
Oppressive regimes	•				•			•
Polluters								•
Pharmaceuticals		•						
Political donations								
South Africa	•	•	•		•	•		•
Tobacco	•	•	•	•	•	•	•	•

TABLE 58-1

SOCIAL CRITERIA APPLIED BY U.K. FUNDS, CONT.

Areas of Avoidance	FUND NAME						
	HE	ME	NM	SE	SO	TA	EIF
Advertising standards				•			•
Alcohol	•		•	•	•	•	•
Animals:							
Cosmetics				•			•
Medical research				•			•
Fur			•	•			•
General			•	•	•		•
Armaments	•	•	•	•	•	•	•

NOTE: See key on p. 665.

Areas of Avoidance	HE	ME	NM	SE	SO	TA	EIF
Banks				•			•
CFC production							
Gambling	•		•	•	•	•	•
Nuclear processing/power		•		•	•		•
Oppressive regimes			•	•	•		•
Pharmaceuticals				•			•
Political donations				•			•
Polluters							
South Africa		•	•	•	•	•	•
Tobacco	•	•	•	•	•	•	•

TABLE 58-1

SOCIAL CRITERIA APPLIED BY U.K. FUNDS, CONT.

Areas of Support	AL	AC	AM	CL	EN	FE	FI	FR
Charitable donations								
Community involvement								•
Ecology				•				
Education	•		•					
Employee welfare								•
Energy conservation			•					
Protection of the environment	•			•	•			
Health care	•		•		•			
Housing	•		•					
Pollution control			•					•
Quality of life					•			
Safety/security	•		•		•			
Third world projects	•							
Waste management			•					
General positive criteria							•	

NOTE: See key on p. 665.

TABLE 58-1

SOCIAL CRITERIA APPLIED BY U.K. FUNDS, CONT.

Areas of Support	FUND NAME						
	HE	ME	NM	SE	SO	TA	EIF
Charitable donations			•				
Community involvement			•	•			•
Ecology		•					
Education							
Employee welfare			•	•		•	•
Energy conservation		•					
Protection of the environment	•	•	•	•			•
Health care	•						
Housing							
Pollution control		•		•			
Quality of life							
Safety/security				•			
Third world projects							
Waste management							
General positive criteria					•	•	

TABLE 58-1: SOCIAL CRITERIA APPLIED BY U.K. FUNDS, CONT.

KEY

AL—Abbey Life Ethical
AC—Acorn Ethical
AM—Allchurches Amity
CL—Clerical Evergreen
EIF—Ethical Investment Fund
EN—CIS Environ
FE—Buckmaster Fellowship
FI—Fidelity Famous Names

FR—Friends Stewardship
HE—Medical Investments Health
ME—Merlin Ecology
NM—NM Conscience
SE—Scottish Equitable Ethical
SO—Sovereign Ethical
TA—Target Global

socially screened investment market. They screen primarily on South Africa but increasingly on environmental issues. The Pensions Investment Research Consultants (PIRC) provides advice and social screening to a number of local authorities. PIRC has established the U.K. Ethical Index, which is screened for South Africa, political donations, and companies that were nationalized industries—such as British Telecom. Very recently PIRC launched the U.K. Environmental Code, which establishes environmental assessment criteria in a way similar to the U.S. Valdez Principles.

Local authorities are also at the forefront of community developments and urban renewal programs, although this area is still in its infancy. Venture capital is most developed among local authorities. A February 1989 survey by PIRC of local authorities found that local authority pension funds had invested £179.1 in venture capital enterprise and allocated a further £475.7 million for future venture capital investments.

| CHURCHES AND CHARITIES

Some church and charity funds are SRI managed. But the statutory duties of trustees of both charities and pension funds require that a trustee maximize the fund's investment return. Despite a number of legal rulings, many organizations avoid SRI because they perceive the legal duty to mean that no investment restrictions should be applied.

The Megarry Judgment

The duties of trustees became less clear with the 1984 law case of *Cowan v. Scargill*. The Mineworkers Pension Fund, led by union president Arthur Scargill, sought to apply geographic restrictions on the pension fund's investment. The case went against the Mineworkers Pension Fund. Sir Robert Megarry held that trustees must put aside personal interests and views in considering which investments to make. The court also ruled that trustees must act in the best financial interest of the trust and beneficiaries and not limit the scope of investments available to them.

Still, Megarry did state that in certain circumstances trustees might consider matters other than financial benefit. He was not asserting that

> the benefit of the beneficiaries which a trustee must make his paramount concern inevitably and solely means their financial benefit even if the only object of the trust is to provide financial benefits. Thus if the only actual or potential beneficiaries of a trust are all adults with very strict views on moral and social matters condemning all forms of alcohol, tobacco and popular entertainment, as well as armaments, I can well understand that it might not be for the "benefit"

of such beneficiaries to know that they are obtaining rather larger financial returns under the trust by reason of investments in those activities than they would have received if the trustees had invested the trust funds in other investments.

Since the Megarry judgment, some trustees have restricted divestment action. However, by demonstrating good performance and taking account of the perspectives of members, pension and charity fund trustees can apply social criteria to their investment funds.

A number of subsequent rulings have failed to clarify the position of trustees. In the latest case, the bishop of Oxford, Richard Harries, is seeking a ruling that the church commissioners (government-appointed charitable trustees established to further the nationwide work of the Church of England) have a Christian as well as a financial duty, and therefore church investors should not put financial gain before Christian values.

Bishop Harries' action does not arise from a dispute within the church establishment. Rather, he is seeking a clear ruling concerning the duties of trustees. The resolution of this case will have implications not only for the Church of England but for all charities and trustee-managed investments.

Shareholder Action

Due to legislation, shareholder action is more difficult in the United Kingdom than it is in the United States. As in the United States, churches have been at the forefront of this approach to SRI. One successful action was the eighteen-year campaign to get Barclays Bank out of South Africa. Currently attempts are continuing (as yet unsuccessfully) to persuade the church commissioners to sell their investments in Shell Oil because of its South Africa interests.

PIRC has joined with the Investor Responsibility Research Center in the United States to offer a worldwide proxy voting and intelligence service.

| MARKET SUSTAINABILITY

Today's SRI market provides opportunities for individual and institutional investment across a wide range of social issues and with social screens based on positive and negative criteria.

Companies are beginning to recognize their responsibilities to the communities in which they do business and to their staff, and their ultimate accountability to their shareholders. While many companies with real conviction have accepted corporate responsibility, many others recognize only that the influence of the SRI market can undermine the very share price and profitability of a group. Similarly, companies have conformed with changes in public attitudes on such issues as South Africa or the environment and have altered their attitudes, realizing that otherwise they would be denied government contracts.

Perhaps the most revealing aspect of the growth of SRI in the United Kingdom is its increased acceptance among the mainstream financial institutions, led mainly by unions and local authority pension funds. They joined first in divestment from South Africa and now are adding their considerable influence to environmental issues.

Social Investment Forum

Founded in 1990, the U.K. Social Investment Forum will promote the development of socially responsible investment throughout the United Kingdom. Similar in its emphasis and appeal to the U.S. Social Investment Forum, it hopes to be representative of all aspects of socially responsible and socially directed investment.

| THE FUTURE

The concept of ethical investments is shaking its "crank" image and gaining wide acceptance in the United Kingdom. The total amount invested in accordance with some form of social charter is now in excess of £100 billion. The *Economist* and the *Financial Times* have commissioned major analytical reports on SRI.

Environmental issues dominate both the domestic agenda and the political agenda for the 1990s. It was Margaret Thatcher who said in 1988, "No generation has a freehold on this earth. All we have is a life tenancy—with a full repairing lease." The popular impetus of environmentalism has impacted SRI more than most investment approaches.

With the worldwide emergence of new government-sponsored environmental initiatives and pressure for environmental responsibility increasing, the prospects for the continued growth of SRI throughout the 1990s are very good indeed. Socially responsible investment in the United Kingdom has come of age.

U.K. RESEARCH SERVICES AND NEWSLETTERS

Ed. Note: *This chapter consists of descriptions of social research services and publications submitted, unless otherwise indicated, by the services. Those that chose not to submit material are listed in the directory in appendix B.*

| THE ETHICAL INVESTMENT RESEARCH INFORMATION SERVICE (EIRIS)

401 Bondway Business Centre
71 Bondway
London SW8 1SQ United Kingdom
(011) 44 71 833 4432

The Ethical Investment Research Information Service (EIRIS) is a not-for-profit U.K. organization providing information on a wide range of issues to help concerned investors apply ethical criteria to investment. EIRIS also promotes debate toward a wider understanding of corporate responsibility issues through publications, conferences, and seminars.

EIRIS reports on U.K. corporate activity in the areas of advertising, alcohol, animal experiments, arms, cosmetics and pharmaceuticals, fur, leather and meat, gambling, nuclear power, nuclear weapons, political contributions, South Africa and Namibia, and tobacco. EIRIS also is researching U.K. corporate involvement in the third world, the environment, employment conditions, and pollution.

EIRIS is supported mainly by subscription fees for the following services:

- Summary reports pinpointing those companies in a portfolio that are involved in the activities indicated by the subscriber.
- "Acceptable" lists giving the name and stock exchange grouping of all companies in the Financial Times All-Share Index that are not involved in the activities indicated by the subscriber.

- Fact sheets giving detailed information on individual companies.
- The *Ethical Investor*, EIRIS's quarterly newsletter.
- Periodic publications and briefings, which currently include a guide to ethical funds in the United Kingdom; and briefing papers on South Africa, nuclear weapons, and advertising.

Contact
Peter Webster, executive secretary.

| MERLIN RESEARCH UNIT

Jupiter Tarbutt Merlin Ltd.
197 Knightsbridge
London SW7 1RB United Kingdom
(011) 44 71 581 8015
(011) 44 71 581 3857 (fax)
269705 JUPITG (telex)

Services
The Merlin Research Unit specializes in the assessment of company performance on environmental and social issues. It was established initially to service the Merlin Jupiter Ecology Fund. Since then its scope has expanded and it now services the Merlin International Green Investment Trust (MIGIT) and a growing number of private clients.

Many institutions are beginning to develop green investment policies. The Research Unit is able to assist in the development of appropriate investment strategies, offering portfolio reviews and supporting research and fund management services. During 1990 major reviews of this type were carried out for several prestigious organizations.

The Research Unit has a rapidly expanding international data base on companies. In addition to the information summarized in the charts (see table 59-1), the unit builds detailed profiles on the environmental and social records of each company.

To complement these assessments, the unit undertakes reviews of industrial sectors and examines the comparative performance of companies operating in the same field. To date the unit has done a worldwide survey of gas companies and U.K. surveys of supermarket, water, and electricity distribution companies.

TABLE 59-1

MERLIN RESEARCH UNIT CHART

Company	ENVIRONMENTAL			South Africa	Defense	Nuclear	Tobacco	Charitable Donations	Watch
	Policy	Audit	Coordinator						
Abbott Mead Vickers	No	Yes	No	<.1%	<.1%	<.1%	<.1%	1.04%	
Alan Paul	Yes	No	Yes	0	0	0	0	2	
Argyll Group	Yes	No	Yes	0	0	0	0	1	
Bimec	No	No	No	0	9	0	0	0	Defense contracts
Body Shop International	Yes	Yes	Yes	0	0	0	0	?	
Eurotherm	No	No	No	<1	0	<1	0	.5	
Haden Mclennan Holdings	Yes	No	No	<1	<1	<1	<1	.5	
Halma	Yes	No	Yes	0	<1	<1	0	0	
Ocean Group	Yes	U/C	Yes	<1	<1	0	0	.75	
RPS Group	Yes	Yes	0	0	0	0	?	?	
Rotork	No	No	Yes	<1	0	<1	?	.1	
Servomex	Yes	No	Yes	<.1	<10	<1	<.1	.1	Defense contracts
Shanks & McEwan	Yes	Yes	Yes	0	0	0	0	<.1	
Sheffield Insulations	No	No	No	0	0	0	0	?	
Siebe	Yes	Yes	Yes	<1	<10	0	0	.1	Defense contracts

SOURCE: Merlin Research Unit.

Newsletter
The *Merlin Research Bulletin* is published in the recognition that unitholders have a right to know about the environmental and social nature of their investments. It is produced with each six-monthly fund managers' report and includes details of companies in the Merlin Jupiter Ecology Fund portfolio and related commentary and graphics. The newsletter was the first to be published by an ethical or green fund in the United Kingdom and set a precedent that other funds have now followed.

The newsletter is available to nonunitholders. Currently there is no charge.

Contact
Tessa Tennant, cofounder of the Merlin Jupiter Ecology Fund and head of the Merlin Research Unit, joined Jupiter Tarbutt Merlin in 1988. Prior to that she worked in the United States for Franklin Research & Development Corporation, where she developed criteria for the assessment of corporate environmental performance. As one of the first environmental science graduates from Kings College, London, she worked on industry and parliamentary affairs for the Green Alliance from 1983 until 1987.

I PENSIONS INVESTMENT RESEARCH CONSULTANTS LTD.*

40 Bowling Green Lane
London EC1R 0NE United Kingdom
(011) 44 71 833 4432
(011) 44 71 837 7612 (fax)

Pensions Investment Research Consultants Ltd. (PIRC) is an independent company that provides professional services for institutional investors concerned with developing socially responsible investment strategies.

Services
PIRC offers a comprehensive range of independent professional services to enable socially responsible investors to achieve their financial and social objectives. These services include:

*Prepared by the editorial staff from materials supplied by PIRC.

- Strategic investment advice—advice to investors on the establishment of goals, criteria, management, and monitoring systems that enable them to realize their SRI objectives;
- Shareholder action—assistance to investors in using their voting rights and influence in a positive and informed manner;
- Research—custom-tailored research reports designed for trustees. PIRC also is working on a variety of special projects, including a local ownership data base that charts current and potential links between a pension fund's portfolio and the local economy;
- Intelligence service—a comprehensive information service for pension fund trustees on key investment issues;
- Training—professional training for lay trustees, including comprehensive briefing material;
- Union pension services—information, analysis, and advice for trade unionists negotiating on pensions; and
- Investment projects—development of new investment vehicles for institutional investors with SRI objectives.

The Greening of Global Investment

PIRC's finance director (and one of its cofounders), Anne Simpson, has recently published *The Greening of Global Investment* (Economist Publications, 1991, £150/$270). Simpson offers a clear overview of environmental investing with extended case studies on the corporate response. Her lengthy overview of ethical investment deserves close reading by Americans. It would be a pity if a mass market publisher did not buy the rights to this invaluable book.

Contact
Alan MacDougall, managing director.

U.K. UNIT TRUSTS
AND INVESTMENT TRUSTS

Ed. Note: *This chapter consists of descriptions of ethical unit trusts and investments trusts in the United Kingdom. The descriptions were prepared, unless otherwise indicated, by Alan Miller of Financial Platforms Ltd. Those that did not choose to submit material are listed in the directory in appendix B.*

Several SRI unit trusts offer personal equity plans (PEPs) using the unit trust solely as the vehicle for investment—namely CIS Environ, Friends Provident Stewardship Income, NM Conscience, and Sovereign Ethical unit trusts. Another SRI PEP, First Charter, offers direct investment in equities. It is included in this chapter.

| ACORN ETHICAL UNIT TRUST

One White Hart Yard
London Bridge
London SE1 1NX United Kingdom
(011) 44 71 407 5966

Launched in November 1988, the Acorn Unit Trust is a small fund of just £600,000.

Research
No independent mechanism exists, and Acorn has no advisory committee.

Minimum Investment
The minimum investment in this fund is £1,000.

| AMITY FUND

Allchurches Investment Management Services
19/21 Billiter Street
London EC3M 2RY United Kingdom
(011) 44 71 528 7364

The manager of the Amity Fund, Allchurches Investment Management Services Ltd., is ultimately owned by Allchurches Trust Ltd., a charitable trust company whose surplus profits are channeled back for use in the church and community. The Amity Fund was launched in February 1988.

Research
Amity conducts its research in-house, assisted by an advisory committee.

Minimum Investment
Minimum investment in the Amity Fund is £500 and £25 monthly. Monthly investments in excess of £100 attract a 1 percent extra allocation of units.

| ETHICAL TRUST*

Abbey Unit Trust Managers Ltd.
80 Holdenhurst Road
Bournemouth BH8 8AL United Kingdom
(011) 44 0202 292373
(011) 44 0345 717373 (dealing)

Fee Structure and Restrictions on Potential Investors
The minimum initial and subsequent investments in £750. The fees are 6 percent initially on investments and 1.25 percent annually from the property of the trust. The trust is open to investment by individuals or institutions.

Investment Objective and Policy
The investment objective of the trust is capital growth mainly from firms quoted on the U.K. stock market with ethically sound attitudes and practices. Investments also are made in some selected overseas opportunities, to a maximum of 25 percent of the trust. There is no restriction on investment opportunities in convertibles provided that they meet the ethical criteria for the trust.

Liquidity: maximum 30 percent.
Number of holdings: minimum 40, maximum 60.

*Submitted by the Ethical Trust.

Yield: minimum 75 percent of Financial Times (FT) All-Share
yield.

Accounting date: May 31.

Income allocation date: allocations of income are made on July 31
in each year and the grouping period for equalization is June 1
to May 31.

Social Criteria

The trust will exclude the following areas altogether:

- armaments
- nuclear processing
- alcohol production
- gambling
- animal exploitation for cosmetics
- exploitation of endangered species
- tobacco production

Certain areas are allowed as long as they account for less than 10
percent of the company's sales, profits, and capital employed. These
include:

- the sale of alcohol and tobacco products
- involvement in nondemocratic regimes

The trust will actively seek companies involved in the promotion
of an improved, safer, and more healthy standard of living for current
or future generations. These will include companies in:

- health care
- environmental control and conservation
- security services or products
- safety equipment
- financial protection
- construction

In addition, stock selection will pay particular attention to companies with the following:

- a high standard of conduct by the management
- progressive labor relations policy

- good consumer relations
- good-quality products
- good safety standards

The portfolio will be structured toward the United Kingdom and will aim to secure as broad a representation in the market as the ethical criteria allow. The overseas content will be composed mainly of more specialist areas, with particular emphasis on the positive selection criteria, such as health care and environmental control.

TABLE 60-1

THE ETHICAL TRUST PERFORMANCE DATA

Trust Size (£M)	Offer Price (P)	PERFORMANCE*			
		6 Months	1 Year	2 Years	3 Years
7.1	53.86	22.9%	6.7%	5.6%	31.8%

SOURCE: Micropal.

*Offer to offer, net income reinvested.

Manager

Abbey Unit Trust Managers Ltd. (AUTM), one of the leading unit trust groups in the United Kingdom, with more than £650 million under management, offers a comprehensive range of authorized unit trusts to meet most investors' needs.

AUTM is part of the Lloyds Abbey Life plc group, which provides a wide range of financial services both in the United Kingdom and in Europe.

Day-to-day investment management is carried out by Abbey Life Investment Services Ltd., a dedicated team of investment managers and analysts with a wealth of experience across U.K. and international markets.

The Advisory Board

Ethical Trust's advisory board is a committee formed from eminent and respected members of the community with a strong and active interest in improving the quality of life. Every three months the managers of the Ethical Trust report to this board, which reviews the overall performance and scrutinizes the suitability of existing and potential investments. The board is highly active.

I FELLOWSHIP TRUST

Credit Suisse Buckmaster & Moore
Beaufort House
15 St. Botolph Street
London EC3A 7JJ United Kingdom
(011) 44 71 247 7474

Credit Suisse Buckmaster & Moore have managed ethical funds for many years, including funds for trade unions, churches, charities, hospitals, and health authorities. It launched the Fellowship Trust in July 1986.

Research
No independent research mechanism exists. The trust has an advisory committee.

Minimum Investment
The minimum investment is £1,000 or £25 a month.

I FIDELITY FAMOUS NAMES TRUST

Fidelity Investment Services Ltd.
Oakhill House
130 Tonbridge Road
Hildenborough, Tonbridge
Kent TN11 9DZ United Kingdom
(011) 44 73 236 1144

Fidelity Investment Services Ltd. is one of the largest unit trust groups in the United Kingdom, with over £2.6 thousand million under management (as of September 1990). Although many do not consider it an SRI fund, Fidelity Famous Names Trust does avoid major tobacco producers in the United Kingdom and Europe.

Research
The trust has no advisory committee, although its list of unacceptable companies is compiled in conjunction with the British Medical Association.

Minimum Investment
The minimum investment is £1,000, or £50 per month.

I FIRST CHARTER ETHICAL PEP

First Charter Investment Management Ltd.
Graylands
High Street
Chipping Ongar, Essex CM5 9LD United Kingdom

Formerly managed by Dominion Investment Management Ltd., which launched the personal equity plan in July 1988, the Ethical PEP was acquired by First Charter Investment Management Ltd. in 1989.

Criteria for Investment
Fifty percent of the funds invested in the PEP will be invested in the Fellowship Trust (see page 678) and the remainder will be in a spread of U.K. equities chosen by reference to the same criteria as the Fellowship Trust.

Minimum Investment
The minimum investment is £500 (£25 monthly) and the maximum is the statutory limit, currently £6,000.

I FRIENDS PROVIDENT STEWARDSHIP FUNDS

Friends Provident Unit Trust Managers
72/122 Castle Street
Salisbury SP1 3SH United Kingdom
(011) 44 72 241 1622

Launched in June 1984, the Stewardship Unit Trust was the first U.K. investment fund to apply social principles to investment. Founded in 1832 by the Society of Friends (Quakers), the Friends Provident has over £8 thousand million under management worldwide.

Friends Provident added two funds in October 1987. The North American Stewardship and Stewardship Income Trusts share identical ethical criteria, although with different investment objectives. An Australian Stewardship Fund also is available in Australia. Its criteria are less restrictive and totally different from the other funds.

Research

The Ethical Investment Research Information Service (EIRIS) provides the research. An advisory committee gives guidance to the managers and helps establish the ethical criteria of the trust.

Minimum Investment

The minimum investment is £1,000 initially and thereafter £500 or £30 monthly. The Stewardship Income Trust is offered as a personal equity plan with lump-sum or regular contributions. The minimum monthly investment in that trust is £40.

| HEALTH FUND

Medical Investments Ltd.
10 Queen Street
Mayfair
London W1X 7PD United Kingdom
(011) 44 71 495 1511

The Health Fund was launched in April 1987 by Medical Investments Ltd. Medical Investments does not manage any other funds at this time. The fund is targeted for growth, although it is a distribution (income-paying) trust.

Social Criteria of the Trust

The trust is primarily a health and medical technology fund. Its ethical criteria include:

Positive Issues	Avoidance Issues
Health care	Manufacture or sale of alcohol
Environment	Production or sale of tobacco products
	Manufacture, distribution, or sale of weapons
	Gambling
	Companies that do not observe the Animals Scientific Procedures Act 1986

Research

An advisory panel made up of leading doctors provides advice to the manager. The fund specializes in biotechnology and noninvasive technology stocks.

Minimum Investment
The minimum investment is £500.

Investment Manager
Framlington Group
155 Bishopsgate
London EC2 United Kingdom
(011) 44 71 374 4100

| NM CONSCIENCE FUND

NM Investment Management
Regal House
14 James Street
London WC2E 8BT United Kingdom
(011) 44 71 537 2222

The Conscience Fund was launched in October 1987. Its managers, NM Investment Management, have assets under management of over £1.5 billion in the United Kingdom and over £10 thousand million worldwide. It has a strong presence in Australia and New Zealand as well as in the United Kingdom.

Research
NM conducts research in-house and also uses information derived from external stockbrokers and the fund's advisory committee.

Minimum Investment
The minimum investment is £500 or £25 per month. The fund can be linked to a personal equity plan (minimum £500, maximum £3,000 lump sum or £50 a month). The PEP carries charges of .5 percent in addition to the standard unit trust charges.

| SCOTTISH EQUITABLE ETHICAL UNIT TRUST*

28 St. Andrew Square
Edinburgh EH2 1YF United Kingdom
(011) 44 31 556 9101

*Submitted by Scottish Equitable Ethical Unit Trust.

Fee Structure and Restrictions on Potential Investors

The initial charge to be retained by the managers is 6 percent and is included in the offer price of units. This is a one-off charge applied at the commencement of the investment. The maximum initial charge by the trust deed is 7.5 percent. In addition, an annual charge of 1.25 percent value-added tax (VAT) of the value of the trust is deducted from the property of the trust, out of which managers' expenses are met. Part of this charge (.5 percent) is payable to the investment adviser, reflecting the extra costs involved in operating the ethical selection criteria. In accordance with the terms of the trust deed, the total annual charge may be increased up to a maximum of 2.5 percent on the managers' giving three months' notice in writing to unitholders.

The Ethical Unit Trust, an international unit trust, is open for investment to any individual (except U.S. nationals).

Investment Objective and Philosophy

The investment objective of Scottish Equitable Ethical Unit Trust is to achieve capital growth by investment worldwide in any economic sector. Investment will be conducted with regard to ethical consideration determined from time to time and by considering the advice of the ethical adviser. The trust will invest largely in equity securities meeting the requisite ethical considerations. Convertible securities, warrants, and options also may be suitable for investment, and the manager would seek appropriate ethical advice from the investment adviser, who monitors the behavior and activities of publicly quoted companies according to the ethical criteria determined by the trust.

Social Screens

Ethical investment with Scottish Equitable Ethical Unit Trust offers investors the chance to receive a return on their money without compromising their principles.

To ensure that the investment truly is ethical, the behavior and activities of publicly quoted companies are monitored by Financial Platforms Ltd. with the support of the Ethical Investment Research Information Service (EIRIS) according to the criteria laid down for the trust. Companies are assessed for positive attitudes toward their work force and the extent to which they protect the natural environment in their communities.

The following are not considered suitable for investment:

- Any company that manufactures *armaments* or *nuclear weapons*.
- Any company that conducts any kind of *experiments on animals* or that manufactures or sells animal-tested cosmetics or pharmaceuticals.
- Any company with subsidiaries or associates in *South Africa*.
- Any company, or a subsidiary of it, that is involved in the production of nuclear fuels or that supplies the *nuclear power industry*.
- Any company that makes *political donations* of more than £10,000 per annum.
- *Advertising complaints*—any company that has had repeated public complaints upheld against it by the Advertising Standards Authority in the last two years.
- *Gambling*—any company whose involvement in casinos, amusement arcades, betting shops, or the fruit machine industry accounts for more than 10 percent of its total business.
- Any company for which the brewing, distilling, or sale of *alcoholic beverages* accounts for more than 10 percent of its total business.
- Any company for which the growing, processing, or sale of *tobacco products* accounts for more than 10 percent of its total business.
- *Banking*—as we are unable to obtain sufficient information on the companies, organizations, or institutions to which banks lend money, all banks are excluded.

TABLE 60-2

SCOTTISH EQUITABLE ETHICAL UNIT TRUST PERFORMANCE DATA

Since Launch (April 1989)	1 Year (March 1990–March 1991)
+6.6%	+18.4%

NOTE: We measure the Unit Trust's performance against others in its sector (that is, other ethical unit trusts).

Scottish Equitable

Scottish Equitable Fund Managers Ltd. is a wholly owned subsidiary of Scottish Equitable Life Assurance Society, which has been in business for more than 150 years and is one of the most highly regarded and successful investment institutions in the United Kingdom today.

In recent years the Society has become established as one of the leaders in the area of unit-linked investment management. Total group assets exceed £3.7 thousand million.

| SOVEREIGN ETHICAL FUND

Sovereign Unit Trust Managers Ltd.
12 Christchurch Road
Bournemouth BH1 3LW United Kingdom
(011) 44 20 229 1111

Sovereign Unit Trust Managers are members of the Teachers Assurance Group, part of the TAC Corporation. The Sovereign Ethical Fund was launched in May 1989.

Research
The fund does not maintain an independent research organization. An advisory committee provides advice to the fund manager.

Minimum Investment
The minimum initial investment is £500, and £100 thereafter. Monthly contributions of £20 minimum also can be invested.

| TARGET GLOBAL OPPORTUNITIES TRUST

Target Trust Managers
Alton House
174/177 High Holborn
London WC1V 7AA United Kingdom
(011) 44 71 836 8040

The Target Group is a substantial investment group with funds under management exceeding £1,000 million. The Global Opportunities Trust was launched in November 1987.

Research
No external research facility exists. Target selects the investments, but an advisory panel provides advice and monitors the companies in which the fund invests.

Minimum Investment
The minimum investment is £500 initially and £100 subsequently.

U.K. ENVIRONMENTAL
UNIT TRUSTS

Ed. Note: *This chapter consists of descriptions of ethical unit trusts and investment trusts in the United Kingdom. The descriptions were prepared, unless otherwise indicated, by Alan Miller of Financial Platforms Ltd.*

Most of the ethical trusts seek first to avoid particular issues and then look for positive qualities in those ethically acceptable companies that remain. Environmental funds primarily seek environmentally conscious companies while maintaining negative social screens that are often less restrictive than ethical funds. A number of environmental sector funds have appeared, most of them in the wake of the explosive "green consumerism." Some of these funds do not apply any social assessment to their investments and, simply because of the environmental nature of their products, may invest in companies unacceptable to ethical investors.

| CIS ENVIRON FUND*

c/o CIS Unit Managers Ltd.
Box 105
Manchester M60 OAH United Kingdom
(011) 61 837 4043
(011) 61 837 5067

This unit trust was launched on May 28, 1990. It was the third unit trust to be introduced by CIS Unit Managers Ltd., a wholly owned subsidiary of the Co-operative Insurance Society Ltd. (CIS). The CIS is one of the largest personal insurers in the U.K. and is itself a subsidiary of the Co-operative Wholesale Society Ltd. (CWS). CIS Unit Managers was inaugurated in May 1989 with the express purpose of managing and marketing unit trusts.

*Submitted by the CIS Environ Fund.

The trustee of the scheme is the governor and Company of the Bank of Scotland, a company constituted in Scotland by act of Parliament in 1695. (Head office: The Mound, Edinburgh EH1 1YZ.)

Fee Structure and Restrictions on Potential Investors

Minimum initial investment: £500.
Subsequent investments: £250.
Charges on dividend reinvestments: none.
Investment in the trust is open to individuals and institutions.

Investment Objective and Philosophy

The CIS Environ Trust is an authorized securities scheme constituted by a trust deed made between the manager and the trustee dated April 27, 1990. The investment objective is to provide capital growth from a diverse portfolio of equities, mainly in the United Kingdom drawn from any economic sector.

Investment will be limited to companies that are likely to benefit from measures taken to improve the environment, human welfare, and the quality of life. The majority of the scheme's assets are represented by investments in quoted U.K. companies and the remainder in quoted overseas securities. The core of the investment portfolio consists of shares in companies involved wholly or in part in the manufacture of products, industrial processes, or the provision of services associated with improving the environment and the enhancement of human health and safety. In addition, investments may be made in companies considered likely to be medium- to long-term beneficiaries of changing attitudes toward a cleaner and safer environment, including those seen to be making above-average efforts to minimize environmental damage caused by their activities. The investment strategy of the scheme is concentrated on specific stocks, including those of companies based overseas, and as a consequence, its portfolio is not represented in many areas of industry and commerce.

Social Screens

ENVIRONMENTAL CRITERIA. The principal environmental criteria will be positive ones, with selection of companies along the following lines:

- Companies whose activities are totally involved in improving the environment, human health, safety, and the quality of life. Because these are generally one-product companies, they are usually small, and hence due regard has to be given to poor marketability of the shares and the risk associated with lack of diversification.
- Companies whose overall activities comply with the basic criteria and that have a significant subsidiary or division involved in the type of activity described above. This kind of company forms the core of the portfolio of stocks and will insure that a large part of it is in more marketable and diversified, and hence less-risky, stocks.
- Companies that are expected to be long-term beneficiaries of the changing attitudes toward the protection of the environment and the enhancement of human health and safety. Examples of such companies may be those producing railway equipment and cleaner forms of energy, such as natural gas.

Care will be needed when considering companies known to be liable to produce significant amounts of pollution. Such companies should not necessarily be excluded altogether, although investments would be made only in exceptional circumstances where it could be established that the management has shown a constructive attitude toward environmental issues and is making efforts, significantly greater than those required merely to comply with advancing legislation, to clean up the company's processes. It is expected, however, that these stocks will form only a small proportion of the portfolio of the trust, at least until there is more public appreciation of the attitudes of their management.

ETHICAL CRITERIA. The proposed ethical criteria are intended to define the types of companies in which the trust should refrain from investing because they participate to a significant extent in areas or activities with which most of the potential investors would not wish to be associated. The principal areas and activities selected are the following:

- Countries with oppressive political regimes.
- Experiments on animals, except for those conducted for the benefit of human or animal health.

- The manufacture, distribution, or sale of products that have predominantly military application.
- The manufacture of tobacco and tobacco-related products.

In order to enable the ethical screening to be carried out, it is necessary to decide on the degree of participation in such areas and activities that is to be regarded as significant. The levels chosen are likely to be between 3 and 10 percent of the company's turnover.

Advisers and Subadvisers
All stocks are screened by an independent researcher, Bromage Ethical Services, to ensure that they meet the environmental and ethical criteria of the trust. Approved stocks are then reviewed regularly by an independent advisory committee comprised of ethical and environmental experts and public figures.

Performance Data
The trust was launched in May 1990 and currently has 5,764,000 units in issue representing a fund value of approximately £5.8 million.

Contact
R. G. Taylor is the environmental and ethical officer of CIS Unit Managers. (This appointment relates only to the CIS Environ Trust, not to the other trusts in the company.)

| CLERICAL MEDICAL EVERGREEN FUND

Clerical Medical Unit Trust Managers
Narrow Plain
Bristol BS2 0JH United Kingdom
(011) 44 27 226 9050

Established in 1824, Clerical Medical Unit Trust Managers manages over £5,000 million. It claims to be the first company to provide a comprehensive range of green investment products: bond, personal, and executive pension plans, a mortgage repayment plan, and unit trust plans. Evergreen was launched in February 1990.

Research
Research appears to come mainly from subscriptions to research magazines. There is no advisory committee.

Minimum Investment

The minimum investment is £500 initially and £250 subsequently, although regular contributions also may be invested in the fund, subject to the minimum £25.

I EAGLE STAR ENVIRONMENTAL OPPORTUNITIES TRUST*

Eagle Star Unit Managers Ltd.
Eagle Star House
Bath Road
Cheltenham, Gloucestershire GL53 7LQ United Kingdom
(011) 44 0242 221311

Fee Structure and Restrictions on Potential Investors

Initial costs, which include any remuneration paid to qualified intermediaries, are met by a charge of 6 percent, which is taken into account in the calculation of the buying and selling prices. Ongoing investment management and administrative costs are met by a charge, currently 1.25 percent, deducted from the trust's income.

The managers have the power under the trust deed to increase the annual charge to a maximum of 3 percent, with not less than a three-month notice period, and the initial charge up to a maximum of 7.5 percent, although they have no intention of doing so at present.

Minimum investment is £1,000, or £400 if an investor is adding to an existing holding in the trust. There are no restrictions on types of investor.

Investment Objective and Philosophy

The fund's objective is to invest for long-term capital appreciation in companies that take a positive attitude to, or that benefit from, environmental issues and to share in their success. While the fund will invest not less than 80 percent in the United Kingdom, it also will seek out opportunities in Europe.

The managers will actively search for promising investment situations in companies whose directors are seeking to respond positively to the growing concern for environmentally "pure" companies as well as those that are just beginning to adapt.

Social Screens

The Eagle Star Environmental Opportunities Trust only has one social screen. We do not make moral or ethical judgments. The EOT

*Submitted by the Eagle Star Environmental Opportunities Trust.

is a vehicle for those wishing to benefit from investing in environmentally oriented stocks. These stocks will not all be "pure" green; some will be taking their first steps along the environmental route. For inclusion in the Environmental Opportunities Trust, the stock must have an environmental activity that will enhance earnings per share and be important to the business—changing the company car fleet over to lead-free gasoline is hardly adequate.

Advisers and Subadvisers
The main advice on investments comes from in-house research based on company visits, and so forth, and analysis of stockbroker research. As we do not make moral judgments, we feel that it is unnecessary to have independent advisers.

Performance Data
See table 61-1.

Contact
Graham Beschizza, CIS, joined Eagle Star in 1972 and has gained a great deal of experience dealing in all of the world's major markets, starting in the fixed-interest area before moving through the equity markets of the United Kingdom, North America, the Far East, and (since 1982) Europe. Appointed investment manager in 1989, he is responsible for the European component of the Environmental Opportunities Trust. (Telephone [011] 44 71 929 1111, extension 55310.)

Fiona Cutting has a bachelor's degree from Exeter University. She

TABLE 61-1

EAGLE STAR ENVIRONMENTAL OPPORTUNITIES
TRUST PERFORMANCE DATA

	PERFORMANCE RECORD AS OF APRIL 3, 1991			
	1 year	*Rank*	*Since Launch**	*Rank*
EOT	+1.70%	57/204	+7.62%	17/186
U.K. Equity Growth Sector Average	−6.56%		−12.90%	
FTA All-Share Index	+6.96%		+10.30%	

SOURCE: Micropal.

NOTE: Offer to offer, income reinvested.

*The Eagle Star EOT was launched on June 29, 1989.

joined Eagle Star as fund manager (U.K. equities) in 1988 after working for a stockbroker and merchant bank. She is responsible for U.K. unit trusts, including the U.K. component of the Environmental Opportunities Trust. (Telephone [011] 44 71 929 1111, extension 55312.)

| MERLIN JUPITER ECOLOGY FUND*

Jupiter Tarbutt Merlin Ltd.
197 Knightsbridge
London SW7 1RB United Kingdom
(011) 44 71 581 8015
(011) 44 71 581 3857 (fax)
269705 JUPITG (telex)

Investment Objective and Philosophy

The fund is an authorized unit trust investing principally in equities and classified as an international growth fund. Its objective is to actively seek out and invest worldwide in companies making a positive commitment to social well-being and the protection and wise use of the natural environment. The fund aims to provide medium- and long-term capital growth while steadily increasing income.

Social Screens

The central principle of the fund is concern for the environment. Criteria vary with each industrial sector. However, assessment observes four broad areas: product, manufacturing process, management policies, and corporate track record. A full description of the Merlin assessment process and environmental and social criteria is contained in the publication "Assessment Process for Green Investment," available from the Merlin Research Unit (see chapter 59).

In addition to environmental concerns, the fund also considers various social criteria and seeks to avoid investment in companies directly involved with South Africa (although this is currently under review) and the armaments, nuclear power, and the tobacco industries.

---

*Supplied by the Merlin Jupiter Ecology Fund.

Advisers

The fund is managed by Merlin Jupiter Unit Trust Managers Ltd., a member of Investment Management Regulatory Organisation (IMRO) and Life Assurance and Unit Trust Regulatory Organisation (LAUTRO), and a wholly owned subsidiary of Jupiter Tarbutt Merlin. The company conducts all investment advice and management and has established a specialist research department, the Merlin Research Unit, to advise on environmental and social matters.

With the establishment of the Research Unit, Jupiter Tarbutt Merlin set two important precedents in the U.K. unit trust industry. First, it allocated not less than 10 percent of the standard management fee to go toward this research. No other U.K. fund is supported in this way. Second, the managers recognized that unitholders had a right to know about the companies in the fund and the reasons for their inclusion. Therefore, a research bulletin is published with every semi-annual managers' report.

The fund also benefits from the guidance of an advisory committee, the members of which have been described as "three of the wisest environmentalists around" *(The Independent)*—John Elkington, Robin Grove-White, and Nigel Haigh.

Performance Data

The fund was launched in April 1988. The fund's performance is summarized in table 61-2. The portfolio is split approximately 40 percent U.K., 45 percent U.S., and the remainder Far East, Europe,

TABLE 61-2

MERLIN JUPITER ECOLOGY FUND, April 1988 to March 1991

	April 18, 1988	*April 17, 1989*	*April 18, 1990*	*March 6, 1991*
Fund offer price (pence)	50.00	60.11	63.97	58.18
Dividends paid (pence)	0.93	0.81	0.50	
FT Actuaries World Index (£)	100.74	124.96	123.35	115.27
FT 100 Index	1787.80	2054.70	2205.90	2420.10
Dow Jones Index	2008.12	2337.79	2732.88	2972.52
£/$	1.9050	1.7150	1.6390	1.892

and cash. The relevant comparable statistics are, therefore, the Financial Times (FT) 100 Index and the Dow Jones Index, with adjustments for currency fluctuations.

Contact

Derek Childs is deputy chairman of Jupiter Tarbutt Merlin and co-founder of the Merlin Jupiter Ecology Fund, for which he is the fund manager. Previously he was a partner of Rowe & Pitman and, when that company merged into Warburgs', a director of Warburg Securities. His directorships include the Merlin International Green Investment Trust. Childs is a member of the finance committee of the Council for the Protection of Rural England.

FIGURE 61-1
MERLIN JUPITER ECOLOGY FUND OFFER PRICE
COMPARED TO FT-SE AND FT-WORLD INDEXES

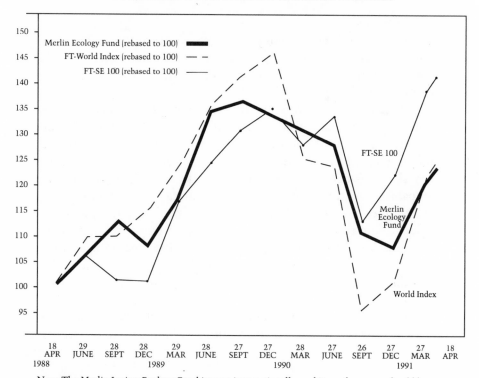

NOTE: The Merlin Jupiter Ecology Fund invests internationally, and its performance should be compared to the Financial Times World (FT-World) Index.

| MERLIN INTERNATIONAL GREEN INVESTMENT TRUST*

197 Knightsbridge
London SW7 1RB United Kingdom
(011) 44 71 581 8015
(011) 44 71 581 3857 (fax)
269705 JUPITG (telex)

Investment Objective and Philosophy

The Merlin International Green Investment Trust (MIGIT) is a public limited company listed on the London Stock Exchange. It invests worldwide. The trust's principal objective is similar to that of the Merlin Jupiter Ecology Fund providing shareholders with capital appreciation and a growing income by investing in environmentally and socially responsible companies. The main difference is that MIGIT was designed primarily for institutional investors whereas the unit trust was designed primarily for private investors.

Social Screens

One of MIGIT's fundamental principles is concern for the environment. Numerous factors—legislation, liability, material costs, and green consumerism—are converging to a degree that makes green business good business.

Criteria for the environmental assessment of a company varies according to the industrial sector but is designed to focus on the following areas of the company's activities: product, manufacturing process, management policies, and corporate track record. The company also considers social policies and seeks to avoid investment in companies directly involved with South Africa (although this is currently under review), and the armaments, nuclear power, and the tobacco industries. MIGIT invests in a wide range of companies, including those in such environmentally sensitive sectors as energy, chemicals, and mining. In these cases companies are selected on the basis that they are leaders in environmental protection in their particular field.

A full criteria paper explaining the research methodology of green investment was published by the Merlin Research Unit in December 1990 and is available by request.

*Supplied by the Merlin International Green Investment Trust.

Advisers

MIGIT has contracted Jupiter Tarbutt Merlin Ltd. to act as invest-ment manager. Derek Childs, who is responsible for the day-to-day investment management, is supported by the Merlin Research Unit, which advises on environmental and social matters. However, the directors have overall responsibility for the company and the deter-mination of its investment policy.

MIGIT also benefits from the guidance of the advisory committee to the Merlin Research Unit.

Performance Data

MIGIT was launched in November 1989 and raised approximately £25 million during the offer period.

The net asset value (NAV) as of December 31, 1990, amounts to 83.2d per share. This compares with 96.1d per share, which was the money available per share after launch expenses (a fall of 13.4 per-cent). The fall in NAV per share is attributable mainly to adverse market conditions worldwide as well as to the fall in the U.S. dollar relative to sterling, since 46.7 percent of MIGIT's investments are in North America. In the calendar year 1990, the FT Actuaries World Index fell by 32.5 percent in sterling terms.

Contact

Derek Childs, deputy chairman of Jupiter Tarbutt Merlin, is co-founder and fund manager of the Merlin Jupiter Ecology Fund and MIGIT. Previously a partner of Rowe & Pitman, when that company merged into Warburgs', he became a director of Warburg Securities. He is a member of the Council for the Protection of Rural England's finance committee.

| TSB ENVIRONMENTAL INVESTOR FUND*

Unit Trust Marketing
Charlton Place
Andover, Hants SP10 1RE United Kingdom
(011) 44 264 345678

Fee Structure

Initial management charge: 6 percent (deducted monthly from the fund's income).

*Submitted by the Environmental Investor Fund.

Annual management charge: 1.5 percent.
Minimum initial investment: £500.
Subsequent investments: £100.

Investments may be made by individuals over the age of eighteen, by corporate bodies, and on behalf of children.

Investment Objectives

The objectives of this fund are long-term capital growth together with an increasing income by investing in companies that demonstrate a positive commitment to conserving the natural environment.

Social Screens

Companies are initially selected by the fund manager for compliance with TSB's eleven areas of consideration (listed below) and their investment potential. As soon as the initial investment is made, the Conservation Foundation sends a preliminary questionnaire to determine the company's environmental policy and major areas of activity. This is followed up by a more detailed questionnaire specific to those areas of activity.

The Conservation Foundation then makes a report to the committee on each company and the committee makes a final decision on whether the investment should stay within the fund. This committee is chaired by Dr. David Bellamy, the well-known environmentalist. The decisions of the committee are binding on the fund managers.

TSB has identified eleven areas of consideration. Some companies may qualify in one only, some in several.

1. Forestry—companies that use acceptably and sustainably managed forest plantations to supply wood as raw materials. They would be unlikely to manage or retail tropical rain forest woods.
2. Ozone layer—companies that have taken steps to stop the use of chlorofluorocarbons (CFCs) in aerosols or foam packing

or who have controlled CFC emissions from refrigeration plants.

3. Recycling—companies that have taken initiatives in the following areas: recycled paper or cardboard; bottle banks or refundable glass bottles; recycling waste; biodegradable packaging; the use of reverse vending machines.

4. Sensitive land use—companies that demonstrate leadership in the use of derelict inner-city land; the screening of sites; or the reinstatement of the environment after extraction or development.

5. Acid rain—companies that make efforts to significantly reduce sulphur dioxide emissions; that actively prevent or clean up acid rain; or that look for new production methods to avoid the problem.

6. Energy conservation—these companies fall into two categories: those that have achieved a significant reduction in fuel bills by efficient energy conservation, and those that use energy efficiently in the production of goods—for example, those using insulation materials or solar heating.

7. Transport—this could range from the use of lead-free gasoline in company cars; the production and/or sale of more energy-efficient or environmentally friendly transportation, such as cars with fuel-efficient engines and corrosion-free bodies.

8. Pollution control—companies involved in the control of emissions of nitrates, oil, chemicals, and so on into waterways or the atmosphere; controlling the use of bleaches for paper products; or water or sewage treatment.

9. Animal and plant welfare—companies that actively avoid the use of endangered species of raw material for, for example, jewelry or cosmetics, and companies that take steps to preserve the natural habitats of flora and fauna threatened by developments of that company and others.

10. Healthy eating—is the company involved in growing, producing, or retailing organic produce to Soil Association standards? Does the company actively avoid the production or use of drugs or hormones used to promote yields through intensive farming?

11. Community—does the company sponsor environmental projects? Does it have evidence of comprehensive employee health and safety initiatives?

Performance Data

The fund was founded in June 1989. The percentage of growth offer-to-bid-income reinvested is:

June 1989 to June 1990: -1.7 percent

FT All-Share: $+6.57$ percent

Contact

Julie Linehan, B.A. Hons, MSC, M.Ch. Inst. Marketing, is the fund's originator and product manager.

U.K. LIFE ASSURANCE BOND FUNDS

Ed. Note: *This chapter consists of descriptions of ethical unit trusts and investment trusts in the United Kingdom. Unless otherwise indicated, the descriptions were prepared by Alan Miller of Financial Platforms Ltd.*

A number of the socially responsible investment (SRI) funds (Clerical Medical, Eagle Star, Fellowship Fund, Friends Provident, NM Conscience, and Scottish Equitable) offer a bond facility. The Ethical Investment Fund and the Homeowners Green Chip Fund are available only as bonds.

| ETHICAL INVESTMENT FUND

D. J. Bromige & Partners Ltd.
Ethical Investment Fund
10 Queen Street
Mayfair
London W1X 7PD United Kingdom
(011) 44 71 491 0558

Launched in January 1986, the Ethical Investment Fund (EIF) was the United Kingdom's second definitive SRI fund. It differs in structure from all other SRI funds in that it is a single-premium, broker-managed life assurance bond.

Investment Policy and Social Criteria of the Trust
The Ethical Investment Fund seeks to invest in companies that are conscious of their role in the community and their obligation to protect and preserve our natural heritage. The social criteria of this fund are the most clearly stated and stringent of all ethical funds in the United Kingdom.

Positive values—the fund aims to select companies that have
 exemplary health and safety standards, that have equal

opportunity practices, and whose products make for a better and environmentally safer world.

Armaments—No investment is made in any company that manufactures armaments of any description.

Nuclear power—The EIF avoids investment in companies involved in the production of nuclear power and also those that supply the nuclear power industry.

Alcohol and tobacco—investment is not made in any company in which the production or sale of alcohol and tobacco accounts for more than 10 percent of its business.

Experiments on animals—the EIF is the only fund in the United Kingdom that imposes a total ban on companies that conduct experiments on animals and those that produce fur goods. It goes a step further by avoiding companies that produce animal-tested cosmetics and pharmaceuticals.

South Africa and Namibia—any subsidiaries or associations in South Africa and Namibia will disqualify a company. Most ethical funds have a stance on South Africa, but a recent survey proved conclusively that the EIF is the only fund that manages to avoid this area of investment completely.

Gambling—investment is not made in any company whose involvement in casinos, betting shops, or amusement arcades accounts for more than 10 percent of its total business.

Advertising—the EIF would not invest in any company that in the last two years has had repeated public complaints upheld against it by the Advertising Standards Authority.

Political donations—companies will not meet our investment criteria if they make political donations of more than £10,000 per annum.

Banks—as we are unable to obtain sufficient information on the companies, organizations, or institutions to which banks lend money, all banks are excluded.

Research
Social screening is provided by EIRIS and supplemented by in-house research. A newsletter, issued to investors biannually, gives details of ethical developments. An advisory committee monitors the investments and maintains the ethical standards of the fund.

Joint Fund Managers

Ethical Investment Services Ltd. and stockbrokers Teather & Greenwood are the managers of the Ethical Investment Fund.

| HOMEOWNERS FRIENDLY SOCIETY GREEN CHIP FUND

Homeowners Friendly Society
Box 94
Homeowners House
Springfield Avenue
Harrogate, North Yorks
HG1 2HN
United Kingdom
(011) 44 42 352 2070

The Homeowners Friendly Society is (like all friendly societies) owned by its members. Homeowners has more than £375 million invested on behalf of its 240,000 members.

Launched in January 1990 (after a trial period with its own members), the Green Chip Fund is a single-premium life assurance bond. In the event of the death of the investor, 101 percent of the investment value (the number of units held at the bid price) of the units held would be payable as a lump sum.

Social Criteria

The Green Chip Fund has no stated ethical criteria, but it aims to invest in companies that practice positive ecological policies and avoid companies with poor environmental records.

Research

EIRIS identifies companies that meet the specified criteria, although the exact criteria are not known.

Minimum Investment

The minimum investment is £1,000. Regular income is available for investments in excess of £2,000.

U.K. PENSION FUNDS

Ed. Note: *This chapter consists of descriptions of ethical unit trusts and in-vestment trusts in the United Kingdom. The descriptions were prepared, un-less otherewise indicated, by Alan Miller of Financial Platforms Ltd.*

A number of funds offer links to retirement plans. These include: Abbey Ethical, Allchurches Amity Fund, Clerical Evergreen, NM Conscience Fund, Eagle Star Environmental Opportunity Fund, Fidelity Famous Names, Fellowship Trust, Friends Provident Stewardship, and the Global Opportunity Fund. Two funds specifically target the large pension fund investments.

| FRIENDS PROVIDENT STEWARDSHIP MANAGED FUND

Friends Provident Unit Trust Managers
72/122 Castle Street
Salisbury SP1 3SH United Kingdom
(011) 44 72 241 1622

The Stewardship Fund, described earlier (see page 679), is available as a managed fund. A fund often is the form of a unit trust that is managed by a life assurance company. The Managed Fund is particularly attractive for large pension fund investments, since the charges are lower. Funds under management in the Managed Fund amount to £35.5 million (as of December 1990).

Charges
Initial charge: 1 percent of first £500,000; .5 percent of next
   £500,000; no further charge over £1 million.
Annual charge: .2 percent of fund value.
Bid-offer spread: 2 percent.

| COMMERCIAL UNION ENVIRONMENTAL EXEMPT FUND

Commercial Union Asset Management
St. Helens
One Undershaft
London EC2P 3DQ United Kingdom
(011) 44 71 283 7500

The Commercial Union Environmental Exempt Fund, launched in December 1989, is available only as an exempt unit trust pension fund. The fund had grown to £6.2 million by December 1990.

Social Criteria
The fund applies no socially responsible investment (SRI) criteria but targets specific environmental concerns. It aims to invest in companies directly involved in the provision of products and services that improve the environment. This includes such areas as water treatment, recycling, emissions control, waste collection and treatment, hazardous waste disposal, and energy conservation.

Charges
Initial charge: 3 percent.
Annual management charge: .5 percent.
Bid-offer spread: 3 percent.

Minimum Investment
The minimum initial investment in this fund is £25,000.

| SCOTTISH EQUITABLE ETHICAL PENSION FUND*

28 St. Andrew Square
Edinburgh EH2 1YF United Kingdom
(011) 44 031 556 9101

Fund Management Fees
When making an investment in the fund, one does so at the offer price. Should the investor wish to cash it, this is done at the bid

*Submitted by the Scottish Equitable Ethical Pension Fund.

price. The offer and bid prices differ by 5 percent. This difference covers the administrative costs in operating the fund. A management charge at a rate equivalent to 1.25 percent per annum is debited directly from the fund on a daily basis.

Investment Objective and Philosophy

The investment objective of the Scottish Equitable Ethical Pension Fund is to achieve capital growth by investment worldwide in any economic sector. Investment will be conducted with regard to ethical consideration determined from time to time and by considering the advice of the ethical adviser. The fund will invest largely in equity securities meeting the requisite ethical considerations. Convertible securities, warrants, and options also may be suitable for investment, and the manager would seek appropriate ethical advice from the investment adviser, who monitors the behavior and activities of publicly quoted companies according to the specified ethical criteria.

Social Screens

Investment with the Scottish Equitable Ethical Pension Fund offers investors the chance to receive a return on their money without compromising their principles.

To ensure that the investment truly is ethical, the behavior and activities of publicly quoted companies are monitored by Ethical Investment Services Ltd. with the support of the Ethical Investment Research Service (EIRIS) according to the ethical criteria laid down for the fund. Companies are assessed for positive attitudes toward their workforce and the extent to which they protect the natural environment in their communities.

The following are considered unsuitable for investment:

Armaments—any investment that manufactures armaments or nuclear weapons.

Experiments on animals—any company that conducts any kind of experimentation on animals or that manufactures or sells animal-tested cosmetics or pharmaceuticals.

South Africa—any company with subsidiaries or associates in South Africa or Namibia.

Nuclear power—any investment, or subsidiary of it, that is involved in the production of nuclear fuels or that supplies the nuclear power industry.

Political donations—any company that makes political donations of more than £10,000 per annum.

Advertising—any company that has had repeated public complaints upheld against it by the Advertising Standards Authority in the last two years.

Gambling—any company whose involvement in casinos, amusement arcades, betting shops, or the fruit machine industry accounts for more than 10 percent of its total business.

Alcohol—any company for which the brewing, distilling, or sale of alcoholic beverages accounts for more than 10 percent of its total business.

Tobacco—any company for which the growing, processing, or sale of tobacco products accounts for more than 10 percent of its total business.

Banks—as we are unable to obtain sufficient information on the companies, organizations, or institutions to which banks lend money, all banks are excluded.

Advisers

The fund is managed by Scottish Equitable Fund Managers Ltd., a wholly owned subsidiary of Scottish Equitable Life Assurance Society. The Society has been in business for more than 150 years and is one of the most highly regarded and successful investment institutions in the United Kingdom today. In recent years the Society has become established as one of the leaders in the area of unit-linked investment management. Total group assets exceed £3.7 thousand million.

Performance Data

Since Launch (April 1988)	1 Year (March 1990–March 1991)
13.7%	5.5%

NOTE: The fund measures its performance against others in its sector (that is, other ethical pension funds).

U.K. COMMUNITY INVESTMENT VEHICLES

Ed. Note: This chapter consists of descriptions of community investment vehicles in the United Kingdom. The descriptions were prepared, unless otherwise indicated, by Alan Miller of Financial Platforms Ltd.

| COMMUNITY BANKING

Community banks are not developed in the United Kingdom to the same extent as they are in the United States. But there are examples of local and community banks and investment institutions where the sole motive is not profit and the social dividend (the social enhancement to the community of a company's products and services) is also an applied value.

MERCURY PROVIDENT PLC

Orlington House
Lewers Road
Forest Row, East Sussex RH18 5AA United Kingdom
(011) 44 0342 823779

Mercury Provident, established in 1974, is a nonprofit deposit-taking institution. Mercury raises funds in the form of banking deposits and then lends the money out on beneficial terms to worthy causes.

Mercury was founded on the principles of Dr. Rudolf Steiner, who saw money as a tool that should be used in a socially conscious way. Mercury's lending extends beyond Steiner's anthroposophy to other projects and ventures. Those making deposits are asked to define the interest rate they wish to receive and the social projects they wish to support.

Mercury recently has launched a new variable deposit interest plan that has already raised in excess of £1 million, but investors cannot identify specific projects to sponsor. Mercury also has started a tax-exempt special savings plan (TESSA), a scheme introduced in the 1990 budget to encourage regular savings by offering tax-free savings—up to £9,000 invested over five years.

Loans granted are normally subject to security. But where conventional security (a mortgage, for example) is not available, Mercury may accept human support-group security in the form of a group of individual investors who each provide up to £1,000 of security. In its first ten years Mercury helped to fund more than a hundred small-scale social enterprises, including organic farming, alternative medicine, housing associations, schools, and publishing.

Mercury encourages projects to develop socially beneficial structures where ownership and control is as widely distributed as possible.

SHARED INTEREST

52 Elwick Road
Newcastle Upon Tyne NE4 6JH United Kingdom
(011) 44 091 272 4979

Launched in April 1990 to help fund sustainable third world enterprises, Shared Interest describes itself as "the first social investment society" in the United Kingdom. It aims to invest in sustainable enterprises that serve the interests of the poor, usually through charitable, cooperative, or community ownership.

At least half of the first £4 million raised through a public share offering will be invested via the Ecumenical Development Cooperative Society, an international agency started by the World Council of Churches fifteen years ago. The remainder will go to help alternative trading organizations in the United Kingdom and Europe that buy goods from third world businesses that benefit people in need.

The minimum investment is £250 (£1 shares), and the maximum holding is ten thousand shares. Each holding has an entitlement to one vote, regardless of the size of the holding, and shares are non-transferable (although they can be redeemed at the original purchase price with six months' notice).

Investors receive 6.75 percent interest without any deduction of tax at the source, which is credited as new shares.

INDUSTRIAL COMMON OWNERSHIP FINANCE LTD.*

12–14 Gold Street
Northampton NN1 1RS United Kingdom
(011) 44 0604 37563

In 1973 ICOF was born out of the Industrial Common Ownership Movement (ICOM) to provide finance and guidance to common ownership and cooperative enterprises in their start-up, expansion, or conversion stages. It was felt that cooperatives would benefit from having their own financial institution that would recognize their special needs and different objectives—in particular their emphasis on fellowship in the workplace, their commitment to their local economy, their democratic working practices, and their subordination of capital as a resource to be hired by labor.

ICOF's Growth

In 1975 Scott Bader Commonwealth, the charitable holding company of the largest common ownership company in the United Kingdom, appointed ICOF to act as managing agents for its Commonwealth Development Fund, which had been created to stimulate the growth of other common ownerships like Scott Bader.

In 1976 the Industrial Common Ownership Act provided £250,000 for lending to common ownership and cooperative enterprises via ICOF. This established ICOF as the "relevant national body for cooperative finance" with the Department of Trade and Industry.

In 1982 attention focused on the support being provided to cooperatives by some local authorities. ICOF carried out a number of consultancy assignments for metropolitan authorities, such as the Greater London Council. West Midlands County Council created, over a two-year period, a £500,000 loan fund for West Midlands coops and entrusted it to ICOF to manage.

In 1987 Northamptonshire Cooperative Development Agency (CDA) invited ICOF to manage their loan fund. In the same year West Glamorgan County Council entrusted £100,000 to ICOF, which enabled us to establish an office in Swansea that now serves cooperatives throughout Wales and the southwest of England. Other loan funds, in Luton, York, Milton Keynes, and Wakefield, have

*Submitted by ICOF.

since been established. Most recently, ICOF took over management of the London Cooperative finance's loan funds.

In 1987 ICOF created a subsidiary company, ICOF plc, to carry out a public share issue. More than £500,000 was raised from five hundred members of the public in the form of nonvoting redeemable preference shares. The share issue attracted widespread attention and has become a model for innovative fund-raising that other organizations have used.

Since 1989 ICOF has expanded its fee-earning consultancy services for cooperatives, local authorities, trade unions, and cooperative development agencies. A growing area of work is for employee buyout teams wishing to bid for their company and convert it into a cooperative. This opens up the exciting possibility of creating much larger cooperative enterprises.

A new subsidiary company, ICOF Consultants Ltd., has been established to carry out all of ICOF's "investment business" under the terms of the Financial Services Act of 1986. ICOF Consultants recently became a member of the Securities Association.

Structure and Staff

ICOF Ltd. is a private company limited by guarantee without share capital. There are presently 120 members, most being individual supporters but also a few organizations, such as the Co-operative Union, the ultimate membership body for the traditional cooperative movement.

ICOF is managed by an elected board of thirteen nonexecutive directors, known as trustees. Trustees serve for three years but may seek reelection. They include members of cooperatives, representatives of affinity organizations, such as the Co-operative Union and the Trades Union Council, and an elected representative of the ICOF plc shareholders. There is provision for another three co-opted trustees. There are no executive directors.

The ultimate controlling body of ICOF is the quarterly trustees' meeting. Authority is delegated to regional subcommittees of trustees, which approve loan applications and receive progress reports on cooperatives in their region and on the general health of the sector.

ICOF currently employs seven staffers based in Northampton, Birmingham, London, and West Glamorgan. The chief executive, to whom staff are accountable, is based in the Northampton head office. In 1990 ICOF added a chartered accountant to meet the more complex demands of larger cooperatives and employee buyouts.

Lending Philosophy and Practice

Our lending policy and practice varies from fund to fund, but for our own national funds, including the plc fund created in 1987, loans are made to:

- start-up cooperative and common-ownership enterprises;
- existing cooperative and common-ownership enterprises wishing to expand;
- recoveries of failed or nearly failed existing enterprises, normally shareholder-controlled and requiring conversion, provided that there is a very good chance of commercial success under worker ownership;
- conversions of existing profitable shareholder-controlled enterprises.

We lend only where there is strong chance of commercial success based on a viable business proposal. There also must be a clear demonstration of cooperative practice as well as a cooperative constitution.

By agreeing to lend to a cooperative, ICOF has often unlocked the door to other financing institutions. We prefer to lend up to one half of a cooperative's total financial requirements—and seldom more than 75 percent—so that our funds can go further and in order to encourage cooperatives to seek matching finance from other sources.

Typical loans range in size from £5,000 to £25,000, usually over five or six years. Interest is paid quarterly on the reducing balance of the loan outstanding. The interest rate is fixed to cover ICOF's own costs rather than to shadow the money market rates, and is currently 12.5 percent per year. An arrangement fee of up to 5 percent also is charged. We aim to make between ten and twenty loans each year.

Security is taken in the form of a fixed and floating charge over the co-op's assets, but we do not take personal security from individual members of a co-op.

As of December 31, 1989, loans of approximately £1.6 million had been made to 178 cooperatives, of which £692,000 (41 percent) has been repaid and £332,000 (19.8 percent) has been written off.

MONITORING OF BORROWERS. ICOF devotes a lot of time and energy to the monitoring and support of cooperative borrowers. We work at establishing a constructive relationship with the cooperative, paying regular visits and providing free advice on financial control, marketing, and planning. Where training or expert advice is needed, we can either provide it from our own staff team or arrange for it to be provided.

| THE FUTURE

Looking to the future, ICOF plans to raise more capital for lending to cooperatives so that the supply of funds keeps pace with the growing demands of the sector, especially from established cooperatives. A second share issue is being considered.

| NEIGHBORHOOD INITIATIVES

Socially directed investment in the United Kingdom is a fast-developing initiative, where investments in people are yielding very high social dividends, not just for the incumbent citizens of poor neighborhoods today, but for the future of the social infrastructure as we know it.

In the United Kingdom such organizations as the Birmingham Settlement have targeted neighborhood initiatives in poor communities. Birmingham Settlement has been involved in developing many areas of social and community work since 1899. The Settlement employs seventy staffers and operates more than twenty programs out of a budget of £1.1 million, its income coming from government as well as industry. The work of the settlement falls into three broad sectors: Neighborhood Services, Money Advice Services, and Social Enterprise initiatives. To help provide affordable credit, the Birmingham Credit Development Agency was formed, and since 1986 fourteen community credit unions have been successfully established in poor areas of the city. This has helped reintroduce credit to one of the poorest neighborhoods in Birmingham, and at a time when the traditional banks have withdrawn from the neighborhood.

The settlement operates in Aston, a deprived neighborhood with a high ethnic concentration. Recognizing the economic regeneration needs of the area, the Aston Commission was established in 1989 to consider the possibility of establishing a local finance vehicle. Following intensive discussions with varying groups, a consultative report was published. The leading recommendation of the report is the establishment of a community bank or community development trust, and work is now under way to put the plan into action.

SCREENED INVESTMENT: THE ACTIVITIES AND PLAYERS IN EUROPE

Alison MacDonald Concorde KGaA iG

The UCITS (Undertakings for Collective Investments in Transferable Securities) Directive of the European Community (EC), which came into force in October 1989, allows unit trusts and other collective forms of investment vehicles to be sold across European frontiers while leaving the control of marketing to host countries.

This chapter describes the operation and marketing of UCITS funds in EC member states. Luxembourg is omitted from the analysis because, although many funds are operated from Luxembourg, the home sales market hardly exists. This article also analyzes screened investment products and the companies that offer them. Also covered are banks specializing in environmental and ethical concerns, and research organizations serving social investors.

Investment vehicles are described synoptically.

Alison MacDonald, one of Europe's leading figures in screened investment, is chair of Concorde International. Concorde, which exclusively sells screened financial and investment products, has more than thirty-seven hundred tied agents throughout Europe, the majority of whom operate in its domestic market, Germany.

MacDonald has been an active contributor to the development of the industry in Europe, where she has designed and launched a large number of the major screened funds. She currently advises financial corporations and governments on the creation and implementation of financial services products and legislation.

TABLE 65-1

SELLING UCITS IN THE EUROPEAN COMMUNITY

Country	Sales Method
Belgium	100% direct sales
Denmark	99% banks and savings banks
France	90% banks
	10% other
Germany	80% banks
	15% insurance companies
	5% other
Holland	90% banks (and tied agents) and Robeco
	10% independent intermediaries and direct sales
Ireland	60% independent intermediaries
	25% banks
	15% direct sales
Italy	82% networks of tied intermediaries
	18% banks
Portugal	100% banks
Spain	50% intermediaries
	30% banks
	20% direct sales
United Kingdom	35–45% independent intermediaries
	25–35% insurance companies
	5–10% direct sales
	5–10% banks

| AUSTRIA

RAIFFEISEN-UMWELTFONDS

Raiffeisen-Kapitalanlage Gesellschaft GmbH.
Am Stadtpark 9
A-1030 Vienna, Austria
(011) 43 222 71707

Launch date: November 1989.
Fund type: open-ended mutual fund.
Current size: öS 85 million (Austrian shillings).
Minimum investment: öS 5,000.
Charges: initial 4 percent (minimum öS 200); annual .6 percent.
Positive criteria: environmental protection, maintenance and
improvement of global environments, pollution control, waste
recycling, and alternative energy.
Contact: Dr. Matthew Bauer.

Raiffeisen-Kapitalanlage is the investment management subsidiary of Austria's Raiffeisen Bank. It is the largest investment management company in Austria (thirty-seven funds/öS 36 billion). It is 50 percent owned by the Raiffeisen Zentralbank a.G. Austria and 50 percent owned by nine other Raiffeisen banks throughout the country.

Z-UMWELTFONDS

Z-INVEST Gesellschaft
Invalidenstrasse 3
A-1030 Vienna, Austria
(011) 43 222 71 25 454

Launch date: November 1989.
Fund type: open-ended mutual fund.
Current size: öS 15 million (Austrian shillings).
Minimum investment: öS 1,000.
Charges: initial 3 percent; annual .48 percent.
Positive criteria: environmental protection, environmental technology, pollution control, waste recycling, alternative energy, and alternative environmental products.

Z-INVEST is the investment management subsidiary of the large Viennese bank Zentralsparkasse und Kommerzial Bank AG, Vienna. Research information comes from broker sources.

ÖKO-INVEST ETHISCHE-ÖKOLOGISCHER INVESTMENTKLUB, AUSTRIA

Lindengrasse 43/17
A-1070 Vienna, Austria
(011) 43 22 52 62 555

Launch date: August 1990.
Fund type: investment club.
Current size: öS 3 million (Austrian shillings).
Minimum investment: öS 10,000.
Charges: none (redemption fee of up to 2 percent).

Criteria: the funds currently are invested in shares and bonds of twenty to twenty-five selected companies in Europe and the United States.

The investment club meets monthly to decide on investment matters. Research information is received from FIFEGA (described below) and members' own sources. No salaries are paid.

FORSCHUNGSINSTITUT FÜR ETHISCH-ÖKOLOGISCHE GELDANLAGEN

Lindengasse 43/17
A-1070 Vienna
(011) 43 1 52 62 555
(011) 43 1 52 62 555 16 (fax)

Launched in autumn 1990, Forschungsinstitut für ethisch-ökologische Geldanlagen (FIFEGA)* provides a public information resource on environmental issues. It networks with other environmental research organizations and universities. It also:

- conducts research into companies on the social and environmental impact of products, innovative new technologies, employee relations, equal employment practices, shareholder democracy, and freedom of information.
- conducts research into the data of worldwide ethical and environmental funds (activities, performance, and so on);
- maintains and builds an archive of press articles, legislative papers, books, publications, research reports and studies, and company financial reports on environmental issues;
- provides technical information for fund managers and investors on the stock markets of German-speaking countries; and
- gives seminars and talks on environmental issues.

I BELGIUM

Belgian UCITS are managed by banks and stockbrokers, who also sell the products. Banks are the dominant sales force in the market,

*FIFEGA is discussed in a different context in the following chapter.

and sales through both intermediary channels and retail outlets are prohibited.

Financial services are not advertised on television in Belgium, the main advertising medium being newspapers. "Off-the-page" advertising is prohibited, as are telephone and door-to-door selling.

DENMARK

More than 5 percent of the Danish population invest in UCITS, most of them in the higher-income groups. The Danes tend to prefer domestic products, which they purchase through the investment management subsidiaries of the banks. Currently no foreign UCITS are sold in Denmark. There are no independent intermediaries in the country, nor are there financial retail outlets. To the extent that funds are advertised, newspapers are the preferred medium.

Ed. Note: *At press time we learned of two funds in Denmark: Aktier Miljö (Bikubem) and Aktier Miljö (Denska Invest). No further information was available.*

CENTER FOR ALTERNATIVE SOCIAL ANALYSIS

Linnesgade 14
DK-1361 Copenhagen K, Denmark
(011) (45) 33 32 05 55

The Center for Alternative Social Analysis (CASA) is a cooperative society, founded in 1986, that conducts research and consultancy on environmental issues. The CASA network combines university personnel, environmentalists, and researchers. CASA is currently active in the following areas:

- green investments for pension funds;
- analysis of clean technologies and waste problems;
- sustainable development in both rich and poor countries;
- green cities;
- traffic and the environment;
- tropical woods and the rain forest; and
- ecology and the economy.

| FRANCE

UCITS funds have proved extremely popular with French savers, with 12 percent of the population owning such an investment by the end of 1987. Indeed, France singularly accounts for 43 percent of the entire UCITS market.

UCITS are managed by banks, insurance companies, and brokers, with banks being the dominant force in the market, accounting for more than 90 percent of sales. Independent intermediaries account for a negligible proportion of sales. Newspaper advertising is increasingly and competitively used and some funds have started to include television in their campaigns.

The most common form of collective investment vehicle in both France and Luxembourg is a SICAV (Société d'Investissement à Capital Variable). SICAVs are different from unit trusts in that they are not products, but companies in their own right, constituted by articles of association and controlled by a board of directors.

BIOSPHERE

Cyril Finance Gestion
20, rue de la Ville l'Eveque
F-75008 Paris, France
(011) (1) 4266 6888

Launch date: October 1989.
Fund type: SICAV (international open-ended mutual fund).
Current size: Fr 200 million.
Minimum investment: one share (currently Fr 986).
Charges: initial: 1–3.75 percent sliding (Fr 1–1,000, 3.75 percent;
    Fr 1,000–1 million, 2.75 percent; Fr 1 million–5 million, 1.75
    percent; Fr 5 million or more, 1 percent); annual: 1 percent.
Positive criteria: biotechnology, water and air purification, waste
    recycling, and environmental technologies.
Contact: Didier Jened or Xavier D'ornellas.

Cyril Finance Gestion (CFG) is a subsidiary of Les Mutuelles Du Mans Assurance, the sixth-largest insurance company in France. Research into companies is done largely through its broker contacts, but company visits are made to national companies. The portfolio is spread 50 percent France, 50 percent international.

| GERMANY

West Germany enjoys an almost avant-garde reputataion for some of the most pioneering environmental legislation in Europe. Yet less than half of East German households are supplied with drinkable water and only 73 percent have main sewerage. This inequality will cost the unified government more than DM 2 billion by the year 2000 and create a wake of opportunity for all areas of environmental technology.

East Germany has experienced a heyday of nonregulation in waste management and pollution control. Carbon dioxide emissions have reached a European high at twenty-two tons per person each year, while most domestic heating still uses soft coal. The consequences to forestry and health are alarming. The Elbe is the most polluted river in Europe, and chemical disposal has caused unknown levels of groundwater pollution. Many fear that the import of Western levels of consumption will compound the existing waste-management crisis.

Unification has created an unprecedented opportunity for alternative energy, emissions control, and waste-management companies. Such industries are strategically placed for dramatic growth, and their investors should enjoy a performance that is consistent against stock market trends.

Ironically, Germany is a country whose financial market is dominated by major banks and whose controlling authority has been single-mindedly reluctant to authorize screened investment funds.

German investors may select from seventy-five domestic investment funds offered by forty-three investment companies. To date only one fund has been authorized to strategically select environmental stocks. The Bundesaufsichtsamt für das Kreditwesen (BAK), a government agency, is responsible for authorizing both domestic and foreign funds within the republic. So far it has been reluctant to give authorization to screened investment products. BAK has refused to license ethically or environmentally geared funds, arguing that it cannot accurately measure, and, by inference, neither can the managers themselves measure, nonfinancial performance criteria.

As a consequence those companies offering green investment funds in Germany have headed offshore to Luxembourg, only to reimport them for sale in the domestic market. Another creative solution was made by Artus in Köln (Cologne), which in 1989 launched a screened product in the form of a unitized investment club.

In Germany, UCITS are managed predominantly by special management companies, KAGs, which are usually subsidiaries of banks or, in some cases, insurance companies. Banks account for 80 percent of the sales activity, insurance companies for 15 percent, and independent sales companies for the remaining 5 percent. The central role of banks in the German market is thought likely to exclude any real threat of foreign competition.

SECURA-RENT LUX

BFG Luxinvest Management S.A.
2 Rue Jean Bertholet
1-1233 Luxembourg
(011) (352) 4522551

Launch date: October 1989.
Fund type: SICAV (open-ended bond fund).
Current size: DM 44 million.
Minimum investment: one share (currently DM 95).
Charges: initial 3 percent; annual .5 percent.
Positive criteria: public authorities supporting or considering human rights, environmentally beneficial products, and those changing toward environmentally less-damaging production.
Negative criteria: countries that violate human rights, armaments, pollution, nuclear power and their suppliers, tobacco and alcohol, and gambling.
Contact: Claus Pyter.

Secura-Rent Lux is a joint venture between two German banks, the Bank für Sozialwirtshaft in Köln and the Bank für Gemeinwirtshaft in Frankfurt. The fund invests internationally, but not in equities, only in bonds.

HCM ECO TECH

Hypo Capital Management
27 Boulevard du Prince Henri
L-1724 Luxembourg
(011) (352) 474 979

Denninger Strasse 130–132
8000 Munich 81, Germany
(011) 49 (89) 9279701

Launch date: April 1990.

Fund type: SICAV (open-ended mutual fund).

Current size: DM 31 million.

Minimum investment: one share (currently DM 85).

Charges: initial 5 percent; annual 1 percent.

Positive criteria: environmental protection, pollution control technologies, alternative energy, recycling, waste management, water purification, and biotechnology.

Contact: Dieter Wimmer (Luxembourg).

Created by the Bavarian Hypo-Bank and operated by its Luxembourg subsidiary, Hypo Capital Management (HCM), HCM Eco Tech invests internationally in environmental stocks.

FOCUS UMWELTTECHNOLOGIE

Focus
Gunther Strasse 21
8000 Munich 19, Germany
(011) 49 (89) 1784010

Launch date: October 1990.

Fund type: unit trust.

Current size: DM 16 million.

Minimum investment: DM 8,000.

Charges: initial: sliding scale 4.5 percent–.9 percent over DM 1 million; annual: 1.2 percent.

Positive criteria (at least 51 percent of a company's earnings or turnover must be in one of these): environmental technology, waste recycling, air or water purification, or waste management.

Negative criteria: armaments, tobacco, and the chemical industry.

Contact: Carl Fischer.

Focus is currently the only screened German fund to have been authorized by the German Banking Federation. It succeeded in its application by defining its investment policy as specific to the area of environmental technology, while observing certain negative criteria in an informal way. It relies on broker sources for company research.

CS ÖEKO PROTEC

Credit Suisse
Kaiserstrasse 30
6000 Frankfurt, Germany
(011) 49 (69) 26912625

Launch date: October 1990.
Fund type: SICAV (open-ended mutual fund).
Current size: DM 5 million.
Minimum investment: ten shares (currently DM 2,650).
Charges: initial 3 percent; annual 1.56 percent.
Criteria: invests in companies that have more than 50 percent of
   their earnings or turnover in environmental technology. The
   remaining percentage must be environmentally benign.

The portfolio includes stocks from well-known green companies,
such as the Body Shop, Waste Management, and Magma Power.
Stocks are selected on the basis of broker research and company
reports.

CONCORDE INTERNATIONAL

Concorde KGaA iG, Germany
Weidenauer Strasse 179
D-5900 Siegen, Germany
(011) 49 (271) 403721

Launch date: April 1991.
Fund type: SICAV (open-ended mutual fund).
Current size: DM 10 million start-up capital.
Minimum investment: DM 1,000; savings plans minimum is DM
   50 per month.
Charges: initial 6 percent equity fund, 3 percent bond fund;
   annual 1.5 percent equity fund, .75 percent bond fund.
Positive criteria: environmental technology, environmental
   energy, employee relations, waste management, natural
   processes and products in the health service and food sector,
   and pollution control.
Negative criteria: armaments and military goods, animal testing,
   tobacco and alcohol, countries with oppressive regimes, unfair
   competition, and racial, political, and social discrimination.

Contact: Alison MacDonald.

Concorde International offers two funds, an equity fund and a bond fund. Both invest internationally for capital growth. Stocks for the equity fund are researched by the Merlin Research Unit in London (described earlier, in chapter 59) and, for the bond fund, Privates Institute für Umweltschutz GmbH in Berlin (dscribed later in this chapter).

CONCORDE-ARTUS ETHISCHE VERMÖGENSVERWALTUNG GmbH

Concorde Ethische Vermögensverwaltung GmbH
Weidenauer Strasse 179
D-5900 Siegen, Germany
(011) 49 (271) 40370

Launch date: December 1989.
Fund type: equity investment club.
Current size: DM 20 million single premiums; DM 1 billion accumulated savings plan volume.
Minimum investment: DM 1,000; savings plan minimum is DM 50 per month.
Charges: initial 7.25 percent (savings plan 5.26 percent); annual 1.6 percent.
Positive criteria: environmental technology, environmental energy, employee relations, waste management, natural processes and products in the health service and food sector, and pollution control.
Negative criteria: armaments and military goods, animal testing, tobacco and alcohol, countries with oppressive regimes, unfair competition, racial, political, and social discrimination.

This savings club was the first to offer screened investment to the German public. It is unitized in the same way as an investment fund.

ARTUS ETHISCHE RENTEN GbR

Artus Ethische Vermögensverwaltung GmbH
von-Werth-Strasse 20-22
D-5000 Cologne 1, Germany
(011) 49 (221) 135056

Launch date: February 1991.
Fund type: bond investment club.
Current size: DM 1 million.
Minimum investment: DM 500.
Charges: initial 3.09 percent; annual .75 percent.
Positive criteria: environmental technology, environmental
   energy, employee relations, waste management, natural
   processes and products in the health service and food sector,
   and pollution control.
Negative criteria: armaments and military goods, animal testing,
   tobacco and alcohol, countries with oppressive regimes, unfair
   competition, and racial, political, and social discrimination.
Contact: Jurgen Conrads.

This is the counterpart to the Concorde-Artus savings club. It invests
internationally in bonds.

ERSTER ETHISCHER INVESTMENTCLUB KÖLN

Maria-Hilf-Strasse 6
D-5000 Cologne 1, Germany
(011) (221) 325272

Launch date: 1989.
Fund type: equity investment club.
Current size: DM 2 million.
Minimum investment: DM 5,000.
Charges: initial 0–1 percent (0–1 percent redemption fee); annual
   1.2 percent, plus profit share.
Positive criteria: environmental protection, alternative energy,
   social justice, and human and animal dignity.
Negative criteria: armaments, production of chemicals, South
   Africa, environmentally damaging products and processes,
   unfair trading with third world countries, and companies that
   give inadequate employee care.
Contact: Hans Berner.

The club invests internationally and currently is invested predominantly in American stocks. It seeks to maximize performance by
active portfolio management, including the sale of call options.

ÖKOBANK

Bronnerstrasse 9
D-6000 Frankfurt, Germany
(011) 49 69 299870

Founded in 1988, the Ökobank offers a traditional banking system of current accounts, deposit accounts, and fixed-interest savings certificates. By mid-1990 it had more than thirty-five thousand accounts and twenty-three thousand clients.

Savers with the Ökobank can nominate for their savings to support a particular project and may decline to take interest in such investments in favor of the borrower. Past projects have included solar energy (housing), an animal welfare project, an alternative radio station, and a women's magazine for the over-forties. It favors projects with a high level of autonomy and selects ecologically oriented projects—innovative environmental technologies, youth opportunities projects, children's homes, third world projects, health care, and the like.

The bank's success has created an unusual problem: it has more funds than projects. These surplus funds are placed with other social and anthroposophical banks. Due to this surplus, the bank also has extended the geographical range of its projects beyond Frankfurt and financed projects that are considered only 50 percent or more socially or environmentally defined.

STEYLER MISSIONSSPARINSTITUT SANKT AUGUSTIN GmbH

Arnold-Jansen-Strasse 22
D-5205 Sankt Augustin, Germany
(011) 49 (2241) 237 337

Founded in 1964 as a limited company, the bank currently has more than twenty thousand investors and DM 190 million in funds. The board of directors coordinates the choice of projects. Investors commit their capital for up to four years and may decline to take interest. Additionally, they may bequeath their capital to the bank.

The bank finances projects that accord to the philosophy of the Steyler missionaries, mostly for religious and social purposes in third world countries. Past projects have included sewing schools in Manila and the building of schools in Ecuador.

GLS GEMEINSCHAFTSBANK eG

Oskar-Hoffman-Strasse 25
D-4630 Bochum 1, Germany
(011) 49 (234) 37653

Launched in 1974 as an anthroposophical cooperative society, GLS Bank currently has seven thousand investors and funds of DM 100 million. It does not operate current accounts.

The bank funds projects, firms, and institutions that have an anthroposophical philosophy—for example, Waldorf schools, organic farms, creches, and human development projects.

Interest rates for borrowers are based on their individual financial situations, favoring lower rates for poorer borrowers. Many projects are financed with a zero interest rate, with the bank making a small charge to cover its administrative costs. The bank's philosophy is to act as an intermediary between lenders and borrowers, matching the needs and intentions of both. Investors receive a regular information bulletin from the bank that describes specific projects needing finance.

BANK FÜR SOZIALWIRTSCHAFT

Worthstrasse 15–17
5000 Cologne 1, Germany
(011) 49 (221) 77680

Established in 1923, Bank für Socialwirtschaft (BfS) offers traditional banking services. It is, however, unique in that it was founded and is owned by various German welfare organizations, such as the Red Cross. The nature of its ownership characterizes the spirit of the bank, which offers savings bonds and financial consulting for charity boards to organize such projects as workshops for handicapped people and cooperative projects with third world countries.

This Cologne-based social bank has been trying to launch the first German bond fund to apply SRI restrictions on South Africa and armaments. The bank has experienced difficulty with regulators who will not permit the use of "ethical," "alternative," or similar terms, since by definition they discriminate against other funds by defining them as unethical.

PRIVATES INSTITUTE FÜR UMWELTSCHUTZ GmbH

Kurfstendamm 180
W-1000 Berlin 15, Germany
(011) 49 (30) 88 32 818

The IFU, which has thirty-two specialist staffers, is owned by Concorde KGaA iG in Germany and supports Concorde's green funds with environmental research. Additionally, it conducts independent environmental research, consultancy and development, project management, market research, public relations, and the transfer of environmental technologies. The institute also:

- assesses new products for their environmental impact;
- publishes research and technical reports on environmental issues;
- conducts environmental project management in such fields as water purification, groundwater pollution, nature and the countryside, noise reduction, and waste recycling;
- conducts environmental consultancy to solve and reduce existing environmental problems;
- gives seminars and offers training programs for international members of industry and commerce; and
- conducts research and development into new and innovative environmental technologies and industries.

| IRELAND

In Ireland UCITS generally are managed by the investment banking subsidiaries of the main clearing banks and life insurance companies. Selling is mainly through independent intermediaries, which account for 60 percent of sales, while banks account for 25 percent and direct sales forces 15 percent.

There are no restrictions on selling methods in Ireland. Direct sales, telephone, and door-to-door sales are permitted.

| ITALY

In Italy UCITS must be managed by special management companies, but they are very rarely sold by the same organizations. Instead sales activity heavily favors sales networks and intermediaries. There are approximately fifteen major sales networks in Italy, most of them selling an exclusive range of products from one management company.

There is no best-advice legislation in the country, and the public response to UCITS, at first very favorable, has suffered somewhat from sales having been made on fairly unscrupulous bases. Advertising is mainly through newspapers (33 percent) and magazines (41 percent), but television (21 percent), radio, and billboards also are used.

At present the only foreign UCITS for sale in the country are those operated from Luxembourg.

| NETHERLANDS

In the Netherlands, UCITS are managed by banks and insurance companies, which sell mainly through bank branches, direct mail, advertising, and telephone contact. Indeed, the most common form of sale is a result of customers telephoning their banks. Bank sales account for over 90 percent of the market, the remainder being split between direct sales and sales by intermediaries.

Some foreign funds are already sold in Holland, where there is a mixed reaction to the threat of foreign competition. U.K. funds are seen to pose the largest threat, but it is argued that the Dutch will continue to favor domestic products.

Ed. Note: *At press time we learned of a Dutch social fund, the Pierson Environment Growth Fund. No other information was available.*

| NORWAY

MILJÖINVEST ENVIRONMENT FUND

Miljölnvest
5020 Bergen, Norway
(011) (5) 17 20 50

Launch date: November 1989.
Fund type: international open-ended mutual fund.
Current size: 65 million Norwegian kroner (Kr).
Minimum investment: Kr 2,000.
Charges: initial 3 percent (1 percent redemption charge); annual 2 percent.

Positive criteria: environmental protection, recycling, pollution
control, waste management, and energy conservation.
Negative criteria: nuclear power, armaments, and tobacco.
Contact: Carlos Jolly.

MiljöInvest is Norway's only environmentally screened fund. It supports companies actively engaged in environmental protection and
invests internationally for long-term capital growth.

| PORTUGAL

In Portugal UCITS are managed by specialized management companies and may be sold only by the depository banks. As a result
there is no intermediary activity in the country. In addition, the
depository banks prefer to sell their other products over UCITS,
which has resulted in a very low demand.

The UCITS directive, which has inspired most recent financial
legislation in Portugal, will not be fully implemented until the deadline of 1992. In the meantime there is no foreign competition, nor
is there any major concern about it.

| SPAIN

The public attitude to UCITS is very favorable in Spain, even if it
has declined a little since the crash of 1987. In general the Spanish
saver prefers funds that offer a regular savings facility. UCITS are
managed by banks and savings banks and sold through tied and
independent sales forces. Intermediaries account for 50 percent of
the sales, banks 30 percent, and direct sales 20 percent.

The marketing of financial services has become more aggressive
recently, with considerable interest being shown via new forms of
media, such as satellite TV.

Some foreign funds are already sold in Spain, but no foreign company has yet established there. The implementation of the UCITS
directive is slow, but it is expected that current laws will be updated
within the correct time period.

SWEDEN

See chapter 66.

SWITZERLAND

ALTERNATIVE BANK SCHWEIZ

Leberngasse 17
CH-4001 Olten, Switzerland
(011) (062) 32 00 85

Alternative Bank Schweiz (ABS) is a public company, launched in October 1990, with two thousand shareholders (including Greenpeace and Anti-Apartheid). Its initial share capital of SFr 9 million is currently full and it is looking to increase it shortly.

Shareholders must commit their investments for periods of up to five years, during which time they will not receive interest. After the five-year term, investors may continue to decline interest in favor of financed projects. Investment is made in, for example, the following areas: alternative energy, reusable products, organic agriculture, community transport systems, community housing, housing for the elderly, third world trade, and energy-saving housing.

The bank avoids investment in the following areas: the chemical industry, genetic engineering, armaments, agricultural chemicals, nuclear power, services or products that go against environmental interests, and companies that are unsocial or undemocratic.

UNITED KINGDOM

The United Kingdom is the most mature of all European markets in the screened investment field. During the early 1980s a few individual managers were inspired by America's already-developed industry and sought to emulate such investment approaches in their domestic market. However, it was not until 1984 that Friends Provident launched Britain's first screened fund, the Stewardship Fund.

The Stewardship Fund had Quaker roots and a clearly described investment philosophy that sought to avoid companies involved in socially or ethically unacceptable practices, such as the armaments industry, tobacco, alcohol, and gambling.

As is usually the case in developing industries, subsequent funds were launched with investment philosophies that emulated the pioneering project. During the following years a number of funds, mostly unit trusts, were launched with investment philosophies that sought to avoid an ever-increasing number of areas deemed to be socially or morally unacceptable.

During this period these new funds attracted an unrepresentative amount of media coverage, largely due to their "human interest" value in the conventionally mundane field of financial reportage. This had the dual effect of educating the buying public as to the issues involved and giving the investment management companies support in the marketing of such funds.

However, as investors became better informed, and therefore more critical, and investigative journalism began to hone in on the facts behind the marketing literature, several issues became subject to criticism. One major issue concerned the practical relevance of simply avoiding investment in companies that engaged in certain practices. Over and above the obvious problem of creating a restricted universe of stocks, thus endangering performance and increasing risk, these funds were increasingly seen as failing against their overall philosophies.

In response to such issues, the Merlin Ecology Fund launched in 1987 the first screened fund to extend the practice of negative screening to favor investment in companies that were making an actual contribution to social or environmental well-being. The launch of Merlin had the effect of redirecting the development of the U.K. screened investment industry toward positive stock selection and introduced such words as *green*, *environmental*, and *ecological* into the marketing vocabulary. Since the launch of Merlin, all subsquent funds have emphasized a green-environmental approach and many of the existing funds added positive criteria to their existing philosophies.

In the United Kingdom, UCITS are managed by independent investment management houses and the associated companies of insurance companies, banks, and stockbrokers. They are a well-established and popular saving medium sold mainly by independent intermediaries (of which there are ten thousand full time) and tied sales forces. UCITS are regulated by the Securities and Investment Board, the Investment Management Regulatory Organisation, and the Life Insurance and Unit Trust Regulatory Organisation. The main pressure for change in the country is the need to simplify the cumbersome provisions of the Financial Services Act (1986). The UCITS directive has already been enacted in the United Kingdom as part of the Financial Services Act.

SOME NOTES ON SOCIAL BANKING INITIATIVES, SCREENING, AND SHAREHOLDER ACTIVISM IN EUROPE

Alan Miller Financial Platforms Ltd.

The socially responsible investment (SRI) movement in mainland Europe is beginning to be felt, largely as an environmental force. With the developing capital markets in Europe and the unified European Community (EC) market of 1992, SRI influences seem set to continue.

For legal reasons, banks play a much larger role in social investing in Europe than they do in the United States. The International Association of Investors in the Social Economy (INAISE) was formed to foster and support the development of social finance organizations primarily in Europe. Some other banks have begun to address the needs of social investors.

Another difference between the United States and the United Kingdom on the one hand and Europe on the other is the lack of emphasis on screening and shareholder activism. Both of these seem in the process of change, however.

This chapter describes INAISE, its members, and some of the other social banking innovators in Europe. It also describes the nascent screening and shareholder activist movements on the continent.

| INTERNATIONAL ASSOCIATION OF INVESTORS IN THE SOCIAL ECONOMY

Vassali House
Twenty Central Road
Leeds LS1 6DE United Kingdom
(011) 44 0532 429600

In early 1989 the European founding members of INAISE began to supplement the cooperation that had existed among them for many years with more formal ties. From this work came INAISE, which was established in November 1989 as a company limited by guarantee. Its memorandum and articles of association states its purpose:

> The members of INAISE wish, in the conduct of the Association, to foster and support the development of finance organizations primarily in Europe, but not to the exclusion of non-European countries, which invest in undertakings of an ethical, ecological, cultural, and self-managing nature, including women's undertakings, undertakings of ethnic minorities, in undertakings whose aims are concerned with people with disabilities, healthier living, peace and the third world, and in undertakings within the social economy generally.
>
> The members wish to support the development of finance organizations which not only invest in ethical undertakings but also in the conduct of their own affairs and their approach to money, organize themselves in such a way as to develop working practices which are supportive of the promotion of social investments for which the Association is established.

Throughout Europe, and the German-speaking countries in particular, banks have a significant role in the investment market. But it is important to note the European Commission's Directive DG23 will require (as of 1993) organizations to have a minimum of five million ECUs (European currency units) to establish financial bodies, except for cooperative banks. This requirement will create problems for the launching of new social economy organizations.

INAISE will facilitate cooperation among financial institutions involved in community banking, social investment, and other ethical saving activities that encourage people to handle their savings in a more conscious way. It will contribute to the development of trust and cooperation that will enable joint investments across European boundaries by its members.

INAISE will start as an information desk for organizations and people. Its newsletter for members will promote mutual understanding and knowledge. INAISE also will play an active role in representing the expanding movement of social investment organizations in the EC and other international bodies. And it will conduct seminars and educational exchanges to improve the quality of the services of its members.

INAISE will arrange professional assistance for new banking initiatives with social objectives. Poland, Hungary, and third world pose great challenges for INAISE to prove the viability of "ethical banking."

INAISE's members are described in the following pages.

BP GUARANTEE COMPANY

Box 159
28 Baldwin Street
Bristol BS99 7NP United Kingdom
(011) 44 0272 253007

Established in 1988 as a private company limited by guarantee, BP guarantees bank loans to small businesses, taking high-risk projects with low security. Its prime objective is to promote social and economic development in Dorset and Avon today, and later to expand into all of the southwest of the United Kingdom.

ECOLOGY BUILDING SOCIETY

18 Station Road
Cross Hills
Keighley, West Yorkshire BD20 7EH United Kingdom
(011) 44 0535 635933

A relatively small building society (similar in structure to U.S. savings and loan institutions), the Ecology Building Society lends money for housing that is ecologically sound, primarily to those who wish to renovate rather than replace property.

GLS GEMEINSCHAFTSBANK eG

Oskar-Hoffman-Strasse 25
D-4630 Bochum 1, Germany
(011) 49 234 313883

Established in 1974, the main activity of GLS Gemeinschaftsbank eG is banking, including project consulting and development of new forms of loans, shares, and donations.

INBERCOP

Plaza Urquinaona 6
7a Planta
0810 Barcelona, Spain
(011) 34 3173616

INBERCOP was established in 1982 by the Co-operative Federations of Catalonia and is one of the founding members of INAISE. It acts as a principal financial and commercial adviser and investor in co-operative organizations in Catalonia. It is active in the worker, consumer, housing, and agricultural cooperative sectors and invests in cooperatives by way of loan and share capital.

L'INSTITUT DE DÉVELOPPEMENT DE L'ÉCONOMIE SOCIALE

24 Avenue Hoche
75008 Paris, France
(011) 33 4359 9494

L'Institut de Développement de l'Économie Sociale (IDES) was formed in 1983 with the objective of providing financial assistance to cooperatives and other organizations involved in the social economy. IDES is a leading organization in investment in the French social economy and a founding member of INAISE.

It invests in enterprises by way of subscription to the *Titre Participatif* (long-term cumulative partly participative loan stock) by worker cooperatives, by way of share capital, and by way of medium-term loans.

The capital of IDES has been subscribed by cooperatives, banks, and mutual insurance organizations (70 percent) and by the French government (30 percent).

INDUSTRIAL COMMON OWNERSHIP FINANCE LTD.

12–14 Gold Street
Northampton NN1 1RS United Kingdom
(011) 44 0604 375563

Industrial Common Ownership Finance Ltd. (ICOF), a founding member of INAISE, is described in chapter 64.

MERCURIUS

Oude Houtlei 2—9000
Gent Ledeberg, Belgium
(011) 32 2 091 313371

Established in 1983, the prime purpose of Mercurius is the provision of low-interest loans, loan mediation, and fund administration.

MERCURY PROVIDENT PLC

Orlingbury House
Lewes Road
Forest Row, East Sussex RH18 5AA United Kingdom
(011) 44 0342 823739

Mercury Provident, a founding member of INAISE, is described in chapter 64.

NETWERK VLAANDEREN

Harenheidestraat 9
B-1130 Brussels, Belgium
(011) 02 241 1997

Established in 1982 in Flanders, Netwerk Vlaanderen is a membership-based finance organization. It invests in cooperative and social enterprises by way of loans, guarantees, and in some cases grants. It obtains its finance from the public by way of member contributions, donations, and by a novel arrangement with a public savings bank called "Cricket-Saving." It is a founding member of INAISE.

ÖKOBANK eG

Bornheimer Landstrasse 22
D-6000 Frankfurt 1, Germany
(011) 49 69 500 910 00

A founding member of INAISE, the Ökobank was launched in 1988. The name *Öko* is derived from both "ecology" and "economy." Ökobank applies SRI values to its overall banking policy.

Ökobank is a cooperative. Its charter lists what it will support and what it will not:

- No investment in the armaments industry or nuclear industry.
- No money for investment in apartheid.
- Money for research, development, and the use of ecologically beneficial products or production processes.
- Money for firms trying new forms of cooperation and social responsibility.

Ökobank has obtained its capital from private investors, by way of shares and savings bonds, largely drawn from the environmental, peace, and women's movements.

In addition to traditional banking services, Ökobank gives its investors a choice of projects to support with their savings. Low-interest loans are made to finance small owner-operated companies and cooperatives.

Through Ökobank's savings bond program investors can determine which savings bond they will support. Specific social savings bonds that support enterprises targeting education, women-managed enterprise, the mentally ill, cooperatives, and ecology. Minimum investment is DM 500 and is invested for a fixed period of from two to five years. Interest is payable at competitive rates, although investors may specify a lower rate.

In addition, Ökobank offers project savings bonds. This facilitates funding of a specific, clearly defined project requiring funding of at least DM 100,000. The first project bond is for the Verkehrs Club Deutschland, an organization committed to a more ecologically aware transportation policy for all transportation users.

S.A. SOFIGA/C.V. FIMABO

Rue Montoyer 63
1040 Brussels, Belgium
(011) 02 237 0692

S.A. Sofiga/C.V. Fimabo was established in 1983 to finance enterprises in the Belgium social economy. It invests by way of shares, loans, and guarantees in cooperative and social enterprises and is a specialist in cofunding employee buyouts. It is funded by the Belgian National Investment Company, a Belgian state holding company. It is a founding member of INAISE.

STICHTUNG STIMULANS

Van der Does de Willebois—Singel 1
5211 CA 'S-Hertogenbosch, Netherlands
(011) 073 144249

Stichtung Stimulans was established in 1980 to provide venture capital to worthy social ventures.

TRIODOSBANK N.V.

Triodosbank N.V.
Stationslaan 4
Box 55
3700 AB Zeist, Netherlands
(011) 31 3404 16544

Established in 1980, the Triodosbank is a licensed bank. Its two main lending criteria are financial feasibility and a positive contribution toward society. Its aim is to contribute to fruitful innovation in social, technological, economic, and cultural fields. Triodos is based on Rudolf Steiner's anthroposophy. It is a founding member of INAISE.

DEN ALMENNYTTIGE ANDELSKASSE TRION MERKUR

Sonnenupvej 41
DK-3300 Fredericksverk, Denmark
(011) 4212 44227

Licensed under the Danish banking laws in 1986, the prime purpose of Den Almennyttige Andelskasse is to work as a bank toward developing the threefold social order (based on the anthroposophy of Rudolf Steiner). Loans go directly to ethical and ecological initiatives.

| OTHER BANKING INITIATIVES: GERMANY

BAYERISCHE HYPOTHEKEN UND WECHSEL BANK (HYPOBANK)

Postfach 20 05 27
8000 Munich 2, Germany
(011) 49 8992 448209

To satisfy demand from substantial investors, Hypobank established an SRI portfolio service in November 1990. (Hypobank is described in chapter 65 as well.) The bank looks for companies that set ecological or social examples and fit the following criteria:

- development, production, or distribution of environmentally friendly products, or using environmentally friendly production methods;
- reduction or elimination of pollution;
- energy-saving or environmentally friendly methods of energy production;
- recycling;
- natural methods of production of health care and nutrition;
- particular recognition of human rights and exemplary working conditions;
- limitation of experiments on animals, and livestock breeding, providing a natural environment;
- engagement in publicly useful projects.

The bank avoids investment in companies that:

- discriminate on grounds of race, ethnic origins, or sex;
- produce or sell weapons and military goods;
- produce or sell environmentally dangerous products;
- have proven pollution violations;
- produce nuclear energy or provide services to nuclear energy companies;
- conduct experiments on animals or are involved in factory farming or fur-breeding farms;
- produce, sell, or distribute alcohol or tobacco;
- are involved in the gambling industry; or
- maintain a production operation in South Africa.

| OTHER BANKING INITIATIVES: SWEDEN

In November 1988 a Swedish national conference was held on socially responsible investing by the Spardelegationen (Commission for the Promotion of Savings). Initiated by research analyst Sören

Bergstrom, it marked a national recognition that peace and environmental issues were at the forefront of Swedish political thinking.

STIFTELSEN ANSVARSFULL PENNINGPLACERING

c/o Marit Lindstein
Lonnvagen 5 A
135 52 Tyreso, Sweden
(011) 46 08 7426330

The "Responsible Investment Foundation" was established in 1986 to provide a screening service to the banks while leaving them to continue to manage the investments. (Banks in Sweden, like those in Germany, control most of the investment management.)

A socially screened investment fund was announced in 1989 but has not yet been launched. It was planned as a joint venture with Save the Children, the Swedish Red Cross, and the Farmers Bank, but it has not yet satisfied the minimum capital requirement of £100,000.

Its social screens include positive records on environmental issues, energy saving, organic farming, and alternative health care; and avoidance of South Africa, weapons, nuclear power and other "ecologically inferior techniques," and unnecessary experimentation on animals.

JAK

Brunnsgatan 15
Stockholm, Sweden
(011) 46 18 202445

For more than fifteen years the organization "Land Labor Capital" (JAK) has operated a savings scheme outside the traditional banking system. JAK employs extensive social screening. Investors do not receive interest.

| SOCIAL SCREENING

A number of screening initiatives are planned in Europe, but only one initiative has as yet been launched.

FORSCHUNGSINSTITUT FÜR
ETHISCH-ÖKOLOGISCHE GELDANLAGEN

Lindengasse 43/17
A-1070 Vienna, Austria
(011) 43 1 52 62 555
(011) 43 1 52 62 555 16 (fax)

Forschungsinstitut für ethisch-ökologische Geldanlagen (FIFEGA),
a nonprofit research institute, was launched in September 1990.
Started with the financial support of green businesses, its purpose
is to provide a research institute for the German-speaking countries.

FIFEGA is sponsoring an environmental research project in Austria that is still in its infancy. A joint project with the Institut fuer
oekologische Wirtschaftsforschung, Vienna, it is expected to be completed in September 1991. The proposal is to produce an environmental rating guide for companies. Issues being considered include:
pollution control, products and processes, waste management, environmental damage, and environmental audit.

One of the founders of FIFEGA, Max Deml, has already published
a handbook for ethical and ecological investors in October 1990
called *Grunes geld* (Green money).

(FIFEGA is discussed in chapter 65 as well.)

| SHAREHOLDER ADVOCACY

Under German law, a shareholder has a statutory right to vote at
annual meetings, a right to information, and a right to speak at
annual meetings.

Max Deml also has written a German language guide to shareholder activism, part of an effort to rekindle the almost defunct
practice of using proxy voting to apply pressure for social change in
company behavior in Austria, Germany, and Switzerland. *Wider-
spruch zu Protokoll* (Against the Record), which Deml coauthored
with Josef Wallner, is aimed at environmental, peace, and antiapartheid activists. The guide discusses how annual meetings are
run, how to interpret annual reports, and tax information, as well
as how to apply for a proxy. A detailed checklist designed to help
activists avoid legal and technical errors is also included.

The most successful activist group in corporate governance is
the Dusseldorf-based Deutsche Schutzvereinigung für Wertpapier-

besitzer (German Association of Shareholders). Founded in 1947, DSW advocates shareholders' rights on behalf of ten thousand investors ranging from small shareholders to institutional investors.

A group called Critical Shareholders of Deutsche Bank confronted the management in early 1990 on issues ranging from the bank's loans to South Africa to its financing of nuclear power plants to its participation in the Daimler-Benz/MBB arms manufacturing merger. Commerz and Dresdner banks also have faced questions at annual meetings over third world debt and apartheid. All chemical companies and major utilities companies, such as Bayer, BASF, VEBA, and RWE, now have their own organized critical shareholder groups, many of them led by members of the Green party.

CHAPTER 67

AUSTRALIAN INVESTMENT FUNDS AND ADVISERS

Ed. Note: *At press time we received some information about Australian social investment firms. Additional addresses appear in the directories in appendix B.*

MONEYMATTERS FINANCIAL GROUP PTY. LTD.

Suite 3, 4–8 Waters Road
Neutral Bay, NSW 2089 Australia
(011) 61 2 953-0599

MoneyMatters is a group of investment consultants specializing in ethical investment. They offer independent consulting that combines investment methodology with in-depth social and environmental research.

FRIENDS' PROVIDENT LIFE OFFICE

Eighty Alfred Street
Milsons Point, NSW 2061 Australia
(011) 61 2 925-9255

Friends' Provident was established by and for Quakers in 1832 in the United Kingdom. Since 1986 it has offered ethical products that aim to provide an avenue for investors to translate their principles into investment action while providing financial gain. Friends' Provident offers three ethical financial vehicles:

- Ethical ordinary insurance bond
- Superannuation and roll-over bonds
- Ethical growth/income trust

All three of these are managed with broad social criteria, avoiding investment in alcohol, tobacco, some animal-tested products, fur products, meat products, uranium and chlorofluorocarbons, gambling, armament production, nuclear power, banking (unless lending is primarily for housing), and trade with South Africa.

ENVIRONMENTAL OPPORTUNITIES FUND

Occidental Life Insurance Company of Australia
Occidental Centre
601 Pacific Highway
St. Leonards, 2065 Australia
(011) 61 2 957-0957

This fund employs a broad range of social criteria and particularly seeks out the following activities:

- recycling and waste management;
- technologies and processes that reduce global warming and pollution;
- processes that reduce usage of fossil fuels and employ renewable energy sources;
- resource- and energy-efficient housing;
- appropriate public transportation systems;
- eucalypt afforestation;
- the production of durable, environmentally benign, resource-efficient essential goods;
- financial institutions that apply environmentally acceptable lending criteria.

EARTHRISE INVESTMENT POOL
MERCATOR MASTER SUPERANNUATION PLAN

Purvis, van Eyk & Company Ltd.
43 Phillip Street
Sydney NSW 2000 Australia
(011) 61 2 247-6000

The fund is invested only in companies that meet a broad range of social criteria; it avoids investments in companies involved in:

- mining, processing, distribution, or sale of uranium;
- logging or importation of primary rain forest timbers;

- wood chipping;
- large-scale chemical-based pulp and paper mills;
- direct or indirect killing of whales, dolphins, or seals;
- logging, mining, or exploration likely to disturb areas of environmental significance;
- tobacco growing, processing, or distribution;
- major defense contracting;
- nuclear armaments;
- trade or presence in countries that are subjects of United Nations sanctions;
- manufacture or distribution of herbicides;
- manufacture of ozone-depleting substances;
- animal experimentation;
- alcohol;
- gambling.

SELECTED U.S. CORPORATIONS' SOCIAL PERFORMANCE

THE CHECKOFF RATINGS AND WHAT THEY REPRESENT

Between July 1990 and June 1991, Kinder, Lydenberg, Domini & Company (KLD), published a series of *Company Reviews* of the four hundred corporations on the Domini Social Index.

Each review contains a summary graph indicating—with a "checkoff" rating—those areas that, in KLD's judgment, a social investor might view as one of strength or one for concern. The reviews also contain a prose explanation of each issue that received a checkoff rating.

The tables in this appendix represent the ratings from those four hundred reviews. (Space considerations precluded reproducing the accompanying text.) In the paragraphs below, preceding the tables, is a sort of "key" to the checkoff ratings: a list for each issue of the topics on which KLD focused. For each topic, KLD set a threshold for corporate involvement that triggered the assigning of the checkoff ratings.

The reviews are reappraised annually, as are the standards on which they are based.

THE COMMUNITY

Areas of Strength
1. The company has consistently given more than 1.5 percent of pretax earnings to charity in recent years.
2. The company's giving goes in substantial amounts to innovative programs, such as affordable housing, job training, and AIDS support groups.
3. The company has taken a leadership role in participation in public-private partnerships directed toward the economically disadvantaged, such as the National Equity Fund.
4. Other.

Areas of Concern

1. The company is the subject of fines, civil settlements, or major controversies relating to communities in which it has operations.
2. The company has developed strained relations with the communities in which it operates due to a long history of plant closings.
3. The company is a bank recently subject to a substantive Community Reinvestment Act challenge.
4. Other.

| EMPLOYEE RELATIONS

Areas of Strength

1. The company has a reputation for high-quality union relations relative to others in its industry.
2. The company has maintained a consistent no-layoff policy.
3. The company has maintained a consistent policy of cash profit sharing.
4. The company encourages substantial worker involvement through a combination of gain-sharing, quality bonuses, bonuses tied to profits, employee stock ownership plans (ESOPs), and employee ownership programs.
5. The company hires and promotes the handicapped, the elderly, or other disadvantaged groups at levels above the average for its industry.
6. The company has the highest compensation or benefits in its industry, innovative benefits programs (such as flexible spending accounts, work-at-home programs, and fitness centers), or a consistent record of superior programs related to worker health and safety.
7. Other.

Areas of Concern

1. The company has a reputation for poor union relations relative to others in its industry.
2. The company is the subject of recent fines, civil suits, or major controversies relating to employee safety.
3. The company has instituted major layoffs recently (more than 15 percent of the total headcount in a twelve-month period).
4. Other: lawsuits or controversies related to human resources and other employment policies.

Note: affirmative action issues are covered under "Women and Minorities," p. 748.

| THE ENVIRONMENT

Areas of Strength

1. The company derives more than 4 percent of revenues from products or services in cleaning up the environment.
2. The company has instituted substantial companywide programs or commitments (over and above regulatory requirements) to reduce hazardous waste and emissions.
3. The company is a substantial user of recycled materials as raw materials in a manufacturing process or is a major player in the recycling business.
4. The company is a substantial developer, user, or marketer of fuels with environmental advantages (over 4 percent of revenues) or is a major player in the cogeneration market.
5. The company has a record of investing in property, plants, and equipment that has above average environmental performance for its industry.
6. Other: exceptional philanthropy related to the environment; environmentally beneficial use of company lands and facilities; innovative products with environmental benefits.

Areas of Concern

1. The company currently faces substantial liabilities at hazardous waste disposal sites (more than $20 million or more than twenty sites) or has Superfund sites at company facilities.
2. The company has a recent record of fines, civil suits, or major controversies relating to air, water, noise, or land pollution.
3. The company is among the top emitters of chlorofluorocarbons (CFCs) or methyl chloroform.
4. The company is one of the largest legal emitters of toxic chemicals or its emissions play a substantial role in the formation of acid rain.
5. The company is a major producer of agricultural chemicals.
6. Other.

| PRODUCT

Areas of Strength

1. The company has a reputation for high-quality products or services relative to others in its industry (multiple mentions by outside sources; outside recognition for quality programs; consistently high performance in customer satisfaction studies) or has instituted credible companywide quality programs.
2. The company has a reputation for outstanding low cost or high quality in products or services relative to others in industry.

3. The company is among the leaders in its industry in research and development spending as a percentage of sales on a consistent basis. The company has a reputation for exceptional innovation or inventiveness in new product development.
4. The company serves or targets the economically disadvantaged.
5. Other: recognition for marketing practices that reflect sensitivity in areas of social concern.

Areas of Concern

1. The company is the subject of recent major life-threatening product liability cases.
2. The company is the subject of recent major non-life-threatening product liability cases.
3. The company derives more than 4 percent of revenues from the manufacture of alcohol, gambling, tobacco, or firearms. (Double X.)
4. The company is the subject of fines, civil settlements, or major controversies relating to the firm's advertising, marketing, or production practices.
5. The company is the subject of fines, civil settlements, or major controversies relating to price fixing, antitrust violations, or consumer fraud.
6. The company's business practices have resulted in accidents or mishaps posing substantial hazards to local communities.
7. Other.

| WOMEN AND MINORITIES

Areas of Strength

1. The company's chief executive officer is a woman or a minority.
2. The company has made notable progress in the promotion of women or minorities, particularly in line and operating positions. The company has received substantial recognition for its progress in the hiring of women and minorities from women's and minorities' organizations.
3. The company has strong representation of women, minorities, or the physically challenged on its board of directors (a total of four in these categories—without double counting—or one third of the board if the board is less than twelve).
4. The company has outstanding benefits relating to child care, elder care, flexible work schedules, and other programs that address work and family concerns. The company has received substantial recognition for its progress in these areas from women's groups.

5. The company has a long and consistent record of exceptional support for women- and minority-owned businesses.
6. Other.

Areas of Concern
1. The company is the subject of fines, civil settlements, or major controversies relating to its affirmative action record.
2. Other.

| OTHER

Areas of Strength

A variety of issues are considered in this category, including:

1. The company has exceptional policies on limiting compensation of board members or other innovative policies in relation to its board.
2. The company has taken exceptional initiatives in pursuing alternatives to animal testing.
3. The company has taken exceptional steps in calling for high standards of business practice relative to its industry.
4. The company is more than 20 percent owned by a company with areas of social strength, or it owns more than 20 percent of companies with areas of social strength.
5. Other.

Areas of Concern

This category contains a variety of issues, including the following:

1. The company has operations in Northern Ireland.
2. The company has a record of excessive compensation for board members.
3. The company has been involved in controversies relating to foreign countries other than South Africa or Northern Ireland or relating to native Americans.
4. The company is involved in major controversies relating to animal testing.
5. The company is involved in major disputes over nonpayment of federal or local taxes.
6. The company is more than 20 percent owned by a company with areas of social concern, or it owns more than 20 percent of companies with areas of social concern.
7. Other.

MILITARY

Areas of Concern

1. The company has substantial involvement in weapons-related contracting (over 2 percent of sales; among the top fifty Defense Department contractors; over $10 million in nuclear weapons-related contracts).
2. The company has minor involvement in weapons-related work (less than 2 percent of sales; nuclear contracts under $10 million; off-the-shelf components used in weapons systems through subcontracting account for more than 10 percent of revenues).
3. The company received more than $50 million in fuel contracts or other commodity products related to weapons from the Department of Defense within the past fiscal year.
4. Other.

NUCLEAR POWER

Areas of Concern

1. The company is an electric utility deriving more than 2 percent of its electricity from nuclear fuels, or it owns more than 20 percent of a nuclear power plant under construction. (Double X.)
2. The company is an electric utility deriving less than 2 percent of its electricity from nuclear fuels, or it owns less than 20 percent of a nuclear power plant under construction.
3. The company derives more than 2 percent of sales from the construction or management of nuclear power plants. (Double X.)
4. The company is involved in the mining, processing, or enriching of uranium or is otherwise involved in the nuclear fuel cycle.
5. The company derives more than 4 percent of sales from the sale of specialized parts or equipment for nuclear power generation.
6. Other.

SOUTH AFRICA

Areas of Concern

1. The company currently has equity interest in South Africa. (Double X.)
2. The company is involved in recent controversies relating to substantial nonequity involvement in South Africa in areas of strategic importance to the government. (Double X.)

3. The company is involved in recent controversies relating to nonequity interests in South Africa in nonstrategic industries.
4. Other.

Note: under KLD's current rating system, a company that has licensing or sales agreements in South Africa in nonstrategic industries will not receive an X unless there have been controversies of some substance relating to this involvement.

TABLE A-1

STRENGTHS AND CONCERNS OF DOMINI 400 SOCIAL INDEX—AS OF JUNE 1991

Company	Community	Employee Relations	Environment	Product	Women/ Minorities	Other	Military Contracts	Nuclear Power	South Africa
ACUSON									
ADVANCED MICRO DEVICES		X	X				X		
AETNA	XX	X		X	X				
AFFILIATED PUBLICATIONS	XX								
AHMANSON	X								
AIR PRODUCTS	X		XX						
AIRBORNE FREIGHT			X						
ALBERTO-CULVER		X							
ALBERTSON'S		X							
ALCO STANDARD			XX						
ALCOA		X	X				X		

No concern =   Concern = X   Major concern = XX

No strength =   Strength = X   Major strength = XX

TABLE A-2

STRENGTHS AND CONCERNS OF DOMINI 400 SOCIAL INDEX—AS OF JUNE 1991

Company	Community	Employee Relations	Environment	Product	Women/Minorities	Other	Military Contracts	Nuclear Power	South Africa
ALEXANDER & ALEXANDER				X		X			
ALLWASTE			X						
ALZA					X				
AMDAHL				X					X
AMERITECH	X	X			X				
AMERICA WEST AIRLINES		X	X		X	X			
AMERICAN EXPRESS	XX			X	X	XX			
AMERICAN GENERAL									
AMERICAN GREETINGS									
AMERICAN INT'L GROUP				X					
AMERICAN STORES									

No concern =   Concern = X   Major concern = XX

No strength =   Strength = X   Major strength = XX

TABLE A-3

STRENGTHS AND CONCERNS OF DOMINI 400 SOCIAL INDEX—AS OF JUNE 1991

Company	Community	Employee Relations	Environment	Product	Women/ Minorities	Other	Military Contracts	Nuclear Power	South Africa
AMERICAN WATER WORKS									
AMERITRUST	X				X				
AMOCO	XX	X	XX		XX		X		
AMP			XX	X			X		
AMR	X	X			X				
ANADARKO		X	X		X		X		
ANALOG DEVICES	X	X							
ANGELICA									
APACHE	X		X						
APOGEE		X					X		
APPLE COMPUTER	X	X		X	XX				

No concern = □   No strength = ▨

Concern = X   Strength = X (shaded)

Major concern = XX   Major strength = XX (shaded)

TABLE A-4

STRENGTHS AND CONCERNS OF DOMINI 400 SOCIAL INDEX—AS OF JUNE 1991

Company	Community	Employee Relations	Environment	Product	Women/ Minorities	Other	Military Contracts	Nuclear Power	South Africa
APPLIED MATERIALS		X	X		X				
ARCHER-DANIELS-MIDL'D			X			X			
ARCO CHEMICAL	X	XX	XX			X			
ARKLA	X		X						
ASK COMPUTER SYSTEMS					X	X			
ATLANTA GAS LIGHT			X						
ATLANTIC RICHFIELD	XX		XX	X	XX	XX	X		
AUTODESK		X			X				
AUTOMATIC DATA PROCESSING		X							
AVNET							X		
AVON					XX	X			

No concern = ☐ No strength = ▨

Concern = ☐X Strength = ▨X

Major concern = ☐XX Major strength = ▨XX

TABLE A-5

STRENGTHS AND CONCERNS OF DOMINI 400 SOCIAL INDEX—AS OF JUNE 1991

Company	Community	Employee Relations	Environment	Product	Women/ Minorities	Other	Military Contracts	Nuclear Power	South Africa
BALDOR ELECTRIC									
BANC ONE	X		X		X				
BANK OF BOSTON	X	X		X					
BANKAMERICA	X	X		X					
BANKERS TRUST	X	X							X
BARNETT BANKS									
BASSETT FURNITURE		X							
BATTLE MOUNT'N GOLD						X			
BAXTER INT'L	XX	X		X	X				
BECTON DICKINSON									
BELL ATLANTIC				X					

No concern = □   Concern = □ X   Major concern = □ XX

No strength = ▨   Strength = ▨ X   Major strength = ▨ XX

TABLE A-6

STRENGTHS AND CONCERNS OF DOMINI 400 SOCIAL INDEX—AS OF JUNE 1991

Company	Community	Employee Relations	Environment	Product	Women/ Minorities	Other	Military Contracts	Nuclear Power	South Africa
BELLSOUTH	X								
BEMIS									
BEN & JERRY'S	XX	XX	X			X			
BENEFICIAL									
BERGEN BRUNSWIG				X					
BETZ LABS		X	X	X					
BIOMET		X		X					
BLOCK, H&R	X	X			X				
BOB EVANS FARMS					X				
BRIGGS & STRATTON									
BROOKLYN UNION GAS	XX		X						

No concern = ☐ Concern = X Major concern = XX

No strength = ▨ Strength = X Major strength = XX

TABLE A-7

STRENGTHS AND CONCERNS OF DOMINI 400 SOCIAL INDEX—AS OF JUNE 1991

Company	Community	Employee Relations	Environment	Product	Women/ Minorities	Other	Military Contracts	Nuclear Power	South Africa
BROWN GROUP	X								
BURLINGTON RESOURCES						X			
CABOT			X	X					
CALGON CARBON		X	X						
CALIFORNIA ENERGY		X	X	X					
CAMPBELL SOUP		X		X					
CAP CITIES/ABC	X	X		X	XX				
CAPITAL HOLDINGS									
CAROLINA FREIGHT				X					
CBS	X			X	X	X			
CENTEX									

No concern = ☐   Concern = X   Major concern = XX

No strength = ▨   Strength = X   Major strength = XX

STRENGTHS AND CONCERNS OF DOMINI 400 SOCIAL INDEX—AS OF JUNE 1991

Company	Community	Employee Relations	Environment	Product	Women/Minorities	Other	Military Contracts	Nuclear Power	South Africa
CHAMBERS DEVELOPMENT	X		X	X					
CHEMICAL BANKING	XX			X					X
CHUBB									
CHURCH & DWIGHT			X						
CIGNA	X								
CINCINNATI MILACRON									
CINTAS									
CIRCUIT CITY STORES	X	X							
CITIZENS UTILITIES									
CLAIRE'S STORES	X				X				
CLARCOR	X								

No concern =
No strength =

Concern = X
Strength = X

Major concern = XX
Major strength = XX

TABLE A-9

STRENGTHS AND CONCERNS OF DOMINI 400 SOCIAL INDEX—AS OF JUNE 1991

Company	Community	Employee Relations	Environment	Product	Women/ Minorities	Other	Military Contracts	Nuclear Power	South Africa
CLARK EQUIPMENT									
CLOROX	X	X							
COCA-COLA	X				X				
COMCAST									
COMMERCE CLEARING HOUSE		X							
COMMUNITY PSYCHIATRIC					X				
COMPAQ COMPUTERS		X							
COMPUTER ASSOCIATES									
CONNECTICUT ENERGY			X		X				
CONSOLIDATED FREIGHTWAYS									
CONSOLIDATED NAT'L GAS	X	X	XX						

No concern = (blank) No strength = (shaded)

Concern = X Strength = X (shaded)

Major concern = XX Major strength = XX (shaded)

TABLE A-10

STRENGTHS AND CONCERNS OF DOMINI 400 SOCIAL INDEX—AS OF JUNE 1991

Company	Community	Employee Relations	Environment	Product	Women/Minorities	Other	Military Contracts	Nuclear Power	South Africa
CONSOLIDATED PAPERS		XX	X						
CONSOLIDATED RAIL		X	XX	X					
CONTINENTAL CORP	X	X			X				
COOPER TIRE		X							
CORESTATES FINANCIAL	X				X				
CORNING	X			X	XX		X		
CPC INTERNATIONAL									
CPI CORP	X								
CRITICAL CARE AMERICA		X		XX					
CROSS, A.T.		XX		X					
CROSS & TRECKER									

No concern = [ ]   Concern = X   Major concern = XX

No strength = [ ]   Strength = [ ]   Major strength = [ ]

TABLE A-11

STRENGTHS AND CONCERNS OF DOMINI 400 SOCIAL INDEX—AS OF JUNE 1991

Company	Community	Employee Relations	Environment	Product	Women/ Minorities	Other	Military Contracts	Nuclear Power	South Africa
CSX		X	X						
CUMMINS ENGINE	XX	X					X		X
CYPRUS MINERALS		X							
DANA		XX		X					
DAYTON HUDSON	XX	X	X			X			
DELTA AIR LINES		XX		X					
DELUXE	X	XX		X					
DIGITAL EQUIPMENT	X	X	XX		XX	X	X		X
DILLARD						X			
DIME SAVINGS BANK OF N.Y.	XX	X			XX				
DIONEX			X						

No concern = [ ]   Concern = [X]   Major concern = [XX]

No strength = [▓]   Strength = [▓X]   Major strength = [▓XX]

TABLE A-12

STRENGTHS AND CONCERNS OF DOMINI 400 SOCIAL INDEX—AS OF JUNE 1991

Company	Community	Employee Relations	Environment	Product	Women/Minorities	Other	Military Contracts	Nuclear Power	South Africa
DISNEY, WALT	X		X						
DOLLAR GENERAL				X					
DONNELLEY, RR	X	X	X	X					
DOW JONES				X					
DSC COMMUNICATION						X			
ECHO BAY MINE			X		X				
EDWARDS, AG		X		X					
EGGHEAD		X			X	X			
ENERGEN	X		X						
ENRON	X		X						
EQUITABLE RESOURCES			X						

No concern = ☐ Concern = X Major concern = XX

No strength = ▨ Strength = X Major strength = XX

TABLE A-13

STRENGTHS AND CONCERNS OF DOMINI 400 SOCIAL INDEX—AS OF JUNE 1991

Company	Community	Employee Relations	Environment	Product	Women/ Minorities	Other	Military Contracts	Nuclear Power	South Africa
FASTENAL	X	X		X					
FEDDERS		X							
FEDERAL EXPRESS	X	XX		XX	X	X			
FEDERAL HOME LOAN	X			X					
FEDERAL-MOGUL	X			X					
FEDERAL NAT'L MORTGAGE ASSN	XX			X	X				
FIRST CHICAGO	XX								
FIRST FIDELITY									
FIRST WACHOVIA	X			X	X				
FLEET/NORSTAR	X		X	X					
FLEETWOOD ENTERPRISES									

No concern = ☐   Concern = ☐ X   Major concern = ☐ XX

No strength = ▓   Strength = ▓ X   Major strength = ▓ XX

TABLE A-14

STRENGTHS AND CONCERNS OF DOMINI 400 SOCIAL INDEX—AS OF JUNE 1991

Company	Community	Employee Relations	Environment	Product	Women/Minorities	Other	Military Contracts	Nuclear Power	South Africa
FLEMING									
FOREST LABS									
FULLER, H.B.	X	X	X						
GANNETT	X				XX				
THE GAP	X								
GATX	X								
GEICO				X		X			
GENERAL CINEMA	X								
GENERAL MILLS	XX	X			XX				
GENERAL RE CORPORATION									
GENERAL SIGNAL							X		

No concern = Major concern = XX

No strength = Major strength = XX

Concern = X

Strength = X

TABLE A-15

STRENGTHS AND CONCERNS OF DOMINI 400 SOCIAL INDEX—AS OF JUNE 1991

Company	Community	Employee Relations	Environment	Product	Women/ Minorities	Other	Military Contracts	Nuclear Power	South Africa
GENUINE PARTS				X					
GERBER PRODUCTS				X					
GIANT FOOD	X		X						
GIBSON GREETINGS		X	X						
GOLDEN WEST FINANCIAL				X	X				
GOULD PUMPS									
GRACO	X								
GRAINGER, W.W.						X			
GREAT ATLANTIC PACIFIC		X	X						
GREAT WESTERN FINANCIAL	X								
GROUNDWATER TECHNOLOGY			XX						

No concern = (white) No strength = (shaded)
Concern = X (white) Strength = X (shaded)
Major concern = XX (white) Major strength = XX (shaded)

TABLE A-16

STRENGTHS AND CONCERNS OF DOMINI 400 SOCIAL INDEX—AS OF JUNE 1991

Company	Community	Employee Relations	Environment	Product	Women/ Minorities	Other	Military Contracts	Nuclear Power	South Africa
HANDLEMAN									
HANNAFORD BROS.			X						
HARLAND, JOHN H.									
HARMAN INT'L		X		X					
HARTFORD STEAM							X		
HARTMARX									
HASBRO	X								
HECHINGER					XX				
HEINZ			X	X		X			
HELMERICH & PAYNE									
HERSHEY									

No concern = (blank)   Concern = X   Major concern = XX
No strength = (shaded)   Strength = X (shaded)   Major strength = XX (shaded)

TABLE A-17

STRENGTHS AND CONCERNS OF DOMINI 400 SOCIAL INDEX—AS OF JUNE 1991

Company	Community	Employee Relations	Environment	Product	Women/Minorities	Other	Military Contracts	Nuclear Power	South Africa
HILLENBRAND									
HOME DEPOT	XX		X						
HON INDUSTRIES		X		X					
HOUSEHOLD INTERNATIONAL									
HUBBELL									
HUFFY	X	X		X					
HUMANA	X								
HUNT MANUFACTURING	XX		X						
IDAHO POWER			X						
ILLINOIS TOOL WORKS				X		X			
INB FINANCIAL	XX				X				

No concern = □   Concern = X   Major concern = XX

No strength = ▨   Strength = X   Major strength = XX

STRENGTHS AND CONCERNS OF DOMINI 400 SOCIAL INDEX—AS OF JUNE 1991

Company	Community	Employee Relations	Environment	Product	Women/Minorities	Other	Military Contracts	Nuclear Power	South Africa
INLAND STEEL		X	XX						
INTEL		X	X				X		
INTERNATIONAL DAIRY QUEEN			X						
IONICS			X				X	X	
ISCO		X	X						
JAMES RIVER CORP		X	XX			X			
JEFFERSON-PILOT			X						
JOHNSON PRODUCTS					X				
JOSTENS	X								
KANSAS POWER & LIGHT			X						
KAUFMAN & BROAD	X								

No concern =   No strength =

Concern = X   Strength = X

Major concern = XX   Major strength = XX

TABLE A-19

STRENGTHS AND CONCERNS OF DOMINI 400 SOCIAL INDEX—AS OF JUNE 1991

Company	Community	Employee Relations	Environment	Product	Women/ Minorities	Other	Military Contracts	Nuclear Power	South Africa
KELLY SERVICES					X				
KING WORLD PRODUCTIONS									
KMART			X						
KNIGHT-RIDDER	X	X	X		X				
KROGER	X	X	X	X	X				
LAND'S END		X		X					
LAWSON PRODUCTS				X					
LEE ENTERPRISES									
LEGGETT & PLATT									
LG&E ENERGY			X						
LILLIAN VERNON	X			X	XX				

No concern =   Concern = X   Major concern = XX

No strength =   Strength = X   Major strength = XX

TABLE A-20

STRENGTHS AND CONCERNS OF DOMINI 400 SOCIAL INDEX—AS OF JUNE 1991

Company	Community	Employee Relations	Environment	Product	Women/Minorities	Other	Military Contracts	Nuclear Power	South Africa
THE LIMITED					X	X			
LINCOLN NATIONAL	XX				XX				
LIZ CLAIBORNE					X				
LONGS DRUG		X							
LOTUS DEVELOPMENT	X				X				
LOUISIANA LAND & EXPLORATION			X						
LOWE'S COS		X							
LUBY'S CAFETERIA									
MAGMA POWER		X	XX			X			
MANOR CARE									
MARRIOTT		X		X	X				

No concern = □   Concern = X   Major concern = XX

No strength = ▨   Strength = ▨   Major strength = ▨

TABLE A-21

STRENGTHS AND CONCERNS OF DOMINI 400 SOCIAL INDEX—AS OF JUNE 1991

Company	Community	Employee Relations	Environment	Product	Women/Minorities	Other	Military Contracts	Nuclear Power	South Africa
MARSH & MCLENNAN						X			
MATTEL									
MAY DEPT STORES	X								
MAYTAG		X		X					
MCCAW CELLULAR						X			
MCDONALD'S			X	X	XX				
MCGRAW-HILL									
MCI							X		
MCKESSON	X		X						
MEAD	X		X						
MEASUREX		X		X					

No concern =
No strength =

Concern = X
Strength = X

Major concern = XX
Major strength = XX

TABLE A-22

STRENGTHS AND CONCERNS OF DOMINI 400 SOCIAL INDEX—AS OF JUNE 1991

Company	Community	Employee Relations	Environment	Product	Women/ Minorities	Other	Military Contracts	Nuclear Power	South Africa
MEDCO CONTAINMENT				X					
MEDIA GENERAL	X		X						
MEDTRONIC	X	X							
MELLON BANK	XX								
MELVILLE	X								
MERCANTILE STORES									
MERCK	X	X	X	X	XX				
MEREDITH									
MERRILL LYNCH	X			X	X				
MICRON TECHNOLOGY				X			X		
MICROSOFT									

No concern = [ ]
No strength = [ ]

Concern = X
Strength = X

Major concern = XX
Major strength = XX

TABLE A-23

STRENGTHS AND CONCERNS OF DOMINI 400 SOCIAL INDEX—AS OF JUNE 1991

Company	Community	Employee Relations	Environment	Product	Women/Minorities	Other	Military Contracts	Nuclear Power	South Africa
HERMAN MILLER		XX	X	X	X				
MILLIPORE		X	X						
MODINE MANUFACTURING		X		X					
MONARCH MACHINE TOOL									
MOORE									
J.P. MORGAN	XX	X							
MORRISON									
MORTON INT'L				X			X		
MYLAN LABORATORIES									
NAT'L EDUCATION CORP									
NAT'L MEDICAL ENTERPRISE									

No concern = [ ]   Concern = X   Major concern = XX
No strength = [shaded]   Strength = X [shaded]   Major strength = XX [shaded]

TABLE A-24

STRENGTHS AND CONCERNS OF DOMINI 400 SOCIAL INDEX—AS OF JUNE 1991

Company	Community	Employee Relations	Environment	Product	Women/Minorities	Other	Military Contracts	Nuclear Power	South Africa
NATIONAL SERVICE IND						X			
NBD BANCORP									
NCR CORP						X	X		
NEUTROGENA									
NEW ENGLAND BUSINESS SER		X							
NEW YORK TIMES	X			X					
NEWELL	X								
NICOR			X						
NIKE	X								
NORDSON	X								
NORDSTROM		X		X	X				

No concern =   Concern = X   Major concern = XX

No strength =   Strength = X   Major strength = XX

TABLE A-25

STRENGTHS AND CONCERNS OF DOMINI 400 SOCIAL INDEX—AS OF JUNE 1991

Company	Community	Employee Relations	Environment	Product	Women/ Minorities	Other	Military Contracts	Nuclear Power	South Africa
NORFOLK SOUTHERN		X	X						
NORTHERN TELECOM		X	X						
NORTHWESTERN PUBLIC SER			X						
NORWEST	XX								
NUCOR		X							
NWNL	X	XX	X	X					
OMNICOM		X							
ONEIDA		X		X		X			
ONEOK	X		X						
ORYX ENERGY		X	X						
OSHKOSH B'GOSH									

No concern = (white box) Concern = X Major concern = XX

No strength = (shaded box) Strength = X (shaded) Major strength = XX (shaded)

TABLE A-26

STRENGTHS AND CONCERNS OF DOMINI 400 SOCIAL INDEX—AS OF JUNE 1991

Company	Community	Employee Relations	Environment	Product	Women/Minorities	Other	Military Contracts	Nuclear Power	South Africa
PACIFIC ENTERPRISES			X						
PACIFIC TELESIS	X	X	X						
PENNEY, J.C.	XX	X			X				
PENNZOIL	X		X						
PEOPLES ENERGY	X		X		XX				
PEP BOYS				X					
PEPSICO	X	X		X	X				
PETRIE STORES					XX				
PHILLIPS-VAN HEUSEN						X			
PIPER JAFFRAY	XX	X				X			
PITNEY BOWES	X	X			X				

No concern = (white box)   Concern = X   Major concern = XX

No strength = (shaded box)   Strength = X   Major strength = XX

TABLE A-27

STRENGTHS AND CONCERNS OF DOMINI 400 SOCIAL INDEX—AS OF JUNE 1991

Company	Community	Employee Relations	Environment	Product	Women/ Minorities	Other	Military Contracts	Nuclear Power	South Africa
PNC FINANCIAL	X								
POLAROID	XX	XX	X						
POTOMAC ELECTRIC	X		X		XX				
PREMIER INDUSTRIAL	XX								
PRICE									
PRIMERICA						X			
PROCTER & GAMBLE	XX	X	X		X	X			
QUAKER OATS	XX			X		X			
RALSTON PURINA			X	X					
REEBOK	X					X			
ROADWAY SERVICES									

No concern = □   Concern = X   Major concern = XX

No strength = ▦   Strength = X   Major strength = XX

STRENGTHS AND CONCERNS OF DOMINI 400 SOCIAL INDEX—AS OF JUNE 1991

Company	Community	Employee Relations	Environment	Product	Women/Minorities	Other	Military Contracts	Nuclear Power	South Africa
ROCHESTER TELEPHONE	X								
ROUSE	XX			XX					
ROWAN									
RUBBERMAID	X			XX					
RUSSELL	X	X			X				
RYAN'S FAMILY STEAKS									
RYDER SYSTEM				X	X				
SAFECO	XX								
SAFETY-KLEEN			X / XX	X					
SANTA FE PACIFIC		X	X	X					
SANTA FE RESOURCES			X						

No concern = ☐ Concern = X Major concern = XX

No strength = ▨ Strength = X̲ Major strength = X̲X̲

TABLE A-29

STRENGTHS AND CONCERNS OF DOMINI 400 SOCIAL INDEX—AS OF JUNE 1991

Company	Community	Employee Relations	Environment	Product	Women/Minorities	Other	Military Contracts	Nuclear Power	South Africa
SARA LEE	XX				X	X			
SCOTT PAPER	X	X	X						
SEALED AIR			X	X		X			
SEARS, ROEBUCK	X	XX		X	XX				
SECURITY PACIFIC	X			X		X			
SERVICE CORP INTERNATIONAL									
SHARED MEDICAL SYSTEMS									
SHAW INDUSTRIES									
SHAWMUT NATIONAL	XX				X				
SHERWIN-WILLIAMS				X					
SIGMA-ALDRICH				X					

No concern = (white)
No strength = (shaded)

Concern = X (white)
Strength = X (shaded)

Major concern = XX (white)
Major strength = XX (shaded)

TABLE A-30

STRENGTHS AND CONCERNS OF DOMINI 400 SOCIAL INDEX—AS OF JUNE 1991

Company	Community	Employee Relations	Environment	Product	Women/ Minorities	Other	Military Contracts	Nuclear Power	South Africa
SKYLINE									
A.O. SMITH	X	X							
J.M. SMUCKER									
SNAP-ON-TOOLS						X			
SOFTWARE TOOLWORKS					X				
SOUTHERN NE TELECOM	X				X				
SOUTHWEST AIRLINES			X	XX					
SOUTHWESTERN BELL									
SPEC'S MUSIC					XX				
SPRINGS INDUSTRIES	X	X							
SPX									

No concern =
No strength =

Concern = X
Strength = X

Major concern = XX
Major strength = XX

TABLE A-31

STRENGTHS AND CONCERNS OF DOMINI 400 SOCIAL INDEX—AS OF JUNE 1991

Company	Community	Employee Relations	Environment	Product	Women/ Minorities	Other	Military Contracts	Nuclear Power	South Africa
SQUARE D	●								
ST. JUDE MEDICAL		X							
ST. PAUL COMPANIES	XX	X							
STANDARD REGISTER									
STANHOME	X								
STANLEY WORKS	X	X							
STRATUS COMPUTER									
STRIDE RITE	X				XX				
STRYKER									
STUDENT LOAN MARKETING									
SUN CO	X		X				X		

No concern =   No strength =   Concern =   Strength =   Major concern = XX   Major strength = XX

TABLE A-32

STRENGTHS AND CONCERNS OF DOMINI 400 SOCIAL INDEX—AS OF JUNE 1991

Company	Community	Employee Relations	Environment	Product	Women/ Minorities	Other	Military Contracts	Nuclear Power	South Africa
SUN MICROSYSTEMS						X	X		
SUNTRUST BANKS									
SUPERVALU	X			X					
SYSCO									
TAMBRANDS					X				
TANDEM COMPUTERS		X							
TANDY		X							
TCBY									
TEKTRONIX	X	X					X		
TELEPHONE & DATA SYSTEMS									
TELE-COMMUNICATION									

No concern =   No strength =

Concern = X   Strength = X

Major concern = XX   Major strength = XX

TABLE A-33

STRENGTHS AND CONCERNS OF DOMINI 400 SOCIAL INDEX—AS OF JUNE 1991

Company	Community	Employee Relations	Environment	Product	Women/ Minorities	Other	Military Contracts	Nuclear Power	South Africa
TELLABS		X		X					
TENNANT	X	X	X	X					
THERMO ELECTRON			X				X	X	
THOMAS INDUSTRIES									
THOMAS & BETTS									
TIMES MIRROR	XX		X						
TJ INTERNAT'L		X	X	X					
TJX COMPANIES									
TONKA									
TOOTSIE ROLL					X				
TORCHMARK					X				

No concern = ☐ Concern = ☐ Major concern = ☐

No strength = ▨ Strength = ▨ Major strength = ▨

TABLE A-34

STRENGTHS AND CONCERNS OF DOMINI 400 SOCIAL INDEX—AS OF JUNE 1991

Company	Community	Employee Relations	Environment	Product	Women/Minorities	Other	Military Contracts	Nuclear Power	South Africa
TORO		X							
TOYS R US		X			X				
TRANSAMERICA	X				X				
TRAVELERS	X				X				
UAL		XX		X	X				
UNITED TELECOM				X					
UNUM	X	X			X				
USF&G				X					
US HEALTHCARE									
US LIFE						X			
US WEST	X				XX				

No concern =   Concern = X   Major concern = XX
No strength =   Strength = X   Major strength = XX

TABLE A-35

STRENGTHS AND CONCERNS OF DOMINI 400 SOCIAL INDEX—AS OF JUNE 1991

Company	Community	Employee Relations	Environment	Product	Women/Minorities	Other	Military Contracts	Nuclear Power	South Africa
VALUE LINE					X				
VAN DORN				X					
VERMONT FINANCIAL	X	X			X				
VF CORP						X			
VIACOM									
WALGREEN	X								
WALLACE COMPUTER									
WAL-MART		X	X	X					
WANG LABS		X			X		X		
WASHINGTON GAS LIGHT		X	X		X				
WASHINGTON POST	X			X	X				

No concern = [ ]   Concern = X   Major concern = XX

No strength = [ ]   Strength = X   Major strength = XX

TABLE A-36

STRENGTHS AND CONCERNS OF DOMINI 400 SOCIAL INDEX—AS OF JUNE 1991

Company	Community	Employee Relations	Environment	Product	Women/Minorities	Other	Military Contracts	Nuclear Power	South Africa
WATTS INDUSTRIES			X	X					
WELLMAN			X						
WELLS FARGO	XX	X							
WESCO		X				XX			
WESTVACO			X						
WETTERAU			X						
WHIRLPOOL	X	X							
WHITMAN				X					
WILLIAMS COS	X								
WOOLWORTH									
WORTHINGTON		XX							

No concern = Concern = X Major concern = XX

No strength = Strength = X Major strength = XX

TABLE A-37

STRENGTHS AND CONCERNS OF DOMINI 400 SOCIAL INDEX—AS OF JUNE 1991

Company	Community	Employee Relations	Environment	Product	Women/ Minorities	Other	Military Contracts	Nuclear Power	South Africa
WRIGLEY, WM.									
XEROX	XX	X	X			X	X		
YELLOW FREIGHT	X	XX		X	XX				
ZENITH ELECTRONICS									

No concern =   Concern = X   Major concern = XX

No strength =   Strength = X   Major strength = XX

DIRECTORIES

Banks
Brokers, Financial Planners, and Money Managers
Community Development Investments
Consulting Firms
Information Providers
Institutional Investors
Mutual and Money Market Funds
Venture Capital

The following directories include all of the organizations mentioned in the text. Inclusion here, or for that matter in the text, is not a recommendation of them or a verification of their abilities in the field of socially responsible investing. The almanac should be only a starting place in your due diligence.

We have made an effort to identify and include all that offer investment products and services to socially responsible investors. We mailed out questionnaires, we made phone calls, and we sent follow-up letters. The result is the most complete listing of SRI providers in North America and Europe ever assembled. We owe special thanks to Alan Miller of Ethical Investment Services Ltd. for his help in marshaling entries for the United Kingdom and Europe.

In any directory, errors and omissions are inevitable. Please send us corrections and additions for the next edition.

A final note of caution: beware of non-U.S. telephone numbers. We have attempted to conform European telephone numbers to North American dialing practices. Therefore, there will be inconsistencies between the city codes as they appear in the directory and as they appear in correspondence from European companies. For example, a London company will list its city code as 071. The zero will prevent the call from being completed from the United States. Therefore, we have omitted the extraneous zeros. Also, the number of digits in telephone numbers, even within a country, can vary by a digit or two. Putting together this directory has been an education in international telephone lore!

| BANKS

Ed. Note: *Some European financial institutions that are active in community investing do not fit comfortably in an American concept of what a bank is. These institutions will be found in the section on community development investments, pp. 802–808.*

United States

ARIZONA
Elk Horn Bank & Trust Company
Box 258
Arkadelphia, Ark. 71923-0248
Contact: Phyllis Stiffler

ILLINOIS
South Shore Bank & Trust Company
Seventy-first and Jeffery Boulevard
Chicago, Ill. 60649
(800) NOW-SSBK
(312) 753-5636
Contact: Joan Shapiro, Senior Vice
President

IOWA
Dubuque Bank & Trust
Box 747
Dubuque, Iowa 52004-0747
(800) 397-3268
(319) 589-2030 (fax)
Contact: Mel Miller, C.F.A.

NEW YORK
Community Capital Bank
111 Livingston Street
Brooklyn, N.Y. 11201
(718) 768-9344
Contact:Lyndon B. Comstock,
Chairman
Amy S. Nolan, Vice President

PENNSYLVANIA
Fidelity Bank
Charitable/Corporate Funds
Management
1700 Market, Ninth Floor
Philadelphia, Pa. 19103
(215) 496-1918
Contact: David P. Harrison, Vice
President

Germany

Bank für Sozialwirtschaft (BfS)
Worthstrasse 15–17
5000 Cologne 1, Germany
(011) 49 221 77680

GLS Gemeinschaftsbank eG
Oskar-Hoffman-Strasse 25
D-4630 Bochum 1, Germany
(011) 49 234 313883
Contact: Thomas Jorberg

Hypobank
(Bayerische Hypotheken und Weschel
Bank)
Postfach 20 05 27
8000 Munich 2, Germany
(011) 49 8992 448209

Ökobank
Bronnerstrasse 9
D-6000 Frankfurt, Germany
(011) 49 69 299870

Ökobank EG
Bornheimer Landstrasse 22
D-6000 Frankfurt 1, Germany
(011) 49 69 500 910 00

Privates Institute für Umweltschutz
   (IFU) GmbH
Kurfstendamm 180
W-1000 Berlin 15, Germany
(011) 49 30 88 32 818

Steyler Missionssparinstitut Sankt
   Augustin GmbH
Arnold-Jansen-Strasse 22
D-5205 Sankt Augustin, Germany
(011) 49 2241 237 337

Switzerland

Alternative Bank Schweiz
   (ABS)
Leberngasse 17
CH-4001 Olten, Switzerland
(011) 41 62 32 00 85

Netherlands

Triodosbank N.V.
Stationslaan 4
Box 55
3700 AB Zeist, Netherlands
(011) 31 3404 16544
Contact: Peter Blom

I BROKERS, FINANCIAL PLANNERS, AND MONEY MANAGERS

United States

CALIFORNIA

Advisory Financial Consultants
505 Durham Road
Fremont, Calif. 94539
(415) 656-1357
Contact: Ruthe P. Gomez, C.F.P.

ALBION Financial Associates
2550 Ninth Street, Suite 209B
Berkeley, Calif. 94710
(415) 486-8333
Contact: Bonnie Albion, C.F.P.

Robert Berend, Esq.
6611 West Fifth Street
Los Angeles, Calif. 90048-4601
(213) 651-2375
(213) 480-7724 (fax)

Joan P. Cudhea, C.F.P., R.I.A.
1860 Oliver Avenue
San Diego, Calif. 92109-5441
(619) 272-4118
(619) 223-3143

Financial Network Investment
   Corporation
9724 Washington Boulevard, No. 203
Culver City, Calif. 90232
(213) 836-4166
Contact: Gay Abarbanell

First Affirmative Financial Network
Walnut Street Securities
1510E Walnut Street
Berkeley, Calif. 94709
(415) 525-1230
Contact: Lincoln Pain

First Affirmative Financial Network
Box 900037
San Diego, Calif. 92190
(619) 582-7717
Contact: Jack A. Brill

First Pacific Financial Services
5290 Overpass Road, Suite 217
Santa Barbara, Calif. 93111
(805) 682-8282
(805) 682-5478 (fax)
Contact: Henry Sharp

Foothill Securities
2213 Vine Street
Berkeley, Calif. 94709
(415) 841-2202
(415) 841-5713
Contact: Michele K. Martin,
C.F.P.

Franklin Research & Development
Corporation
65K Gate Five
Sausalito, Calif. 94965
(415) 332-5822
Contact: Melanie Burnett

Harrington Investments
1001 Second Street, Suite 325
Napa, Calif. 94558
(707) 252-6166
(707) 257-7923 (fax)
Contact: John C. Harrington

Lieberman Associates Financial
Planning
100 Larkspur Landing Circle, No. 214
Larkspur, Calif. 94939
(415) 925-9055
Contact: Anne M. Lieberman,
Director

Paine Webber
William Morris Plaza
150 El Camino Drive, Suite 300
Beverly Hills, Calif. 90212
(213) 274-8441
(213) 272-8321
Contact: Marlene Share
Stuart Sieroty

Portfolio Advisory Services
444 South Flower Street, Thirty-ninth
Floor
Los Angeles, Calif. 90017
(213) 645-5667
(213) 216-9934 (fax)
Contact: Cedd Moses

Progressive Asset Management
1814 Franklin Street, Suite 710
Oakland, Calif. 94612
(800) 527-8627
(415) 834-3722
Contact: John Harrington, Chair, Board
of Directors
Peter Camejo, President
James Nixon, Director, Institutional
Investing
Eric Leenson
Duncan Meaney
Maryann Simpson, C.F.P.
Eileen Stromberg

Progressive Asset Management of Palo
Alto
459 Hamilton Avenue, Suite 207
Palo Alto, Calif. 94301
(415) 323-3700
Contact: Curt Weil, C.F.P.

Progressive Benefits
309 Santa Monica Boulevard, No. 221
Santa Monica, Calif. 90401
(213) 450-2020
Contact: James C. Pursley, C.F.P.

Sava Financial Advisory Services
8808 Las Tunas Drive
San Gabriel, Calif. 91776
(818) 285-3664
Contact: Manny Sandoval

Schmitz & Associates
655 Redwood Highway, Suite 160
Mill Valley, Calif. 94941
(415) 332-4584
(415) 331-5387 (fax)
Contact: Steven J. Schmitz

Scudder, Stevens & Clark
101 California Street, Suite 4100
San Francisco, Calif. 94111-5886
(800) 654-5777
(513) 621-2733
Contact: Brian Beitner

Sutro and Company
555 South Flower Street, Suite 3400
Los Angeles, Calif. 90071
(800) 252-9051 (southern Calif. only)
(213) 362-3900
Contact: Abe S. Ohanian

Walnut Street Securities
7829 Melrose Avenue, No. 351
Los Angeles, Calif. 90046
(213) 393-9066
Contact: Carolyn Woosley, C.F.P.

Venture Analysis
Box 3551
Santa Barbara, Calif. 93130
(805) 966-2503
(805) 528-8166 (fax)
Contact: Michael K. Harris

COLORADO

Boettcher & Company
1919 Fourteenth Street
Boulder, Colo. 80302
(800) 228-1026
(303) 441-0628
(303) 441-0656 (fax)
Contact: Kathy Leonard

Conover Investment Counsel
90 Madison Street, No. 501
Denver, Colo. 80206
(303) 321-9454
(303) 394-4848 (fax)
Contact: Katie Conover

First Affirmative Financial Network
1040 South Eighth Street, Suite 200
Colorado Springs, Colo. 80906
(800) 422-7284
(719) 636-1045
Contact: George Gay
    Ed Winslow, C.P.A.

Norman A. Hirsch, C.F.P.
1715 Pearl Street, Suite C
Boulder, Colo. 80302
(303) 440-7300

CONNECTICUT

William M. Banks Associates
12 Cob Drive
Westport, Conn. 06880
(800) 762-4435
(203) 454-2735
Contact: James Stephen Luce

Brody & Weiser
21 Woodland Street
New Haven, Conn. 06511
(203) 777-5375
(203) 782-9764 (fax)
Contact: Frances L. Brody

First Affirmative Financial Network
One River Oaks Road
Westport, Conn. 06880
(203) 454-3577
Contact: S. David Bue

Money Matters
38 Ranger Lane
West Hartford, Conn. 06117
(203) 233-2829
Contact: Marilyn S. Steinmetz, C.F.P.

Paine Webber
Two Union Plaza
New London, Conn. 06320
(800) 247-9488
(203) 444-6500
Contact: Laurel Butler

WASHINGTON, D.C.

Co-op America
2100 M Street NW, Suite 403
Washington, D.C. 20063
(202) 872-5307
Contact: Diane Keefe

Ferris, Baker, Watts
1720 I Street NW
Washington, D.C. 20006
(202) 429-3632 (call collect)
(202) 429-3645 (fax)
Contact: Sacha Millstone

FLORIDA

Money Plans
1017-A Thomasville Road
Tallahassee, Fla. 32303
(904) 222-5313
Contact: Marylyn Mitsuo Feaver,
C.F.P.

Paine Webber
100 South Ashley Drive, No. 1800
Tampa, Fla. 33602
(813) 221-5555
(813) 227-2878
Contact: Gary Moore

GEORGIA

Interstate/Johnson Lane
945 East Paces Ferry Road
Box 4103
Atlanta, Ga. 30302
(404) 240-5054
(404) 240-5111 (fax)
Contact: Dennis Scully

Social Responsibility Investment Group
Candler Building, Suite 622
127 Peachtree Street NE
Atlanta, Ga. 30303
(404) 577-3635
(404) 577-4496 (fax)
Contact: Hugh J. Kelley, President

ILLINOIS

Ariel Capital Management
307 North Michigan Avenue
Chicago, Ill. 60601
(312) 726-0140
Contact: Darice Wright

Chicago Corporation
208 South LaSalle Street
Chicago, Ill. 60604
(800) 621-0686
(312) 855-7714
Contact: Michael P. McGillicuddy,
C.F.P.

Ron Freund & Associates
835 Judson Avenue, Suite 507
Evanston, Ill. 60202
(708) 869-2424
Contact: Ron Freund

KENTUCKY
First Affirmative Financial Network
800 Brown & Williamson Tower
Louisville, Ky. 40202
(800) 422-7284
(502) 581-1122
(502) 582-0124 (fax)
Contact: Mary Becker, C.F.P.

MASSACHUSETTS

Bromfield & Bickling Financial
Services
Nine Meriam Street, Suite 25
Lexington, Mass. 02173
(617) 862-9779
Contact: Sandra Bromfield

A. G. Edwards & Sons
101 Derby Street
Hingham, Mass. 02043
(800) 543-8010 (New England only)
(617) 749-8010
(617) 749-8170 (fax)
Contact: Douglas John XXIII
Calnan

Falcon Capital Management
10 Tremont Street
Boston, Mass. 02108
(617) 227-8234
Contact: Karen Pratt

Financial Strategies
124 Wendy Lane
North Attleboro, Mass. 02760
(617) 695-6766
Contact: Elizabeth Hafkin, Ph.D.,
   C.F.P.

Franklin Management Corporation
531 Lewis Wharf
Boston, Mass. 02111
(617) 423-6655
(617) 482-6179 (fax)
Contact: Don Falvey

Franklin Research & Development
   Corporation
711 Atlantic Avenue, Fourth Floor
Boston, Mass. 02111
(617) 423-6655
(617) 482-6179 (fax)
Contact: Patrick McVeigh

Frontier Capital Management Company
90 Sumner Street
Boston, Mass. 02210
(617) 261-0777
Contact: Grace Keeney Fey

Interactive Investments
129 South Street
Boston, Mass. 02111
(617) 426-5786
Contact: David Ennis

Loring, Wolcott & Coolidge
230 Congress Street
Boston, Mass. 02110
Contact: Amy Domini
   Elizabeth Glenshaw

Linda Marks
785 Centre Street
Newton, Mass. 02158
(508) 842-3050
(617) 965-7846

New York Life
40 William Street, Suite 220
Wellesley Office Park
Wellesley, Mass. 02181
(617) 239-0732
Contact: David L. Levington,
   Ch.F.C.

NorthStar Asset Management
Six Enfield Street
Boston, Mass. 02130
(617) 522-3919 (home)
(617) 522-2635 (office)
Contact: Julie Wendrich, President

PanAgora Asset Management
260 Franklin Street, Twenty-second
   Floor
Boston, Mass. 02110
(800) 423-6041
(617) 439-6300
Contact: Richard Wilk, Senior
   Manager, U.S. Equities

Seaward Management Company
10 Post Office Square
Boston, Mass. 02109
(617) 426-1196
Contact: Roger D. Scoville

Smith Barney, Harris Upham &
   Company
Exchange Place
53 State Street
Boston, Mass. 02109
(800) 235-1205
(617) 570-9519
(617) 570-9458 (fax)
Contact: Anne Greenwood

U.S. Trust Company
Asset Management Division
40 Court Street
Boston, Mass. 02108
(617) 627-7000

Contact: James McPartland
   Geeta Bhide
   Lawrence Litvak
   Robert Zevin

WOMONEY
76 Townsend Road
Belmont, Mass. 02178
(617) 489-3601
Contact: Sharon Rich, Ed.D.

Yates Capital Management Corporation
Eight Louisburg Square
Boston, Mass. 02108
(617) 227-0314
Contact: Susannah W. Sears

MARYLAND
First Financial Group
401 Washington Avenue, Sixth Floor
Baltimore, Md. 21204-9705
(301) 828-5400
Contact: Stephen J. Siegel, C.F.P.

MAINE
H. M. Payson & Company
One Portland Square
Box 31
Portland, Me. 04112
(800) 456-6710
(207) 772-3761
(207) 772-7456
Contact: Laura McDill

MICHIGAN

First Affirmative Financial Network
2336 Oakland Drive, Suite 2
Kalamazoo, Mich. 49008
(616) 357-7222
Contact: Gordon Mitchell

First of Michigan Corporation
10850 Traverse Highway
Box 1068
Traverse City, Mich. 49685

(800) 543-7535
(616) 947-2200
(616) 947-7047 (fax)
Contact: William E. Corbett, C.F.P.

Worldview Financial Services
18245 Devonshire
Box 2200
Birmingham, Mich. 48012
(315) 540-6442
Contact: Joel M. Diskin, C.F.P.

MINNESOTA

AMG Advisors
1915 Highway 52 North, Suite 206
Rochester, Minn. 55901
(507) 286-9130
(507) 289-8105 (fax)
Contact: Mark Breneman, C.F.P.

Dean Witter Reynolds
170 Pillsbury Center
Minneapolis, Minn. 55402
(800) 328-4902
(612) 340-6700
Contact: Kim Dewey

Ethical Investments
430 First Avenue North, Suite 204
Minneapolis, Minn. 55401
(612) 339-3939
Contact: John E. Schultz, President

Paine Webber
3737 Multifoods Tower
33 South Sixth Street
Minneapolis, Minn. 55402
(800) 937-2463
(612) 371-5025
(612) 371-9430 (fax)
Contact: Roberta Cole, C.F.P.

Robert Doran Shepard, C.F.P.
430 First Avenue North, Suite 204
Minneapolis, Minn. 55401
(612) 338-1728
(612) 342-2212 (fax)

Whittlinger Capital Management
743B Butler Square
100 North Sixth Street
Minneapolis, Minn. 55403
(612) 341-2218
Contact: Erica Whittlinger

NORTH CAROLINA

Advent Advisors
104 East Main Street
Durham, N.C. 27701
(919) 682-0308
Contact: F. Farnum Brown, Jr., Vice
  President

Interstate/Johnson Lane
BB & T Building
Asheville, N.C. 28801
(800) 627-3111
(704) 252-5252
(704) 254-3286
Contact: Joel B. Adams, Jr.

NEW HAMPSHIRE

Clean Yield Asset Management
224 State Street
Portsmouth, N.H. 03801
(603) 436-0820
(603) 436-7721 (fax)
Contact: Ben Lovell, President

A. G. Edwards & Sons
Nobles Island
Portsmouth, N.H. 03801
(800) 422-1030
(603) 430-8000
(603) 433-1625 (fax)
Contact: David E. Hills, Vice President

NEW JERSEY

Merrill Lynch Asset Management
800 Scudders Mill Road
Plainsboro, N.J. 08536
(609) 282-2458
Contact: Deborah Osgood

Tucker Anthony
100 Nassau Street
Princeton, N.J. 08542
(800) 624-0642 (N.J.)
(800) 221-1683
(609) 924-0314
Contact: Robert Turoff, Investment
  Executive

NEW MEXICO

First Affirmative Financial Network
151 Gonzales Road, Suite 18
Santa Fe, N.M. 87501
(800) 487-4732
(505) 988-4732 (Santa Fe)
(505) 265-2151 (Albuquerque)
Contact: Richard Barr

Merrill Lynch
123 East Marcy Street
Santa Fe, N.M. 87501
(800) 456-0305
(505) 982-6542
(505) 982-6584
Contact: James E. Dean
  Robert A. Morgart

NEW YORK

Discriminating Investor Financial
  Network
370 East Seventy-sixth Street, Suite A-
  704
New York, N.Y. 10021
(212) 628-1108
Contact: Judith M. Turof

ERIAC
555 Madison Avenue
New York, N.Y. 10022
(800) 223-5211
(212) 371-3950
(212) 758-4967
Contact: Bernard Herold

GAMCO Investors
655 Third Avenue
New York, N.Y. 10017
(212) 972-6479
Contact: Robin Prever, Vice President

Frederick Osborn III
Cat Rock Road
Box 187
Garrison, N.Y. 10524
(914) 424-3396
(914) 424-8338 (fax)

Shearson Lehman Brothers
Schwank Drive
Box 3965
Kingston, N.Y. 12401
(914) 331-1900
Contact: Brooks Jackson

Shearson Lehman Brothers
666 Fifth Avenue, Thirteenth Floor
New York, N.Y. 10103
(212) 603-6113
(212) 765-1057 (fax)
(800) 843-0211
Contact: David B. Crocker, Financial
  Consultant

Shearson Lehman Brothers
Box 1086
14 Wall Street, Ninth Floor
New York, N.Y. 10005
(800) 221-5734
(212) 306-0600
Contact: Arline Segal, Financial
  Consultant

Shearson Lehman Brothers
14 Wall Street, Ninth Floor
New York, N.Y. 10005
(800) 221-5734
(212) 306-0695
Contact: Michael Moffitt, Portfolio
  Manager

Windmill Group
Four Evergreen Row
Armonk, N.Y. 10504
(914) 273-1700
Contact: Marshall Scott Belkin, Vice
  President

OHIO

Bartlett & Company
36 East Fourth Street
Cincinnati, Ohio 45202
(800) 543-0863
(513) 621-4612
(513) 621-6462 (fax)
Contact: Susan J. Hickenlooper,
  C.F.A.
  Mark Motley, C.F.A.

Scudder, Stevens & Clark
600 Vine Street, Suite 2000
Cincinnati, Ohio 45202
(513) 621-2733
Contact: Marilyn R. Ericksen, Director

OREGON

Black & Company
One Columbia Street SW
Portland, Oreg. 97258
(503) 248-9600
(503) 228-0818
Contact: Allen T. Denison

Dain Bosworth
One Columbia Street SW, Suite 1400
Portland, Oreg. 97258
(800) 547-4795
(503) 241-7020
Contact: Shelly McFarland

First Affiliated Securities
10136 Washington SW
Portland, Oreg. 97225
(800) 248-1173
(503) 297-1173
Contact: Troy W. Horton

Garner, Monosoff, Rumer, Datz &
Associates
1380 Oleander Street, Suite C
Medford, Oreg. 97504
(503) 779-4088
(503) 779-7938 (fax)
Contact: Barbara Rumer
Linda Datz

Progressive Benefits
Route 1, Box 184M
Banks, Oreg. 97106
(503) 324-4040
Contact: James C. Pursley,
C.F.P.

Progressive Securities Financial
Services
767 Willamette, Suite 307
Eugene, Oreg. 97401
(800) 659-5669
(503) 345-5669
(503) 343-2723 (fax)
Contact: Laurie McClain
Scott Pope
Darrell Reeck, C.F.A.

Progressive Securities Financial
Services
5200 Macadam SW, Suite 350
Portland, Oreg. 97201
(800) 776-4737
(503) 224-7828
Contact: Carsten Henningsen
Jan Schorey
Rob Baird

Smith Barney
200 Market Street SW, Suite
1200
Portland, Oreg. 97201
(800) 547-1526
(503) 221-7614
(503) 221-7647 (fax)
Contact: Martin Weber

PENNSYLVANIA

Allegheny Investments, Ltd.
3000 McKnight East Drive
Pittsburgh, Pa. 15237
(800) 899-3880
(412) 367-3880
(412) 367-8353 (fax)
Contact: Raymond Schutzman

Financial Planning Advisors
510 Park Road North
Wyomissing, Pa. 19610
(215) 376-6334 (Wyomissing)
(215) 323-3374 (Pottstown)
Contact: Nancy M. Hanna, C.F.P.

Lincoln Investment Planning
101 West Avenue
Jenkintown, Pa. 19046
(800) 242-1421, ext. 1338
(215) 887-3029 (fax)
Contact: Jim Rowley

Rightime Social Awareness Fund
Forst Pavilion, Suite 3000
Wyncote, Pa. 19095
(800) 242-1421
(215) 887-8111
Contact: David J. Rights
Anthony W. Soslow, C.F.A.

SOUTH CAROLINA
Litchfield Financial Services
4123 Litchfield Executive Center
Pawleys Island, S.C. 29585
(800) 333-3764
(803) 237-9798
Contact: E. Dean Berry, C.F.P.

TEXAS
Acacia Group and Calvert Securities
Corporation
11 Greenway Plaza, Suite 626
Houston, Tex. 77046

(713) 626-5261
(713) 871-2084 (fax)
Contact: James A. Shields, Investment
Advisory Associate

Dean Witter Reynolds
1990 Post Oak Boulevard, Suite 2000
Houston, Tex. 77056
(800) 359-4358
(713) 850-1708
Contact: William M. Goodykoontz,
Ph.D.

A. G. Edwards & Sons
4800 Lakewood Drive, Suite 5
Waco, Tex. 76710
(800) 234-8410
(817) 776-8410
(817) 776-1551 (fax)
Contact: Skip Londos

VERMONT

Prentiss Smith and Company
103 Main Street
Brattleboro, Vt. 05391
(802) 254-2913
Contact: Trudy Campbell
Jay Falk

A. G. Edwards & Sons
126 College Street
Box 790
Burlington, Vt. 05401
(800) 639-8000
(802) 864-8000
(802) 864-6397 (fax)
Contact: Robert D. Guthrie

VIRGINIA

Cecil, Welsh & Welsh
1001 Boulders Parkway, Suite 315
Richmond, Va. 23112
(804) 330-2777
(804) 330-9879 (fax)
Contact: Timothy T. Welsh, C.F.P.

WASHINGTON

M2, Inc.
7811 Twenty-seventh SE, Suite 113
Mercer Island, Wash. 98040
(206) 889-2333
Contact: George (Chip) Feiss, C.F.P.,
R.I.A., President

Dean Witter Reynolds
601 Union Street, No. 2900
Seattle, Wash. 98101
(800) 922-2037 (in Wash.)
(800) 453-4873 (outside Wash.)
(206) 464-4005
Contact: Macon (Mimi) Simonds

Financial Network Investment
Corporation
605 First Avenue, Suite 505
Seattle, Wash. 98104
(206) 292-8483
Contact: Kathleen M. Kendziorski,
C.F.P.
C. Keith Wentworth, M.S.W., C.F.P.

Financial Network Investment Corporation
4321 Powell Place South
Seattle, Wash. 98108
(206) 763-4350
Contact: Helene Robertson, C.F.P.

Informed Investors Group
2025 First Avenue, Suite 750
Seattle, Wash. 98121
(206) 441-4211
Contact: Steve Koenig

KMS Investment Advisors
KMS Financial Services
1125 Denny Building
Seattle, Wash. 98121
(206) 448-7737 (collect)
(206) 441-2885
(206) 448-4764 (fax)
Contact: Eric A. Smith

R. D. Lamson & Associates
2611 Eastlake Avenue E, Suite 405
Seattle, Wash. 98102
(206) 322-7575
Contact: Robert D. Lamson

WISCONSIN

ACS Financial Group
110 East Main Street, Suite 515
Madison, Wisc. 53703
(608) 251-7772
(608) 257-0489 (fax)
Contact: Edward Celnicker

Buttonwood Partners
6411 Mineral Point Road
Madison, Wisc. 53717
(608) 277-1776
(608) 277-1790 (fax)
Contact: Allen Jacobson, Ph.D.

Shearson Lehman Brothers
411 East Wisconsin Avenue, Suite 2000
Milwaukee, Wisc. 53202
(800) 289-4888
Contact: Dean Muller

Australia

MoneyMatters Financial Group Pty.
  Ltd.
Suite 3, 4–8 Waters Road
Neutral Bay, NSW 2089 Australia
(011) 61 2 953-0599
Contact: Robert Rosen

Canada

Odlum Brown Ltd.
Box 357
Chilliwack, B.C. V2P 6J4 Canada
(800) 663-5251 (in B.C.)
(604) 795-9477
(604) 795-4617 (fax)
Contact: Larry Trunkey

United Kingdom

Barchester Insurance and Investment
Phoenix Buildings
32 Market Place
Salisbury
Wiltshire SP1 1HE United Kingdom
(011) 44 722 331241

Canadian Imperial Bank of Commerce
  Investment Management Ltd.
Cottons Centre
Cottons Lane
London SE1 2QL United Kingdom
(011) 44 71 234 6000

James Capel & Company
James Capel House
Box 551
Six Bevis Marks
London EC3A 7JQ United Kingdom
(011) 44 71 621 0011

Capital House Investment Management
  Ltd.
24 Chiswell Street
London EC1Y 4SP United Kingdom
(011) 44 71 638 1233

Charities Official Investment Fund
Two Fore Street
London EC2Y 5AQ United Kingdom
(011) 44 71 588 1815

Ethical Investment Services Ltd.
22 Aylesford Avenue
Beckenham, Kent BR3 3SD United
  Kingdom
(011) 44 81 650 4511
Contact: Alan Miller

Holden Meehan
57 Park Street
Bristol BS1 5NU United Kingdom
(011) 44 272 252733

Leopold Joseph Merchant Bankers
31–45 Gresham Street
London EC2V 7EA United Kingdom
(011) 44 71 588 2323

London & Bishopsgate International
  Investment Management PLC
76 Shoe Lane, Twelfth Floor
London EC4A 3JB United Kingdom

Pall Mall Money
125 Pall Mall
London SW1Y 5EA United Kingdom
(011) 44 71 839 4272

Paribas Capital Markets Group
33 Wigmore Street
London W1H 0BN United Kingdom
(011) 44 71 355 2000

Phillips & Drew Fund Management
  Ltd.
Triton Court
14 Finsbury Square
London EC2A 1PD United Kingdom
(011) 44 71 901 9050

I COMMUNITY DEVELOPMENT INVESTMENTS

United States

ARKANSAS

Elk Horn Bank & Trust Company
Box 258
Arkadelphia, Ark. 71923-0248
Contact: Phyllis Stiffler

Good Faith Fund
1210 Cherry Street, Suite 9
Pine Bluff, Ark. 71601
(501) 535-6233
Contact: Julia Vindasius, Director

CALIFORNIA

CANNICOR Research
Box 6819
San Francisco, Calif. 94101-6819
(415) 885-5102
Contact: John E. Lind, Executive Director

Low Income Housing Fund
605 Market Street, Suite 709
San Francisco, Calif. 94105
(415) 777-9804
Contact: Daniel M. Leibsohn, President

Sand County Venture Fund
1010 El Camino Real, Suite 300
Menlo Park, Calif. 94025
(415) 324-4414
Contact: Michael Kieschnick

CONNECTICUT

Cooperative Fund of New England
108 Kenyon Street
Hartford, Conn. 06105
(203) 523-4305
Contact: Rebecca Dunn, Executive
  Director

Toni A. Gold
96 Kenyon Street
Hartford, Conn. 06105
(203) 232-9018

Save the Children
54 Winton Road
Box 950
Westport, Conn. 06881
(203) 226-7272
Contact: Betsy Campbell

Technoserve
148 East Avenue
Norwalk, Conn. 06851
(203) 852-0377
Contact: Ed Bullard, Director

WASHINGTON, D.C.
Consumers United Group
2100 M Street NW, Suite 207
Washington, D.C. 20063
(800) 242-9711
(202) 872-5709
Contact: James P. Gibbons, Jr.,
 President

GEORGIA
Southeastern Reinvestment Ventures
159 Ralph McGill Boulevard, Room 505
Atlanta, Ga. 30308
(404) 659-0002, ext. 241
Contact: Jonathan Jones, Director

ILLINOIS

Continental Community Development
 Corporation
231 South LaSalle Street
Chicago, Ill. 60697
(312) 828-4167
Contact: Frances R. Grossman,
 Executive Director

Ecumenical Development Corporation,
 U.S.A.
155 North Michigan Avenue, Suite 627
Chicago, Ill. 60601
(312) 938-0884
Contact: Elwyn Ewald, Executive
 Director

Opportunity International
360 West Butterfield Road, Suite 225
Elmhurst, Ill. 60126
(708) 279-9300
Contact: Larry Reed

South Shore Bank of Chicago
Seventy-first and Jeffery Boulevard
Chicago, Ill. 60649
(800) NOW-SSBK
(312) 753-5636
(312) 753-5699 (fax)
Contact: Joan Shapiro, Senior Vice
 President

Women's Self Employment Project
166 West Washington Street, Suite 730
Chicago, Ill. 60602
(312) 606-8257
Contact: Connie Evans, Director

MARYLAND

Calvert Social Venture Partners
7201 Wisconsin Avenue, Suite 310
Bethesda, Md. 20814
(202) 659-0142
Contact: John May

Marianist Sharing Fund
4301 Roland Avenue
Baltimore, Md. 21210-2793
(301) 366-1324
Contact: Richard Ullrich, Executive
 Secretary

Partners for the Common Good Loan
 Fund
8300 Colesville Road, Third Floor
Silver Spring, Md. 20910
(301) 565-0053
Contact: Carol Coston, O.P.

MASSACHUSETTS
AI Group
129 South Street
Boston, Mass. 02111
(617) 350-0250
Contact: Barbara Ann Cleary

ACCION International
130 Prospect Street
Cambridge, Mass. 02139
(617) 492-4930
(617) 876-9509 (fax)
Contact: William Burrus, Director
  Sonia Saltzman

Boston Community Loan Fund
30 Germania Street, Second Floor
Jamaica Plain, Mass. 02130
(617) 273-4666
(617) 277-3596
Contact: DeWitt Jones, Fund Manager

Commonwealth Capital Partners
334 Broadway
Cambridge, Mass. 02139
(617) 491-0988
Contact: David F. Sand, Managing
  Director

First Trade Union Savings Bank
10 Drydock Avenue
Box 9063
Boston, Mass. 02205
(617) 951-1401
Contact: Wayne Sharpe

Highland Financial Group
1030 Massachusetts Avenue
Cambridge, Mass. 02138
(617) 661-4852
Contact: William Ware

Industrial Cooperative Association
58 Day Street, Suite 200
Somerville, Mass. 02144
(617) 629-2700

Institute for Community Economics
57 School Street
Springfield, Mass. 01105
(413) 746-8660
Contact: Louise Foisey, Revolving
  Loan Fund Manager
  Mr. Greg Ramm, ICE Director

Neighborhood Reinvestment
Department of Commercial and
  Economic Development
80 Boylston Street, Suite 1207
Boston, Mass. 02116
(617) 565-8240
Contact: Margaret Barringer, Director

Philanthropic Initiative
160 State Street
Boston, Mass. 02109
Contact: H. Peter Karoff, President

MICHIGAN
Michigan Housing Trust Fund
3401 East Saginaw, Suite 212
Lansing, Mich. 48912
(517) 336-9919
Contact: Judith Transue, Executive
  Director

MINNESOTA
Women's Enterprise Development
  Corporation (WEDCO)
2324 University Avenue
St. Paul, Minn. 55114
(612) 646-3808
Contact: Kathy Keeley, Director

NEW HAMPSHIRE
Working Capital
2500 North River Road
Manchester, New Hampshire 03104
(617) 547-9109
(603) 644-3124
Contact: Jeffrey Ashe, Director

NEW YORK
Alternatives Federal Credit Union
301 West State Street
Ithaca, N.Y. 14850
(607) 273-4666
(607) 277-6391 (fax)
Contact: Bill Myers

Brooklyn Union Gas Company
Area Development Fund
195 Montague Street
Brooklyn Heights, N.Y. 11201
(718) 403-2583
(718) 522-1433 (fax)
Contact: Jan C. Childress,
  Administrator

CARE
660 1st Avenue
New York, N.Y. 10016
(212) 686-3110
Contact: Larry Frankel

Community Capital Bank
111 Livingston Street
Brooklyn, N.Y. 11201
(718) 768-9344
Contact: Lyndon B. Comstock,
  Chairman
  Amy S. Nolan, Vice President

Leviticus 25:23 Alternative Fund
Marinadale Center, Box 1200
Ossining, N.Y. 10562
(914) 941-9422
Contact: George C. Schmitz, CSC,
  Executive Director

Nonprofit Facilities Fund
12 West 31st Street
New York, N.Y. 10001
(212) 868-6710
(212) 268-8653 (fax)
Contact: Clara Miller

Trickle Up Program
54 Riverside Drive
PHE
New York, N.Y. 10024
(212) 362-7958
Contact: Glen and Mildred Leet,
  Directors

NORTH CAROLINA
Self-Help Credit Union
Box 3619
Durham, North Carolina 27702
(919) 683-3016
(800) 476-7428
(919) 688-3615 (fax)
Contact: Bonnie Wright, Manager

OHIO
Cornerstone Loan Fund
Box 8974
Cincinnati, Ohio 45208
(513) 871-3899
Contact: Greg Buening, President,
  Board of Directors

SOUTH DAKOTA
The Lakota Fund
Box 340
Kyle, South Dakota 57752
(605) 455-2500
Contact: Gerald Sherman, Director

VIRGINIA
FINCA
901 King Street, 4th floor
Alexandria, Va. 22314
(703) 836-5516
Contact: John Hatch, Director

Oweesta Fund
First Nation Financial Project
69 Kelley Road
Falmouth, Va. 22405
(703) 371-5615
(703) 371-3505 (fax)
Contact: Bruce King

VERMONT
Catalyst Group
139 Main Street, Suite 614
Brattleboro, Vermont 05301

(802) 254-8144
(802) 254-8591 (fax)
Contact: Blake Ross

WISCONSIN
Credit Union National Association
(CUNA)
Box 431
Madison, Wisc. 53701-0431
(608) 231-4000

Australia

Ethical Deposit Fund
Community Aid Abroad
156 George Street
Fitzroy, 0365 Australia
(011) 61 419-7111

Housing Co-operative Ethical Bonds
The ANA Friendly Society
Suite 46, Benson House
2 Benson Street, Toowong
PO Box 323, Toowong 4066
(011) 61 6 870-9947

North Coast Ethical Credit Union
FREEPOST 60
Box 402, Lismore 2480 Australia
(011) 61 66 221 511

YWCA Ethical Investment Trust
Level 18, 99 Mount Street
North Sydney NSW 2060 Australia
(011) 61 2 957-5820

Belgium

Mercurius
Oude Houtlei 2
9000 Gent Ledeberg, Belgium
(011) 32 2 91 313371
Contact: Kurt Degrieck

Netwerk Vlaanderen
Harenheidestraat 9

B-1130 Brussels, Belgium
(011) 32 2 241 1997
Contact: Hugo Wanner

S.A. Sofiga/C.V. Fimabo
Rue Montoyer 63
1040 Brussels, Belgium
(011) 32 2 237 0692
Contact: J. P. Feldbusch
Frans de Clerck

Canada

Canadian Alternative Investment
Cooperative
146 Laird Drive, Suite 101
Toronto, Ontario, M4G 3V7 Canada
(416) 467-7798

CARE Canada
Box 9000
1550 Carling Road
Ottawa, Ontario, K1G 4X6 Canada
(613) 521-7081
Contact: Doris Wong

Ecumenical Development Society of
Canada
147 Chedoke Avenue
Hamilton, Ontario L8P 4P2 Canada

First People's Fund
304–334 Adelaide Street
East Toronto, Ontario M5C 1K9
Canada
(416) 360-1708
Contact: Shelle Brant, Manager

Denmark

Den Almennyttige Andelskasse Trion
Merkur
Sonnenupvej 41
DK-3300 Frederiksverk, Denmark
(011) 45 4212 4422
Contact: Erik Nielsen

Germany

GLS Gemeinschaftsbank eG
Oskar-Hoffman-Strasse 25
D-4630 Bochum 1, Germany
(011) 49 234 313883
Contact: Thomas Jorberg

Ökobank EG
Bornheimer Landstrasse 22
D-6000 Frankfurt 1, Germany
(011) 49 69 500 910 00

Privates Institute für Umweltschutz
   (IFU) GmbH
Kurfstendamm 180
W-1000 Berlin 15, Germany
(011) 49 30 88 32 818

Netherlands

Stichting Stimulans
Van der Does de Willebois—
   Singel 1
5211 CA 'S-Hertogenbosch,
   Netherlands
(011) 31 73 144249
Contact: T. J. Van Rooy

Triodosbank N.V.
Stationslaan 4
Box 55
3700 AB Zeist, Netherlands
(011) 31 3404 16544
Contact: Peter Blom

New Zealand

Cooperative Enterprise Loan Trust
   (CELT)
Box 68-091
Auckland, New Zealand
(011) 64 9 773 196

Spain

INBERCOP
Plaza Urquinaona 6
7a Planta
0810 Barcelona, Spain
(011) 34 3 3173616
Contact: Joan Peiro Prodoum

Sweden

JAK
Brunnsgatan 15
Stockholm, Sweden
(011) 46 8 202445

Spardelegationen
(Commission for the Promotion of
   Savings)
Hybrogatan 6
Box 7547
10393 Stockholm, Sweden
(011) 46 8 226860

Stiftelsen Ansvarsfull Penningplacering
Lonnvagen 5A
135 52 Tyreso, Sweden
(011) 46 8 448463
Contact: Marit Lindstein

United Kingdom

Association of British Credit Unions Ltd.
Unit 307
Westminster Business Square
339 Kennington Lane
London SE11 56QY United Kingdom
(011) 44 71 582 2626

Birmingham Settlement
318 Summer Lane
Birmingham B19 3RL United Kingdom
(011) 44 21 359 3562

BP Guarantee Company
Box 159
28 Baldwin Street

Bristol BS99 7NP United Kingdom
(011) 44 272 253007
Contact: Glen Saunders

Cooperative Bank
(ICOF Ethical Savings Account)
Box 101
One Balloon Street
Manchester M60 4EP United Kingdom
(011) 44 61 829 5359

Ecology Building Society
18 Station Road
Cross Hills
Keighley
West Yorkshire BD20 7EH United
    Kingdom
(011) 44 535 635933
Contact: Bob Lowman
    Tony Weekes

ICOF Consultants Ltd.
318 Summer Lane
Birmingham B19 3RL United Kingdom

(011) 44 21 3590188
(011) 44 21 3596357 (fax)

International Association of Investors
    in the Social Economy (INAISE)
Vassali House
20 Central Road
Leeds Ls1 6DE United Kingdom
(011) 44 532 429600
Contact: Malcolm Lynch, Secretary

Mercury Provident PLC
Orlingbury House
Lewes Road
Forest Row
East Sussex RH18 5AA United
    Kingdom
(011) 44 342 823739
Contact: Duncan Power

Shared Interest
52 Elswick Road
Newcastle Upon Tyne NE4 6JH United
    Kingdom
(011) 44 91 272 4979

| CONSULTING FIRMS

United States

CALIFORNIA
Paragon Consulting Group
2426 Thirty-third Avenue
San Francisco, Calif. 94116
(415) 564-5956
Contact: Frank Tsai

CONNECTICUT
Shore & Reich Ltd.
Mariner Square, Suite 110
Eugene O'Neill Drive
New London, Conn. 06320
(800) 733-2540
(203) 444-7015
Contact: Robert Doss

DELAWARE
Consulting Group
A Division of Shearson Lehman
    Brothers
222 Delaware Avenue, Ninth Floor
Wilmington, Del. 19806
Contact: Kenneth Nemery, Senior Vice
    President

ILLINOIS
Marquette Associates
Quaker Tower, Suite 950
Chicago, Ill. 60610
(312) 527-5500
Contact: Brien O'Brien,
    President

MASSACHUSETTS

New England Pension
  Consultants
253 Summer Street, Suite 210
Boston, Mass. 02210
(617) 737-1960
Contact: Richard M. Charlton

Nonprofit Consultants
23 John Alden Road
Holden, Mass. 01520-1924
(508) 852-5164
Contact: Edmund T. Bennett

Peabody & Arnold
50 Rowes Wharf
Boston, Mass. 02110
(617) 951-2000
Contact: Ralph Tuller

MINNESOTA

Jeffrey Slocum & Associates
430 First Avenue North, Suite 720
Minneapolis, Minn. 55401-1746
(612) 338-7020
Contact: Jeffrey C. Slocum

NEW YORK

Kidder, Peabody & Company
20 Exchange Place
New York, N.Y. 10005
Contact: Neil Wolfson

Sentinel Investment Management
  Corporation
34 South Broadway
White Plains, N.Y. 10601
Contact: L. B. Eichler

PENNSYLVANIA

Yanni, Bilkey Investment Consulting
  Company
2500 Grant Building
Pittsburgh, Pa. 15219
(412) 232-1000
Contact: James E. Yanni, Principal
    Keith Goldner, Senior Consultant

TEXAS

Lehrer Development and Investments
5555 Del Monte Drive, Suite 802
Houston, Tex. 77056
(800) 364-1400
Contact: Dr. Kenneth Eugene Lehrer

I INFORMATION PROVIDERS

United States

CALIFORNIA

Mitja V. Hinderks
1015 Gayley Avenue, No. 1228
Los Angeles, Calif. 90024
(213) 208-6606
(213) 208-3335 (fax)

Ocean Rudee Company
Box 4234
791 Eighth Street, Suite M
Arcata, Calif. 95521

(707) 822-2665
(707) 822-4134
Contact: Paul Ennis

Public Advocates
1535 Mission Street
San Francisco, Calif. 94103
(415) 431-7430

Save the Dolphins Project
Earth Island Institute
300 Broadway, Suite 28
San Francisco, Calif. 94133
Contact: Deborah Flagg

Vanguard Public Foundation
14 Precita Avenue
San Francisco, Calif. 94110
(415) 285-2005
(415) 285-2519 (fax)
Contact: Dan Geiger

WASHINGTON, D.C.

ACORN
739 Eighth Street SE
Washington, D.C. 20003
(202) 547-9292

Amalgamated Clothing and Textile
  Workers Union
1818 Swann Street NW
Washington, D.C. 20009
(202) 745-1710

BankWatch
215 Pennsylvania Avenue SE
Washington, D.C. 20003
(202) 546-4996

Building Economic Alternatives
Co-op America
2100 M Street NW, Suite 310
Washington, D.C. 20036
(800) 424-2667
(202) 872-5307

Center for Community Change
1000 Wisconsin Avenue NW
Washington, D.C. 20007
(202) 342-0567

Consumer Federation of America
1424 Sixteenth Street NW, Suite 604
Washington, D.C. 20036
(202) 387-6121

ESOP Association
1100 Seventeenth Street, Suite 1207
Washington, D.C. 20036
(202) 293-2971

Institutional Shareholders Services
333 K Street NW, Suite 730
Washington, D.C. 20007
(202) 333-0339
(202) 333-5747 (fax)
Contact: James E. Heard

Justice for Janitors
Service Employees International Union
1313 L Street NW
Washington, D.C. 20005
(202) 898-1505

National Credit Union Administration
  (NCUA)
1776 G Street NW
Washington, D.C. 20456
(202) 682-9600

GEORGIA

Fund for Southern Communities
552 Hill Street SE
Atlanta, Ga. 30312
(404) 577-3178

ILLINOIS

Crossroads Fund
3411 West Diversey, Suite 20
Chicago, Ill. 60647
(312) 227-7676
Contact: Jacqueline Schad, Executive
  Director

National Training and Information
  Center
810 North Milwaukee
Chicago, Ill. 60622-4103
(312) 243-3035

Woodstock Institute
407 South Dearborn, Suite 550
Chicago, Ill. 60605
(312) 427-8070

MARYLAND

Calvert Social Investment Foundation
7205 Pomander Lane
Chevy Chase, Md. 20815
Contact: John G. Guffey, President

Institute for Policy Studies
Johns Hopkins University
Baltimore, Md. 21218
Contact: Anne Shlay

McAuley Institute
8300 Colesville Road, Suite 310
Silver Spring, Md. 20910
(301) 588-8110
Contact: Josephine Ann Kane,
   Executive Director

MASSACHUSETTS

Mark Albion
27 Draper Road
Dover, Mass. 02030
(508) 785-2065

Jeffrey Ashe
1039 Massachusetts Avenue, No. 6B
Cambridge, Mass. 02138

Haymarket People's Fund
42 Seaverns Avenue
Boston, Mass. 02130
Contact: Hillary Smith

Kinder, Lydenberg, Domini &
   Company
Seven Dana Street
Cambridge, Mass. 02138
(617) 547-7479
Contact: Steven D. Lydenberg

Northeastern University
Hayden Hall 414
360 Huntington Avenue
Boston, Mass. 02115
(617) 437-3620
Contact: Professor Dove Izraeli

MINNESOTA

Business Ethics Magazine
1107 Hazeltine Boulevard, Suite 530
Chaska, Minn. 55318
(612) 448-8864
Contact: Miriam Kniaz

Hubert H. Humphrey Institute
University of Minnesota
Minneapolis, Minn. 55411
(612) 625-8302
Contact: Chuck Finn

Philanthrofund Foundation
607 Marquette Avenue, Suite 101
Minneapolis, Minn. 55402-1709

NEW HAMPSHIRE

Investor Responsibility Research
   Center (IRRC)
Box 50
Plainfield, New Hampshire 03781
(603) 675-9274
Contact: Douglas G. Cogan, Senior An-
   alyst

NEW YORK

Council on Economic Priorities
30 Irving Place
New York, N.Y. 10003
(212) 420-1133
(212) 420-0988 (fax)
Contact: Alice Tepper Marlin,
   Executive Director

Funding Exchange
National Office
666 Broadway, Fifth Floor
New York, N.Y. 10012
(212) 529-5300

Interfaith Center on Corporate Responsibility (ICCR)
475 Riverside Drive, Room 566
New York, N.Y. 10115

(212) 870-2936
(212) 870-2023 (fax)
Contact: Tim Smith, Executive
Director

Left Business Observer
250 West Eighty-fifth Street
New York, N.Y. 10024
(212) 874-4020
Contact: Doug Henwood, Editor and
Publisher

National Federation of Community
Development Credit Unions
(NFCDCU)
59 John Street, Eighth Floor
New York, N.Y. 10038
(800) 437-8711
(212) 513-7191

New York Center for Employee
Ownership and Participation
1515 Broadway, Fifty-second Floor
New York, N.Y. 10036
(212) 930-0108

Strub Media Group
270 West Seventeenth Street,
No. PII-C
New York, N.Y. 10011
(212) 242-1900
(212) 242-1963 (fax)
Contact: Sean O. Strub

Lillian Vernon Corporation
510 South Fulton Avenue
Mount Vernon, N.Y. 10550
(914) 699-4131
Contact: David Hochberg, Vice
President of Public Affairs

NORTH CAROLINA

Financial Democracy Campaign
604 W. Chapel Hill Street

Durham, North Carolina 27702
(919) 687-4004

Southern Finance Project
329 Rensselaer
Charlotte, North Carolina 28203
(704) 372-7072

OHIO

Northeast Ohio Employee Ownership
Center
Kent State University
Kent, Ohio 44242
(216) 672-3028

Northeast Ohio Employee Ownership
Center (Publications)
Kent Popular Press
P.O. Box 905
Kent, Ohio 44240
Contact: Leon Boros

PENNSYLVANIA

National Association of Community
Development Loan Funds
924 Cherry Street, Third Floor
Philadelphia, Pa. 19107-2405
(215) 923-4754
(215) 923-4764 (fax)
Contact: Martin Paul Trimble,
Executive Director

TEXAS

Texas Center for Policy Studies
1300 East Twenty-eighth Street
Austin, Tex. 78722
(512) 474-0811

VERMONT

Clean Yield Publications
Box 1880
Greensboro Bend, Vermont 05842
(802) 533-7178
(802) 533-2907 (fax)

Austria

Forschunginstitut für ethisch-ökologische Geldanlagen (FIFEGA)
Lindengrasse 43/17
A-1070 Vienna, Austria
(011) 43 1 52 62 55

Verband osterreichischer
Investmentklubs
(Association of Austrian Investment
Clubs)
Prominade 11–13
A 4041 Linz, Austria
(011) 43 732 2391

Denmark

Center for Alternative Social Analysis
(CASA)
Linnesgade 14
DK-1361 Copenhagen K, Denmark
(011) 45 33 32 05 55

France

L'Institut de Développement de
l'Économie Sociale (IDES)
24 Avenue Hoche
75008 Paris, France
(011) 33 4359 9494
Contact: Jean Jacques Samuel

Netherlands

Ecumenical Development Cooperative
Society
Utrechtseweg 91
3818 EB Amersfoort, Netherlands
(011) 31 33 63 3122

Sweden

Research on Business and Society
Urvadersgrand 6B

116 46 Stockholm, Sweden
(011) 46 8 44 8463
Contact: Sören Bergstrom

United Kingdom

Church Commissioners for England
One Millbank
London SW1P 3JZ United Kingdom
(011) 44 71 222 7010

Church of England, General Synod
Board for Social Responsibility
Church House
Great Smith Street
London SW1P 3NZ United Kingdom
(011) 44 71 222 9011

End Loans to South Africa
56 Camberwell Road
London SE5 0EN United Kingdom
(011) 44 71 708 4702

Ethical Consumer
ERCA Publishing Ltd.
100 Gretney Walk
Manchester M15 5ND United Kingdom
(011) 44 61 226 6683

Ethical Investment Services Ltd.
22 Aylesford Avenue
Beckenham, Kent BR3 3SD United
Kingdom
(011) 44 81 650 4511
Contact: Alan Miller

Green Alliance
60 Chandos Place
London WC2N 4HG United Kingdom
(011) 44 71 836 0341

Industrial Common Ownership Finance
Ltd. (ICOF)
12–14 Gold Street
Northampton NN1 1RS United Kingdom
(011) 44 604 375563
Contact: David Ralley

International Association of Investors in the Social Economy (INAISE)
Vassali House
20 Central Road
Leeds LS1 6DE United Kingdom
(011) 44 532 429600
Contact: Malcolm Lynch, Secretary

Methodist Church
Division of Social Responsibility
Central Hall
Westminster
London SW1H 9NH United Kingdom
(011) 44 71 222 8010
Contact: John Kennedy

New Consumer
52 Elswick Road
Newcastle Upon Tyne NE4 6JH United Kingdom
(011) 44 91 272 1148

Pensions & Investment Research Consultants Ltd.
40 Bowling Green Lane
London EC1R 0NE United Kingdom

(011) 44 71 833 4432
Contact: Alan MacDougall, Managing Director
  Anne Simpson, Director

Religious Society of Friends
Communication Services Department
Friends House
Euston Road
London NW1 2BJ United Kingdom
(011) 44 71 387 3601

Scottish Churches Action for World Development Investments Association
(Ecumenical Development Cooperative Society)
41 George IV Bridge
Edinburgh, Scotland EH1 1EL United Kingdom
(011) 44 31 225 1772

Traidcraft Exchange
Kingsway
Gateshead NE11 0NE United Kingdom
(011) 44 91 491 0591

| INSTITUTIONAL INVESTORS

United States

ILLINOIS

Evangelical Lutheran Church in America
8765 West Higgins Road
Chicago, Ill. 60631
(312) 380-2863
Contact: Edgar Crane

MASSACHUSETTS

Choate, Hall & Stewart
Exchange Place
53 State Street

Boston, Mass. 02109
(617) 227-5020
Contact: Stephen P. Boyle, Managing Director, Fiduciary and Investment Services

MINNESOTA

Evangelical Lutheran Church in America
Board of Pensions
800 Marquette Avenue, Suite 1050
Minneapolis, Minn. 55402
(612) 334-5356
Contact: Michael L. Troutman

NEW YORK

City of New York
Department of Finance
One Centre Street, Room 500
New York, N.Y. 10007
(212) 669-4855
Contact: Dr. Carol O'Cleireacain

Ford Foundation
Program-Related Investments
320 East Forty-third Street
New York, N.Y. 10017
(212) 573-4760

(212) 573-4904
Contact: Thomas F. Miller, Director,
  Program-Related Investments
  Judith F. Samuelson, Program
  Investment Officer

New York City Comptroller's Office
Chambers & Centre Streets
Municipal Building
New York, N.Y. 10007
(212) 669-2672 (direct)
Contact: Gelvin Stevenson, Director,
  Investment Responsibility

| MUTUAL AND MONEY MARKET FUNDS

United States

CALIFORNIA

American Funds Group
  American Mutual Fund
  Washington Mutual Investors Fund
333 South Hope Street
Los Angeles, Calif. 90071
(800) 421-9900
(213) 486-9200

Muir California Tax-Free Bond Fund
One Sansone Street, Suite 810
San Francisco, Calif. 94104
(800) 648-3448
(415) 616-8500

Parnassus Fund
244 California Street, Suite 210
San Francisco, Calif. 94111
(800) 999-3505
Contact: Jerome L. Dodson, President

Pacific Investment Management
  Company
840 Newport Center Drive
Newport Beach, Calif. 92660
(714) 760-4456

Wells Fargo Nikko Investment
  Advisors
45 Fremont Street
San Francisco, Calif. 94105
(415) 597-2700

WASHINGTON, D.C.

Calvert Social Investment Fund
1715 Eighteenth Street NW
Washington, D.C. 20009
(202) 232-0798
Contact: D. Wayne Silby,
  Chairman

FLORIDA

Templeton Investment Counsel
Broward Financial Centre
Suite 2100
Fort Lauderdale, Fla. 33394-3091
(305) 764-7390
(305) 462-1230 (fax)

ILLINOIS

Ariel Capital Management
  Calvert-Ariel Appreciation Fund
  Calvert-Ariel Growth Fund

307 North Michigan Avenue
Chicago, Ill. 60601
(312) 726-0140
Contact: Darice Wright

INDIANA

Lincoln National Life Insurance
  Lincoln National Social Awareness
  Fund
1300 South Clinton Street
Fort Wayne, Ind. 46801
(219) 427-2000

MARYLAND

Calvert Group
  Calvert Bond Portfolio
  Calvert Managed Growth Portfolio
  Calvert Money Market Fund
4550 Montgomery Avenue
Bethesda, Md. 20814
(800) 368-2748
(301) 951-4820
(301) 654-7820 (fax)
Contact: Steve Schueth, Vice President,
  Socially Responsible Investing

MASSACHUSETTS

Babson-Steward, Ivory
One Memorial Drive
Cambridge, Mass. 02142
(617) 225-3800

Colonial Management Associates
  Colonial Advanced Strategies Gold
  Trust
One Financial Center
Boston, Mass. 02111
(800) 426-3750

Environmentally Responsible Mutual
  Funds
28 Temple Place
Boston, Mass. 02111-1305
(617) 292-4800
Contact: Mindy S. Lubber

Fidelity Investments
  Fidelity Select American Gold
  Portfolio
  Fidelity Select Environmental
  Services Portfolio
82 Devonshire Street
Boston, Mass. 02109
(800) 544-8888

Freedom Capital Management
  Corporation
  Freedom Environmental Fund
One Beacon Street
Boston, Mass. 02108
(800) 225-6258

Grantham, Mayo, van Otterloo
40 Rowes Wharf
Boston, Mass. 02110-3300
(617) 330-7500

The Pioneer Group
  Pioneer Bond Fund
  Pioneer Fund
  Pioneer Fund II
  Pioneer Fund III
  Pioneer Money Market Trust
  Pioneer Municipal Bond Fund
60 State Street
Boston, Mass. 02109
(800) 225-6292
(617) 742-7825

Standish, Ayre & Wood
One Financial Center
Boston, Mass. 02111-2621
(617) 350-6100

State Street Bank & Trust Company
Asset Management Division
225 Franklin Street, Third Floor
Boston, Mass. 02110
(617) 786-3000

NEW HAMPSHIRE

Pax World Fund
224 State Street

Portsmouth, New Hampshire 03801
(800) 767-1729
(603) 431-8022
(603) 436-7721 (fax)

NEW YORK

Alliance Capital Management
  Alliance Global Environment Fund
1345 Avenue of the Americas
New York, N.Y. 10105
(212) 969-1432

Christian Brothers Investment Services
  Catholic United Investment Trust
  Balanced Fund
  Catholic United Investment Trust
  Growth Fund
  Religious Communities Trust
  Certificates of Deposit Fund
  Religious Communities Trust
  College Fund
  Religious Communities Trust
  Intermediate Bond Fund
  Religious Communities Trust Money
  Market Fund
675 Third Avenue, Thirty-first Floor
New York, N.Y. 10017
(800) 592-8890
(212) 490-0800
(212) 490-6092 (fax)
Contact: Gerard Frendreis, F.S.C.,
  Director, Socially Responsible
  Investment

Dreyfus Third Century Fund
EAB Plaza, East Tower
144 Glenn Curtiss Boulevard
Uniondale, N.Y. 11556-0144
(800) 782-6620
Contact: Diane M. Coffey, Vice
  President

New Alternatives Fund
295 Northern Boulevard

Great Neck, N.Y. 11021
(516) 466-0808

Monitrend Mutual Funds
  Monitrend Mutual Fund Gold Series
272 Closter Dock Road, Suite 1
Closter, N.J. 07624
(800) 251-1970
(201) 886-2300

PENNSYLVANIA

Miller, Anderson & Sherrerd
  MAS Select Equity Portfolio
  MAS Select Fixed Income Portfolio
  MAS Select Growth Portfolio
  MAS Select Value Portfolio
One Tower Bridge
West Conshohoken, Pa. 19428
(215) 940-5000

SFT Environmental Awareness Fund
Box 926
King of Prussia, Pa. 19406
(800) 523-2044
(215) 337-8422

TEXAS

United Services Advisors
  United Services New Prospector
  Fund
Box 29467
San Antonio, Tex. 78229
(800) 873-8637
(512) 523-2453

WASHINGTON

Saturna Capital Corporation
  Amana Mutual Funds Trust Income
  Fund
520 Herald Building
1155 North State Street
Bellingham, Wash. 98225
(800) 728-8762
(207) 734-9900

Australia

Directed Financial Management Ltd.
  (August Investments)
Suite 614
Ultimo NSW 2007 Australia
(011) 61 2 281-1440

Earthrise Investment Pool
  Mercator Master Superannuation
  Plan
Purvis, van Eyk & Company Ltd.
43 Phillip Street
Sydney NSW 2000 Australia
(011) 61 2 247-6000

Friends' Provident Life Office
80 Alfred Street
Milsons Point, NSW 2061 Australia
(011) 61 2 925-9255
Contact: Susan Gavan

Occidental Life Insurance Company of
  Australia Environmental Opportunities Fund
Occidental Centre
601 Pacific Highway
St. Leonards NSW 2065 Australia
(011) 61 2 957-0957

Austria

ÖKO-INVEST Ethische-ökologischer
  Investmentklub
Lindengrasse 43/17
A-1070 Vienna, Austria
(011) 43 22 52 62 555

Raiffeisen-Umweltfonds
Raiffeisen-Kapitalanlage Gesellschaft
  GmbH.
Am Stadtpark 9
A-1030 Vienna, Austria
(011) 43 222 71 707
Contact: Dr. Mathew Bauer

Z-Umweltfonds
Z-INVEST Gesellschaft

Invalidenstrasse 3
A-1030 Vienna, Austria
(011) 43 222 71 25 454

Canada

CEDAR Investment Services
  CEDAR Balanced Fund
902 Kapilano 100, Park Royal
West Vancouver, B.C. V7T 1A2 Canada
(604) 926-7355

Crown Life Insurance Company
  Crown Commitment Fund
120 Bloor Street East
Toronto, Ontario M4W 1B8 Canada
(416) 928-5722

EIF Fund Management Ltd.
  Environmental Investment Canada
  Fund
  Environmental Investment
  International Fund
225 Brunswick Avenue
Toronto, Ontario M5S 2M6 Canada
(416) 978-7014

Fonds Desjardins Environment
  Desjardins Trust
One Complex Desjardins
Box 34
Montreal, Quebec H5B 1E4 Canada
(418) 835-4403

Investors Group
  Investors Summa Fund Ltd.
One Canada Centre
447 Portage Avenue
Winnipeg, Manitoba R3C 3B6 Canada
(204) 956-8536

Vancouver City Savings Credit
  Union
  Ethical Growth Fund
515 West Tenth Avenue
Vancouver, B.C. V5Z 4A8 Canada
(604) 877-7613

France

Biosphere
Cyril Finance Gestion (CFG)
20, rue de la Ville l'Eveque
F-75008 Paris, France
(011) 33 14 266 6888
Contact: Didier Jened
Xavier D'ornellas

Germany

Artus Ethische Vermogensverwaltung
GbR
Beethovenplatz 1
5300 Bonn 1, Germany
(011) 49 2286 52112

Artus Ethische Renten GbR
Artus Ethische Vermögensverwaltung
GmbH von-Werth-Strasse 20–22
D-5000 Cologne 1, Germany
(011) 49 221 135056
Contact: Jurgen Conrads

Concorde-Artus Ethische
Vermogensverwaltung GmbH
Concorde Ethische
Vermogensverwaltung GmbH
Weidenauer Strasse 179
D-5900 Siegen, Germany
(011) 49 271 40370

Concorde International
Concorde KGaA iG, Germany
Weidenauer Strasse 179
D-5900 Siegen, Germany
(011) 49 271 40370
(011) 49 271 403733 (fax)
Contact: Alison MacDonald

CS Oeko Protec
Credit Suisse
Kaiserstrasse 30
6000 Frankfurt, Germany
(011) 49 69 26912625

CS Oeko Protec
Credit Suisse
Denninger Strasse 130–132
8000 Munich 81, Germany
(011) 49 89 9279701

DG Capital Öko 2000
DG Capital Management GmbH
Platz der Republik
D-6000 Frankfurt 1, Germany
(011) 49 69 744701
Contact: Hartmut Korn

EthiK (Erster Ethischer Investmentclub
Koln)
Maria-Hilf-Strasse 6
D-5000 Cologne 1, Germany
(011) 49 221 325272
Contact: Hans Berner

Focus Umwelttechnologie
Gunther Strasse 21
8000 Munich 19, Germany
(011) 49 89 1784010
Contact: Carl Fischer

HCM Eco Tech
Denninger Strasse 130–132
8000 Munich 81, Germany
(011) 49 89 9279701

Luxembourg

HCM Eco Tech
Hypo Capital Management
27 Boulevard de Prince Henri
L-1724 Luxembourg
(011) 352 474 979
Contact: Dieter Wimmer

Secura-Rent Lux
BFG Luxinvest Management S.A.
2 Rue Jean Bertholet
1-1233 Luxembourg
(011) 352 4522551
Contact: Claus Pyter

Norway

MiljoInvest Environment Fund
MiljoInvest
5020 Bergen, Norway
(011) 47 5 17 20 50
Contact: Carlos Jolly

Sweden

Fria Kulturfonden
Robyggehuset
153 00 Jarna, Sweden
(011) 46 7 55 50450

Svenska Kyrkansfond AB
St. Eriksgatan 63
112 34 Stockholm, Sweden
(011) 46 8 7377000

United Kingdom

Abbey Unit Trust Managers
 Ethical Trust
80 Holdenhurst Road
Bournemouth BH8 8AL United
 Kingdom
(011) 44 20 229 2373
Contact: Trevor Forbes

Acorn Unit Trust Managers Ltd.
 Acorn Ethical Unit Trust
One White Hart Yard
London Bridge
London SE1 1NX United Kingdom
(011) 44 71 407 5966
Contact: Roger Noddings

Allchurches Investment Management
 Services
 Amity Fund
19/21 Billiter Street
London EC3M 2RY United Kingdom
(011) 44 71 528 7364
Contact: G. A. Prescott

Allied Provincial
 Allied Provincial Green PEP
Town Centre House
Merrion Centre
Leeds LS2 8LA United Kingdom
(011) 44 532 420303

D. J. Bromige & Partners
 Ethical Investment Fund
10 Queen Street
London W1X 7PD United Kingdom
(011) 44 71 491 0558
Contact: Alan Miller

Clerical Medical Unit Trust Managers
 Evergreen Trust
Narrow Plain
Bristol BS2 0JH United Kingdom
(011) 44 27 226 9050
Contact: Peter Hill

Commercial Union Asset Management
 Environmental Exempt Pension Fund
St. Helens
One Undershaft
London EC2P 3DQ United Kingdom
(011) 44 71 283 7500
Contact: Ian Williams

Cooperative Insurance Society
 Environ Trust
CIS Unit Managers
Miller Street
Manchester M60 0AL United Kingdom
(011) 44 61 832 8686
Contact: Philip Deverel Smith

Credit Suisse Buckmaster & Moore
 Fellowship Trust
Beaufort House
15 St. Botolph Street
London EC3A 7JJ United Kingdom
(011) 44 71 247 7474
Contact: Tony Franks

Eagle Star Unit Trust Managers
 Environmental Opportunities Trust

Eagle Star House
Bath Road
Cheltenham
Glos GL53 7RN United Kingdom
(011) 44 24 222 1311
Contact: Fiona Cutting

Fidelity Investment Services Ltd.
  Fidelity Famous Names Trust
Oakhill House
130 Tonbridge Road
Hildenborough, Tonbridge
Kent TN11 9DZ United Kingdom
(011) 44 73 236 1144
Contact: Peter Holland

First Charter Investment Management
  Ltd.
  First Charter Ethical PEP
Graylands
High Street
Chipping Ongar
Essex CM5 9LD United Kingdom
(011) 44 277 364949

Friends Provident Unit Trust Managers
  North American Stewardship Trust
  Stewardship Income Trust
  Stewardship Unit Trust
  Stewardship Pension Fund
72/122 Castle Street
Salisbury SP1 3SH United Kingdom
(011) 44 72 241 1622
Contact: Richard Lowman

Henderson Financial Management Ltd.
  Henderson Green PEP
Three Finsbury Avenue
London EC2M 2PA United Kingdom
(011) 44 71 638 5757

Homeowners Friendly Society
  Green Chip Investment Fund
Box 94
Homeowners House
Springfield Avenue

Harrogate
North Yorkshire HG1 2HN United
  Kingdom
(011) 44 42 352 2070

Medical Investments Ltd.
  Health Fund
One White Hart Yard
London Bridge
London SE1 1NX United Kingdom
(011) 44 71 407 5966
Contact: Roger Noddings

Merlin Jupiter Unit Trust Management
  Ltd.
  Merlin Ecology Fund
  Merlin International Green
  Investment Trust
197 Knightsbridge
London SW7 1RB United Kingdom
(011) 44 71 581 3857
Contact: Tessa Tennant

NM Investment Management
  Conscience Fund
Regal House
14 James Street
London WC2E 8BT United Kingdom
(011) 44 70 537 222
Contact: Carol Smith

Scottish Equitable Fund Managers
  Ethical Pension Fund
  Ethical Unit Trust
28 St. Andrew Square
Edinburgh EH2 1YF United Kingdom
(011) 31 556 9101
Contact: Tom Copeland

Sovereign Unit Trust Managers Ltd.
  Sovereign Ethical Fund
12 Christchurch Road
Bournemouth BH1 3LW United
  Kingdom
(011) 44 20 229 1111
Contact: Ron Spack

Target Trust Managers
  Target Global Opportunities Trust
Alton House
174/177 High Holborn
London WC1V 7AA United Kingdom
(011) 44 71 836 8040
Contact: Quentin Toalster

Touche Remnant
  TR Ecotec Environmental Fund
Mermaid House
Two Puddle Dock

London EC4V 3AT United Kingdom
(011) 44 71 236 6565
Contact: Peter Wolf

TSB Unit Trusts
  Environmental Investor Fund
Charlton Place
Andover
Hants SP10 1RE United Kingdom
(011) 44 26 456 789
Contact: Julie Lineham

| VENTURE CAPITAL

United States

CALIFORNIA

Ally Capital Corporation
Environmental Allies Fund
85 Liberty Ship Way, Suite 403
Schoonmaker Point Marina
Sausalito, Calif. 94965
(415) 331-5500
(415) 331-1212 (fax)
Contact: Gordon Davidson, Vice
  President

Sand County Ventures
One Sansone Street, Suite 810
San Francisco, Calif. 94104
(800) 648-3448
(415) 616-8500
Contact: Michael Hall Kieschnick,
  President

MARYLAND

Calvert Social Investment Foundation
7205 Pomander Lane
Chevy Chase, Md. 20815
(301) 951-9426
(301) 907-8728 (fax)
Contact: John G. Guffey, President

Calvert Social Venture Partners, L.P.
7201 Wisconsin Avenue, Suite 310
Bethesda, Md. 20814
(202) 657-0142
Contact: John May, Managing General
  Partner

MAINE

Sandy River Group
183 Middle Street
Portland, Me. 04101
(207) 774-8444
(207) 774-9643
Contact: David L. Friedman

MASSACHUSETTS

Alterra Group
1030 Massachusetts Avenue
Cambridge, Mass. 02138
(617) 661-4852
Contact: William Ware

MINNESOTA

i e Associates
3704 Eleventh Avenue South
Minneapolis, Minn. 55407
(612) 823-3154
(612) 825-6865 (fax)
Contact: Dr. Tom P. Abeles, President

United Kingdom

Financial Initiative Ltd.
Barchester House
5A Brown Street
Salisbury
Wiltshire SP1 1HE United Kingdom
(011) 44 722 338900

Global Money Placement Ltd.
Collier House

163–169 Brompton Road
Knightsbridge
London SW3 1HW United
   Kingdom
(011) 44 71 589 4567

TR Ecotech Fund
Mermaid House
Two Puddle Dock
London EC4V 3AT United Kingdom
(011) 44 71 236 6565

This glossary consists of terms used in *The Social Investment Almanac*. Many of the terms are unique to the social investment field. The glossary itself is unique in its coverage of terms from the United Kingdom and the European Community (EC). While this glossary may be more complete than most, it is no substitute for a dictionary.

Where we felt it necessary, we have gone beyond the traditional limits of the glossary form by supplying somewhat longer explanations for terms of art, especially for those unique to social investing. It is our goal over time to create a lexicon of terms used in social investing. We invite your suggestions. Another distinguishing feature of the glossary is its grouping of terms under the common word contained in each. For example, under "bank" appears "commercial bank" and several other types of banks. Among the words treated in this fashion are "bond," "risk," "security," and "yield."

In a real sense, all of the contributors to the almanac also contributed to the glossary. However, certain of them deserve special recognition. Diane Keefe painstakingly defined dozens of terms relating to bonds. Jean Pogge of the Woodstock Institute in Chicago generously shared with us her work in defining terms relating to community development. *The Bankers of Today, the Banks of Tomorrow: The Financial Services Industry and Its Role in Community Reinvestment* (Woodstock Institute, 1987), by Jean Pogge and David Flax-Hatch, is an indispensable resource. Martin Trimble, executive director of the National Association of Community Development Loan Funds, gave us permission to use its glossary of terms.

In developing the definitions for this book, and therefore for the glossary, the authors looked to the *American Heritage Dictionary*, 2d ed. (Houghton Mifflin, 1984); *Ballentine's Law Dictionary*, 3d ed. (Lawyers Co-op/Bancroft Whitney, 1969); *Black's Law Dictionary*, 5th ed. (West Publishing, 1979); M. Brett, *How to Read the Financial Pages* (Hutchinson Business Books, 1990); *Chambers Etymological English Dictionary*, new ed. (Pyramid Books, 1966); *Cochran's Law Lexicon*, 5th ed. (Anderson Publishing Company, 1977); *A Concise Dictionary of Business* (Oxford University Press, 1990); Coopers and Lybrand, *Guide to Financial Instruments* (Coopers & Lybrand, 1990); J. Downes and J. E. Goodman, *Barron's Finance and Investment Handbook*, 3d ed. (Barron's, 1990); *English Business Dictionary* (Peter Collin, 1986); S. Lee, *ABZs of Money and Finance* (Poseidon Press, 1988); *The*

Oxford Companion to Law (Oxford University Press, 1980); *The Oxford English Dictionary* (Oxford University Press, 1971); *The Oxford Dictionary of English Etymology* (Oxford University Press, 1966); M. J. Wallace and P. J. Flynn, *Collins Business English Dictionary* (Collins Educational, 1984); *Webster's New Collegiate Dictionary*, 8th ed. (G + C Merriam Co., 1980); and *Webster's New World Dictionary*, 3d college ed. (Simon & Schuster, 1988). Certain definitions in the Glossary are adapted from L. S. Clark and P. D. Kinder, *Law and Business: The Regulatory Environment* (McGraw-Hill, 1991).

AB or **Aktb:** *Aktiebolaget*, a joint stock company in Sweden.

accountant: A person who performs accounting work.
> **certified public accountant (C.P.A.):** An individual who has satisfied a state's educational and experiential requirements, has passed the examination prepared by the American Institute of Certified Public Accountants (AI-C.P.A.), and is not an employee of those for whom he or she performs accounting services.
> **management accountant:** A private accountant.
> **private accountant:** Usually a person who has met the same requirements as a C.P.A. but provides advice only to an employer, such as a government agency or a business.

accrued interest: In bonds, the interest due from the last interest payment to the day the bond is sold, which the buyer of a bond must pay the seller.

additional voluntary contribution (AVC): *U.K.* Individual contributions to pension plans whose purpose is to build up later benefits.

adjustable-rate mortgage securities (ARMS): *see* securities

administrator: A person responsible to a probate court who takes charge of an intestate's estate, pays off its debts, distributes what remains of the estate to the persons the law says should inherit, and renders a final accounting to the court. *See also* executor

administratrix: A female administrator.

Advertising Standards Authority (ASA): *U.K.* An independent board established and paid for by the advertising industry to enforce the British Code of Advertising Practice (BCAP), which regulates nonbroadcast advertising.

AG: *Aktien-Gesellschaft*, a joint stock company in Germany.

agency: A bond or note issued under statutory authorization by an agency of the federal or a state government that sometimes is guaranteed by the government itself.

agent: Someone who has the authority to represent another person, called a principal.

All-Share: *see* Financial Times All-Share Index

alternative investment: A catch-all term formerly used to describe any social investment that did not fit into the category of a publicly traded security or mutual fund. *See* community investment

appraisal: An estimation, usually in writing, of the value of property that is made by a disinterested person qualified to make such a judgment.

appraiser: A person qualified to make an appraisal.

ARMS: Adjustable-rate mortgage securities. *See* securities

Articles of Association: *U.K.* One of two organic documents governing a corporation, in this case the internal operations of the company, including such matters as the transfer of shares, the holding of general meetings, and the duties of directors. *See* memorandum of association

AS or **Akts:** *Aktieselskabet,* a joint stock company in Denmark and Norway.

asked: The price at which securities on certain markets and commodities are offered to potential buyers; the price sellers offer to take; the asking price. *See also* bid

asking price: The price at which commodities and securities on certain markets are offered to potential buyers; the price sellers offer to take.

asset: Anything one owns that another would buy; something one owns that has commercial or exchange value.
> **financial asset:** An intangible asset held for its monetary benefits; a security.

auction: A method of sale in which an auctioneer invites bids from prospective buyers.

authority: An agent's legal ability to act for another.

bank: A corporation licensed by either the state or federal government that is in the business of taking money on deposit, cashing checks and drafts, issuing promissory notes, making loans, and the like.
> **commercial bank:** A financial institution that accepts demand deposits and makes commercial loans. Its principal banking functions are the collection of deposits, lending, and the servicing of checking accounts, and its principal source of funds is deposits. It uses these funds for commercial, consumer, and residential loans. Its principal source of income is the interest on these loans and fees for its services.
> **community development bank:** A financial institution regulated by either a state agency or a federal agency whose business is the per-

manent, long-term economic development of low- and moderate-income communities and that targets loan resources to residents of its primary service area.

development bank: An insured depository facility whose corporate mission establishes community development as its key organizational goal. Development banks are proactive lenders that use subsidiaries and affiliates to provide technical assistance for borrowers, advocate for new resources, and develop housing and small business. Development banks sometimes create lending subsidiaries that can make loans to borrowers outside the parameters of the depository institution's lending guidelines because they are too small, too risky, or do not offer bankable collateral.

bank draft: *see* draft

basis: In tax law, generally the amount for which an asset was purchased by its current owner and that, after certain adjustments are made, will be used to calculate a gain or loss.

basis point: *see* point

BCAP: British Code of Advertising Practice.

bear: A person whose behavior on the securities markets indicates that he or she expects the markets to decline generally or the price of a particular issue to fall. (Adjective: *bearish.*)

bear market: A condition in which a market for securities is in a persistent decline, usually for a period of months.

bearer paper: Commercial paper payable to the person who has physical possession of it.

beneficial interest: A beneficiary's right to income or principal under a trust.

beneficiary: (1) A person receiving or who is designated to receive an interest or a benefit, as under a trust, a will, or an insurance policy; one for whose benefit property is held in trust. (2) *U.K.* A person in whose favor a draft is drawn or a letter of credit is opened.

bid: (1) An offer to buy at an auction or on an auction market as for securities or commodities. (2) The price at which sellers may dispose of securities or commodities on an auction market. (3) The price offered by a unit trust to a unitholder in the cashing in of his or her units.

bid-offer spread: The difference between the selling bid and buying (offer) prices of a unit in a unit trust or an investment trust that accounts for the dealing and administration expenses, including the initial charge, of a unit trust or investment trust.

bid price: *see* bid

Blue List: Bond dealers' offering sheets issued daily listing municipal bonds for sale nationwide.

bond: A security evidencing a loan to a company or to a government unit that contains a written promise by a borrower to repay a fixed amount on a specified date and, usually, in the meantime to pay a set annual rate of interest at semiannual intervals. *See also* debt; debenture

> **bearer bond:** A bond issued in blank that is presumed to be owned by the person who holds it. In the United States, new corporate bonds of this type are not being issued. *See* coupon bond
>
> **convertible bond:** A corporate bond that may be converted at a specified exchange rate into a stated number of shares of the corporation's common stock. Its price tends to fluctuate with the price of the stock as well as with changes in interest rates.
>
> **corporate bond:** Evidence of debt issued by a corporation.
>
> **coupon bond:** A type of bond, so called because a part of it is detachable coupons that the holder exchanges after established dates for interest payments. *See* bearer bond
>
> **fully registered bond:** *see* registered bond
>
> **government bond:** Evidence of debt of the U.S. Treasury.
>
> **high-grade corporate bond:** A bond issued by a company with a rating of BBB- and Baa3 or better.
>
> **housing authority bond:** A municipal bond issued by a local public housing authority and backed by a U.S. government guarantee.
>
> **industrial development bond (IDB):** Municipal bonds issued for commercial or industrial purposes secured by revenues from the companies that use the facilities.
>
> **life assurance bond:** *U.K.* A vehicle resembling a variable annuity in the United States.
>
> **limited tax bond:** A bond that is secured by a tax that is limited as to rate and amount.
>
> **mortgage bond:** A bond secured by a lien on a specific property.
>
> **municipal bond:** A bond issued by governmental units that are not part of the federal government. Unlike corporate bonds, municipals pay interest that is exempt from U.S. income tax and sometimes state and local income taxes in the state in which they are issued.
>
> **registered bond:** A bond may be registered in the name of the owner as to principal or interest or both. A bond registered as to principal can be transferred only with the endorsement of the registered owner, but interest is paid by presentation of the appropriate coupon. A bond may provide in its indenture that interest is to be paid to the owner by a check from the issuer's agent. Most new corporate bond issues are available only in fully registered form.
>
> **reset bonds:** Bonds whose coupon payments are adjusted periodically based on a formula defined at issuance.

revenue bond: A municipal bond backed by revenues from a specified source, such as a power authority or a hospital.

serial bond: A municipal or equipment trust issue that is segmented into a series of maturities.

special tax bond: A municipal bond backed by revenues produced from a particular tax.

step-up bond: A bond whose coupon rate increases on a specified date.

term bond: A municipal bond issue that has a single maturity.

bond fund: (1) *U.S.* A mutual fund that invests exclusively in debt securities. (2) *U.K.* A life insurance bond whose underlying vehicle may be a portfolio of securities or a unit trust.

bond rating: A formal opinion expressed in letter values by an outside professional service on the credit worthiness of an issuer and the investment quality of its securities.

bottom-up: A money management style in which asset allocation is based exclusively on the client's objectives and constraints.

BP: Basis point.

British Code of Advertising Practice (BCAP): *U.K.* Industry regulations governing nonbroadcast advertising. *See* Advertising Standards Authority

broker: A person acting as an agent for buyers and sellers.

broker-dealer: Under the Securities Exchange Act of 1934, a person who deals in securities issued by others.

bull: A person whose behavior on the securities markets indicates that he or she expects the markets to rise generally or the price of a particular issue to rise. (Adjective: bullish.)

bull market: A condition in which a market for securities is rising generally for a period of months.

bulldog: A bond denominated in sterling but not issued in the United Kingdom.

business judgment rule: A rule of law that a court will not question the judgment of the board of a corporation so long as the board acts with due diligence and in the absence of bad faith, fraud, or conflict of interest.

business loans: In community development loan funds, all loans to nonprofit organizations, for-profit corporations, and individuals for business purposes.

bylaws: A rule adopted by a board or, rarely, shareholders for the internal governance of a corporation.

call: A method an issuer may use to retire debt prior to maturity, if it is allowed by the terms of the indenture. *See* refunding

call provision: A provision in an indenture that permits the issue to be redeemed at the option of the issuer before maturity, usually at a premium.

callable: Redeemable at the issuer's option before maturity under conditions detailed in the bond's indenture.

capital: (1) Wealth; assets that produce income. (2) In banking, the difference between the market price of a bank's assets and the market costs of its liabilities.

> **capital contribution:** The amount of property or cash or both provided in exchange for a partnership interest or shares of stock in a corporation.

capitalization: *See* market capitalization

CAR: *U.K.* Compound annual rate.

cash: (1) Money in the form of coins, bills, or notes. (2) To exchange for money in the form of coins, bills, or notes.

> **cash in:** To terminate an insurance policy in exchange for its cash value.

cash equivalents: Assets that are essentially as liquid as cash.

cash flow: A figure calculated by subtracting expenses from income; the amount of money coming into a business (its receipts) less the amount of money leaving (its expenditures).

certificate of deposit (CD): An interest-bearing negotiable promissory note issued by a bank (the maker) to a customer (the payee) against funds deposited in the bank for a definite period. The minimum maturity is fourteen days at commercial banks. Interest rates are in line with money market rates current at the time of issuance and are governed by limits set by the Federal Reserve's Regulation Q.

certificate of incorporation: A document issued by a secretary of state of a state that signifies that a corporation has come into existence.

certificate of limited partnership: A document filed with the secretary of state of a state that brings a limited partnership into existence.

certified public accountant: *see* accountant

charges: *U.K.* A fee levied on the trust property of a unit trust to meet its expenses.

> **annual charge:** *U.K.* A yearly charge, normally deducted at each valuation date and included in the unit price, that is levied on the property of the trust and from which the managers' expenses are met.

> **initial charge:** *U.K.* A one-off charge included in the offer price of units that covers a unit trust's initial expenses, including commission payments.

one-off charge: *U.K.* A charge made only once.

other charges: *U.K.* A catch-all term for charges that may be paid out of the property of an investment scheme that may include registrars' fees, trustees' fees, audit fees, regulatory costs, and dealing expenses.

charitable institution: A broad category of nonprofit organizations, including: schools and other educational entities; social service organizations; foundations; churches; arts organizations; and entities organized to relieve the burdens of government.

charity: An activity for the public good undertaken without expectation of profit that may include improving the economic conditions of the poor, maintaining educational or religious establishments, or other activities for the public good.

chartered financial analyst (CFA): A person who has passed a series of tests related to financial services and who, over the period during which he or she took the tests, also held a job related to security analysis and selection.

church commissioners: *U.K.* Government-appointed charitable trustees established to further the work of the Church of England.

closed-end: A type of mutual fund that issues only a fixed number of shares which are listed on stock exchanges rather than redeemed by the fund.

CLT: Community land trust.

collateral: An asset a borrower pledges to a lender which the lender may seize and sell if the borrower defaults.

commercial bank: *See* bank

commercial paper: Unsecured promissory notes issued to finance short-term credit needs in conjunction with bank loans. Commercial paper is generally backed by unused bank credit lines to refund the notes in the event of an adverse market. Commercial paper is usually bought and sold on a discount basis figured for the actual number of days to maturity on a 360-day basis, in the same manner as Treasury bills and bankers acceptances. Interest-bearing commercial paper is often available. Commercial paper is normally available in multiples of $25,000, with no maximum amount, but the usual minimum round-lot transaction size is $100,000 in maturity value. The Securities Act of 1933 exempts these notes from registration.

commingle: To mix; to merge a principal's funds with an agent's.

commission-only financial planner: *see* financial planner

community development bank: *see* bank

community development credit union (CDCU): *see* credit union

community development investment: A grant, loan, or equity investment made primarily to support or encourage community development that is paid back and may produce income.

community foundation: *see* foundation

community land trust (CLT): A democratically structured nonprofit corporation with an open membership and an elected board organized to acquire land and remove it from the speculative market whose purpose is to make land permanently accessible to community residents in need of affordable housing.

company: (1) A term used to indicate a for-profit enterprise. (2) *U.K.* An enterprise formed and registered in accordance with the Companies Act that has a legal identity separate from that of its members.

> **limited company (Ltd.):** *U.K.* (1) A privately held corporation whose shareholders' liability for the company's debts is limited to their investment in the company's shares. (2) Usually an enterprise in the form of a society or trade association whose members' liability is limited by a memorandum to a certain amount that the members commit to contribute on the winding-up of the company.
>
> **proprietary company (pty.):** *Australia, Republic of South Africa or RSA.* A private limited company.
>
> **public limited company (Plc):** *U.K.* A publicly owned company whose shareholders' liability for the debts of the company is limited to the value of their shares.

control: In a corporation, the ability of a shareholder or a group of shareholders to run a corporation.

controlled persons: In finance, persons who work directly for a controlling person, including financial advisers, brokers, and the like.

controlling person: Under the Securities Act of 1933, a person who can greatly influence decisions of a corporation, regardless of the amount of stock in the corporation he or she holds.

corporation: (1) A form of business that comes into existence when, upon an application by one or more persons, the secretary of state of a state issues a certificate of incorporation and whose owners' liability for its debts ordinarily is limited to the amount of their investment. (2) *U.K.* A limited company.

> **close corporation:** A small corporation, usually with less than fifty shareholders.
>
> **closely held corporation:** Under federal securities regulations, a corporation with less than five hundred shareholders whose stock is not otherwise subject to registration with the Securities and Exchange Commission.

foreign corporation: A corporation incorporated under laws of another state.

for-profit corporation: A private corporation generally engaged in a business.

nonprofit corporation: A corporation not organized to make profits.

privately held corporation: A corporation whose stock is not publicly traded.

professional corporation: A corporation whose shareholders have joined together to offer legal, medical, architectural, or other professional services.

public corporation: A corporation created by an act of Congress or of a state legislature.

publicly traded corporation: A corporation whose stock or debt or both can be bought and sold on an exchange.

coupon: Evidence of interest due on a bond. The coupon is detached from the bond and presented to the issuer's agent or the bondholder's bank for payment of interest.

coupon bond: *see* bond

coupon rate: The annual rate of interest that the borrower promises to pay the bondholder.

covenant: (1) A promise; a clause in a contract. (2) A contract.

cover note: *U.K.* Binder.

credit risk: *see* risk

credit union: (1) A nonprofit, federally regulated, cooperative financial institution owned and controlled by its members, the borrowers and savers who use the institution. By law the members must share a "common bond," such as a church affiliation, a profession, or a common employer. Each member has one vote, regardless of the amount of his or her deposit. All surplus is either returned to members as dividends on shares (interest on savings accounts) or retained as reserves. Sixty to ninety percent of a credit union's deposits usually are invested in consumer or mortgage loans to members with the balance in government securities, certificates of deposits, or other nonspeculative instruments. (2) *Canada. Caisse populaire.*

community development credit union (CDCU): A credit union chartered specifically to serve low-income communities. Its legal structure is identical to that of other credit unions, except that a 1970 statute allows a CDCU to raise deposits from nonmembers, such as foundations, churches, banks, and corporations. These deposits are insured on the same basis as member deposits, up to $100,000 per depositor per institution as of January 1991. Nonmember depositors do not have a vote in the credit union's affairs, nor may they borrow from it.

current yield: *see* yield

custodian: A person or institution holding funds on another's behalf.

dealer: A person or firm acting as a principal in buying and selling securities.

debenture: A bond that is not secured by a particular asset but rather is backed by the general credit of the issuing corporation.

debt capital: In community development loan funds, that portion of a fund's total capitalization provided by the fund's creditors.

debt: In terms of securities, corporate borrowings in the form of bonds, debentures, or commercial paper.

derivative: In terms of securities, a product derived from a type of securities or another financial vehicle.

development bank: *see* bank

development banking: A for-profit business enterprise organized to accelerate local economic activity and to stimulate market forces where they have stalled or ceased to function.

development deposits: Market rate bank deposits combining competitive returns with the social dividend of renewing distressed minority neighborhoods.

discount: (1) The difference between the value of a bond at maturity and its price when the price is lower than the maturity value. (2) A deduction from the face value of commercial paper in consideration of the seller's receipt of cash before the maturity date. (3) An allowance from the quoted price of goods, usually made by the deduction of a certain percentage from the invoice price.

> **discount rate:** The interest rate that the Federal Reserve charges to lend money to its member banks.

discretionary expense: *See* expense

distribution trust: An income-paying unit trust.

dividend: (1) A portion of a corporation's earnings distributed pro rata among the shares outstanding in a class of stock. (2) In credit unions, the interest paid on shares.

> **property dividend:** A distribution to shareholders of corporate assets or stock in another corporation.
> **stock dividend:** A distribution to shareholders of additional shares of the corporation's own stock.

DPSP: *Canada.* Deferred profit-sharing plan.

draft: Bill of exchange; bill.

> **bank draft:** A draft by one bank on another, usually to provide a customer with funds payable at a distant bank.

clean draft: A draft to which no documents are attached.

date draft: A draft so drawn as to mature on a fixed date, irrespective of acceptance.

time draft: A draft so drawn as to mature at a certain fixed time after presentation or acceptance.

duty: (1) A standard of care society imposes on reasonable persons in similar circumstances. (2) A tax imposed on imported goods, usually at the port of entry.

EC: European Community.

economic risk: *see* risk

economic conversion: The planned transfer of production resources from military or weapons to more stable, diversified operations.

economically targeted investing: Investments by pension funds that are intended to achieve a market rate of return and confer a benefit (social or economic) to the public at large. *See also* alternative investment

EEC: *See* European Community

effective after-tax current yield: *see* yield

EFTA: European Free Trade Association.

eleemosynary: Charitable.

employee benefit: A form of compensation, other than direct wages or salary, that an employee receives because he or she is a member of an employer-established group.

employee stock ownership plan (ESOP): (1) A mechanism by which employees receive shares of the company for which they work. In general, to create an ESOP, a company sets up a trust fund that borrows money to buy company stock. The company makes tax-deductible contributions to the trust, which uses the money to repay the loan. As the loan is repaid, the trust releases shares from a "suspense account" and allocates them to accounts for individual employees, who receive their shares when they leave the company. (2) A trust fund established to implement an ESOP.

encashment value: *U.K.* The amount paid by a unit trust to a holder on the redemption of his or her shares is calculated:

Number of units held x Bid price per unit = Encashment value

endorsement: A signature on the back of a negotiable instrument made primarily for the purpose of transferring the rights of the holder to another person. It constitutes a contract between the holder and all parties to the instrument by which an endorser orders the maker to pay his or her transferee and promises the transferee that if the maker does not pay, he or she will.

endowment: Assets held by a charitable institution that may be invested; funds with respect to which the donor has required the principal not to be consumed but to be invested to produce return.

> **endowment fund:** A fund or any part of a fund that is not wholly expendable by a charitable institution on a current basis under the terms of the applicable gift instrument.

entity: A being; an organization or group.

equipment trust certificate (ETC): A type of debt used to finance the purchase of railroad cars and locomotives under which a trustee holds title to the equipment for ETC owners until the debt is paid. Unlike most corporate bonds, ETCs offer serial maturities.

equities: Equity securities.

equity: Ownership.

> **equity securities:** Ownership interests in a corporation; stock; intangible personal property, ownership of which usually is represented by a share certificate or stock certificate.

ESOP: Employee stock ownership plan.

ETC: Equipment trust certificate.

ethical investment: A social investment.

ethics: Standards of conduct or of moral judgment.

estate: All of a decedent's property, both personal and real, that his or her heirs will inherit.

Eurodollars: U.S. dollars owned by foreigners and placed on deposit in banks outside the United States, principally in Europe. Such deposits are available for lending to corporations and other banks.

European Community (EC): An economic and political federation consisting of Belgium, Denmark, France, Germany, Greece, the Republic of Ireland, Italy, Luxembourg, Netherlands, Portugal, Spain, and the United Kingdom; formerly, with different membership, the European Economic Community.

European Economic Community: *see* European Community

European Free Trade Association (EFTA): An economic federation whose members include Austria, Finland, Iceland, Norway, Sweden, and Switzerland. Liechtenstein, through its customs union with Switzerland, is also a participant.

event risk: *see* risk

Eximbank: Export-Import Bank.

expense: (1) Cost. (2) To account for a payment as a current charge rather than as an investment to be amortized.
    discretionary expense: An expenditure that an individual has a real choice about making.
    fixed expense: A cost of everyday life that most people cannot avoid.

Export-Import Bank: A U.S. government agency authorized to make medium- and long-term project and development loans to foreign businesses and government.

Fannie Mae: (1) Federal National Mortgage Association (FNMA). (2) A security issued by FNMA.

federal funds rate: A misnomer for the interest that banks charge each other for short-term loans.

Federal National Mortgage Association (FNMA, or Fannie Mae): A publicly owned, but federally sponsored, corporation established in 1938 to buy mortgages from lenders and to resell them to investors.

fee-based financial planner: *see* financial planner

fee-only financial planner: *see* financial planner

fiduciary: (1) A person who has undertaken to act for another person's benefit in a circumstance in which the law imposes a duty of trust; a person having the character or nature of a trustee as to a particular undertaking. (2) Characterized by trust.
    fiduciary duties: A person's responsibilities of trust to another.

FIMBRA: *U.K.* Financial Intermediaries, Managers and Brokers Regulatory Association.

finance company: A state licensed and regulated corporation that makes loans to individuals or businesses but does not accept deposits. Its principal sources of funds are corporate capital, loans from other financial institutions, and the sale of loans and securities. Its principal uses of funds are consumer loans, commercial loans, and mortgages. Its principal sources of income from banking activities come from fees and interest on loans.

financial planner: An individual who holds himself or herself out to the public as someone who will assist in managing their assets and liabilites.
    commission-only financial planner: A financial planner who receives commissions from the investment vehicles his or her clients buy.
    fee-based financial planner: A financial planner who charges both a per-hour fee and receives a commission on what a client buys.

fee-only financial planner: A financial planner who charges a fixed fee for services, regardless of what those services involve.

Financial Intermediaries, Managers and Brokers Regulatory Association (FIMBRA): *U.K.* A self-regulating industry group designed to police independent financial advisors.

Financial Times (FT) All-Share Index: *U.K.* A market capitalization-weighted index consisting of approximately 650 companies.

Financial Times–Stock Exchange 100-Share (FT 100) Index: *U.K.* An index that measures the performance of the one hundred largest companies in terms of market capitalization on the London Stock Exchange.

fixed expense: *see* expense

floating rate notes: Bonds whose payments change in line with changes in LIBOR or another rate.

FNMA: Federal National Mortgage Association.

for-profit: In community development loan funds, a business incorporated without prohibitions regarding its earnings or profits, including worker or member cooperatives that pay dividends to the members based on earnings.

foreign exchange: Transactions involving the purchase and sale of currencies.

fraud: (1) An intentional misrepresentation intended to deceive, whether by misstating or concealing the truth. (2) A statement made with reckless disregard for whether or not it is true.

freeze out: (1) The denial of the rights of a minority shareholder to participate in a close corporation's management in violation of the majority's fiduciary duties. (2) To deny the rights of a minority shareholder.

freeze-out merger: A merger designed to eliminate public ownership of a corporation by means of corporate processes and corporate assets.

full-time equivalent (FTE): In community development loan funds, an accounting device under which each staff person who works full time (thirty-five to forty hours a week, year-round) is counted as 1 FTE. Each contracted person who works forty hours a week is 1 FTE. Persons working less than full time are accounted for as a percentage of FTE. If someone works ten hours a week, that individual is equivalent to .25 FTE.

future exchange contract: A contract, usually between a bank and a customer, for the purchase or sale of foreign exchange at a fixed rate with delivery at a specified time. It is used to avoid the risk of fluctuations in the foreign exchange rates.

G7: *see* Group of Seven

general obligation: A municipal bond backed by the general taxing powers of the issuer.

GIC: *U.K.* Guaranteed investment contract.

gift: A voluntary transfer of ownership without consideration.
  gift inter vivos: A gift made by one living person to another living person.
  gift causa mortis: A gift made by a donor who anticipates imminent death.
  testamentary gift: A gift made by will.

gilt-edged: *U.K.* securities of high quality in debt securities.

gilts: *U.K.* High-quality debt securities.

GmbH: Gesellschaft mit beschraenkter Haftung. A limited liability company in Germany.

Government National Mortgage Association (GNMA, or Ginnie Mae): (1) A corporate agency of the Department of Housing and Urban Development that guarantees the mortgage-backed securities of private issuers. (2) A mortgage-backed security that represents a portion of a pool of government-guaranteed Federal Housing Administration and Veterans Association mortgages. Its holders are guaranteed against loss by the U.S. government. Unlike a bond, a Ginnie Mae does not repay the principal at maturity. Instead the issuer makes principal payments each month with interest payments.

go public: To sell shares of what was a close corporation in a public offering.

good faith: "Honesty in fact in the conduct or transaction concerned" (Uniform Commercial Code, sec. 1–201[19]).

governing board: The body responsible for the management of a charitable institution or of such an institution's funds.

Group of Seven (G7): The self-designated seven leading industrial nations in the nonsocialist world, comprising Canada, France, Germany, Italy, Japan, the United Kingdom, and the United States. The group holds an annual economic summit, usually in the late spring or early summer.

group RRSP: *Canada.* An individual registered retirement savings plan operated by the employer on a group basis.

guarantor: A person who conditionally promises to pay a creditor if the principal debtor does not.

housing loans: In community development loan funds, all loans to both nonprofit and for-profit developers and to individuals for housing development and home purchase.

IFA: Independent financial adviser.

illiquid: Difficult or impossible to turn into cash.

IMRO: *U.K.* Investment Management Regulatory Organisation.

income: (1) Money received in the form of dividends, interest, rent, commissions, and salary. (2) Money earned by the principal of a trust.

> **disposable income:** Personal income that remains after paying taxes.
>
> **income statement:** A financial report that identifies where money came from and where it went.
>
> **net income:** The amount of money that remains after meeting, or making provisions for, all expenses.

incorporation: The act of forming a corporation.

incorporator: An individual or agent who signs the articles of incorporation and files them with the secretary of state of a state.

indemnify: To secure against damage or loss; to reimburse.

independent financial adviser (IFA): *U.K.* An independent contractor who is not tied, like a salesperson, to a particular vendor of securities or other financial products. He or she must exercise independent judgment on financial products.

index: (1) A means of measuring the performance of a financial market through the combined prices of some or all of that market's constituents. (2) To manage assets with the objective of approximating the performance of an index.

indirect compensation: Something of tangible value, other than cash, that an employee receives by virtue of being a member of an employer-established group.

individual retirement account (IRA): A federal savings incentive program that permits a self-employed person or an employee earning up to a certain amount to set aside a portion of his or her income each year without paying taxes on it. If the money is left in the plan until after the holder reaches fifty-nine and one-half years of age, the money is taxed at the rate applicable at the time of withdrawal, which is presumably a lower rate than when the monies were earned. *See* Keogh plan

industrial development bond: *see* bond

insider: (1) Generally, under the securities laws, a person with access to confidential corporate information. (2) Under SEC reporting requirements, an officer or director of a person holding 10 percent of the corporation's stock.

institution: (1) An incorporated or unincorporated entity organized and operated exclusively for educational, religious, charitable, or other eleemosynary purposes. (2) An organization—such as a pension fund, mutual fund, bank, or insurance company—that invests in securities.

insurance: A means of indemnifying the risks of individuals and businesses in return for a premium that is calculated by evaluating experience with similar risks. It is risk shifting from the insured to the insurer and risk spreading among the insured by the insurer. *See* insurance company

>**insurance policy:** The contract between an insurer and an insured.

>**term insurance:** A type of life insurance that is bought for certain periods (usually of one year), though generally it is renewable.

>**whole life insurance:** A type of life insurance that pays a benefit if the insured dies but also has a "savings" feature that accumulates value over the life of the policy. Such policies may be cashed in at any time prior to the insured's death.

>**umbrella insurance policy:** An insurance policy designed to cover losses in excess of the limits of other liability policies or to cover events not covered by the other policies.

insurance company: A state-regulated financial intermediary that facilitates the sharing of the risk of financial loss among a large group so that the risk of loss for each group member is less. It contracts with individuals or businesses to pay losses from unexpected events or catastrophes in return for set premiums. Because it collects premiums from a large, diverse group, only a small number of which will experience losses, and it has expertise in evaluating the probabilities of losses, the total collected should exceed the amount needed to pay losses. It derives funds from its policy premiums, reserves, and investment income, and it uses those funds to make loans to policy holders, commercial loans, and residential mortgages.

insured: A person whose life or property is covered by a life insurance policy.

insurer: An insurance carrier or company.

interest: Money paid for the use of another's money.

interest rate risk: *see* risk

inter vivos trust: *see* trust

intestate: (1) A person who dies not leaving a valid will. (2) The state of dying and not leaving a valid will.

investment advisor: A person in the business of advising others, either directly or through publications, on the value of securities or on whether to buy, hold, or sell securities.

investment club: *Europe.* A financial vehicle, similar in structure to an investment trust in the United Kingdom, in which there is a set number of investment units. When all of the units have been purchased, the club is closed and a new club opened. In legal form, they are associations or societies that collect money from their members to buy securities. Each member's investment is reflected in unit holdings. Investments are pooled to reduce capital risk and charges.

Investment Management Regulatory Organisation (IMRO): *U.K.* A self-regulating organization consisting of those who manage the principal forms of pooled investment.

investment securities: Negotiable instruments issued by a corporation that evidence ownership interests or debt obligations.

investment supervisory services: The giving of continuous investment advice to a client (or making investments for a client) based on the individual needs of the client.

IRA: Individual retirement account.

irrevocable trust: *see* trust

issue: (1) To sell a security to its first holders; to deliver commercial paper to its first holder. (2) A particular group of securities.

junior: Subordinated to other lenders' interests.

Keogh plan: A tax-advantaged savings plan for self-employed individuals that resembles an individual retirement account.

LAUTRO: *U.K.* Life Assurance and Unit Trust Regulatory Organisation.

lease: A contract by which a person owning property (the lessor) grants another (the lessee) the right to possess and use it for a specified period at a set price.

legal opinion: As to bonds, an opinion, usually issued by a law firm specializing in public borrowing, about the legality of a bond issue.

lending fees: In community development loan funds, application, origination, or other one-time payments received from borrowers or applicants. The term usually does not include fees charged to cover direct costs, as for appraisals.

liability: (1) The assignment of financial responsibility for the violation of a legal duty. (2) A debt; an obligation enforceable in a legal action; a person's claim on another's assets that arises from a transfer of goods or services that has already occurred.

LIBOR: The London Interbank offered rate.

Life Assurance and Unit Trust Regulatory Organisation (LAUTRO): *U.K.* A self-regulating organization established under the Financial Services Act that supervises the retail marketing of life assurance and unit trusts.

life assurance bond: *see* bond

limited partnership: A business form organized under a state statute that consists of one or more general partners and one or more limited partners.

liquidate: To turn an asset into cash.

listed: Traded on a securities exchange.

litigation: Adversary proceedings before either a court or an administrative agency.

load: A charge in the amount of a percentage of an investment added to the price of a mutual fund. It is paid to the fund but usually goes to an intermediary who facilitated the transaction.

loan-loss reserves: In community development loan funds, that portion of a fund's permanent capital designated by the board as a reserve against possible loan losses and, as such, unavailable for lending purposes. Generally, permanent capital plus loss reserves will equal equity.

loan-to-value (LTV): A ratio describing the relationship between a loan and the value of the security for the loan.

London Interbank offered rate (LIBOR): A benchmark rate of interest representing what the most creditworthy banks charge each other for funds. LIBORs are expressed in various currencies for three- and six-month terms.

low income: In community development loan funds, at or below the federal standard of 80 percent of area's median income, based on family size.

Ltd.: *U.K.* Private limited company.

LTV: Loan-to-value.

make-whole provision: A provision in an ESOP or a contract for the sale of an interest in a corporation that guarantees the seller a floor price for his or her shares.

management accountant: *see* accountant

manager: A person who manages money for others.

margin: In banking, the difference between the market value of collateral pledged to secure a loan and the amount of the loan.
> **margin loan:** An account set up with a brokerage house that allows a customer to borrow, depending on Federal Reserve Board regulations, up to 90 percent of the value of securities the customer puts up as collateral.

market capitalization: The total value of a corporation's issued and outstanding common stock, which is calculated by multiplying the total number of shares by the price per share.

market price: The last reported price at which the security actually changed hands on a specified date.

market value: The price a willing buyer would pay a willing seller; the market price.

maturity: (1) The date on which bond principal or stated value becomes due and payable in full to the bondholder. (2) The date on which a draft or acceptance becomes due for payment.

> **maturity value:** In bonds and notes, the amount the issuer promises to pay the holder at the end of the instrument's term.

maximum commissions agreement: *U.K.* A device designed to limit the commission payable to independent financial advisers so that they would not have a bias toward a particular financial product because it paid a greater commission.

memorandum of association: *U.K.* One of two organic documents for companies, this one covering the company's public face and including the name of the company, its stated capital, and its objectives. *See also* articles of association

microenterprise: In microlending, the smallest size of businesses.

microlending: A type of loan program directed at microenterprises that relies on peer support and pressure.

minipermanent: In community development loan funds, a loan that is amortized as if made for fifteen to thirty years but with a balloon repayment of remaining principal expected in a much shorter period of time, such as three to five years.

minor: A person under the age of eighteen.

minority: An ethnic group in the United States that is not considered, by law, to have participated in the benefits of being a part of the Western European majority.

misrepresentation: A false or misleading statement or inference.

money manager: Portfolio manager.

mortgage: A voluntary security interest in real property that a debtor gives a creditor to secure an obligation.

> **adjustable-rate mortgage (ARM):** A mortgage that stipulates that the interest rate payable by the borrower will be adjusted at specific intervals according to a formula set out in the mortgage.

> **mortgage-backed securities (MBS):** Bonds issued by agencies of the federal government.

> **mortgage banker:** A lender that originates, sells, and services residential and commercial mortgages but does not collect deposits. Its principal

sources of funds are the sale of mortgages, company capital, loans from other financial institutions, and the sale of securities. Its principal source of income from banking activities comes from fees.

mutual funds: Pools of money managed by investment companies that are used to buy securities. Shares in a mutual fund are, themselves, securities.

net asset value (NAV): For mutual funds, the bid price or market value of a fund share.

net worth: A figure reached by subtracting the value of all liabilities from the value of all assets. Net worth appears on the bottom right of the balance sheet.

new issue: Securities offered to the public for the first time, usually equities in a company that has not been listed before.

noncallable: As to bonds, not redeemable by the issuer prior to the maturity date.

nonprofit: An organization whose purpose is other than making profits; a corporation so chartered under the laws of its state of incorporation.

nonprofit corporation: *see* corporation

note: (1) A writing evidencing a debt. (2) A short-term bond.
> **corporate note:** A bond issued by a corporation maturing in seven years or less.
> **municipal note:** The shortest-term municipal obligation, generally maturing in five years or less.
> **Treasury note:** *see* Treasury

OPIC: Overseas Private Investment Corporation.

odd lot: (1) In equities, a quantity of shares that does not exceed one hundred. (2) In bonds, a quantity whose par amount does not exceed $250,000.

offer: An offeror's proposal stating what he or she is willing to do or not to do in exchange for a specified action or promise by the offeree.
> **bid-offer spread:** *see* bid
> **offer price:** *U.K.* The price at which an investor buys units in a pension trust or an investment trust.

offeree: A party who receives an offer.

offeror: A party who makes an offer.

operating expenses: In community development loan funds, the actual expenses incurred in the operation of a core lending program. The term encompasses overall program activities, such as fund-raising and capitalization, administration, promotion, loan underwriting and monitoring, and basic technical assistance. However, it does not necessarily include special training programs and educational efforts.

OTC: Over-the-counter securities.

Overseas Private Investment Corporation (OPIC): A U.S. government corporation that guarantees or insures U.S. private investment in less-developed countries.

over the counter (OTC): *see* security

PA: *U.K.* Per annum.

PAC: Political action committee.

Par: (1) In bonds, the principal amount of a bond; the amount of money due at maturity. (2) The stock's value, printed for historic reasons on a stock certificate, which usually bears no relationship to either the stock's original sale price or its current worth.

partnership: A voluntary association of two or more persons to carry on a business for profit as co-owners; also called a general partnership.

peace conversion: The movement to encourage more government support for civilian economic development instead of military programs.

peer lending groups: In microlending, groups of borrowers organized to provide mutual support and to increase the stability of the microlending effort.

pension funds: A retirement benefits program funded by an employee's deferred wages.

PEP: *U.K.* Personal equity plan.

permanent capital: In community development loan funds, that portion of a fund's total capitalization exclusive of loss reserves not provided by creditors.

permanent loan: In community development loan funds, a loan that is fully amortized over its term and does not require refinancing or repayment of a balloon; generally a longer-term loan.

personal equity plan (PEP): *U.K.* A tax-advantaged personal investment vehicle designed to encourage individuals to invest in the stocks of companies in the United Kingdom. The program is designed to encourage direct investment, so only a limited percentage of the PEP may be invested in unit or investment trusts.

PLC: *U.K.* Public limited company.

point: One percent; in bond prices a point is worth $10, since bond prices are quoted as percentages of $1,000 maturity value.

basis point: One tenth of 1 percent. Thus, in bond prices quoted in $1,000 maturity value, a basis point is worth $1.

policy loan: A loan made by an insurance company to a policy holder against the equity in the policy. In essence, a policy loan allows the insured to borrow money paid as premiums without canceling the policy.

political action committee (PAC): An organization sanctioned by federal campaign financing laws that permits corporations and affinity groups to funnel individual contributions into state and federal election campaigns.

political risk: *see* risk

poison pill: A type of shareholder rights plan incorporated in the company's bylaws that is intended to ward off hostile takeovers and that, upon some triggering event, such as the acquisition by a tender offeror of a certain percentage of a corporation's common stock, entitles the remaining shareholders to receive additional shares of common stock (or other securities) at bargain prices.

portfolio: A metaphor for an owner's investments.
    portfolio management: The management of financial assets for the benefit of another.
    portfolio manager: A person (or firm) who, for a fee, assumes responsibility for managing part or all of a client's portfolio; a money manager.

power of attorney: A legal document that authorizes an agent to act on behalf of the principal who has executed the document.

preferred stock: *see* stock

premium: (1) Money to be paid by an insured to an insurer as the consideration for insurance. (2) The difference between the price of a bond and its value at maturity when the price is higher than the maturity value; a price greater than $100 per $100 of bond value.

PRI: Program-related investment.

primary market: In securities, the new issue market.

principal: (1) An amount invested exclusive of earnings. (2) The property a grantor places in trust. (3) A person who employs an agent.

private accountant: *see* accountant

private placement: A sale of securities to a qualified investor that does not have to be registered with the SEC, as a public offering would.

privately held: As to corporations, not publicly traded.

program-related investment (PRI): Community development investment.

proprietary (pty.): *Australia, Republic of South Africa or RSA.* The abbreviation *pty.* following a company name signifies a corporation whose shares are not publicly traded.

proxy: A power of attorney often used to vote shares in a corporation.

> **proxy statement:** A booklet sent by a corporation and accompanied by a proxy describing candidates for election to the board of directors and all other matters to be dealt with at a shareholders' meeting.

prudent man rule: "A duty to the beneficiary [of a trust] . . . to make such investments and only such investments as a prudent man would make of his own property having in view the preservation of the estate and the amount and regularity of the income to be derived." (Restatement (2d) of Trusts, sec. 227.)

prudent person rule: *see* prudent man rule

pty.: *Australia, Republic of South Africa or RSA.* Proprietary company.

public limited company (PLC): *see* company

publicly traded securities: *see* securities

put: A contracted provision requiring repurchase of securities at or after a certain date at a predetermined price.

quant: A qualitative money manager; a person who uses money-management techniques relying primarily or solely on mathematical techniques (slang).

quotation: The price quoted for a security.

rate of exchange: The basis on which the money of one country will be exchanged for that of another.

realized gains and losses: A category on a portfolio manager's or a trustee's report reflecting which assets have been sold and whether they were sold at a profit or a loss.

reasonable man: A judicial fiction who always acts prudently and does the right thing; an expression of the conduct society demands.

reasonable person: *see* reasonable man

rebate rate: The percent deductible if a bill of exchange or draft is paid before its maturity date.

redemption: The forced exchange of outstanding bonds for cash on or before maturity at a price set when the bond is initially offered to the public; a call.

> **redemption protection:** A clause in a bond indenture protecting the holder against an early call.

redlining: The practice of removing poor or minority communities from a bank's lending area. The practice is generally forbidden by law and so is de facto.

refunding: The sale of a new issue of securities whose proceeds are applied to the redemption of an outstanding issue of bonds. *See also* call

> **refunding protection:** A provision in a bond indenture that prohibits for a period of five or ten years redemption with funds raised through the sale of an issue having an interest cost lower than that on the outstanding bond. Bonds with refunding protection are subject to regular redemption and provide for a sinking fund.

register: To file a report describing an offering under the Securities Act of 1933.

related person: Under U.S. securities regulations, any officer, director, or partner of an investment adviser or any person directly or indirectly controlling, controlled by, or under common control with an investment adviser, including nonclerical, nonministerial employees.

resolution: A statement authorizing an action adopted by a formal vote of a board of directors.

return: Profit, usually expressed as a percentage, on an investment in securities or other assets.

revaluation: An official increase in the value of one nation's currency expressed in the terms of another.

revenue bond: *see* bond

revolving credit: A letter of credit in which the issuing bank notifies a seller of merchandise that the amount involved when used will again become available, usually under the same terms and without issuance of another letter.

risk: (1) Price fluctuation. (2) The danger that a bond will have been expensively priced relative to other bonds in the market; the possibility that a bond price will fluctuate or that interest payments will be delayed or suspended.

> **credit risk:** In bonds, the probability that an issuer will not repay the principal and interest in a timely fashion or at all.
>
> **economic risk:** In bonds, the probability that economic conditions will deteriorate and thereby affect the safety of the principal and interest payments.
>
> **event risk:** The probability that an event, such as a leveraged buyout, will affect the value of a bond.
>
> **interest rate risk:** In bonds, the probability that a bond's price will rise when interest rates fall and will decline when interest rates rise.

liquidity risk: The degree of difficulty in buying and selling bonds that is a function of issue size, credit quality, and quantity for sale. It is measured by the spread between bid and ask quotes. A spread of one-quarter to one-half point represents ample liquidity while a 2 to 3 percent spread suggests less liquidity.

political risk: The probability that a bond will lose its tax-exempt status.

roll-up: A merger of several limited partnerships into a single publicly traded company, often to the disadvantage of the limited partners.

RPP: *Canada.* Registered pension plan.

RRIF: *Canada.* Registered retirement investment fund.

RRSP: *Canada.* Registered retirement savings plan.

S.A.: (1) *Sociedad anonima;* a joint stock company in Spanish-speaking countries. (2) *Societa anonima;* a joint stock company in Italy.

Sallie Mae: Nickname for the Student Loan Marketing Association (SLMA) or a bond it issues.

samurai: Bonds denominated in yen of non-Japanese issuers.

screen: (1) To look for securities or issuers that meet certain defined criteria. (2) A criterion or a group of criteria used to select securities or issuers.

SEC: Securities and Exchange Commission.

secondary market: An over-the-counter market or an exchange where existing issues are bought and sold by subsequent owners and purchasers.

securities: A security is an instrument, issued in bearer or registered form, that is of a type commonly dealt in upon securities exchanges or markets or dealt in as a medium for investment. It is either one of a class or series or by its terms is divisible into a class of series of instruments, and evidences a share, participation, or other interest in property or in an enterprise or evidences an obligation of the issuer (UCC, sec. 8–102[1][a]).

    adjustable-rate mortgage security (ARMS): A debt security based on a portfolio of adjustable-rate mortgages.

    over-the-counter (OTC) security: A security usually not listed on a major exchange that trades by means of a computer network linking brokerages across the country.

    publicly traded security: A security commonly bought and sold on a defined market.

    support-group security: *U.K.* A community investment device whereby a group of individuals each provide up to £1,000 of security for another's loan.

Securities and Exchange Commission (SEC): An administrative agency of the U.S. government that regulates publicly traded securities and securities markets.

Securities and Investments Board (SIB): *U.K.* An industry group established under the Financial Services Act that supervises the self-regulating investor protection organizations, such as LAUTRO.

securities firm: A corporation regulated by either the Securities and Exchange Commission (SEC) or a state securities regulator, or both, that underwrites investment securities or serves as an intermediary or broker in the sale of securities. Its principal source of income is fees on transactions it conducts for clients.

SEP: Simplified employee pension plans.

serial structure: An issue of bonds that is divided into a series of individual bonds, each of which is due on the same date for a series of years and each of which has different coupons and yields.

share: A unit of ownership in a corporation, mutual fund, or money market mutual fund; stock.
    share certificate: (1) Evidence of ownership of equity securities; stock certificate. (2) In credit unions, the equivalent of a certificate of deposit in banks.
    share draft account: In credit unions, the equivalent of a checking account in banks.

shareholder: The owner of a share, or ownership interest, in a corporation.

SIB: *U.K.* Securities and Investment Board.

sinking-fund provision: A provision in a bond indenture that requires the issuer to redeem a portion of a bond issue prior to maturity, allowing the issuer to repay the debt gradually.

SLMA: Student Loan Marketing Association.

Soc. Anon.: *Societe anonyme;* a joint stock company in France.

social investment: An investment that combines an investor's financial objectives with his or her commitment to social concerns, such as peace, social justice, economic development, or a healthy environment; an investment, which may or may not have economic return as its principal goal, made with an intent to take into account the impact of the investment on the society in which the investment is made.

social screen: A nonfinancial criterion or set of criteria applied in the investment decision-making process. *See* screen

socially responsible investment (SRI): *see* social investment

Societe d'Investissement a Capital Variable (SICAV): An open-end investment fund similar to a unit trust in the United Kingdom that is the most common form of collective investment vehicle in France and Luxembourg. It differs from a unit trust in that it is not a product, but a company in its own right, constituted by articles of association and controlled by a board of directors.

spot exchange contract: A contract between a bank and its customers for the purchase or sale of foreign exchange at a fixed rate for immediate delivery.

spread: The difference between what a dealer pays for a security and the price at which he or she offers to sell it.
> **spread between sectors:** The risk premium required to invest in a sector as expressed in basis points of yield over the Treasury curve.

stakeholder: A person or organization whom the activities of a corporation impact directly or indirectly and who therefore has an interest in the corporation's future.

stated value: A value sometimes placed on shares by a corporation's board of directors to fulfill outdated capital requirements by state statutes; par value.

statement of transactions: A category on a portfolio manager's or trustee's report reflecting the changes that have taken place in the portfolio during the period covered by the report.

statement savings account: In credit unions, the equivalent of a passbook savings account in banks.

step up bond: *see* bond

sterling: *U.K.* The currency of the United Kingdom. Used in this context, the word has nothing to do with silver.

stock: An ownership share in a corporation. *See* share
> **common stock:** Equity securities; shares in a corporation that typically have voting rights but have the lowest priority when the corporation makes distributions of earnings or in liquidation.
> **outstanding stock:** Stock held by shareholders.
> **preferred stock:** An equity security that has preference over common stock as to dividends or asset distributions on dissolution of the company.
> **privately held stock:** Stock not held by mutual funds, pensions, and other institutions.
> **stock certificate:** Evidence of ownership of equity securities; share certificate.

stock dividend: *see* dividend

stock split: The exchange by a corporation of one existing share for two or more new shares.

treasury stock: Issued shares that the corporation has reacquired and not canceled.

stockholder: *see* shareholder

street name: The name of a brokerage recorded as the nominal owner of shares it purchased for the account of one of its clients.

Student Loan Marketing Association (SLMA, or Sallie Mae): A publicly traded corporation established by the federal government in 1972 to guarantee student loans traded on a secondary market that it operates.

syndicate: A group of underwriters.

take-me-along provision: A provision in a stock purchase agreement that prevents the founders from selling any of their stock unless the investors can sell a proportionate amount.

tax basis: As used in a portfolio manager's, trustee's, or brokerage's report, the price paid for a stock or bond. *See* basis

Tax-exempt special savings account (TESSA): *U.K.* A tax deferral program authorized by legislation intended to encourage saving, roughly similar to a Keogh account in the United States.

T-bill: Treasury bill.

tender: (1) An offer of delivery; the act of making goods available to the buyer. (2) To be ready, willing, and able to perform; to offer to perform.

tender offer: An offer to acquire stock for a certain period at a stated price that is made either to an issuer or to its shareholders, who may accept by delivering the stock to the offeror.

term insurance: *see* insurance

TESSA: *U.K.* Tax-exempt special savings account.

third party: A person whose relationship to a contract is not that of being the offeror or the offeree.

thrift institution: A savings and loan association, a federal savings bank, or a state-chartered savings bank or industrial bank that accepts deposits and makes loans. Its main banking functions are deposit collection, lending, and servicing checking accounts. Its principal source of funds is deposits, which it uses for residential mortgages, consumer loans, and commercial loans. Its principal source of income from banking activities comes from the interest on loans and fees for its services.

time draft: *see* draft

top-down: A money-management style that begins with an assessment of economic conditions and an ideal asset allocation and then moves toward an ideal allocation of the client's assets.

total compensation: The combination of all forms of direct and indirect compensation provided by an employer.

trade acceptance: *see* acceptance

Treasury: A bond issued by the U.S. Treasury; any obligation issued by the U.S. Treasury.
> **Treasury bill (T-bill):** A short-term U.S. obligation, maturing in as little as ninety days after issue, that does not pay interest but is sold at a discount from its face value.

treasury stock: *see* stock

trust: (1) A fiduciary relationship created by one person (the creator) in which a second person (the trustee) holds title for the benefit of a third (the beneficiary). (2) The assured reliance on another's integrity.
> **investment trust:** *U.K.* A company that invests its shareholders' contributions in publicly traded securities. They are closed-end investments traded on exchanges in the same way as equities. Investment trusts are different from unit trusts in that unitholders are not shareholders.
> **unit trust:** *see* unit trust

trustee: A person who holds, manages, and invests assets for the benefit of a trust's beneficiary.

UCC: Uniform Commercial Code.

UCITS: *E.C.* Undertakings for Collective Investments in Transferable Securities.

umbrella insurance policy: *see* insurance

Undertakings for Collective Investments in Transferable Securities (UCITS): *E.C.* A 1989 directive of the European Community that allows unit trusts and other collective forms of investments to be sold across European frontiers while leaving control of marketing to host countries.

underwriter: An investment banker who buys part or all of an issue of securities from the issuer for resale to individual and institutional investors.

Uniform Commercial Code (UCC): A statutory scheme adopted with minor variations by each of the states (except Louisiana) that covers a broad range of transactions, including the sale of goods over $500, negotiable instruments, investment securities, and commercial paper.

unit trust: *U.K.* An organization operating under a trust deed that takes money from investors and invests it in a range of stocks, thereby spreading the risk.

unitholder: *U.K.* An owner of one or more units (shares) in a unit trust.

VAT: *U.K.* Value-added tax.

vehicle: A financing or investment option, such as equity or debt.

weighted average: In community development loan funds, the weighted average is the average based on the frequency of occurrence, calculated as follows:

$$\frac{\text{Total \$ @ same term}}{\text{Total \$}} \times \text{term} + \frac{\text{Total \$ @ same term}}{\text{Total \$}} \times \text{term} + = \text{Weighted average}$$

whole life insurance: *see* insurance.

yield: Return on an investment in debt. The two components of yield are interest payments and price (depreciation or appreciation).

> **current yield:** In bonds, the percent relation of the annual interest received to the price of the bond:
>
> **effective after-tax current yield:** The return on a bond that is not exempt from taxation. It is expressed as:
>
> $$\frac{\text{Interest PA}}{\text{Current price}} = \text{Current yield}$$
>
> $$\frac{\text{Tax exempt current yield}}{(1 - \text{federal tax rate})}$$
>
> **realized yield:** Actual return received by the investor who holds a bond for a defined period of time.
>
> **yield to maturity:** The average annual return on an investment based on the interest rate, price, and length of time to maturity. It differs from current yield in that it takes into consideration the increase to par of a bond bought at a discount and the decrease to par of a bond bought at a premium.

COMPANIES, FUNDS, AND BONDS

GENERAL INDEX